Racial and Ethnic Groups

Fourteenth Edition

Racial and Ethnic Groups

Fourteenth Edition

Richard T. Schaefer

DePaul University

Boston   Columbus   Indianapolis   New York   San Francisco   Upper Saddle River
Amsterdam   Cape Town   Dubai   London   Madrid   Milan   Munich   Paris   Montréal   Toronto
Delhi   Mexico City   São Paulo   Sydney   Hong Kong   Seoul   Singapore   Taipei   Tokyo

Editor in Chief: Dickson Musslewhite
Publisher: Charlyce Jones Owen
Program Manager: Seanna Breen
Editorial Assistant: Maureen Diana
Marketing Manager: Brittany Pogue-Mohammed
Marketing Assistant: Karen Tanico
Project Manager: Fran Russello
Procurement Manager: Mary Fischer
Procurement Specialist: Diane Peirano
Design Interior: Irene Ehrmann
Digital Media Project Manager: Claudine Bellanton

Senior Art Director: Blair Brown
Art Director: Maria Lange
Cover Designer: Lumina Datamatics, Inc.
Manager, Rights and Permissions: Carolyn Cruthirds
Photo Researcher: Carolyn Arcabascio/PreMediaGlobal
Cover Art: Peter M. Fisher/Corbis
Full-Service Project Management: George Jacob/Integra
Printer/Binder: Courier Kendallville
Cover Printer: Courier Kendallville
Text Font: 10/12, ITC New Baskerville Std

Library of Congress Cataloging-in-Publication Data
Schaefer, Richard T.
    Racial and ethnic groups / Richard T. Schaefer, DePaul University.—Fourteenth edition.
        pages cm
    Includes bibliographical references and index.
    ISBN-13: 978-0-13-377099-5
    ISBN-10: 0-13-377099-0
    1. Minorities—United States.   2. United States—Race relations.   3. United States—Ethnic relations.
4. Prejudices.   I. Title.
    E184.A1S3 2014
    305.800973—dc23

                                                                2013041297

10 9 8 7 6 5 4 3 2

Student Edition ISBN-10:   0-13-377099-0
ISBN-13: 978-0-13-377099-5
À la Carte ISBN-10:   0-13-377365-5
ISBN-13: 978-0-13-377365-1

To my grandson, may he grow to flourish

in our multicultural society

Brief Contents

Contents

PART I   Perspectives on Racial and Ethnic Groups

x Contents

PART III Major Racial and Ethnic Minority Groups in the United States

Features

Research Focus

- Multiracial Identity (Chapter 1)
- Virtual Prejudice and Anti-Prejudice (Chapter 2)
- The Unequal Wealth Distribution (Chapter 3)
- The Hispanic Dairyland (Chapter 4)
- Immigrants: Yesterday and Today (Chapter 5)
- Sovereignty of the Shinnecock Nation (Chapter 6)
- Sundown Towns, USA (Chapter 7)
- Moving on Up, or Not (Chapter 8)
- English-Language Acquisition (Chapter 9)
- The Latino Family Circle: Familism (Chapter 10)
- Self-Identifying as "Arab American" (Chapter 11)
- Arranged Marriages in America (Chapter 12)
- Tiger Mothers (Chapter 13)
- Intermarriage: The Final Step to Assimilation? (Chapter 14)
- Give Me a Male Boss (Chapter 15)
- Intergroup Contact and South Africa (Chapter 16)
- The Three Maxes (Chapter 17)

Speaking Out

- Problem of the Color Line, by W. E. B. Du Bois (Chapter 1)
- Gangsters, Gooks, Geishas, and Geeks, by Helen Zia (Chapter 2)
- The Conversation We're *Not* Having When We Talk About Affirmative Action, by Gail Christopher (Chapter 3)
- Chinese Exclusion Act of 1882, by Judy Chu (Chapter 4)
- The Next Americans, by Tomás Jiménez (Chapter 5)
- Holocaust Museum of the Indigenous People Should Be Built at Wounded Knee, by Tim Giago (Chapter 6)
- The New Jim Crow, by Michelle Alexander (Chapter 7)
- On the 50th Anniversary of the March on Washington, by Charles Rangel (Chapter 8)
- Leaving Cuba, by J. Alfredo Jimenez (Chapter 9)
- Puerto Ricans Cannot Be Silenced, by Luis Gutierrez (Chapter 10)
- Arab Problem, by Moustafa Bayoumi (Chapter 11)
- Recognizing Native Hawaiians, by Daniel Akaka (Chapter 12)
- Anti-Bullying, by Mike Honda (Chapter 13)
- Night, by Elie Wiesel (Chapter 14)
- What Do Women and Men Want?, by Kathleen Gerson (Chapter 15)
- Africa, It Is Ours!, by Nelson Mandela (Chapter 16)
- My Journey Into the Deaf World, by Erik Olin Wright (Chapter 17)

A Global View

- The Roma: A Thousand Years of Discrimination (Chapter 3)

- Immigration and South Africa (Chapter 4)

- Australia's Aboriginal People (Chapter 6)

- France Noire: Black France (Chapter 7)

- The Salvadoran Connection (Chapter 9)

- Muslims in France (Chapter 11)

- Argentina's Jewish Community (Chapter 14)

- Gender Inequality in Japan (Chapter 15)

Preface

The first fifteen years of the 21st century have witnessed significant changes. The heavily written about growth in the Latino population has overtaken the African American population with the Asian American population growing faster than either. Meanwhile, the number of White non-Hispanic youth has actually become a numerical minority when compared collectively to the other racial and ethnic groups. Yet alongside these demographic changes has been a series of events that serve to underscore the diversity of the American people.

People cheered on May 1, 2011, upon hearing that Osama bin Laden had been found and killed. However, the always patriotic American Indian people were very troubled to learn that the military had assigned the code name "Geronimo" to the infamous terrorist. The Chiricahua Apache of New Mexico were particularly disturbed to learn the name of their freedom fighter was used in this manner.

Barack Obama may be the son of an immigrant and the first African American president, but that is not the end of his ethnicity. On an official state visit to Ireland, the president made a side trip to the village of Moneygall in County Offaly from where his great-great-grandfather Falmouth Kearney, a shoemaker's son, came to the United States in 1850.

Race and ethnicity are an important part of the national agenda. Thirty years ago, when the first edition of this book was being written, it was noted that race is not a static phenomenon and that, although it is always a part of the social reality, specific aspects change. At that time, the presence of a new immigrant group, the Vietnamese, was duly noted, and the efforts to define affirmative action were described. Today, we seek to describe the growing presence of Salvadorans, Haitians, Tongans, Somalis, Hmong, and Arab Americans.

Specific issues may change over time, but they continue to play out against a backdrop of discrimination that is rooted in the social structure and changing population composition as influenced by immigration and reproduction patterns. One unanticipated change is that the breakup of the Soviet Union and erosion of power of totalitarian leaders in the Middle East have made ethnic, language, and religious divisions even more significant sources of antagonism between and within nations. The old ideological debates about communism and capitalism have been replaced by emotional divisions over religious dogma and cultural traditions.

Changes in the Fourteenth Edition

We continue to take full advantage of the most recent data releases from the Census Bureau through the annual American Community Survey. This allows the timelier updating of information, instead of waiting for the results of the census every ten years. The reader will find updated and revised tables, figures, maps, and Internet sources. As one example of the thorough updating, we note that over 30 percent of the citations in the references are new since the last edition.

Learning Objectives are explicitly identified at the beginning of each chapter with the numbered Summary points and Review Questions at the conclusion of each chapter tied specifically to each objective.

Relevant scholarly findings in a variety of disciplines, including economics, anthropology, social psychology, and communication sciences, have been incorporated. The

Speaking Out feature appears in every chapter. These selections provide firsthand commentaries on race and ethnicity in America. This helps us appreciate the expression and passion of racial and ethnic groups in response to prejudice and challenges. Excerpts are included from the writings or speeches of noted members of racial and ethnic groups, such as Elie Wiesel, W. E. B. DuBois, Tomás R. Jiménez, Helen Zia, and Nelson Mandela. Their writings will help students appreciate the emotional and the intellectual energies felt by subordinate groups.

New to this edition are Key Terms of environmental refugees, feminism, kanaka maoli, medical apartheid, religion, segmented assimilation, and two-state solution. Previous users will see a definite increase in the effort to introduce key terms throughout the book in an effort to make them a part of the reader's working vocabulary.

Along with the Speaking Out feature, the Research Focus and Global View boxes offer new insights into the ever-changing nature of race and ethnicity. Eighteen of these boxes are new to the fourteenth edition.

The Spectrum of Intergroup Relations figure now appears in sixteen of the chapters. Included among these is a large, comprehensive Spectrum at the end of the final chapter, which ties the observations together from throughout the textbook.

The fourteenth edition includes entirely new sections on why hate crimes carry harsher penalties, avoiding racial and ethnic groups through the Internet, the African American middle class, the state of education among Hispanics, and contemporary feminism.

We continue and update the new feature added in the twelfth edition called A Global View, consisting of boxes that profile racial and ethnic issues in other nations. This edition features an entirely new one on "France Noire: Black France." These discussions are intended to create a dialogue between the student reader and the material in this book concerning the similarities in racial and ethnic issues globally.

Chapter-by-Chapter Changes

As with all previous editions, every line, every source, and every number has been rechecked for its currency. We pride ourselves on providing the most current information possible to document the patterns in intergroup relations both in the United States and abroad. In addition to all these revisions and new material, we now detail the major changes chapter by chapter:

Chapter 1

- New opening examples
- New Jeff Parker cartoon on changing racial and ethnic landscape
- Latest American Community Survey 2010 data update all statistics
- New census data now allows listing of Arab Americans among major racial groups.
- Table of metropolitan segregation data for African Americans, Hispanics, and Asian Americans
- 2012 map of minority population by counties
- Proposed census changes for racial/ethnic categories for 2020
- Racial and ethnic population projections for 2060 including data for Arab and Biracial Americans

Chapter 2

- New opening example on impact of racial names on allocating public assistance
- Research Focus: Virtual Prejudice and Anti-Prejudice
- Speaking Out: Gangsters, Gooks, Geishas, and Geeks, by Helen Zia
- 2012 data on police profiling in New York City

- New section on avoidance of racial and ethnic groups via the Internet
- New cartoon on workplace diversity
- 2012 data on foreign-born workers

Chapter 3

- Actions in Czech republic taken on Roma schooling
- Section: What Are Hate Crimes?
- Section: Why Do Hate Crimes Carry Harsher Penalties?
- Figure on hate crimes (updated to 2012 release)
- Map of voter identification laws illustrates institutional discrimination
- 2013 HUD study of housing discrimination
- Tables and figure on income by race and sex, holding education constant, updated through 2013 Census reports
- Wealth inequity data updated through the recent economic slowdown
- Research Focus: The Unequal Wealth Distribution
- Implications of *Fisher v. University of Texas* 2013 decision outlined
- Speaking Out: The Conversation We're *Not* Having When We Talk About Affirmative Action, by Gail Christopher
- Recent changes in Craigslist policy on discriminatory advertisements

Chapter 4

- Opener on the success of Dr. Alfredo Quiñones-Hinojosa
- Two figures and map on immigration updated through 2012
- Speaking Out: Chinese Exclusion Act of 1882, by Judy Chu
- Table on immigrant adaptation to the USA
- Research Focus: The Hispanic Dairyland
- Updated figure on languages most frequently spoken at home from 2013 census report
- Cartoons on bilingual language and "border-line schizophrenia"
- Table on refugees updated to 2012
- Key terms of occupational segregation and environmental refugees

Chapter 5

- Opening on Little Italy and Chinese Americans in Manhattan's Little Italy
- Head "Studying Whiteness" rephrased
- More states enact "moment of silence" as a stand-in for prayer in schools
- Romanian language newspaper persists
- New key term of religion and key term of White privilege re-introduced

Chapter 6

- Opener on tribal language use
- Table of major tribal languages
- National map on population of American Indians by county
- Cartoon on destruction of indigenous people of North America
- Table on largest American Indian groupings

- Snapshot table of major social indicators comparison with total population
- Background on policies on Alaskan Natives
- Table of poverty rates of American Indians in cities with largest populations
- Speaking Out: Holocaust Museum of the Indigenous People Should Be Built at Wounded Knee, by Tim Giago
- End of growth in tribal casinos
- Research Focus: Sovereignty of the Shinnecock Nation
- Another look at the Washington NFL team's nickname

Chapter 7

- Obama's family connection to slavery
- Locating of Gee's Bend on Civil Rights Movement map
- Global View: France Noire: Black France
- Speaking Out: The New Jim Crow, by Michelle Alexander

Chapter 8

- Speaking Out: On the 50th Anniversary of the March on Washington, by Charles Rangel
- Reintroducing key term color-blind racism to describe Acting White theory
- Section on "The Middle Class" within Economic Picture
- Research Focus: Moving on Up, or Not
- Reformulation of table on Black presence in selected occupations
- Key term of medical apartheid
- Figure of Black–White voter turnout comparison over time
- Challenge in fundraising faced by Black politicians
- Map on changes in Black population by county 2000–2010

Chapter 9

- Opener on growth of Latinos in rural America
- Figure comparing Hispanic versus White non-Hispanic worker wages
- Section on Education
- Figure comparing Hispanic versus White non-Hispanic going to college
- Comparison of Irish and Cuban immigration
- Speaking Out: Leaving Cuba, by J. Alfredo Jimenez
- Map on Latin American countries
- Survey data on how Salvadorans feel about the USA

Chapter 10

- The Borderlands moved to this chapter from Chapter 9
- Map of the Borderlands

Chapter 11

- Introduction by Marvel Comics of a Muslim American superhero character
- The impact of Islamophobia on the 9/11 generation

- 2012 Arab and Muslim political party preferences
- Figure on Arab American household income data

Chapter 12

- Chapter opener on the diversity of Asian American life
- Key term chain immigration reintroduced
- Table comparing six Asian American groups with USA population on four social indicators
- Discussion of bhanga dancing among Indian Americans
- New cartoon of Japanese American artist Tak Toyoshima
- New heading under Hawai'i: Sovereignty Movement
- Key term of kanaka maoli
- Speaking Out: Recognizing Native Hawaiians, by Daniel Akaka
- Updated map and pie graph of major Asian and Pacific Islander American groups based on 2010 population reports

Chapter 13

- Emergence of Chinese outside of old Chinatowns
- Research Focus: Tiger Mothers
- Key term tiger mother
- Key term of familism reintroduced within context of tiger mother
- Closer look at the "No, No" internees
- Key term xenophobia reintroduced
- Four factors explaining persistence of anti-Asian American prejudice
- Speaking Out: Anti-Bullying, by Mike Honda

Chapter 14

- Blatant anti-Semitism in an upstate New York school
- National and world maps of Jewish population updated to 2012
- Figure on anti-Semitic incidents updated to 2012 report
- Results of 2012 multi-nation anti-Semitism survey
- Results of a 2013 European survey on anti-Semitism
- Results of a 2013 USA survey comparing Jewish denominations
- Efforts of some Jewish faiths to reach out

Chapter 15

- Twitter, and other IT corporations, lack of female board director members
- Research Focus: Give Me a Male Boss
- Section on Feminism with key term added
- Updated figure on women's labor force participation in selected countries
- Updated figure on ratio of women's to men's earnings in selected occupations
- Updated figure on income by sex, holding education constant
- Figure on Labor Department data on allocation of housework between men and women
- Women entrepreneurs in Japan

Chapter 16

- Updated table comparing four nations
- Recent Canada discrimination study
- Critical look at Two-state solutions for Israel and Palestine

Chapter 17

- Research Focus: The Three Maxes
- Figure: Actual and Projected Growth of the Elderly Population of the United States, 1960–2060
- Figure: Changes in Minority Population under Age 18, 2000–2010
- Key term "matrix of domination" reintroduced
- USA map on same-sex households
- Updated look at gays in television
- Results of 2013 national survey on gays and lesbians
- Latest on gay marriage policy
- Speaking Out: My Journey Into the Deaf World, by Erik Olin Wright

Complete Coverage in Four Parts

Any constructive discussion of racial and ethnic minorities must do more than merely describe events. Part I, "Perspectives on Racial and Ethnic Groups," includes the relevant theories and operational definitions that ground the study of race and ethnic relations in the social sciences. We specifically present the functionalist, conflict, and labeling theories of sociology in relation to the study of race and ethnicity. We show the relationship between subordinate groups and the study of stratification. We also introduce the dual labor market theory and the irregular economy theory from economics and the reference group theory from psychology. The extensive treatment of prejudice and discrimination covers anti-White prejudice as well as the more familiar topic of bigotry aimed at subordinate groups. Discrimination is analyzed from an economic perspective, including the latest efforts to document discrimination in environmental issues such as location of toxic waste facilities and the move to dismantle affirmative action.

In Part II, "Ethnic and Religious Sources of Conflict," we examine some often-ignored sources of intergroup conflict in the United States: White ethnic groups and religious minorities. Diversity in the United States is readily apparent when we look at the ethnic and religious groups that have resulted from waves of immigration. Refugees, now primarily from Haiti and Central America, also continue to raise major issues.

Any student needs to be familiar with the past to understand present forms of discrimination and subordination. Part III, "Major Racial and Ethnic Minority Groups in the United States," brings into sharper focus the history and contemporary status of Native Americans, African Americans, Latinos, Arab and Muslim Americans, Asian Americans, and Jews in the United States. Social institutions such as education, economy, family, housing, the criminal justice system, healthcare, and politics receive special attention for the subordinate groups. The author contends that institutional discrimination, rather than individual action, is the source of conflict between the subordinate and dominant elements in the United States.

Part IV, "Other Patterns of Dominance," includes topics related to American racial and ethnic relations. The author recognizes, as have Gunnar Myrdal and Helen Mayer Hacker before, that relations between women and men resemble those between Blacks and Whites. Therefore, in this book, we consider the position of women as a subordinate group. Since the first edition of *Racial and Ethnic Groups*, published more than 25 years ago, debates over equal rights and abortion have shown no sign of resolution. For women of color, we document the matrix of domination suffered because of their subordinate status of race and gender.

Perhaps we can best comprehend intergroup conflict in the United States by comparing it with the ethnic hostilities in other nations. The similarities and differences between the United States and other societies treated in this book are striking. We examine the tensions in Mexico, Brazil, Israel, Palestine, and South Africa to document further the diversity of intergroup conflict.

The final chapter highlights other groups that have been the subject of exclusion: the aged, people with disabilities, and gay men and lesbians. This chapter also includes a concluding section that ties together thematically the forces of dominance and subordination and the persistence of inequality that have been the subject of this book.

Features to Aid Students

Several features are included in the text to facilitate student learning. A short introductory section alerts students to important issues and topics to be addressed. To help students review, each chapter ends with a Conclusion and the new feature of a numbered Summary list. The Key Terms are highlighted in bold when they are first introduced in the text and are listed with page numbers at the end of each chapter. Periodically throughout the book, the Spectrum of Intergroup Relations first presented in Chapter 1 is repeated to reinforce major concepts while addressing the unique social circumstances of individual racial and ethnic groups.

In addition, there is an end-of-book Glossary with full definitions referenced to page numbers. This edition includes both Review Questions and Critical Thinking Questions. The Review Questions are intended to remind the reader of major points, whereas the Critical Thinking Questions encourage students to think more deeply about some of the major issues raised in the chapter. An extensive illustration program, which includes maps and political cartoons, expands the text discussion and provokes thought.

Ancillary Materials

This book is accompanied by an extensive learning package to enhance the experience of both instructors and students.

Supplementary Material for Instructors

Instructor's Manual and Test Bank Each chapter in the Instructor's Manual offers a variety of the following types of resources: Chapter Summary, Chapter Outline, Learning Objectives, Critical Thinking Questions, Activities for Classroom Participation, Key Terms, Suggested Readings, and Suggested Films. Designed to make your lectures more effective and to save preparation time, this extensive resource gathers useful activities and strategies for teaching your course.

Also included in this manual is a test bank offering multiple-choice, true/false, fill-in-the-blank, and/or essay questions for each chapter. The Instructor's Manual and Test Bank is available to adopters at www.pearsonhighered.com/irc.

MyTest This computerized software allows instructors to create their own personalized exams, to edit any or all of the existing test questions, and to add new questions. Other special features of this program include random generation of test questions, creation of alternate versions of the same test, scrambling question sequence, and test preview before printing. For easy access, this software is available within the instructor section of the *MySocLab for Racial and Ethnic Groups* or at www. pearsonhighered.com/irc.

PowerPoint Presentation The PowerPoint presentations are informed by instructional and design theory. You have the option in every chapter of choosing from Lecture and Illustration (figures, maps, and images) PowerPoints. The Lecture PowerPoint slides follow the chapter outline and feature images from the textbook integrated with the text. They are available to adopters via the MySocLab website for the text or www.pearsonhighered.com.

Supplementary Material for Students

MySocLab™ **MySocLab** is a state-of-the-art interactive and instructive solution, designed to be used as a supplement to a traditional lecture course, or to completely administer an online course. MySocLab provides access to a wealth of resources all geared to meet the individual teaching and learning needs of every instructor and every student. Highlights of MySocLab include:

- **MySocLab** for *Racial and Ethnic Groups* provides all the tools you need to engage every student before, during, and after class. An assignment calendar and gradebook allow you to assign specific activities with due dates and to measure your students' progress throughout the semester.
- The **Pearson eText** lets students access their textbook anytime, anywhere, and anyway they want, including *listening online*. The eText for *Racial and Ethnic Groups* features integrated videos, Social Explorer activities, additional readings and interactive self-quizzes.
- A **Personalized Study Plan** for each student, based on Bloom's Taxonomy, arranges activities from those that require less complex thinking—like remembering and understanding—to more complex critical thinking—like applying and analyzing. This layered approach promotes better critical thinking skills, helping students succeed in the course and beyond.

New Features of MySocLab Two exciting new features of MySocLab are Social Explorer and MySocLibrary.

- **Social Explorer** activities connect with topics from the text, engaging students with data visualizations, comparisons of change over time, and data localized to their own communities.
- **MySocLibrary** available in the Pearson eText are 200 classic and contemporary articles that enable students to explore the discipline more deeply. Multiple choice questions for each reading help students review what they've learned—and allow instructors to monitor their performance.

Acknowledgments

The fourteenth edition was improved by the suggestions of:

Tanetta Andersson, Central Connecticut State University
Michelle Bentz, Central Community College-Columbus Campus
Mary Donaghy, Arkansas State University
Elena Ermolaeva, Marshall University
Mominka Filey, Davenport University
Dr. Lloyd Ganey, College of Southern Nevada

Malcolm Gold, Malone University

Lisa Munoz, Hawkeye Community College

Jose Soto, Southeast Community College

Gerald Titchener, Des Moines Area Community College

I would also like to thank my publisher at Pearson, Charlyce Jones-Owen, for developing this fourteenth edition. Her long experience, love of history, and appreciation of books combine to enrich this and every academic book with which she is associated. My appreciation also extends to Editor in Chief Dickson Musslewhite for his encouragement and support for my textbooks on race and ethnicity.

The truly exciting challenge of writing and researching has always been for me an enriching experience, mostly because of the supportive home I share with my wife, Sandy. She knows so well my appreciation and gratitude, now as in the past and in the future.

Richard T. Schaefer
schaeferrt@aol.com
www.schaefersociology.net

About the Author

Richard T. Schaefer grew up in Chicago at a time when neighborhoods were going through transitions in ethnic and racial composition. He found himself increasingly intrigued by what was happening, how people were reacting, and how these changes were affecting neighborhoods and people's jobs. In high school, he took a course in sociology. His interest in social issues caused him to gravitate to more sociology courses at Northwestern University, where he eventually received a B.A. in sociology.

"Originally as an undergraduate I thought I would go on to law school and become a lawyer. But after taking a few sociology courses, I found myself wanting to learn more about what sociologists studied and was fascinated by the kinds of questions they raised," Dr. Schaefer says. "Perhaps most fascinating and, to me, relevant to the 1960s was the intersection of race, gender, and social class." This interest led him to obtain his M.A. and Ph.D. in sociology from the University of Chicago. Dr. Schaefer's continuing interest in race relations led him to write his master's thesis on the membership of the Ku Klux Klan and his doctoral thesis on racial prejudice and race relations in Great Britain.

Dr. Schaefer went on to become a professor of sociology. He has taught sociology and courses on multiculturalism for 30 years. He has been invited to give special presentations to students and faculty on racial and ethnic diversity in Illinois, Indiana, Missouri, North Carolina, Ohio, and Texas.

Dr. Schaefer is the author of *Racial and Ethnic Diversity in the USA* (Pearson 2014) and *Race Matters,* seventh edition (Pearson, 2012). Dr. Schaefer is the general editor of the three-volume *Encyclopedia of Race, Ethnicity, and Society* (2008). He is also the author of the thirteenth edition of *Sociology* (2012), the eleventh edition of *Sociology: A Brief Introduction* (2015), third edition *Sociology: A Modular Approach* (2015), and the sixth edition of *Sociology Matters* (2013). Schaefer coauthored with William Zellner the ninth edition of *Extraordinary Groups* (2011), which, in 2014, was translated into Japanese. His articles and book reviews have appeared in many journals, including *American Journal of Sociology, Phylon: A Review of Race and Culture, Contemporary Sociology, Sociology and Social Research, Sociological Quarterly,* and *Teaching Sociology.* He served as president of the Midwest Sociological Society from 1994 to 1995. In recognition of his achievements in undergraduate teaching, he was named Vincent de Paul Professor of Sociology in 2004.

Racial and Ethnic Groups

Fourteenth Edition

1

Exploring Race and Ethnicity

1-1 Explain how groups are ranked.

1-2 Describe the different types of groups.

1-3 Explain what is meant by race being socially constructed.

1-4 Define biracial and multiracial identity.

1-5 Describe how sociology helps us understand race and ethnicity.

1-6 Restate the creation of subordinate groups.

1-7 Use the Spectrum of Intergroup Relations.

1-8 Restate the consequences of subordinate groups.

1-9 Articulate how change occurs in racial and ethnic relations.

Lewiston, Maine, was dying. Now Lewiston is thriving, even in the midst of a national recession. This city changed its future. In 2000, the community of about 36,000, of which 96 percent were White, mostly of French and Irish descent, was going nowhere. The textile mills were shuttered and massive social welfare programs were created locally to meet the needs of the people. It was little wonder that nearby resident Stephen King often chose its abandoned mills and other buildings as inspiration for his suspense novels.

In February 2001, Black Africans, originally from Somalia and of the Muslim faith, began to settle in Lewiston from other areas throughout the United States. With few job opportunities and well-known long, cold winters, it seemed an unlikely destination for people whose homeland was hot and mostly arid. Better schools, little crime, cheap housing, and good social welfare programs attracted the initial arrivals. Once a small group was established, more and more Somalis arrived as the first group shared their positive experiences with friends and relatives. Not everyone stayed because of the winters or unrelated explanations, yet they continued to come.

The numbers of arrivals ebbed and flowed—the increased immigration regulations after 9/11 made entry difficult for Arab Muslims such as the Somali immigrants. One mayor in 2002 issued a public letter encouraging Somalis not to come; his actions were widely denounced. Another man threw a pig's head into a local mosque during evening prayers. Muslims by tradition cannot touch, much less eat, pork. Politicians continue to make unwelcoming comments, but they are quickly drowned out by those who are supportive of the 6,000-plus Somali community. For their part, the Somalis have settled in and are raising their children, but they are concerned that their sons and daughters identify more with being American than with being Somali. Despite their limited resources, as a community they send about $300,000 a month to friends and relatives in Somalia who continue to face incredible hardship.

For over ten years, they have come to Lewiston—10 to 30 *every week*. Lewiston is thriving in a state that continues to face many challenges. A decade is not a long time to reach conclusions about race, religion, and immigration. Somalis, who now account for about 15 percent of the population, have graduated from the local community college, run for office, and opened up dozens of previously shuttered businesses. Others commute the 20 miles to L.L.Bean warehouses to work (Canfield 2012; Cullen 2011; Hammond 2010; Huisman et al. 2011; Tice 2007).

The struggles of racial, ethnic, language, and religious minorities have often required their organized efforts to overcome inequities. Significant White support but also organized resistance typically mark these struggles. The various groups that make the United States diverse do not speak with one voice. For example, the Somalis of Maine are made up of different ethnic or tribal groups. Most are Bantu, who were targeted during the 1991 civil war, fled to refugee camps in Kenya, came to the United States, and resettled in Maine. They still see themselves as different from other ethnic groups from Somalia.

One aspect of the struggle to overcome inequality is the continuing effort to identify strategies and services to assist minorities in their struggle to overcome prejudice and discrimination. Among the beneficiaries of programs aimed at racial and ethnic minorities are White Americans, who, far from all being affluent themselves, have also experienced challenges in their lives.

The election and reelection of the nation's first African American president (who incidentally carried three states of the former Confederacy) presents the temptation to declare that issues of racial inequality are past or racism is limited to a few troublemakers. Progress has been made and expressions of explicit

Lewiston, Maine, a town undergoing difficult economic times over the last 20 years, received a boost from the arrival of Somalis from Africa who have now established a viable community.

TABLE 1.1
Racial and Ethnic Groups in the United States

Classification	Number in Thousands	Percentage of Total Population
RACIAL GROUPS		
Whites (non-Hispanic)	195,371	60.3
Blacks/African Americans	37,686	12.2
Native Americans, Alaskan Natives	2,247	0.7
Asian Americans	15,553	5.0
Chinese	3,347	1.1
Asian Indians	2,843	0.9
Filipinos	2,556	0.8
Vietnamese	1,548	0.5
Koreans	1,424	0.5
Japanese	763	0.2
Pacific Islanders, Native Hawaiians	1,847	0.6
Other Asian Americans	1,225	0.5
Arab Americans	1,517	0.5
Two or more races	9,009	2.9
ETHNIC GROUPS		
White ancestry		
Germans	49,341	16.0
Irish	35,664	11.6
English	26,873	8.7
Italians	17,486	5.7
Poles	9,757	3.2
French	9,159	3.0
Scottish and Scots-Irish	9,122	3.0
Jews	5,425	1.8
Hispanics (or Latinos)	50,478	16.4
Mexican Americans	31,798	10.3
Puerto Ricans	4,624	1.5
Cubans	1,785	0.6
Salvadorans	1,648	0.5
Dominicans	1,415	0.5
Guatemalans	1,044	0.3
Other Hispanics	8,164	2.7
TOTAL (ALL GROUPS)	308,746	

Note: Arab American population excluded from White total. All data are for 2010. Percentages do not total 100 percent, and when subcategories are added, they do not match totals in major categories because of overlap between groups (e.g., Polish American Jews or people of mixed ancestry such as Irish and Italian).

Source: American Community Survey 2011b: Table C04006; Asi and Beaulieu 2013; DellaPergola 2012; Ennis, Rosc Vargas and Albert 2011; Hixson, Hepler, and Kim 2012; Hoeffel, Rastogi, Kim, and Shahid 2012; Humes, Jones, and Ramirez 2011; Norris, Vines, and Hoeffel 2012.

racism are rarely tolerated, yet challenges remain for immigrants of any color and racial, ethnic, and religious minorities (Massey 2011).

The United States is a diverse nation and is becoming even more so, as shown in Table 1.1. In 2010, approximately 40 percent of the population were members of racial minorities or were Hispanic. This represents one out of three people in the United States, without counting White ethnic groups or foreign-born Whites.

As shown in Figure 1.1, between 2010 and 2060, the Black, Hispanic, Asian, Arab, and Native American population along with those identifying as biracial or multiracial in the United States is expected to increase to about 63 percent. Although the composition of the population is changing, problems of prejudice, discrimination, and mistrust remain.

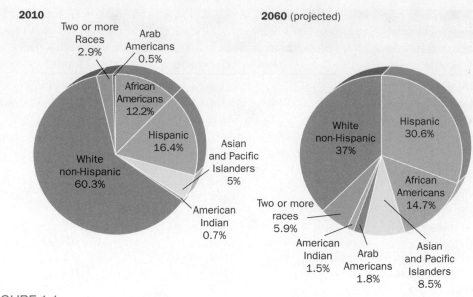

FIGURE 1.1

Population of the United States by Race and Ethnicity, 2010 and 2060 (Projected)

According to projections by the Census Bureau, the proportion of residents of the United States who are White and non-Hispanic will decrease significantly by the year 2060. By contrast, the proportion of both Hispanic Americans and Asian Americans will rise significantly.

Source: Bureau of the Census 2013b: Table 4, sources listed in Table 1.1, and author estimates.

This trend toward "majority-minority" got underway noticeably in 2011 when Latino and non-White babies outnumbered White newborns for the first time in the United States (Bureau of the Census 2012d).

Ranking Groups

1-1 Explain how groups are ranked.

In every society, not all groups are treated or viewed equally. Identifying a subordinate group or a minority in a society seems to be a simple task. In the United States, the groups readily identified as minorities—Blacks and Native Americans, for example—are outnumbered by non-Blacks and non–Native Americans. However, having minority status is not necessarily a result of being outnumbered. A social minority need not be a mathematical one. A **minority group** is a subordinate group whose members have significantly less control or power over their own lives than do the members of a dominant or majority group. In sociology, *minority* means the same as *subordinate*, and *dominant* is used interchangeably with *majority*.

Confronted with evidence that a particular minority in the United States is subordinate to the majority, some people respond, "Why not? After all, this is a democracy, so the majority rules." However, the subordination of a minority involves more than its inability to rule over society. A member of a subordinate or minority group experiences a narrowing of life's opportunities—for success, education, wealth, the pursuit of happiness—that goes beyond any personal shortcoming he or she may have. A minority group does not share in proportion to its numbers what a given society, such as the United States, defines as valuable.

Being superior in numbers does not guarantee a group has control over its destiny or ensure majority status. In 1920, the majority of people in Mississippi and South Carolina were African Americans. Yet African Americans did not have as much control over their lives as did Whites, let alone control of the states in which they lived. Throughout the United States today are counties or neighborhoods in which the majority of people are African American, Native American, or Hispanic, but White Americans are the dominant force. Nationally, 50.7 percent of the population is female, but males still dominate positions of authority and wealth well beyond their numbers.

A minority or subordinate group has five characteristics: unequal treatment, distinguishing physical or cultural traits, involuntary membership, awareness of subordination, and in-group marriage (Wagley and Harris 1958):

1. Members of a minority experience unequal treatment and have less power over their lives than members of a dominant group have over theirs. Prejudice, discrimination, segregation, and even extermination create this social inequality.

2. Members of a minority group share physical or cultural characteristics such as skin color or language that distinguish them from the dominant group. Each society has its own arbitrary standard for determining which characteristics are most important in defining dominant and minority groups.

3. Membership in a dominant or minority group is not voluntary: People are born into the group. A person does not choose to be African American or White.

4. Minority-group members have a strong sense of group solidarity. William Graham Sumner, writing in 1906, noted that people make distinctions between members of their own group (the in-group) and everyone else (the out-group). When a group is the object of long-term prejudice and discrimination, the feeling of "us versus them" often becomes intense.

5. Members of a minority generally marry others from the same group. A member of a dominant group often is unwilling to join a supposedly inferior minority by marrying one of its members. In addition, the minority group's sense of solidarity encourages marriage within the group and discourages marriage to outsiders.

Although "minority" status is not about numbers, there is no denying that the White American majority is diminishing in size relative to the growing diversity of racial and ethnic groups, as illustrated in Figure 1.2.

Using available population projects, which are heavily influenced by estimating future immigration patterns, the White population will be outnumbered by other racial groups and Hispanics somewhere between 2040 and 2045 or before the time people born now turn 30 years of age. The move to a more diverse nation—one in which no

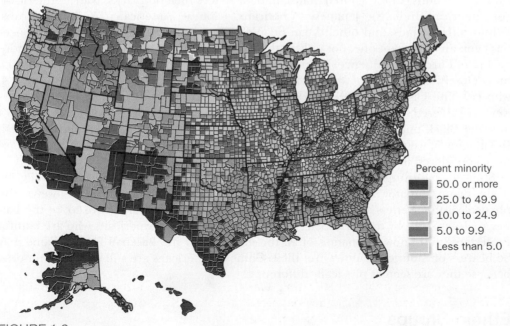

Percent minority
- 50.0 or more
- 25.0 to 49.9
- 10.0 to 24.9
- 5.0 to 9.9
- Less than 5.0

FIGURE 1.2
Minority Population by County

In four states (California, Hawaii, New Mexico, and Texas) and the District of Columbia, as well as in about one out of every nine of counties, minorities constitute the numerical majority.

Source: Jones-Puthoff 2013: slide 5.

group is the numerical minority—will have social impact in everything from marriage patterns, housing, political party politics, health care delivery, and education (Bureau of the Census 2013b).

Types of Groups

1-2 Describe the different types of groups.

There are four types of minority or subordinate groups. All four, except where noted, have the five properties previously outlined. The four criteria for classifying minority groups are race, ethnicity, religion, and gender.

Racial Groups

The term **racial group** is reserved for minorities and the corresponding majorities that are socially set apart because of obvious physical differences. Notice the two crucial words in the definition: *obvious* and *physical*. What is obvious? Hair color? Shape of an earlobe? Presence of body hair? To whom are these differences obvious, and why? Each society defines what it finds obvious.

In the United States, skin color is one obvious difference. People in the United States have learned informally that skin color is important. In the United States, people have traditionally classified themselves as either Black or White. There is no in-between state except for people readily identified as Native Americans or Asian Americans. Later in this chapter, we explore this issue more deeply and see how such assumptions about race have complex implications.

Other societies use skin color as a standard but may have a more elaborate system of classification. In Brazil, where hostility between races is less prevalent than in the United States, numerous categories identify people on the basis of skin color or tone. In the United States, a person is Black or White. In Brazil, a variety of terms such as *cafuso*, *mazombo*, *preto*, and *escuro* are used to describe various combinations of skin color, facial features, and hair texture.

The designation of a racial group emphasizes physical differences as opposed to cultural distinctions. In the United States, minority races include Blacks, Native Americans (or American Indians), Japanese Americans, Chinese Americans, Arab Americans, Filipinos, Hawaiians, and other Asian peoples. The issue of race and racial differences has been an important one, not only in the United States but also throughout the entire sphere of European influence. Later in this chapter, we examine race and its significance more closely. We should not forget that Whites are a race, too. As we consider in Chapter 4, who is White has been subject to change over history when certain European groups were considered not worthy of being considered White. Partly to compete against a growing Black population, the "Whiting" of some European Americans has occurred. In Chapter 5, we will consider how Italians and Irish for all intents and purposes were once considered not to be White by others.

Some racial groups also may have unique cultural traditions, as we can readily see in the many Chinatowns throughout the United States. For racial groups, however, the physical distinctiveness and not the cultural differences generally prove to be the barrier to acceptance by the host society. For example, Chinese Americans who are faithful Protestants and know the names of all the members of the Baseball Hall of Fame may be bearers of American culture. Yet these Chinese Americans are still part of a minority because they are seen as physically different.

Ethnic Groups

Ethnic minority groups are differentiated from the dominant group on the basis of cultural differences such as language, attitudes toward marriage and parenting, and food habits. **Ethnic groups** are groups set apart from others because of their national origin or distinctive cultural patterns.

1-2

Ethnic groups in the United States include a grouping that we call *Hispanics* or *Latinos*, which, in turn, include Mexican Americans, Puerto Ricans, Cubans, and other Latin American residents of the United States. Hispanics can be either Black or White, as in the case of a dark-skinned Puerto Rican who may be taken as Black in central Texas but may be viewed as Puerto Rican in New York City. The ethnic group category also includes White ethnics such as Irish Americans, Polish Americans, and Norwegian Americans.

The cultural traits that make groups distinctive usually originate from their home-lands or, for Jews, from a long history of being segregated and prohibited from becoming a part of a host society. Once living in the United States, an immigrant group may maintain distinctive cultural practices through associations, clubs, and worship. Ethnic enclaves such as a Little Haiti or a Greektown in urban areas also perpetuate cultural distinctiveness.

Ethnicity and race has been long recognized as an important source of differentiation. More than a century ago, African American sociologist W. E. B. Du Bois, addressing an audience at a world antislavery convention in London in 1900, called attention to the overwhelming importance of the color line throughout the world. In "Listen to Our Voices," we read the remarks of Du Bois, the first Black person to receive a doctorate from Harvard, who later helped to organize the National Association for the Advancement of Colored People (NAACP). Du Bois's observations give us a historic perspective on the struggle for equality. We can look ahead, knowing how far we have come and speculating on how much farther we have to go.

🎙 Speaking Out

Problem of the Color Line

In the metropolis of the modern world, in this the closing year of the nineteenth century, there has been assembled a congress of men and women of African blood, to deliberate solemnly upon the present situation and outlook of the darker races of mankind. The problem of the twentieth century is the problem of the color line, the question as to how far differences of race—which show themselves chiefly in the color of the skin and the texture of the hair—will hereafter be made the basis of denying to over half the world the right of sharing to their utmost ability the opportunities and privileges of modern civilization....

To be sure, the darker races are today the least advanced in culture according to European standards. This has not, however, always been the case in the past, and certainly the world's history, both ancient and modern, has given many instances of no despicable ability and capacity among the blackest races of men.

In any case, the modern world must remember that in this age when the ends of the world are being brought so near together, the millions of black men in Africa, America, and Islands of the Sea, not to speak of the brown and yellow myriads elsewhere, are bound to have a great influence upon the world in the future, by reason of sheer numbers and physical contact. If now the

W. E. B. Du Bois

world of culture bends itself towards giving Negroes and other dark men the largest and broadest opportunity for education and self-development, then this contact and influence is bound to have a beneficial effect upon the world and hasten human progress. But if, by reason of carelessness, prejudice, greed, and injustice, the black world is to be exploited and ravished and degraded, the results must be deplorable, if not fatal—not simply to them, but to the high ideals of justice, freedom and culture which a thousand years of Christian civilization have held before Europe....

Let the world take no backward step in that slow but sure progress which has successively refused to let the spirit of class, of caste, of privilege, or of birth, debar from life, liberty, and the pursuit of happiness a striving human soul.

Let not color or race be a feature of distinction between White and Black men, regardless of worth or ability....

Thus we appeal with boldness and confidence to the Great Powers of the civilized world, trusting in the wide spirit of humanity, and the deep sense of justice of our age, for a generous recognition of the righteousness of our cause.

Source: From W. E. B. Du Bois 1900 [1969a], *An ABC of Color*, pp. 20–21, 23. Copyright 1900 by International Publishers.

1-3

We also should appreciate the context of Du Bois's insight. He spoke of his "color-line" prediction in light of then-contemporary U.S. occupation of the Philippines and the relationship of "darker to lighter races" worldwide. So today, he would see race matters not only in the sporadic hate crimes we hear about but also in global conflicts (Roediger 2009).

Religious Groups

Association with a religion other than the dominant faith is the third basis for minority-group status. In the United States, Protestants, as a group, outnumber members of all other religions. Roman Catholics form the largest minority religion. For people who are not a part of the Christian tradition, such as followers of Islam, allegiance to their faith often is misunderstood and stigmatizes people. This stigmatization became especially widespread and legitimated by government action in the aftermath of the attacks of September 11, 2001.

Religious minorities include groups such as the Church of Jesus Christ of Latter-day Saints (the Mormons), Jehovah's Witnesses, Amish, Muslims, and Buddhists. Cults or sects associated with practices such as animal sacrifice, doomsday prophecy, demon worship, or the use of snakes in a ritualistic fashion also constitute religious minorities. Jews are excluded from this category and placed among ethnic groups. Culture is a more important defining trait for Jewish people worldwide than is religious doctrine. Jewish Americans share a cultural tradition that goes beyond theology. In this sense, it is appropriate to view them as an ethnic group rather than as members of a religious faith.

Gender Groups

Gender is another attribute that creates dominant and subordinate groups. Males are the social majority; females, although numerous, are relegated to the position of the social minority. Women are considered a minority even though they do not exhibit all the characteristics outlined earlier (e.g., there is little in-group marriage). Women encounter prejudice and discrimination and are physically distinguishable. Group membership is involuntary, and many women have developed a sense of sisterhood.

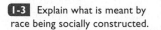
1-3 Explain what is meant by race being socially constructed.

Women who are members of racial and ethnic minorities face special challenges to achieving equality. They suffer from greater inequality because they belong to two separate minority groups: a racial or ethnic group plus a subordinate gender group.

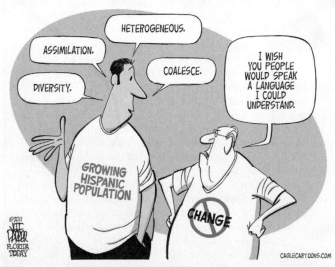

The changing landscape of the United States is hard to miss, but not all people equally embrace it.

Other Subordinate Groups

This book focuses on groups that meet a set of criteria for subordinate status. People encounter prejudice or are excluded from full participation in society for many reasons. Racial, ethnic, religious, and gender barriers are the main ones, but there are others. Age, disability status, physical appearance, and sexual orientation are among the factors that are used to subordinate groups of people.

Does Race Matter?

We see people around us—some of whom may look quite different from us. Do these differences matter? The simple answer is no, but because so many people have for so long acted as if differences in physical characteristics as well as geographic origin and shared culture do matter, distinct groups have been created in people's minds. Race has many meanings for many people. Often these meanings are inaccurate and based on theories scientists discarded generations ago. As we will see, race is a socially constructed concept (Young 2003).

Biological Meaning

The way the term *race* has been used by some people to apply to human beings lacks any scientific basis. Distinctive physical characteristics for groups of human beings cannot be identified the same way that scientists distinguish one animal species from another. The idea of **biological race** is based on the mistaken notion of a genetically isolated human group.

Absence of Pure Races   Even past proponents of the belief that sharp, scientific divisions exist among humans had endless debates over what the races of the world were. Given people's frequent migration, exploration, and invasions, pure genetic types have not existed for some time, if they ever did. There are no mutually exclusive races. Skin tone among African Americans varies tremendously, as it does among White Americans. There is even an overlapping of dark-skinned Whites and light-skinned African Americans. If we grouped people by genetic resistance to malaria and by fingerprint patterns, then Norwegians and many African groups would be the same race. If we grouped people by lactose intolerance some Africans, Asians, and southern Europeans would be of one group and West Africans and northern Europeans of another (Leehotz 1995; Shanklin 1994).

Biologically, no pure, distinct races exist. Research as a part of the Human Genome Project mapping human deoxyribonucleic acid (DNA) has served to confirm genetic diversity only, with differences within traditionally regarded racial groups (e.g., Black Africans) much greater than that between groups (e.g., between Black Africans and Europeans). Contemporary studies of DNA on a global basis have determined that about 90 percent of human genetic variation is within "local populations," such as within the French or within the Afghan people. The remaining 10 percent of total human variation is what we think of today as constituting races and accounts for skin tone, hair texture, nose shape, and so forth (Feldman 2010).

Research has also been conducted to determine whether personality characteristics such as temperament and nervous habits are inherited among minority groups. It is no surprise that the question of whether races have different innate levels of intelligence has led to the most explosive controversies (Bamshad and Olson 2003; El-Haj 2007).

Intelligence Tests   Typically, intelligence is measured as an **intelligence quotient (IQ)**, which is the ratio of a person's mental age to his or her chronological age, multiplied by 100, with 100 representing average intelligence and higher scores representing greater intelligence. It should be noted that there is little consensus over just what intelligence is, other than as defined by such IQ tests. Intelligence tests are adjusted for a person's age so that 10-year-olds take a different test from someone 20 years old. Although research shows that certain learning strategies can improve a person's IQ, generally IQ remains stable as one ages.

A great deal of debate continues over the accuracy of IQ tests. Are they biased toward people who come to the tests with knowledge similar to that of the test writers? Skeptics argue that questions in IQ tests do not truly measure intellectual potential. The

question of cultural bias in tests remains a concern. The most recent research shows that differences in intelligence scores between Blacks and Whites are almost eliminated when adjustments are made for social and economic characteristics (Brooks-Gunn, Klebanov, and Duncan 1996; Kagan 1971; Young 2003).

In 1994, an 845-page book unleashed another national debate on the issue of IQ. The research efforts of psychologist Richard J. Herrnstein and social scientist Charles Murray, published in *The Bell Curve* (1994), concluded that 60 percent of IQ is inheritable and that racial groups offer a convenient means to generalize about any differences in intelligence. Unlike most other proponents of the race–IQ link, the authors offered policy suggestions that included ending welfare to discourage births among low-IQ poor women and changing immigration laws so that the IQ pool in the United States is not diminished. Herrnstein and Murray even made generalizations about IQ levels among Asians and Hispanics in the United States, groups subject to even more intermarriage. In spite of *The Bell Curve* "research," it is not possible to generalize about absolute differences between groups, such as Latinos versus Whites, when almost half of Latinos in the United States marry non-Hispanics.

More than a decade later, the mere mention of the "bell curve" still signals to many people a belief in a racial hierarchy, with Whites toward the top and Blacks near the bottom. The research present then and repeated today points to the difficulty in definitions: What is intelligence, and what constitutes a racial group, given generations (if not centuries) of intermarriage? How can we speak of definitive inherited racial differences if there has been intermarriage between people of every color? Furthermore, as people on both sides of the debate have noted, regardless of the findings, we would still want to strive to maximize the talents of each individual. All research shows that the differences within a group are much greater than any alleged differences between group averages.

Why does such IQ research reemerge if the data are subject to different interpretations? The argument that "we" are superior to "them" is appealing to the dominant group. It justifies receiving opportunities that are denied to others. We can anticipate that the debate over IQ and the allegations of significant group differences will continue. Policymakers need to acknowledge the difficulty in treating race as a biologically significant characteristic.

Social Construction of Race

If race does not distinguish humans from one another biologically, then why does it seem to be so important? It is important because of the social meaning people have attached to it. The 1950 (UNESCO) Statement on Race maintains that the scientific use of race is not a biological phenomenon (Montagu 1972:118).

Race is a social construction, and this process benefits the oppressor, who defines which groups of people are privileged and which groups are not. The acceptance of race in a society as a legitimate category allows racial hierarchies to emerge to the benefit of the dominant "races." For example, inner-city drive-by shootings are now seen as a race-specific problem worthy of local officials cleaning up troubled neighborhoods. Yet school shootings are viewed as a societal concern and placed on the national agenda.

People could speculate that if human groups have obvious physical differences, then they could have corresponding mental or personality differences. No one disagrees that people differ in temperament, potential to learn, and sense of humor, among other characteristics. In its social sense, race implies that groups that differ physically also bear distinctive emotional and mental abilities or disabilities. These beliefs are based on the notion that humankind can be divided into distinct groups. We have already seen the difficulties associated with pigeonholing people into racial categories. Despite these difficulties, belief in the inheritance of behavior patterns and in an association between physical and cultural traits is widespread. It is called **racism** when this belief is coupled with the feeling that certain groups or races are inherently superior to others. Racism is a doctrine of racial supremacy that states one race is superior to another (Bash 2001; Bonilla-Silva 1996).

We questioned the biological significance of race in the previous section. In modern complex industrial societies, we find little adaptive utility in the presence or absence of prominent chins, epicanthic eye fold associated with Eastern and Central Asian peoples, or the comparative amount of melanin in the skin. It is of little importance that people are genetically different; what is important is that they approach one another with dissimilar perspectives. It is in the social setting that race is decisive. Race is significant because people have given it significance.

Race definitions are crystallized through what Michael Omi and Howard Winant (1994) called **racial formation**, a sociohistorical process by which racial categories are created, inhabited, transformed, and destroyed. Those in power define groups of people in a certain way that depends on a racist social structure. As in the United States, these definitions can become systematic and embedded in many aspects of society for a significant length of time. No one escapes the extent and frequency to which we are subjected to racial formation. The Native Americans and the creation of the reservation system for Native Americans in the late 1800s is an example of this racial formation. The federal American Indian policy combined previously distinctive tribes into a single group (Feagin, Cobas, and Elias 2012).

With rising immigration from Latin America in the latter part of the twentieth century, the fluid nature of racial formation is evident. As if it happened in one day, people in the United States have spoken about the Latin Americanization of the United States or stated that the biracial order of Black and White has been replaced with a *triracial* order. We examine this social context of the changing nature of diversity to understand how scholars have sought to generalize about intergroup relations in the United States and elsewhere (Bonilla-Silva and Dietrich 2011; Frank, Akresh, and Lu 2010).

In the southern United States, the social construction of race was known as the "one-drop rule." This tradition stipulated that if a person had even a single drop of "Black blood," that person was defined and viewed as Black. Today, children of biracial or multiracial marriages try to build their own identities in a country that seems intent on placing them in some single, traditional category—a topic we look at next.

Biracial and Multiracial Identity: Who Am I?

People are now more willing to accept and advance identities that do not fit neatly into mutually exclusive categories. Hence, increasing numbers of people are identifying themselves as biracial or multiracial or, at the very least, explicitly viewing themselves as reflecting a diverse racial and ethnic identity. Barack Obama is the most visible person with a biracial background. President Obama has explicitly stated he sees himself as a Black man, although his mother was White and he was largely raised by his White grandparents. Yet in 2010, he chose only to check the "Black, African American, or Negro) box on his household's census form. Obviously, biracial does not mean biracial identity.

1-4 Define biracial and multiracial identity.

The diversity of the United States today has made it more difficult for many people to place themselves on the racial and ethnic landscape. It reminds us that racial formation continues to take place. Obviously, the racial and ethnic landscape, as we have seen, is constructed not naturally but socially and, therefore, is subject to change and different interpretations. Although our focus is on the United States, almost every nation faces the same problems.

The United States tracks people by race and ethnicity for myriad reasons, ranging from attempting to improve the status of oppressed groups to diversifying classrooms. But how can we measure the growing number of people whose ancestry is mixed by anyone's definition? In the Research Focus, we consider how the U.S. Bureau of the Census dealt with this issue.

Besides the increasing respect for biracial identity and multiracial identity, group names undergo change as well. Within little more than a generation during the twentieth century, labels that were applied to subordinate groups changed from *Negroes* to *Blacks* to *African Americans*, from *American Indians* to *Native Americans* or *Native Peoples*. However, more Native Americans prefer the use of their tribal name, such as *Seminole*, instead of

1-4 **Q** Research Focus

Multiracial Identity

Approaching Census 2000, a movement was spawned by people who were frustrated by government questionnaires that forced them to indicate only one race. Take the case of Stacey Davis in New Orleans. The young woman's mother is Thai and her father is Creole, a blend of Black, French, and German. People seeing Stacey confuse her for a Latina, Filipina, or Hawaiian. Officially, she has been "White" all her life because she looks White. The census in 2000 for the first time gave people the option to check off one or more racial groups. "Biracial" or "multiracial" was not an option because pretests showed very few people would use it. This meant that in Census 2000 the government recognized different social constructions of racial identity—that is, a person could be Asian American and White.

Most people did select one racial category in Census 2000 and again in 2010. Overall, approximately 9 million people, or 2.9 percent of the total population, selected two or more racial groups in 2010. This was a smaller proportion than many observers had anticipated. In fact, not even the majority of mixed-race couples identified their children with more than one racial classification. As shown in Figure 1.3, Whites and African Americans were the most common multiple identity, with 1.8 million people or so selecting that response. As a group, American Indians were most likely to select a second category and Whites least likely. Race is socially defined.

Complicating the situation is that, in the Census, people are asked separately whether they are Hispanic or non-Hispanic. So a Hispanic person can be any race. In the 2010 Census, 94 percent indicated they were one race, but 6 percent indicated two or more races; this proportion was twice as high than among non-Hispanics. Therefore, Latinos are more likely than non-Hispanics to indicate a multiracial ancestry.

Changes in measuring race and ethnicity is not necessarily over. Already Bureau officials are considering for 2020 adding categories for people of Middle Eastern, North African, or Asian descent. "Hispanic" may even be added as a "race category" along with White, African-American, Asian, and American Indian/Alaska Native and Pacific Islander.

Regardless of government definitions, we know that people do change their racial identity over time, choosing to self-identify as something different. This fluidity in individual actions could well be increased if the nation as a whole appears to be more accepting of biracial and multiracial categories.

The Census Bureau's decision does not necessarily resolve the frustration of hundreds of thousands of people such as Stacey Davis, who daily face people trying to place them in some racial or ethnic category that is convenient. However, it does underscore the complexity of social construction and trying to apply arbitrary definitions to the diversity of the human population. A symbol of this social construction of race can be seen in President Barack Obama, born of a White woman and a Black immigrant from Kenya. Although he has always identified himself as a Black man, it is worthy to note he was born in Hawaii, a state in which 23.6 percent of people see themselves as more than one race, compared to the national average of 2.9 percent.

Sources: DaCosta 2007; Dade 2012a; Grieco and Cassidy 2001; Humes, Jones, and Ramirez 2011: 2–11; Jones and Smith 2001; Saperstein and Penner 2012; Saulny 2011; Welch 2011; Williams 2005.

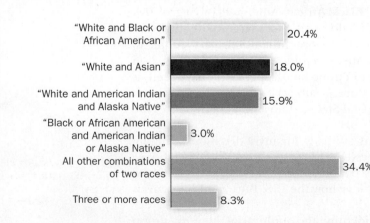

"White and Black or African American" — 20.4%
"White and Asian" — 18.0%
"White and American Indian and Alaska Native" — 15.9%
"Black or African American and American Indian or Alaska Native" — 3.0%
All other combinations of two races — 34.4%
Three or more races — 8.3%

FIGURE 1.3
Multiple-Race Choices in Census 2010

This figure shows the percentage distribution of the 9 million people who chose two or more races (out of the total population of 309 million).

Source: Humes, Jones, and Ramirez 2011:10.

a collective label. The old 1950s statistical term of "people with a Spanish surname" has long been discarded, yet there is disagreement over a new term: *Latino* or *Hispanic*. Like Native Americans, Hispanic Americans avoid such global terms and prefer their native names, such as *Puerto Ricans* or *Cubans*. People of Mexican ancestry indicate preferences for a variety of names, such as *Mexican American*, *Chicano*, or simply *Mexican*.

In the United States and other multiracial, multiethnic societies, **panethnicity**, the development of solidarity between ethnic subgroups, has emerged. The coalition of tribal groups as Native Americans or American Indians to confront outside forces, notably the federal government, is one example of panethnicity. Hispanics or Latinos and Asian Americans are other examples of panethnicity. Although it is rarely recognized by the dominant society, the very term *Black* or *African American* represents the descendants of many different ethnic or tribal groups, such as Akamba, Fulani, Hausa, Malinke, and Yoruba (Lopez and Espiritu 1990).

Is panethnicity a convenient label for "outsiders" or a term that reflects a mutual identity? Certainly, many people outside the group are unable or unwilling to recognize ethnic differences and prefer umbrella terms such as *Asian Americans*. For some small groups, combining with others is emerging as a useful way to make them heard, but there is always a fear that their own distinctive culture will become submerged. Although many Hispanics share the Spanish language and many are united by Roman Catholicism, only one in four native-born people of Mexican, Puerto Rican, or Cuban descent prefers a panethnic label to nationality or ethnic identity. Yet the growth of a variety of panethnic associations among many groups, including Hispanics, continues into the twenty-first century (de la Garza et al. 1992; Espiritu 1992; Steinberg 2007).

Another challenge to identity is **marginality**: the status of being between two cultures, as in the case of a person whose mother is a Jew and father a Christian. A century ago, Du Bois (1903) spoke eloquently of the "double consciousness" that Black Americans feel—caught between being a citizen of the United States but viewed as something quite apart from the dominant social forces of society. Incomplete assimilation by immigrants also results in marginality. Although a Filipino woman migrating to the United States may take on the characteristics of her new host society, she may not be fully accepted and may, therefore, feel neither Filipino nor American. Marginalized individuals often encounter social situations in which their identities are sources of tension, especially when the expression of multiple identities is not accepted, and they find themselves being perceived differently in different environments, with varying expectations (Park 1928; Stonequist 1937; Townsend, Markos, and Bergsieker 2009).

Yet another source of marginality comes from children of biracial or multiracial parental backgrounds and children adopted by parents of a different racial or ethnic background. For these children or adolescents, developing their racial or ethnic identity says more about society's desire to fix labels onto their own actions. (Fryer et al. 2012).

As we seek to understand diversity in the United States, we must be mindful that ethnic and racial labels are just that: labels that have been socially constructed. Yet these social constructs can have a powerful impact, whether self-applied or applied by others.

Sociology and the Study of Race and Ethnicity

Before proceeding further with our study of racial and ethnic groups, let us consider several sociological perspectives that provide insight into dominant–subordinate relationships. **Sociology** is the systematic study of social behavior and human groups, so it is aptly suited to enlarge our understanding of intergroup relations. The study of race relations has a long, valuable history in sociology. Admittedly, it has not always been progressive; indeed, at times it has reflected the prejudices of society. In some instances, sociology scholars who are members of racial, ethnic, and religious minorities, as well as women, have not been permitted to make the kind of contributions they are capable of making to the field.

1-5 Describe how sociology helps us understand race and ethnicity.

Stratification by Class and Gender

That some members of society have unequal amounts of wealth, prestige, or power is a characteristic of all societies. Sociologists observe that entire groups may be assigned less or more of what a society values. The hierarchy that emerges is called **stratification**. Stratification is the structured ranking of entire groups of people that perpetuates unequal rewards and power in a society.

Much discussion of stratification identifies the **class**, or social ranking, of people who share similar wealth, according to sociologist Max Weber's classic definition. Mobility from one class to another is not easy to achieve. Movement into classes of greater wealth may be particularly difficult for subordinate-group members faced with lifelong prejudice and discrimination (Banton 2008; Gerth and Mills 1958).

Recall that the first property of subordinate-group standing is unequal treatment by the dominant group in the form of prejudice, discrimination, and segregation. Stratification is intertwined with the subordination of racial, ethnic, religious, and gender groups. Race has implications for the way people are treated; so does class. One also must add the effects of race and class together. For example, being poor and Black is not the same as being either one by itself. A wealthy Mexican American is not the same as an affluent Anglo American or Mexican Americans as a group.

Public discussion of issues such as housing or public assistance often is disguised as a discussion of class issues, when, in fact, the issues are based primarily on race. Similarly, some topics such as the poorest of the poor or the working poor are addressed in terms of race when the class component should be explicit. Nonetheless, the link between race and class in society is abundantly clear (Winant 2004).

Another stratification factor that we need to consider is gender. How different is the situation for women as contrasted with men? Returning again to the first property of minority groups—unequal treatment and less control—women do not receive treatment that equals that received by men. Whether the issue is jobs or poverty, education or crime, women typically have more difficult experiences. In addition, the situations women face in areas such as health care and welfare raise different concerns than they do for men. Just as we need to consider the role of social class to understand race and ethnicity better, we also need to consider the role of gender.

Theoretical Perspectives

Sociologists view society in different ways. Some see the world basically as a stable and ongoing entity. The endurance of a Chinatown, the general sameness of male–female roles over time, and other aspects of intergroup relations impress them. Some sociologists see society as composed of many groups in conflict, competing for scarce resources. Within this conflict, some people or even entire groups may be labeled or stigmatized in a way that blocks their access to what a society values. We examine three theoretical perspectives that are widely used by sociologists today: the functionalist, conflict, and labelling perspectives.

Functionalist Perspective In the view of a functionalist, a society is like a living organism in which each part contributes to the survival of the whole. The **functionalist perspective** emphasizes how the parts of society are structured to maintain its stability. According to this approach, if an aspect of social life does not contribute to a society's stability or survival, then it will not be passed on from one generation to the next.

It seems reasonable to assume that bigotry between races offers no such positive function, and so we ask, Why does it persist? Although agreeing that racial hostility is hardly to be admired, the functionalist would point out that it serves some positive functions from the perspective of the racists. We can identify five functions that racial beliefs have for the dominant group:

1. Racist ideologies provide a moral justification for maintaining a society that routinely deprives a group of its rights and privileges.

2. Racist beliefs discourage subordinate people from attempting to question their lowly status and why they must perform "the dirty work"; to do so is to question the very foundation of the society.

3. Racial ideologies not only justify existing practices but also serve as a rallying point for social movements, as seen in the rise of the Nazi party or present-day Aryan movements.

4. Racist myths encourage support for the existing order. Some argue that if there were any major societal change, the subordinate group would suffer even greater poverty, and the dominant group would suffer lower living standards.

5. Racist beliefs relieve the dominant group of the responsibility to address the economic and educational problems faced by subordinate groups.

As a result, racial ideology grows when a value system (e.g., that underlying a colonial empire or slavery) is being threatened (Levin and Nolan 2011:115–145; Nash 1962).

Prejudice and discrimination also cause definite dysfunctions. **Dysfunctions** are elements of society that may disrupt a social system or decrease its stability. Racism is dysfunctional to a society, including to its dominant group, in six ways:

1. A society that practices discrimination fails to use the resources of all individuals. Discrimination limits the search for talent and leadership to the dominant group.

2. Discrimination aggravates social problems such as poverty, delinquency, and crime and places the financial burden of alleviating these problems on the dominant group.

3. Society must invest a good deal of time and money to defend the barriers that prevent the full participation of all members.

4. Racial prejudice and discrimination undercut goodwill and friendly diplomatic relations between nations. They also negatively affect efforts to increase global trade.

5. Social change is inhibited because change may assist a subordinate group.

6. Discrimination promotes disrespect for law enforcement and for the peaceful settlement of disputes.

That racism has costs for the dominant group as well as for the subordinate group reminds us that intergroup conflict is exceedingly complex (Bowser and Hunt 1996; Feagin, Vera, and Batur 2000; Rose 1951).

Conflict Perspective In contrast to the functionalists' emphasis on stability, conflict sociologists see the social world as being in continual struggle. The **conflict perspective** assumes that the social structure is best understood in terms of conflict or tension between competing groups. The result of this conflict is significant economic disparity and structural inequality in education, the labor market, housing, and health care delivery. Specifically, society is in a struggle between the privileged (the dominant group) and the exploited (the subordinate group). Such conflicts need not be physically violent and may take the form of immigration restrictions, real estate practices, or disputes over cuts in the federal budget.

The conflict model often is selected today when one is examining race and ethnicity because it readily accounts for the presence of tension between competing groups. According to the conflict perspective, competition takes place between groups with unequal amounts of economic and political power. The minorities are exploited or, at best, ignored by the dominant group. The conflict perspective is viewed as more radical and activist than functionalism because conflict theorists emphasize social change and the redistribution of resources.

Those who follow the conflict approach to race and ethnicity have remarked repeatedly that the subordinate group is criticized for its low status. That the dominant group

1-5

From the conflict perspective, the emphasis should not be primarily on the attributes of the individual (i.e., "blaming the victim") but on structural factors such as the labor market, affordable housing, and availability of programs to assist people with addiction or mental health issues.

is responsible for subordination is often ignored. William Ryan (1976) calls this an instance of **blaming the victim**: portraying the problems of racial and ethnic minorities as their fault rather than recognizing society's responsibility.

Conflict theorists consider the costs that come with residential segregation. Besides the more obvious cost of reducing housing options, racial and social class isolation reduces for people (including Whites) all available options in schools, retail shopping, and medical care. People, however, can travel to access services and businesses, and it is more likely that racial and ethnic minorities will have to make that sometimes costly and time-consuming trip (Carr and Kutty 2008).

Labeling Theory   Related to the conflict perspective and its concern over blaming the victim is **labeling theory**, a concept introduced by sociologist Howard Becker to explain why certain people are viewed as deviant and others engaging in the same behavior are not. Students of crime and deviance have relied heavily on labeling theory. According to labeling theory, a youth who misbehaves may be considered and treated as a delinquent if he or she comes from the "wrong kind of family." Another youth from a middle-class family who commits the same sort of misbehavior might be given another chance before being punished.

The labeling perspective directs our attention to the role that negative stereotypes play in race and ethnicity. The image that prejudiced people maintain of a group toward which they hold ill feelings is called a **stereotype**. Stereotypes are unreliable generalizations about all members of a group that do not take individual differences into account. The warrior image of Native American (American Indian) people is perpetuated by the frequent use of tribal names or even names such as "Indians" and "Redskins" for sports teams. In Chapter 2, we review some of the research on the stereotyping of minorities. This labeling is not limited to racial and ethnic groups, however. For instance, age can be used to exclude a person from an activity in which he or she is qualified to engage. Groups are subjected to stereotypes and discrimination in such a way that their treatment resembles that of social minorities. Social prejudice as a result of stereotyping exists toward ex-convicts, gamblers, alcoholics, lesbians, gays, prostitutes, people with AIDS, and people with disabilities, to name a few.

The labeling approach points out that stereotypes, when applied by people in power, can have negative consequences for people or groups identified falsely. A crucial aspect of the relationship between dominant and subordinate groups is the prerogative of the dominant group to define society's values. U.S. sociologist William I. Thomas (1923), an early critic of racial and gender discrimination, saw that the "definition of the situation" could mold the personality of the individual. In other words, Thomas observed that people respond not only to the objective features of a situation (or person) but also to the meaning these features have for them. So, for example, a lone walker seeing a young Black man walking toward him may perceive the situation differently than if the oncoming person is an older woman. Sociologist Elijah Anderson (2011) has long seen passers-by scrutinize him and other African American males more closely and suspiciously than they would women or White males. In this manner, we can create false images or stereotypes that become real in their social consequences.

In certain situations, we may respond to negative stereotypes and act on them, with the result that false definitions become accurate. This is known as a **self-fulfilling prophecy**. A person or group described as having particular characteristics

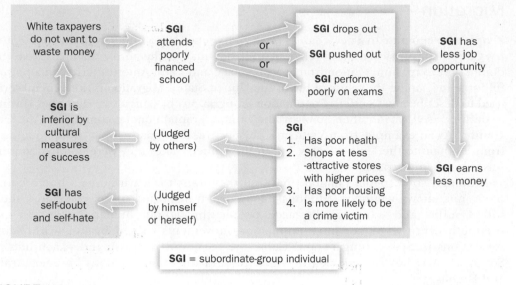

SGI = subordinate-group individual

FIGURE 1.4
Self-Fulfilling Prophecy

The self-validating effects of dominant-group definitions are shown here. The subordinate-group individual attends a poorly financed school and is left unequipped to perform jobs that offer high status and pay. He or she then gets a low-paying job and must settle for a much lower level of society's standard of living. Because the person shares these societal standards, he or she may begin to feel self-doubt and self-hatred.

begvins to display the very traits attributed to him or her. Thus, a child who is praised for being a natural comic may focus on learning to become funny to gain approval and attention.

Self-fulfilling prophecies can be devastating for minority groups (Figure 1.4). Such groups often find that they are allowed to hold only low-paying jobs with little prestige or opportunity for advancement. The rationale of the dominant society is that these minority people lack the ability to perform in more important and lucrative positions. Training to become scientists, executives, or physicians is denied to many subordinate-group individuals (SGIs), who are then locked into society's inferior jobs. As a result, the false definition of the self-fulfilling prophecy becomes real. The subordinate group becomes inferior because it was defined at the start as inferior and was, therefore, prevented from achieving the levels attained by the majority.

Because of this vicious circle, a talented subordinate-group person may come to see the fields of entertainment and professional sports as his or her only hope for achieving wealth and fame. Thus, it is no accident that successive waves of Irish, Jewish, Italian, African American, and Hispanic performers and athletes have made their mark on culture in the United States. Unfortunately, these very successes may convince the dominant group that its original stereotypes were valid—that these are the only areas of society in which subordinate-group members can excel. Furthermore, athletics and the arts are highly competitive areas. For every LeBron James and Jennifer Lopez who makes it, many, many more SGIs will end up disappointed.

The Creation of Subordinate-Group Status

Three situations are likely to lead to the formation of a relationship between a subordinate group and the dominant group. A subordinate group emerges through migration, annexation, and colonialism.

1-6 Restate the creation of subordinate groups.

Migration

People who emigrate to a new country often find themselves a minority in that new country. Cultural or physical traits or religious affiliation may set the immigrant apart from the dominant group. Immigration from Europe, Asia, and Latin America has been a powerful force in shaping the fabric of life in the United States. **Migration** is the general term used to describe any transfer of population. **Emigration** (by emigrants) describes leaving a country to settle in another. **Immigration** (by immigrants) denotes coming into the new country. As an example, from Vietnam's perspective, the "boat people" were emigrants from Vietnam to the United States, but in the United States they were counted among this nation's immigrants.

Although some people migrate because they want to, leaving one's home country is not always voluntary. Millions have been transported as slaves against their will. Conflict and war have displaced people throughout human history. In the twentieth century, we saw huge population movements caused by two world wars; revolutions in Spain,Hungary, and Cuba; the partition of British India; conflicts in Southeast Asia, Korea, and Central America; and the confrontations between Arabs and Israelis.

In all types of movement, even when a U.S. family moves from Ohio to Florida, but especially regarding emigration, two sets of forces operate: push factors and pull factors. Push factors discourage a person from remaining where he or she lives. Religious persecution and economic factors such as dissatisfaction with employment opportunities are possible push factors. Pull factors, such as a better standard of living, friends and relatives who have already emigrated, and a promised job, attract an immigrant to a particular country.

Although generally we think of migration as a voluntary process, much of the population transfer that has occurred in the world has been involuntary. Such forced movement of people into another society guarantees a subordinate role. Involuntary migration is no longer common; although enslavement has a long history, all industrialized societies today prohibit such practices. Of course, many contemporary societies, including the United States, bear the legacy of slavery.

Migration has taken on new significance in the twenty-first century partly because of **globalization**, or the worldwide integration of government policies, cultures, social movements, and financial markets through trade and the exchange of ideas. The increased movement of people and money across borders has made the distinction between temporary and permanent migration less meaningful. Although migration has always been fluid, people in today's global economy are connected across societies culturally and economically as never before. Even after they have relocated, people maintain global linkages to their former country and with a global economy (Richmond 2002).

Annexation

Nations, particularly during wars or as a result of war, incorporate or attach land. This new land is contiguous to the nation, as in the German annexation of Austria and Czechoslovakia in 1938 and 1939 and in the U.S. Louisiana Purchase of 1803. The Treaty of Guadalupe Hidalgo that ended the Mexican–American War in 1848 gave the United States California, Utah, Nevada, most of New Mexico, and parts of Arizona, Wyoming, and Colorado. The indigenous peoples in some of this huge territory were dominant in their society one day, only to become minority-group members the next.

When annexation occurs, the dominant power generally suppresses the language and culture of the minority. Such was the practice of Russia with the Ukrainians and Poles and of Prussia with the Poles. Minorities try to maintain their cultural integrity despite annexation. Poles inhabited an area divided into territories ruled by three countries but maintained their own culture across political boundaries.

Colonialism

Colonialism has been the most common way for one group of people to dominate another. **Colonialism** is the maintenance of political, social, economic, and cultural dominance over people by a foreign power for an extended period (Bell 1991). Colonialism is rule by outsiders but, unlike annexation, does not involve actual incorporation into the dominant people's nation. The long-standing control that was exercised by the British Empire over much of North America, parts of Africa, and India is an example of colonial domination (see Figure 1.5).

Societies gain power over a foreign land through military strength, sophisticated political organization, and investment capital. The extent of power may also vary according to the dominant group's scope of settlement in the colonial land. Relations between the colonizing nation and the colonized people are similar to those between a dominant group and exploited subordinate groups. Colonial subjects generally are limited to menial jobs and the wages from their labor. The natural resources of their land benefit the members of the ruling class.

By the 1980s, colonialism, in the sense of political rule, had become largely a phenomenon of the past, yet industrial countries of North America and Europe still dominated the world economically and politically. Drawing on the conflict perspective, sociologist Immanuel Wallerstein (1974) views the global economic system of today as much like the height of colonial days. Wallerstein has advanced the **world systems theory**, which views the global economic system as divided between nations that control wealth and those that provide natural resources and labor. The limited economic resources available in developing nations exacerbate many of the ethnic, racial, and religious conflicts noted at the beginning of this chapter. In addition, the presence of massive inequality between nations only serves to encourage immigration generally and, more specifically, the movement of many of the most skilled from developing nations to the industrial nations.

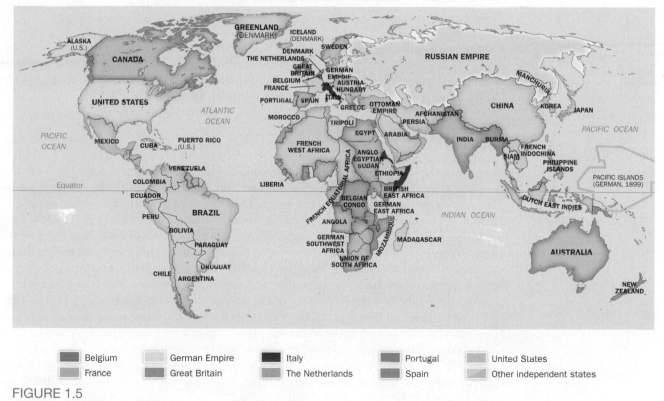

FIGURE 1.5

World Colonial Empires (1900)

Events of the nineteenth century increased European dominance over the world. By 1900, most independent African nations had disappeared, and the major European powers and Japan took advantage of China's internal weakness to gain both trading ports and economic concessions.

Source: Divine, Breen, Williams, Gross & Brands, *America: Past and Present,* Volume 2, 10/e ©2013 | Pearson.

Spectrum of Intergroup Status

1-7 Use the Spectrum of Intergroup Relations.

Relationships between and among racial, ethnic, and religious groups as well as other dominate-subordinate relationships are not static. These relations change over time, sometimes in one's own lifetime. To better illustrate this, we can use the Spectrum of Intergroup Relations illustrated here.

SPECTRUM OF INTERGROUP RELATIONS

EXPULSION	SEGREGATION	ASSIMILATION

INCREASINGLY UNACCEPTABLE   MORE TOLERABLE

EXTERMINATION	SECESSION	FUSION	PLURALISM
or genocide	or partitioning	or amalgamation or melting pot	or multiculturalism

These relationships can be viewed among a continuum from those largely unacceptable to the subordinate group such as extermination and expulsion to those that are more tolerant such as assimilation and pluralism. In the next section we will explore these consequences of group inequality in more detail.

The Consequences of Subordinate-Group Status

1-8 Restate the consequences of subordinate groups.

A group with subordinate status is faced with several consequences. These differ in their degree of harshness, ranging from physical annihilation to absorption into the dominant group. In this section, we examine six consequences of subordinate-group status: extermination, expulsion, secession, segregation, fusion, and assimilation.

Extermination

The most extreme way to deal with a subordinate group is to eliminate it. Today, the term **genocide** is used to describe the deliberate, systematic killing of an entire people or nation. This term is often used in reference to the Holocaust, Nazi Germany's extermination of 12 million European Jews and other ethnic minorities during World War II. The **Holocaust** was the state-sponsored systematic persecution and annihilation of European Jewry by Nazi Germany and its collaborators. The move to eliminate Jews from the European continent started slowly, with Germany gradually restricting the rights of Jews: preventing them from voting, living outside the Jewish ghetto, and owning businesses. Much anti-Semitic cruelty was evident before the beginning of the war. Dramatically, *Kristallnacht*, or the "Night of Broken Glass," in Berlin on November 9, 1938, was a turning point toward genocide. Ninety Berlin Jews were murdered, hundreds of homes and synagogues were set on fire or ransacked, and thousands of Jewish store windows were broken.

Despite the obvious intolerance they faced, Jews desiring to immigrate were often turned back by government officials in Europe and the Americas (Institute for Jewish and Community Research 2008; DellaPergola 2007).

The term **ethnic cleansing** refers to the forced deportation of people, accompanied by systematic violence including death. The term was introduced in 1992 to the world's vocabulary as ethnic Serbs instituted a policy intended to "cleanse"—eliminate—Muslims from parts of Bosnia. Again in 1994, a genocidal war between the Hutu and Tutsi people in Rwanda left 300,000 school-age children orphaned (Chirot and Edwards 2003; Naimark 2004).

Genocide also appropriately describes White policies toward Native Americans in the nineteenth century. In 1800, the American Indian population in the United States was approximately 600,000; by 1850, it had been reduced to 250,000 through warfare with the U.S. Army, disease, and forced relocation to inhospitable environments.

In 2008, the Australian government officially apologized for past treatment of its native people, the Aboriginal population. Not only did this involve brutality and neglect, but also a quarter of their children, the so-called lost generation, were taken from their families and places in orphanages, foster homes, or put up for adoption by White Australians until the policy was finally abandoned in 1969 (Johnston 2008).

Expulsion

Dominant groups may choose to force a specific subordinate group to leave certain areas or even vacate a country. Expulsion, therefore, is another extreme consequence of minority-group status. European colonial powers in North America and eventually the U.S. government itself drove almost all Native Americans out of their tribal lands and into unfamiliar territory.

More recently, beginning in 2009, France expelled over 10,000 ethnic Roma (or Gypsies), forcing their return to their home countries of Bulgaria and Romania. This appeared to violate the European Union's (EU) ban against targeting ethnic groups as well as Europe's policy of "freedom of movement." In 2011, the EU withdrew its threat of legal action against France when the government said it would no longer expel Roma in particular but only those living in "illegal camps," which many observers felt was only a technical way for the country to get around long-standing human rights policies.

Secession

A group ceases to be a subordinate group when it secedes to form a new nation or moves to an already-established nation, where it becomes dominant. After Great Britain withdrew from Palestine, Jewish people achieved a dominant position in 1948, attracting Jews from throughout the world to the new state of Israel. Similarly, Pakistan was created in 1947 when India was partitioned. The predominantly Muslim areas in the north became Pakistan, making India predominantly Hindu. Throughout this century, minorities have repudiated dominant customs. In this spirit, the Estonian, Latvian, Lithuanian, and Armenian peoples, not content to be merely tolerated by the majority, all seceded to form independent states after the demise of the Soviet Union in 1991. In 1999, ethnic Albanians fought bitterly for their cultural and political recognition in the Kosovo region of Yugoslavia.

Some African Americans have called for secession. Suggestions dating back to the early 1700s supported the return of Blacks to Africa as a solution to racial problems. The settlement target of the American Colonization Society was Liberia, but proposals were also advanced to establish settlements in other areas. Territorial separatism and the emigrationist ideology were recurrent and interrelated themes among African Americans from the late nineteenth century well into the 1980s. The Black Muslims, or Nation of Islam, once expressed the desire for complete separation in their own state or territory within the modern borders of the United States. Although a secession of Blacks from the United States has not taken place, it has been proposed.

Stigmatizing and expelling minority groups is not an action of the distance past. Here, police in Paris round up Roma (Gypsies) for subsequent expulsion from the country.

Segregation

Segregation is the physical separation of two groups in residence, workplace, and social functions. Generally, the dominant group imposes segregation on a subordinate group. Segregation is rarely complete; however, intergroup contact inevitably occurs even in the most segregated societies.

Sociologists Douglas Massey and Nancy Denton wrote *American Apartheid* (1993), which described segregation in U.S. cities on the basis of 1990 data. The title of their book was meant to indicate that neighborhoods in the United States resembled the segregation of the rigid government-imposed racial segregation that prevailed for so long in the Republic of South Africa.

Analysis of census data shows continuing segregation despite racial and ethnic diversity in the United States. Scholars use a segregation index to measure separation. This index ranges from 0 (complete integration) to 100 (complete segregation), where the value indicates the percentage of the minority group that needs to move to be distributed exactly like Whites. So a segregation index of 60 for Blacks–Whites would mean that 60 percent of all African Americans would have to move to be residing just like Whites.

In Table 1.2, we look at the most segregated metropolitan areas with large African American, Latino, and Asian American populations. Blacks and Whites are most separated from each other in Detroit; the Los Angeles/Long Beach metropolitan area finds Whites and Latinos most living apart; and the New Brunswick, New Jersey, area is where Asians and Whites are most segregated from each other. Typically half to three-quarters

TABLE 1.2
Segregated Metro America

BLACK–WHITE	
1. Detroit	79.6
2. Milwaukee	79.6
3. New York/White Plains	79.1
4. Newark	78.0
5. Chicago/Naperville	75.9
6. Philadelphia	73.7
7. Miami/Miami Beach	73.0
8. Cleveland	72.6
HISPANIC–WHITE	
1. Los Angeles/Long Beach	63.4
2. New York/White Plains	63.1
3. Newark	62.6
5. Boston	62.0
6. Salinas, CA	60.0
7. Philadelphia	58.8
8. Chicago/Naperville	57.0
9. Oxford/Venture, CA	54.5
ASIAN–WHITE	
1. Edison/New Brunswick, NJ	53.7
2. New York/White Plains	49.5
3. Houston	48.7
4. Los Angeles/Long Beach	47.6
5. Boston	47.4
6. Sacramento, CA	46.8
7. San Francisco	46.7
8. Warren/Farmington Hills MI MI	46.3

Note: The higher the value, the more segregated the metropolitan area.
Source: Logan and Stults 2011.

of the people would have to move to achieve even distribution throughout the city and surrounding suburbs.

Over the last 40 years, Black–White segregation has declined modestly. Hispanic–White segregation, while lower, has not changed significantly in the last 30 years. Asian–White segregation is even a bit lower but also has been mostly unchanged over the three decades. Even when we consider social class, the patterns of minority segregation persist. Despite the occasional multiracial neighborhood, segregation prevails (Bureau of the Census 2010b; Frey 2011; Iceland, Sharp, and Timberlake 2013; Krysan, Farley, and Couper 2008).

This focus on metropolitan areas should not cause us to ignore the continuing legally sanctioned segregation of Native Americans on reservations. Although the majority of our nation's first inhabitants live outside these tribal areas, the reservations play a prominent role in the identity of Native Americans. Although it is easier to maintain tribal identity on the reservation, economic and educational opportunities are more limited in these areas, which are segregated from the rest of society.

A particularly troubling pattern has been the emergence of **resegregation**, or the physical separation of racial and ethnic groups reappearing after a period of relative integration. Resegregation has occurred in neighborhoods and schools after a transitional period of desegregation. For example, in 1954, only 1 in 100,000 Black students attended a majority White school in the South. Thanks to the civil rights movement and a series of civil rights measures, by 1968, the percentage of Black students in White majority schools rose to 23 percent and then to 47 percent by 1988.

The latest analysis, however, shows continuing racial isolation. A 2012 report documents that nationwide, 43 percent of Latinos and 38 percent of Blacks attend schools in which fewer than 10 percent of their classmates are White (Orfield 2007; Orfield, Kucsera and Siegel-Hawley 2012; Orfield and Lee 2005; Rich 2008).

Given segregation patterns, many Whites in the United States have limited contact with people of other racial and ethnic backgrounds. In one study of 100 affluent powerful White men that looked at their experiences past and present, it was clear they had lived in a "White bubble"—their neighborhoods, schools, elite colleges, and workplaces were overwhelmingly White. The continuing pattern of segregation in the United States means our diverse population grows up in very different nations. For many urban Blacks and Latinos, segregation in neighborhoods with limited job opportunities is a social fact (Bonilla-Silva and Embrick 2007; Feagin and O'Brien 2003; Massey 2012).

Segregation by race, ethnicity, religion, tribal or clan affiliation, and sometimes even language grouping occurs throughout the world. The most dramatic government-engineered segregation in recent memory was in South Africa. In 1948, the Great Britain granted South Africa its independence, and the National Party, dominated by a White minority, assumed control of the government. The rule of White supremacy, well under way as the custom in the colonial period, became more and more formalized into law. To deal with the multiracial population, the Whites devised a policy called apartheid to ensure their dominance. **Apartheid** (in Afrikaans, the language of the White Afrikaners, it means *separation* or *apartness*) came to mean a policy of separate development, euphemistically called *multinational development* by the government. Black South Africans were relegated to impoverished urban townships or rural areas and their mobility within the country strictly regulated. Events took a significant turn in 1990, when the South African Prime Minister legalized once-banned Black organizations and freed Nelson Mandela, leader of the African National Congress (ANC), after 27 years of imprisonment. Mandela's triumphant return was soon followed by him becoming head of the government, and a half-century of apartheid came to an end.

Fusion

Fusion occurs when a minority and a majority group combine to form a new group. This combining can be expressed as $A + B + C \rightarrow D$, where A, B, and C represent the groups present in a society and D signifies the result, an ethnocultural–racial group that shares some of the characteristics of each initial group. Mexican people are an example of fusion, originating as they do from the mixing of Spanish and indigenous Indian cultures. Theoretically, fusion does not entail intermarriage, but it is very similar to **amalgamation**, or the process by which a dominant group and a subordinate group combine through intermarriage into a new people. In everyday speech, the words *fusion* and *amalgamation* are rarely used, but the concept is expressed in the notion of a human **melting pot** in which diverse racial or ethnic groups form a new creation, a new cultural entity (Newman 1973).

The analogy of the cauldron, the "melting pot," was first used to describe the United States by the French observer Crèvecoeur in 1782. The phrase dates back to the Middle Ages, when alchemists attempted to change less-valuable metals into gold and silver. Similarly, the idea of the human melting pot implied that the new group would represent only the best qualities and attributes of the different cultures contributing to it. The belief in the United States as a melting pot became widespread in the early twentieth century. This belief suggested that the United States had an almost divine mission to destroy artificial divisions and create a single kind of human. However, the dominant group had indicated its unwillingness to welcome such groups as Native Americans, Blacks, Hispanics, Jews, Asians, and Irish Roman Catholics into the melting pot. It is a mistake to think of the United States as an ethnic mixing bowl. Although superficial signs of fusion are present, as in a cuisine that includes sauerkraut and spaghetti, most contributions of subordinate groups are ignored (Gleason 1980).

Marriage patterns indicate the resistance to fusion. People are unwilling, in varying degrees, to marry outside their own ethnic, religious, and racial groups. Until relatively recently, interracial marriage was outlawed in much of the United States. At the time that President Barack Obama's White mother and Black father were married in Hawaii, their union would have been illegal and unable to occur in 22 other states. Surveys show that 20 to 50 percent of various White ethnic groups report single ancestry. When White ethnics do cross boundaries, they tend to marry within their religion and social class. For example, Italians are more likely to marry Irish, who are also Catholic, than they are to marry Protestant Swedes.

Although it may seem that interracial matches are everywhere, there is only modest evidence of a fusion of races in the United States. Racial intermarriage has been increasing. In 1980, there were 651,000 interracial marriages, but by 2010, there were 5.4 million. That is still less than 7 percent of married couples but it is increasing significantly. Among unmarried couples it rises to 14 percent and among same-sex couples to 15 percent.

Among couples in which at least one member is Hispanic, marriages with a non-Hispanic partner account for 28 percent. Taken together, all interracial and Hispanic–non-Hispanic marriages account for 10 percent of married opposite-sex couples today. But this includes decades of marriages. Among new couples, about 15 percent of marriages are between people of different races or between Hispanics and non-Hispanics (Bureau of the Census 2010a: Table 60; Lofquist et al. 2012; Passel, Wang, and Taylor 2010).

Assimilation

Assimilation is the process by which a subordinate individual or group takes on the characteristics of the dominant group and is eventually accepted as part of that group. Assimilation is a majority ideology in which A + B + C → A. The majority (A) dominates in such a way that the minorities (B and C) become indistinguishable from the dominant group. Assimilation dictates conformity to the dominant group, regardless of how many racial, ethnic, or religious groups are involved (Newman 1973:53).

To be complete, assimilation must entail an active effort by the minority-group individual to shed all distinguishing actions and beliefs and the

While still not typical, more couples are crossing racial and ethnic boundaries in the United States today than any generation before. Clearly this will increase the potential for their children to identify as biracial or multiracial rather than in a single category.

1-8

One aspect of assimilation is when immigrants seek to learn the language of the host society, as shown in this adult English as a Second Language class in Minneapolis, Minnesota.

unqualified acceptance of that individual by the dominant society. In the United States, dominant White society encourages assimilation. The assimilation perspective tends to devalue alien culture and to treasure the dominant. For example, assimilation assumes that whatever is admirable among Blacks was adapted from Whites and that whatever is bad is inherently Black. The assimilation solution to Black–White conflict has been typically defined as the development of a consensus around White American values.

Assimilation is very difficult. The person being assimilated must forsake his or her cultural tradition to become part of a different, often antagonistic culture. However, assimilation should not be viewed as if immigrants are extraterrestrials. Cross-border movement is often preceded by adjustments and awareness of the culture that awaits the immigrant (Skrentny 2008).

Assimilation does not occur at the same pace for all groups or for all individuals in the same group. Typically, the assimilation process is not completed by the first generation— the new arrivals. Assimilation tends to take longer under the following conditions:

- The differences between the minority and the majority are large.
- The majority is not receptive, or the minority retains its own culture.
- The minority group arrives over a short period of time.
- The minority-group residents are concentrated rather than dispersed.
- The arrival is recent, and the homeland is accessible.

Assimilation is not a smooth process (Warner and Srole 1945).

Segmented assimilation describes the outcome of immigrants and their descendants moving in to different classes of the host society. It emphasizes that there is not a single, uniform lifestyle in the United States and that much of the assimilation is into the working or even lower classes. For a very small portion, such as high level and elite engineers and other professionals, the movement might be into the higher reaches of class divisions. However, for many assimilation may be into a lower class than that enjoyed in their home country and may represent downward mobility even while assimilation progresses (Haller, Portes, and Lynch 2011).

Many people view assimilation as unfair or even dictatorial. However, members of the dominant group see it as reasonable that subordinate people shed their distinctive cultural traditions. In public discussions today, assimilation is the ideology of the dominant group in forcing people how to act. Consequently, the social institutions in the United States—the educational system, economy, government, religion, and medicine—all push toward assimilation, with occasional references to the pluralist approach.

The Pluralist Perspective

Thus far, we have concentrated on how subordinate groups cease to exist (removal) or take on the characteristics of the dominant group (assimilation). The alternative to these relationships between the majority and the minority is pluralism. **Pluralism** implies that various groups in a society have mutual respect for one another's culture, a respect that allows minorities to express their own culture without suffering prejudice or discrimination. Whereas the assimilationist or integrationist seeks the elimination of ethnic boundaries, the pluralist believes in maintaining many of them.

There are limits to cultural freedom. A Romanian immigrant to the United States cannot expect to avoid learning English and still move up the occupational ladder. To survive, a society must have a consensus among its members on basic ideals, values, and beliefs. Nevertheless, there is still plenty of room for variety. Earlier, fusion was described as $A + B + C \rightarrow D$ and assimilation as $A + B + C \rightarrow A$. Using this same scheme, we can think of pluralism as $A + B + C \rightarrow A + B + C$, with groups coexisting in one society (Manning 1995; Newman 1973; Simpson 1995).

In the United States, cultural pluralism is more an ideal than a reality. Although there are vestiges of cultural pluralism—in the various ethnic neighborhoods in major cities, for instance—the rule has been for subordinate groups to assimilate. Yet as the minority becomes the numerical majority, the ability to live out one's identity becomes a bit easier. African Americans, Hispanics, American Indians, and Asian Americans already outnumber Whites in most of the largest cities. The trend is toward even greater diversity. Nonetheless, the cost of cultural integrity throughout the nation's history has been high. The various Native American tribes have succeeded to a large extent in maintaining their heritage, but the price has been bare subsistence on federal reservations.

The United States is experiencing a reemergence of ethnic identification by groups that had previously expressed little interest in their heritage. Groups that make up the dominant majority also are reasserting their ethnic heritages. Various nationality groups are rekindling interest in almost forgotten languages, customs, festivals, and traditions. In some instances, this expression of the past has taken the form of a protest against exclusion from the dominant society. For example, Chinese youths chastise their elders for forgetting the old ways and accepting White American influence and control.

The most visible expression of pluralism is language use. As of 2008, nearly one in every five people (19.1 percent) over age five spoke a language other than English at home. Later, in Chapter 4, we consider how language use figures into issues relating to immigration and education (American Community Survey 2009: Table S1601).

Facilitating a diverse and changing society affects just about every aspect of that society. Yet another nod to pluralism, although not nearly so obvious as language to the general population, has been the changes within the funeral industry. Where Christian and Jewish funeral practices once dominated, funeral home professionals are now being trained to accommodate a variety of practices. Latinos often expect 24-hour viewing of their deceased, whereas Muslims may wish to participate in washing the deceased before burial in a grave pointing toward Mecca. Hindu and Buddhist requests to participate in cremation are now being respected (Brulliard 2006).

Resistance and Change

1-9   Articulate how change occurs in racial and ethnic relations.

By virtue of wielding power and influence, the dominant group may define the terms by which all members of society operate. This is particularly evident in a slave society, but even in contemporary industrialized nations, the dominant group has a disproportionate role in shaping immigration policy, the curriculum of the schools, and the content of the media.

Subordinate groups do not merely accept the definitions and ideology proposed by the dominant group. A continuing theme in dominant–subordinate relations is the minority group's challenge to its subordination. Resistance by subordinate groups is well documented as they seek to promote change that will bring them more rights and privileges, if not true equality. Often, traditional notions of racial formation are overcome not only

Through recent efforts of collective action, African American farmers successfully received Congressional approval in 2010 for compensation denied them in the latter 1900s by the Department of Agriculture.

through panethnicity but also because Black people, along with Latinos and sympathetic Whites, join in the resistance to subordination (Moulder 1996; Winant 2004).

Resistance can be seen in efforts by racial and ethnic groups to maintain their identity through newspapers and organizations and in today's technological age through cable television stations, blogs, and Internet sites. Resistance manifests itself in social movements such as the civil rights movement, the feminist movement, and gay rights efforts. The passage of such legislation as the Age Discrimination Act or the Americans with Disabilities Act marks the success of oppressed groups in lobbying on their own behalf.

Resistance efforts may begin through small actions. For example, residents of a reservation question why a toxic waste dump is to be located on their land. Although it may bring in money, they question the wisdom of such a move. Their concerns lead to further investigations of the extent to which American Indian lands are used disproportionately as containment areas for dangerous materials. This action in turn leads to a broader investigation of the ways in which minority-group people often find themselves "hosting" dumps and incinerators. As we discuss later, these local efforts eventually led the Environmental Protection Agency to monitor the disproportionate placement of toxic facilities in or near racial and ethnic minority communities. There is little reason to expect that such reforms would have occurred if the reservation residents had relied on traditional decision-making processes alone.

Change has occurred. At the beginning of the twentieth century, lynching was practiced in many parts of the country. At the beginning of the twenty-first century, laws punishing hate crimes were increasingly common and embraced a variety of stigmatized groups. Although this social progress should not be ignored, the nation still must focus concern on the significant social inequalities that remain. It is too easy to look at the accomplishments of Barack Obama and Hillary Clinton and conclude "mission accomplished" in terms of racial and gender injustices (Best 2001).

An even more basic form of resistance is to question societal values. In this book, we avoid using the term *American* to describe people of the United States because geographically, Brazilians, Canadians, and El Salvadorans are Americans as well. It is easy to overlook how our understanding of today has been shaped by the way institutions and even the very telling of history have been presented by members of the dominant group. African American studies scholar Molefi Kete Asante (2007, 2008) has called for an **Afrocentric perspective** that emphasizes the customs of African cultures and how they have pervaded the history, culture, and behavior of Blacks in the United States and around the world. Afrocentrism seeks to balance Eurocentrism and works toward a multiculturalist or pluralist orientation in which no viewpoint is suppressed. The Afrocentric approach could become part of our school curriculum, which has not adequately acknowledged the importance of this heritage.

The Afrocentric perspective has attracted much attention in education. Opponents view it as a separatist view of history and culture that distorts both past and present. Its supporters counter that African peoples everywhere can come to full self-determination only when they are able to overthrow the dominance of White or Eurocentric intellectual interpretations (Conyers 2004).

The remarkable efforts by members of racial and ethnic minorities working with supportive White Americans beginning in the 1950s through the early 1970s successfully targeted overt racist symbols or racist and sexist actions. Today's targets are more intractable and tend to emerge from institutional discrimination. Sociologist Douglas Massey (2011) argued that a central goal must be to reform the criminal justice system by demanding repeal of the following: the three-strikes law, mandatory minimum sentencing, and harsher penalties for crack than for powdered cocaine. Such targets are quite different from laws that prevented Blacks and women from serving on juries.

In considering the inequalities present today, as we do in the chapters that follow, it is easy to forget how much change has taken place. Much of the resistance to prejudice and discrimination in the past, either to slavery or to women's prohibition from voting, took the active support of members of the dominant group. The indignities still experienced by subordinate groups continue to be resisted as subordinate groups and their allies among the dominant group seek further change.

Conclusion

One hundred years ago, sociologist and activist W. E. B. Du Bois took another famed Black activist, Booker T. Washington, to task for saying that the races could best work together apart, like fingers on a hand. Du Bois felt that Black people had to be a part of all social institutions and not create their own. With an African American elected and now reelected to the presidency, Whites, African Americans, and other groups continue to debate what form society should take. Should we seek to bring everyone together into an integrated whole? Or do we strive to maintain as much of our group identities as possible while working as cooperatively as necessary?

In this chapter, we have attempted to organize our approach to subordinate–dominant relations in the United States. We observed that subordinate groups do not necessarily contain fewer members than the dominant group. Subordinate groups are classified into racial, ethnic, religious, and gender groups. Racial classification has been of interest, but scientific findings do not explain contemporary race relations. Biological differences of race are not supported by scientific data. Yet as the continuing debate over standardized tests demonstrates, attempts to establish a biological meaning of race have not been swept entirely into the dustbin of history. However, the social meaning given to physical differences is very significant. People have defined racial differences in such a way as to encourage or discourage the progress of certain groups.

Subordinate-group members' reactions include the seeking of an alternative avenue to acceptance and success: "Why should we give up what we are, to be accepted by them?" In response to this question, there continues to be strong ethnicity identification. A result of this maintenance of ethnic and racial identity, complimentary, and occasionally competing, images of what it means to be a productive member of a single society persist. Pluralism describes a society in which several different groups coexist, with no dominant or subordinate groups. People individually choose what cultural patterns to keep and which to let go.

Subordinate groups have not and do not always accept their second-class status passively. They may protest, organize, revolt, and resist society as defined by the dominant group. Patterns of race and ethnic relations are changing, not stagnant. Indicative of the changing landscape, biracial and multiracial children present us with new definitions of identity emerging through a process of racial formation, reminding us that race is socially constructed.

In the twenty-first century, we are facing new challenges to cooperation. There has been a marked increase in the population of minority racial and ethnic groups to the point that collectively they will be in the majority well before today's college students reach 40 years of age. Society is not static, but dynamic and evolving. Little wonder that scholars are now talking about "super-diversity" and considering whether past notions of race and ethnicity are passé (Bobo 2013).

Continuing immigration and the explosive growth of the Hispanic population—more than double since 1990, fuels this growth. Latinos are now settling in to the point that the Spanish-language Telemundo network is now introducing English-language subtitles to ensure their Latino viewers can fully comprehend their programming.

Barack Obama's historic campaign and becoming the 44th president of the United States in January 2009 marks a significant time in U.S. history. The fact that he is the first African American (and also the first non-White person) to serve as president demonstrates how much progress has been achieved in race relations in this country. It also underscores both how long it has taken and how much more needs to be accomplished for the United States to truly be "a more perfect union" as stated in the Constitution.

The two significant forces that are absent in a truly pluralistic society are prejudice and discrimination. In an assimilation society, prejudice disparages out-group differences, and discrimination financially rewards those who shed their past. In the next two chapters, we explore the nature of prejudice and discrimination in the United States.

Summary

1. When sociologists define a minority group, they are concerned primarily with the economic and political power, or powerlessness, of the group.

2. A racial group is set apart from others primarily by physical characteristics; an ethnic group is set apart primarily by national origin or cultural patterns.

3. People cannot be sorted into distinct racial groups, so race is best viewed as a social construct that is subject to different interpretations over time.

4. A small but still significant number of people in the United States—more than 7 million—readily see themselves as having a biracial or multiracial identity.

5. The study of race and ethnicity in the United States often considers the role played by class and gender.

6. Subordinate-group status has emerged through migration, annexation, and colonialism.

7. The Spectrum of Intergroup Relations illustrates the patterns between racial and ethnic groups ranging from those extremely harsh to more tolerant.

8. The social consequences of subordinate-group status include extermination, expulsion, secession, segregation, fusion, assimilation, and pluralism.

9. Racial, ethnic, and other minorities maintain a long history of resisting efforts to restrict their rights.

Key Terms

Afrocentric perspective, p. 27

amalgamation, p. 24

apartheid, p. 23

assimilation, p. 24

biological race, p. 9

blaming the victim, p. 16

class, p. 14

colonialism, p. 19

conflict perspective, p. 15

dysfunction, p. 15

emigration, p. 18

ethnic cleansing, p. 20

ethnic group, p. 6

functionalist perspective, p. 14

fusion, p. 23

genocide, p. 20

globalization, p. 18

Holocaust, p. 20

immigration, p. 18

intelligence quotient (IQ), p. 9

labeling theory, p. 16

marginality, p. 13

melting pot, p. 24

migration, p. 18

minority group, p. 4

panethnicity, p. 13

pluralism, p. 26

racial formation, p. 11

racial group, p. 6

racism, p. 10

resegregation, p. 23

segmented assimilation, p. 25

segregation, p. 22

self-fulfilling prophecy, p. 16

sociology, p. 13

stereotype, p. 16

stratification, p. 14

world systems theory, p. 19

Review Questions

1. What are the characteristics of subordinate and minority groups?

2. Distinguish between racial and ethnic groups.

3. In what different ways is race viewed?

4. How do biracial and multiracial categories call into question traditional groupings in the United States?"

5. How do the conflict, functionalist, and labeling approaches apply to the social construction of race?

6. How do subordinate groups emerge?

7. Describe the Spectrum of Intergroup Relations.

8. Characterize the range of intergroup relations from those which are most tolerant to those that are most unacceptable to minority groups.

9. What role do subordinate groups play in their own destiny?

Critical Thinking

1. How do the concepts of "biracial" and "multiracial" relate to W. E. B. Du Bois's notion of a "color line"?

2. How diverse is your city? Can you see evidence that some group is being subordinated? What social construction of categories do you see that may be different in your community as compared to elsewhere?

3. Select a racial or ethnic group and apply the Spectrum of Intergroup Relations. Can you provide an example today or in the past where each relationship occurs?

4. Identify some protest and resistance efforts by subordinated groups in your area. Have they been successful? Even though some people say they favor equality, why are they uncomfortable with such efforts? How can people unconnected with such efforts either help or hinder such protests?

2

Prejudice

2-1 Differentiate between prejudice and discrimination.

2-2 Apply White privilege.

2-3 Paraphrase the theories of prejudice.

2-4 Describe stereotyping.

2-5 Put into your own words color-blind racism.

2-6 Discuss how members of subordinate groups respond to prejudice.

2-7 Explain how hostility is present among racial and ethnic groups.

2-8 Illustrate research on reducing prejudice.

2-9 Identify ways to reduce hate.

These are tough economic times—hard to find jobs and when one does find a job they often are part-time and do not pay a good wage. Government funds to help the jobless make it while they look for work or training opportunities are limited. So imagine you are in the difficult position to allocate government assistance and you want the money to be effective.

A study published in 2013 gave people the choice to extend $1,500 of assistance to applicants based on a completed questionnaire—some with an excellent work ethic, others with a poor work ethic. You also had the alternative not to spend the money and help reduce the state's budget deficit—another very real challenge. Oh, there was more piece of information you were given besides the assessment of the person's work ethic: their name—either Laurie and Emily or Keisha and Latoya.

Looking at how the nationwide sample of 1,000 adults responded to this task, the results were clear. Not surprisingly hard workers were given more assistance than those judged to be poor. Faced with a "lazy" recipient, the hypothetical decision makers were more likely to use the money to offset the budget deficit. However what seemed to make the real difference was the name. Hard-working Emily was given ten times as much money as hard-working Keisha. Similarly idle Emily received much more than lazy Latoya. In fact, money allocated to the lazy White-sounding name applicant started to approach what the hard-working Black could expect to be awarded.

In summary, Keisha and Latoya were not given the same credit as Emily and Latoya and were more likely to be punished where it hurt with assistance withheld (DeSante 2013).

Prejudice is so prevalent that it is tempting to consider it inevitable or, even more broadly, part of human nature. Such a view ignores its variability from individual to individual and from society to society. Not everyone punished "Keisha" and rewarded "Emily." People learn prejudice as children before they exhibit it as adults. Therefore, prejudice is a social phenomenon, an acquired characteristic. A truly pluralistic society would lack unfavorable distinctions made through prejudicial attitudes among racial and ethnic groups.

Holding ill feelings based on a person's race or ethnicity is more of an issue because our nation is so increasingly diverse. In Figure 2.1, we look at the increase in minority

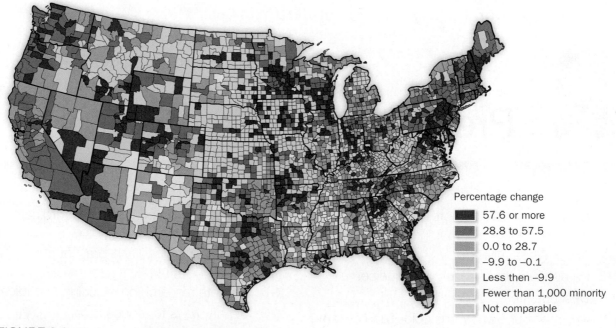

Percentage change

- ■ 57.6 or more
- ■ 28.8 to 57.5
- ■ 0.0 to 28.7
- ■ −9.9 to −0.1
- □ Less then −9.9
- ■ Fewer than 1,000 minority
- ■ Not comparable

FIGURE 2.1

Change in Minority Population by County, 2000–2010

Growth in the minority population has occurred in the last decade across the country, including in many areas that previously had few members of racial and ethnic minorities.

Source: Humes, Jones, and Ramirez 2011:21.

presence in the first decade of the twenty-first century. Many counties far removed from urban centers or historic areas with Black and Latino populations saw population increases in the years from 2000 to 2010. The likelihood that prejudices will be expressed, dealt with, or hidden is beginning to become a truly nationwide phenomenon as majority-minority interaction pervades more and more communities.

Ill feeling among groups of different races, ethnicities, or cultures may result from **ethnocentrism,** or the tendency to believe that one's culture and way of life are superior to all others'. The ethnocentric person judges other groups and other cultures by the standards of his or her own group. This attitude makes it quite easily for people to view other cultures as inferior. We see a woman wearing a veil and may regard it as strange and backward, yet we are baffled when other societies think U.S. women in short skirts are dressed inappropriately. Ethnocentrism and other expressions of prejudice are often voiced; but unfortunately, such expressions sometimes become the motivation for criminal acts.

Prejudice and Discrimination

Prejudice and discrimination are related concepts but are not the same. **Prejudice** is a negative attitude toward an entire category of people. The important components in this definition are *attitude* and *entire category*. Prejudice involves attitudes, thoughts, and beliefs—not actions. Prejudice often is expressed using **ethnophaulisms,** or ethnic slurs, which include derisive nicknames such as *honky*, *gook*, and *wetback*. Ethnophaulisms also include speaking to or about members of a particular group in a condescending way, such as saying, "José does well in school for a Mexican American" or referring to a middle-aged woman as "one of the girls."

2-1   Differentiate between prejudice and discrimination.

Research Focus

Virtual Prejudice and Anti-Prejudice

More and more of our daily lives are spent not directly talking or seeing other people but in time online. Sometimes this may include indirectly communicating with friends through social media, but it includes a large amount of time spent in some virtual world separated from our reality. What impact can this have on reinforcing or undercutting prejudice?

Researchers have looked at video games and found minorities are vastly underrepresented, and when they do appear it is usually as thugs or athletes. Even when given the opportunity to interact with games, White players are more likely to recall Black characters as violent and aggressive.

Yet like real society, virtual society can seek to have a positive impact. User-generated video sites like YouTube abound with videos reflecting all sorts of representations of racial and ethnic groups. However, one study found that generally images of American Indians provoke positive responses in online comments. However, there were some important qualifications. Viewers seemed most positive when videos were historical rather than dealing with present-day situations. And if ill treatment toward today's Native Americans was central to the video, negative comments began to escalate.

The complexity of online representations and prejudice is highlighted in the May 2013 Cheerios advertisement. In the 30-second spot a White Mom is shown telling her biracial daughter that is it true that Cheerios is heart-healthy. The six-year-old then scampers into the next room spilling Cheerios on her Black father's chest while he is napping on the living room couch. People weighed in to General Mills with comments 10-1 favorable toward the biracial household but the company was forced to disable the comment section because of all the racist remarks that were left.

Not to be outdone, a parody was mounted within days on YouTube by comedian Kenji America showing a girl dumping the breakfast cereal on her Black mother in a household of biracial lesbian parents with their cute biracial daughter. Humor was used to deflect prejudice aimed at earlier video.

Researchers of online prejudice admit the depth of hostility is difficult to assess since many commercial venues and news outlets monitor, at some expense, comments and selectively delete them, giving to the casual online user an inaccurate view of how the general public is responding to racially charged topics. It also appears that those who wish to express racist views are retreating to online sites where such rhetoric will not be challenged. As in everyday life, one cannot assume the absence of overt prejudice means tolerance.

Sources: Burgess et al. 2011; Hughley and Daniels 2013; Kenji America 2013; Kopacz and Lawton 2013; Nudd 2013)

A prejudiced belief also leads to categorical rejection. Prejudice means you dislike someone not because you find his or her behavior objectionable; it means you dislike an entire racial or ethnic group, even if you have had little or no contact with that group. A college student is not prejudiced because he requests a room change after three weeks of enduring his roommate's sleeping all day, playing loud music all night, and piling garbage on his desk. However, he is displaying prejudice if he requests a change after arriving at school and learning his new roommate is of a different nationality.

Prejudice is a belief or attitude; discrimination is action. **Discrimination** is the denial of opportunities and equal rights to individuals and groups because of prejudice or for other arbitrary reasons. Unlike prejudice, discrimination involves *behavior* that excludes members of a group from certain rights, opportunities, or privileges. Like prejudice, it is categorical, except for a few rare exceptions. If an employer refuses to hire an illiterate Italian American as a computer analyst, that is not discrimination. If an employer refuses to hire all Italian Americans because he or she thinks they are incompetent and makes no effort to determine if an applicant is qualified, that is discrimination.

Prejudice is a complicated aspect of our behavior and has been extensively researched as you will see in this chapter. To give you just a sample, consider the Research Focus dealing with online expressions of prejudice.

Merton's Typology

Prejudice does not necessarily coincide with discriminatory behavior. In exploring the relationship between negative attitudes and negative behavior, sociologist Robert Merton (1949, 1976) identified four major categories (Figure 2.2). The label added to each of Merton's categories may more readily identify the type of person described:

1. The unprejudiced nondiscriminator—or all-weather liberal
2. The unprejudiced discriminator—or reluctant liberal
3. The prejudiced nondiscriminator—or timid bigot
4. The prejudiced discriminator—or all-weather bigot

As the term is used in types 1 and 2, liberals are committed to equality among people. The all-weather liberal believes in equality and practices it. Merton was quick to observe that all-weather liberals may be far removed from any real contact with subordinate groups such as African Americans or women. Furthermore, such people may be content with their own behavior and do little to change it. The reluctant liberal is not completely committed to equality between groups. Social pressure may cause such a person to discriminate. Fear of losing employees may lead a manager to avoid promoting women to supervisory capacities. Equal-opportunity legislation may be the best way to influence a reluctant liberal.

Types 3 and 4 do not believe in equal treatment for racial and ethnic groups, but they vary in their willingness to act. The timid bigot, type 3, will not discriminate if discrimination costs money or reduces profits or if peers or the government apply pressure against doing so. The all-weather bigot acts without hesitation on the prejudiced beliefs he or she holds.

LaPiere's Study

Merton's typology points out that attitudes should not be confused with behavior. People do not always act as they believe. More than a half-century ago, Richard LaPiere (1934, 1969) exposed the relationship between racial attitudes and social conduct. From 1930 to 1932, LaPiere traveled throughout the United States with a Chinese couple. Despite an alleged climate of intolerance of Asians, LaPiere observed that the couple was treated courteously at hotels, motels, and restaurants. He was puzzled by the good reception they received; all the conventional attitude surveys showed extreme prejudice by Whites toward the Chinese.

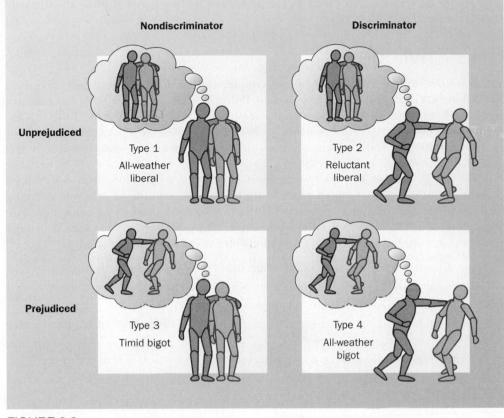

FIGURE 2.2

Prejudice and Discrimination

As sociologist Robert Merton's formulation shows, prejudice and discrimination are related but are not the same.

Was it possible that LaPiere was fortunate during his travels and consistently stopped at places operated by tolerant members of the dominant group? To test this possibility, he sent questionnaires asking the places at which they had been served whether the owner would "accept members of the Chinese race as guests in your establishment." More than 90 percent responded no, even though LaPiere's Chinese couple were treated politely at all of these establishments. How can this inconsistency be explained? People who returned questionnaires reflecting prejudice were unwilling to act based on those asserted beliefs; they were timid bigots.

The LaPiere study is not without flaws. First, he had no way of knowing whether the respondent to the questionnaire was the person who had served him and the Chinese couple. Second, he accompanied the couple, but the questionnaire suggested that the guests would be unescorted (and, in the minds of some, uncontrolled) and might consist of many Chinese people. Third, personnel may have changed between the time of the visit and the mailing of the questionnaire (Deutscher, Pestello, and Pestello 1993).

The LaPiere technique has been replicated with similar results. This technique questions whether attitudes are important if they are not reflected in behavior. But if attitudes are not important in small matters, they are important in other ways: Lawmakers legislate and courts may reach decisions based on what the public thinks.

This is not just hypothetical. Legislators in the United States often are persuaded to vote a certain way by what they perceive are changed attitudes toward immigration, affirmative action, and prayer in public schools. Sociologists have enumerated some of prejudice's functions. For the majority group, prejudice maintains privileged occupations and more power for its members.

2-2

The following sections examine theories of why prejudice exists and discuss the content and extent of prejudice today.

White Privilege

2-2 Apply White privilege.

White travelers, unlike LaPiere's Chinese couple, rarely, if ever, would be concerned about second-class treatment because of race. Being White in the United States may not assure success and wealth, but it does limit encounters with intolerance.

White privilege refers to the rights or immunities granted as a particular benefit or favor for being White. This advantage exists unconsciously and is often invisible to the White people who enjoy it (Ferber 2008).

Scholar Peggy McIntosh of the Wellesley College Center for Research on Women looked at the privilege that comes from being White and the added privilege of being male. The other side of racial oppression is the privilege enjoyed by dominant groups. Being White or being successful in establishing a White identity carries with it distinct advantages. Among those that McIntosh (1988) identified were the following:

- Being considered financially reliable when using checks, credit cards, or cash
- Taking a job without having coworkers suspect it came about because of race
- Never having to speak for all the people of your race
- Watching television or reading a newspaper and seeing people of your own race widely represented
- Speaking effectively in a large group without being called a credit to your race
- Assuming that if legal or medical help is needed, your race will not work against you

Whiteness does carry privileges, but most White people do not consciously think of them except on the rare occasions when they are questioned. Returning to the research described at the beginning of the chapter, we saw how easily "Emily" and "Laurie" were privileged over "Latoya" and "Keisha" in being awarded government assistance.

Being White means having distinct advantages, which has been called *White privilege*. For example, one can seek assistance and assume your race will not work against you.

Typically, White people do not see themselves as privileged in the way many African Americans and Latinos see themselves as disadvantaged. When asked to comment on their "Whiteness," White people most likely see themselves devoid of ethnicity ("no longer Irish," for example), stigmatized as racist, and victims of reverse discrimination. Privilege for many White people may be easy to exercise in one's life, but it is difficult to acknowledge (McKinney 2008).

Theories of Prejudice

Prejudice is learned. Friends, relatives, newspapers, books, movies, television, and the Internet all teach it. Awareness of the differences among people that society judges to be important begins at an early age. Several theories have been advanced to explain the rejection of certain groups in a society. We examine four theoretical explanations. The first two, scapegoating and authoritarian personality, are psychological and emphasize why a particular person harbors ill feelings. The second two, exploitation and normative, are sociological and view prejudice in the context of our interaction in a larger society.

2-3 Paraphrase the theories of prejudice.

Scapegoating Theory

People use some expressions of prejudice so they can blame others and refuse to accept responsibility. **Scapegoating theory** says that prejudiced people believe they are society's victims.

The term *scapegoat* comes from a biblical injunction telling the Hebrews to send a goat into the wilderness to symbolically carry away the people's sins. Similarly, the theory of scapegoating suggests that, rather than accepting guilt for some failure, a person transfers the responsibility for failure to a vulnerable group.

In the major tragic twentieth century example, Adolf Hitler used the Jews as the scapegoat for all German social and economic ills in the 1930s. This premise led to the passage of laws restricting Jewish life in pre–World War II Germany and eventually escalated into the mass extermination of Europe's Jews. Scapegoating of Jews persists. A national survey in 2009 showed that one out of four people in the United States blame "the Jews" for the recent financial crisis. **Anti-Semitism**—anti-Jewish prejudice and discrimination—remains a very real phenomenon (Malhotra and Margalit 2009).

Today in the United States, both legal and illegal immigrants often are blamed by "real Americans" for their failure to secure jobs or desirable housing. The immigrant becomes the scapegoat for one's own lack of skills, planning, or motivation. It is so much easier to blame someone else.

Authoritarian Personality Theory

Prejudice may be influenced by one's upbringing and the lessons taught—and learned—early in life. Several efforts have been made to detail the prejudiced personality, but the most comprehensive effort culminated in a volume titled *The Authoritarian Personality* (Adorno et al. 1950). Using a variety of tests and relying on more than 2,000 respondents, ranging from middle-class Whites to inmates of San Quentin State Prison (California), the authors claimed they had isolated the characteristics of the authoritarian personality.

In Adorno and colleagues' (1950) view, the **authoritarian personality** has basic characteristics that mean it is a personality type that is likely to be prejudiced. It encompasses adherence to conventional values, uncritical acceptance of authority, and concern with power and toughness. With obvious relevance to the development of intolerance, the authoritarian personality also was characterized by aggressiveness toward people who did not conform to conventional norms or obey authority. According to the researchers, this personality type developed from the experience of harsh discipline in early childhood.

A child with an authoritarian upbringing was obedient to authority figures and then later treated others as he or she had been raised.

This study has been widely criticized, but the very existence of such wide criticism indicates the influence of the study. Critics have attacked the study's equation of authoritarianism with right-wing politics (although liberals also can be rigid); its failure to see that prejudice is more closely related to other individual traits, such as social class, than to authoritarianism as it was defined; the research methods used; and the emphasis on extreme racial prejudice rather than on more-common expressions of hostility.

Despite these concerns about specifics in the study, which was completed 60 years ago, annual conferences continue to draw attention to how authoritarian attitudes contribute to racism, sexism, and even torture (Kinloch 1974; O'Neill 2008).

Exploitation Theory

Racial prejudice is often used to justify keeping a group in a subordinate economic position. Conflict theorists, in particular, stress the role of racial and ethnic hostility as a way for the dominant group to keep its position of status and power intact. Indeed, this approach maintains that even the less-affluent White working class uses prejudice to minimize competition from upwardly mobile minorities.

This **exploitation theory** is clearly part of the Marxist tradition in sociological thought. Karl Marx emphasized exploitation of the lower class as an integral part of capitalism. Similarly, the exploitation or conflict approach explains how racism can stigmatize a group as inferior to justify the exploitation of that group. As developed by Oliver Cox (1942), exploitation theory saw prejudice against Blacks as an extension of the inequality faced by the entire lower class.

The exploitation theory of prejudice is persuasive. Japanese Americans were the object of little prejudice until they began to enter occupations that brought them into competition with Whites. The movement to keep Chinese out of the country became strongest during the late nineteenth century, when Chinese immigrants and Whites fought over dwindling numbers of jobs. Both the enslavement of African Americans and the removal westward of Native Americans were to a significant degree economically motivated.

Normative Approach

Although personality factors are important contributors to prejudice, normative or situational factors also must be given serious consideration. The **normative approach** takes the view that prejudice is influenced by societal norms and situations that encourage or discourage the tolerance of minorities.

Analysis reveals how societal influences shape a climate for tolerance or intolerance. Societies develop social norms that dictate not only what foods are desirable (or forbidden) but also what racial and ethnic groups are to be favored (or despised). Social forces operate in a society to encourage or discourage tolerance. The force may be widespread, such as the pressure on White Southerners to oppose racial equality even though there was slavery or segregation, which would seem to make concerns about equality irrelevant. The influence of social norms may be limited, as when one man finds himself becoming more sexist as he competes with three women for a position in a prestigious law firm.

The four approaches to prejudice summarized in Table 2.1 are not mutually exclusive. Social circumstances provide cues for a person's attitudes; personality determines the extent to which people follow social cues and the likelihood that they will encourage others to do the same. Societal norms may promote or deter tolerance; personality traits suggest the degree to which a person will conform to norms of intolerance. To understand prejudice, we must use all four approaches together.

TABLE 2.1
Theories of Prejudice

No single explanation of why prejudice exists is satisfactory, but several approaches taken together offer insight.

Theory	Explanation	Example
Scapegoating	People blame others for their own failures.	An unsuccessful applicant assumes that a minority member or a woman got "his" job.
Authoritarian	Childrearing leads one to develop intolerance as an adult.	The rigid personality type dislikes people who are different.
Exploitation	People use others unfairly for economic advantage.	A minority member is hired at a lower wage level.
Normative	Peer and social influences encourage tolerance or intolerance.	A person from an intolerant household is more likely to be openly prejudiced.

Stereotypes

On Christmas Day 2001, Arab American Walied Shater boarded an American Airlines flight from Baltimore to Dallas carrying a gun. The cockpit crew refused to let him fly, fearing that Shater would take over the plane and use it as a weapon of mass destruction. However, Walied Shater carried documentation identifying him as a Secret Service agent, and calls to Washington, DC, confirmed that he was flying to join a presidential protection force at President George W. Bush's ranch in Texas. Nevertheless, the crew could not get past the stereotype of Arab American men posing a lethal threat (Leavitt 2002).

2-4 Describe stereotyping.

What Are Stereotypes?

In Chapter 1, we saw that stereotypes play a powerful role in how people come to view dominant and subordinate groups. **Stereotypes** are unreliable generalizations about all members of a group and do not take individual differences into account. Numerous scientific studies have been made of these exaggerated images. This research has shown the willingness of people to assign positive and negative traits to entire groups of people, which are then applied to particular individuals. Stereotyping causes people to view Blacks as superstitious, Whites as uncaring, and Jews as shrewd. Over the last 80 years of such research, social scientists have found that people have become less willing to express such views openly, but prejudice persists, as we will see later in this chapter (Quillian 2006).

If stereotypes are exaggerated generalizations, then why are they so widely held, and why are some traits assigned more often than others? Evidence for traits may arise out of real conditions. For example, more Puerto Ricans live in poverty than Whites, so the prejudiced mind associates Puerto Ricans with laziness. According to the New Testament, some Jews were responsible for the crucifixion of Jesus, so, to the prejudiced mind, all Jews are Christ killers. Some activists in the women's movement are lesbians, so all feminists are seen as lesbians. From a kernel of fact, faulty generalization creates a stereotype.

In "Speaking Out," journalist Helen Zia, born in New Jersey of parents who emigrated from Shanghai, comments about how immigrant parents grapple with the prejudice their children feel. Should they teach their children their language and perhaps heighten stereotypes and ill feelings from others or push them to become American as fast as possible?

Labeling individuals through negative stereotypes has strong implications for the self-fulfilling prophecy. Studies show that people are all too aware of the negative

2-4 🎙 Speaking Out

Gangsters, Gooks, Geishas, and Geeks

Ah so. No tickee, no washee. So sorry, so sollee.

Chinkee, Chink. Jap, Nip, zero, kamikaze. Dothead, flat face, flat nose, slant eye, slope. Slit, mamasan, dragon lady. Gook, VC, Flip, Hindoo.

Helen Zia

By the time I was ten, I'd heard such words so many times I could feel them coming before they parted lips. I knew they were meant in the unkindest way. Still, we didn't talk about these incidents at home; we just accepted them as part of being in America, something to learn to rise above.

The most common taunting didn't even utilize words but a string of unintelligible gobbledygook that kids—and adults—would spew as they pretended to speak Chinese or some other Asian language. It was a mockery of how they imagined my parents talked to me.

Truth was that Mom and Dad rarely spoke to us in Chinese, except to scold or call us to dinner. Worried that we might develop an accent, my father insisted that we speak English at home. This, he explained, would lessen the hardships we might encounter and make us more acceptable as Americans.

I'll never know if my father's language decision was right. On the one hand, I, like most Asian Americans, have been complimented countless times on my spoken English by people who assumed I was a foreigner. "My, you speak such good English," they'd cluck. "No kidding, I ought to," I would think to myself, then wonder: should

I thank them for assuming that English isn't my native language? Or should I correct them on the proper usage of "well" and "good"?

More often than feeling grateful for my American accent, I've wished that I could jump into a heated exchange of rapid-fire Chinese, volume high and spit flying. But with a vocabulary limited to "Ni hao?" (How are you?) and "Ting bu dong" (I hear but don't understand), meaningful exchanges are woefully impossible. I find myself smiling and nodding like a dashboard ornament. I'm envious of the many people I know who grew up speaking an Asian language yet converse in English beautifully.

Armed with standard English and my flat New Jersey "a," I still couldn't escape the name-calling. I became all too familiar with other names and faces that supposedly matched mine—Fu Manchu, Suzie Wong, Hop Sing, Madame Butterfly, Charlie Chan, Ming the Merciless—the "Asians" produced for mass consumption. Their faces filled me with shame whenever I saw them on TV or in the movies. They defined my face to the rest of the world: a sinister Fu, Suzie the whore, subservient Hop Sing, pathetic Butterfly, cunning Chan, and warlike Ming. Inscrutable Orientals all, real Americans none.

Source: Excerpt from pp. 109–110 in *Asian-American Dreams* by Helen Zia. Copyright (c) 2000 by Helen Zia. Reprinted by permission of Farrar, Straus and Giroux.

images others have of them. When asked to estimate the prevalence of hard-core racism among Whites, one in four Blacks agrees that more than half "personally share the attitudes of groups like the Ku Klux Klan toward Blacks"; only one Black in ten says "only a few" share such views. Stereotypes not only influence how people feel about themselves but also, and perhaps equally important, affect how people interact with others. If people feel that others hold incorrect, disparaging attitudes toward them, then it undoubtedly makes it difficult to have harmonious relations (Sigelman and Tuch 1997).

Although explicit expressions of stereotypes are becoming less common, it is much too soon to write the obituary of racial and ethnic stereotypes. In addition, stereotyping is not limited to racial and ethnic groups. Other groups are subjected to stereotyping. Probably easiest to see in daily life and the mass media is sexism. **Sexism** is the ideology that one sex is superior to the other. Images and descriptions of women and even girls often reinforce sexism. **Homophobia**, the fear of and prejudice toward homosexuality, is present in every facet of life: the family, organized religion, the workplace, official policies, and the mass media. Like the myths and stereotypes of race and gender, those about homosexuality keep gay men and lesbian women oppressed as a group and may also prevent sympathetic members of the dominant group, the heterosexual community, from supporting them. We next consider the use of stereotypes in the contemporary practice of racial profiling.

Stereotyping in Action: Racial Profiling

A Black dentist, Elmo Randolph, testified before a state commission that he was stopped dozens of times in the 1980s and 1990s while traveling the New Jersey Turnpike to work. Invariably state troopers asked, "Do you have guns or drugs?" "My parents always told me, be careful when you're driving on the turnpike," said Dr. Randolph, age 44. "White people don't have that conversation" (Purdy 2001:37; see also Fernandez and Fahim 2006).

Little wonder that Dr. Randolph was pulled over. Although African Americans accounted for only 17 percent of the motorists on that turnpike, they were 80 percent of the motorists pulled over. Such occurrences gave rise to the charge that a new traffic offense was added to the books: DWB, or "driving while Black" (Bowles 2000).

In recent years, the government has given its attention to a social phenomenon with a long history: racial profiling. According to the Department of Justice, **racial profiling** is any police-initiated action based on race, ethnicity, or national origin rather than the person's behavior. Generally, profiling occurs when law enforcement officers, including customs officials, airport security, and police, assume that people fitting certain descriptions are likely to be engaged in something illegal. In 2012, national attention was drawn to the incident of a man on a neighborhood watch patrol shooting dead 17-year-old Trayvon Martin, a black youth visiting his father's fiancée in a gated Florida community. While the legal system slowly investigated, many felt the boy would still be alive had he been White and the shooter immediately arrested if Black. So unsettling was the event that it prompted President Obama in the midst of his public nomination of the head of the World Bank to express sympathy for Martin's parents and say, "If I had a son, he'd look like Trayvon" (White House 2012).

Racial profiling persists despite overwhelming evidence that it not a predictive approach toward identifying potential troublemakers. Whites are more likely to be found with drugs in the areas in which minority group members are disproportionately targeted. A federal study made public in 2005 found little difference nationwide in the likelihood of being stopped by law enforcement officers, but African Americans were twice as likely to have their vehicles searched, and Latinos were five times more likely. A similar pattern emerged in the likelihood of force being used against drivers: It was

The majority of people in the United States think that ethnic and religious profiling should be taken into account to maintain security.

three times more likely for Latinos and Blacks than White drivers. A study of New York City police officers describing some 4.43 million stops between 2004 and mid-2012 found that Blacks and Latinos accounted for 83 percent of people who were stopped and frisked, and a related study found that Whites were 50 percent more likely to be carrying weapons (Center for Constitutional Rights 2011; Goldstein 2013;Herbert 2010; Tomaskovic-Devey and Warren 2009).

Back in the 1990s, increased attention to racial profiling led not only to special reports and commissions but also to talk of legislating against it. This proved difficult. The U.S. Supreme Court in *Whren v. United States* (1996) upheld the constitutionality of using a minor traffic infraction as an excuse to stop and search a vehicle and its passengers. Nonetheless, states and other government units are discussing policies and training that would discourage racial profiling. At the same time, most law enforcement agencies reject the idea of compiling racial data on traffic stops, arguing that it would be a waste of money and staff time.

Efforts to stop racial profiling came to an abrupt end after the September 11, 2001, terrorist attacks on the United States. Suspicions about Muslims and Arabs in the United States became widespread. Foreign students from Arab countries were summoned for special questioning. Legal immigrants identified as Arab or Muslim were scrutinized for any illegal activity and were prosecuted for routine immigration violations that were ignored for people of other ethnic backgrounds and religious faiths (Withrow 2006).

National surveys have found little change since 2001 in support for profiling Arab Americans at airports. In 2010, 53 percent of Americans favored "ethnic and religious profiling," even for U.S. citizens, and wanted requirements that Arab Americans undergo special and more-intensive security checks before boarding planes in the United States (Zogby 2010).

Color-Blind Racism

2-5 Put into your own words color-blind racism.

Over the last three generations, nationwide surveys have consistently shown growing support by Whites for integration, interracial dating, and having members of minority groups attain political office, including becoming president of the United States. Yet how can this be true when the hatred described at the beginning of the chapter persists and thousands of hate crimes occur annually?

Color-blind racism refers to the use of race-neutral principles to defend the racially unequal status quo. Yes, "no discrimination for college admission" should exist, yet the disparity in educational experiences means that formal admissions criteria will privilege White high school graduates. "Healthcare is for all," but if you do not have workplace insurance, you likely cannot afford it.

Color-blind racism has also been referred to as laissez-faire, postracialism, or aversive racism, but the common theme is that notions of racial inferiority are rarely expressed and that proceeding color-blind into the future will perpetuate inequality. In the post–civil rights era and with the election of President Barack Obama, people are more likely to assume discrimination is long past and express views that are more proper—that is, lacking the overt expressions of racism of the past.

An important aspect of color-blind racism is the recognition that race is rarely invoked in public debates on social issues. Instead, people emphasize lower social class, the lack of citizenship, or illegal aliens; these descriptions serve as proxies for race. Furthermore, the emphasis is on individuals failing rather than on recognizing patterns of groups being disadvantaged. This leads many White people to declare they are not racist and that they do not know anyone who is racist. It also leads to the mistaken conclusion that more progress has been made toward racial and ethnic equality and even tolerance than has really taken place.

When we survey White attitudes toward African Americans, three conclusions are inescapable. First, attitudes are subject to change; during periods of dramatic social upheaval, dramatic shifts can occur within one generation. Second, less progress was made in the late twentieth and beginning of the twenty-first centuries than was made in the relatively brief period of the 1950s and 1960s. Third, the pursuit of a color-blind agenda has created lower levels of support for politics that could reduce racial inequality if implemented.

Economically less-successful groups such as African Americans and Latinos have been associated with negative traits to the point that issues such as urban decay, homelessness, welfare, and crime are viewed as race issues even though race is rarely mentioned explicitly. Besides making it harder to resolve difficult social issues, this is another instance of blaming the victim. These perceptions come at a time when the willingness of the government to address domestic ills is limited by increasing opposition to new taxes and continuing commitments to fight terrorism here and abroad. The color line remains, even if more people are unwilling to accept its divisive impact on everyone's lives (Ansell 2008; Bonilla-Silva 2006; Bonilla-Silva and Embrick with Seamster 2011; Kang and Lane 2010; Mazzocco et al. 2006; Quillian 2006; Winant 2004:106–108).

The Mood of the Oppressed

Sociologist W. E. B. Du Bois relates an experience from his youth in a largely White community in Massachusetts. He tells how, on one occasion, the boys and girls were exchanging cards, and everyone was having a lot of fun. One girl, a newcomer, refused his card as soon as she saw that Du Bois was Black. He wrote:

2-6 Discuss how members of subordinate groups respond to prejudice.

> *Then it dawned upon me with a certain suddenness that I was different from others . . . shut out from their world by a vast veil. I had therefore no desire to tear down that veil, to creep through; I held all beyond it in common contempt and lived above it in a region of blue sky and great wandering shadows.* (1903:2)

In using the image of a veil, Du Bois describes how members of subordinate groups learn they are being treated differently. In his case and that of many others, this leads to feelings of contempt toward all Whites that continue for a lifetime.

Opinion pollsters have been interested in White attitudes on racial issues longer than they have measured the views of subordinate groups. This neglect of minority attitudes reflects, in part, the bias of the White researchers. It also stems from the contention that the dominant group is more important to study because it is in a better position to act on its beliefs. The results of a nationwide survey conducted in the United States offer insight into sharply different views on the state of race relations today (Figure 2.3). Latinos, African Americans, and Asian Americans all have strong reservations about the state of race relations in the United States. They are skeptical about the level of equal opportunity and perceive a lot of discrimination. It is interesting to note that Hispanics and Asian Americans, overwhelmingly immigrants, are more likely to feel they will succeed if they work hard. Yet the majority of all three groups have a positive outlook for the next ten years (New America Media 2007; Preston 2007).

National surveys showed that the 2008 successful presidential bid of Senator Barack Obama led to a sense of optimism and national pride among African Americans, even though political observers noted that Obama ran a race-neutral campaign and rarely addressed issues specifically of concern to African Americans. Unlike Whites or Hispanics, Black voters still saw President Obama's campaign as addressing issues important to the Black community. Survey researchers closely followed these perceptions after the 2008 election.

Optimism about the present and future increased significantly among African Americans during the Obama campaign and first year of his presidency. Ironically, White optimism about positive racial change was even more optimistic during the early period of the Obama administration. Yet other data show little evidence of a new nationwide perspective on race following the election. For example, only 35.3 percent of first-year

2-6

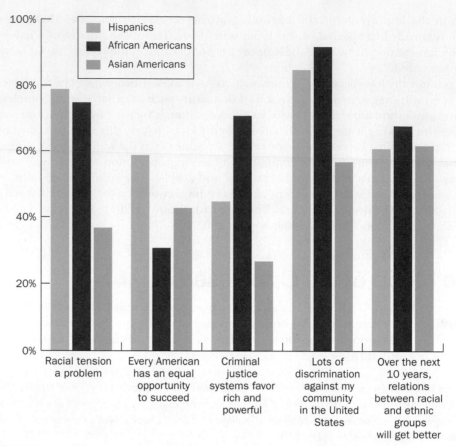

FIGURE 2.3
What Is the State of Race Relations? Three Views

Note: Answers mean respondent believes "very important problem" or "strongly agree" regarding the statements listed. Based on 1,105 interviews in August–September 2007, with bilingual questioners used as necessary.

Source: New America Media 2007:6, 12, 14, 24, 26.

college students in September 2012 indicated a goal of "helping to promote racial understanding" compared to 46 percent in 1992 (Pew Research Center 2010; Pryor et al. 2012:43).

We have focused so far on what comes to mind when we think about prejudice: one group hating another group. But there is another form of prejudice that has been proposed in the past: A group may come to hate itself. Members of groups held in low esteem by society may, as a result, either hate themselves or have low self-esteem, as many social scientists once believed. Research literature of the 1940s through the 1960s emphasized the low self-esteem of minorities. Usually, the subject was African American, but the argument also has been generalized to include any subordinate racial, ethnic, or nationality group.

This view is no longer accepted. We should not assume that minority status influences personality traits in either a good or a bad way. First, such assumptions may create a stereotype. We cannot describe a Black personality any more accurately than we can a White personality. Second, characteristics of minority-group members are not entirely the result of subordinate racial status; they also are influenced by low incomes, poor neighborhoods, and so forth. Third, many studies of personality imply that certain values are normal or preferable, but the values chosen are those of dominant groups.

If assessments of a subordinate group's personality are so prone to misjudgements, then why has the belief in low self-esteem been so widely held? Much of the research rests on studies with preschool-age Black children who were asked to express their

2-7

How do children come to develop an image about themselves? Toys and playthings have an important role, and for many children of racial and ethnic minorities, it is unusual to find toys that look like them. In 2005, a new doll was released called Fulla—an Arab who reflects modesty, piety, and respect, yet underneath she wears chic clothes that might typically be worn by a Muslim woman in private.

preferences for dolls with different facial colors. Indeed, one such study by psychologists Kenneth and Mamie Clark (1947) was cited in the arguments before the U.S. Supreme Court in the landmark 1954 case *Brown v. Board of Education*. The Clarks' study showed that Black children preferred White dolls, a finding that suggested the children had developed a negative self-image. Although subsequent doll studies have sometimes shown Black children's preference for white-faced dolls, other social scientists contend that this shows a realization of what most commercially sold dolls look like rather than documenting low self-esteem (Bloom 1971; Powell-Hopson and Hopson 1988).

Because African American children, as well as other subordinate groups' children, realistically see that Whites have more power and resources and, therefore, rate them higher does not mean that they personally feel inferior. Children who experience overt discrimination are more likely to continue to display feelings of distress and anxiety later in life. However, studies, even those with children, show that when the self-images of middle-class or affluent African Americans are measured, their feelings of self-esteem are more positive than those of comparable Whites (Coker et al. 2009; Gray-Little and Hafdahl 2000).

Intergroup Hostility

Prejudice is as diverse as the nation's population. It exists not only between dominant and subordinate peoples but also among specific subordinate groups. Unfortunately, until recently little research existed on this subject except for a few social distance scales administered to racial and ethnic minorities.

Do we get along? Although this question often is framed in terms of the relationships between White Americans and other racial and ethnic groups, we should recognize the prejudice between groups. In a national survey, people were asked whether they felt they could generally get along with members of other groups. In Figure 2.4, we can see that Whites felt they had the most difficulty getting along with Blacks. We also see the different views that Blacks, Latinos, Asian Americans, and American Indians hold toward other groups.

It is curious finding that some groups feel they get along better with Whites than with other minority groups. Why would that be? Often, low-income people compete daily with

2-7 Explain how hostility is present among racial and ethnic groups.

2-7

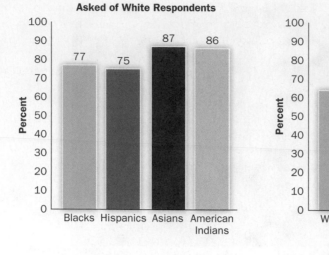

Asked of White Respondents

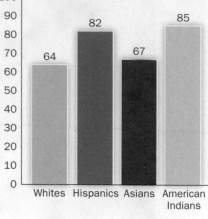

Asked of Black Respondents

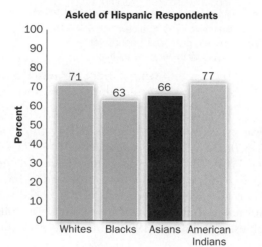

Asked of Hispanic Respondents

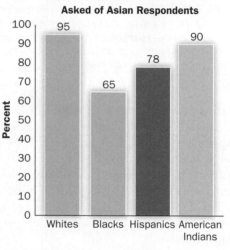

Asked of Asian Respondents

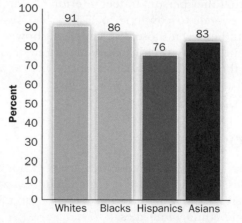

Asked of American Indian Respondents[1]

FIGURE 2.4
Do We Get Along?

Percentage saying groups get along with each other ("Don't Knows" excluded).[1]

[1]Sample size for American Indians is very small and subject to large sample variance.

Note: The wording of the question was, "We hear a lot these days about how various groups in society get along with each other. I'm going to mention several groups and ask whether you think they generally get along with each other or generally do not get along with each other." So, in the "Asked of White Respondents" graph, Whites are asked how Whites get along with each ethnic group; in the "Asked of Black Respondents" graph, Blacks are asked how Blacks get along with each ethnic group, and so on.

Source: Smith 2006:65. Reprinted by permission of the author.

other low-income people and do not readily see the larger societal forces that contribute to their low status. The survey results reveal that many Hispanics are more likely to believe Asian Americans are getting in their way than the White Americans who are the real decision makers in their community.

Most troubling is when intergroup hostility becomes violent. Ethnic and racial tensions among African Americans, Latinos, and immigrants may become manifest in hate crimes. Violence can surface in neighborhoods where people compete for scarce resources such as jobs and housing. Gangs become organized along racial lines, much like private clubs "downtown." In recent years, Los Angeles has been particularly concerned about rival Black and Hispanic gangs. Conflict theorists see this violence as resulting from larger structural forces, but for the average person in such areas, life itself becomes more of a challenge (Archibold 2007).

Reducing Prejudice

Focusing on how to eliminate prejudice involves an explicit value judgment: Prejudice is wrong and causes problems for those who are prejudiced and for their victims. As individuals, we can act to stop prejudice, as indicated in Table 2.2. The important thing to remember is not to ignore prejudice when you witness it.

2-8 Illustrate research on reducing prejudice.

The obvious way to eliminate prejudice is to eliminate its causes: the desire to exploit, the fear of being threatened, and the need to blame others for one's own failure. These might be eliminated by personal therapy, but therapy, even if it works for every individual, is no solution for an entire society in which prejudice is a part of everyday life.

The answer appears to rest with programs directed at society as a whole. Prejudice is attacked indirectly when discrimination is attacked. Despite prevailing beliefs to the contrary, we *can* legislate against prejudice: Statutes and decisions do affect attitudes. In the past, people firmly believed that laws could not overcome norms, especially racist ones.

TABLE 2.2
Ways to Fight Prejudice

1. *Act.* Do something. In the face of hatred, apathy will be taken as acceptance, even by the victims of prejudice themselves.
2. *Unite.* Call a friend or coworker. Organize a group of like-thinking friends from school or your place of worship or club. Create a coalition that is diverse and includes the young, the old, law enforcement representatives, and the media.
3. *Support the victims.* Victims of hate crimes are especially vulnerable. Let them know you care by words, in person, or by e-mail. If you or your friend is a victim, report it.
4. *Do your homework.* If you suspect a hate crime has been committed, do your research to document it.
5. *Create an alternative.* Never attend a rally where hate is a part of the agenda. Find another outlet for your frustration, whatever the cause.
6. *Speak up.* You, too, have First Amendment rights. Denounce the hatred, the cruel jokes. If you see a news organization misrepresenting a group, speak up.
7. *Lobby leaders.* Persuade policymakers, business heads, community leaders, and executives of media outlets to take a stand against hate.
8. *Look long term.* Participate or organize events such as annual parades or cultural fairs to celebrate diversity and harmony. Supplement it with a Web site that can be a 24/7 resource.
9. *Teach acceptance.* Prejudice is learned, and parents and teachers can influence the content of curriculum. In a first-grade class in Seattle, children paint self-portraits, mixing colors to match their skin tone.
10. *Dig deeper.* Look into the issues that divide us—social inequality, immigration, and sexual orientation. Work against prejudice. Dig deep inside yourself for prejudices and stereotypes you may embrace. Find out what is happening and act!

Source: Author, based on Southern Poverty Law Center 2010; Willoughby 2004.

Recent history, especially after the civil rights movement began in 1954, has challenged that once-common belief. Laws and court rulings that have equalized the treatment of Blacks, and Whites have led people to reevaluate their beliefs about what is right and wrong. The increasing tolerance by Whites during the civil rights era from 1954 to 1965 supports this conclusion.

Much research has been done to determine how to change negative attitudes toward groups of people. The most encouraging findings point to education, mass media, intergroup contact, and workplace training programs.

Education

Research on education and prejudice considers special programs aimed at promoting mutual respect as well as what effect more formal schooling generally has on expressions of bigotry.

Most research studies show that well-constructed programs have a positive effect on reducing prejudice, at least temporarily. The reduction is rarely as much as one might want, however. The difficulty is that a single program is insufficient to change life-long habits, especially if little is done to reinforce the program's message once it ends. Persuasion to respect other groups does not operate in a clear field because, in their ordinary environments, people are still subjected to situations that promote prejudicial feelings. Children and adults are encouraged to laugh at Polish jokes and cheer for a team named the *Redskins*. Black adolescents may be discouraged by peers from befriending a White youth. All this undermines the effectiveness of prejudice-reduction programs (Allport 1979).

Studies document that increased formal education, regardless of content, is associated with racial tolerance. Research data show that highly educated people are more likely to indicate respect and liking for groups different from themselves. Why should more education have this effect? It might promote a broader outlook and make a person less likely to endorse myths that sustain racial prejudice. Formal education teaches the importance of qualifying statements such as "even though they have lower test scores, you need to remember the neighborhoods from which they come." Education introduces one to the almost indefinite diversity of social groups and the need to question rigid categorizations, if not reject them altogether. Colleges increasingly include a graduation requirement that students complete a course that explores diversity or multiculturalism. Another explanation is that education does not reduce intolerance but instead makes people more careful about revealing it. Formal education may simply instruct people in the appropriate responses. Despite the lack of a clear-cut explanation, either theory suggests that the continued trend toward a better-educated population will contribute to a reduction in overt prejudice.

However, college education may not reduce prejudice uniformly. For example, some White students might believe that minority students did not earn their admission into college. Students may feel threatened to see large groups of people of different racial and cultural backgrounds congregating and forming their own groups. Racist confrontations do occur outside the classroom and, even if they involve only a few individuals, the events will be followed by hundreds more. Therefore, some aspects of the college experience may only foster "we" and "they" attitudes (Schaefer 1986, 1996).

Mass Media

Mass media, like schools, may reduce prejudice without requiring specially designed programs. Television, radio, motion pictures, newspapers, magazines, and the Internet present only a portion of real life, but what effect do they have on prejudice if the content is racist or antiracist, sexist or antisexist? As with measuring the influence of programs designed to reduce prejudice, coming to strong conclusions on mass media's effect is hazardous, but the evidence points to a measurable effect.

Today, over 56 percent of all youth less than 14 years of age in the United States are children of color, yet few faces they see on television reflect their race or cultural heritage. What is more, the programs shown earlier in the evening, when young people are most likely to watch television, are the least diverse of all. It is not surprising that young people quickly develop expectations of the roles that various racial and ethnic group members play in mass media such as television and motion pictures. A national survey of teens (ages 12–18) asked what characters members of racial and ethnic groups would be likely to play. The respondents' perception of media, as shown in Table 2.3, shows a significant amount of stereotyping occurring in their minds, in the media, or both.

Why the underrepresentation? Incredibly, network executives seemed surprised by the research demonstrating an all-White season. Producers, writers, executives, and advertisers blamed each other for the alleged oversight. In recent years, the rise of cable television and the Internet has fragmented the broadcast entertainment market, siphoning viewers away from the general-audience sitcoms and dramas of the past. With the proliferation of cable channels such as Black Entertainment Television (BET) and the Spanish-language Univision and Web sites that cater to every imaginable taste, there no longer seems to be a need for broadly popular series such as *The Cosby Show*, whose tone and content appealed to Whites as well as Blacks in a way that newer series do not. The result of these sweeping technological changes has been a sharp divergence in viewer preferences. Black comedian and director Tyler Perry is an immensely popular and successful actor, director, and producer but his popularity is largely limited to the African American community.

The absence of racial and ethnic minorities in television is well documented. They are less likely to play recurring roles and are far underrepresented in key decision making positions such as directors, producers, and casting agents. Television series are only part of the picture. News broadcasting is done predominantly by Whites, and local news emphasizes crime, often featuring Black or Hispanic perpetrators; print journalism is nearly the same (Media Matters for America 2013; Writers Guild of America West 2013).

This is especially troubling given another finding in a research study creating simulations where the participants can choose to act in a possible crime situation. Research showed that people were quicker to "shoot" an armed Black person than a White man in a video simulation. In another variation of that same study, the researchers showed subjects fake newspaper articles describing a string of armed robberies that showed either Black or White suspects. The subjects were quicker to "shoot" the armed suspect if he was Black but reading the articles had no impact on their willingness to "shoot" the

---

TABLE 2.3
Stereotyping in the Twenty-First Century

When asked to identify the role a person of a particular ethnic or racial background would be most likely to play in a movie or on television, teenagers cited familiar stereotypes.

Group	Media Roles Identified
African American	Athlete, gang member, police officer
Arab American	Terrorist, convenience store clerk
Asian American	Physician, lawyer, CEO, factory worker
Hispanic	Gang member, factory worker
Irish American	Drunkard, police officer, factory worker
Italian American	Crime boss, gang member, restaurant worker
Jewish American	Physician, lawyer, CEO, teacher
Polish American	Factory worker

Note: Based on national survey of 1,264 people between ages 13 and 18.

Source: Zogby 2001.

Who does the guy pick on *The Bachelor*? Who does the gal pick on *The Bachelorette*? If the first 24 seasons of the two shows are any indication, the person choosing will definitely be White and the choices will most likely be White.

armed White criminal. This is a troubling aspect of the potential impact of media content (Correll et al. 2007a, 2007b).

Reality or unscripted television programs have dominated prime time television for the last few years. Popular with consumers and relatively inexpensive to produce, broadcast and cable networks alike rushed into production shows that featured everyday people or, at least, C-list celebrities thrust into challenges. While unscripted shows have been routinely criticized on many artistic grounds, it is hard not to see the diverse nature of the participants. Reality programs have been analyzed as representing the diversity of the population. They represent a new and significant exception to television dominated by White actors and actresses.

In one area of unscripted television, the color line remains in place. Reality shows that promote creation of romantic partnerships such as *The Bachelor* and *The Bachelorette* do so in an all-white dating gallery—at least that has been the case for the first 24 seasons through late 2012. Meanwhile, back on scripted television, in a recent year, only four of the nearly 70 pilot projects under development by the four major networks had a minority person cast in a starring role (Belton 2009; Braxton 2009; NAACP 2008; Ratledge 2012; Wyatt 2009).

Avoidance Versus Friendship

Is prejudice reduced or intensified when people cross-racial and ethnic boundaries? Two parallel paths have been taken to look at this social distance and equal-status contact.

The Social Distance Scale Robert Park and Ernest Burgess (1921:440) first defined **social distance** as the tendency to approach or withdraw from a racial group. Emory

2-8

Bogardus (1968) conceptualized a scale that could measure social distance empirically. His social distance scale is so widely used that it is often called the **Bogardus scale**.

The scale asks people how willing they would be to interact with various racial and ethnic groups in specified social situations. The situations describe different degrees of social contact or social distance. The items used, with their corresponding distance scores, follow. People are asked whether they would be willing to work alongside someone or be a neighbor to someone of a different group, and, showing the least amount of social distance, be related through marriage. Over the 70-year period in which the tests were administered, certain patterns emerged. In the top third of the hierarchy are White Americans and northern Europeans. Held at greater social distance are eastern and southern Europeans, and generally near the bottom are racial minorities (Bogardus 1968; Song 1991; Wark and Galliher 2007).

Generally, the researchers also found that among the respondents who had friends of different racial and ethnic origins, they were more likely to show greater social distance— that is, they were less likely to have been in each other's homes, shared in fewer activities, and were less likely to talk about their problems with each other. This is unlikely to promote mutual understanding.

Equal Status Contact   An impressive number of research studies have confirmed the **contact hypothesis**, which states that intergroup contact between people of equal status in harmonious circumstances causes them to become less prejudiced and to abandon previously held stereotypes. The importance of equal status in interaction cannot be stressed enough. If a Puerto Rican is abused by his employer, little interracial harmony is promoted. Similarly, the situation in which contact occurs must be pleasant, making a positive evaluation likely for both individuals. Contact between two nurses, one Black and the other White, who are competing for one vacancy as a supervisor may lead to greater racial hostility. On the other hand, being employed together in a harmonious workplace or living in the same neighborhood would work against harboring stereotypes or prejudices (Krysan, Farley, and Couper 2008; Schaefer 1976).

The key factor in reducing hostility, in addition to equal-status contact, is the presence of a common goal. If people are in competition, as already noted, contact may heighten tension. However, bringing people together to share a common task has been shown to reduce ill feelings when these people belong to different racial, ethnic, or religious groups. A study released in 2004 traced the transformations that occurred over the generations in the composition of the Social Service Employees Union in New York City. Always a mixed membership, the union was founded by Jews and Italian Americans, only to experience an influx of Black Americans. More recently in other parts of the United States, it comprises Latin Americans, Africans, West Indians, and South Asians. At each transformation, the common goals of representing the workers effectively overcame the very real cultural differences among the rank and file of Mexican and El Salvadoran immigrants in Houston. The researchers found that when the new arrivals had contact with African Americans, intergroup relations generally improved, and the absence of contact tended to foster ambivalent, even negative, attitudes (Fine 2008; Foerster 2004; Paluck and Green 2009).

The limited amount of intergroup contact is of concern given the power of the contact hypothesis. If there is no positive contact, then how can we expect a decrease in prejudice? National surveys show prejudice directed toward Muslim Americans, but social contact bridges that hatred. In a 2006 survey, 50 percent of people who were not acquainted with a Muslim favored special identification for Muslim Americans, but only 24 percent of those who knew a Muslim embraced that same view. Similarly, people personally familiar with Muslims are more than one-third less likely to endorse special security checks just for Muslims and are less nervous to see Muslim men on the same flight with themselves. Although negative views are common toward Muslim Americans today, they are much less likely to be endorsed by people who have had intergroup contact (Saad 2006).

As African Americans and other subordinate groups slowly gain access to better-paying and more-responsible jobs, the contact hypothesis takes on greater significance. Usually, the availability of equal-status interaction is taken for granted; yet in everyday life, inter-group contact does not conform to the equal-status idea of the contact hypothesis. Furthermore, as we have seen, in a highly segregated society such as the United States, contact tends to be brief and superficial, especially between Whites and minorities. The apartheid-like friendship patterns prevent us from learning firsthand not just how to get along but also how to revel in interracial experiences (Bonilla-Silva and Embrick 2007; Miller 2002).

Avoidance Via the Internet   The emergence of the Internet, smartphones, and social media are often heralded as transforming social behavior, allowing us to network globally. While this may be the case in some instances, avoiding people online who are racially, ethnically, and religiously different is just another means of doing what one's parents and grandparents did face-to-face.

Take dating, for example. While in the past, one avoided people who looked different at social occasions, Internet daters have a new tool for such avoidance. Studies document that people who use Internet dating services typically use filters or respond to background questions to exclude contact with people different from themselves. While many daters use such means, Whites are least open to dating racial and ethnic groups different from themselves, African Americans are most open, and Latinos and Asian Americans are somewhere between the two extremes (Robnett and Feliciano 2011).

Sometimes the avoidance is not necessarily initiated by people but by the helpful technology. There is growing concern that because of an increasingly wired world, in a more subtle fashion we are less likely to benefit from intergroup contacts, not to mention friendships, in the future. Through Facebook, Classmate, and LinkedIn, the Internet allows us to reach out to those who are different from ourselves—or does it? The search engines we use to navigate the Internet are personalized. Google, for example, uses as many as 57 sources of information, including a person's location and past searches, to make calculated guesses about the sites a person might like to visit. Its searches have been personalized in this way since 2009. Keep in mind that Google accounts for 82 percent of the global Internet searches and captures 98 percent of the mobile phone searches. In 2012, Google carried the process one step further by collecting information from the websites that people "friend" or "like" through social media, and then use that information to direct their web searches.

Although Google's approach may at first sound convenient, critics charge that it can trap users in their own worlds by routing them ever more narrowly in the same direction. In his book, *The Filter Bubble,* online political activist Eli Pariser (2011a, 2011b) contends that when a search engine filters our searches, it encloses us in a kind of "invisible bubble" or "walled garden" that limits what we see to what we are already familiar with. Thus, we are not likely to discover people, places, and ideas that are outside our comfort zone. Secure in our online bubble, which we may not even realize is there, we have little interaction with people different from ourselves (Katz 2012; Zitrain 2008).

What is wrong with that? Given a choice, most of us go only to restaurants whose food we enjoy and read and listen to only those books and radio programs we know we like. Yet, wasn't the Internet supposed to open new vistas to us? If we are investigating a major news event, shouldn't we all see the same information when we search for it? Pariser describes what happened when two friends searched for the term "BP" in the spring of 2010, during the Deepwater Horizon oil rig's accidental discharge of crude oil into the Gulf of Mexico. Using the same browser, the two friends got very different results. One saw links to information about the oil spill; the other saw links to information about BP's CEO, intended for investors.

Corporate Response: Diversity Training

Prejudice carries a cost. This cost is not only to the victim but also to any organization that allows prejudice to interfere with its functioning. Workplace hostility can lead to lost productivity and even staff attrition. Furthermore, if left unchecked, an

We often are unaware of all the social situations that allow us to meet people of different ethnic and racial backgrounds. Such opportunities may increase understanding.

organization—whether a corporation, government agency, or nonprofit enterprise—can develop a reputation for having a "chilly climate."

If a business has a reputation that it is unfriendly to people of color or to women, qualified people are discouraged from applying for jobs there and potential clients might seeking products or services elsewhere.

In an effort to improve workplace relations, most organizations have initiated some form of diversity training. These programs are aimed at eliminating circumstances and relationships that cause groups to receive fewer rewards, resources, or opportunities. Typically, programs aim to reduce ill treatment based on race, gender, and ethnicity. In addition, diversity training may deal with (in descending order of frequency) age, disability, religion, and language as well as other aspects, including citizenship status, marital status, and parental status (Society for Human Resource Management 2010, 2011.

It is difficult to make broad generalization about the effectiveness of diversity-training programs because they vary so much in structure between organizations. At one extreme are short presentations that seem to have little support from management. People file into the room feeling it is something they need to get through quickly. Such training is unlikely to be effective and may be counterproductive by heightening social tensions. At the other end of the continuum is a diversity training program that is integrated into initial job training, reinforced periodically, and presented as part of the overall mission of the organization, with full support from all levels of management. In such businesses, diversity is a core value, and management demands a high degree of commitment from all employees.

Remarkably, the prevalence of any diversity programs in organizations remains slow (10 to 30 percent), even in the 30 plus years after the diversity-management paradigm was first widely viewed as good for business. Even inexpensive steps are not widely adopted. Unfortunately, corporations with lower representation of women and minorities are less likely to embrace diversity programs.

Research into different corporate policies have found two that are particularly effective. Diversity task forces that bring together people from different departments to brainstorm about opening up hiring opportunities appear to eventually increase the diversity in upper management. A second successful policy is the diversity mentoring programs designed for aspiring women and minorities, as well as White men, to

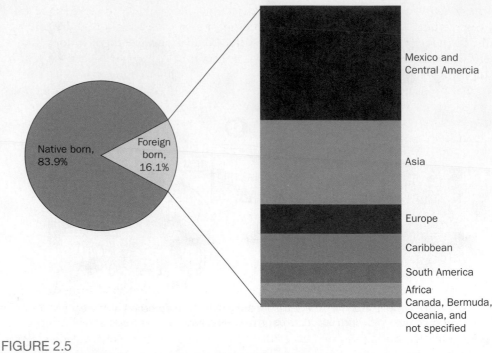

Mexico and
Central Amercia

Asia

Europe

Caribbean

South America

Africa
Canada, Bermuda,
Oceania, and
not specified

Native born,
83.9%

Foreign
born,
16.1%

FIGURE 2.5
Foreign-Born Workers in the United States, by Country
About 16 percent of the civilian labor force is foreign-born, with Mexico the largest source.

Source: Data for 2012 from Mosisa 2013:2.

2-9 Identify ways to reduce hate.

achieve their career goals. Unfortunately, research suggests that if White men perceive African Americans are the primary organizers of such efforts, networking progress can actually have a negative impact.

As shown in Figure 2.5, the workforce is becoming more diverse, and management is taking notice. An increasing proportion of the workforce is foreign-born, and the numbers of U.S.-born African Americans, Latinos, and Asian Americans also are growing. Growing research in business and the social sciences documents that diversity is an asset in bringing about creative changes. The benefits of workplace diversity are especially true at management levels where leadership teams can develop innovative solutions and creative ideas. However, it is troubling to note that organizations that have the least diverse leadership are less likely to adopt any kind of diversity program, whatever its effectiveness (DiTomaso, Post, and Parks-Yancy 2007; Dobbin and Kalev 2013; Dobbin, Kalev, and Kelly 2007; Dobbin, Kim, and Kalev 2011; Gose 2013; Kalev, Dobbin, and Kelly 2006; Leung et al. 2008; Page 2007).

It is not in an organization's best interests if employees start to create barriers based on, for example, racial lines. Earlier, we learned that equal-status contact can reduce hostility. However, in the workplace, people compete for promotions, desirable work assignments, and better office space, to name a few sources of friction. When done well, an organization undertakes diversity training to remove ill feelings among workers, which often reflect the prejudices present in larger society.

To have a lasting impact, diversity training also should not be separated from other aspects of the organization. For example, even the most inspired program will have little effect on prejudice if the organization promotes a sexist or ethnically offensive image in its advertising. The University of North Dakota launched an initiative in 2001 to become one of the top institutions for Native Americans in the nation. Yet at almost the same time, the administration reaffirmed its commitment, despite tribal objections, to have the "Fighting Sioux" as its mascot for athletic teams. In 2005, the National Collegiate Athletic Association began to review logos and mascots that could be considered insulting to Native Americans. Some colleges have resisted suggestions to change or alter their publicity images, although others have abandoned the practice. Finally, 68 percent of the voters of the state voted to abandon the logo. It does little to present diversity training if overt actions by an organization propel it in the opposite direction. (Kolpack 2012).

Despite the problems inherent in confronting prejudice, an organization with a comprehensive, management-supported program of diversity training can go a long way toward reducing prejudice in the workplace. The one major qualifier is that the rest of the organization must also support mutual respect.

Conclusion

This chapter has examined theories of prejudice and measurements of its extent. Prejudice has a long history in the United States. Whispering campaigns suggested that presidents Martin Van Buren and William McKinley were secretly working with the Pope. This whispering emerged into the national debate when John F. Kennedy became the first Roman Catholic to become president. Much more recently, in 2010, 18 percent of Americans believed President Obama to be a Muslim and only 34 percent a Christian (Kristof 2010; Pew Forum on Religion and Public Life 2010).

Are some minority groups now finally being respected? People cheered on May 1, 2011, on hearing that Osama bin Laden had been found and killed. However, the always-patriotic American Indian people were troubled to learn that the military had assigned the code name "Geronimo" to the operation to capture the terrorist. The Chiricahua Apache of New Mexico were particularly disturbed to learn that the name of their freedom fighter was associated with a global terrorist. In response, the U.S. Defense Department said no disrespect was meant to Native Americans. Of course, one can imagine that the operation never would have been named "Operation Lafayette" or "Operation Jefferson" (Dally 2011).

Several theories try to explain why prejudice exists. Theories for prejudice include two that tend to be psychological scapegoating and authoritarian personality—and emphasize why a particular person harbors ill feelings. Others are more sociological-exploitation and normative—and view prejudice in the context of our interaction in a larger society.

Surveys conducted in the United States over the past 60 years point to a reduction of prejudice as measured by the willingness to express stereotypes or maintain social distance. Survey data also show that African Americans, Latinos, Asian Americans, and American Indians do not necessarily feel comfortable with each other. They have adopted attitudes toward other oppressed groups similar to those held by many White Americans.

The absence of widespread public expression of prejudice does not mean prejudice itself is absent. Recent prejudice aimed at Hispanics, Asian Americans, and large recent immigrant groups such as Arab Americans and Muslim Americans is well documented. Issues such as immigration and affirmative action reemerge and cause bitter resentment. Furthermore, ill feelings exist between subordinate groups in schools, on the streets, and in the workplace. Color-blind racism allows one to appear to be tolerant while allowing racial and ethnic inequality to persist.

Equal-status contact may reduce hostility between groups. However, in a highly segregated society defined by inequality, such opportunities are not typical. The mass media can help reduce discrimination, but they have not done enough and may even intensify ill feelings by promoting stereotypical images.

Even though we can be encouraged by the techniques available to reduce intergroup hostility, sizable segments of the population still do not want to live in integrated neighborhoods, do not want to work for or be led by someone of a different race, and certainly object to the idea of their relatives marrying outside their own group. People still harbor stereotypes toward one another, and this tendency includes racial and ethnic minorities having stereotypes about one another.

Reducing prejudice is important because it can lead to support for policy change. There are steps we can take as individuals to confront prejudice and overcome hatred. Another real challenge and the ultimate objective are to improve the social condition of oppressed groups in the United States. To consider this challenge, we turn to discrimination in Chapter 3. Discrimination's costs are high to both dominant and subordinate groups. With this fact in mind, we examine some techniques for reducing discrimination.

Summary

1. Prejudice consists of negative attitudes, and discrimination consists of negative behavior toward a group.

2. Typically unconsciously, White people accept privilege automatically extended to them in everyday life.

3. Among explanations for prejudice are the theories of scapegoating, authoritarian personality, and exploitation as well as the normative approach.

4. Stereotypes present the content or images that prejudiced people hold but also become accepted as reality.

5. Although evidence indicates that the public expression of prejudice has declined, ample evidence exists that people are expressing race-neutral principles or color-blind racism that still serves to perpetuate inequality in society.

6. Typically, members of minority groups have a significantly more negative view of social inequality and are more pessimistic about the future compared to Whites.

7. Not only do people in dominant positions direct prejudice at racial and ethnic minorities but intergroup hostility among the minorities themselves also persists and may become violent.

8. Various techniques are utilized by the corporate sector to reduce prejudice, including educational programs, mass media, friendly intergroup contact, and diversity-training programs.

9. Ten steps have been identified that individuals can take to reduce or end prejudice.

Key Terms

anti-Semitism, p. 37

authoritarian personality, p. 37

Bogardus scale, p. 51

color-blind racism, p. 42

contact hypothesis, p. 51

discrimination, p. 34

ethnocentrism, p. 33

ethnophaulisms, p. 33

exploitation theory, p. 38

homophobia, p. 40

normative approach, p. 38

prejudice, p. 33

racial profiling, p. 41

scapegoating theory, p. 37

sexism, p. 40

social distance, p. 50

stereotypes, p. 39

White privilege, p. 36

Review Questions

1. How are prejudice and discrimination both related and unrelated to each other?

2. If White people are privileged, how do we explain the presence of poverty among Whites?

3. How do theories of prejudice relate to different expressions of prejudice?

4. What is the impact of stereotypes on how we interact with others?

5. How is color-blind racism expressed?

6. What toll can prejudice take on the people subjected to bigotry?

7. How would you describe the presence or absence of prejudice expressed between racial and ethnic subordinate groups?

8. Describe the efforts to reduce prejudice through education and the mass media.

9. Describe the ways that a community or individual can combat prejudice and hatred.

Critical Thinking

1. What might a contemporary version of the LaPiere study look like? Instead of using a Chinese couple, one might look at the treatment of a Muslim man accompanied by his veiled wife.

2. What privileges do you have that you do not give much thought to? Are they in any way related to race, ethnicity, religion, or social class?

3. Identify stereotypes associated with a group of people such as older adults or people with physical disabilities.

4. Consider the television programs you watch the most. In terms of race and ethnicity, how well do the programs you watch reflect the diversity of the population in the United States?

5. Can you identify any steps that have been taken against prejudice in your community?

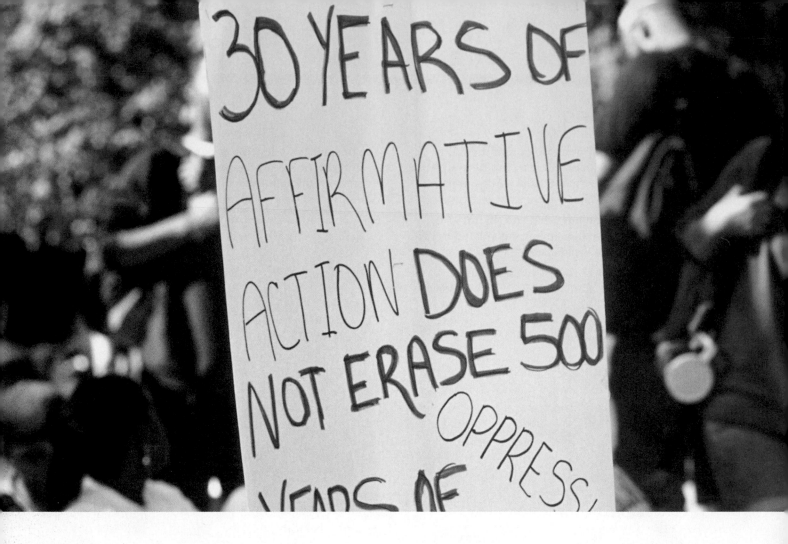

3

Discrimination

3-1 Distinguish between relative and absolute deprivation.

3-2 Define hate crimes.

3-3 Summarize how institutions discriminate.

3-4 Describe how discrimination can be documented today.

3-5 Illustrate how wealth inequality is discrimination's legacy.

3-6 Discuss environmental justice.

3-7 Explain affirmative action.

3-8 Analyze reverse discrimination.

3-9 Put into your own words the glass ceiling.

"I didn't get the job" is a frequent complaint that soon leads to reasons "I" did not get the job for which I applied. Sometimes people think it's because of their race. Is discrimination still the case?

A dramatic confirmation of discrimination came with research begun by sociologist Devah Pager in 2003. She sent White, Black, and Latino men out as trained "testers" to look for entry-level jobs in Milwaukee and New York City that required no experience or special training. Each tester was in his twenties and was college educated, but each one presented himself as having only a high school diploma and similar job history.

The job-seeking experiences with different employers were vastly different among the men. Why? Besides having different racial and ethnic background, some testers indicated in the job application that they had served 18 months in jail for a felony conviction (possession of cocaine with intent to distribute). As you can see in Figure 3.1, applicants with a prison record received significantly fewer callbacks. Although a criminal record made a dramatic difference, race was clearly more important. In another study, Pager documented that Latino job applicants were at a disadvantage similar to that of the African American testers (Pager, Western, and Bonikowski 2009; Pager and Western 2012).

The differences were so pointed that a White job applicant with a jail record received more callbacks for further consideration than a Black man with no criminal record. Whiteness has a privilege even when it comes to jail time; race, it seems, was more of a concern to potential employers than a criminal background. It is no surprise that an analysis of labor patterns after release from prison finds that wages grow at a 21 percent slower rate for Black compared to White ex-inmates.

"I expected there to be an effect of race, but I did not expect it to swamp the results as it did," Pager told an interviewer. Her finding was especially significant because one in three African American men and one in six Hispanic men are expected to serve time in prison during their lifetime compared to one in 17 White men (Greenhouse 2012; Kroeger 2004).

Pager's research, which was widely publicized, eventually contributed to a change in public policy. In his 2004 State of the Union address, and specifically referring to Pager's work, President George W. Bush announced a $300 million monitoring program for ex-convicts who are attempting to reintegrate into society.

Discrimination has a long history, right up to the present, of taking its toll on people. Discrimination is the denial of opportunities and equal rights to individuals and groups because of prejudice or other arbitrary reasons. We examine the many faces of discrimination, its many victims, and the many ways scholars have documented its presence today in the United States. We not only return to more examples of discrimination in housing but also look at differential treatment in employment opportunities, wages, voting, vulnerability to environmental hazards, and even access to membership in private clubs.

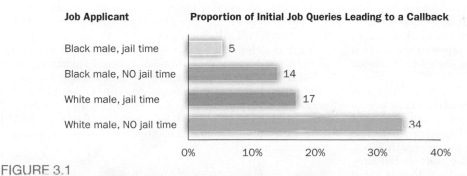

Job Applicant   **Proportion of Initial Job Queries Leading to a Callback**

Black male, jail time — 5
Black male, NO jail time — 14
White male, jail time — 17
White male, NO jail time — 34

0%   10%   20%   30%   40%

FIGURE 3.1
Discrimination in Job Seeking

Source: Pager 2003:958. Reprinted by permission of the University of Chicago.

3-1

3-1 Distinguish between relative and absolute deprivation.

Understanding Discrimination

People in the United States find it difficult to see discrimination as a widespread phenomenon. "After all," it is often said, "these minorities drive cars, hold jobs, own their homes, and even go to college." Discriminatory practices are not limited to any one nation and its victims include a broad array of groups. In the A Global View, we consider how the Roma (or Gypsies) have been victimized.

Relative vs. Absolute Deprivation

An understanding of discrimination in modern industrialized societies such as the United States must begin by distinguishing between relative and absolute deprivation.

Conflict theorists have said correctly that it is not absolute, unchanging standards that determine deprivation and oppression. Although minority groups may be viewed as having adequate or even good incomes, housing, health care, and educational opportunities, it is their position relative to some other group that offers evidence of discrimination.

Relative deprivation is defined as the conscious experience of a negative discrepancy between legitimate expectations and present actualities. After settling in the United States, immigrants often enjoy better material comforts and more political freedom than was possible in their old countries. If they compare themselves with most other people in the United States, however, they will feel deprived because, although their standards have improved, the immigrants still perceive relative deprivation.

Absolute deprivation, on the other hand, implies a fixed standard based on a minimum level of subsistence below which families should not be expected to exist. Discrimination does not necessarily mean absolute deprivation. A Japanese American who is promoted to a management position may still be a victim of discrimination if he or she had been passed over for years because of corporate reluctance to place an Asian American in a highly visible position.

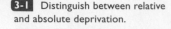 **A Global View**

The Roma: A Thousand Years of Discrimination

The Roma people (also referred to as Gypsies) are members of a minority group numbering 12 to 15 million people who are dispersed over many countries. The people originated in India, but most Roma now live in Europe, with perhaps as many as 1 million in North America. They continue to be characterized by a nomadic lifestyle, often in response to prejudice and discrimination. Certain common activities such as fortune telling, traveling together in large caravans, and arranged marriages create hostile responses to their arrival in communities. Although the Roma speak their own distinctive language, they have usually adopted the religion of their home region, such as Roman Catholic, Orthodox Christian, or Muslim.

The Roma are the largest ethnic minority in the European Union and are the objects of that organization's efforts to address their poor housing levels, little formal schooling, and high levels of unemployment. Progress is evident in a decline in racially motivated murders of Roma since the early 1990s. Historically, they had been subjected to expulsion, but large numbers died in the Holocaust as a part of Hitler's racial purification efforts. In reference to this genocide, a mayor in France in response to complaints about Roma in his area responded by saying, "Maybe Hitler didn't kill enough of them" (Corbert 2013).

In addition to the efforts of the European Union, Gypsies themselves have begun to work through established channels to confront discrimination. Simply being Roma makes many authorities assume a child is ill prepared, as in the Czech Republic, where the majority of children in special schools for the learning disabled are Roma. The Roma brought legal action to stop this practice. In a case compared to the 1954 *Brown v. Board of Education* decision in the United States, the European Court of Human Rights ruled in 2007 in *D.H. and Others v. Czech Republic* that the Czech practice was discriminatory, with Gypsy children receiving inappropriate placements and substandard education. Actions taken by the Czech Republic finally in 2011 were greeted with muted enthusiasms with many seeing little change.

Sources: European Roma Rights Centre 2008, 2012; Hacek 2008; Schaefer and Zellner 2011.

3-2

Dissatisfaction also is likely to arise from feelings of relative deprivation. The members of a society who feel most frustrated and disgruntled by the social and economic conditions of their lives are not necessarily worse off in an objective sense. Social scientists have long recognized that what is most significant is how people perceive their situations. Karl Marx pointed out that although the misery of the workers was important in reflecting their oppressed state, so was their position relative to the ruling class. In 1847, Marx wrote, "Although the enjoyment of the workers has risen, the social satisfaction that they have has fallen in comparison with the increased enjoyment of the capitalist" (Marx and Engels 1955:94).

This statement explains why the groups or individuals who are most vocal and best organized against discrimination are not necessarily in the worst economic and social situation. However, they are likely to be those who most strongly perceive that, relative to others, they are not receiving their fair share. Resistance to perceived discrimination, rather than the actual amount of absolute discrimination, is the key.

Hate Crimes

Although prejudice certainly is not new in the United States, it is receiving increased attention as it manifests itself in hate crimes in neighborhoods, at meetings, and on college campuses. The Hate Crime Statistics Act, which became law in 1990, directs the Department of Justice to gather data on hate or bias crimes.

3-2 Define hate crimes.

What Are Hate Crimes?

The government defines an ordinary crime as a **hate crime** when offenders are motivated to choose a victim because of some characteristic—for example, race, ethnicity, religion, sexual orientation, or disability—and provide evidence that hatred prompted them to commit the crime. Hate crimes also are sometimes referred to as *bias crimes*.

The Hate Crime Statistics Act created a national mandate to identify such crimes, whereas previously only 12 states had monitored hate crimes. The act has since been amended to include disabilities, physical and mental, as well as sexual orientation as factors that could be considered a basis for hate crimes.

In 2013, law enforcement agencies released hate crime data submitted by police agencies. Even though many hate crimes are not reported (less than one in seven participating agencies reported an incident), a staggering number of offenses that come to law agencies' attention were motivated by hate. While most incidents receive relatively little attention, some become the attention of headlines and online sites for days. Such was the case in 2009 when a Maryland man with a long history of ties to neo-Nazi groups walked into the U.S. Holocaust Memorial Museum in Washington, DC, and opened fire, killing a security guard.

Official reports noted more than 6,700 hate crimes and bias-motivated incidents in 2012. As indicated in Figure 3.2, race was the apparent motivation for the bias in

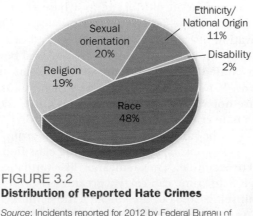

FIGURE 3.2
Distribution of Reported Hate Crimes

Source: Incidents reported for 2012 by Federal Bureau of Investigation 2013.

approximately 48 percent of the reports, and religion, sexual orientation, and ethnicity accounted for 11 to 20 percent each. Vandalism against property and intimidation were the most common crimes, but among the more than 4,600 crimes directed against people, 44 percent involved assault, rape, or murder.

The vast majority of hate crimes are directed by members of the dominant group toward those who are, relatively speaking, powerless. Only one in five bias incidents based on race are anti-White. Hate crimes, except for those that are most horrific, receive little media attention, and anti-White incidents probably receive even less. Hostility based on race knows no boundaries (Department of Justice 2013; Witt 2007).

The official reports of hate or bias crimes appear to be only the tip of the iceberg. Government-commissioned surveys conducted over a national cross section indicate that 192,000 people annually report they have been victims of hate crimes, but only half of these are reported to police. Of these, only one out of ten, according to the victims, are confirmed as hate crimes. Although definitions vary, a considerable amount of racial hostility in this country becomes violent (Harlow 2005; Perry 2003).

National legislation and publicity have made *hate crime* a meaningful term, and we are beginning to recognize the victimization associated with such incidents. A current proposal would make a violent crime a federal crime if it were motivated by racial or religious bias. Although passage is uncertain, the serious consideration of the proposal indicates a willingness to consider a major expansion of federal jurisdiction. Currently, federal law prohibits crimes motivated by race, color, religion, or national origin only if they violate a federally guaranteed right such as voting.

Victimized groups do more than experience and observe hate crimes and other acts of prejudice. Watchdog organizations play an important role in documenting bias-motivated violence; among such groups are the Anti-Defamation League, the National Institute Against Prejudice and Violence, the Southern Poverty Law Center, and the National Gay and Lesbian Task Force.

To further their agenda, established hate groups have even set up propaganda sites on the World Wide Web. This also creates opportunities for previously unknown haters and hate groups to promote themselves. However, hate crime legislation does not affect such outlets because of legal questions involving freedom of speech. An even more recent technique of hate groups has been to use instant messaging software, which enables Internet users to create a private chat room with another individual. Enterprising bigots use directories to target their attacks through instant messaging, much as harassing telephone calls were placed in the past. Even more creative and subtle are people who have constructed Web sites to attract people who are surfing for information on Martin Luther King, Jr., only to find a site that looks educational but savagely discredits the civil rights activist. A close inspection reveals that a White-supremacist organization hosts the site (Davis 2008; Simon Wiesenthal Center 2008; Working 2007).

Why Do Hate Crimes Carry Harsher Penalties?

Frequently, one hears the identification of a crime as a hate crime being questioned. After all, is not hate involved in every assault or act of vandalism? While many non-hate crimes may include a motivation of hatred toward an individual or organization, a hate or bias crime toward a minority is intended to carry a message well beyond the individual victim. When a person is assaulted because they are gay or lesbian, the act is meant to terrorize all gay and lesbians. Vandalizing a mosque or synagogue is meant to warn all Muslims or Jews that they are not wanted and their religious faith is considered inferior.

In many respects, today's hate crimes are like the terrorist efforts of the Ku Klux Klan of generations ago. Targets may be randomly selected, but the group being terrorized is carefully chosen. In many jurisdictions, having a crime being classified as a hate crime can increase the punishment. For example, a misdemeanor like vandalism can be increased to a felony. A felony that is a hate crime can carry a greater prison sentence. These sanctions were upheld by the Supreme Court in the 1993 decision *Mitchell v. Wisconsin*, which recognized that greater harm may be done by hate-motivated crimes (Blazak 2011).

Institutional Discrimination

3-3

Individuals practice discrimination in one-on-one encounters, and institutions practice discrimination through their daily operations. Indeed, a consensus is growing today that institutional discrimination is more significant than acts committed by prejudiced individuals.

3-3 Summarize how institutions discriminate.

Social scientists are particularly concerned with how patterns of employment, education, criminal justice, housing, health care, and government operations maintain the social significance of race and ethnicity. **Institutional discrimination** is the denial of opportunities and equal rights to individuals and groups that results from the normal operations of a society.

Civil rights activist Stokely Carmichael and political scientist Charles Hamilton are credited with introducing the concept of institutional racism. *Individual discrimination* refers to overt acts of individual Whites against individual Blacks; Carmichael and Hamilton reserved the term *institutional racism* for covert acts committed collectively against an entire group. From this perspective, discrimination can take place without an individual intending to deprive others of privileges and even without the individual being aware that others are being deprived (Ture and Hamilton 1992).

How can discrimination be widespread and unconscious at the same time? A few documented examples of institutional discrimination follow:

1. Standards for assessing credit risks work against African Americans and Hispanics who seek to establish businesses because many lack conventional credit references. Businesses in low-income areas where these groups often reside also have much higher insurance costs.

2. IQ testing favors middle-class children, especially the White middle class, because of the types of questions included.

3. The entire criminal justice system, from the patrol officer to the judge and jury, is dominated by Whites who find it difficult to understand life in poverty areas.

4. Hiring practices often require several years' experience at jobs only recently opened to members of subordinate groups.

5. Many jobs automatically eliminate people with felony records or past drug offenses, a practice that disproportionately reduces employment opportunities for people of color.

Institutional discrimination is so systemic that it takes on the pattern of what has been termed "woodwork racism" in that racist outcomes become so widespread that African Americans, Latinos, Asian Americans, and others endure them as a part of everyday life (Feagin and McKinney 2003).

At the beginning of this chapter, we noted how employers routinely pass over job applicants who are felons. To casual observers, this may seem reasonable; however, Black and Latino job applicants are more likely to be passed over than Whites. This is a form of institutional discrimination. Recognizing this, the Equal Opportunity Commission ruled in 2012 that while employers may consider criminal records, a policy that excludes all applicants with a conviction could violate employment discrimination laws because of this differential impact. This does not mean employers must hire ex-felons, only that blanket exclusions are to be avoided (Greenhouse 2012).

Despite the positive step, concern grows over another potential example of institutional discrimination in the area of voting requirements. How do we establish the authenticity of a person's right to vote? States are now considering requiring a government-issued ID *with the person's photograph* to vote. Numerous states (see Figure 3.3) have enacted laws requiring voters to show a photo ID, presumably to prevent voter fraud. However, there is little evidence that people have been impersonating eligible voters at the polls.

Courts have been reluctant to uphold such laws, contending that accessibility is not ensured for all eligible voters to obtain such a credential. Such laws disproportionately disenfranchise members of minority groups, as well as the elderly, simply because they do

3-4

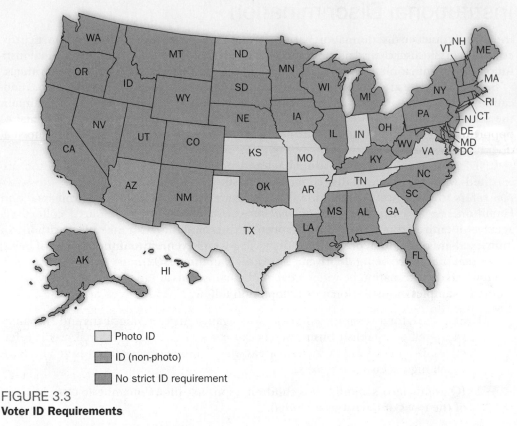

FIGURE 3.3
Voter ID Requirements

Legend:
- Photo ID
- ID (non-photo)
- No strict ID requirement

Source: National Conference of State Legislatures 2013.

not have a driver's license. National surveys found 25 percent of African Americans and 16 percent of Latino citizens do not have a valid government-issued photo ID, compared to 8 percent of White citizens. So, court decisions aside, what we have is another case of institutional discrimination in that through the normal operation of voting regulations equal rights are more likely to be denied to people of color (Brennan Center 2006, 2013; Dade 2012b).

In other situations, even apparently neutral institutional standards can lead a college's policy to have discriminatory effects. African American students at a Midwestern state university protested a policy under which fraternities and sororities that wanted to use campus facilities for a dance were required to post a security deposit to cover possible damage. The Black students complained that this policy had a discriminatory impact on minority student organizations. Campus police countered that the university's policy applied to all student groups interested in using these facilities. However, because almost all White fraternities and sororities at the school had their own houses, which they used for dances, the policy affected only African American and other subordinate groups' organizations.

Institutional discrimination continuously imposes more hindrances on and awards fewer benefits to certain racial and ethnic groups than it does to others. This is the underlying and painful context of American intergroup relations.

Discrimination Today

3-4 Describe how discrimination can be documented today.

Discrimination continues to be widespread in the United States. It sometimes results from prejudices held by individuals but, more significantly, it is found in institutional discrimination. We will look first at measuring discrimination in terms of income and then efforts that are being made to eliminate or at least reduce it.

Discrimination Hits the Wallet

How much discrimination is there? As in measuring prejudice, problems arise when trying to quantify discrimination. Measuring prejudice is hampered by the difficulties in assessing attitudes and by the need to take many factors into account. It is further limited by the initial challenge of identifying different treatment. A second difficulty of measuring discrimination is assigning a cost to discrimination.

An important measure of economic well-being for any household is their annual income and the wealth they have to draw upon in cases of emergency. **Income** refers to salaries, wages, and other money received; **wealth** is a more inclusive term that encompasses all of a person's material assets, including land and other types of property. We first consider income and then look at wealth later in this chapter.

Some tentative conclusions about discrimination can be made looking at income and wealth data. Figure 3.4 uses income data to show the vivid disparity in income between African Americans and Whites and also between men and women. This encompasses all full-time workers. White men, with a median income of $55,989, earn one-third more than Black men and almost twice what Hispanic women earn in wages.

Yet Asian American men are at the top and edge out White males by almost $5,000 a year. Why do Asian American men earn so much if race serves as a barrier? The economic picture is not entirely positive. Some Asian American groups such as Laotians and Vietnamese have high levels of poverty. We might be drawn to the fact that Asian American income appears to slightly overtake that of Whites. However, a significant number of Asian Americans with advanced educations have high-earning jobs, which brings up the median income. However, as we will see, given their high levels of schooling, their incomes should be even higher.

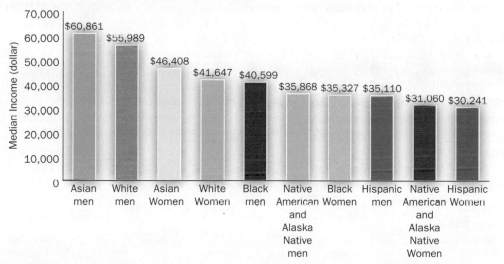

FIGURE 3.4
Median Income by Race, Ethnicity, and Gender

Even at the very highest levels of schooling, the income gap remains between Whites and Blacks. Education also has little apparent effect on the income gap between male and female workers. Even a brief analysis reveals striking differences in earning power between White men and other groups in the United States. Furthermore, greater inequality is apparent for African American and Hispanic women.

Note: Data released in 2013 for income earned in 2012. Median income is from all sources and is limited to year-round, full-time workers at least 25 years old (American Indian data for 16 years or older). Data for White men and women are for non-Hispanics.

Source: American Community Survey American A 2013a: Table B20017C; DeNavas-Walt, Proctor, and Smith 2013 PINC-03.

3-4

Clearly, regardless of race or ethnicity, men outpace women in annual income. This disparity between the incomes of Black women and White men has remained unchanged over the more than 50 years during which such data have been tabulated. It illustrates yet another instance of the greater inequality experienced by minority women. Also, Figure 3.4 includes data only for full-time, year-round workers; it excludes homemakers and the unemployed. Even in this comparison, the deprivation of Blacks, Hispanics, and women is confirmed again.

Are these differences entirely the result of discrimination in employment? No. Individuals within the four groups are not equally prepared to compete for high-paying jobs. Past discrimination is a significant factor in a person's current social position. Taxpayers, predominantly White, were unwilling to subsidize the public education of African Americans and Hispanics at the same levels as White pupils. Even as these actions have changed, today's schools show the continuing results of this uneven spending pattern from the past. Education clearly is an appropriate variable to control.

In Table 3.1, median income is compared, holding education constant, which means that we can compare Blacks and Whites and men and women with approximately the same amount of formal schooling. More education means more money, but the disparity remains. The gap between races does narrow somewhat as education increases. However, both African Americans and women lag behind their more affluent counterparts. The contrast remains dramatic: Women with a master's degree typically receive $60,927, which means they earn more than $5,000 *less* than men who complete only a bachelor's degree.

Thinking over the long term, a woman with a bachelor's degree will work full-time three years to earn $150,000. The typical male can work a little more than 27 months, take over 9 months off without pay, and still exceed the woman's earnings. Women, regardless of race, pay at every point. They are often hired at lower starting salaries in jobs comparable to those held by men. Salary increases come slower. And by their 30s, they rarely recover from even short maternity leaves.

Note what happens to Asian American households. Although highly educated Asian Americans earn a lot of money, they trail well behind their White counterparts. With a

TABLE 3.1
Median Income by Race and Sex, Holding Education Constant

Even at the very highest levels of schooling, the income gap remains between Whites and Blacks. Education also has little apparent effect on the income gap between male and female workers (income values in dollars).

	Race				Sex	
	White Families	Black Families	Asian Families	Hispanic Families	Male	Female
Total	72,404	41,737	80,046	41,970	50,955	39,777
High School						
Nongraduate	35,648	20,537	34,030	30,992	30,329	21,387
Graduate	55,037	32,075	48,734	39,145	40,351	30,406
College						
Associate Degree	71,633	48,813	70,110	55,580	50,961	37,321
Bachelor's degree	100,412	72,724	95,654	76,647	66,153	50,173
Master's degree	112,503	84,164	119,290	101,083	85,116	60,927
Doctorate degree	140,303	108,333	124,515	126,048	106,467	77,902

Note: Data released in 2013 for income earned in 2012. Figures are median income from all sources except capital gains. Included are public assistance payments, dividends, pensions, unemployment compensation, and so on. Incomes are for all workers 25 years of age and older with earnings. High school graduates include those with GEDs. Data for Whites are for White non-Hispanics. Family data for Hispanic doctorate-holders' families are author's estimate.
Source: DeNavas-Walt, Proctor, and Smith 2013 FINC-01, PINC-03.

doctorate degree holder in the family, the typical Asian American household earns an estimated $124,515, compared to $140,303 in a White household.

This is the picture today, but is it getting better? According to a Census Bureau report released in 2011, the answer is no. During the early years of the twenty-first century, Blacks were more likely to stay poor than Whites and those African Americans in the top rung of income were more likely to fall than their White counterparts among the wealthy. The inequality is dramatic and the trend is not diminishing (Hisnanick and Giefer 2011).

Now that education has been held constant, is the remaining gap caused by discrimination? Not necessarily. Table 3.1 uses only the amount of schooling, not its quality. Racial minorities are more likely to attend inadequately financed schools. Some efforts have been made to eliminate disparities between school districts in the amount of wealth available to tax for school support, but they have met with little success.

The inequality of educational opportunity may seem less important in explaining sex discrimination. Although women usually are not segregated from men, educational institutions encourage talented women to enter fields that pay less (nursing or elementary education) than other occupations that require similar amounts of training. Even when they do enter the same occupation, the earnings disparity persists. Even controlling for age, a study of census data showed that female physicians and surgeons earned 69 percent of what their male counterparts did. Looking at broad ranges of occupations, researchers in the last few years have attributed between one-quarter and one-third of the wage gap to discrimination rather than personal choices, skill preparation, and formal schooling (Reskin 2012; Weinberg 2004).

Eliminating Discrimination

Two main agents of social change work to reduce discrimination: voluntary associations organized to solve racial and ethnic problems and the federal government, including the courts. The two are closely related: Most efforts initiated by the government were urged by associations or organizations that represent minority groups, following vigorous protests by African Americans against racism. Resistance to social inequality by subordinate groups has been the key to change. Rarely has any government on its own initiative sought to end discrimination based on such criteria as race, ethnicity, and gender.

All racial and ethnic groups of any size are represented by private organizations that are, to some degree, trying to end discrimination. Some groups originated in the first half of the twentieth century, but most have been founded since World War II or have become significant forces in bringing about change only since then. These include church organizations, fraternal social groups, minor political parties, and legal defense funds, as well as more militant organizations operating under the scrutiny of law enforcement agencies. The purposes, membership, successes, and failures of these resistance organizations dedicated to eliminating discrimination are discussed throughout this book.

The judiciary, charged with interpreting laws and the U.S. Constitution, has a much longer history of involvement in the rights of racial, ethnic, and religious minorities. However, its early decisions protected the rights of the dominant group, as in the 1857 U.S. Supreme Court's *Dred Scott* decision, which ruled that slaves remained slaves even when living or traveling in states where slavery was illegal. Not until the 1940s did the Supreme Court revise earlier decisions and begin to grant African Americans the same rights as those held by Whites. The 1954 *Brown v. Board of Education* decision, which stated that "separate but equal" facilities—including education—were unconstitutional, heralded a new series of rulings, arguing that distinguishing between races in order to segregate was inherently unconstitutional.

The most important legislative effort to eradicate discrimination was the Civil Rights Act of 1964. This act led to the establishment of the Equal Employment Opportunity Commission (EEOC), which had the power to investigate complaints against employers and to recommend action to the Department of Justice. If the justice department sued and discrimination was found, then the court could order appropriate compensation. The act covered employment practices of all businesses with more than 25 employees and nearly all employment agencies and labor unions. A 1972 amendment broadened the coverage to employers with as few as 15 employees.

The Civil Rights Act of 1964 prohibited discrimination in public accommodations—that is, hotels, motels, restaurants, gasoline stations, and amusement parks. Publicly owned facilities such as parks, stadiums, and swimming pools were also prohibited from discriminating. Another important provision forbade discrimination in all federally supported programs and institutions such as hospitals, colleges, and road construction projects.

The Civil Rights Act of 1964 was not perfect. Since 1964, several acts and amendments to the original act have been added to cover the many areas of discrimination it left untouched, such as criminal justice and housing. Even in areas singled out for enforcement in the act, discrimination still occurs. Federal agencies charged with enforcement complain that they are underfunded or are denied wholehearted support by the White House. Also, regardless of how much the EEOC may want to act in a particular case, the person who alleges discrimination has to pursue the complaint over a long time that is marked by lengthy periods of inaction. Despite these efforts, devastating forms of discrimination persist. African Americans, Latinos, and others fall victim to **redlining**, or the pattern of discrimination against people trying to buy homes in minority and racially changing neighborhoods.

While overt discriminatory practices may have largely ended, home seekers are not treated alike. The race of the home seeker makes a difference. The Department of Housing and Urban Development (HUD) issued a report based on testing 8,000 times in 28 metropolitan areas. Testers were matched gender and age, and presented themselves as equally well-qualified to rent or buy the advertised unit. Overall Blacks, Hispanics, and Asian Americans were all told about and shown fewer units than their White counterparts. HUD has done such studies since 1977 and the latest study shows a decline in the disparity in housing opportunities offered to minorities but the gap persists. Minority home seekers continue to be asked more questions about their finances, experience unkept appointments, are quoted higher rents for the same unit, and, in the case of home purchases, are expected to be prequalified for a loan. Discrimination against Blacks, Latinos, and Asians persists in housing even in a more subtle form from the days of the redlining (Turner et al 2013).

People living in predominantly minority neighborhoods have found that companies with delivery services refuse to go to their area. In one case that attracted national attention in 1997, a Pizza Hut in Kansas City refused to deliver 40 pizzas to an honors program at a high school in an all-Black neighborhood. A Pizza Hut spokesperson called the neighborhood unsafe and said that almost every city has "restricted areas" to which the company will not deliver. This admission was particularly embarrassing because the high school already had a $170,000-a-year contract with Pizza Hut to deliver pizzas as a part of its school lunch program. Service redlining covers everything from parcel deliveries to repair people as well as food deliveries. The red pencil continues to exist in cities throughout the United States (Fuller 1998; Rusk 2001; Schwartz 2001; Turner et al. 2002; Yinger 1995).

Although civil rights laws often have established rights for other minorities, the Supreme Court made them explicit in two 1987 decisions involving groups other than African Americans. In the first of the two cases, an Iraqi American professor asserted that he had been denied tenure because of his Arab origins; in the second, a Jewish congregation brought suit for damages in response to the defacement of its synagogue with derogatory symbols. The Supreme Court ruled unanimously that, in effect, any member of an ethnic minority might sue under federal prohibitions against discrimination. These decisions paved the way for almost all racial and ethnic groups to invoke the Civil Rights Act of 1964 (Taylor 1987).

A particularly insulting form of discrimination seemed finally to be on its way out in the late 1980s. Many social clubs had limitations that forbade membership to minorities, Jews, and women. For years, exclusive clubs argued that they were merely selecting friends, but, in fact, a principal function of these clubs is as a forum to transact business. Denial of membership meant more than the inability to attend a luncheon; it also seemed to exclude certain groups from part of the marketplace. In 1988, the Supreme Court ruled unanimously in *New York State Clubs Association v. City of New York* that states and cities might ban sex discrimination by large private clubs where business lunches and similar activities take place. Although the ruling does not apply to all clubs and leaves the issue of racial and ethnic barriers unresolved, it did chip away at the arbitrary exclusiveness of private groups (Steinhauer 2006; Taylor 1988).

Memberships and restrictive organizations remain perfectly legal. The rise to national attention of professional golfer Tiger Woods, of mixed Native American, African, and Asian ancestry, made the public aware that he would be prohibited from playing at a minimum of 23 golf courses by virtue of race. In 2002, women's groups tried unsuccessfully to have the golf champion speak out because the Master's and British Open were played on courses closed to women as members. Ten years later, the Augusta National Golf Club, home of the Masters, opened its membership to women (Martin, Dawsey, and McKay 2012; Scott 2003; Sherwood 2010).

A setback in antidiscrimination lawsuits came when the Supreme Court told Lilly Ledbetter, in effect, that she was "too late." Ledbetter had been a supervisor for many years at the Gadsden, Alabama, Goodyear Tire Rubber plant when she realized that she was being paid $6,500 less per year than the lowest-paid male supervisor. The Court ruled that she must sue within 180 days of the initial discriminatory paycheck even though it had taken years before she even knew of the differential payment. Congress later enacted legislation eliminating the 180-day restriction.

Proving discrimination, even as outlined for generations in legislation, continues to be difficult. In the 2007 *Ledbetter v. Goodyear Tire and Rubber Co.* ruling, the Supreme Court affirmed that victims had to file a formal complaint within 180 days of the alleged discrimination. This set aside thousands of cases where employees learned their initial pay was lower to comparably employed White or male workers only after they had been in a job for years. Given the usual secrecy in workplaces around salaries, it would have made it difficult for potential cases of pay disparity to be effectively advanced. Two years later, Congress enacted the Lilly Ledbetter Fair Pay Act, which gives victims more time to file a lawsuit.

The inability of the Civil Rights Act, similar legislation, and court decisions to end discrimination does not result entirely from poor financial and political support, although it does play a role. The number of federal employees assigned to investigate and prosecute bias cases is insufficient. Many discriminatory practices, such as those described as institutional discrimination, are seldom subject to legal action.

Wealth Inequality: Discrimination's Legacy

Discrimination that has occurred in the past carries into the present and future. African American and other minority groups have had less opportunity to accumulate assets such as homes, land, and savings that can insulate them, and later their children, from economic setbacks.

3-5 Illustrate how wealth inequality is discrimination's legacy.

Wealth is a more inclusive term than income and encompasses all of a person's material assets, including land, stocks, and other types of property. Wealth allows one to live better; even modest assets provide insurance against the effects of job layoffs, natural disasters, and long-term illness, and they afford individuals much better interest rates when they need to borrow money. Wealth allows children to graduate from college with little or no debt. This reminds us that for many people, wealth is not always related to assets but also can be measured by indebtedness.

Studies document that the disparities in income we have seen are even greater when wealth is considered. In 2010, only 6 percent of homebuyers were African Americans and another 6 percent Latino. This is, unfortunately, to be expected, because if individuals experience lower incomes throughout their lives, they are less likely to be able to put anything aside for a down payment. They are more likely to have to pay for today's expenses rather than save for their future or their children's future.

In the Research Focus "The Unequal Wealth Distribution," we consider findings regarding the relative assets among White, Black, and Latino Americans.

The wealth gap continues. The economic slowdown of 2007 through 2009 has only increased the disparity between White households as a group and Black and Latino

Research Focus

The Unequal Wealth Distribution

There is widespread consensus that African Americans typically have fewer assets and other wealth than Whites. However, recent research suggests that the gap is widening.

Using government data, a team of researchers at Brandeis University found that over two decades, the difference in wealth (excluding homes) grew from $20,000 less for the typical Black household to $95,000 less, as shown in Figure 3.5. This growing gap is the result of long-term economic affects but also recent policy changes such as lowering taxes on investment income and inheritances that benefit the more affluent, who are more likely to be White.

While the wealth gap has grown, so has debt. As indicated in Figure 3.6, among the least wealthy—the bottom 10 percent—the African American typically is $3,600 in debt, while the least wealthy White families are able to average $100 to the good. Other researchers have confirmed these findings and show further that the recession of the last few years has made the gaps even greater. A key to most people's wealth is home ownership and there is a long-standing fundamental gap in home ownership between Whites and minorities. The recent disaster in home loans has led many people to lose their homes—the most significant asset for most families—the proportion of Black homeowners who lost homes through foreclosure or bankruptcy is much higher than among White families.

Sources: Bernard 2012; Kochhar, Fry, and Taylor 2011; Kuebler 2013; Shapiro, Meschede, and Sullivan 2010.

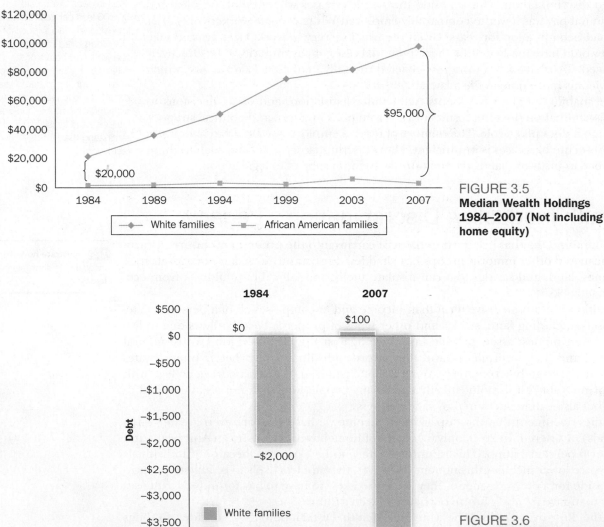

FIGURE 3.5
Median Wealth Holdings 1984–2007 (Not including home equity)

FIGURE 3.6
Bottom 10 Percent of Wealth Holdings 1984 and 2007

households. While the pace has wealth accumulation has varied, economists declared in 2013 that wealth disparity has increased steadily for 27 years. It is now approaching three decades of increased wealth of Whites compared to other households.

It is little wonder then that White children are more likely to surpass their parents' income than Black children. Furthermore, White children are more likely to move up the economic social class ladder than are Black children, who also are more likely to fall back in absolute terms. As adults, well-off Black Americans are less likely to have acquired knowledge from their parents about how to invest wisely and more likely will make "safe" economic decisions for the future of themselves and their children.

Wealth is not just money in the bank, but insurance against joblessness, homelessness, and ill health. On the positive side, wealth accumulation serves as a springboard to the middle class or higher. African American and Latinos households are much less likely to anticipate such a positive future.

A close analysis of wealth shows that African American families typically have $95,000 less in wealth than their White counterparts, even when households are comparably educated and employed. The median wealth of White households is 20 times that of Black households and 18 times that of Latino households (McKernan et al. 2013).

Environmental Justice

Discrimination takes many forms and is not necessarily apparent, even when its impact can be far reaching. Take the example of Old Smokey, a massive incinerator shut down in 1970 in Miami after operating for 45 years in the segregated area that for a generation was cut out from public water and sewage systems leaving residents to rely on wells and outhouses. While older residents of the West Grove remember well the soiled laundry from the old incinerator days, recent revelations show a hazardous legacy.

3-6 Discuss environmental justice.

Soil samples neighborhood reveal contamination from carcinogens like arsenic and heavy metals. The findings only became public in 2013 even though city officials new two years earlier that a fire fighting facility in the area had detected the dangerous levels two years earlier. The environmental impact is now being closely examined given a cluster of cancer cases detected in West Grove (Madigan 2013).

The conflict perspective sees the case of the Miami neighborhood of West Grove as one in which pollution harms minority groups disproportionately. **Environmental justice** refers to the efforts to ensure that hazardous substances are controlled so that all communities receive protection regardless of race or socioeconomic circumstance. After the Environmental Protection Agency and other organizations documented discrimination in the location of hazardous waste sites, an executive order

3-7

was issued in 1994 that requires all federal agencies to ensure that low-income and minority communities have access to better information about their environment and have an opportunity to participate in shaping government policies that affect their communities' health. Initial efforts to implement the policy have met widespread opposition, including criticism from some proponents of economic development who argue that the guidelines unnecessarily delay or altogether block locating new industrial sites.

Low-income communities and areas with significant minority populations are more likely to be adjacent to waste sites, landfills, incinerators, and polluting factories than are affluent White communities. Studies in California show the higher probability that people of color live closer to sources of air pollution. Another study concluded that grade schools in Florida nearer to environmental hazards are disproportionately Black or Latino. People of color jeopardized by environmental problems also lack the resources and political muscle to do something about it (Pastor, Morello-Frosch, and Saad 2005; Pellow and Brehm 2013; Pellow and Brulle 2007;   Stretesky and Lynch 2002).

Issues of environmental justice are not limited to metropolitan areas. Another continuing problem is abuse of Native American reservation land. Many American Indian leaders are concerned that tribal lands are too often regarded as toxic waste dumping grounds that go to the highest bidder. On the other hand, the economic devastation faced by some tribes in isolated areas has led one tribe in Utah to seek out becoming a depot for discarded nuclear waste (Jefferies 2007).

As with other aspects of discrimination, experts disagree. There is controversy within the scientific community over the potential hazards, and there is even some opposition within the subordinate communities being affected. This complexity of the issues in terms of social class and race is apparent; as some observers question the wisdom of an executive order that may slow economic development coming to areas in dire need of employment opportunities. On the other hand, some observers counter that such businesses typically employ only a few unskilled workers and make the environment less liveable for those left behind. Despite such varying viewpoints, environmental justice is an excellent example of resistance and change in the 1990s that the civil rights workers of the 1950s could not have foreseen.

Affirmative Action

3-7 Explain affirmative action.

Affirmative action is the positive effort to recruit subordinate-group members, including women, for jobs, promotions, and educational opportunities. The phrase *affirmative action* first appeared in an executive order issued by President John F. Kennedy in 1961. The order called for contractors to "take affirmative action to ensure that applicants are employed, and that employees are treated during employment, without regard to their race, creed, color, or national origin." However, at that time, no enforcement procedures were specified. Six years later, the order was amended to prohibit discrimination on the basis of sex, but affirmative action was still defined vaguely.

Today, affirmative action has become a catchall term for racial preference programs and goals. It also has become a lightning rod for opposition to any programs that suggest special consideration of women or racial minorities.

Affirmative Action Explained

Affirmative action has been viewed as an important tool for reducing institutional discrimination. Whereas previous efforts were aimed at eliminating individual acts of discrimination, federal measures under the heading of affirmative action have been aimed at procedures that deny equal opportunities, even if they are not intended to be overtly discriminatory. This policy has been implemented to deal with both current discrimination and past discrimination, outlined earlier in this chapter.

Affirmative action has been aimed at institutional discrimination in areas such as the following:

- Height and weight requirements that are unnecessarily geared to the physical proportions of White men without regard to the actual characteristics needed to perform the job and that therefore exclude women and some minorities.

- Seniority rules, when applied to jobs historically held only by White men, that make more recently hired minorities and females more subject to layoff—the "last hired, first fired" employee—and less eligible for advancement.

- Nepotism-based membership policies of some unions that exclude those who are not relatives of members who, because of past employment practices, are usually White.

- Restrictive employment leave policies, coupled with prohibitions on part-time work or denials of fringe benefits to part-time workers, that make it difficult for the heads of single-parent families, most of whom are women, to get and keep jobs and also meet the needs of their families.

- Rules requiring that only English be spoken at the workplace, even when not a business necessity, which result in discriminatory employment practices toward people whose primary language is not English.

- Standardized academic tests or criteria geared to the cultural and educational norms of middle-class or White men when these are not relevant predictors of successful job performance.

- Preferences shown by law and medical schools in admitting children of wealthy and influential alumni, nearly all of whom are White.

- Credit policies of banks and lending institutions that prevent granting mortgages and loans in minority neighborhoods or that prevent granting credit to married women and others who have previously been denied the opportunity to build good credit histories in their own names.

Employers also have been cautioned against asking leading questions in interviews, for example, "Did you know you would be the first Black to supervise all Whites in that factory?" or "Does your husband mind your working on weekends?" Furthermore, the lack of minority-group or female employees may in itself represent evidence for a case of unlawful exclusion (Commission on Civil Rights 1981; see also Bohmer and Oka 2007).

The Legal Debate

How far can an employer go in encouraging women and minorities to apply for a job before it becomes unlawful discrimination against White men? Since the late 1970s, several bitterly debated cases on this difficult aspect of affirmative action have reached the U.S. Supreme Court. The most significant cases are summarized in Table 3.2.

In the 1978 *Bakke* case (*Regents of the University of California v. Bakke*), by a narrow 5–4 vote, the Court ordered the medical school of the University of California at Davis to admit Allan Bakke, a qualified White engineer who had originally been denied admission solely on the basis of his race. The justices ruled that the school had violated Bakke's constitutional rights by establishing a fixed quota system for minority students. However, the Court added that it was constitutional for universities to adopt flexible admission programs that use race as one factor in making decisions.

Colleges and universities responded with new policies designed to meet the *Bakke* ruling while broadening opportunities for traditionally underrepresented minority students. The Supreme Court heard arguments in *Fisher v. University of Texas at Austin* arguing that a White woman, Abigail Fisher, missed out on automatic admission under a Texas provision that extended admissions to the top 10 percent of a high school graduating class. While she was not in the top tenth, she contended that non-Whites who did not have comparable academic preparation were admitted and that the top 10 percent provision leaves any further racial consideration unnecessary. In 2013, the Court set aside

3-7

TABLE 3.2
Key Decisions on Affirmative Action

In a series of split and often very close decisions, the Supreme Court has expressed a variety of reservations in specific situations.

Year	Favorable (+) or Unfavorable (−) to Policy	Case	Vote	Ruling
1971	+	*Griggs v. Duke Power Co.*	9–0	Private employers must provide a remedy where minorities were denied opportunities, even if unintentional.
1978	−	*Regents of the University of California v. Bakke*	5–4	Prohibited holding a specific number of places for minorities in college admissions.
1979	+	*United Steelworkers of America v. Weber*	5–2	Okay for union to favor minorities in special training programs.
1984	−	*Firefighters Local Union No. 1784 (Memphis, TN) v. Stotts*	6–1	Seniority means recently hired minorities may be laid off first in staff reductions.
1986	+	*International Association of Firefighters v. City of Cleveland*	6–3	May promote minorities over more-senior Whites.
1986	+	*New York City v. Sheet Metal*	5–4	Approved specific quota of minority workers for union.
1987	+	*United States v. Paradise*	5–4	Endorsed quotas for promotions of state troopers.
1987	+	*Johnson v. Transportation Agency, Santa Clara, CA*	6–3	Approved preference in hiring for minorities and women over better-qualified men and Whites.
1989	−	*Richmond v. Croson Company*	6–3	Ruled a 30 percent set-aside program for minority contractors unconstitutional.
1989	−	*Martin v. Wilks*	5–4	Ruled Whites may bring reverse discrimination claims against Court-approved affirmative action plans.
1990	+	*Metro Broadcasting v. FCC*	5–4	Supported federal programs aimed at increasing minority owner-ship of broadcast licenses.
1995	−	*Adarand Constructors Inc. v. Peña*	5–4	Benefits based on race are constitutional only if narrowly defined to accomplish a compelling interest.
1996	−	*Texas v. Hopwood*	*	Let stand a lower court decision covering Louisiana, Mississippi, and Texas that race could not be used in college admissions.
2003	+	*Grutter v. Bollinger*	5–4	Race can be a limited factor in admissions at the University of Michigan Law School.
2003	−	*Gratz v. Bollinger*	6–3	Cannot use a strict formula awarding advantage based on race for admissions to the University of Michigan.
2009	−	*Ricci v. DeStefano*	5–4	May not disregard a promotion test because Blacks failed to qualify for advancement.
2013	−	*Davis v. University of Texas at Austin*	7-1	The college must show compelling evidence that racial prefer-ences are justified as one of the admissions criteria.

*U.S. Court of Appeals Fifth Circuit decision.

a lower court's decision upholding the admissions policy arguing that the university must make a stronger case for race-based admissions policies. The ruling did not have any direct impact on any other institution's policies although other schools probably would re-examine their procedures in light of the *Fisher* decision. Given the various legal actions, further challenges to affirmative action can be expected.

So what has happened to minority enrolment? Since the African American and Latino college-age population is increasing, it makes analysis difficult. However, in states such as California, Florida, Michigan, and Texas, that have been barred from using race explicitly in admissions, Black and Latino enrollment has dropped. Sometimes pre-ban levels have begun to be approached after much maneuvering with new criteria but often these none-race specific criteria have been called in to question as well by opponents to affirmative action (Hoover 2013).

Has affirmative action actually helped alleviate employment inequality on the basis of race and gender? This question is difficult to answer, given the complexity of the labor market and the fact that other anti-discrimination measures are in place, but it does appear that affirmative action has had a significant impact in the sectors where it has been

Speaking Out

3-7

The Conversation We're *Not* Having When We Talk About Affirmative Action

GAIL CHRISTOPHER

An affirmative action case now before the U.S. Supreme Court provides renewed proof of the urgent need for communities across the country to engage openly in developing deeper understanding about the issue of racism.

Before the successes of the civil rights movement, discrimination against people of color was easy to spot in the United States. Today, many Americans find racist beliefs and attitudes abhorrent, and there's no question that we have made great progress as a country in addressing overt and legalized racism. But these changes in our laws and culture do not mean that racial bias is a thing of the past....

Before the court recesses at the end of June, it will issue a decision in Fisher v. University of Texas at Austin. At immediate stake in the case is the university's policy of considering race as one factor among many in its admissions. Even with the policy, the school's student body is not representative of the state's high school graduates. Striking it down would further harm efforts to create diversity in Texas' flagship public university.

If the university prevails, it will be partly a result of the court's recognition of the compelling educational benefits that all students receive when they are part of a diverse student body. These benefits are undeniable and well-documented. For example, when students from different walks of life come together in the classroom, they are able to challenge each other to think critically about their own worldviews.

But a focus on the educational benefits of diversity puts aside the fact that students of color still confront, and must overcome, hidden racial biases in order to succeed in school and in life. That's why a deeper understanding about racism is necessary. As Ronald Brownstein so capably emphasized in a recent *National Journal* story, the state of race in America has changed dramatically since the last time the Supreme Court considered the issue of affirmative action.

Racial bias can manifest itself in far more subtle ways today, and sometimes in far more overt ways... (W)e have witnessed the racist reactions to a simple television commercial that leads with a child of an interracial relationship, and shows both parents. The flood of racist comments to the

YouTube page led General Mills to remove the comments section for that video.

And we know that two-thirds of broadcast media about Muslims portrays them as extremists. School teachers may have lower expectations for Hispanic or black students than they have for white students. Doctors may diagnose and treat black patients differently from white patients, even when they present the same symptoms. Mortgage lenders may be more likely to steer homebuyers of color to subprime loans even when they qualify for lower-cost prime loans....

These biases abound in other realms, from art to commerce to the justice system, exacting a toll on the health of people of color which has an impact upon the future viability of the nation. The point is that they are not necessarily—or even typically—conscious decisions on the part of the teachers, doctors, and lenders...

We must expand the narrative by laying bare the hidden racial biases that act as obstacles in the paths of young people of color who want to go to college. A broader narrative would help us understand the abilities and grit that minority applicants required in order to put themselves on the path to college despite these obstacles. It would move all of us beyond a constrained idea of what prepares students for college success.

African Americans comprise 12 percent of the working-age population in the U.S., yet only five percent of doctors and dentists and three percent of architects are black, proportions that have not changed in over two decades.

If we fail to finally open the doors of opportunity to all students in the U.S., regardless of skin color, then we all lose. By the middle of this century, the Census Bureau tells us, the U.S. population will be majority minority. Our ability to compete in the global economy demands that we prepare students from every background for success in college and careers. Our nation's long struggle for equality demands that our campuses come to look more like our communities.

If nothing else, the Supreme Court's impending decision will give us a reason to address the nation's unique legacy of racism and its continuing impact, even in the 21st century. Let's not miss that chance.

Source: Christopher 2013.

---

applied. Sociologist Barbara Reskin (2012) reviewed available studies looking at workforce composition in terms of race and gender in light of affirmative action policies. She found that gains in minority employment could be attributed to affirmative action policies. This includes firms mandated to follow affirmative action guidelines and those that took them on voluntarily. There is also evidence that some earnings gains can be attributed to affirmative action. Economists M. V. Lee Badgett and Heidi Hartmann (1995), reviewing 26 other research studies, came to similar conclusions: Affirmative action and other federal compliance programs have had a modest impact, but it is difficult to assess,

3-8

given larger economic changes such as recessions or the rapid increase in women in the paid labor force.

Scholars of the debate over affirmative action in higher education acknowledge that many issues need to be addressed beyond its legal ramifications. In the Speaking Out section, W. K. Kellogg Foundation vice president Gail Christopher makes the case for the necessity of this broader perspective.

Reverse Discrimination

3-8 Analyze reverse discrimination.

Although researchers debated the merit of affirmative action, the public—particularly Whites but also some affluent African Americans and Hispanics—questioned the wisdom of the program. Particularly strident were the charges of reverse discrimination: that government actions cause better-qualified White men to be bypassed in favor of women and minority men. **Reverse discrimination** is an emotional term, because it conjures up the notion that somehow women and minorities will subject White men in the United States to the same treatment received by minorities during the last three centuries. Such cases are not unknown, but they are uncommon.

Increasingly, critics of affirmative action call for color-blind policies that would end affirmative action and, they argue, allow all people to be judged fairly. However, will that end institutional practices that favored Whites? For example, according to the latest data, 40 percent of applicants who are children of Harvard's alumni, who are almost all White, are admitted to the university, compared to 11 percent of nonalumni children.

By contrast, at the competitive California Institute of Technology, which specifically does not use legacy preferences, only 1.5 percent of students are children of alumni. Ironically, studies show that students who are children of alumni are far more likely than either minority students or athletes to run into academic trouble (Kahlenberg 2010; Massey and Mooney 2007; Pincus 2003, 2008).

Is it possible to have color-blind policies prevail in the United States in the twenty-first century? Supporters of affirmative action contend that as long as businesses rely on informal social networks, personal recommendations, and family ties, White men will have a distinct advantage built on generations of being in positions of power. Furthermore, an end to affirmative action should also mean an end to the many programs that give advantages to certain businesses, homeowners, veterans, farmers, and others. Most of these preference holders are White.

Consequently, by the 1990s and into the twenty-first century, affirmative action had emerged as an increasingly important issue in state and national political campaigns. As noted earlier, in 2003, the Supreme Court reviewed the admission policies at the University of Michigan, which may favor racial minorities (see Table 3.2). In 2006, Michigan citizens, by a 58 percent margin, voted to restrict all their state universities from using affirmative action in their admissions policies. Generally, discussions have focused on the use of quotas in hiring practices. Supporters of affirmative action argue that hiring goals establish "floors" for minority inclusion but do not exclude truly qualified candidates from any group. Opponents insist that these "targets" are, in fact, quotas that lead to reverse discrimination (Lewin 2006; Mack 1996).

The State of California, in particular, was a battleground for this controversial issue. The California Civil Rights Initiative (Proposition 209) was placed on the ballot in 1996 as a referendum to amend the state constitution and prohibit any programs that give preference to women and minorities for college admission, employment, promotion, or government contracts. Overall, 54 percent of the voters backed the state proposition.

In 2009, the Supreme Court ruled 5–4 in the *Ricci v. DeStefano* case in favor of White firefighters. Many observers felt this outcome recognized reverse racism. In 2003, in New Haven, Connecticut, firefighters took an examination to identify possible promotions but no African Americans taking the test qualified to be eligible for advancement. Rather than select all White (including one Hispanic) firefighters, the city threw out the test results. The qualifying firefighters sued that they were victims of discrimination and

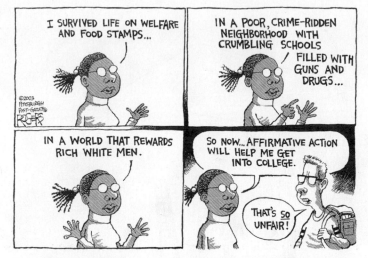

Does affirmative action represent an overdue just solution to a centuries-old problem or an undeserved outright reward for the current generation?

the Court eventually concurred. The decision was limited in its applications because the justices seemed to say that possible test bias could be considered in the design stage of a test, but others saw it as "impeding" the use of race in hiring even advantaged minorities.

The Glass Ceiling

We have discussed racial and ethnic groups primarily as if they have uniformly failed to keep pace with Whites. Although this notion is accurate, tens of thousands of people of color have matched and even exceeded Whites in terms of income. For example, in 2012, more than 395,000 Black households and over 541,000 Hispanic households earned more than $200,000. What can we say about financially better-off members of subordinate groups in the United States (DeNavas-Walt, Proctor, and Smith 2013:Table HINC-03)?

Prejudice does not necessarily end with wealth. Black newspaper columnist De Wayne Wickham (1993) wrote of the subtle racism he had experienced. He heard a White clerk in a supermarket ask a White customer whether she knew the price of an item the computer would not scan; when the problem occurred while the clerk was ringing up Wickham's groceries, she called for a price check. Affluent subordinate-group members routinely report being blocked as they move toward the first-class section aboard airplanes or seek service in upscale stores. Another journalist, Ellis Cose (1993), has called these insults the soul destroying slights to affluent minorities that lead to the "rage of a privileged class."

Discrimination persists for even educated and qualified people from the best family backgrounds. As subordinate-group members are able to compete successfully, they sometimes encounter attitudinal or organizational bias that prevents them from reaching their full potential. They have confronted what has come to be called the **glass ceiling**. This refers to the barrier that blocks the promotion of a qualified worker because of gender or minority membership (see Figure 3.7). Often, people entering nontraditional areas of employment become marginalized and are made to feel uncomfortable, much like the situation of immigrants who feel like they are part of two cultures, as we discussed in Chapter 1.

Reasons for glass ceilings are as many as the occurrences. It may be that one Black or one woman vice president is regarded as enough, so the second potential candidate faces a block to movement up through management. Decision makers may be concerned that their clientele will not trust them if they have too many people of color or may worry that

3-9 Put into your own words the glass ceiling.

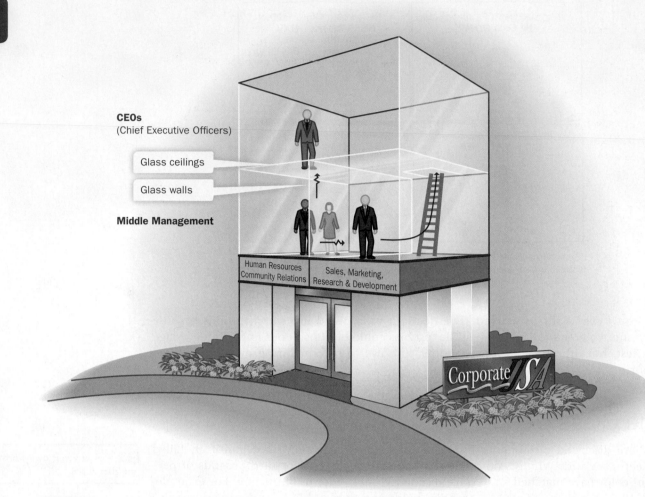

CEOs
(Chief Executive Officers)

Glass ceilings

Glass walls

Middle Management

Human Resources
Community Relations

Sales, Marketing,
Research & Development

Corporate USA

FIGURE 3.7
Glass Ceilings and Glass Walls

Women and minority men are moving up in corporations but encounter glass ceilings that block entry to top positions. In addition, they face glass walls that block lateral moves to areas from which executives are promoted. These barriers contribute to women and minority men not moving into the ultimate decision-making positions in the nation's corporate giants.

a talented woman could become overwhelmed with her duties as a mother and wife and thus perform poorly in the workplace.

Concern about women and minorities climbing a broken ladder led to the formation in 1991 of the Glass Ceiling Commission, with the U.S. secretary of labor chairing the 21-member group. Initially, it regarded the following as some of the glass ceiling barriers:

- Lack of management commitment to establishing systems, policies, and practices for achieving workplace diversity and upward mobility
- Pay inequities for work of equal or comparable value
- Sex-, race-, and ethnicity-based stereotyping and harassment
- Unfair recruitment practices
- Lack of family-friendly workplace policies
- "Parent-track" policies that discourage parental leave policies
- Limited opportunities for advancement to decision-making positions

This significant underrepresentation of women and minority males in managerial positions results in large part from the presence of glass ceilings. Sociologist Max Weber wrote more than a century ago that the privileged class monopolizes the purchase of high-priced consumer goods and wields the power to grant or withhold opportunity from others. To grasp just how White and male the membership of this elite group is, consider the following: 71 percent of the 1,219 people who serve on the boards of directors of *Fortune* 100 corporations are White non-Hispanic males. For every 82 White men on these boards, there are two Latinos, two Asian Americans, three African Americans, and eleven White women (Alliance for Board Diversity 2009; Weber 1947).

Glass ceilings are not the only barriers. Glass walls also block minorities. Catalyst, a nonprofit research organization, conducted interviews in 1992 and again in 2001 with senior and middle managers from larger corporations. The study found that even before glass ceilings are encountered, women and racial and ethnic minorities face **glass walls** that keep them from moving laterally. Specifically, the study found that women tend to be placed in staff or support positions in areas such as public relations and human resources and are often directed away from jobs in core areas such as marketing, production, and sales. Women are assigned to and, therefore, trapped in jobs that reflect their stereotypical helping nature and encounter glass walls that cut off access to jobs that might lead to broader experience and advancement (Bjerk 2008; Catalyst 2001; Lopez 1992).

Researchers have documented a differential impact the glass ceiling has on White males. It appears that men who enter traditionally female occupations are more likely to rise to the top. Male elementary teachers become principals, and male nurses become supervisors. The **glass escalator** refers to the White male advantage experienced in occupations dominated by women. Whereas females may become tokens when they enter traditionally male occupations, men are more likely to be advantaged when they move out of sex-typical jobs. In summary, women and minority men confront a glass ceiling that limits upward mobility and glass walls that reduce their ability to move into fast-track jobs leading to the highest reaches of the corporate executive suite. Meanwhile, White men who do choose to enter female-dominated occupations are often rewarded with promotions and positions of responsibility coveted by their fellow female workers (Budig 2002; Cognard-Black 2004).

SPECTRUM OF INTERGROUP RELATIONS

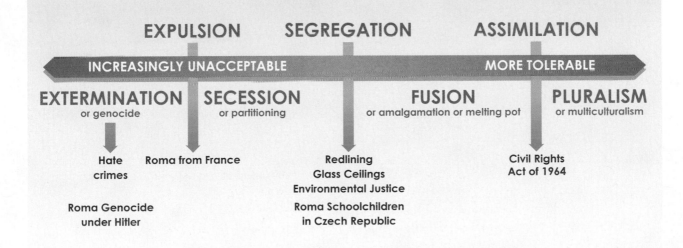

Conclusion

What is it like to experience discrimination over and over again? Not just an occasional slight or a possible instance of discrimination but constantly seeing yourself dealt with differently because of race, ethnicity, or gender? W. E. B. Du Bois (1903:9) wrote in his classic *The Souls of Black Folks,* "To be a poor man is hard, but to be a poor race in a land of dollars is the very bottom of hardships." Not all members of racial and ethnic minorities, much less all women, are poor, of course, but virtually all can recall instances where they were treated as second-class citizens, not necessarily by White men, but even by members of their own group or by other women.

One job advertisement read "African Americans and Arabians tend to clash with me so that won't work out." Sound like it was from your grandfather's era? Actually, it appeared on the popular Craigslist Web site in 2006 and is just one example of how explicit discrimination thrives even in the digital age. Similar charges have been made concerning "no minorities" wording in housing advertisements. Courts have not held Craigslist responsible and accepted the Web site's argument that it cannot screen out all racism in online advertising. Nonetheless, Craigslist finally posted in 2012 a policy forbidding ads that violated state or federal laws ensuring equal access to housing (American Financial Resources 2012; Oliveri 2009).

Discrimination takes its toll, whether or not a person who is discriminated against is part of the informal economy or looking for a job on the Internet. Even members of minority groups who are not today overtly discriminated against continue to fall victim to past discrimination. We also have identified the costs of discrimination to members of the privileged group.

From the conflict perspective, it is not surprising to find the widespread presence of the informal economy proposed by the dual labor market model and even an underclass. Derrick Bell (1994), an African American law professor, has made the sobering assertion that "racism is permanent." He contends that the attitudes of dominant Whites prevail, and society is willing to advance programs on behalf of subordinate groups only when they coincide with needs as perceived by those Whites.

The surveys presented in Chapter 2 show gradual acceptance of the earliest efforts to eliminate discrimination, but that support is failing as color-blind racism takes hold, especially as it relates to affirmative action. Indeed, concerns about doing something about alleged reverse discrimination are as likely to be voiced as concerns about racial or gender discrimination or glass ceilings and glass walls.

Institutional discrimination remains a formidable challenge in the United States. Attempts to reduce discrimination by attacking institutional discrimination have met with staunch resistance. Partly as a result of this outcry from some of the public, especially White Americans, the federal government gradually de-emphasized its affirmative action efforts, beginning in the 1980s and continuing into the twenty-first century. Most of the material in this chapter has been about racial groups, especially Black and White Americans. It would be easy to see intergroup hostility as a racial phenomenon, but that would be incorrect. Throughout the history of the United States, relations between some White groups have been characterized by resentment and violence. The next two chapters examine the ongoing legacy of immigration and the nature and relations of White ethnic groups.

Summary

1. Discrimination is likely to result in feeling of relative deprivation, not necessarily absolute deprivation.
2. Hate crimes highlight hostility that culminates in a criminal offense.
3. Institutional discrimination results from the normal operations of a society.
4. Discrimination in hiring is documented through job-testing experiments.
5. Inequality continues to be apparent in the analysis of annual incomes, controlling for the amount of education attained and wealth, and even in the absence of environmental justice.
6. Presidential executive orders, legislative acts, and judicial decisions have all played a part in reducing discrimination.
7. For over 60 years, affirmative action as a remedy to inequality has been a hotly contested issue, with its critics contending it amounts to reverse discrimination.
8. Upwardly mobile professional women and minority males may encounter a glass ceiling and be thwarted in their efforts by glass walls to become more attractive candidates for advancement.

Key Terms

absolute deprivation, p. 60

affirmative action, p. 72

discrimination, p. 59

environmental justice, p. 71

glass ceiling, p. 77

glass escalator, p. 79

glass wall, p. 79

hate crime, p. 61

income, p. 65

institutional discrimination, p. 63

redlining, p. 68

relative deprivation, p. 60

reverse discrimination, p. 76

wealth, p. 65

Review Questions

1. Why might people feel disadvantaged even though their incomes are rising and their housing circumstances have improved?
2. How do hate crimes differ from other types of felony crimes?
3. Why does institutional discrimination sometimes seem less objectionable than individual discrimination?
4. In what way might national income data point to discrimination?
5. What is the wealth disparity among racial and ethnic groups and what is the trend in this disparity?
6. Explain how the concept of environmental justice relates to understanding racial and ethnic groups.
7. Why are questions raised about affirmative action even though inequality persists?
8. Describe what is meant by reverse discrimination.
9. Distinguish among glass ceilings, glass walls, and glass escalators. How do they differ from more obvious forms of discrimination in employment?

Critical Thinking

1. What are the purposes of hate crimes? Do you think they serve those purposes?

2. Discrimination can take many forms. Select a case of discrimination that you think almost everyone would agree is wrong. Then describe another incident in which the alleged discrimination was subtler. Who is likely to condemn and who is likely to overlook such situations?

3. Discuss the social implications that wealth disparity between racial and ethnic groups has for social mobility.

4. Analyse what is meant by environmental justice can be understood in terms of institutional discrimination.

5. Resistance is a continuing theme of intergroup race relations. Discrimination implies the oppression of a group, but how can discrimination also unify the oppressed group to resist such unequal treatment? How can acceptance, or integration, for example, weaken the sense of solidarity within a group?

6. Voluntary associations such as the National Association for the Advancement of Colored People (NAACP) and government units such as the courts have been important vehicles for bringing about a measure of social justice. In what ways can the private sector—corporations and businesses—also work to bring about an end to discrimination?

4 Immigration

4-1

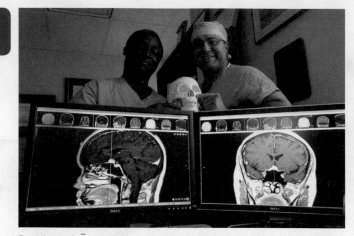

Dr. Alfredo Quiñones-Hinojosa (on the right)

The story of Alfredo the immigrant is not typical, but then every immigrant who comes to the United States has a unique story. Alfredo Quiñones-Hinojosa came to the United States as an illegal immigrant in 1987 at the age of nineteen. Caught the first time, he succeeded the second time on the same day. (The majority of immigrants apprehended at the border have been caught previously.) One of six children, Alfredo had frequently come across the border from his native Mexico to work as a farmhand pulling weeds in the fields to help support his five younger brothers and sisters. Eventually, he settled with relatives in Stockton, California. He tried other jobs: sweeping floors, shoeing horses, and soldering metal. He learned English and eventually applied and was accepted to the local San Joaquin Delta College.

His next big step was when he accepted an offer to study at the University of California at Berkeley. Alfredo dreamed of becoming a doctor, and nothing was going to stop him.

After graduating from Berkeley, Alfredo was accepted to Harvard Medical School, where he graduated with honors, but he also became a citizen along the way.

While Quiñones-Hinojosa, and later his parents, had entered the United States as an undocumented worker, under an amnesty provision passed under President Reagan, he was able to secure a green card legally allowing him to work and continue his education. In 1997, he became a U.S. citizen.

Today, married with three children, he heads the Brain Tumor Surgery Program at Johns Hopkins Medical Center and is actively engaged in research as to the causes of brain cancer. It has not been easy. His hands now perform brain surgery, but they bear the scars of farmwork. He endured prejudice: People strongly suggested he change his name to something easier to pronounce. While reluctant to speak out in the immigration debate, he recognizes that many people today want to exclude from the United States people exactly like he was fewer than 30 years ago (Cave 2011; Gupta 2012; Ramos 2010; Quiñones-Hinojosa with Rivas 2011).

The world is now a global network. The core and periphery countries, described in world systems theory (see page 19 in Chapter 1), link not only commercial goods but also families and workers across political borders. Social forces that cause people to emigrate are complex. The most important have been economic, such as the case of Alfredo Quiñones-Hinojosa: financial failure in the old country and expectations of higher incomes and standards of living in the new land. Other factors include dislike of new political regimes in their native lands, being victims of racial or religious bigotry, and a desire to reunite families. All these factors push people from their homelands and pull them to other nations such as the United States. Immigration into the United States, in particular, has been facilitated by cheap ocean transportation and by other countries' removal of restrictions on emigration.

Scholars of immigration often point to *push* and *pull factors.* For example, economic difficulties, religious or ethnic persecution, and political unrest may push individuals from their homelands. Immigration to a particular nation, the pull factors, may be a result of perceptions of a better life ahead or a desire to join a community of their fellow nationals already established abroad.

A potent factor contributing to immigration anywhere in the world is chain immigration. **Chain immigration** refers to an immigrant who sponsors several other immigrants who, on their arrival, may sponsor still more. Laws that favor people desiring to enter a given country who already have relatives there or someone who can vouch for them financially may facilitate this sponsorship. But probably the most important aspect of chain immigration is that immigrants anticipate knowing someone who can help them adjust to their new surroundings and find a new job, place to live, and even the kinds of foods that are familiar to them. Later in this chapter, we revisit the social impact of worldwide immigration.

Patterns of Immigration to the United States

Immigration to the United States has three unmistakable patterns: (1) the number of immigrants has fluctuated dramatically over time largely because of government policy changes; (2) settlement has not been uniform across the country but centered in certain regions and cities; and (3) the immigrants' countries of origin have changed over time. First, we look at the historical picture of immigrant numbers.

4-1 Summarize the general patterns of immigration to the United States.

Vast numbers of immigrants have come to the United States. Figure 4.1 indicates the high but fluctuating number of immigrants who arrived during every decade from the 1820s through the beginning of the twenty-first century. The United States received the largest number of legal immigrants during the first decade of the 1900s; that number likely will be surpassed in the first decade of the twenty-first century. However, the country was much smaller in the period from 1900 through 1910, so the numerical impact was even greater then.

Immigrants to this country have not always received a friendly reception. Open bloodshed, restrictive laws, and the eventual return of almost one-third of immigrants and their children to their home countries attest to some Americans' uneasy feelings toward strangers who want to settle here. Generally surveys show immigration viewed negatively but with some ambivalence. Opinion polls in the United States beginning in 1965 through 2013 have never shown more than 23 percent of the public in favor of more immigration, and usually about 35 to 40 percent want less, but the trend over the last decade has been slowly moving to welcoming *more* immigrants. Nationally border enforcement remains a concern, but support for deporting illegal immigrants already here has declined (Jones and Saad 2013; Muste 2013).

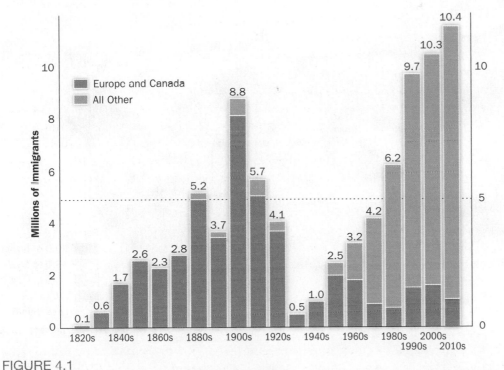

FIGURE 4.1
Legal Immigration to the United States, 1820–2020

Source: Office of Immigration Statistics 2013 and author's estimates for projection out to 2020.

Before considering the sweep of past immigration policies, let us consider today's immigrant population. About 13 percent of the nation's people are foreign-born—a level not reached since the 1920s. As recently as 1979, this proportion was just 4.7 percent. By global comparisons, the foreign-born population in the United States is large but not unusual. Whereas most industrial countries have a foreign population of around 5 percent, Canada's foreign population is 19 percent and Australia's is 25 percent.

As noted earlier, immigrants have not settled evenly across the nation. As shown in the map in Figure 4.2, six states—California, New York, Texas, Florida, New Jersey, and Illinois—account for two-thirds of the nation's total foreign-born population but less than 40 percent of the nation's total population.

Cities in these states are the destinations of the foreign-born population. Almost half (43.3 percent) live in the central city of a metropolitan area, compared with about one-quarter (27 percent) of the nation's population. More than one-third of residents in the cities of Miami, Los Angeles, San Francisco, San Jose, and New York are now foreign-born.

The source countries of immigrants have changed. First, settlers came from Europe, then Latin America, and, now, increasingly, Asia. The majority of today's 38.5 million foreign-born people are from Latin America rather than Europe, as was the case through the 1950s. Primarily, they are from Central America and, more specifically, Mexico. By contrast, Europeans, who dominated the early settlement of the United States, now account for fewer than one in seven of the foreign-born today. The changing patterns of immigration have continued into the twenty-first century. Beginning in 2010, the annual immigration from Asia exceeded the level of annual immigration from Latin America for the first time (Grieco et al. 2012; Pew Social and Demographic Trends 2012; Semple 2012).

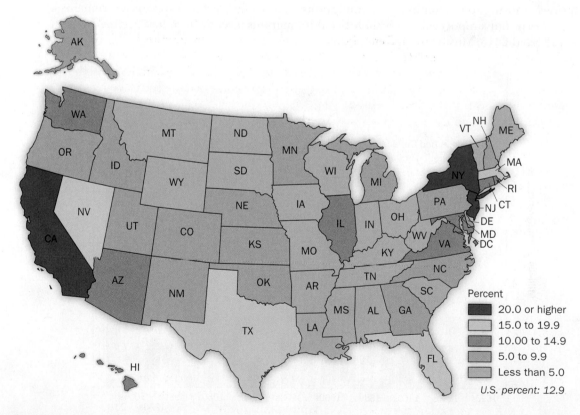

Percent

- 20.0 or higher
- 15.0 to 19.9
- 10.00 to 14.9
- 5.0 to 9.9
- Less than 5.0

U.S. percent: 12.9

FIGURE 4.2
Foreign-Born Population in the United States

Source: Grieco et al. 2012: 4.

Early Immigration

4-2

Settlers, the first immigrants to the Western Hemisphere, soon followed the European explorers of North America. The Spanish founded St. Augustine, Florida, in 1565, and the English founded Jamestown, Virginia, in 1607. Protestants from England emerged from the colonial period as the dominant force numerically, politically, and socially. The English accounted for 60 percent of the 3 million White Americans in 1790. Although exact statistics are lacking for the early years of the United States, the English were soon outnumbered by other nationalities as the numbers of Scotch-Irish and Germans, in particular, swelled. However, the English colonists maintained their dominant position, as Chapter 5 examines.

4-2 Characterize how immigration was controlled in the nineteenth century.

Throughout American history, immigration policy has been politically controversial. The policies of the English king, George III, were criticized in the U.S. Declaration of Independence for obstructing immigration to the colonies. Toward the end of the nineteenth century, the American republic itself was criticized for enacting immigration restrictions. In the beginning, however, the country encouraged immigration. Legislation initially fixed the residence requirement for naturalization at five years, although briefly, under the Alien Act of 1798, it was 14 years, and so-called dangerous people could be expelled. Despite this brief harshness, immigration was unregulated through most of the 1800s, and naturalization was easily available. Until 1870, naturalization was limited to "free white persons" (Calavita 2007).

Although some people hold the mistaken belief that concern about immigration is something new, some people also assume that immigrants to the United States rarely reconsider their decision to come to a new country. Analysis of available records, beginning in the early 1900s, suggests that about 35 percent of all immigrants to the United States eventually emigrated back to their home country. The proportion varies, with the figures for some countries being much higher, but the overall pattern is clear: About one in three immigrants to this nation eventually choose to return home (Wyman 1993).

The relative absence of federal legislation from 1790 to 1881 does not mean that all new arrivals were welcomed. **Xenophobia** (the fear or hatred of strangers or foreigners) led naturally to **nativism** (beliefs and policies favoring native-born citizens over immigrants). Although the term *nativism* has largely been used to describe nineteenth-century sentiments, anti-immigration views and organized movements have continued into the twenty-first century. Political scientist Samuel P. Huntington (1993, 1996) articulated the continuing immigration as a "clash of civilizations" that could be remedied only by significantly reducing legal immigration, not to mention closing the border to illegal arrivals. His view, which enjoys support, is that the fundamental world conflicts of the new century are cultural in nature rather than ideological or even economic (Citrin et al. 2007; Schaefer 2008b).

The most dramatic outbreak of nativism in the nineteenth century was aimed at the Chinese. If any doubt remained by the mid-1800s that the United States could harmoniously accommodate all and was some sort of melting pot, debate on the Chinese Exclusion Act negatively ended that doubt.

The Anti-Chinese Movement

Before 1851, official records show that only 46 Chinese had immigrated to the United States. Over the next 30 years, more than 200,000 came to this country, lured by the discovery of gold and the opening of job opportunities in the West. Overcrowding, drought, and warfare in China also encouraged them to take a chance in the United States. Another important factor was improved oceanic transportation; it was cheaper to travel from Hong Kong to San Francisco than from Chicago to San Francisco. The frontier communities of the West, particularly in California, looked on the Chinese as a valuable resource to fill manual jobs. As early as 1854, so many Chinese wanted to emigrate that ships had difficulty handling the volume.

4-2

Chinese workers, such as these pictured in 1844, played a major role in building railroads in the West.

In the 1860s, railroad work provided the greatest demand for Chinese labor until the Union Pacific and Central Pacific railroads were joined at Promontory Summit, Utah, in 1869. The Union Pacific relied primarily on Irish laborers, but 90 percent of the Central Pacific's labor force was Chinese because Whites generally refused to do the backbreaking work over the Western terrain. Despite the contribution of the Chinese, White workers physically prevented them from attending the driving of the golden spike to mark the joining of the two railroads.

With the dangerous railroad work largely completed, people began to rethink the wisdom of encouraging Chinese to immigrate to do the work no one else would do. Reflecting their xenophobia, White settlers found the Chinese immigrants, their customs, and religion difficult to understand. Indeed, few people tried to understand these immigrants from Asia. Although they had had no firsthand contact with Chinese Americans, Easterners and legislators soon jumped on the anti-Chinese bandwagon as they read sensationalized accounts of the lifestyle of the new arrivals.

Even before the Chinese immigrated, stereotypes of them and their customs were prevalent. American traders returning from China, European diplomats, and Protestant missionaries consistently emphasized the exotic and sinister aspects of life in China. **Sinophobes**, people who fear anything associated with China, appealed to the racist theory developed during the slavery controversy that non-Europeans were subhuman. Americans also were becoming more conscious of biological inheritance and disease, so it was not hard to conjure up fears of alien genes and germs. The only real challenge the anti-Chinese movement faced was convincing people that the negative consequences of unrestricted Chinese immigration outweighed any possible economic gain. Earlier, racial prejudice was subordinated to industrial dependence on Chinese labor for the work that Whites shunned, but acceptance of the Chinese was short-lived. The fear of the "yellow peril" overwhelmed any desire to know more about Asian peoples and their customs (Takaki 1998).

Employers were glad to pay the Chinese low wages, but non-Chinese laborers began directing their resentment against the Chinese rather than against their compatriots' willingness to exploit the Chinese. Only a generation earlier, the same concerns were felt about the Irish, but with the Chinese, the hostility reached new heights because of another factor.

Although many arguments were voiced, racial fears motivated the anti-Chinese movement. Race was the critical issue. The labor market fears were largely unfounded, and most advocates of restrictions at that time knew that. There was no possibility of the Chinese immigrating in numbers that would match those of Europeans at that time, so it is difficult to find any explanation other than racism for their fears (Winant 1994).

From the sociological perspective of conflict theory, we can explain how the Chinese immigrants were welcomed only when their labor was necessary to fuel growth in the United States. When that labor was no longer necessary, the welcome mat for the immigrants was withdrawn. Furthermore, as conflict theorists point out, restrictions were not applied evenly: Americans focused on a specific nationality (the Chinese) to reduce the number of foreign workers in the nation. Because decision making at that time rested in the hands of the descendants of European immigrants, the steps taken were most likely to be directed against the least powerful: immigrants from China who, unlike Europeans seeking entry, had few allies among legislators and other policymakers.

In 1882, Congress enacted the Chinese Exclusion Act, which outlawed Chinese immigration for ten years. It also explicitly denied naturalization rights to the Chinese in the United States; that is, they were not allowed to become citizens. There was little debate in Congress, and discussion concentrated on how to best handle suspending Chinese immigration. No allowance was made for spouses and children to be reunited with their husbands and fathers in the United States. Only brief visits of Chinese government officials, teachers, tourists, and merchants were exempted.

The rest of the nineteenth century saw the remaining loopholes allowing Chinese immigration closed. Beginning in 1884, Chinese laborers could not enter the United States from any foreign place, a ban that also lasted ten years. Two years later, the Statue of Liberty was dedicated, with a poem by Emma Lazarus inscribed on its base. To the Chinese, the poem welcoming the tired, the poor, and the huddled masses must have seemed a hollow mockery.

In 1892, Congress extended the Exclusion Act for another ten years and added that Chinese laborers had to obtain certificates of residence within a year or face deportation. After the turn of the century, the Exclusion Act was extended again. With immigration restrictions, like many other laws, the ill effects last generations. Judy Chu,

((•)) Speaking Out

Chinese Exclusion Act of 1882

A century ago, the Chinese came here in search of a better life; but they faced harsh conditions, particularly in the Halls of Congress. Congress passed numerous laws to restrict Chinese Americans, starting from the 1882 Chinese Exclusion Act, to stop the Chinese from immigrating, from becoming naturalized citizens, and from ever having the right to vote.

Judy Chu

These were the only such laws to target a specific ethnic group. The Chinese were the only residents that had to carry papers on them at all times. They were often harassed and detained. If they couldn't produce the proper documents, authorities threw them into prison or out of the country, regardless of their citizenship status. Political cartoons and hateful banners…were hung in towns and cities and printed in papers. At that time of this hateful law, the Chinese were called racial slurs, were spat upon in the streets, and even brutally murdered.

Only after China became an ally of the United States in World War II was this law repealed in 1943, 60 years after its passage. Congress has never formally acknowledged it as incompatible with America's founding principles.

That is why, as the first Chinese American woman elected to Congress, and whose grandfather was a victim of this law, I stand on the very floor where the Chinese Exclusion Act was passed and announce that I have introduced a resolution calling for a formal acknowledgment and expression of regret for the Chinese exclusion laws.

When the exclusion laws were first introduced, there was a great deal of debate in Congress over their merits. The U.S. had just abolished slavery. The 14th and 15th Amendments had recently been ratified. Slavery had been defeated, and freedom seemed more certain. The national atmosphere led many in Congress to stand up against the discriminatory anti-Chinese laws. But over the years, those standing for justice almost all disappeared. By the time 1882 came around, Members of Congress were fighting over who deserved the most credit for getting the most discriminatory laws passed and standing against the "Mongolian horde."….

But there were a brave few, a small minority who fought hard against prejudice and principles of freedom. One such man was Senator George Frisbie Hoar, whose statue now stands proudly in the Capitol. He stood up to all of the Chinese exclusion laws and voted against each. He said in 1904 when the laws were made permanent, "I cannot agree with the principle that this legislation or any legislation on the subject rests. All races, all colors, all nationalities contain persons entitled to be recognized everywhere as equals of other men. I am bound to record my protest, if I stand alone."

And stand alone he did. The final vote against the Chinese in the Senate was 76–1. What Senator Hoar stood up for is what I am asking Congress to stand up for today: that all people, no matter the color of their skin, or the nation of origin, are the equals of every other man or woman.

America came to be what it is today through immigrants who came from all corners of the world. Chinese immigrants were amongst them. They sought a place to live that was founded upon liberty and equality. They came in search of the American Dream—that if you worked hard, you could build a good life. It is why my grandfather came to the United States.

But when the Chinese Exclusion Act was passed, the truths that this Nation holds as self-evident—that all are endowed with the inalienable rights of life, liberty and the pursuit of happiness—were discounted by the very ones elected to uphold them.

And so for a generation of our ancestors, like my grandfather, who were told for six decades by the U.S. government that the land of the free wasn't open to them, it is long past time that Congress officially and formally acknowledges these ugly laws that targeted Chinese immigrants, and express sincere regret for these actions.

With my resolution, Congress will acknowledge the injustice of the Chinese Exclusion Act, express regret for the lives it destroyed, and make sure that the prejudice that stained our Nation is never repeated again. And it will demonstrate that today is a different day and that today we stand side by side for a stronger America.

Chu, 2011.

born of Chinese immigrants, was first elected to Congress in 2009 from suburban Los Angeles. A psychology professor and school board member before going to Washington, she was keenly aware of the toll that one of the most restrictive immigration laws ever passed in the United States had on Chinese Americans. In "Speaking Out," we hear the Congresswoman's case for a resolution apologizing for the passage of the Chinese Exclusion Act. In 2012, Congress passed the resolution unanimously. This marked only the fourth official apology in the last 25 years—the other three were slavery, the internment of Japanese Americans during World War II, and mistreatment of native Hawaiians and the overthrow of their rule of the islands (Chu 2011, Nahm 2012).

Restrictionist Sentiment Increases

4-3 Describe how restrictionist sentiment increased in the twentieth century.

As Congress closed the door to Chinese immigration, the debate on restricting immigration turned in new directions. Prodded by growing anti-Japanese feelings, the United States entered into the so-called gentlemen's agreement, which was completed in 1908. Japan agreed to halt further immigration to the United States, and the United States agreed to end discrimination against the Japanese who had already arrived. The immigration ended, but anti-Japanese feelings continued. Americans were growing uneasy that the "new immigrants" would overwhelm the culture established by the "old immigrants." The earlier immigrants, if not Anglo-Saxon, were from similar groups such as the Scandinavians, the Swiss, and the French Huguenots. These people were more experienced in democratic political practices and had a greater affinity with the dominant Anglo-Saxon culture. By the end of the nineteenth century, however, more and more immigrants were neither English speaking nor Protestant and came from dramatically different cultures.

The National Origin System

Beginning in 1921, a series of measures was enacted that marked a new era in American immigration policy. Whatever the legal language, the measures were drawn up to block the growing immigration from southern Europe (from Italy and Greece, for example) and also to block all Asian immigrants by establishing a zero quota for them.

Ellis Island
Although it was not opened until 1892, New York Harbor's Ellis Island—the country's first federal immigration facility—quickly became the symbol of all migrant streams to the United States. By the time it closed in late 1954, it had processed 17 million immigrants. Today, their descendants number over 100 million Americans.

To understand the effect of the national origin system on immigration, it is necessary to clarify the quota system. Quotas were deliberately weighted to favor immigration from northern Europe. Because of the ethnic composition of the country in 1920, the quotas placed severe restrictions on immigration from the rest of Europe and other parts of the world. Immigration from the Western Hemisphere (i.e., Canada, Mexico, Central and South America, and the Caribbean) continued unrestricted. The quota for each nation was set at 3 percent of the number of people descended from each nationality recorded in the 1920 census. Once the statistical manipulations were completed, almost 70 percent of the quota for the Eastern Hemisphere went to just three countries: Great Britain, Ireland, and Germany.

The absurdities of the system soon became obvious, but it was nevertheless continued. British immigration had fallen sharply, so most of its quota of 65,000 went unfilled. However, the openings could not be transferred, even though countries such as Italy, with a quota of only 6,000, had 200,000 people who wanted to enter. However one rationalizes the purpose behind the act, the result was obvious: Any English person, regardless of skill and whether related to anyone already here, could enter the country more easily than, say, a Greek doctor whose children were American citizens. The quota for Greece was 305, with the backlog of people wanting to come reaching 100,000.

By the end of the 1920s, annual immigration had dropped to one-fourth of its pre–World War I level. The worldwide economic depression of the 1930s decreased immigration still further. A brief upsurge in immigration just before World War II reflected the flight of Europeans from the oppression of expanding Nazi Germany. The war virtually ended transatlantic immigration. The era of the great European migration to the United States had been legislated out of existence.

The Immigration and Nationality Act

The national origin system was abandoned with the passage of the 1965 Immigration and Nationality Act (also called the Hart-Cellar Act), signed into law by President Lyndon B. Johnson at the foot of the Statue of Liberty. The primary goals of the act were to reunite families and to protect the American labor market. The act also initiated restrictions on immigration from Latin America. After the act, immigration increased by one-third, but the act's influence was primarily on the composition rather than the size of immigration. The sources of immigrants now included Italy, Greece, Portugal, Mexico, the Philippines, the West Indies, and South America.

The lasting effect is apparent when we compare the changing sources of immigration over the last 190 years, as shown in Figure 4.3. The most recent period shows that Asian and Latin American immigrants combined to account for 78 percent of the people who were permitted entry. This contrasts sharply with early immigration, which was dominated by arrivals from Europe.

The nature of immigration laws is exceedingly complex and is subjected to frequent, often minor, adjustments. From 2000 to 2010, between 840,000 and 1,270,000 people were legally admitted each year. For 2010, people were admitted for the following reasons:

- Relatives of citizens   57%
- Relatives of legal residents   9%
- Employment based   14%
- Refugees/people seeking political asylum   13%
- Diversity (lottery among applications from
  nations historically sending few immigrants)   5%
- Other   2%

Overall, two-thirds of immigrants come to join their families, one-seventh because of skills needed in the United States, and another one-seventh because of special refugee status. However, it would be a mistake for thinking family reunions are easy to accomplish.

4-4

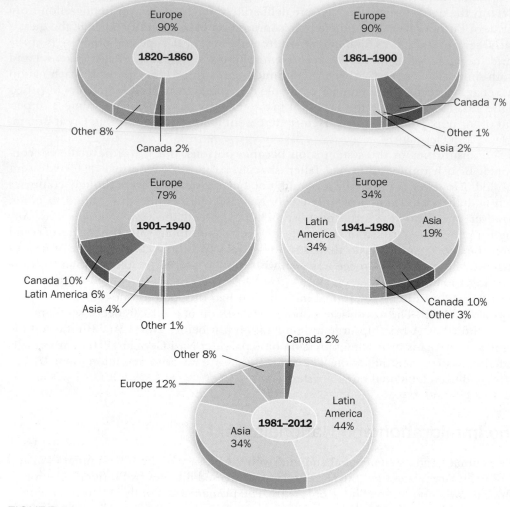

FIGURE 4.3

Legal Immigrants Admitted to the United States by Region of Last Residence, 1820–2012

Source: Office of Immigration Statistics 2013.

Because there are limits on how many people can enter legally each year for any one country, backlogs exist for such nations as China, India, Mexico, and Philippines. So, for example, as of 2013, there was a *13-year* backlog for adult children from the Philippines to join their American citizen parents. Similarly, there was a *17-year* backlog for the Mexican brothers and sisters of American citizens to join their siblings (Martin and Yankay 2013; Preston 2013b).

Contemporary Social Concerns

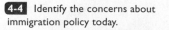 Identify the concerns about immigration policy today.

Although our current immigration policies are less restrictive than other nations', they are the subjects of great debate. Table 4.1 summarizes the benefits and concerns regarding immigration to the United States. We now consider five continuing criticisms relating to our immigration policy: the brain drain, population growth, mixed status, English language acquisition, economic impact, and illegal immigration. All five, but particularly illegal immigration, have provoked heated debates on the national level and continuing efforts to resolve them with new policies.

TABLE 4.1
Immigration Benefits and Concerns

Potential Benefits	Areas of Concern
Provide needed skills	Drain needed resources from home country
Contribute to taxes	Send money home
May come with substantial capital to start business	Less-skilled immigrants compete with already disadvantaged residents
Maintain growth of consumer market	Population growth
Diversify the population (intangible gain)	Language differences
Maintain ties with countries throughout the world	May complicate foreign policy by lobbying the government
	Illegal immigration

4-4

The Brain Drain

How often have you identified your science or mathematics teacher or your physician as someone who was not born in the United States? This nation has clearly benefited from attracting human resources from throughout the world, but this phenomenon has had its price for the nations of origin.

Brain drain is the immigration to the United States of skilled workers, professionals, and technicians who are desperately needed by their home countries. In the mid-twentieth century, many scientists and other professionals from industrial nations, principally Germany and Great Britain, came to the United States. More recently, however, the brain drain has pulled emigrants from developing nations, including India, Pakistan, the Philippines, and several African nations. They are eligible for H-1B visas that qualify them for permanent work permits.

Currently 65,000 foreigners with at a least a bachelor's degree and a specialized skill receive the H-1B visa. Another 20,000 such visas go to foreign nationals with advanced degrees from U.S. universities. In these cases, a person comes to the United States on a student visa, secures a degree, say in engineering, and then may apply for the H-1B.

More than one out of four physicians (27 percent) in the United States is foreign-born and plays a critical role in serving areas with too few doctors. Thousands of doctors have sought to enter the United States, pulled by the economic opportunity. Persons born in India, the Philippines, and China account for the largest groups of foreign-born physicians. The pay differential is so great that, beginning in 2004, when foreign physicians were no longer favored with entry to the United States, physicians in the Philippines retrained as nurses so that they could immigrate to the United States where, employed as nurses, they would make four times what they would as doctors in the Philippines. By 2010, one-third of the foreign born workers employed as registered nurses were born in the Philippines (McCabe 2012; *New York Times* 2005).

Many foreign students say they plan to return home. Fortunately for the United States, many do not and make their talents available in the United States. One study showed that the majority of foreign students receiving their doctorates in the sciences and engineering remain here four years later. Critics note, however, that this foreign supply means that the United States overlooks its own minority scholars. Currently, for every African American and Latino doctorate a foreign citizen receives this degree in the United States. More encouragement must be given to African Americans and Latinos to enter high-tech career paths.

Conflict theorists see the current brain drain as yet another symptom of the unequal distribution of world resources. In their view, it is ironic that the United States gives foreign aid to improve the technical resources of African and Asian countries while maintaining an immigration policy that encourages professionals in such nations to migrate to our shores. These very countries have unacceptable public health conditions and need native scientists, educators, technicians, and other professionals. In addition, by relying on foreign talent, the United States is not encouraging native members of subordinate groups to enter these desirable fields of employment (National Center for Education Statistics 2013: Table 307; Pearson 2006; Wessel 2001; West 2010).

4-4

Population Growth

The United States, like a few other industrial nations, continues to accept large numbers of permanent immigrants and refugees. Although such immigration has increased since the passage of the 1965 Immigration and Nationality Act, the nation's birth rate has decreased. Consequently, the contribution of immigration to population growth has become more significant. As citizen "baby boomers" age, the country has increasingly depended on the economically younger population fueled by immigrants (Meyers 2007).

Immigration, legal and illegal, is projected to account for nearly 50 percent of the nation's growth from 2005 to 2050 with the children and grandchildren of immigrants accounting for another 35 percent. To some observers, the United States is already over-populated. Environmentalists have weighed in on the immigration issue, questioning immigration's possible negative impact on the nation's natural resources. We consider that aspect of the immigration debate later in this chapter. Thus far, the majority of environmentalists have indicated a desire to keep a neutral position rather than enter the politically charged immigration debate (Kotkin 2010; Livingston and Cohn 2012).

The patterns of uneven settlement by immigrants in the United States are expected to continue, so future immigrants' impact on population growth will be felt much more in certain areas, for example, California and New York rather than Wyoming or West Virginia. Although immigration and population growth may be viewed as national concerns, their impact is localized in certain areas, such as Southern California and large urban centers nationwide (Camarota and Jensenius 2009; Passel and Cohn 2009).

Mixed-Status Families

Little is simple when it comes to immigration. This is particularly true regarding the challenge of the estimated 9 million people living in mixed status families. **Mixed status** refers to families in which one or more members are citizens and one or more are non-citizens. This especially becomes problematic when the noncitizens are illegal or undocumented immigrants.

The problem of mixed status emerges on two levels. On the macro level, when policy debates are made about issues that seem clear to many people—such as whether illegal immigrants should be allowed to attend state colleges or whether illegal immigrants should be immediately deported—the complicating factor of mixed-status families quickly emerges. On the micro level, the daily toll on members of mixed-status households is difficult. Often, the legal resident or even the U.S. citizen in a household finds daily life limited for fear of revealing the undocumented status of a parent or brother or even a son.

About three-quarters of illegal immigrants' children were born in the United States and thus are citizens. This means that perhaps half of all adult illegal immigrants have a citizen in their immediate family. This proportion has grown in recent years. Therefore, some of the issues facing illegal immigrants, whom we discuss later, also affect the citizens in the families because they avoid bringing attention to themselves for fear of revealing the illegal status of their mother or father. Immigration issues aside, one can only begin to imagine the additional pressure this places upon families beyond the usual ones of balancing work and home, school, and children moving through adolescent to adulthood (Gonzales 2011; mixed-status; Gonzalez 2009; Passel and Cohn 2009; Pew Hispanic Center 2011b).

Language Barriers

For many people in the United States, the most visible aspects of immigration are non-English speakers, businesses with foreign-language storefronts, and even familiar stores assuring potential customers that their employees speak Spanish or Polish or Chinese or another foreign language. Non-English speakers cluster in certain states, but bilingualism attracts nationwide passions. The release in 2006 of "Nuestro Himno," the Spanish-language version of "The Star-Spangled Banner," led to a strong reaction, with 69 percent of people saying it was appropriate to be sung only in English. Yet at least one congressman who decried the Spanish version sang the anthem himself in English with incorrect lyrics (Carroll 2006; Koch 2006).

About 21 percent of the population speaks a language other than English at home, as shown in Figure 4.4. Indeed, 39 different languages are spoken at home by at least 90,000 residents. Spanish accounts for 62 percent of the foreign language speakers at home. As of 2011, about half of the 61 million people speaking a foreign language at home abroad spoke English less than "very well." Since 1980, the largest growth has been in speakers of Spanish, Chinese, Korean, Vietnamese, Tagalog, Russian, and Persian. The largest decreases have all been in European-based languages such as Italian, Greek, German, Yiddish, and Polish (Ryan 2013).

The myth of Anglo superiority has rested in part on language differences. (The term *Anglo* in the following text means all non-Hispanics but primarily Whites.) First, the criteria for economic and social achievement usually include proficiency in English. By such standards, Spanish-speaking pupils are judged less able to compete until they learn English. Second, many Anglos believe that Spanish is not an asset occupationally. Only

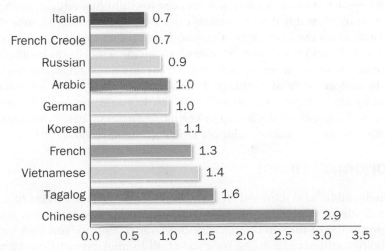

FIGURE 4.4

Ten Languages Most Frequently Spoken at Home, Other Than English and Spanish

By comparison, of 291 million people over 5 years of age, 231 million only speak English at home, 38 million Spanish, and about 22 million some other language.

Source: Data for 2011 in Ryan 2013:3.

4-4

recently, as government agencies belatedly began serving Latino people and as businesses recognized the growing Latino consumer market, have Anglos recognized that knowing Spanish is not only useful but also necessary to carry out certain tasks.

Until the last 40 years, a conscious effort was made to devalue Spanish and other languages and to discourage the use of foreign languages in schools. In the case of Spanish, this practice was built on a pattern of segregating Hispanic schoolchildren from Anglos. In the recent past in the Southwest, Mexican Americans were assigned to Mexican schools to keep Anglo schools all-White. These Mexican schools, created through de jure school segregation resulting from residential segregation, were substantially underfunded compared with the Anglo public schools. Legal action against such schools dates back to 1945, but it was not until 1970 that the U.S. Supreme Court ruled, in *Cisneros v. Corpus Christi Independent School District*, that segregation of Mexican Americans was unconstitutional. Appeals delayed implementation of that decision, and not until September 1975 was the de jure plan forcibly overturned in Corpus Christi, Texas (Commission on Civil Rights 1976).

Is it essential that English be the sole language of instruction in schools in the United States? **Bilingualism** is the use of two or more languages in places of work or educational facilities and accords each language equal legitimacy. Thus, a program of **bilingual education** may instruct children in their native language (such as Spanish) while gradually introducing them to the language of the dominant society (English). If such a program also is bicultural, it will teach children about the culture of both linguistic groups. Bilingual education allows students to learn academic material in their own language while they learn a second language. Proponents believe that, ideally, bilingual education programs should also allow English-speaking pupils to be bilingual, but generally they are directed only at making non-English speakers proficient in more than one language.

Do bilingual programs help children learn English? It is difficult to reach firm conclusions on the effectiveness of the bilingual programs in general because they vary so widely in their approach to non-English-speaking children. The programs differ in the length of the transition to English and how long they allow students to remain in bilingual classrooms. A major study analyzed more than three decades of research, combining 17 different studies, and found that bilingual education programs produce higher levels of student achievement in reading. The most successful are paired bilingual programs—those offering ongoing instruction in a native language and English at different times of the day (Slavin and Cheung 2003; Soltero 2008).

Attacks on bilingualism in voting and education have taken several forms and have even broadened to question the appropriateness of U.S. residents using any language other than English. Federal policy has become more restrictive. Local schools have been given more authority to determine appropriate methods of instruction; they also have been forced to provide more of their own funding for bilingual education. Adding to the difficulty is that increasingly school districts outside the central city in suburbs and rural agricultural areas face the challenge of serving non-English-speaking schoolchildren.

In the United States, as of 2013, 30 states have made English their official language. Repeated efforts have been made to introduce a constitutional amendment declaring English as the nation's official language. Even such an action would not completely outlaw bilingual or multilingual government services. It would, however, require that such services be called for specifically as in the Voting Rights Act of 1965, which requires voting information to be available in multiple languages (U.S. English 2013).

The Economic Impact

There is much public and scholarly debate about the economic effects of immigration, both legal and illegal. Varied, conflicting conclusions have resulted from research ranging from case studies of Korean immigrants' dominance among New York City greengrocers to mobility studies charting the progress of all immigrants and their children. The confusion results in part from the different methods of analysis. For example, the studies do not always include political refugees, who generally are less prepared than other refugees to become assimilated. Sometimes, the research focuses only on economic effects, such as whether people are employed or are on welfare; in other cases, it also considers cultural factors such as knowledge of English.

Perhaps the most significant factor in determining the economic impact of immigration is whether a study examines the national impact of immigration or only its effects on a local area. Overall, we can conclude from the research that immigrants adapt well and are an asset to the local economy. In some areas, heavy immigration may drain a community's resources. However, it can also revitalize a local economy. Marginally employed workers, most of whom are either themselves immigrants or African Americans, often experience a negative impact by new arrivals. With or without immigration, competition for low-paying jobs in the United States is high, and those who gain the most from this competition are the employers and the consumers who want to keep prices down (Steinberg 2005; Zimmerman 2008).

Research Focus

The Hispanic Dairyland

Dairyland Wisconsin invokes images of rolling hills and pastures, black and white Holstein cows, and roadside shops selling cheese. But now an indispensable part of this portrayal is the important role played by Latino workers.

Just since the beginning of the twenty-first century, immigrant workers, almost entirely Hispanic and largely Mexican, have become the majority of laborers on large dairy farms and overall at least 40 percent of all hired dairy employees on the more than 14,000 dairy farms in Wisconsin. Latinos working in agriculture is not new—nationally they accounted in 2012 for 24 percent of all employed persons in animal and crop production—but their rapid presence in dairy farming is a recent twenty-first century phenomenon. Dairy farmers turned to immigrant workers when they found it difficult to locate U.S.-born workers who were "reliable," to use their often-expressed criteria. Dairy farms have also grown larger, requiring additional milking shifts and more workhands.

As one typical dairy farmer with 150 cows said in 2009,

So as our last two children entered high school, and I realized that soon I would have no family labor to rely on, we moved our farm to all hired labor. I have not been able to hire an American citizen since 1997. I have tried! The way I see it, if we didn't have Hispanics to rely on for a work force, I don't believe I could continue farming. (Harrison, Lloyd, and O'Kane 2009:2–3)

The important role that Latinos now play on dairy farms is not limited to the Midwest but is repeated in places like California, Texas, New York state, and Vermont, which also used to depend on local workers.

The use of immigrant labor on dairy farms is an example of **occupational segregation**. This refers to the concentration of one particular group of people to a particular job. In this case we see occupational segregation with respect to Latinos, largely male, to the more manual labor on these farms. They are not involved in caring for the herd, distribution of the product, or equipment maintenance managing, much less owning the farm. They are limited to the "milking parlors" or the large barns where cows are milked. The Latinos work as "milkers" typically hooking the cows to hoses, "pushers" getting the cows in and out of the salon, or "cleaners" scraping manure from the parlors. Cows are milked two to three times a day, every day, so the labor demand is continuous.

The low-level jobs are now often even described as "Mexican" work, regardless of the nationality of the laborer, even though little more than a decade or two ago it was all done by family or local workers. So associated are Latinos with this hard labor that farm operators now speak of the U.S.-born workers as being too weak to do the immigrant labor. Hispanic laborers are so well-regarded for working the long hours at tough work that when a worker seems reluctant to do it, they are derisively referred to as now being "Americanized" in a reference to the local people unwilling to do labor in the milk parlors. Occupation segregation is growing so well-defined that now Latinos are seen as suited for the job and unsatisfactory for any more skilled and higher paying work on the farm. For the workers, their "success" as milkers has led to chain migration to the area through family and friendship networks as more and more workers are needed.

Pay is about $9 an hour as of 2013 with few non-wage benefits, and jobs are year-round, but this often means working at split intervals in the same day totalling 55–60 hours a week. Even though they may work for several years on the same farm, there is little interest in training the workers to do more highly skilled labor. The farm owners recognize that many of these workers may be illegal and do not wish to "invest" in their future. From the workers' standpoint, they rarely complain, fearing that their illegal status or that of their friends and family members, even if they themselves are legal, may be disclosed. Given that they labor in rural areas doing work that no one else wants to do, there is little incentive to investigate their legal status and dairy farms are rarely investigated.

Dairy farms represent a very small aspect of Latino life in the United States but for dairy farmers, Latinos are all important. Therefore, through agriculture lobbying organizations, farm operators and owners are well heard on any immigration bill that may jeopardize their continuing to access their "reliable," if illegal, workforce.

Sources: Department of Agriculture 2010; Campion 2013; Dorschner 2013; Harrison and Lloyd 2012; Jordan 2009; Kohli 2013.

4-4

There is no one portrait, or even a dozen portraits, of the typical situation that describes the economic role of immigrants in the United States. Similarly, there are many explanations for whey unauthorized immigration persists. In the Research Focus, we show that labor on dairy a farm has been dominated by Latino workers, many of them undocumented.

The impact of immigration on African Americans deserves special attention. Given that African Americans are a large minority and many continue to be in the underclass, many people, including some Blacks themselves, perceive immigrants as advancing at the expense of the African American community. There is evidence that in the very lowest paid jobs—for example, workers in chicken-processing plants—wages have dropped with the availability of unskilled immigrants to perform them, and Blacks have left these jobs for good. Many of these African Americans do not necessarily move to better or even equivalent jobs. This pattern is repeated in other relatively low-paying, undesirable employment sectors, so Blacks are not alone in being impacted; but given other job opportunities, the impact is longer lasting (Borjas, Grogger, and Hanson 2006; Holzer 2008).

About 70 percent of illegal immigrant workers pay taxes of one type or another. Many of them do not file to receive entitled refunds or benefits. For example, in 2005, the Social Security Administration identified thousands of unauthorized workers contributing about $7 billion to the fund but that could not be credited properly. Supporters of immigration reform point to increased tax revenue and even more net financial benefits to all local governments if illegal immigrants move toward legal residency (Institute on Taxation and Economic Policy 2013; Lipman 2008; Porter 2005).

Social science studies generally contradict many of the negative stereotypes about the economic impact of immigration. A variety of recent studies found that immigrants are a net economic gain for the population in times of economic boom as well as in periods of recession. But despite national gains, in some areas and for some groups, immigration may be an economic burden or create unwanted competition for jobs (Kochhar 2006).

What about the immigrants themselves? Considering contemporary immigrants as a group, we can make the following conclusions in Table 4.2. They represent a mix of successes and challenges to adaptation. These positive trends diverge among specific immigrant groups, with Asian immigrants doing better than European immigrants, who do better than Latino immigrants (Capps, Leighton, and Fix 2002; Farkas 2003; Myers, Pitkin, and Park 2004; Zimmerman 2008).

One economic aspect of immigration that has received increasing attention is the role of **remittances**, or the monies that immigrants return to their countries of origin. The amounts are significant and measure in the hundreds of millions of dollars flowing from the United States to a number of countries where they provide substantial support for

---

TABLE 4.2
Immigrant Adaptation to the USA

Less Encouraging	Positive Signs
■ Although immigrants have lower divorce rates and are less likely to form single-parent households than natives, their rates equal or exceed these rates by the second generation.	■ Immigrant families and, more broadly, noncitizen households are more likely to be on public assistance, but their time on public assistance is less and they receive fewer benefits. This is even true when considering special restrictions that may apply to noncitizens.
■ Children in immigrant families tend to be healthier than U.S.-born children, but the advantage declines. We consider this in greater detail later in this chapter.	■ Second-generation immigrants (i.e., children of immigrants) are overall doing as well as or better than White non-Hispanic natives in educational attainment, labor force participation, wages, and household income.
■ Immigrant children attend schools that are disproportionately attended by other poor children and students with limited English proficiency, so they are ethnically, economically, and linguistically isolated.	■ Immigrants overwhelmingly (65 percent) continue to see learning English as an ethical obligation of all immigrants.

The immigration debates range from loosening to tightening the flow of immigrants, whether illegal immigrants who came here as children and went to school should be allowed a pathway to citizenship (the proposed DREAM act), and whether states such as Arizona have overstepped their bounds in trying to identify illegal immigrants by empowering any person stopped or arrested if they have reason to believe they have immigrated illegally.

families and even venture capital for new businesses. Although some observers express concern over this outflow of money, others counter that it probably represents a small price to pay for the human capital that the United States is able to use in the form of the immigrants themselves. Immigrants in the United States send annually about 31 billion to their home countries and worldwide remittances bring about $530 billion to all the world's countries, easily surpassing all other forms of foreign aid. While this cash inflow is integral to the economics of many nations, it also means that during the global economic recession that occurred recently, this resource drops off significantly (World Bank 2013a, 2013b).

The concern about immigration today is both understandable and perplexing. The nation has always been uneasy about new arrivals, especially those who are different from the more affluent and the policymakers. In most of the 1990s, we had paradoxical concerns about immigrants hurting the economy despite strong economic growth. With the economic downturn beginning in 2008, it was clear that low-skilled immigrants (legal or illegal) took the hardest hit and, as a result, remittances immediately declined.

Illegal Immigration

The most bitterly debated aspect of U.S. immigration policy has been the control of illegal or undocumented immigrants. These immigrants and their families come to the United States in search of higher-paying jobs than their home countries can provide. While some people contend there are differences in their meaning, we will use the terms illegal, undocumented, or unauthorized interchangeably to refer to people who have entered the country without the proper documents as well as people who entered legally as students or tourists but then remained illegally.

Because by definition illegal immigrants are in the country illegally, the exact number of these undocumented or unauthorized workers is subject to estimates and disputes. Based on the best available information in late 2013, more than 11.7 million illegal or unauthorized immigrants live in the United States. This compares with about 3.5 million in 1990 and a peak of 12.2 million in 2007. With employment opportunities drying up during the economic downturn beginning in 2008, significantly fewer people tried to

4-5 Discuss the scope of and issues related to illegal immigration.

4-5

enter illegally, and many unauthorized immigrants returned to their countries (Passel, Cohn and Gonzalez-Barrera 2013).

The public has tied illegal immigrants, and even legal immigrants, to almost every social problem in the nation. They become the scapegoats for unemployment; they are labeled "drug runners" and, especially since September 11, 2001, "terrorists." Arrest, detention, and deportation of illegal immigrants greatly increased. Their vital economic and cultural contribution to the United States is generally overlooked, as it has been for more than a hundred years. Considering it from the perspective of the immigrant, the possibility of apprehension and punishment are not significant deterrents. However, the decision to enter illegally is affected by the assessment of the employment possibilities in the home country and, as we will see later, the dangers of border crossing (Ryo 2013).

There are significant costs for aliens—that is, foreign-born noncitizens—and for other citizens. Civil rights advocates have expressed concern that the procedures used to apprehend and deport people are discriminatory and deprive many aliens of their legal rights. American citizens of Hispanic or Asian origin, some of whom were born in the United States, may be greeted with prejudice and distrust, as if their names automatically imply that they are illegal immigrants. Furthermore, these citizens and legal residents of the United States may be unable to find work because employers wrongly believe that their documents are forged.

In the context of this illegal immigration, Congress approved the Immigration Reform and Control Act of 1986 (IRCA) after debating it for nearly a decade. The act marked a historic change in immigration policy compared with earlier laws, as summarized in Table 4.3. Amnesty was granted to 2.7 million illegal immigrants who could document that they had established long-term residency in the United States. Under the IRCA, hiring illegal aliens became illegal, and employers became subject to fines and even prison sentences. Little workplace enforcement occurred for years, but beginning in 2009, federal agents concentrated on auditing large employers rather than raiding workplaces (Massey and Pren 2012; Siegal 2013).

Many illegal immigrants continue to live in fear and hiding, subject to even more severe harassment and discrimination than before. From a conflict perspective, these immigrants, primarily poor and Hispanic or Asian, are being firmly lodged at the bottom of the nation's social and economic hierarchies. However, from a functionalist perspective, employers, by paying low wages, are able to produce goods and services that are profitable for industry and more affordable to consumers. Despite the poor working conditions often experienced by illegal immigrants, they continue to come because it is still in their best economic interest to work here in disadvantaged positions rather than seek wage labor unsuccessfully in their home countries.

Illegal aliens or undocumented workers are not necessarily transient. One estimate indicates 63 percent had been here for at least ten years. Many have established homes, families, and networks with relatives and friends in the United States whose legal status

TABLE 4.3
Major Immigration Policies

Policy	Target Group	Impact
Chinese Exclusion Act, 1882	Chinese	Effectively ended all Chinese immigration for more than 60 years
National origin system, 1921	Southern Europeans	Reduced overall immigration and significantly reduced likely immigration from Greece and Italy
Immigration and Nationality Act, 1965 (Hart-Cellar Act)	Western Hemisphere and the less skilled	Facilitated entry of skilled workers and relatives of U.S. residents
Immigration Reform and Control Act of 1986	Illegal immigrants	Modest reduction of illegal immigration
Illegal Immigration Reform and Immigrant Responsibility Act of 1996	Illegal immigrants	Greater border surveillance and increased scrutiny of legal immigrants seeking benefits

might differ. These are the mixed-status households noted earlier. For the most part, their lives are not much different from legal residents, except when they seek services that require documentation proving citizenship status (Pew Hispanic Center 2011).

Policymakers continue to avoid the only real way to stop illegal immigration: discourage employment opportunities. This has certainly been the approach in recent years. The Immigration and Customs Enforcement (ICE) notifies major companies that it will soon audit its employment records looking for illegal immigrants. If found, civil and criminal penalties can be levied against the business. The workers themselves are subject to deportation. This has led corporations such as American Apparel and Chipotle Mexican Grill to look more closely at and fire hundreds of employees lacking sufficient documentation. In 2012, about 410,000 people had been deported, a similar number to the year before—this is equivalent to deporting the people of San Diego during a two-year period (Migration News 2012b; Preston 2013a).

The public often thinks in terms of controlling illegal immigration through greater surveillance at the border. After the terrorist attacks of September 11, 2001, greater control of border traffic took on a new sense of urgency, even though almost all the hijackers had entered the United States legally. It also is very difficult to secure the vast boundaries that mark the United States on land and sea. The cost of the federal government's attempt to police the nation's borders and locate illegal immigrants is sizable. The federal government spends $18 billion annually with costs of proposed enhancements of border security ranging from fencing to drones easily reaching another 4.5 billion dollars (*Economist* 2013; Preston 2013a).

Numerous civil rights groups and migrant advocacy organizations have expressed alarm regarding people who cross into the United States illegally and perish in the attempt. Some die in deserts, in isolated canyons, and while concealed in containers or locked in trucks during smuggling attempts. Several hundred die annually in the Southwest by seeking ever more dangerous crossing points because border control has increased. However, this toll has received so little attention that one journalist likened it to several jumbo jets crashing between Los Angeles and Phoenix every year without anyone giving it much notice. Approximately 2,269 immigrant deaths were record for the 2 ½ year period from October 1999 through March 2012. The immigration policy debate was largely absent from the 2008 and 2012 presidential races and was replaced by concerns over the economy (Del Olmo 2003; Helmore 2013).

An immigration-related issue that began being raised recently has been concern over illegal immigrants' children who are born here and thus regarded as citizens at birth. Public opinion polls reveal that about half of the population has concerns regarding these children. Some people want to alter the Fourteenth Amendment to revise the "birthright citizenship" that was intended for children of slaves but has long been interpreted to cover anyone born in the United States regardless of their parents' legal status. While such a movement is unlikely to succeed, it is yet another example of a relatively minor issue that sidetracks any substantive discussion of immigration reform (Gomez 2010).

So what is the future of immigration reform? It is unlikely to be resolved in any satisfying way because the issues are complex and are wrapped up in economic interests, humanitarian concerns, party politics, constitutional rights, and even foreign policy. Alongside immigration policy is how the nation is to accommodate people escaping political and religious persecution.

When it comes to issues of race and ethnicity, South Africa usually evokes past images of apartheid and the struggle to overcome generations of racial separation—both important topics to be considered in Chapter 16. However, in the Global View, we consider the contemporary challenge of dealing with immigration.

4-6 **A Global View**

Immigration and South Africa

With its over 52 million people, the Republic of South Africa is not rich by global standards, but its economy is very attractive to most of the African continent. For example, South Africa has a gross national income per person of $10,360, compared to well under $2,000 in neighboring Zimbabwe. Even when South Africa was ruled by a White-supremacist government, Black Africans from throughout the continent came to the country fleeing violence and poverty in their home countries and to work, often in the mining of coal and diamonds. In the post-apartheid era, the numbers of immigrants, legal and illegal, have skyrocketed. Today's government is caught between compassion for those seeking entry and the growing inability of the economy to absorb those who seek work and shelter.

In 2008, the world took notice as riots broke out between poor South Africans taking out their rage on even more impoverished foreigners. The growing xenophobia took the government, which advocates racial harmony, by surprise as it tried to quell violence among Black Africans divided by citizenship status and nationality. In a matter of months in early 2008, some 32,000 immigrants had been driven from their homes, with attackers seizing all of their belongings. Some immigrants returned to their home countries—including Burundi, Ethiopia, Ghana, Malawi, Mozambique, and Zimbabwe—but most settled temporarily in camps.

South Africa, with limited government resources, deported over 310,000 immigrants in 2007–2008, a proportion nearly comparable to that of the United States (with six times the population). However, estimates of the total number of illegal immigrants in South Africa range from 3 million to 5 million—a much higher proportion than estimated in the United States.

The scapegoating of immigrants, or "border jumpers" as they often are called in South Africa, is not unique to this nation. The tension between South Africans and foreigners has led to concerns over continuing xenophobia with threats toward foreign-owned shops. For the global community that still relishes Nelson Mandela's peaceful ascent to power, it has been a reminder of immigration's challenge throughout the world.

Sources: Dixon 2007; Forced Migration Studies Programme 2010; Haub and Kaneda 2013; Koser 2008; Nevin 2008; Roodt 2008; South African Institute of Race Relations 2011.

Path to Citizenship: Naturalization

4-6 Outline the process of naturalization.

In **naturalization**, citizenship is conferred on a person after birth, a process that has been outlined by Congress and extends to foreigners the same benefits given to native-born U.S. citizens. Naturalized citizens, however, cannot serve as president.

Until the 1970s, most people who were naturalized had been born in Europe. Reflecting changing patterns of immigration, Asia and Latin America are now the largest sources of new citizens. In fact, the number of naturalized citizens from Mexico has come close to matching those from all of Europe. In recent years, the number of new citizens going through the naturalization process has been close to one million a year (Baker 2009).

To become a naturalized U.S. citizen, a person must meet the following general conditions:

- be 18 years of age;
- have continually resided in the United States for at least five years (three years for the spouses of U.S. citizens);
- have good moral character as determined by the absence of conviction of selected criminal offenses;
- be able to read, write, speak, and understand words of ordinary usage in the English language; and
- pass a test in U.S. government and history administered orally in English.

Table 4.4 offers the types of questions immigrants face on the citizenship test. This is a sample of the actual questions used; you must get six out of ten correct to pass. If a person fails, he or she can immediately retake it with different questions. If failed a second time, typically the person must wait 90 days to retake the test. As of 2013, the fee for applying for citizenship is $680, compared with $95 in 1998.

TABLE 4.4
So You Want to Be a Citizen?

Try these sample questions from the naturalization test (answers below).

1. What do the stripes on the flag represent?
2. How many amendments are there to the Constitution?
3. Who is the chief justice of the Supreme Court?
4. Who was president during World War I?
5. What do we call the first 10 amendments to the Constitution?
6. What are two rights in the Declaration of Independence?
7. Name one right or freedom from the First Amendment.
8. When was the Constitution written?

Answers:
(1) The first 13 states; (2) 27; (3) John Roberts; (4) Woodrow Wilson; (5) Bill of Rights; (6) life, liberty, and the pursuit of happiness; (7) The rights are freedom of speech, religion, assembly, and press, and freedom to petition the government; (8) 1787.

Source: Department of Homeland Security 2013.

Although we often picture the United States as having a very insular, nativistic attitude toward foreigners living here, the country has a rather liberal policy toward people maintaining the citizenship of their old countries. Although most countries do not allow people to maintain dual (or even multiple) citizenships, the United States does not forbid it. Dual citizenship is most common when a person goes through naturalization after already being a citizen of another country or is a U.S.-born citizen and goes through the process of becoming a citizen of another country—for example, after marrying a foreigner (Department of State 2013).

The continuing debate about immigration reform often includes calls for some type of "amnesty" or pathway to citizenship for illegal immigrants. Details in proposals vary but usually include proof of long-term residence in the USA, absence of criminal activity, and willingness to accept a waiting period before actual citizenship can occur. Critics of such proposals question the wisdom of "rewarding illegals" but also argue that if legal residency is acquired than their relatives will also apply for legal residency. Current policy as earlier noted has created long waiting periods for those abroad trying to join their relatives, but surveys also show that, as in 1986 when some type of amnesty was offered, not all qualified illegal immigrants will seek legal status. For example, in recent years only 46 percent of Hispanic immigrants eligible to naturalize have chosen to become citizens, compared with 71 percent of non-Hispanic immigrants. Typical difficulties with the English language and the costs of application serve as a barrier to the path to citizenship. Other special one-time programs since 1986 also show only about half taking advantage of naturalization (Lopez and Gonzalez-Barrera 2013).

Women and Immigration

Immigration is presented as if all immigrants are similar, with the only distinctions being made concerning point of origin, education, and employment prospects. Another significant distinction is whether immigrants travel with or without their families. We often think that historical immigrants to the United States were males in search of work. Men dominate much of the labor migration worldwide, but because of the diversified labor force in the United States and some policies that facilitate relatives coming, immigration to the United States generally has been fairly balanced. Actually, most immigration historically appears to be families. For example, from 1870 through 1940, men entering the United States exceeded women by only about 10 to 20 percent. Since 1950, women immigrants have actually exceeded men by a modest amount (Gibson and Jung 2006).

4-7 Understand the special role of women in immigration.

4-8

Immigration is a challenge to all family members. But immigrant women must navigate a new culture and a new country not only for themselves but also for their children, such as in this household in Colorado.

The second-class status women normally experience in society is reflected in immigration. Most dramatically, women citizens who married immigrants who were not citizens actually lost their U.S. citizenship from 1907 through 1922 with few exceptions. However, this policy did not apply to men (Johnson 2004).

Immigrant women face not only all the challenges faced by immigrant men but also additional ones. Typically, they have the responsibility of navigating the new society when it comes to services for their family and, in particular, their children. Many new immigrants view the United States as a dangerous place to raise a family and therefore remain particularly vigilant of what happens in their children's lives.

Male immigrants are more likely to be consumed with work, leaving the women to navigate the bureaucratic morass of city services, schools, medical facilities, and even everyday concerns such as stores and markets. Immigrant women are often reluctant to seek outside help, whether they are in need of special services for medical purposes or they are victims of domestic violence. Yet immigrant women are more likely to be the liaison for the household, including adult men, to community associations and religious organizations (Hondagneu-Sotelo 2003; Jones 2008).

Women play a critical role in overseeing the household; for immigrant women, the added pressures of being in a new country and trying to move ahead in a different culture heighten this social role.

The Global Economy and Immigration

4-8 Illustrate the relationship of globalization with respect to immigrants.

Immigration is defined by political boundaries that bring the movement of peoples crossing borders to the attention of government authorities and their policies. Within the United States, people may move their residence, but they are not immigrating. For residents in the member nations of the European Union, free movement of people within the union is also protected.

Yet, increasingly, people recognize the need to think beyond national borders and national identity. As noted in Chapter 1, **globalization** is the worldwide integration of government policies, cultures, social movements, and financial markets through trade, movement of people, and the exchange of ideas. In this global framework, even immigrants are less likely to think of themselves as residents of only one country. For generations, immigrants have used foreign-language newspapers to keep in touch with events in their home countries. Today, cable channels carry news and variety programs from their

SPECTRUM OF INTERGROUP RELATIONS

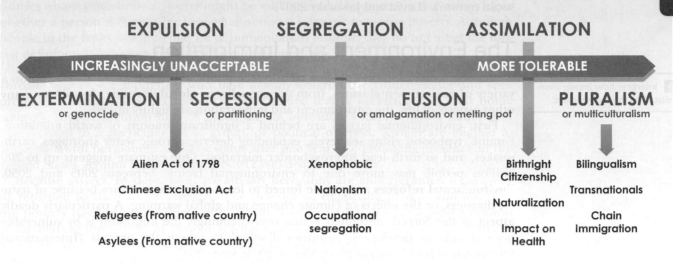

EXPULSION	SEGREGATION	ASSIMILATION

INCREASINGLY UNACCEPTABLE → MORE TOLERABLE

EXTERMINATION	SECESSION	FUSION	PLURALISM
or genocide	or partitioning	or amalgamation or melting pot	or multiculturalism

Alien Act of 1798	Xenophobic	Birthright Citizenship	Bilingualism
Chinese Exclusion Act	Nationlsm		Transnationals
Refugees (From native country)	Occupational segregation	Naturalization	Chain Immigration
Asylees (From native country)		Impact on Health	

home countries, and the Internet offers immediate access to the homeland and kinfolk thousands of miles away.

Although it helps in bringing the world together, globalization has also highlighted the dramatic economic inequalities between nations. Today, people in North America, Europe, and Japan consume 32 times more resources than the billions of people in developing nations. Thanks to tourism, media, and other aspects of globalization, the people of less-affluent countries are aware of such affluent lifestyles and, of course, often aspire to enjoy them (Diamond 2003).

Transnationals are immigrants who sustain multiple social relationships that link their societies of origin and settlement. Immigrants from the Dominican Republic, for example, not only identify themselves with Americans but also maintain very close ties to their Caribbean homeland. They return for visits, send remittances, and host extended stays of relatives and friends. Back in the Dominican Republic, villages reflect these close ties, as shown in billboards promoting special long-distance services to the United States and by the presence of household appliances sent by relatives. The volume of remittances worldwide is easily the most reliable source of foreign money going to poor countries, far outstripping foreign aid programs.

The presence of transnationals would be yet another example of pluralism, as illustrated in the Spectrum of Intergroup Relations. Since transnationals move back and forth, it is not unusual for any given moment that different generations of the same family will find themselves residing in different countries (Foner and Dreby 2011).

The growing number of transnationals, as well as immigration in general, directly reflects the world systems analysis we considered in Chapter 1. Transnationals are not new, but the ability to communicate and transfer resources makes the immigration experience today different from that of the nineteenth century. The sharp contrast between the industrial "have" nations and the developing "have-not" nations only encourages movement across borders. The industrial haves gain benefits from such movement even when they seem to discourage it. The back-and-forth movement only serves to increase globalization and help create informal social networks between people who seek a better life and those already enjoying increased prosperity.

The transnationals themselves maintain a multithreaded relationship between friends and relatives in the United Sates, their home country, and perhaps other countries where relatives and friends have resettled. Besides the economic impact of remittances

Conclusion

The immigrant presence in the United States can often be heard on the streets and the workplace as people speak in different languages, Check out your radio. As of 2011, radio stations broadcast in 35 languages other than English, including Albanian, Creole, Welsh, Yiddish, and Oji—a language spoken in Ghana. The Internet in 2013 expands it to over 90 languages via online radio stations aimed at the USA (Keen 2011; Omniglot 2013).

Throughout the history of the United States, as we have seen, there has been intense debate over the nation's policies that bring the immigrants who speak these and other languages to the country. In a sense, this debate reflects the deep value conflicts in the U.S. culture and parallels the "American dilemma" identified by Swedish social economist Gunnar Myrdal (1944). One strand of our culture—epitomized by the words "Give us your tired, your poor, your huddled masses"—has emphasized egalitarian principles and a desire to help people in their time of need. One could hardly have anticipated at the time the Statue of Liberty was dedicated in 1886 that more than a century later Barack Obama, the son of a Kenyan immigrant, would be elected President of the United States.

At the same time, however, hostility to potential immigrants and refugees—whether the Chinese in the 1880s, European Jews in the 1930s and 1940s, or Mexicans, Haitians, and Arabs today—reflects not only racial, ethnic, and religious prejudice but also a desire to maintain the dominant culture of the in-group by keeping out those viewed as outsiders. The conflict between these cultural values is central to the American dilemma of the twenty-first century.

The current debate about immigration is highly charged and emotional. Some people see it in economic terms, whereas others see the new arrivals as a challenge to the very culture of our society. Clearly, the general perception is that immigration presents a problem rather than a promise for the future.

Today's concern about immigrants follows generations of people coming to settle in the United States. This immigration in the past produced a very diverse country in terms of both nationality and religion, even before the immigration of the last 60 years. Therefore, the majority of Americans today are not descended from the English, and Protestants are just more than half of all worshipers. This diversity of religious and ethnic groups is examined in Chapter 5.

Summary

1. Immigration to the United States has changed over time from unrestricted to restricted, with the sending nations now in Latin America and Asia rather than Europe.

2. Immigration began being regulated by the United States in the nineteenth century; the first significant restriction was the Chinese Exclusion Act in 1882.

3. Subsequent legislation through the national origins system favored northern and western Europeans. Not until 1965 were quotas by nation largely lifted.

4. Issues including the brain drain, population growth, mixed-status households, English-language acquisition, and economic impact influence contemporary immigration policy.

5. Often more of a concern than legal immigration has been the continuing presence of a large number of illegal immigrants.

6. Naturalization is a complex process that is still pursued by those abroad as well as by unauthorized immigrants.

7. While immigrant men may typically dominate the workers, women play a critical role in the household formation and increasingly in the workforce.

8. The worldwide integration of societies has been facilitated by transnationals who sustain multiple social relationships across borders.

9. Environment affects and, in turn, is influenced by global immigration.

10. Refugees present a special challenge to policymakers who balance humanitarian values against an unwillingness to accept all those who are fleeing poverty and political unrest.

Key Terms

asylees, p. 107

bilingual education, p. 96

bilingualism, p. 96

brain drain, p. 93

chain immigration, p. 84

environmental refugees, p. 106

globalization, p. 104

mixed status, p. 94

nativism, p. 87

naturalization, p. 102

occupational segregation, p. 97

refugees, p. 106

remittances, p. 98

sinophobes, p. 88

transnationals, p. 105

xenophobia, p. 87

Review Questions

1. How would you describe the general patterns of immigration?

2. What were the social and economic issues when public opinion mounted against Chinese immigration to the United States?

3. How did restrictionist immigration policies develop in the twentieth century?

4. What are the contemporary social concerns about legal immigration today?

5. What are the main issues surrounding illegal immigration?

6. How can one become a naturalized citizen?

7. How do women play a critical role in global immigration?

8. How are the physical environment and immigration interrelated?

9. How is globalization furthered by immigration?

10. What principles appear to guide U.S. refugee policy?

Critical Thinking

1. What are the functions and dysfunctions of immigration?

2. Ultimately, what do you think is the major concern people have about contemporary immigration to the United States: the numbers of immigrants, their legal status, or their nationality?

3. What challenge does the presence of people in the United States speaking languages other than English present for them? For schools? For the workplace? For you?

4. What is your family's immigrant root story? Consider how your ancestors arrived in the United States and also how other immigrant groups have shaped your family's past.

5

Ethnicity and Religion

5-1 Understand what is meant by "Whiteness."

5-2 Describe how people rediscover ethnicity.

5-3 Recall the German American experience.

5-4 Identify the major periods of the Irish American immigration.

5-5 Put into your own words the Italian American experience.

5-6 Restate the Polish American immigration story.

5-7 State what is meant by religious pluralism.

5-8 Interpret how the courts have ruled on religion.

When China and the United States established diplomatic relations in 1868, Chinese were allowed to legally immigrate to the United States. Most settled in California but some made their way to New York City and settled around Mott Street just south of Canal Street. Italians began immigrating in large numbers about the same time, settling in several areas including along Mulberry Street one street over from Mott but north of Canal. For 150 years Italian and Chinese Americans lived in adjoining densely populated neighborhoods.

By 1940, Little Italy was a tourist destination as was neighboring Chinatown. A decade later few Italians immigrated and those already in Little Italy began to move out. A few years later the Chinese community and its Chinatown expanded and by 1980 the population had surpassed that of San Francisco.

The character of Little Italy changed. In 1950, half of the residents were Italian American, with 20 percent of those born in Italy. By 2000 it was only 6 percent Italian American with very few born in Italy. Ten years later the proportion of Italian Americans had edged down to 5 percent with not a single Italian-born resident living in Little Italy. While the area along Mulberry remained a powerful symbol to ethnic Italians, today it is defined not as a place to live but by two elements. One is food, as represented by 50 or so restaurants and cafes as well as an occasional bakery. The other is religion.

Going to church? The Zion English Lutheran Church established in 1801 became in 1853 the Church of the Transfiguration, as the Catholic Church took over the facility to serve the poor Irish. By 1891, it served the Italian neighborhood, but a couple of generations later Chinese Catholics began to attend and now its congregation is almost entirely Chinese with masses offered in English, Mandarin, and Cantonese.

Looking for the Chinese American Planning Council? Its offices are in Little Italy. Looking for the Museum of Chinese in America? Little Italy. By 2010, the 38-block area of Little Italy and Chinatown were listed in a single historic district on the National Register of Historic Places. So is it, "Arrivederci, Little Italy"?

Not yet. Near the Church of the Transfiguration, an annual 11-day festival of San Gennaro takes over several blocks and honors the Patron Saint of Naples—the point of origin for many of the Italian immigrants. The festival's climactic parade runs on both Mott and Mulberry Streets, where most of the residents are Chinese. Some follow Catholicism but others are of the Protestant, Buddhist, and Daoist faiths.

Yes, the Italian Americans express concern over the visible Chinese American presence, but often they work with their ethnic neighbors to maintain an Italian presence. What really worries the Italian and even the much more numerous Chinese Americans about losing their ethnic neighborhood and religious institutions? It is the encroachment of boutiques, fancy little restaurants prepared to pay higher rents, and the dreaded arrival of a Starbucks. There is no negotiating the maintenance of ethnic ties with these agents of social change, so the Italian and Chinese Americans work together. For example, the two groups organized the annual Marco Polo Day, now in its fifth year, which honors the explorer from Venice who journeyed in the thirteenth century through Central Asia to China (Guest 2003; Krase 2006; National Park Service 2009, 2010; Roberts 2011; Tonelli 2004; Two Bridges 2013).

It's May, ready for the National Day of Prayer? Congress formalized this observance in 1952. While 83 percent of people in the United States indicate there is a God who answers prayers, the increasing diversity of believers makes even the observance of this event increasingly contentious. What kind of praying? Some more ecumenical prayers (no reference to Jesus Christ, for example, or even to a supreme being) affront many. Specific Biblical, Talmudic, or Qur'anic references have limited appeals across a nation tolerant of so many faiths. So are we too religious or not religious enough (Grossman 2010)?

One's religious or ethnic experience is unlikely to be identical to the next person, so it is this diversity that we consider in this chapter. Also, with this diversity we consider how one goes about "fitting in" to a new society. First we will consider the social canvas against which this diversity is painted—Whiteness.

The changing nature of ethnicity in America's cities was underscored when the 2010 census showed not a single Italian-born person living in New York City's Little Italy. While many people of Italian descent resided there, one was much more likely to find Chinese-born people than people of any other nationality.

Studying Whiteness

Race is socially constructed, as we learned in Chapter 1. Sometimes we define race in a clear-cut manner. A descendant of a Pilgrim is White, for example. But sometimes race is more ambiguous: Children of an African American and Vietnamese American union are biracial, mixed, or whatever they come to be seen by others. Our recognition that race is socially constructed has sparked a renewed interest in what it means to be White in the United States. Two aspects of the White race are useful to consider: the historical creation of Whiteness and how contemporary White people reflect on their racial identity.

5-1 Understand what is meant by "Whiteness."

When the English immigrants established themselves as the political founders of the United States, they also came to define what it meant to be White. Other groups that today are regarded as White—such as Irish, Germans, Norwegians, or Swedes— were not always considered White in the eyes of the English. Differences in language and religious worship as well as past allegiance to a king in Europe different from the English monarch meant these groups were seen not so much as Whites in the Western Hemisphere but more as nationals of their home country who happened to reside in North America.

The old distrust in Europe, where, for example, the English viewed the Irish as socially and culturally inferior, continued on this side of the Atlantic Ocean. Writing from England, Karl Marx reported that the average English worker looked down on the Irish the way poor Whites in the U.S. South looked down on Black people (Ignatiev 1994, 1995; Roediger 1994).

As European immigrants and their descendants assimilated to the English and distanced themselves from other oppressed groups such as American Indians and African Americans, they came to be viewed as White rather than as part of a particular "alien" culture. Writer Noel Ignatiev (1994:84), contrasting being White with being Polish, argues, "Whiteness is nothing but an expression of race privilege." This strong statement argues that being White, as opposed to being Black or Asian, is characterized by being a member of the dominant group. Whiteness, although it may often be invisible, is aggressively embraced and defended (Giroux 1997).

White people do not think of themselves as a race or have a conscious racial identity. A White racial identity emerges only when filling out a form asking for self-designation of race or when Whites are culturally or socially surrounded by people who are not White.

Many immigrants who were not "White on arrival" had to "become White" in a process long forgotten by today's White Americans. The long-documented transparent racial divide that engulfed the South during slavery let us ignore how Whiteness was constructed.

Therefore, contemporary White Americans give little thought to "being White." Consequently, there is little interest in studying "Whiteness" or considering "being White" except that it is "not being Black." Unlike non-Whites, who are much more likely to interact with Whites, take orders from Whites, and see Whites as leading figures in the mass media, Whites enjoy not being reminded of their Whiteness.

Unlike racial minorities, Whites downplay the importance of their racial identity, although they are willing to receive the advantages that come from being White. This means that advocating a "color-blind" or "race-neutral" outlook permits the privilege of Whiteness to prevail (Bonilla-Silva 2002; Feagin and Cobas 2008; Yancey 2003).

New scholarly interest seeks to view Whiteness but not from the vantage point of a White supremacist. Rather, focusing on White people as a race or on what it means today to be White goes beyond any definition that implies superiority over non-Whites. It also is recognized that "being White" is not the same experience for all Whites, any more than "being Asian American" or "being Black" is the same for all Asian Americans or all Blacks. Historian Noel Ignatiev observes that studying Whiteness is a necessary stage to the "abolition of whiteness"—just as, in Marxist analysis, class-consciousness is a necessary stage to the abolition of class. By confronting Whiteness, society grasps the all-encompassing power that accompanies socially constructed race (Lewis 2004; McKinney 2003; Roediger 2006).

White privilege, introduced in Chapter 2, refers to the rights granted as a benefit or favor of being White and can be an element of Whiteness. However, of course, many Whites consciously minimize exercising this privilege. Admittedly, it is difficult when a White person is more likely than not to see national leaders, celebrities, and role models who also are White. For every Barack Obama, there are hundreds of movers and shakers who are White. For example, many White people champion the cause of the HBCUs (historically Black colleges and universities), conveniently ignoring that their presence is due to the existence of thousands of HWCUs (historically White colleges and universities) (Bonilla-Silva 2012).

When race is articulated or emphasized for Whites, it is more likely to be seen as threatening to Whites than allowing them to embrace their own race or national roots with pride. Behavioral economists Michael Norton and Samuel Sommers (2011) found that Whites view race as a zero-sum game—that is, decreases in bias against African Americans over the last 60 years are associated with increases in what they perceive as bias against Whites. While still seeing anti-Black bias as greater today than anti-White feeling in society, their analysis shows that, in the minds of the White respondents, the two biases are coming closer together. Black respondents also saw a marked decline in anti-Black bias during the same period but perceived only a modest increase in anti-White feelings. While Norton and Sommers's research deals only with perception of reality, it does suggest that race, and not just that of non-Whites, influences one's perception of society.

Rediscovering Ethnicity

5-2 Describe how people rediscover ethnicity.

Robert Park (1950:205), a prominent early sociologist, wrote in 1913, "a Pole, Lithuanian, or Norwegian cannot be distinguished, in the second generation, from an American, born of native parents." At one time, sociologists saw the end of ethnicity as nearly a foregone conclusion. W. Lloyd Warner and Leo Srole (1945) wrote in their often-cited *Yankee City* series that the future of ethnic groups seemed to be limited in the United States and that they would be quickly absorbed. Oscar Handlin's *The Uprooted* (1951) told of the destruction of immigrant values and their replacement by American culture. Although Handlin was among the pioneers in investigating ethnicity, assimilation was the dominant theme in his work.

Many writers have shown almost a fervent hope that ethnicity would vanish. For some time, sociologists treated the persistence of ethnicity as dysfunctional because it meant continuing old values that interfered with the allegedly superior new values. For example, holding on to one's language delayed entry into the larger labor market and the upward social mobility it afforded. Ethnicity was expected to disappear not only because of assimilation but also because aspirations to higher social class and status demanded that it vanish. It was assumed that one could not be ethnic and middle class, much less affluent.

The Third-Generation Principle

Historian Marcus Hansen's (1952) **principle of third-generation interest** was an early exception to the assimilationist approach to White ethnic groups. Simply stated, Hansen maintained that in the third generation—the grandchildren of the original immigrants—ethnic interest and awareness would increase. According to Hansen, "What the son wishes to forget, the grandson wishes to remember."

Hansen's principle has been tested several times since it was first put forth. John Goering (1971), in interviewing Irish and Italian Catholics, found that ethnicity was more important to members of the third generation than to the immigrants themselves. Similarly, Mary Waters (1990)—in her interviews of White ethnics living in suburban areas of San Jose, California, and Philadelphia, Pennsylvania—observed that many grandchildren wanted to study their ancestors' language, even though it would be a foreign language to them. They also expressed interest in learning more of their ethnic group's history and a desire to visit their homeland.

Social scientists in the past were quick to minimize the ethnic awareness of blue-collar workers. In fact, ethnicity was viewed as merely another aspect of White ethnics' alleged racist nature, an allegation examined later in this chapter. Curiously, the same intellectuals and journalists who bent over backward to understand the growing solidarity of Blacks, Hispanics, and Native Americans refused to give White ethnics the academic attention they deserved (Kivisto 2008; Wrong 1972).

The new assertiveness of ethnicity is not limited to Whites of European descent. Many members of third and successive generations of Asian and Latin American immigrants are showing renewed interest in their native languages. The very languages they avoided or even scorned themselves as children, they now want to learn as young adults. "Heritage language" programs have become increasingly common. Even when the descendants may easily communicate in their native language in everyday life, they often find they lack the language tools necessary for more sophisticated vocabulary or to be able to read easily (Nawa 2011).

Ethnic Paradox

While many nearly assimilated Whites are rediscovering their ethnicity (i.e., the principle of third-generation interest); others are at least publicly acknowledging their ethnicity from time to time (i.e., symbolic ethnicity). Yet research confirms that preserving elements of one's ethnicity may advance economic success and further societal acceptance.

Ethnic paradox refers to the maintenance of one's ethnic ties in a manner that can assist with assimilation with larger society. Immigrant youth as well as adults who maintain their ethnicity tend to have more success as indicated by health measures, educational attainment, and lower incidence of behavioral problems such as delinquency and truancy.

Researchers typically measure ethnic maintenance by facility in the mother language (not just conversational or "street" use) and living with others of the same ethnic background. These clear ethnic ties are not an automatic recipe for success. For example, residing with co-ethnics can lead to exploitation such as in neighborhoods where people steer those of their own ethnicity into dead-end, poor-paying, and even unhealthy working

5-2

conditions. Yet for many ethnics, enclaves offer a refuge, sort of a halfway house, between two different cultures. Language maintenance, as noted in the previous chapter, is often critical to being literate and comfortable with English (Desmond and Kubrin 2009).

In Speaking Out, sociologist Tomás Jiménez at Stanford University considers the role that new people arriving has played in the United States in shaping the nation's identity and how immigrants manage life in a new society.

((Q)) Speaking Out

The Next Americans

How immigrants and their descendants see themselves will change over time, and they will simultaneously transform many aspects of what it means to be an American. This is undoubtedly an uncomfortable process, fraught with tension between newcomers and established Americans that can occasionally become explosive. But the real issue is whether the United States can provide opportunities for upward mobility so that immigrants can, in turn, fortify what is most essential to our nation's identity.

Tomás Jiménez

History is instructive on whether immigrants will create a messy patchwork of ethnicities in the U.S. About a century ago, a tide of Southern and Eastern European immigrants arriving on our shores raised fears similar to those we hear today. Then, as now, Americans worried that the newcomers were destroying American identity. Many were certain that Catholic immigrants would help the pope rule the United States from Rome, and that immigrants from Southern Europe would contaminate the American gene pool.

None of this came to pass, of course. The pope has no political say in American affairs, the United States is still a capitalist democracy, and there is nothing wrong with the American gene pool. The fact that these fears never materialized are often cited as proof that European-origin immigrants and their descendants successfully assimilated into an American societal monolith.

However, as sociologists Richard Alba and Victor Nee point out, much of the American identity, as we know it today, was shaped by previous waves of immigrants. For instance, they note that the Christian tradition of the Christmas tree and the leisure Sunday made their way into the American mainstream because German immigrants and their descendants brought these traditions with them. Where religion was concerned, Protestantism was the clear marker of the nonsecular mainstream. But because of the assimilation of millions of Jews and Catholics, we today commonly refer to an American "Judeo-Christian tradition," a far more encompassing notion of American religious identity than the one envisioned in the past....

Even in Los Angeles County, where 36 percent of the population is foreign-born and more than half speak a language other than English at home, English is not losing out in the long run. According to a recent study by social scientists Rubén Rumbaut, Douglas Massey, and Frank Bean, published in the *Population and Development Review*, the use of non-English languages virtually disappears among nearly all U.S.-born children of immigrants in the country. Spanish shows more staying power among the U.S.-born children and grandchildren of Mexican immigrants, which is not surprising given that the size of the Spanish-speaking population provides near-ubiquitous access to the language. But the survival of Spanish among U.S.-born descendants of Mexican immigrants does not come at the expense of their ability to speak English and, more strikingly, English overwhelms Spanish-language use among the grandchildren of these immigrants.

An equally telling sign of how much immigrants and their children are becoming "American" is how different they have become from those in their ethnic homelands. Virtually all of today's immigrants stay connected to their countries of origin. They send money to family members who remain behind. Relatively inexpensive air, rail, and bus travel and the availability of cheap telecommunication and e-mail enable them to stay in constant contact, and dual citizenship allows their political voices to be heard from abroad. These enduring ties might lead to the conclusion that continuity between here and there threatens loyalty to the Stars and Stripes.

But ask any immigrant or their children about a recent visit to their country of origin, and they are likely to tell you how American they felt. The family and friends they visit quickly recognize the prodigal children's tastes for American styles, their American accents, and their declining cultural familiarity with life in the ethnic homeland—all telltale signs that they've Americanized. As sociologist David Fitzgerald puts it, their assimilation into American society entails a good deal of "dissimilation" from the countries the immigrants left behind.

American identity is absorbing something quite significant from immigrants and being changed by them. Language, food, entertainment, and holiday traditions are palpable aspects of American culture on which immigrants today, as in the past, are leaving their mark. Our everyday lexicon is sprinkled with Spanish words. We are now just as likely to grab a burrito as a burger. Hip-hop is tinged with South Asian rhythms. And Chinese New Year and Cinco de Mayo are taking their places alongside St. Patrick's Day as widely celebrated American ethnic holidays.

Source: Jiménez 2007.

Symbolic Ethnicity

Observers comment on both the evidence of assimilation and the signs of ethnic identity that support a pluralistic view of society. How can both be possible?

First, the visible evidence of **symbolic ethnicity** might lead us to exaggerate the persistence of ethnic ties among White Americans. According to sociologist Herbert Gans (1979), ethnicity today increasingly involves symbols of ethnicity, such as eating ethnic food, acknowledging ceremonial holidays such as St. Patrick's Day, and supporting specific political issues or issues confronting the old country. One example was the push in 1998 by Irish Americans to convince state legislatures to make it compulsory that public schools teach about the Irish potato famine—a significant factor in immigration to the United States. This symbolic ethnicity may be more visible, but this type of ethnic heritage does not interfere with what people do, read, or say, or even whom they befriend or marry. By one analysis, only an estimated 7 percent of White non-Hispanics self-express a significant sense of ethnicity (Scully 2012; Torkelson and Hartmann 2010).

The ethnicity of the twenty-first century, as embraced by English-speaking Whites, is largely symbolic. It does not include active involvement in ethnic activities or participation in ethnic-related organizations. In fact, sizable proportions of White ethnics have gained large-scale entry into almost all clubs, cliques, and fraternal groups. Such acceptance is a key indicator of assimilation. Ethnicity has become increasingly peripheral to the lives of members of the ethnic group. Although today's White ethnics may not relinquish their ethnic identity, other identities become more important.

Second, the ethnicity that exists may be more a result of living in the United States than importing practices from the past or the old country. Many so-called ethnic foods or celebrations, for example, began in the United States. The persistence of ethnic consciousness, then, may not depend on foreign birth, a distinctive language, and a unique way of life. Instead, it may reflect the experiences in the United States of a unique group that developed a cultural tradition distinct from that of the mainstream. For example, in Poland, the *szlachta*, or landed gentry, rarely mixed socially with the peasant class. In the United States, however, even with those associations still fresh, *szlachta* and peasants interacted together in social organizations as they settled in concentrated communities segregated physically and socially from others (Lopata 1994; Winter 2008).

Third, maintaining ethnicity can be a critical step toward successful assimilation. This ethnicity paradox facilitates full entry into the dominant culture. The ethnic community may give its members not only a useful financial boost but also the psychological strength and positive self-esteem that will allow them to compete effectively in a larger society. Thus, we may witness people participating actively in their ethnic enclave while trying to cross the bridge into the wider community (Lal 1995).

Therefore, ethnicity gives continuity with the past in the form of an effective or emotional tie. The significance of this sense of belonging cannot be emphasized enough. Whether reinforced by distinctive behavior or by what Milton Gordon (1964) called a sense of *peoplehood*, ethnicity is an effective, functional source of cohesion. Proximity to fellow ethnics is not necessary for a person to maintain social cohesion and in-group identity. Fraternal organizations or sports-related groups can preserve associations between ethnics who are separated geographically. Members of ethnic groups may even maintain feelings of in-group solidarity after leaving ethnic communities in the central cities for the suburban fringe.

The German Americans

Germany is the largest single source of ancestry of people in the United States today, even exceeding the continents of either Africa or Asia. Yet except in a few big-city neighborhood enclaves, the explicit presence of German culture seems largely relegated to bratwurst, pretzels, and Kris Kringle.

5-3 Recall the German American experience.

5-3

Settlement Patterns

In the late 1700s, the newly formed United States experienced the arrival of a number of religious dissenters from Germany (such as the Amish) who were attracted by the proclamation of religious freedom as well as prospects for economic advancement. At the time of the American Revolution, immigrants from Germany accounted for about one in eight White residents. German colonial subjects split their loyalty between the revolutionaries and the British, but were united in their optimistic view of the opportunities the New World would present.

Although Pennsylvania was the center of early settlements, German Americans, like virtually all other Europeans, moved out west (Ohio, Michigan, and beyond), where land was abundant. In many isolated communities, they established churches and parochial schools, and, in some instances, ethnic enclaves that in selected areas spoke of creating "New Germanys."

Beginning in the 1830s through 1890, Germans represented at least one-quarter of the immigrants, ensuring their destiny in the settlement of the United States (see Figure 5.1). Their major urban presence was in Milwaukee, Chicago, Cleveland, Detroit, and Cincinnati.

Early in the history of America, German immigrant cultural influence was apparent. Although the new United States never voted on making German the national language, publications of the proceedings of the Continental Congress were published in German and English. Yet even in those early years, the fear of foreigners—that is, non-Anglos—prevented German, even temporarily, from ever getting equal footing with English.

German Americans, then perhaps representing 10 percent of the population, established bilingual programs in many public schools, but the rise of Germany as a military foe in the twentieth century ended that movement (Harzig 2008; Nelsen 1973).

Twenty First-Century German America

In 1901, the German-American National Alliance (Deutsche-Amerikanischer National-Bund) was founded to speak for all Germans in the United States, especially urban Protestant middle-class German Americans. As time passed, it sought to commemorate the contributions to the nation's development but also sought to block prohibition. With the rise of German military power, many German Americans sought to argue for U.S. neutrality.

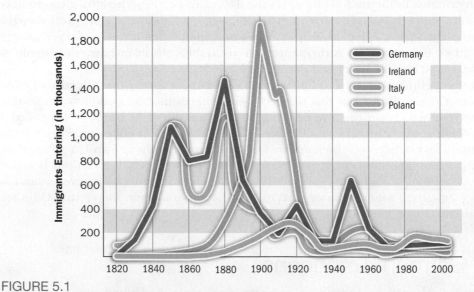

FIGURE 5.1
Immigration from Germany, Ireland, Italy, and Poland

Source: Office of Immigration Statistics 2009: Table 2.

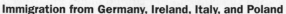

Note: Immigration after 1925 from Northern Ireland is not included. No separate data is included for Poland from 1900 to 1920.

But these efforts ended quickly, and the organization actually disbanded after the United States declared war on Germany in 1917.

With World War I and especially the rise of the Nazi era and the war years of the 1930s and 1940s, most German Americans sought to distance themselves from the politics in their homeland. There were anti-German incidents of harassment and intimidation. About 11,000 German Americans (out of 5 million) were interned, but the stigmatization did not come close to that felt by Japanese Americans. By comparison, many more German Americans enlisted and played important roles (none more so than Dwight Eisenhower, whose ancestors immigrated to Pennsylvania from Germany in 1741).

German Americans made the group transition into core society. Indeed, Horace Kallen, who popularized the term *pluralism*, held up German America as a success in finding a place in the United States. With the end of wartime tensions, German Americans moved from having multiple identities that included being somewhat marginalized as "Germans" to an identity of "American" and, less explicitly, White (Carlson 2003; Kazal 2004; Krammer 1997).

Anti-German sentiment spread in the United States during World War I, escalating dramatically after the United States entered the war in April 1917. A wave of verbal and physical attacks on German Americans was accompanied by a campaign to repress German culture. In this photograph from 1917, a group of children stand in front of an anti-German sign posted in Chicago. As the sign suggests, some people in the United States questioned the loyalty of their German American neighbors.

By the latter half of the twentieth century, the animosity toward Germany seemed a part of the distant past. Germany and its people became emblematic of stalwart friends of the United States, as reflected with appearances beginning with John F. Kennedy in Berlin in 1963 and Ronald Reagan in 1987. Both spoke of the U.S. commitment to uniting Germany, and presidential candidate Barack Obama in 2008 spoke in Berlin of a united Europe.

In the last ten years, immigration from Germany, a country of 82 million, has fluctuated between 6,000 and 10,000 annually. The steady immigration for decades placed Germany in the 2000 census as the tenth-largest source of foreign-born residents, with more than 700,000 (only about 170,000 behind Cuba and Korea). Yet the broad dispersion of these immigrants and their bilingual capability means the numbers are insufficient to create (or re-create) a German cultural presence. Rather, today's German American community is characterized by postwar and historical ties that have long since overshadowed the lingering bitterness of World Wars I and II (Harzig 2008; Office of Immigration Statistics 2012).

Famous German Americans include industrialist John D. Rockefeller, General John Pershing, baseball players Babe Ruth and Lou Gehrig, celebrity Paris Hilton, and actors Clark Gable and Katherine Heigl.

The Irish Americans

The Irish presence in the United States stretches back to the 1600s and reflects a diversity based on time of entry, settlement area, and religion. Irish Americans have been visible both in a positive way in terms of playing a central role in American life and in a negative way at certain historical periods, being victimized like so many other immigrant groups.

5-4 Identify the major periods of the Irish American immigration.

Irish Immigration

The Roman Catholics among the early immigrants were a diverse group. Some were extensions of the privileged classes seeking even greater prosperity. Protestant settlers of all national backgrounds including those coming from Ireland were united in their hatred of Catholicism. In most of the colonies, Catholics could not practice their faith openly and either struggled inwardly or converted to Anglicanism. Other Roman Catholics and some Protestants came from Europe as an alternative to prison or after signing articles of indenture and arriving bound to labor for periods of customarily three to five years and sometimes as long as seven years (Meagher 2005).

The American Revolution temporarily stopped the flow of immigration, but deteriorating economic conditions in Ireland soon spurred even greater movement to North America. British officials, by making passage to the newly formed republic of the United States expensive, diverted many immigrants to British North America (Canada). Yet the numbers to the United States remained significant and, although still primarily Protestant, drew from a broader spectrum of Ireland both economically and geographically.

Many people mistakenly overlook this early immigration and begin with Irish immigration during the Great Famine. Yet the Irish were the largest group after the English among immigrants during the colonial period. The historical emphasis on the famine immigrants is understandable, given the role it played in Ireland and its impetus for the massive transfer of population from Ireland to the United States.

In 1845, a fungus wiped out the potato crop of Ireland, as well as that of much of Western Europe and even coastal America. Potatoes were particularly central to the lives of the Irish, and the devastating starvation did not begin to recede until 1851. Mortality was high, especially among the poor and in the more agricultural areas of the island. Predictably, to escape catastrophe, some 2 million Irish fled mostly to England, but then many continued on to the United States. From 1841 through 1890, more than 3.2 million Irish arrived in the United States (Figure 5.1).

This new migration fleeing the old country was much more likely to consist of families rather than single men. The arrival of entire households and extended kinship networks increased significantly the rapid formation of Irish social organizations in the United States. This large influx of immigrants led to the creation of ethnic neighborhoods called Little Italy such as described in the beginning of the chapter, complete with parochial schools and parish churches serving as focal points. Fraternal organizations such as the Ancient Order of Hibernians, corner saloons, local political organizations, and Irish nationalist groups seeking the ouster of Britain from Ireland rounded out neighborhood social life.

Even in the best of times, the lives of the famine Irish would have been challenging in the United States, but they arrived at a very difficult time. Nativist—that is, anti-Catholic and anti-immigrant—movements were already emerging and being embraced by politicians. Antagonism was not limited to harsh words. From 1834 to 1854, mob violence against Catholics across the country led to death, the burning of a Boston convent, the destruction of a Catholic church and the homes of Catholics, and the use of Marines and state militia to bring peace to American cities as far west as St. Louis.

In retrospect, the reception given to the Irish is not difficult to understand. Many immigrated after the potato crop failure and famine in Ireland. They fled not so much to a better life as from almost certain death. The Irish Catholics brought with them a celibate clergy, who struck the New England aristocracy as strange and reawakened old religious hatreds. The Irish were worse than Blacks, according to the dominant Whites, because unlike the slaves and even the freed Blacks, who "knew their place," the Irish did not suffer their maltreatment in silence. Employers balanced minorities by judiciously mixing immigrant groups to prevent unified action by the laborers. For the most part, nativist efforts only led the foreign born to emphasize their ties to Europe.

Mostly of peasant backgrounds, the arriving Irish were ill prepared to compete successfully for jobs in the city. Their children found it much easier to improve their occupational status over that of their fathers as well as experienced upward mobility in their own lifetimes (Miller 2014: 268–270).

Becoming White

Ireland had a long antislavery tradition, including practices that prohibited Irish trade in English slaves. Some 60,000 Irish signed an address in 1841, petitioning Irish Americans to join the abolitionist movement in the United States. Many Irish Americans already opposed to slavery applauded the appeal, but they were soon drowned out by fellow immigrants who denounced or questioned the authenticity of the petition.

The Irish immigrants, subjected to derision and menial jobs, sought to separate themselves from the even lower classes, particularly Black Americans and especially the slaves. It was not altogether clear that the Irish were "White" during the antebellum period. Irish character was rigidly cast in negative racial typology. Although the shared experiences of oppression could have led Irish Americans to ally with Black Americans, they grasped for Whiteness at the margins of their lives in the United States. Direct competition was not common between the two groups. For example, in 1855, Irish immigrants made up 87 percent of New York City's unskilled laborers, whereas free Blacks accounted for only 3 percent (Greeley 1981; Ignatiev 1995; Roediger 1994).

As Irish immigration continued in the latter part of the nineteenth century until Irish independence in 1921, they began to see themselves favorably in comparison to the initial waves of Italian, Polish, and Slovak Roman

For many Irish American participants in a St. Patrick's Day parade, this is their most visible expression of symbolic ethnicity during the entire year.

Catholic immigrants. The Irish Americans began to assume more leadership positions in politics and labor unions. Loyalty to the church still played a major role. By 1910, the priesthood was the professional occupation of choice for second-generation men. Irish women were more likely than their German and English immigrant counterparts to become schoolteachers. In time, Irish Americans' occupational profiles diversified, and they began to experience slow advancement and gradually were welcomed into the White working class as their identity as "White" overcame any status as "immigrant."

With mobility came social class distinctions within Irish America. The immigrants and their children who began to move into the more affluent urban areas were derogatorily referred to as the "lace-curtain Irish." The lower-class Irish immigrants they left behind, meanwhile, were referred to as the "shanty Irish." But as immigration from Ireland slowed and upward mobility quickened, fewer and fewer Irish qualified as the poor cousins of their predecessors.

For the Irish American man, the priesthood was viewed as a desirable and respected occupation. Irish Americans furthermore played a leadership role in the Roman Catholic Church in the United States. The Irish dominance persisted long after other ethnic groups swelled the ranks of the faithful (Fallows 1979; Lee and Bean 2007; Lee and Casey 2006).

The Contemporary Picture

By 2010, 35.6 million people identified themselves as having Irish ancestry—second only to German ancestry and more than five times the current population of Ireland itself. Massachusetts has the largest concentration of Irish Americans, with 24 percent of the state indicating Irish ancestry.

Irish immigration today is relatively slight, accounting for perhaps one out of 1,000 legal arrivals until because of tough economic times it climbed to 2,800 in 2010. About 122,000 people in the United States were born in Ireland. Today's Irish American typically enjoys the symbolic ethnicity of food, dance, and music. Gaelic language instruction is limited to fewer than 30 colleges. Visibility as a collective ethnic group is greatest with the annual St. Patrick's Day celebrations, when everyone seems to be Irish, or with the occasional fervent nationalism aimed at curtailing Great Britain's role in Northern

Ireland. Yet some stereotypes remain concerning excessive drinking despite available data indicating that alcoholism rates are no higher and sometimes lower among people of Irish ancestry compared to descendants of other European immigrant groups (Bureau of the Census 2011b; Chazan and Tomson 2011).

St. Patrick's Day celebrations, as noted previously, offer an example of how ethnic identity evolves over time. The Feast of St. Patrick has a long history, but public celebrations with parties, concerts, and parades originated in the United States, which were then exported to Ireland in the latter part of the twentieth century. Even today, the large Irish American population often defines what is authentic Irish globally. For example, participants in Irish step dancing in the United States have developed such clout in international competitions that they have come to define many aspects of cultural expression, much to the consternation of the Irish in Ireland (Bureau of the Census 2009b; Hassrick 2007).

Well-known Irish Americans can be found in all arenas of American society, including celebrity chef Bobby Flay, songwriter and musician Kurt Cobain, comedian Conan O'Brien, and author Frank McCourt, as well as the political dynasties of the Kennedys in Massachusetts and the Daleys in Chicago. Reflecting growing rates of intermarriage, Irish America also includes singer Mariah Carey (her mother Irish and her father African American and Venezuelan).

The Irish were the first immigrant group to encounter prolonged organized resistance. However, strengthened by continued immigration, facility with the English language, building on strong community and family networks, and familiarity with representative politics, Irish Americans became an integral part of the United States.

The Italian Americans

5-5 Put into your own words the Italian American experience.

Although each European country's immigration to the United States has created its own social history, the case of Italians, though not typical of every nationality, offers insight into the White ethnic experience. Italians immigrated even during the colonial period, coming from what was a highly differentiated land, because Italian states did not unify as one nation and escaped foreign domination until 1848.

Early Immigration

From the beginning Italian Americans played prominent roles during the American Revolution and the early days of the republic. Mass immigration began in the 1880s, peaking in the first 20 years of the twentieth century, when Italians accounted for one-fourth of European immigration (refer to Figure 5.1).

Italian immigration was concentrated not only in time but also by geography. The majority of the immigrants were landless peasants from rural southern Italy, the Mezzogiorno. Although many people in the United States assume that Italians are a nationality with a single culture, this is not true either culturally or economically. The Italian people recognize multiple geographic divisions reflecting sharp cultural distinctions. These divisions were brought with the immigrants to the New World.

Many Italians, especially in the early years of mass immigration in the nineteenth century, received their jobs through an ethnic labor contractor, the padrone. Similar arrangements have been used by Asian, Hispanic, and Greek immigrants, where the labor contractors, most often immigrants, have mastered sufficient English to mediate for their compatriots. Exploitation was common within the padrone system through kickbacks, provision of inadequate housing, and withholding of wages. By World War I, 90 percent of Italian girls and 99 percent of Italian boys in New York City were leaving school at age 14 to work, but by that time, Italian Americans were sufficiently fluent in English to seek out work on their own, and the padrone system had disappeared. Still, by comparison to the Irish, the Italians in the United States were slower to accept formal schooling as essential to success (Sassler 2006).

Along with manual labor, the Catholic Church was a very important part of Italian Americans' lives at that time. Yet they found little comfort in a Catholic Church dominated by an earlier immigrant group: the Irish. The traditions were different; weekly attendance for Italian Americans was overshadowed by the religious aspects of the feste (or festivals) held throughout the year in honor of saints (the Irish viewed the feste as practically a form of paganism). These initial adjustment problems were overcome with the establishment of ethnic parishes, a pattern repeated by other non-Irish immigrant groups. Thus, parishes would be staffed by Italian priests, sometimes imported for that purpose. Although the hierarchy of the Church adjusted more slowly, Italian Americans were increasingly able to feel at home in their local parish church. Today, more than 70 percent of Italian Americans identify themselves as Roman Catholics (Luconi 2001).

Over the first few generations in the United States, Italian Americans rose up through the social classes largely by acquiring skills in low-skilled occupations rather than acquiring advanced degrees and entering professions. Eventually they began to achieve success in wine and fruit growing as well as entrepreneurs of retail outlets in the urban northeast and Midwest (Llosa 2013).

Constructing Identity

As assimilation proceeded, Italian Americans began to construct a social identity as a nationality group rather than viewing themselves in terms of their village or province. As shown in Figure 5.2, over time, Italian Americans shed old identities for new ones. As immigration from Italy declined, the descendants' ties became more nationalistic. This move from local or regional to national identity was followed by Irish and Greek Americans. The changing identity of Italian Americans reflected the treatment they received in the United States, whereas non-Italians did not make those regional distinctions. However, they were not treated well. For example, in turn-of-the-century New Orleans, Italian Americans established special ties with the Black community because both groups were marginalized in Southern society. Gradually, Italian Americans became White and enjoyed all the privileges that came with it. Today, it would be inconceivable to imagine that Italian Americans of New Orleans would reach out to the African American community as their natural allies on social and political issues (Guglielmo and Salerno 2003; Luconi 2001; Steinberg 2007:126).

A controversial aspect of the Italian American experience involves organized crime, as typified by Al Capone (1899–1947). Arriving in U.S. society in the bottom layers, Italians lived in decaying, crime-ridden neighborhoods. For a small segment of these immigrants, crime was a significant means of upward social mobility. In effect, entering and leading criminal activity was one aspect of assimilation, though not a positive one. Complaints linking ethnicity and crime actually began in colonial times with talk about the criminally inclined Irish and Germans, and they continue with contemporary stereotyping of groups such as Colombian drug dealers and Vietnamese street gangs. Yet the image of Italians as criminals has persisted from Prohibition-era gangsters to the view of mob

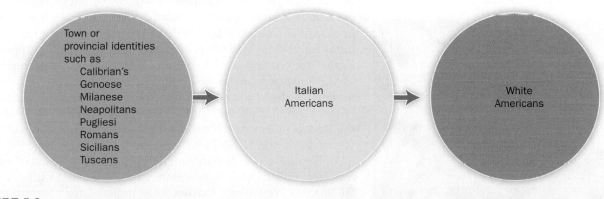

FIGURE 5.2
Constructing Social Identity among Italian Immigrants
Over time, Italian Americans moved from seeing themselves in terms of their provincial or village identity to their national identity, and then they successfully became indistinguishable from other Whites.

families today. As noted earlier, it is not at all surprising that groups have been organized to counter such negative images.

The fact that Italians often are characterized as criminal, even in the mass media, is another example of what we have called respectable bigotry toward White ethnics. The persistence of linking Italians, or any other minority group, with crime probably is attributable to attempts to explain a problem by citing a single cause: the presence of perceived undesirables. Many Italian Americans still see their image tied to old stereotypes. A 2001 survey of Italian American teenagers found that 39 percent felt the media presented their ethnic group as criminal or gang members and 34 percent as restaurant workers (Girardelli 2004; IAAMS 2009; National Italian American Foundation 2006; Parrillo 2008).

The immigration of Italians was slowed by the national origins system, described in Chapter 4. As Italian Americans settled permanently, the mutual aid societies that had grown up in the 1920s to provide basic social services began to dissolve. More slowly, education came to be valued by Italian Americans as a means of upward mobility. Even becoming more educated did not ward off prejudice, however. In 1930, for example, President Herbert Hoover rebuked Fiorello La Guardia, then an Italian American member of Congress from New York City, stating that "the Italians are predominantly our murderers and bootleggers" and recommending that La Guardia "go back to where you belong" because, "like a lot of other foreign spawn, you do not appreciate this country which supports you and tolerates you" (Baltzell 1964: 30).

Although U.S. troops, including 500,000 Italian Americans, battled Italy during World War II, some hatred and sporadic violence emerged against Italian Americans and their property. However, they were not limited to actions against individuals. Italian Americans were even confined by the federal government in specific areas of California by virtue of their ethnicity alone, and 10,000 were relocated from coastal areas. In addition, 1,800 Italian Americans who were citizens of Italy were placed in an internment camp in Montana. The internees were eventually freed on Columbus Day 1942 as President Roosevelt lobbied the Italian American community to gain full support for the impending land invasion of Italy (Department of Justice 2001; Fox 1990).

In the Research Focus we consider how social scientists examine the economic experience of these early Italian immigrants and their children in the United States and compare it to how Mexican immigrants are faring today.

The Contemporary Picture

In politics, Italian Americans have been more successful, at least at the local level, where family and community ties can be translated into votes. However, political success did not come easily because many Italian immigrants anticipated returning to their homeland and did not always take neighborhood politics seriously. It was even more difficult for Italian Americans to break into national politics.

For many people the six seasons of MTVs Jersey Shore represented sheer entertainment, but for some in the Italian American community it stigmatized the Italian American working class as engaged in outrageous behavior.

Not until 1962 was an Italian American named to a cabinet-level position. Geraldine Ferraro's nomination as the Democratic vice presidential candidate in 1984 was every bit as much an achievement for Italian Americans as it was for women. The opposition to the nomination of Judge Samuel Alito to the Supreme Court in 2006 struck many as bordering on anti–Italian American sentiments in the manner the opposition was advanced. Numerous critics used the phrase "Judge Scalito" in obvious reference to the sitting Italian American on the Court, Justice Antonio Scalia (Cornacchia and Nelson 1992).

While as a group Italian Americans are firmly a part of middle America, they frequently continue to be associated with crime. In 2009, three New Jersey mayors were indicted for corruption and not all of them were Italian. At the core of the scandal were five Syrian American rabbis, yet newspapers quickly dubbed it "New Jersey's 'Italian' Problem." MTV's successful reality show *Jersey Shore*, which seems to focus on drinking, hot tubbing, and brawling

Research Focus

Immigrants: Yesterday and Today

Anyone thinking about the future of today's immigrants might reflect back on the experiences of those who came a century ago. It is widely agreed that, despite difficult times and often harsh treatment by those already here, the immigrants of the late nineteenth and early twentieth century ultimately fared well. Certainly their descendants are doing well today. So can we generalize from this experience to today's immigrants?

Sociologist Joel Perlmann and other scholars have considered the experience of immigrants from southern, central, and Eastern Europe who were predominantly low-skilled workers. A significant component were Italian and Poles. Based on his analysis and that of other sociologists, we find that these earlier immigrant workers earned typically only between 60 and 88 percent in wages as that of nonimmigrant Whites in the same occupational groups.

Contrary to an often commonly held belief, these immigrants did not end up in well-paying jobs in manufacturing that led them into the middle class in their own lifetimes. Rather, they firmly remained working class until after World War II. Upward mobility occurred across generations typically, not within the lifetimes of the arriving Italian, Polish, and other southern, central, and eastern European immigrants. This would mean economic parity took about three or four generations and not a decade as some writers have romantically portrayed it.

Taking these data, Perlmann looks at contemporary Mexican immigrants. In many ways the deck is stacked against this current immigrant group, which is by far the largest. Unlike their European counterparts of a century ago, many arrivals from Mexico (about 55 percent) are having to labor as illegal immigrants, which obviously curtail the opportunities available to them and their family members. Today's second-generation Mexicans in the United States are lagging further behind in education compared to the general population than were the comparable generation of the turn-of-the century European immigrants.

The education gap among today's Latinos does not facilitate upward mobility. This is particularly challenging given the much greater importance that formal schooling has today for economic success compared to a century ago.

Language acquisition does not appear to be an issue, even given the large concentrations of Spanish-speaking neighborhoods that might seem to work against Hispanics becoming fluent English speakers. Although 23 percent of Hispanic immigrants as a group speak English very well, the percentage of these immigrants who are fluent in English rises to 88 percent among their U.S.-born children and then to 94 percent in the third generation.

It is early to make firm direct comparisons because the second-generation Mexican American is just coming of age, much less having full labor force experience and creating their own families. Although the complete entry of today's immigrants into the economy is likely to come based on analysis of the situation today, comparisons to White ethnics suggests that it may take the immigrants longer by at least an additional generation.

Sources: Bean and Stevens 2003; Camarota 2007a; Dickson 2006; Hakimzadeh and Cohn 2007; Katz, Stern, and Fader 2007; Perlmann 2005; Portes 2006; Portes and Rumbaut 2006.

stars, did not help. Stereotypes and labeling do not go away and truth is no antidote (Cohen 2010a; McGurn 2009).

There is no paucity of famous Italian Americans. They include athletes such as Joe DiMaggio, politician Rudolph Giuliani, film director Francis Ford Coppola, singer Madonna, comedian Jay Leno, writer Mario Puzo, actor Leonardo DiCaprio, chef Rachel Ray, and auto racing legend Mario Andretti.

Italian Americans still remain the seventh-largest immigrant group. Just how ethnically conscious is the Italian American community? Although the number is declining, 700,000 Americans speak Italian at home; only eight languages are spoken more frequently at home: Spanish, Chinese, Tagalog (Philippines), Vietnamese, Korean, Russian, German, Arabic, Russian, and French Creole. For the 17-plus million Italian Americans, however, the language tie to their culture is absent, and, depending on their degree of assimilation, only traces of symbolic ethnicity may remain. As we saw in the chapter opener describing Little Italy in New York City Italian ethnic enclaves throughout North America are more and more limited to a cluster of Italian restaurants and bakeries. In a later section, we look at the role that language plays for many immigrants and their children (Ryan 2013:3).

The Polish Americans

Immigrants from Poland have had experiences similar to those of the Irish and Italians. They had to overcome economic problems and personal hardships just to make the journey. Once in the United States, they found themselves often assigned to the jobs many

5-6 Restate the Polish American immigration story.

citizens had not wanted to do. They had to adjust to a new language and a familiar yet different culture. And always they were looking back to the family members left behind who either wanted to join them in the United States or, in contrast, never wanted them to leave in the first place.

Like other arrivals, many Poles sought improvement in their lives, a migration that was known as Za Chlebem (For Bread). The Poles who came were, at different times, more likely than many other European immigrants to see themselves as forced immigrants and were often described by, and themselves adopted, the terminology directly reflecting their social roles—exiles, refugees, displaced persons, or émigrés. The primary force for this exodus was the changing political status of Poland through most of the nineteenth and twentieth centuries, which was as turbulent as the lives of the new arrivals.

Early Immigration

Polish immigrants were among the settlers at Jamestown, Virginia, in 1608, to help develop the colony's timber industry, but it was the Poles who came later in that century who made a lasting mark. The successful exploits of Polish immigrants such as cavalry officer Casimir Pulaski and military engineer Thaddeus Kosciuszko are still commemorated today in communities with large Polish American populations. As we can see in Figure 5.1, it was not until the 1890s that Polish immigration was significant in comparison to some other European arrivals. Admittedly, it is difficult to exactly document the size of this immigration because at various historical periods Poland or parts of the country became part of Austria-Hungary, Germany (Prussia), and the Soviet Union so that the migrants were not officially coming from a nation called "Poland."

Many of the Polish immigrants were adjusting not only to a new culture but also to a more urban way of life. Sociologists William I. Thomas and Florian Znaniecki, in their classic study *The Polish Peasant in Europe and America* ([1918] 1996), traced the path from rural Poland to urban America. Many of the peasants did not necessarily come directly to the United States but first traveled through other European countries. This pattern is not unique and reminds us that, even today, many immigrants have crossed several countries, sometimes establishing themselves for a period of time before finally settling in the United States (Abbott and Egloff 2008).

Like the Germans, Italians, and Irish, Poles arrived at the large port cities of the East Coast but, unlike the other immigrant groups, they were more likely to settle in cities further inland or work in mines in Pennsylvania. In such areas, they would join kinfolk or acquaintances through the process of chain migration (described in the previous chapter).

The reference to coal mining as an occupation reflects the continuing tendency of immigrants to work in jobs avoided by most U.S. citizens because they paid little, were dangerous, or both. For example, in September 1897, a group of miners in Lattimer, Pennsylvania, marched to demand safer working conditions and an end to special taxes placed only on foreign-born workers. In the ensuing confrontation with local officials, police officers shot at the protesters, killing 19 people, most of who were Polish, the others Lithuanians and Slovaks (Duszak 1997).

Polonia

With growing numbers, the emergence of Polonia (meaning Polish communities outside of Poland) became more common in cities throughout the Midwest. Male immigrants who came alone often took shelter through a system of inexpensive boarding houses called *tryzmanie bortnków* (brother keeping), which allowed the new arrival to save money and send it back to Poland to support his family. These funds eventually provided the financial means necessary to bring family members over, adding to the size of Polonia in cities such as Buffalo, Cleveland, Detroit, Milwaukee, Pittsburgh, and, above all, Chicago, where the population of Poles was second only to Warsaw, Poland.

Religion has played an important role among Polish immigrants and their descendants. Most of the Polish immigrants who came to the United States before World War I were Roman Catholic. They quickly established their own parishes where new arrivals could feel welcome. Although religious services at that time were in the Latin language, as they had been in Poland, the many service organizations around the parish, not to mention the Catholic schools, kept the immigrants steeped in the Polish language and the latest happenings back home. Jewish Poles began immigrating during the first part of the twentieth century to escape the growing hostility they felt in Europe, which culminated in the Holocaust. Their numbers swelled greatly until movement from Poland stopped with the invasion of Poland by Germany in 1939; it resumed after the war.

Although the Jewish–Catholic distinction may be the most obvious distinguishing factor among Polish Americans, there are other divisions as well. Regional subgroups such as the Kashubes, the Górali, and the Mazurians have often carried great significance. Some Poles emigrated from areas where German was actually the language of origin.

As with other immigrant groups, Polish Americans could make use of a rich structure of voluntary self-help associations that were already well established by the 1890s. Not all organizations smoothly cut across different generations of Polish immigrants. For example, the Poles who came immediately after World War II as political refugees fleeing Soviet domination were quite different in their outlook than the descendants of the economic refugees from the turn of the century. These kinds of tensions in an immigrant community are not unusual, even if they go unnoticed by the casual observer who lumps all immigrants of the same nationality together (Jaroszyn'ska-Kirchmann 2004).

Like many other newcomers, Poles have been stigmatized as outsiders and also stereotyped as simple and uncultured—the typical biased view of working-class White ethnics. Their struggles in manual occupations placed them in direct competition with other White ethnics and African Americans, which occasionally led to labor disputes and longer-term tense and emotional rivalries. "Polish jokes" continue now to have a remarkable shelf life in casual conversation well into the twenty-first century. Jewish Poles suffer the added indignities of anti-Semitism (Dolan and Stotsky 1997).

The Contemporary Picture

Today, Polonia in the United States is nearly 10 million. Although this may not seem significant in a country of more than 300 million, we need to recall that today Poland itself has a population of only about 39 million. Whether it was to support the efforts of Lech Walesa, the Solidarity movement leader who confronted the Soviet Union in the 1980s, or to celebrate the elevation of Karol Józef Wojtyla as Pope John Paul II in 1978, Polish Americans are a central part of the global Polish community.

Many Polish Americans have retained little of their rich cultural traditions and may barely acknowledge even symbolic ethnicity. Data released in 2013 show about 600,000 whose primary language is Polish—a decline from over 800,000 in 1980. For those still immersed in Polonia, their lives revolve around many of the same religious and social institutions that were the center of Polonia a century ago. For example, 54 Roman Catholic churches in the metropolitan Chicago area still offer Polish-language masses. Although in many of these parishes there may be only one service in Polish serving a declining number of celebrants, a few traditional "Polish" churches still have Polish-speaking priests in residence. Even with the decline in Polish-language service, the Roman Catholic Church actively recruits Pole seminarians, although now English-language training is often emphasized.

In the latter part of the twentieth century, some of the voluntary associations relocated or built satellite centers to serve the outlying

Polish-American actress Scarlett Johansonn reflects the multiple ethnic roots of many Americans today. Born in New York City, her father is a Danish immigrant and her mother is a U.S.-born Jew whose parents came from Poland and Belarus, then part of the former Soviet Union. She reports celebrating both Hanukkah and Christmas and holds both American and Danish citizenship.

5-7

Polish American populations. To sustain their activities financially, these social organizations also reached out of the central cities in order to tap into the financial resources of suburban Poles. Increasingly, people of Polish descent also have now made their way into the same social networks populated by German, Irish, Italian, and other ethnic Americans (Bukowcyk 2007; Erdmans 1998, 2006; Lopata 1994; Mocha 1998; Polzin 1973; Shin and Kominski 2010; Stone 2006).

Except for immigrants who fled persecution in their homelands, immigration typically has back-and-forth movement. In the early years of the twenty-first century, there was an identifiable movement of Polish Americans from Polonia to Poland, especially as economic opportunity improved in the home country. One estimate of returnees places it at 50,000 from 2004, when Poland entered the European Union, to 2009, which is a significant number in absolute numbers but is relatively small given the magnitude of the Polish American community (Hundley 2009; Mastony 2013).

Among the many Polish Americans well known or remembered today are home designer Martha (Kostyra) Stewart, comedian Jack Benny (Benjamin Kubelsky), guitarist Richie Sambora of the rock group Bon Jovi, actress Scarlett Johansson, entertainer Liberace, *Wheel of Fortune* host Pat Sajak, baseball star Stan Musial, football star Mike Ditka, novelist Joseph Conrad (Józef Korzeniowski), singer Bobby Vinton (Stanley Ventula, Jr.), polio vaccine pioneer Albert Sabin, and motion picture director Stanley Kubrick.

Religious Pluralism

5-7 State what is meant by religious pluralism.

Religion plays a fundamental role in society and affects even those who do not practice or even believe in organized religion. **Religion** refers to a unified system of sacred beliefs and practices that encompass elements beyond everyday life that inspire awe, respect, and even fear (Durkheim [1912] 2001).

In popular speech, the term *pluralism* has often been used in the United States to refer explicitly to religion. Although certain faiths figure more prominently in the worship scene, the United States has a history of greater religious tolerance than most other nations. Today, religious bodies number more than 1,500 in the United States and range from the more than 66 million members of the Roman Catholic Church to sects with fewer than 1,000 adherents. In every region of the country, religion is being expressed in greater variety, whether it be the Latinization of Catholicism and some Christian faiths or the de-Europeanizing of some established Protestant faiths, as with Asian Americans, or the de-Christianizing of the overall religious landscape with Muslims, Buddhists, Hindus, Sikhs, and others (Roof 2007).

The Greek Orthodox Church is one of 25 Christian faiths with at least a million members.

How do we view the United States in terms of religion? Increasingly, the United States has a non-Christian presence. In 1900, an estimated 96 percent of the nation was Christian; slightly more than 1 percent was nonreligious, and approximately 3 percent held other faiths. In 2013, it was estimated that the nation was 74 percent Christian, 17 percent nonreligious, and another 9 percent all other faiths. The United States has a long Jewish tradition, and Muslims number close to 5 million. A smaller but also growing number of people adhere to such Eastern faiths as Hinduism, Buddhism, Confucianism, and Taoism (Newport 2011).

Sociologists use the word **denomination** for a large, organized religion that is not linked officially with the state or government. By far, the largest denomination in the United States is Catholicism; yet at least 24 other Christian religious denominations have 1 million or more members (Lindner 2011).

At least four non-Christian religious groups in the United States have numbers that are comparable to any of these large denominations: Jews, Muslims, Buddhists, and Hindus. In the United States, each numbers more than 1 million members. Within each of these groups are branches or sects that distinguish themselves from each other. For example, the Judaic faith embraces several factions such as Orthodox, Conservative, Reconstructionist, and Reform that are similar in their roots but marked by sharp distinctions. Continuing the examples, in the United States and the rest of the world, some Muslims are Sunni and others Shia. Further divisions are present within these groups, just as among Protestants and, in turn, among Baptists.

TABLE 5.1
Churches with More Than a Million Members

Denomination Name	Inclusive Membership
Roman Catholic Church	68,503,456
Southern Baptist Convention	16,160,088
United Methodist Church	7,774,931
Church of Jesus Christ of Latter Day Saints	6,058,907
Church of God in Christ	5,499,875
National Baptist Convention, U.S.A., Inc.	5,000,000
Evangelical Lutheran Church in America	4,542,868
National Baptist Convention of America, Inc.	3,500,000
Assemblies of God	2,914,669
Presbyterian Church (U.S.A.)	2,770,730
African Methodist Episcopal Church	2,500,000
National Missionary Baptist Convention of America	2,500,000
Lutheran Church—Missouri Synod (LCMS)	2,312,111
Episcopal Church	2,006,343
Churches of Christ	1,639,495
Greek Orthodox Archdiocese of America	1,500,000
Pentecostal Assemblies of the World, Inc.	1,500,000
African Methodist Episcopal Zion Church	1,400,000
American Baptist Churches in the U.S.A.	1,310,505
Jehovah's Witnesses	1,162,686
United Church of Christ	1,080,199
Church of God (Cleveland, TN)	1,076,254
Christian Churches and Churches of Christ	1,071,616
Seventh-Day Adventist Church	1,043,606
Progressive National Baptist Convention, Inc.	1,010,000

Note: Most recent data as of 2012.

Source: Eileen Lindner (ed.) 2012. *Yearbook of American and Canadian Churches 2011,* Table 2, p. 12. Nashville, TN. Abingdon Press. Reprinted by permission from *Yearbook of American and Canadian Churches 2008.* Copyright © National Council of Churches of Christ in the USA.

5-7

The United States has long been described as a Judeo-Christian nation, but with interest in other faiths and continuing immigration, this description, if ever accurate, is not now. This is especially true with the growth of Muslim Americans.

Islam in the United States has a long history stretching from Muslim Africans who came as slaves to today's Muslim community, which includes immigrants and native-born Americans. President Obama, the son of a practicing Muslim and who lived for years in Indonesia, the country with the largest Muslim population, never sought to hide his roots. However, reflecting the prejudices of many toward non-Christians, his Christian upbringing was stressed throughout his presidential campaigns. Little wonder that a national survey showed that 55 percent believe the U.S. Constitution establishes the country as a "Christian nation" (Cose 2008; Thomas 2007).

Even if religious faiths have broad representation, they tend to be fairly homogeneous at the local church level. This is especially ironic, given that many faiths have played critical roles in resisting racism and in trying to bring together the nation in the name of racial and ethnic harmony.

Broadly defined, faiths represent a variety of ethnic and racial groups. In Figure 5.3, we consider the interaction of White, Black, and Hispanic races with religions. Muslims, Pentecostals, and Jehovah's Witnesses are much more diverse than Presbyterians or Lutherans. Religion plays an even more central role for Blacks and Latinos than Whites. A national survey indicated that 65 percent of African Americans and 51 percent of Latinos attend a religious service every week, compared to 44 percent of White non-Hispanics (Winseman 2004).

It would also be a mistake to focus only on older religious organizations when considering religion's role in society. Local churches that developed into national faiths in the 1990s, such as Calvary Chapel, Vineyard, and Hope Chapel, have a following among Pentecostal believers, who embrace a more charismatic form of worship devoid of many traditional ornaments, with pastors and congregations alike favoring informal attire. New faiths develop with increasing rapidity in what can only be called a very competitive market for individual religious faith. In addition, many people, with or without religious affiliation, become fascinated with spiritual concepts such as angels or become a part of loose-knit fellowships. Religion in the United States is an ever-changing social phenomenon. Other nonmainstream faiths emerge in new arenas, as evidenced by the successful campaign of Mitt Romney, a Mormon, to win the Republican nomination for president in 2012 or the visible role of celebrities promoting the Church of Scientology (Schaefer and Zellner 2011).

Divisive conflicts along religious lines are muted in the United States compared with those in, say, the Middle East. Although not entirely absent, conflicts about religion in the United States seem to be overshadowed by civil religion. **Civil religion** is the religious dimension in the United States that merges public life with sacred beliefs. It also reflects that no single faith is privileged over all others. Indeed, it even encompasses the conversation of nonbelievers regarding the human condition.

Sociologist Robert Bellah (1967) borrowed the phrase *civil religion* from eighteenth-century French philosopher Jean-Jacques Rousseau to describe a significant phenomenon in the contemporary United States. Civil religion exists alongside established religious faiths, and it embodies a belief system that incorporates all religions but is not associated specifically with any one. It is the type of faith to which presidents refer in inaugural speeches and to which American Legion posts and Girl Scout troops swear allegiance. In 1954, Congress added the phrase *under God* to the Pledge of Allegiance as a legislative recognition of religion's significance. Elected officials in the United States, beginning with Ronald Reagan, often conclude even their most straightforward speeches with "God bless the United States of America," which in effect evokes the civil religion of the nation.

Functionalists see civil religion as reinforcing central American values that may be more expressly patriotic than sacred in nature. The mass media, following major societal upheavals, from the 1995 Oklahoma City bombing to the 2001 terrorist attacks, often show church services with clergy praying and asking for national healing. Bellah (1967) sees no sign that the importance of civil religion has diminished in promoting collective identity, but he does acknowledge that it is more conservative than during the 1970s.

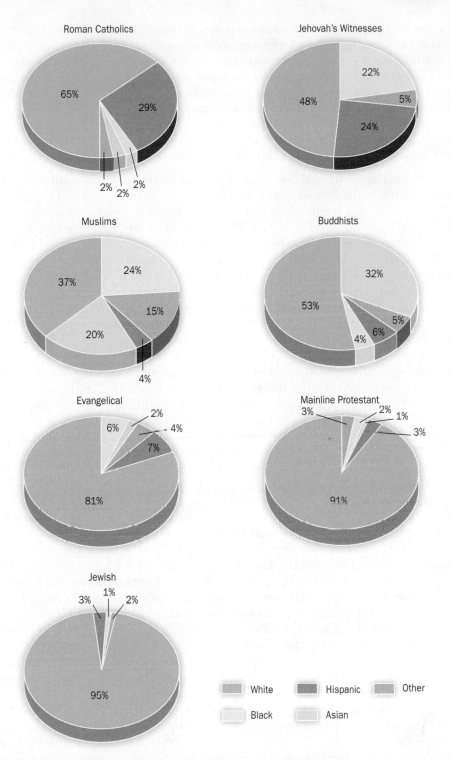

FIGURE 5.3
Racial and Ethnic Makeup of Selected Religions in the United States

Note: "Other" includes self-identified mixed races. Evangelical includes Baptist, Lutheran (Missouri and Wisconsin Synods), and Pentecostal, among others. Mainline Protestant includes Methodist, Lutheran (ELCA), Presbyterian, Episcopal, and United Church of Christ, among others, but excludes historically Black churches. Based on a national survey of 35,556 adults conducted in August 2007.

Source: Pew Forum on Religion and Public Life 2008: 120

Beginning with the Clinton administration, the federal government has made explicit efforts to include religious organizations. The 1996 welfare reform act President Clinton signed provided that religious groups could compete for grants. President George W. Bush created a White House Office of Faith-Based and Community Initiatives to provide for a significant expansion of charitable choice. President Barack Obama has continued the office, naming a Pentecostal minister to oversee it (Jacoby 2009).

In the following sections, we explore the diversity among the major Christian groups in the United States, such as Roman Catholics and Protestants, as well as how Islam has emerged as a significant religious force in the United States and can no longer be regarded as a marginal faith in terms of followers (Gorski 2010).

Diversity among Roman Catholics

Social scientists have persistently tended to ignore the diversity within the Roman Catholic Church in the United States. Recent research has not sustained the conclusions that Roman Catholics are melding into a single group, following the traditions of the American Irish Catholic model, or even that parishioners are attending English-language churches. Religious behavior has been different for each ethnic group within the Roman Catholic Church. The Irish and French Canadians left societies that were highly competitive both culturally and socially. Their religious involvement in the United States is more relaxed than it was in Ireland and Quebec. However, the influence of life in the United States has increased German and Polish involvement in the Roman Catholic Church, whereas Italians have remained largely inactive. Variations by ethnic background continue to emerge in studies of contemporary religious involvement in the Roman Catholic Church (Eckstrom 2001).

Since the mid-1970s, the Roman Catholic Church in America has received a significant number of new members from the Philippines, Southeast Asia, and particularly Latin America. Although these new members have been a stabilizing force offsetting the loss of White ethnics, they have also challenged a church that for generations was dominated by Irish, Italian, and Polish parishes. Perhaps the most prominent subgroup in the Roman Catholic Church is the Latinos, who now account for one-third of all Roman Catholic parishioners. Clearly immigrants are seen as a significant part of the Catholic Church's future. More than 150 immigration-oriented programs are mounted by the Church nationwide. Often a program for a patron saint or national feast begins with two national anthems sung—that of the participant's native country and The Star-Spangled Banner. Some Los Angeles churches in or near Latino neighborhoods must schedule 14 masses each Sunday to accommodate the crowds of worshipers. In 2010, the Pope selected a Latino, Mexican-born archbishop, Jose H. Gomez, to lead the Los Angeles Archdiocese (Dolan 2013; Goodstein and Steinhauer 2010; Navarro-Rivera, Kosmin, and Keysar 2010).

The Roman Catholic Church, despite its ethnic diversity, has clearly been a powerful force in reducing the ethnic ties of its members, making it also a significant assimilating force. The irony in this role of Catholicism is that so many nineteenth-century Americans heaped abuse on Catholics in this country for allegedly being un-American and having a dual allegiance. The history of the Catholic Church in the United States may be portrayed as a struggle within the membership between the Americanizers and the anti-Americanizers, with the former ultimately winning. Unlike the various Protestant churches that accommodated immigrants of a single nationality, the Roman Catholic Church had to Americanize a variety of linguistic and ethnic groups. The Catholic Church may have been the most potent assimilating force after the public school system. Comparing the assimilationist goal of the Catholic Church and the current diversity in it leads us to the conclusion that ethnic diversity has continued in the Roman Catholic Church despite, not because of, this religious institution.

Diversity among Protestants

Protestantism, like Catholicism, often is portrayed as a monolithic entity. Little attention is given to the doctrinal and attitudinal differences that sharply divide the various denominations in both laity and clergy. However, several studies document the diversity. Unfortunately, many opinion polls and surveys are content to learn whether a respondent is a Catholic, a Protestant, or a Jew. Stark and Glock (1968) found sharp differences in religious attitudes within Protestant churches. For example, 99 percent of Southern Baptists had no doubt that Jesus was the divine Son of God as contrasted to only 40 percent of Congregationalists. We can identify four "generic theological camps":

1. *Liberals:* United Church of Christ (Congregationalists) and Episcopalians
2. *Moderates:* Disciples of Christ, Methodists, and Presbyterians
3. *Conservatives:* American Lutherans and American Baptists
4. *Fundamentalists:* Missouri Synod Lutherans, Southern Baptists, and Assembly of God

Roman Catholics generally hold religious beliefs similar to those of conservative Protestants, except on essentially Catholic issues such as papal infallibility (the authority of the spiritual role in all decisions regarding faith and morals). Whether or not there are four distinct camps is not important: The point is that the familiar practice of contrasting Roman Catholics and Protestants is clearly not productive. Some differences between Roman Catholics and Protestants are inconsequential compared with the differences between Protestant sects.

Secular criteria as well as doctrinal issues may distinguish religious faiths. Research has consistently shown that denominations can be arranged in a hierarchy based on social class. As Figure 5.4 reveals, members of certain faiths, such as Episcopalians, Jews, and Presbyterians, have a higher proportion of affluent members. Members of other faiths, including Baptists, tend to be poorer. Of course, all Protestant groups draw members from each social stratum. Nonetheless, the social significance of these class differences is that religion becomes a mechanism for signaling social mobility. A person who is moving up in wealth and power may seek out a faith associated with a higher social ranking. Similar contrasts are shown in formal schooling in Figure 5.5.

Protestant faiths have been diversifying, and many of their members have been leaving them for churches that follow strict codes of behavior or fundamental interpretations of biblical teachings. This trend is reflected in the gradual decline of the five mainline churches: Baptist, Episcopalian, Lutheran, Methodist, and Presbyterian. In 2006, these faiths accounted for about 58 percent of total Protestant membership, compared with 65 percent in the 1970s. With a broader acceptance of new faiths and continuing immigration, it is unlikely that these mainline churches will regain their dominance in the near future (Davis, Smith, and Marsden 2007:171–172).

Although Protestants may seem to define the civil religion and the accepted dominant orientation, some Christian faiths feel they, too, experience the discrimination usually associated with non-Christians such as Jews and Muslims. For example, representatives

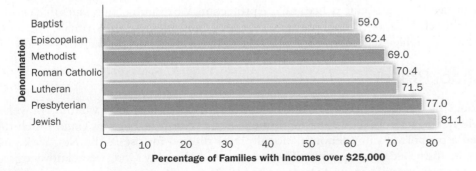

FIGURE 5.4
Income and Denominations

Denominations attract different income groups. All groups have both affluent and poor members, yet some have a higher proportion of members with high incomes whereas others are comparatively poor.

Source: Based on interviews with a representative sample of 35,000 adults conducted May–August and reproduced in the Pew Forum on Religion and Public Life 2008b: 78–79, 84–85.

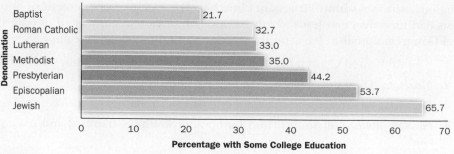

FIGURE 5.5
Education and Denominations

There are sharp differences in the proportion of those with some college education by denomination.

Source: Based on interviews with a representative sample of 35,000 adults conducted May–August and reproduced in the Pew Forum on Religion and Public Life 2008b: 78–79, 84–85.

of the liberal and moderate faiths dominate the leadership of the military's chaplain corps. There are 16 Presbyterian soldiers for every Presbyterian chaplain, 121 Full Gospel worshippers for every Full Gospel chaplain, and 339 Muslim soldiers for every Muslim chaplain (Cooperman 2005).

As another example of denominational discrimination, in 1998, the Southern Baptist Convention amended its basic theological statements of beliefs to include a strong statement on family life. However, the statement included a declaration that a woman should "submit herself graciously" to her husband's leadership. There were widespread attacks on this position, which many Baptists felt was inappropriate because they were offering guidance for their denomination's members. In some respects, Baptists felt this was a form of respectable bigotry. It was acceptable to attack them for their views on social issues even though such criticism would be much more muted for many more liberal faiths that seem free to tolerate abortion (Bowman 1998; Niebuhr 1998).

Religion and the Courts

5-8 Interpret how the courts have ruled on religion.

Religious pluralism owes its existence in the United States to the First Amendment declaration that "Congress shall make no law respecting an establishment of religion, or prohibiting the free exercise thereof." The U.S. Supreme Court has consistently interpreted this wording to mean not that government should ignore religion but that it should follow a policy of neutrality to maximize religious freedom. For example, the government may not help religion by financing a new church building, but it also may not obstruct religion by denying a church adequate police and fire protection. We examine four issues that continue to require clarification: school prayer, secessionist minorities and their rituals, creationism (including intelligent design), and the public display of religious (or sacred) symbols.

School Prayer

Among the most controversial and continuing disputes has been whether prayer has a role in the schools. The 1962 Supreme Court decision in *Engel v. Vitale*, which disallowed a purportedly nondenominational prayer drafted for use in the New York public schools, disturbed many people. The prayer was "Almighty God, we acknowledge our dependence upon Thee, and we beg Thy blessings upon us, our parents, our teachers, and our country." Subsequent decisions overturned state laws requiring Bible reading in public schools, laws requiring recitation of the Lord's Prayer, and laws permitting a daily one-minute period of silent meditation or prayer. Despite such judicial pronouncements, children in many public schools in the United States are led in regular prayer recitation or Bible reading. Contrary to what many people believe, religion has not been hounded out of public schools (Yemma 2013).

What about prayers at public gatherings? In 1992, the Supreme Court ruled 5–4 in *Lee v. Weisman* that prayer at a junior high school graduation in Providence, Rhode Island, violated the U.S. Constitution's mandate of separation of church and state. A rabbi had given thanks to God in his invocation. The district court suggested that the invocation would have been acceptable without that reference. The Supreme Court did not agree with the school board that a prayer at a graduation was not coercive. The Court did say in its opinion that it was acceptable for a student speaker voluntarily to say a prayer at such a program (Marshall 2001).

Public schools and even states have mandated a "moment of silence" at the start of the school day in what critics contend is a transparent attempt to get around *Lee v. Weisman*. While prayer or religious thoughts are clearly intended by legislators when they created these "moments," the courts have to date ruled such policies as constitutional and argued that the policy is secular, rather than sacred. Arkansas in 2013 became the latest state to mandate a minute of silence at the beginning of the school day (ABC Television 2013).

Secessionist Minorities

Several religious groups have been in legal and social conflict with the rest of society. Some can be called **secessionist minorities** in that they reject both assimilation and coexistence in some form of cultural pluralism. The Amish are one such group that comes into conflict with outside society because of its beliefs and way of life. The Old Order Amish shun most modern conveniences and maintain a lifestyle dramatically different from that of larger society.

Are there limits to the free exercise of religious rituals by secessionist minorities? Today, tens of thousands of members of Native American religions believe that ingesting the powerful drug peyote is a sacrament and that those who partake of peyote will enter into direct contact with God. In 1990, the Supreme Court ruled that prosecuting people who use illegal drugs as part of a religious ritual is not a violation of the First Amendment guarantee of religious freedom. The case arose because Native Americans were dismissed from their jobs for the religious use of peyote and were then refused unemployment benefits by the state of Oregon's employment division. In 1991, however, Oregon enacted a new law permitting the sacramental use of peyote by Native Americans (*New York Times* 1991).

In another ruling on religious rituals, in 1993, the Supreme Court unanimously overturned a local ordinance in Florida that banned ritual animal sacrifice. The High Court held that this law violated the free-exercise rights of adherents of the Santeria religion, in which the sacrifice of animals (including goats, chickens, and other birds) plays a

After lobbying by Wiccans, the U.S. Department of Veterans Affairs eventually approved the pentacle symbol for use on the cemetery markers of fallen soldiers who self-identify as Witches.

central role. The same year, Congress passed the Religious Freedom Restoration Act, which said the government may not enforce laws that "substantially burden" the exercise of religion. Presumably, this action will give religious groups more flexibility in practicing their faiths. However, many local and state officials are concerned that the law has led to unintended consequences, such as forcing states to accommodate prisoners' requests for questionable religious activities or to permit a church to expand into a historic district in defiance of local laws (Greenhouse 1996).

The legal acceptance of different faiths has been illustrated in numerous decisions. For example, the courts have allowed Wiccan organizations to enjoy non-profit status. In addition, the U.S. Department of Veterans Affairs approved of the pentacle symbol for use on national cemetery markers of those fallen soldiers who self-identify as Witches.

Creationism and Intelligent Design

The third area of contention has been whether the biblical account of creation should be or must be presented in school curricula and whether this account should receive the same emphasis as scientific theories. In the famous "monkey trial" of 1925, Tennessee schoolteacher John Scopes was found guilty of teaching the scientific theory of evolution in public schools. Since then, however, Darwin's evolutionary theories have been presented in public schools with little reference to the biblical account in Genesis. People who support the literal interpretation of the Bible, commonly known as **creationists**, have formed various organizations to crusade for creationist treatment in U.S. public schools and universities.

In a 1987 Louisiana case, *Edwards v. Aguillard*, the Supreme Court ruled that states may not require the teaching of creationism alongside evolution in public schools if the primary purpose of such legislation is to promote a religious viewpoint. The target to promote creationism is often to influence choice of textbooks by a local school district or, in states with state-wide adoptions, by a state board of education. The teaching of evolution and creationism has remained a controversial issue in many communities across the United States (Applebome 1996; Rich 2013).

Beginning in the 1980s, those who believe in a divine hand in the creation of life have advanced **intelligent design** (ID), the idea that life is so complex it could only have been created by a higher intelligence. Although not explicitly drawn on the biblical account, creationists feel comfortable with ID and advocate that it is a more accurate account than Darwinism or, at the very least, that it be taught as an alternative alongside the theory of evolution. In 2005, a federal judge in *Kitzmiller v. Dove Area School District* ended a Pennsylvania school district intention to require the presentation of ID. In essence, the judge found ID to be "a religious belief" that was only a subtler way of finding God's fingerprints in nature than traditional creationism. Because the issue continues to be hotly debated, future court cases are certain to come (Clemmitt 2005; Goodstein 2005).

Public Displays

The fourth area of contention has been a battle over public displays that depict symbols of religion or appear to others to be sacred representations. Can manger scenes be erected on public property? Do people have a right to be protected from large displays such as a cross or a star atop a water tower overlooking an entire town? In a series of decisions in the 1980s through 1995, the Supreme Court ruled that tax-supported religious displays on public government property may be successfully challenged but may be permissible if made more secular. Displays that combine a crèche—the Christmas manger scene depicting the birth of Jesus—or the Hanukkah menorah and also include Frosty the Snowman or even Christmas trees have been ruled secular. These decisions have been dubbed "the plastic reindeer rules." In 1995, the Court clarified the issue by stating that privately sponsored religious displays may be allowed on public property if other forms of expression are permitted in the same location.

The final judicial word has not been heard, and all these rulings should be viewed as tentative because the Court cases have been decided by close votes. Changes in the Supreme Court's composition in the next few years also may alter the outcome of future cases (Bork 1995; Hirsley 1991; Mauro 1995).

Conclusion

From his cramped basement apartment, Grigore Culian has been producing a biweekly Romanian-language paper called *New York Magazine* since 1997 that provides local news of interest to Romanians in the metro area and beyond. There are over 146,000 adults in the United States for whom Romanian is their primary language. While being a one-person operation is unusual, producing news for a small ethnic community is not. Language newspapers, radio stations, cable outlets, and more recently video streaming keep ethnic ties alive and go beyond symbolic ethnicity. Similar media outlets foster a sense of community for hundreds of religious denominations, Christian and non-Christian alike, to believers in the United States (Lazar 2013).

Considering ethnicity and religion reinforces our understanding of the spectrum of intergroup relations first presented in Chapter 1. The Spectrum of Intergroup Relations figure shows the rich variety of relationships as defined by people's ethnic and religious identities. The profiles of German, Irish, Italian, and Polish Americans reflect the variety of White ethnic experiences.

Any study of life in the United States, especially one that focuses on dominant and subordinate groups, cannot ignore religion and ethnicity. The two are closely related, as certain religious faiths predominate in certain nationalities. Both religious activity and interest by White ethnics in their heritage continue to be prominent features of the contemporary scene. People have been and continue to be ridiculed or deprived of opportunities solely because of their ethnic or religious affiliation. To get a true picture of people's place in society, we need to consider both ethnicity and social class in association with their religious identification.

Religion is changing in the United States. As one commercial recognition of this fact, Hallmark created its first greeting card in 2003 for the Muslim holiday Eid-al-fitr, which marks the end of the month-long fast

SPECTRUM OF INTERGROUP RELATIONS

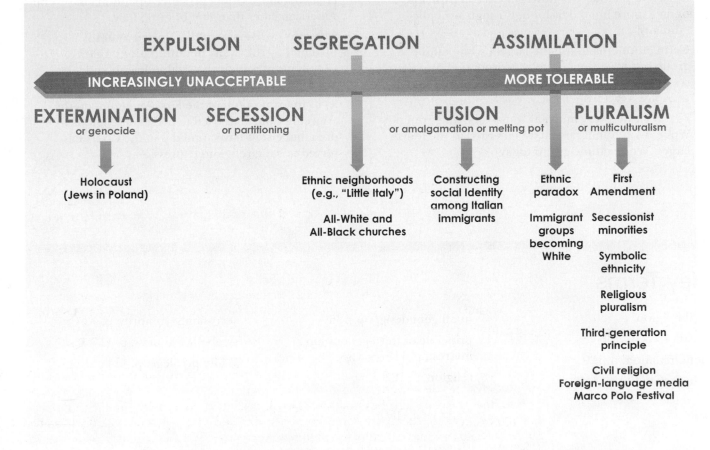

of Ramadan. The issue of the persistence of ethnicity is an intriguing one. Some people may only casually exhibit their ethnicity and practice what has been called symbolic ethnicity. However, can people immerse themselves in their ethnic culture without society punishing them for their will to be different? The tendency to put down White ethnics through respectable bigotry continues. Despite this intolerance, ethnicity remains a viable source of identity for many citizens today. There is also the ethnic paradox, which finds that practicing one's ethnic heritage often strengthens people and allows them to move successfully into the larger society.

The issue of religious expression in all its forms also raises a variety of intriguing questions. How can a country that is increasingly populated by diverse and often non-Christian faiths maintain religious tolerance? How might this change in the decades ahead? How will the courts and society resolve the issues of religious freedom? This is a particularly important issue in areas such as school prayer, secessionist minorities, creationism, intelligent design, and public religious displays. Some examination of religious ties is fundamental to completing an accurate picture of a person's social identity.

Ethnicity and religion are a basic part of today's social reality and of each individual's identity. The emotions, disputes, and debate over religion and ethnicity in the United States are powerful indeed.

Summary

1. While considering race and ethnicity in the United States, we often ignore how White people come to see themselves as a group and in relationship to others.

2. Feelings of ethnicity may be fading among the descendants of Europeans, but it may reemerge as reflected in either the third-generation principle or, in a more limited fashion, through symbolic ethnicity.

3. German Americans are the largest White ethnic group but have been largely incorporated into the core population with little visible distinctive cultural presence apart from food.

4. First regarded very much as "outsiders" and even not White, Irish immigrants have emerged as the fourth largest White ethnic group today.

5. Like the Irish, immigrants from Italy first encountered resistance in the United States but moved up from their lower and working-class place in the American social hierarchy.

6. The more recent immigration from Poland has created a more visible presence of Polonia in several American cities than that of Little Italy.

7. The ethnic diversity of the United States is matched by the many denominations among Christians as well as the sizable Jewish and Muslim presence.

8. In its interpretation of the First Amendment, the Supreme Court has tried to preserve religious freedom, but critics have argued that the Court has served to stifle religious expression.

Key Terms

civil religion, p. 130

creationists, p. 136

denomination, p. 129

ethnic paradox, p. 115

intelligent design, p. 136

principle of third-generation interest, p. 115

religion, p. 128

secessionist minority, p. 135

symbolic ethnicity, p. 117

White privilege, p. 114

Review Questions

1. How is Whiteness social constructed?
2. In what ways can White ethnicity be rediscovered?
3. Explain the impact that World War II had on German Americans both before and after the war.
4. Apply "Whiteness" to Irish Americans.
5. How does stereotyping relate to contemporary Italian Americans?
6. What role does Polonia play in the lives of contemporary Polish Americans?
7. To what extent has a non-Christian tradition been developing in the United States?
8. How have court rulings affected religious expression?

Critical Thinking

1. When do you see ethnicity becoming more apparent? When does it appear to occur only in response to other people's advancing their own ethnicity? From these situations, how can ethnic identity be both positive and perhaps counterproductive or even destructive?
2. How do White people you know seem to be aware or unaware of their ethnic roots? Of their Whiteness?
3. Why do you think we are so often reluctant to show our religion to others? Why might people of certain faiths be more hesitant than others?
4. How does religion reflect conservative and liberal positions on social issues? Consider services for the homeless, the need for childcare, the acceptance or rejection of gay men and lesbians, and a woman's right to terminate a pregnancy versus the fetus's right to survive.

6 Native Americans: The First Americans

6-1 Describe the relationship between Native Americans and the early European immigrants.

6-2 Describe the impact treaties had right up the present.

6-3 Explain how federal policies affect Native Americans.

6-4 Discuss the Native Americans collective action efforts and results.

6-5 Put into your own words the macro and micro levels of American Indian identity.

6-6 Summarize the special challenges Native Americans face today in regards to economic development, education, healthcare, and the environment.

6-7 Discuss how religion and spirituality are expressed.

6-8 Analyze how environmental issues impact Native Americans.

Boozhoo might be the sign that welcomes you at the local coffee shop in this college town. On-campus restroom door signs say *Ikwewag* and *Ininiway*, but fortunately, each is followed by *Women* and *Men*, respectively. No, you're not attending a college in a foreign country: You are in Bemidji, Minnesota, checking out Bemidji State University. The town and college have made an effort to make Native Americans, and in particular members of the Ojibway (or Chippewa) tribe, feel welcomed. Using the language also is an effort to keep it alive because fewer than 1,000 people in the United States speak it fluently.

The battle to keep language alive is fought throughout the United States, from Riverton, Wyoming, to Long Island, New York, to the Florida Everglades. Efforts are underway to significantly increase the numbers of the more than 370,000 Native people who currently speak their native language at home.

In Wyoming, Ryan Wilson is teaching the Arapaho language in the Hinono' Eitinino' Oowuu', the Arapaho language Lodge, because no one under the age of 55 speaks it fluently and thus there are few surviving speakers. The Shinnecock native language on Long Island has not been spoken for nearly 200 years. Drawing on a historical vocabulary list made by Thomas Jefferson during a tribal visit in 1791, linguists are attempting to reintroduce the tribe of 1,700 people to their native language. (Later in this chapter, we will be discussing the Shinnecock's efforts to become recognized as a sovereign tribe.) In Florida, the Miccosukee Indian Schools' efforts to increase speaking their native language are having positive results, as are efforts around the country to increase the low population (only 20.4 percent) of Native people who speak their native language at home.

The languages themselves are threatened because easily 70 of the 139 tribal languages could become extinct in a very few years. In Table 6.1, we highlight the ten most commonly spoken languages, although not necessarily fluently, by Native Americans (Bureau of the Census 2013d; Frosch 2008; T. Lee 2011; National Congress of American Indians 2012; Sturtevant and Cattelino 2004).

Although this chapter focuses on the Native American experience in the United States, the pattern of land seizure, subjugation, assimilation, and resistance to domination has been repeated with indigenous people in nations throughout the world, including the tribal people in Mexico, Canada, and throughout Latin America. Hawaiians, another native people who fell under the political, economic, and cultural control of the United States, are considered in Chapter 12. Later in this chapter we consider the experience of the Aboriginal people of Australia. Indigenous peoples on almost every continent are familiar with the patterns of subjugation and the pressure to assimilate. So widespread is this oppression that the United Nations in 1977 and even its precursor organization, the League of Nations, have repeatedly considered this issue.

The common term *American Indians* tells us more about the Europeans who explored North America than it does about the native people. The label reflects the initial explorers' confusion in believing that they had arrived in "the Indies" of the Asian continent. However, reference to the diverse tribal groups either by *American Indians* or *Native Americans* is a result of the forced subordination to the dominant group. Today, most American Indians prefer to identify themselves using their tribal affiliation, such as Cherokee, or affiliations, such as Cheyenne Arapaho, if one has mixed ancestry. To collectively refer to all tribal people in this book, we use *Native Americans* and *American Indians* interchangeably.

An estimated 2.9 million Native Americans and Alaskan Natives lived in the United States in 2010. This represents an increase of about 18 percent over the year 2000, compared to a growth of about 1 percent among White non-Hispanics. In addition to the 2.9 million people who gave American Indian or Alaskan Native as their sole racial identification, another 2.3 million people listed multiple responses that included American Indian. As shown in Figure 6.1,

TABLE 6.1 Major Tribal Languages	
1. Navajo	169,471
2. Yupik (Alaska)	18,950
3. Dakota (Sioux)	18,616
4. Apache	13,083
5. Keres (Pueblo)	12,945
6. Cherokee	11,610
7. Choctaw	10,343
8. Zuni	9,686
9. Ojibwa	8,371
10. Pima	7,270

Source: 2006–2010 American Community Survey in Siebens and Julian 2011: Table 1.

6-1

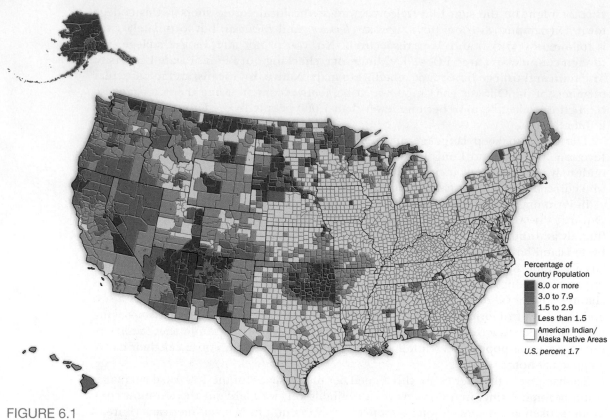

FIGURE 6.1
American Indian and Alaska Native Population

Source: Norris, Vines, and Hoeffel 2012: Figure 4 on p. 9.

Percentage of
Country Population

- 8.0 or more
- 3.0 to 7.9
- 1.5 to 2.9
- Less than 1.5
- American Indian/
  Alaska Native Areas

U.S. percent 1.7

Native Americans are located throughout the United States but are most present in the Southwest, Northwest, northern Great Plains, and Alaska. Fourteen states have at least 100,000 American Indian and Alaska Natives—Alaska, Arizona, California, Colorado, Florida, Michigan, Minnesota, New Mexico, New York, North Carolina, Oklahoma, Oregon, Texas, and Washington (Bureau of the Census 2013d; Norris, Vines, and Hoeffel 2012).

Early European Contacts

6-1 Describe the relationship between Native Americans and the early European immigrants.

Native Americans have been misunderstood and ill-treated by their conquerors for several centuries. Assuming that he had reached the Indies, Christopher Columbus called the native residents "people of India." The European immigrants who followed Columbus did not understand them any more than the Native Americans could have anticipated the destruction of their way of life. But the Europeans had superior weaponry, and the diseases they brought wiped out huge numbers of indigenous people throughout the Western hemisphere.

The first explorers of the Western hemisphere came long before Columbus and Leif Eriksson. The ancestors of today's Native Americans were hunters in search of wild game, including mammoths and long-horned bison. For thousands of years, these people spread through the Western hemisphere, adapting to its many physical environments. Hundreds of cultures evolved, including the complex societies of the Maya, Inca, and Aztec (Deloria 1995, 2004).

It is beyond the scope of this chapter to describe the many tribal cultures of North America, let alone the ways of life of Native Americans in Central and South America and the islands of the Caribbean. We must appreciate that the term *Indian culture* is a convenient way to gloss over the diversity of cultures, languages, religions, kinship systems, and political organizations that existed—and, in many instances, remain—among the peoples referred to collectively as *Native Americans* or *American Indians*. For example, in 1500, an estimated 700 distinct languages were spoken in the area north of Mexico. For simplicity, we refer to these many cultures as *Native American*, but we must be always mindful of the differences this term conceals. Similarly, we refer to non–Native Americans as non-Indians, recognizing in this context that this term encompasses many groups, including Whites, African Americans, and Hispanics in some instances (J. Schwartz 1994; Swagerty 1983).

The number of Native Americans north of the Rio Grande, estimated at about 10 million in 1500, gradually decreased as their food sources disappeared and they fell victim to diseases such as measles, smallpox, and influenza. By 1800, the Native American population was about 600,000; by 1900, it was reduced to fewer than 250,000. This loss of human life can only be described and judged as catastrophic. The United States does not bear total responsibility. The pattern had been well established by the early Spaniards in the Southwest and by the French and English colonists who sought control of the eastern seaboard.

Native Americans did have warfare between tribes, which presumably reduces the guilt for European-initiated warfare. However, their conflicts differed significantly from those of the conquerors. The Europeans launched large campaigns against the tribes, resulting in mass mortality. In contrast, in the Americas, the tribes limited warfare to specific campaigns designed for specific purposes such as recapturing a resource or avenging a loss.

Not all initial contacts led to deliberate loss of life. Some missionaries traveled well in advance of settlement in efforts to Christianize Native Americans before they came into contact with less-tolerant Europeans. Fur trappers, vastly outnumbered by Native Americans, were forced to learn their customs, but these trappers established routes of commerce that more and more non-Indians were to follow (Snipp 1989; Swagerty 1983; Thornton 1991).

Gradually, the policies directed from Europe toward the indigenous peoples of North America resembled the approach described in the world systems theory. As introduced in Chapter 1, the **world systems theory** takes the view that the global economic system is divided between nations that control wealth and those that provide natural resources and labor. The indigenous peoples and, more important to the Europeans, the land they occupied were targets of exploitation by Spain, England, France, Portugal, and other nations with experience as colonizers in Africa and Asia (Chase-Dunn and Hall 1998).

6-2 Describe the impact treaties had right up the present.

Treaties and Warfare

The United States formulated a policy toward Native Americans during the nineteenth century that followed the precedents established during the colonial period. The government policy was not to antagonize the Native Americans unnecessarily. Yet if the needs of tribes interfered with the needs, or even the whims, of non-Indians, then Whites were to have precedence.

Tribes were viewed as separate nations to be dealt with by treaties formed through negotiations with the federal government. Fair-minded as that policy might seem, it was

SCHWADRON

"NOT SO FAST! HOW DO WE KNOW YOU'RE NOT TERRORISTS WITH WEAPONS OF MASS DESTRUCTION?!"

clear from the beginning that the non-Indian government would deal harshly with tribal groups that refused to agree to treaties. Federal relations with the Native Americans were the responsibility of the secretary of war. Consequently, when the Bureau of Indian Affairs (BIA) was created in 1824 to coordinate the government's relations with the tribes, it was part of the Department of War. The government's primary emphasis was to maintain peace and friendly relations along the frontier. Nevertheless, as settlers moved the frontier westward, they encroached more and more on land that Native Americans had inhabited for centuries.

The Indian Removal Act, passed in 1830, called for the relocation of all Eastern tribes across the Mississippi River. The Removal Act was popular with non–American Indians because it opened more land to settlement through annexation of tribal land. Almost all non-Indians felt that the Native Americans had no right to block progress—which was defined as movement by White society. Among the largest groups relocated were the five tribes of the Creek, Choctaw, Chickasaw, Cherokee, and Seminole, who were resettled in what is now Oklahoma. The movement, lasting more than a decade, is called the Trail of Tears because the tribes left their ancestral lands under the harshest conditions. Poor planning, corrupt officials, little attention to those ill from a variety of epidemics, inadequate supplies, and the deaths of several thousand Native Americans characterized the forced migration (Hirsch 2009).

The Removal Act disrupted Native American cultures but didn't move the tribes far enough or fast enough to stay out of the path of the ever-advancing non–American Indian settlers. After the Civil War, settlers moved westward at an unprecedented pace. The federal government negotiated with the many tribes but primarily enacted legislation that affected them with minimal consultation. The government's first priority was almost always to allow the settlers to live and work regardless of Native American claims. Along with the military defeat of the tribes, the federal government tried to limit the functions of tribal leaders. If tribal institutions were weakened, it was felt, the Native Americans would assimilate more rapidly.

The more significant federal actions that continue up to the present are summarized in Table 6.2.

TABLE 6.2
Major Federal Policies

Year	Policy	Central Feature
1830	Removal Act	Relocated Eastern tribes westward
1887	Allotment Act	Subdivided tribal lands into individual household plots
1934	Reorganization Act	Required tribes to develop election-based governments and leaders
1934	Johnson-O'Malley Act	Aided public school districts with Native American enrollments
1946	Indian Claims Commission	Adjudicated litigation by tribes against the federal government
1952	Employment Assistance Program	Relocated reservation people to urban areas for jobs
1953	Termination Act	Closed reservations and their federal services
1971	Alaska Native Settlement Act	Recognized legally the lands of tribal people
1974	Indian Financing Act	Fostered economic development
1975	Indian Self-Determination and Education Assistance Act	Increased involvement by tribal people and governments
1988	Indian Gaming Regulatory Act	Allowed states to negotiate gaming rights to reservations
1990	Native American Graves and Repatriation Act	Returned Native remains to tribes with authentic claims
1990	Indian Arts and Crafts Act	Monitored authenticity of crafts
1994	American Indian Religious Freedom Act	Sought to protect tribal spirituality, including use of peyote

The Allotment Act

The Allotment Act of 1887 bypassed tribal leaders and proposed making individual landowners of tribal members. Each family was given as many as 160 acres under the government's assumption that, with land, Native Americans would become more like the White homesteaders who were flooding the not-yet-settled areas of the West.

The effect of the Allotment Act, however, was disastrous. To guarantee that they would remain homesteaders, the act prohibited the Native Americans from selling the land for 25 years. Yet no effort was made to acquaint them with the skills necessary to make the land productive. Many tribes were not accustomed to cultivating land and, if anything, considered such labor undignified, and they received no assistance in adapting to homesteading.

Much of the land initially deeded under the Allotment Act eventually came into the possession of White landowners. The land could not be sold legally, but it could be leased with the BIA serving as the trustee. In this role, the federal government took legal title that included the duty to collect on behalf of the tribal members any revenues generated by non-Indians through mining, oil, timber operations, grazing, or similar activities. The failure of the government to carry out this duty has been an issue for well over a century.

Large parcels of land eventually fell into the possession of non-Indians. For Native Americans who managed to retain the land, the BIA required that, upon the death of the owner, the land be divided equally among all descendants, regardless of tribal inheritance customs. In documented cases, this division resulted in as many as 30 people trying to live off an 80-acre plot of worthless land. By 1934, Native Americans had lost approximately 90 million of the 138 million acres in their possession before the Allotment Act. The land left was generally considered worthless for farming and marginal even for ranching (Blackfeet Reservation Development Fund 2006; Deloria and Lytle 1983).

The Reorganization Act

The assumptions behind the Allotment Act and the missionary activities of the nineteenth century were that it was best for Native Americans to assimilate into White society, and an individual was best considered apart from his or her tribal identity. Gradually, in the twentieth century, government officials began accepting the importance of tribal identity. The Indian Reorganization Act of 1934, known as the Wheeler-Howard Act, recognized the need to use, rather than ignore, tribal identity. But assimilation, rather than movement toward a pluralistic society, was still the goal.

Many provisions of the Reorganization Act, including revocation of the Allotment Act, benefited Native Americans. Still, given the legacy of broken treaties, many tribes at first distrusted the new policy. Under the Reorganization Act, tribes could adopt a written constitution and elect a tribal council with a head. This system imposed foreign values and structures. Under it, the elected tribal leader represented an entire reservation, which might include several tribes, some hostile to one another. Furthermore, the leader had to be elected by majority rule, a concept alien to many tribes. Many full-blooded Native Americans resented the provision that mixed-bloods had full voting rights. The Indian Reorganization Act did facilitate tribal dealings with government agencies, but the dictation to Native Americans of certain procedures common to White society and alien to the tribes was another sign of forced assimilation.

As was true of earlier government reforms, the Reorganization Act sought to assimilate Native Americans into the dominant society on the dominant group's terms. In this case, the tribes were absorbed within the political and economic structure of the larger society. Apart from the provision that tribal chairmen were to oversee reservations with several tribes, the Reorganization Act solidified tribal identity. Unlike the Allotment Act,

6-3 ## 🌐 A Global View

Australia's Aboriginal People

The indigenous people of Australia have continuously inhabited the continent for at least 50,000 years. Today, they number over 600,000 people constituting about 2.5 percent of the total population and, although small in number, their presence based on this long legacy is highly visible. The terms *Aboriginal* and *indigenous people* are used here interchangeably.

Aboriginals make up many clans, language groups, and communities with little interconnections except those that are occasionally created through kinship or trade. The cultural practices of these indigenous peoples have historically been very diverse. At the time Europeans arrived, an estimated 600–700 groups spoke 200–250 separate languages as distinct from one another as French is to German. In addition, there were many more dialects of a language that could be more or less understood by others.

Reflecting this diversity is the spirituality of the people. Although belief systems vary in ways that reflect the changing terrain from the Outback to rainforests, Aboriginals see themselves as having arisen from the land itself and ultimately returning to the land. Collectively, these beliefs are commonly referred to as *Dreaming* or *Dreamtime* and sometimes take on a style that Westerners view or label as a cosmology or oral folklore.

As was the case with American Indians, the size of Australia's indigenous population declined dramatically after European settlement as a result of the colonialism.

The impact of new diseases, some of which were not life threatening to Europeans, had devastating effects on indigenous communities because they lacked immunity. The number of indigenous people also decreased as a result of their mistreatment, the dispossession of their land, and the disruption and disintegration of their culture.

Legally, there historically was little recognition of indigenous people. Not until 1967 were Australian citizenship and voting rights extended to the indigenous people, allowing them access to welfare and unemployment benefits. It would be misleading to view Aboriginal people as passive either in colonial days or more contemporary times with respect to their position in Australia. They have taken an active part in efforts to secure their rights.

Reflecting the low regard that White Australians had for the indigenous people, thousands of Aboriginal children were forcibly taken from their families and raised by Whites because it was thought that bringing them into the dominant society's culture was best for them. The government program affected somewhere between 10 and 30 percent of all Aboriginal children from 1910 to 1970. Finally in 2008, the Australian government expressed its regret for the "Stolen Generations" and committed to improve the living conditions and future prospects of all Aboriginal people.

Sources: Anderson 2003; Attwood 2003; Australian Bureau of Statistics 2012a, 2012b; Schaefer 2008a.

it recognized the right of Native Americans to approve or reject some actions taken on their behalf. The act still maintained substantial non–Native American control over the reservations. As institutions, the tribal governments owed their existence not to their people but to the BIA. These tribal governments rested at the bottom of a large administrative hierarchy (Cornell 1984; Deloria 1971; McNickle 1973; Washburn 1984; Wax and Buchanan 1975).

In 2000, on the 175th anniversary of the BIA, its director, Kevin Guer, a Pawnee, declared that it was "no occasion for celebration as we express our profound sorrow for what the agency has done in the past." A formal apology followed. The United States is not the only country expressing regret over past actions with its indigenous peoples, as we see in A Global View (Stout 2000).

Reservation Life and Federal Policies

6-3 Explain how federal policies affect Native Americans.

Today, more than one-third of Native Americans live on 557 reservations and trust lands in 33 states, which account for a bit more than 2 percent of the land throughout the United States. Even for those Native Americans who reside far away from the tribal lands, the reservations play a prominent role in their identities (see Figure 6.2).

More than any other segment of the population, with the exception of the military, a Native American living on the reservation finds his or her life determined by the federal government. From the condition of the roads to the level of fire protection to the quality of the schools, the federal government through such agencies as the BIA and the Public Health Service effectively controls reservation life. Tribes and their leaders are

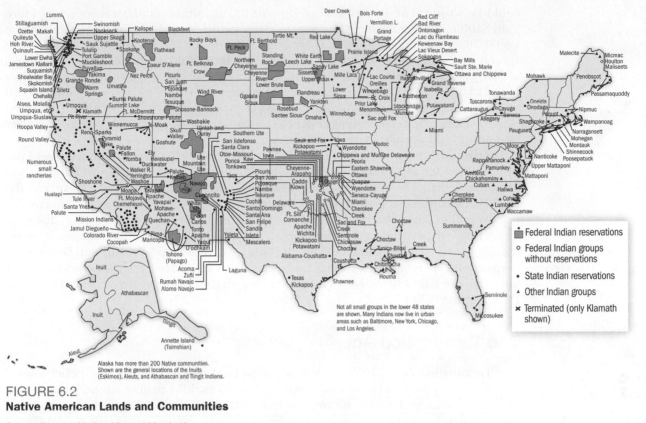

FIGURE 6.2
Native American Lands and Communities

Source: Bureau of Indian Affairs 1986: 12–13.

now consulted more than in the past, but ultimate decisions rest in Washington, DC, to a degree that is not true for the rest of the civilian population.

Many of the policies instituted by the BIA in the twentieth century were designed with giving tribal people more autonomy, but final control resting with the federal government. Most Native Americans and their organizations do not quarrel with this goal. They may only wish that the government and the White people had never gotten into the Indians' business in the first place. Disagreement between the BIA and the tribes and among Native Americans themselves has focused on *how* to reduce federal control and subsidies, not on whether they *should be* reduced. The government has taken three steps in this direction since World War II. Two of these measures have been the formation of the Indian Claims Commission and the passage of the Termination Act. The following section shows how the third step, the Employment Assistance Program, has created a new meeting place for Native Americans in cities, far from their native homelands and the reservations.

Legal Claims

Native Americans have had a unique relationship with the federal government. As might be expected, little provision was ever made for them as individuals or tribes to bring grievances against the government. The U.S. Court of Federal Claims as well as Congress are now hearing cases and trying to resolve disputes.

In 1996, Elouise Cobell, a member of the Blackfeet tribe in Montana, brought a class-action lawsuit on behalf of a half-million American Indians, charging that the government had cheated them of billions of dollars in royalties under the trust arrangements created by the Allotment Act of 1887. The courts ruled that the BIA and other government agencies had extremely poor records even from recent times, much less going back in time. How difficult was the federal government defense in the *Cobell* case? The BIA shut down its Web site over fear that any information it gave out about almost anything

6-3

could be wrong. The Department of Interior, by its own accounts, was spending more than $100 million annually in attempts to clean up the record keeping in a manner that would allow it to defend itself in court eventually. In late 2009, the federal government agreed to a settlement of $3.4 billion, including individual payments of at least $1,000 to 300,000 individual American Indians. Another similar case was settled in 2012 for just over $1 billion to 41 tribes for similar mismanagement (Hevesi 2011; T. Williams 2012a).

In specific land issues apart from the *Cobell* class action lawsuit, Native Americans often express a desire to recover their land rather than accept any financial settlements. After numerous legal decisions favoring the Sioux.

Indians, including a ruling of the U.S. Supreme Court, Congress finally agreed to pay $106 million for the land that was illegally seized in the aftermath of the Battle of the Little Big Horn. The Sioux rejected the money and lobbied for measures, such as the 1987 Black Hills Sioux Nation Act in Congress, to return the land to tribal authority. No positive action has yet been taken on these measures. In the meantime, however, the original settlement, the subsequent unaccepted payments, and the accrued interest brought the 2012 total of funds being held for the Sioux to more than $800 million. Despite the desperate need for housing, food, healthcare, and education, the Sioux would prefer to regain the land lost in the 1868 Fort Laramie Treaty and have not accepted payment (T. Williams 2012b).

The Termination Act

The Termination Act of 1953 initiated the most controversial government policy toward reservation Native Americans in the twentieth century. Like many such policies, the act originated in ideas that were meant to benefit Native Americans. The BIA commissioner, John Collier, had expressed concern in the 1930s over extensive government control of tribal affairs. In 1947, congressional hearings were held to determine which tribes had the economic resources to be relieved of federal control and assistance. The policy proposed at that time was an admirable attempt to give Native Americans greater autonomy while at the same time reducing federal expenditures, a goal popular among taxpayers.

The services the tribes received, such as subsidized medical care and college scholarships, should not have been viewed as special and deserving to be discontinued. These services were not the result of favoritism but merely fulfilled treaty obligations. The termination of the Native Americans' relationship to the government then came to be viewed by Native Americans as a threat to reduce services rather than a release from arbitrary authority. Native Americans might gain greater self-governance, but at a high price.

Unfortunately, the Termination Act as finally passed in 1953 emphasized reducing costs and ignored individual needs. Recommendations for a period of tax immunity were dropped. According to the act, federal services such as medical care, schools, and road equipment were supposed to be withdrawn gradually. Instead, when the Termination Act's provisions began to go into effect, federal services were stopped immediately, with minimal coordination between local government agencies and the tribes to determine whether the services could be continued by other means. The effect of the government orders on the Native Americans was disastrous, with major economic upheaval on the affected tribes, who could not establish some of the most basic services—such as road repair and fire protection—that the federal government had previously provided. The federal government resumed these services in 1975 with congressional action that signaled the end of another misguided policy intended to be good for tribal peoples (Deloria 1969; Ulrich 2010; Wax and Buchanan 1975).

Employment Assistance Program

The depressed economic conditions of reservation life might lead us to expect government initiatives to attract business and industry to locate on or near reservations. The government could provide tax incentives that would eventually pay for themselves. However, such proposals have not been advanced. Rather than take jobs to the Native

Americans, the federal government decided to lead the more highly motivated away from the reservation. This policy has further devastated the reservations' economic potential.

In 1952, the BIA began programs to relocate young Native Americans to urban areas. One of these programs, after 1962, was called the Employment Assistance Program (EAP). The EAP's primary provision was for relocation, individually or in families, at government expense, to urban areas where job opportunities were greater than those on the reservations. The BIA stressed that the EAP was voluntary, but this was a fiction given the lack of viable economic alternatives open to American Indians. The program was not a success for the many Native Americans who found the urban experience unsuitable or unbearable. By 1965, one-fourth to one-third of the people in the EAP had returned to their home reservations. So great was the rate of return that in 1959 the BIA stopped releasing data on the percentage of returnees, fearing that they would give too much ammunition to critics of the EAP (Bahr 1972).

Cities have not proven to serve as a simple solution to Native American economic growth. In Figure 6.3, we see an analysis released in 2013 by the Bureau of the Census of the most recent data available. Nationally at the time White non-Hispanics had an unemployment rate of 9.9 percent, but in each of the 20 cities with the largest Native American population, unemployment levels were higher—ranging from a "low" of 10.6 percent in Anchorage to 50.9 percent in Rapid City, South Dakota. As desperate

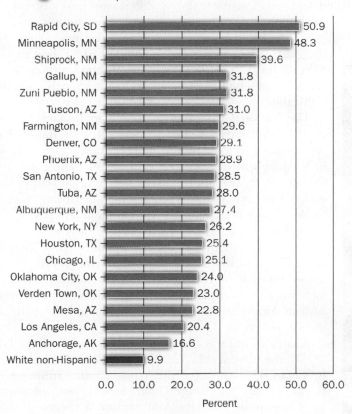

Poverty Rates for the American Indian and Alaska Native Alone Population in the 20 Cities Most Populated by this Group, 2007–2011 ACS

■ Below poverty: American Indian and Alaska Native Alone
■ White non-Hispanic

City	Percent
Rapid City, SD	50.9
Minneapolis, MN	48.3
Shiprock, NM	39.6
Gallup, NM	31.8
Zuni Puebio, NM	31.8
Tuscon, AZ	31.0
Farmington, NM	29.6
Denver, CO	29.1
Phoenix, AZ	28.9
San Antonio, TX	28.5
Tuba, AZ	28.0
Albuquerque, NM	27.4
New York, NY	26.2
Houston, TX	25.4
Chicago, IL	25.1
Oklahoma City, OK	24.0
Verden Town, OK	23.0
Mesa, AZ	22.8
Los Angeles, CA	20.4
Anchorage, AK	16.6
White non-Hispanic	9.9

Percent

FIGURE 6.3
American Indian Poverty Rates

Note: Data from American Community Survey for 2007–2011 for 20 cities most populated by American Indian and Alaska Native Alone population. White non-Hispanic rate is for entire nation.

Source: Macartney, Bishaw, and Fontenot 2013: 10.

6-4

as these data indicate the situation is for urban tribal peoples, it is typically better than on the reservation. Now more than 7 of 10 Native Americans live in metropolitan areas (T. Williams 2013)

The movement of Native Americans into urban areas has had many unintended consequences. It has further reduced the labor force on the reservation. Those who leave tend to be better educated, creating the Native American version of the brain drain. Urbanization unquestionably contributed to the development of an intertribal network, or pan-Indian movement, which we describe later in this chapter. The city became the new meeting place of Native Americans, who learned of their common predicament both in the city and on the 325 federally administered reservations. Government agencies also had to develop a policy of continued assistance to nonreservation Native Americans; despite such efforts, the problems of Native Americans in cities persist.

Collective Action

6-4 Discuss the Native Americans collective action efforts and results.

Native Americans have worked collectively through tribal or reservation government action and across tribal lines. As we noted in Chapter 1, the **panethnicity** of solidarity among ethnic subgroups has been reflected in the use of such terms as *Hispanic, Latino,* and *Asian American*. **Pan-Indianism** refers to intertribal social movements in which several tribes, joined by political goals but not by kinship, unite in a common identity. Today, these pan-Indian efforts are most vividly seen in cultural efforts and political protests of government policies (Cornell 1996; Jolivette 2008).

Proponents of these movements see the tribes as captive nations or even colonies. They generally see the enemy as the federal government. Until recently, pan-Indian efforts usually failed to overcome the cultural differences and distrust among tribal groups. However, some efforts to unite have succeeded. The Iroquois made up a six-tribe confederation dating back to the seventeenth century. The Ghost Dance briefly united the Plains tribes in the 1880s, some of which had earlier combined to resist the U.S. Army. But these were exceptions. It took nearly a century and a half of BIA policies to accomplish a significant level of unification.

The National Congress of American Indians (NCAI), founded in 1944 in Denver, Colorado, was the first national organization representing Native Americans. The NCAI registered itself as a lobby in Washington, DC, hoping to make the Native American perspective heard in the aftermath of the Reorganization Act described earlier. Concern about "White people's meddling" is reflected in the NCAI requirement that non-Indian members pay twice as much in dues. The NCAI has had its successes. Early in its history, it played an important role in creating the Indian Claims Commission, and it later pressured the BIA to abandon termination. It is still the most important civil rights organization for Native Americans and uses tactics similar to those of the NAACP, although the problems facing African Americans and Native Americans are legally and constitutionally different.

A later arrival was the more radical American Indian Movement (AIM), the most visible pan-Indian group. AIM was founded in 1968 by Clyde Bellecourt (of the White Earth Chippewa) and Dennis Banks (of the Pine Ridge Oglala Sioux), both of whom then lived in Minneapolis. Initially, AIM created a patrol to monitor police actions and document charges of police brutality. Eventually, it promoted programs for alcohol rehabilitation and school reform. By 1972, AIM was nationally known not for its neighborhood-based reforms but for its aggressive confrontations with the BIA and law enforcement agencies.

Most reservations today have a measure of self-government through an elected tribal. Pictured is the Navaho tribal council at work.

Protest Efforts

Fish-ins began in 1964 to protest interference by Washington State officials with Native Americans who were fishing, as they argued, in accordance with the 1854 Treaty of Medicine Creek, and were not subject to fine or imprisonment, even if they did violate White society's law. The fish-ins had protesters fishing en masse in restricted waterways. This protest was initially hampered by disunity and apathy, but several hundred Native Americans were convinced that civil disobedience was the only way to bring attention to their grievances with the government. Legal battles followed, and the U.S. Supreme Court confirmed the treaty rights in 1968. Other tribes continued to fight in the courts, but the fish-ins brought increased public awareness of the deprivations of Native Americans. These fishing rights battles continue today with the Chippewa in Wisconsin and Nez Perce in Idaho, among others (Bobo and Tuan 2006; D. Johnson 2005).

((🎙)) Speaking Out

Holocaust Museum of the Indigenous People Should Be Built at Wounded Knee

Since 1492 the history of the Western Hemisphere has been marked by one of the greatest holocausts in the history of the world.

There are no true figures to quote about how many millions of indigenous people have perished in this land that was once their own. Those who wrote the history of the settlement of these lands often reduced the numbers of deaths because they were so high that it would make the invaders of this land appear in history as bloodthirsty barbarians. No culture wants to be remembered like this.

Tim Giago

But somewhere in the books of man there is a compilation of the millions of indigenous people who died at the hands of the invaders whether by guns, knives, or diseases.

In Washington D. C. there is a museum to mark the Holocaust brought upon the Jewish people by Adolf Hitler. It is a place of tragedy and yet it reminds the world of what happened to the Jews in hopes that this will never happen again. More than six million Jews died in the death camps operated by the Nazis and the Holocaust Museum stands as a stark reminder of these tragedies. Perhaps 5 to 10 times that number of indigenous people died beginning in 1492.

It would be prophetic if the Oglala Sioux Tribe would build a holocaust museum to educate and to remind the world of what happened to the indigenous people of the Western Hemisphere. From South America, Central America and North America, millions of indigenous people died protecting and defending what was theirs.

What happened to the Native people everywhere in the Western Hemisphere is one of the most shameful chapters in the history of mankind on this planet called earth.

Wounded Knee may have been the final chapter on this holocaust of indigenous people. It is only right that the Oglala Lakota build a Holocaust Museum of the Indigenous People right here on the grounds where the massacre of the Lakota took place on December 29, 1890.

The museum could house the history of the millions who died from the tip of South America to the top of North America. Every indigenous tribe has its stories of the death and destruction that was visited upon their people. A museum of this nature would draw visitors from around the world and it would inform and educate the masses as to the true history of the Natives of this hemisphere. But more than that, the museum would serve as a stark reminder that the hands of the invaders were not clean, but they were the hands of a people who tried in vain to destroy a culture and a people.

Whether that destruction came in the form of forced religions or in the quest for gold, indigenous people died in its wake. There are hundreds of stories to be told and hundreds of photos and artifacts to substantiate the holocaust of the Native people. It should be a priority venture for the Oglala Sioux Tribe and there should be many wealthy people and the United States government itself that would contribute money and the expertise to make the Holocaust Museum of the Indigenous People a reality.

It is time to stop talking about the genocide foisted upon us and to do something about it. This idea is one that is achievable. We now need the Lakota people of vision to cease upon it and make it happen. It is time to tell the true history of the invasion of the Americas and about the millions of deaths that ensued.

And the Lakota People should be the leaders in this endeavor because for all intent and purposes, the holocaust of the indigenous people ended on the Sacred Grounds at Wounded Knee.

Source: Giago 2013.

6-4

The fish-ins were only the beginning. After the favorable Supreme Court decision in 1968, other events followed in quick succession. In 1969, members of the San Francisco Indian Center seized Alcatraz Island in San Francisco Bay. The 13-acre island was an abandoned maximum-security federal prison, and the federal government was undecided about how to use it. The Native Americans claimed the "excess property" in exchange for $24 in glass beads and cloth, following the precedent set in the sale of Manhattan more than three centuries earlier. With no federal response and the loss of public interest in the demonstration, the protesters left the island more than a year later. The activists' desire to transform it into a Native American cultural center was ignored. Despite the outcome, the event gained international publicity for their cause. Red Power was born, and Native Americans who sympathized with the BIA were labeled *Uncle Tomahawks* or *apples* (red on the outside, white on the inside).

The most dramatic confrontation between Native Americans and the government happened in what came to be called the Battle of Wounded Knee II. In January 1973, AIM leader Russell Means led an unsuccessful drive to impeach Richard Wilson as tribal chairman of the Oglala Sioux tribe on the Pine Ridge Reservation. In the next month, Means, accompanied by some 300 supporters, started a 70-day occupation of Wounded Knee, South Dakota, site of the infamous cavalry assault in 1890 and now part of the Pine Ridge Reservation. The occupation received tremendous press coverage.

In the Speaking Out, journalist Tim Giago, born a member of the Oglala Sioux tribe on the Pine Ridge Reservation, draws attention to the harsh reality of the experience of the Plains Indians at the heads of the U.S. Army. Specifically he calls for a museum at Wounded Knee to recognize the millions of American Indians who lost their lives in the nineteenth century.

However, the media coverage of the protest did not affect the outcome. Negotiations between AIM and the federal government on the occupation itself brought no tangible results. Federal prosecutions were initiated against most participants. AIM leaders Russell Means and Dennis Banks eventually faced prosecution on several felony charges, and both men were imprisoned. AIM had less visibility as an organization then. Russell Means wryly remarked in 1984, "We're not chic now. We're just Indians, and we have to help ourselves" (Hentoff 1984:23; see also Janisch 2008; Nagel 1988, 1996).

The most visible recent AIM activity has been its efforts to gain clemency for one of its leaders, Leonard Peltier. Imprisoned since 1976, Peltier was given two life sentences

Powwows offer an opportunity for Native Americans from many tribes to gather for celebrations, competitive dancing and drumming, and selling goods and food.

for murdering two FBI agents the year before on the embattled Sioux reservation of Pine Ridge, South Dakota. Fellow AIM leaders such as Dennis Banks organized a 1994 Walk for Justice to bring attention in Washington, DC, to the view that Peltier is innocent. This view was supported in two 1992 movie releases: the documentary *Incident at Oglala*, produced by Robert Redford; and the more entertaining but fictionalized *Thunderheart*. To date, clemency appeals to the president to lift the federal sentence have gone unheeded, but this issue remains the rallying point for today's remnants of AIM (Matthiessen 1991; Sandage 2008).

Collective Action: An Overview

Protest activities have created a greater solidarity among Native Americans as they seek solutions to common grievances with government agencies. Research shows that tribal people born since the collective action efforts of the 1960s are more likely to reject negative and stereotypic representations of American Indians than those born before the self-determination efforts. Whether through moderate groups such as the NCAI or the more activist AIM, these pan-Indian developments have awakened Whites to the real grievances of Native Americans and have garnered the begrudging acceptance of even the most conservative tribal members, who are more willing to cooperate with government action (Schulz 1998).

However, the results of collective action have not all been productive, even when viewed from a perspective sympathetic to Native American self-determination. Plains tribes dominate the national organizations, not only politically but also culturally. Powwow styles of dancing, singing, and costuming derived from the Plains tradition are spreading nationwide as common cultural traits (see Table 6.3 for the largest concentrations of Native Americans).

The growing visibility of **powwows** is symbolic of Native Americans in the 1990s. The phrase *pau wau* referred to the medicine man or spiritual leader of the Algonquian tribes, but Europeans who watched medicine men dance thought the word referred to entire events. Over the last hundred years, powwows have evolved into gatherings in which Native Americans of many tribes come to dance, sing, play music, and visit. More recently, they have become organized events featuring competitions and prizes at several thousand locations. The general public sees them as entertainment, but for Native Americans, they are a celebration of their cultures (Eschbach and Applebaum 2000).

6-5

TABLE 6.3
Largest American Indian Groupings

Reservations

1. Navajo (AZ, NM, UT)	169,321
2. Pine Ridge (SO, NE)	16,906
3. Fort Apache (AZ)	13,014
4. Gila River (AZ)	11,251
5. Osage (OK)	9,920
6. San Carlos (AZ)	9,901
7. Rosebud (SD)	9,809
8. Tohono O'oodham (AZ)	9,278
9. Blackfeet (MT)	9,149
10. Flathead (MT)	9,138

Tribes

1. Navajo	286,731
2. Cherokee	284,247
3. Ojibwa/Chippewa	112,757
4. Sioux	112,176
5. Choctaw	103,916
6. Apache	63,193
7. Lumbee	62,306
8. Pueblo	49,695
9. Creek	48,352
10. Iroquois	40,570

Cities

1. New York City	111,749
2. Los Angeles	54,236
3. Phoenix	43,724
4. Oklahoma City	36,572
5. Anchorage	36,062
6. Tulsa	35,990
7. Albuquerque	32,571
8. Chicago	26,933
9. Houston	25,521
10. San Antonio	20,137

Source: 2010 Census in Norris, Vines, and Hoeffel 2012; Tables 4, 6, 7

American Indian Identity

Today, American Indian identity occurs on two levels: macro and micro. At the macro level is the recognition of tribes; at the micro level is how individuals view themselves as American Indian and how this perception is recognized.

6-5 Put into your own words the macro and micro levels of American Indian identity.

Sovereignty

Sovereignty in this context refers to tribal self-rule. Supported by every U.S. president since the 1960s, sovereignty is recognition that tribes have vibrant economic and cultural lives. At the same time, numerous legal cases, including many at the Supreme Court level,

6-5

continue to clarify to what extent a recognized tribe may rule itself and to what degree it is subject to state and federal laws. In 2004, the U.S. Supreme Court ruled 7–2 in *United States v. Lara* that a tribe has the inherent right to prosecute all American Indians, regardless of affiliation, for crimes that occur on the reservation. However, other cases in lower courts continue to chip away at tribal self-government.

This legal relationship can be quite complex. For example, tribal members always pay federal income, Social Security, unemployment, and property taxes but do not pay state income tax if they live and work only on the reservation. Whether tribal members on reservations pay sales, gasoline, cigarette, or motor vehicle taxes has been negotiated on a reservation-by-reservation basis in many states.

Focused on the tribal group, sovereignty remains linked to both the actions of the federal government and the actions of individual American Indians. The government ultimately determines which tribes are recognized, and although tribal groups may argue publicly for their recognition, self-declaration carries no legal recognition. This has always been an issue, but given the rise of casino gambling (discussed shortly), the determination of who constitutes a sovereign tribe and who does not may carry significant economic benefits.

A most significant step resolving sovereignty was taken in 1971 with the passage of the Alaska Native Claims Settlement Act (ANCSA). The indigenous people gave up their collective claims in exchange for 62.5 million dollars and 44 million acres. In addition, new for-profit corporations owned by Alaska Natives, which included large expanses of land with 12 regional associations and over 200 villages, were also established. There was a great deal of debate among the indigenous people but, in the end, this was felt to be the best deal possible given to growing pressure to access valuable resources such as minerals and oil and, importantly, unlike tribal peoples in the lower 48, there were no treaties to govern any settlement. In the more than 40 years since ANCSA, economic progress remains uneven and many issues are unresolved. The act did not address, for example, Native hunting and fishing rights, nor did it address the question of Native government (Native Federation 2011; Huhndorf and Huhndorf 2011).

The federal government takes this gatekeeping role of sovereignty very seriously—the irony of the conquering people determining who are "Indians" in the continental United States is not lost on many tribal activists. In 1978, the Department of the Interior established what it called the *acknowledgment process* to decide whether any more tribes should have a government-to-government relationship. They must show that they were a distinct group and trace continuity since 1900 (Light and Rand 2007).

This is not easy to accomplish as we see in the Research Focus, where we consider the efforts of a tribe of Native Americans on Long Island, New York, seeking official recognition.

Individual Identity

Most people reflect on their ancestry to find roots or to self-identify themselves. For an individual who perceives himself or herself to be an American Indian, the process is defined by legalistic language. Recognized tribes establish a standard of ancestry, or what some tribes call "blood quantum," to determine who is a tribal member or "enrolled," as on the "tribal rolls." Understandably, there is some ambivalence about this procedure because it applies some racial purity measures. Still, tribes see it as an important way to guard against potential "wannabes" (Fitzgerald 2008).

This process may lead some individuals or entire extended families to be disenrolled. For these people, who perceive themselves as worthy of recognition by a tribe but are denied this coveted "enrollment" status, disputes have resulted that are rarely resolved satisfactorily for all parties. This has occurred for generations but has become more contentious recently for tribes that profit from casino gambling and must determine who is entitled to share in any profits that could be distributed to those on tribal rolls (Russell 2011).

Research Focus

Sovereignty of the Shinnecock Nation

One does not think of American Indian tribes on Long Island outside of New York City. The typical person associates tribes with the West, but this ignores the many East Coast indigenous people, which were moved or pushed to make way for European settlers or wiped out by disease. In fact, in 1643 there were 13 different settlements or bands of the Algonquin tribe collectively numbering in the hundreds living on Long Island, or *Paumanok*—"land of tribute."

While area newspapers throughout the nineteenth century would frequently feature the death of a Long Island American Indian as "the last one," only to repeat the statement a decade later with the passing of another, remnants of the Algonquin bands lived on, although not necessarily on Long Island. During the 1800s, the area clans freely intermarried with African Americans, giving the Native people today a decidedly biracial physical appearance. But for some outsiders, this only seemed to undercut their claim to Native American identity because it did not conform to the Hollywood image, much less official recognition as a sovereign American Indian nation.

The largest band present on Long Island today is the Shinnecock Nation, which has maintained an 800-acre reservation with about 600 living in 200 homes since shortly after World War II. Another 1,100 Shinnecock live elsewhere. The area is just outside the very affluent town of South Hampton where single-family homes sell for $30 million. The typical Shinnecock household, in contrast, has a median household income of under $15,000. The Shinnecock have long fought for federal recognition as a tribe as well as adjoining land they argue was wrongfully taken from them. Sit-ins blocking bulldozers followed by court action have been taken to

prevent unlawful annexing of Shinnecock lands as recently as 1997.

An even more significant modern day victory came in 2010 when the Obama administration ended the 32-year political battle for recognition by approving the tribe's petition, making it the 565th federally recognized tribe. Sovereignty officially granted is hardly automatic. At the same time six other tribes were denied recognition. Now the Shinnecock Nation looks ahead to the future.

The key to the economic viability of the Shinnecock people does not to lie in the tradition of three hundred years ago of whaling and jewelry making from seashells. Nor can it rest even on the contemporary annual Labor Day weekend powwow held to attract visitors for nearly 70 years.

Rather, it lies in the very twenty-first century answer of casino gambling. With nearly three million people on Long Island and another eight million in New York City just a train ride away, it is difficult not to embrace the economics of a casino. The tribe has made no decision on whether to seek to build on their land or to seek permission to build one somewhere nearby on Long Island. Feelings run high about the issue, which came to a recent dramatic turn when the tribe's office trailer housing their fledging gaming authority was destroyed in a 2013 fire that the FBI termed suspicious for fire.

The path to federal recognition may be complete but the road to self-sufficiency is still paved with many obstacles.

Sources: Applebome 2010; Buetner 2009; Hakim 2010; Richmond Hill Historical Society 2013; Shinnecock Nation 2013; Strong 1998; Vecsey 2013.

Native Americans Today

The United States has taken most of the land originally occupied by or deeded to Native Americans, restricted their movement, unilaterally severed agreements, created a special legal status for them, and, after World War II, attempted to move them again. As a result of these efforts and generally poor economic conditions of most reservations, substantial numbers of Native Americans live in the nation's most populated urban areas. In Table 6.4, we provide some broad comparisons between the First Americans and the general population of the 50 states.

How are Native Americans treated today? A very public insult is the continuing use of American Indian names as mascots for athletic teams, including high schools, colleges, and many professional sports teams in the United States. Almost all American Indian organizations, including AIM, have brought attention to the insulting use of Native Americans as the mascots of sports teams, such as the Washington Redskins, and to such spectator practices as the "Tomahawk chop" associated with the Atlanta Braves baseball team.

Many sports fans and college alumni find it difficult to understand why Native Americans take offense at a name such as "Braves" or even "Redskins" if it is meant to represent a team about which they have positive feelings. For Native Americans, however, the use of such mascots trivializes their past and their presence today. This at best

6-6 Summarize the special challenges Native Americans face today in regards to economic development, education, healthcare, and the environment.

TABLE 6.4
A Snapshot: Native Americans

	Total Population	Native Americans
Average Family Size	3.17	3.62
Never Married	34.2%	44.2%
High School Graduates	85.0	76.6
College Graduates	27.9	13.0
Veterans	9.9	9.3
Born in United States	85.9%	93.0%
Unemployment Rate (2010)	5.1	12.9
Median Household Income	$51,914	$36,779
Families below Poverty Level	10.1%	22.1%

Source: American Community Survey 2006–2010 American Indian and Alaska Native Tables DP02 and DP03 in Bureau of Census 2012f.

puzzles if not infuriates most Native people, who already face several challenges today. The National Collegiate Athletic Association (NCAA), which oversees college athletics, has asked colleges to "explain" their use of mascot names, nicknames, or logos such as savages, braves, warriors, chieftains, redmen, and Indians, to name a few. In some cases, the NCAA has already banned the appearance of students dressed as such mascots in tournaments. Typically, college alumni and most students wonder what the fuss is about, while most Native people question why they should be so "honored" if they don't want to be (NCAA 2003a, 2003b; Wieberg 2006).

Any discussion of Native American socioeconomic status today must begin with emphasizing the diversity of the people. Besides the variety of tribal heritages already noted, the contemporary Native American population is split between those on and off reservations and those who live in small towns or central cities. Life in these contrasting social environments is quite different, but enough similarities exist to warrant some broad generalizations on the status of Native Americans in the United States.

The sections that follow summarize the status of contemporary Native Americans in economic development, education, healthcare, religious and spiritual expression, and the environment.

Economic Development

Native Americans are an impoverished people. Even to the most casual observer of a reservation, poverty is a living reality, not merely numbers and percentages. Some visitors seem unconcerned, arguing that because Native Americans are used to hardship and lived a simple life before the Europeans arrived, poverty is a familiar and traditional way of life. In an absolute sense of dollars earned or quality of housing, Native Americans are no worse off now. But in a relative sense that compares their position with that of non-Indians, they are dismally behind on all standards of income and occupational status. Bureau of Indian Affairs (2005) surveys show that overall unemployment is about 50 percent.

Given the lower incomes and higher poverty rates, it is not surprising that the occupational distribution of Native Americans is similarly bleak. Those who are employed are less likely to be managers, professionals, technicians, salespeople, or administrators. This pattern of low-wage employment is typical of many racial and ethnic minorities in the United States, but Native Americans differ in three areas: their roles in tourism, casino gambling, and government employment.

Tourism Tourism is an important source of employment for many reservation residents, who either serve the needs of visitors directly or sell souvenirs and craft items. Generally, such enterprises do not achieve the kind of success that improves the tribal economy significantly. Even if they did, sociologist Murray Wax (1971:69) argued, "It requires a special type of person to tolerate exposing himself and his family life to the gaze of tourists, who are often boorish and sometimes offensively condescending in their attitudes."

Tourism, in light of exploitation of tribal people, is a complex interaction of the outside with Native Americans. Interviews with tourists visiting museums and reservations found that, regardless of the presentation, many visitors interpreted their brief experiences to be consistent with their previously held stereotypes of and prejudices toward Native Americans. Yet, at the other extreme, some contemporary tourists conscious of the historical context are uncomfortable taking in Native foods and purchasing crafts at tribal settlements despite the large economic need many reservations have for such commerce (Laxson 1991; Padget 2004).

Craftwork rarely produces the profits that most Native Americans desire and need. The trading-post business has also taken its toll on Native American cultures. Many non-Indian craft workers have produced the items tourists want. Creativity and authenticity often are replaced by mechanical duplication of "genuine Indian" curios. Concern and controversy continue to surround art such as paintings and pottery that may not be produced by real Native Americans. In 1935, the federal government began to officially promote tribal arts. The influx of fraudulent crafts was so great that Congress added to its responsibilities the Indian Arts and Crafts Act in 1990, which severely punishes anyone who offers to sell an object as produced by a Native American artisan when it was not. The price of both economic and cultural survival is very high (Indian Arts and Crafts Board 2013).

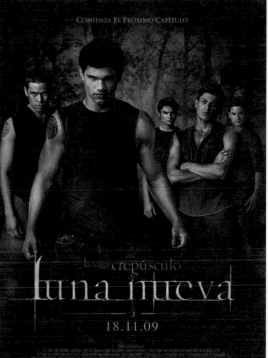

Shown here is the Spanish language version of a poster for *New Moon* released in 2009 as a part of the Twilight series. Perhaps one of the strangest tourist developments has been people trying to experience the book and movie series by seeking out the Quileute Nation in Washington State. Numbering only 750, this tribe is the subject of the fictionalized account of Native Americans who shapeshift into wolves as enemies of vampires. Tourists receive a hospitable welcome from tribal members who show off their picturesque rainforest location and a museum exhibit called "The Real Wolves of the Quileute."

Casino Gambling   A recent source of significant income and some employment has been the introduction of gambling on reservations. Some forms of gambling, originally part of tribal ceremonies or celebrations, existed long before Europeans arrived in the Western hemisphere. Today, however, commercial gambling is the only viable source of employment and revenue available to many tribes.

Under the 1988 Indian Gaming Regulatory Act, states must negotiate gambling agreements with reservations and cannot prohibit any gambling already allowed under state law. By 2011, 242 tribal governments in 28 states were operating a variety of gambling operations, including off-track betting, casino tables such as blackjack and roulette, lotteries, sports betting, video games of chance, telephone betting, slot machines, and high-stakes bingo. The gamblers, almost all non–Native Americans, sometimes travel long distances for the opportunity to wager money. The actual casinos are a form of tribal government enterprise as opposed to private business operations.

The economic impact on some reservations has been enormous, and nationwide receipts amounted to $27.4 billion in 2011 from reservation casino operations—more than Las Vegas and Atlantic City combined. However, the wealth is uneven: About two-thirds of the recognized Indian tribes have no gambling ventures. A few successful casinos have led to staggering windfalls, but reliance on a single industry can prove deadly as in the recent recession when the gaming industry in general, and on reservations, took a major hit. Recently, expansion of gambling outlets, mostly non-tribal, including on the Internet, have led to no growth in receipts on virtually all reservation gaming operations for the first time in 25 years (Meister 2013, T. Williams 2012c).

The more typical picture is of moderately successful gambling operations associated with tribes whose social and economic needs are overwhelming. Tribes that have

6-6

opened casinos have experienced drops in unemployment and increases in household income not seen on nongaming reservations. However, three important factors must be considered:

1. The tribes do pay taxes. They pay $10 billion in gambling-generated taxes to local, state, and federal governments. That still leaves significant profits that can be paid to tribal members or reinvested in collective tribal operations.

2. Nationwide, the economic and social impact of this revenue is limited. The tribes that make substantial revenue from gambling are a small fraction of Native American people.

3. Even on the reservations that benefit from gambling enterprises, the levels of unemployment are substantially higher and the family income significantly lower than for the nation as a whole (Bartlett and Steele 2002; Katel 2006:365; Meister 2013; National Indian Gaming Association 2006; Sahagun 2004; Taylor and Kalt 2005).

Criticism is not hard to find, even among Native Americans, some of whom oppose gambling on moral grounds and because it is marketed in a form that is incompatible with Native American cultures. Opponents are concerned about the appearance of compulsive gambling among some tribal members. The majority of the gamblers are not Native Americans, and almost all of the reservation casinos, though owned by the tribes, are operated by non-Indian-owned businesses. Some tribal members feel that the casinos trivialize and cheapen their heritage. The issue of who shares in gambling profits also has led to heated debates in some tribal communities about who is a member of the tribe. In addition, established White gaming interests lobby Congress to restrict the tribes, which account for about 44 percent of total casino gaming revenue, so they do not compete with nonreservation casinos (Toensing 2011).

Native Americans' voting clout is very weak, even compared to that of African Americans and Latinos, but their lobbying power has become significant. Casino money fueled the 2006 scandal involving lobbyist Jack Abramoff, who cheated several tribes by pretending to lobby on their behalf. Although many of the political donations Native Americans make are aimed at protecting reservation casinos, tribes' political agendas include obtaining federal grants for education, roads, housing, and other projects. By the 2007–2008 election cycle, tribes with casinos accounted for four of the top donors nationwide (Capriccioso 2011b).

Although income from gambling has not dramatically changed the lifestyle of most Native Americans, it has been a magnet of criticism from outsiders. Critics question the special status afforded to Native Americans and contend that the playing field should be even. Tribal members certainly would endorse this view because most government policies over the last 200 years placed tribes at a major disadvantage. Attention is drawn to some tribes that made contributions to politicians involved in policies concerning gambling laws. Although some contributions may have been illegal, the national media attention was far more intense than was warranted in the messy area of campaign financing. In 2012, tribes made over $3.25 million in contributions to the presidential campaigns—ten times that just four years earlier. It is another example of how the notion that Native Americans are now playing the White man's game of capitalism "too well" becomes big news (Gold and Tanfani 2012).

We have examined sources of economic development such as tourism and legalized gambling, but the dominant feature of reservation life is, nevertheless, unemployment. A government report issued by the Full Employment Action Council opened with the statement that such words as *severe, massive,* and *horrendous* are appropriate to describe unemployment among Native Americans. Official unemployment figures for reservations range from 23 to 90 percent. It is little wonder that census data released in 2010 showed that the poorest county in the nation was wholly on tribal lands: Ziebach County, South Dakota, of the Cheyenne River Reservation, had a 62 percent poverty rate. Two of the other poorest six were defined by the Pine Ridge and Rosebud Reservations. The other poor counties were either in the devastated Gulf Coast area or defined largely by a prison facility (Joseph 2010).

The economic outlook for Native Americans need not be bleak. A single program is not the solution; the diversity of Native Americans and their problems demands a multifaceted approach. The solutions need not be unduly expensive; indeed, because the Native American population is very small compared with the total population, programs with major influence may be financed without significant federal expenditures. Murray Wax (1971) observed that reformers viewing the economically depressed position of Native Americans often seize on education as the key to success. As the next section shows, improving educational programs for Native Americans would be a good place to start.

Education

Government involvement in the education of Native Americans dates as far back as a 1794 treaty with the Oneida Indians. In the 1840s, the federal government and missionary groups combined to start the first school for American Indians. By 1860, the government was operating schools that were free of missionary involvement. Today, laws prohibit federal funds for Native American education from going to sectarian schools. Also, since the passage of the Johnson-O'Malley Act in 1934, the federal government has reimbursed public school districts that include Native American children.

Federal control of the education of Native American children has had mixed results from the beginning. Several tribes started their own school systems at the beginning of the nineteenth century, financing the schools themselves. The Cherokee tribe developed an extensive school system that taught both English and Cherokee, the latter using an alphabet developed by the famed leader Sequoyah. Literacy for the Cherokees was estimated by the mid-1800s at 90 percent, and they even published a bilingual newspaper. The Creek, Chickasaw, and Seminole also maintained school systems. But by the end of the nineteenth century, all these schools had been closed by federal order. Not until the 1930s did the federal government become committed to ensuring an education for Native American children. Despite the push for educational participation, by 1948 only one-quarter of the children on the Navajo reservation, the nation's largest, were attending school (Pewewardy 1998).

A serious problem in Native American education has been the unusually low level of enrollment. Nationwide, about 15 percent of 16- to 24-year-old Native Americans were high school dropouts compared to 6.4 among Whites of a similar age. The term *dropout* is misleading because many tribal American schoolchildren have found their educational experience so hostile that they have no choice but to leave. In 2005, the South Dakota Supreme Court ruled that a school serving the Lakota Sioux tribe was routinely calling in the police to deal with the slightest misbehavior. The youth soon developed a juvenile record leading to what was termed a "school-to-discipline pipeline" (Dell'Angela 2005; DeVoe, Darling-Church, and Snyde 2008).

Rosalie Wax (1967) conducted a detailed study of the education among the Sioux on the Pine Ridge Reservation of South Dakota. She concluded that terms such as **kickout** or **pushout** are more appropriate than *dropout*. The children are not so much hostile toward school as they are set apart from it; they are socialized by their parents to be independent and not to embarrass their peers, but teachers reward docile acceptance and expect schoolchildren to correct one another in public. Socialization is not all that separates home from school. Teachers often are happy to find that Native American parents do not "interfere" with their job. Parents do not visit the school, and teachers avoid the homes, a pattern that furthers the isolation of school from home. This lack of interaction results partly from the predominance of non–Native American teachers, many of whom do not recognize the learning styles of American Indian students, although the situation is improving (Hilberg and Tharp 2002).

Do Native Americans need a curriculum that, at the very least, considers the unique aspects of their heritage? It is hoped things have changed since Charles Silberman (1971:173) visited a sixth-grade English class in a school on a Chippewa reservation. The students there were busy writing a composition for Thanksgiving: "Why We Are Happy the Pilgrims Came." Evidence of having Native cultures in the curriculum is uneven. Among teachers of eighth-graders, about one in four reports such presentations more than once a month in any subject among those attending schools that are at least one-fourth American (DeVoe, Darling-Church, and Snyde 2008).

This assimilationist view argues that to succeed in larger White-dominated society, it is important for Native Americans to start shedding the "old ways" as soon as possible. It is interesting that research done in the last ten years has questioned the assimilationist view, concluding that American Indian students can improve their academic performance through educational programs that are less assimilationist and use curricula that build on what the Native American youth learn in their homes and communities.

Representative of this growing research is the study completed by sociologist Angela A. A. Willeto among her fellow Navajo tribal people. She studied a random sample of 451 Navajo high school students from 11 different Navajo Nation schools. She examined the impact of the students' orientation toward traditional Navajo culture on their performance. The prevailing view has been that all that is inherently Navajo in a child must be eliminated and replaced with mainstream White society beliefs and lifestyles.

The Navajo tradition was measured by a number of indicators, such as participating in Navajo dances, consulting a medicine man, entering a sweat bath to cleanse oneself spiritually, weaving rugs, living in a traditional hogan, and using the Navajo language. School performance was measured by grades, commitment to school, and aspirations to attend college. Willeto found that the students who lived a more traditional life among the Navajo succeeded in school just as well and were just as committed to success in school and college as high schoolers leading a more assimilated life.

Today, the Navajo Nation's Department of Dine' Education promotes embracing the past. For example, in 2012, Barboncito held a competition with students reading an 1868 speech. In his speech, the Navajo leader spoke boldly to General Tecumseh Sherman, whom President Andrew Johnson had dispatched to secure the Navajo's agreement to a treaty. Students were invited to write an essay or prepare a painting that indicated what the speech meant to them in 2012.

These results are important because even many Native Americans themselves accept an assimilationist view. Even within the Navajo Nation, where Navajo language instruction has been mandated in all reservation schools since 1984, many Navajos still equate learning only with the mastery of White society's subject matter (Department of Dine' Education 2012; Willeto 1999, 2007).

The picture for Native Americans in higher education is decidedly mixed, with some progress and some promise. Enrollment in college increased steadily from the mid-1970s through the beginning of the twenty-first century, but degree completion, especially the completion of professional degrees, may be declining. The economic and educational backgrounds of Native American students, especially reservation residents, make the prospect of entering a predominantly White college very difficult. Native American students may soon feel isolated and discouraged, particularly if the college does not help them understand the alien world of American-style higher education. Even at campuses with large numbers of Native Americans in their student bodies, only a few Native American faculty members or advisors are present to serve as role models.

Another encouraging development in higher education in recent years has been the creation of tribally controlled colleges, usually two-year community colleges. The Navajo Community College (now called Diné College), the first such institution, was established in 1968, and by 2012 there were 37 tribal colleges in 14 states, with more than 16,000 students enrolled. Besides serving in some rural areas as the only educational institution for many miles, these colleges also provide services such as counseling and childcare. Tribal colleges enable students to maintain their cultural identity while training them to succeed, which means helping with job placement—a major challenge given the economic situation that most tribal colleges find in their immediate vicinity (American Indian Higher Education Consortium 2012; González 2012).

At higher levels, Native Americans largely disappear from the educational scene. In 2009, of the over 50,000 doctorates awarded to U.S. citizens, 332 went to Native Americans, compared with over 16,000 that went to citizens of foreign countries.

This achievement of doctorates among Native Americans has not changed significantly since at least as far back as 1981 (National Center for Educational Statistics 2012).

Healthcare

For Native Americans, *healthcare* is a misnomer, another broken promise in the long line of unmet pledges the government has made. Compared to other groups, Native Americans are more likely to have poorer health and unmet medical needs and not be able to afford healthcare. They more likely have higher levels of diabetes, trouble hearing, and activity limitations and have experienced serious psychological distress. As of 2012, about 28 percent lacked health insurance coverage compared to 15 percent for the nation as a whole (Bureau of the Census 2013d; Frieden 2011).

In 1955, amidst criticism even then, the responsibility for healthcare through the Indian Health Service (IHS) transferred from the BIA to the Public Health Service. Although the health of Native Americans has improved markedly in absolute terms since the mid-1960s, their overall health is comparatively far behind all other segments of the population. With a new administration in 2009, yet another call was made for overhauling healthcare provided to Native Americans. With the pressure toward Native Americans to assimilate in all aspects of their lives, there has been little willingness to recognize their traditions of healing and treating illnesses. Native treatments tend to be noninvasive, with the patient encouraged to contribute actively to the healing benefits and prevent future recurrence. In the 1990s, a pluralistic effort was slowly emerging to recognize alternative forms of medicine, including those practiced by Native Americans. In addition, reservation healthcare workers began to accommodate traditional belief systems as they administered the White culture's medicine (Belluck 2009).

Contributing to the problems of healthcare and mortality on reservations are often high rates of crime, not all of which is reported. For tribal people along the Mexico–U.S. border, the rising amount and associated violence in the drug trade have only furthered their vulnerability. Poverty and few job opportunities offer a fertile environment for the growth of youth gangs and drug trafficking. All the issues associated with crime can be found on the nation's reservations. As with other minority communities dealing with poverty, Native Americans strongly support law enforcement but at the same time contend that the very individuals selected to protect them are abusing their people. As with efforts for improving healthcare, the isolation and vastness of some of the reservations make them uniquely vulnerable to crime (Eckholm 2010).

Religious and Spiritual Expression

Like other aspects of Native American cultures, religious expression is diverse, reflecting the variety of tribal traditions and the assimilationist pressure of the Europeans. Initially, missionaries and settlers expected Native Americans simply to forsake their traditions for European Christianity, and, as was the case in the repression of the Ghost Dance, sometimes force was used. Today, many Protestant churches and Roman Catholic parishes with large tribal congregations incorporate customs such as the sacred pipe ceremony, native incenses, sweat lodges, ceremonies affirming care for the Earth, and services and hymns in native languages.

6-7 Discuss how religion and spirituality are expressed.

Whether traditional in nature or reflecting the impact of Europeans, Native people typically embrace a broad world of spirituality. Whereas Christians, Jews, and Muslims adhere to a single deity and often confine spiritual expression to designated sites, traditional American Indian people see considerably more relevance in the whole of the world, including animals, water, and the wind.

After generations of formal and informal pressure to adopt Christian faiths and their rituals, in 1978, Congress enacted the American Indian Religious Freedom Act, which declares that it is the government's policy to "protect and preserve the inherent right of American Indians to believe, express, and practice their traditional religions." However, the act contains no penalties or enforcement mechanisms. For this reason, Hopi leader

6-8

Vernon Masayesva (1994:93) calls it "the law with no teeth." Therefore, Native Americans are lobbying to strengthen this 1978 legislation. They are seeking protection for religious worship services for military personnel and incarcerated Native Americans, as well as better access to religious relics, such as eagle feathers, and better safeguards against the exploitation of sacred lands (Deloria 1992; Garroutte 2009).

A major spiritual concern is the stockpiling of Native American relics, including burial remains. Contemporary Native Americans are increasingly seeking the return of their ancestors' remains and artifacts, a demand that alarms museums and archeologists. The Native American Graves Protection and Repatriation Act of 1990 requires an inventory of such collections and provides for the return of materials if a claim can be substantiated. In 2010, this was revised to cover all Native American remains—even those without identified ties to a tribe (J. Smith 2011).

In recent years, significant publicity has been given to a Native American expression of religion: the ritual use of peyote, which dates back thousands of years. The sacramental use of peyote was first noted by Europeans in the 1640s. In 1918, the religious use of peyote, a plant that creates mild psychedelic effects, was organized as the Native American Church (NAC). At first a Southwest-based religion, since World War II, the NAC has spread among northern tribes. The use of the substance is a small part of a long and moving ritual. The exact nature of NAC rituals varies widely. Clearly, the church maintains the tradition of ritual curing and seeking individual visions. However, practitioners also embrace elements of Christianity, representing a type of religious pluralism of Indian and European identities.

Peyote is a hallucinogen, however, and federal and state governments have been concerned about its use by NAC members. Several states passed laws in the 1920s and 1930s prohibiting the use of peyote. In the 1980s, several court cases involved the prosecution of Native Americans who were using peyote for religious purposes. Finally, in 1994, Congress amended the American Indian Religious Freedom Act to allow Native Americans the right to use, transport, and possess peyote for religious purposes (J. Martin 2001).

Today's Native Americans are asking that their traditions be recognized as an expression of pluralist rather than assimilationist coexistence. These traditions also are closely tied to religion. The sacred sites of Native Americans, as well as their religious practices, have been under attack. In the next section, we focus on aspects of environmental disputes that are anchored in the spiritualism of Native Americans (Kinzer 2000; Mihesuah 2000).

Environment

6-8 Analyze how environmental issues impact Native Americans.

Environmental issues bring together many of the concerns we have previously considered for Native Americans: stereotyping, land rights, environmental justice, economic development, and spiritualism.

First, in some of today's environmental literature, we can find stereotypes of Native peoples as the last defense against the encroachment of "civilization." This image trivializes native cultures, making them into what one author called a "New Age savage" (Waller 1996).

Second, many environmental issues are rooted in continuing land disputes arising from treaties and agreements more than a century old. Reservations contain a wealth of natural resources and scenic beauty. In the past, Native Americans often lacked the technical knowledge to negotiate beneficial agreements with private corporations—and even when they had this ability, the federal government often stepped in and made the final agreements more beneficial to the non–Native Americans than to the residents of the reservations. The Native peoples have always been rooted in their land. It was their land that was the first source of tension and conflict with the Europeans. At the beginning of the twenty-first century, it is no surprise that land and the natural resources it holds continue to be major concerns. This does not mean that tribal governments are not willing to embrace new technologies. For example, some Plains American Indian tribes are starting to create wind farms that not only provide power for their own needs but also even allow them to sell extra power (Standen 2010).

Third, environmental issues reinforce the tendency to treat the first inhabitants of the Americas as inferior. This is manifested in **environmental justice**—a term introduced in Chapter 3 to describe efforts to ensure that hazardous substances are controlled so that all communities receive protection regardless of race or socioeconomic circumstances. Reservation representatives often express concern about how their lands are used as dumping grounds. For example, the Navajo reservation is home to hundreds of abandoned uranium mines—some are still contaminated. After legal action, the federal government finally provided assistance in 2000 to Navajos who had worked in the mines and showed ill effects from radiation exposure. Although compensation has been less than was felt necessary, the Navajos continue to monitor closely new proposals to use their land. Few reservations have escaped negative environmental impact, and some observers contend that Native American lands are targeted for nuclear waste storage. Critics see this as a de facto policy of nuclear colonialism, whereby reservations are forced to accept all the hazards of nuclear energy, but the Native American people have seen few of its benefits (Macmillan 2012).

The Hualapai (WALL-uh-pie) in the remote Grand Canyon area outside the National Park have long suffered extreme economic poverty. In an effort to overcome this, they commissioned to build this bridge for tourists over the canyon wall offering an amazing view. However, to some observers, it represents an assault on the environment. In response, Native Americans say they should be able to take advantage of the land at times, just like the White man has for centuries.

Fourth, environmental concerns by American Indians often are balanced against economic development needs, just as they are in the larger society. On some reservations, authorizing timber companies access to hardwood forests led to conflicted feelings among American Indians. However, such arrangements often are the only realistic source of needed revenue, even if they mean entering into arrangements that more affluent people would never consider. The Skull Valley Goshute tribe of Utah has tried to attract a nuclear waste dump over state government objections. Eventually, the federal government rejected the tribe's plans. Even on the Navajo reservation, a proposed new uranium mine has its supporters—those who consider the promises of royalty payments coupled with alleged safety measures sufficient to offset the past half-century of radiation problems (Pasternak 2010).

Fifth, spiritual needs must be balanced against demands on the environment. For example, numerous sacred sites lie in such public areas as the Grand Canyon, Zion, and Canyonlands National Parks that, though not publicized, are accessible to outsiders. Tribal groups have in vain sought to restrict entry to such sites. The San Carlos Apaches unsuccessfully tried to block the University of Arizona from erecting an observatory on their sacred Mt. Graham. Similarly, Plains Indians have sought to ban tourists from climbing Devil's Tower, long the site of religious visions, where prayer bundles of tobacco and sage were left behind by Native peoples (Campbell 2008; Martin 2001).

Conclusion

Native Americans have to choose between assimilating to the dominant non-Indian culture and maintaining their identity. In the accompanying figure, we revisit the Spectrum of Intergroup Relations as it relates to Native Americans. Recently, some pluralism is evident, but the desire to improve themselves economically usually drives Native Americans toward assimilation.

Are Native Americans now receiving respect? The controversy over team mascots strikes many sports fans and others as "much ado about nothing." But consider closer the case of the NFL team in the nation's capital. The historical derivation of redskin is not just to skin that is red but also to the practice in the nineteenth century of some local governments of paying bounties for dead American

SPECTRUM OF INTERGROUP RELATIONS

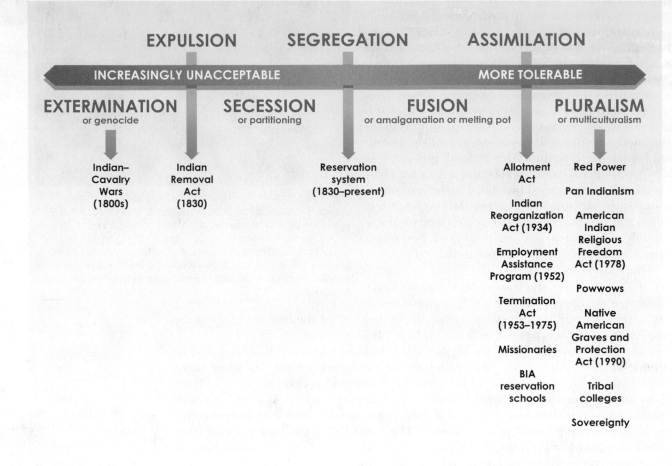

Indians with requesting the "hunters" to present "redskins." The use of Redskins for Washington's professional team dates back to 1937 and was not intended as a slur. Nonetheless, for many American Indians, including the many football fans, it is hateful to see a team so named. Court efforts to remove the offending trademark have failed, saying the Native American plaintiffs waited too long to file the case. But with the start of every football season, the calls to change the Redskins name is renewed (Belson 2013).

Maintaining one's tribal identity outside a reservation is not easy. One's cultural heritage must be consciously sought out while under the pressure to assimilate. Even on a reservation, it is not easy to integrate being Native American with elements of contemporary society. The dominant society needs innovative approaches to facilitate pluralism.

The reservations are economically depressed, but they also are the home of the Native American people spiritually and ideologically, if not always physically. Furthermore, the reservation isolation means that the frustrations of reservation life and the violent outbursts regarding those frustrations do not alarm large numbers of Whites, as do disturbances in urban centers. Native

Americans today, except in motion pictures, are out of sight and out of mind. Since the BIA's creation in 1824, the federal government has had much greater control over Native Americans than over any other civilian group in the nation. For Native Americans, the federal government and White people are synonymous. However, the typical non-Indian tends to be more sympathetic, if not paternalistic, toward Native Americans than toward African Americans.

Subordinate groups in the United States, including Native Americans, have made tremendous gains and will continue to do so in the years to come. But the rest of the population is not standing still. As Native American income rises, so does White income. As Native American children stay in school longer, so do White children. American Indian healthcare improves, but so does White healthcare. Advances have been made, but the gap remains between the descendants of the first Americans and those of later arrivals. Low incomes, inadequate education, and poor healthcare spurred relations between Native Americans and non-Indians to take a dramatic turn in the 1960s and 1970s, when Native Americans demanded a better life in America.

As the next chapter will show, African Americans have achieved a measure of recognition in Washington, DC, that Native Americans have not. Only 5 percent as numerous as the Black population, Native Americans have a weaker collective voice, even with casino money fueling lobbying efforts. Only a handful of Native Americans have ever served in Congress, and many of the non-Indians representing states with large numbers of Native Americans have emerged as their biggest foes rather than their advocates.

The greatest challenge to and asset of the descendants of the first Americans is their land. More than 120 years after the Allotment Act, Native American peoples are still seeking what they feel is theirs. The land they still possess, although only a small slice of what they once occupied, is an important asset. It is barren and largely unproductive agriculturally, but some of it is unspoiled and rich in natural resources. It is no wonder that many large businesses, land developers, environmentalists, and casino managers covet Native American land for their own purposes. For Native Americans, the land they still occupy, as well as much of that occupied by other Americans, represents their roots, their homeland.

One Thanksgiving Day, a scholar noted that, according to tradition, at the first Thanksgiving in 1621 the Pilgrims and the Wampanoag ate together. The descendants of these celebrants increasingly sit at distant tables with equally distant thoughts of equality. Today's Native Americans are the "most undernourished, most short-lived, least educated, least healthy." For them, "that long-ago Thanksgiving was not a milestone, not a promise. It was the last full meal" (Dorris 1988:A23).

Summary

1. Early European Americans usually did not intend to antagonize the Native peoples unnecessarily, but the needs of the settlers always ruled.

2. Policies created out of warfare and treaties such as the Allotment and Reorganization Acts reflected a treatment of tribal people inferior to that of the White Europeans.

3. Reservation life in the first half of the twentieth century was made even more difficult following outcomes in legal claims and the passage of the Termination Acts and the Employment Assistance Program.

4. Native Americans have consistently resisted mistreatment through their tribes and reservation organizations and collectively across boundaries through pan-Indian efforts.

5. American Indians' identity issues emerge today through sovereignty questions at the macro level and self-identification and tribal enrollment at the micro level.

6. Despite gains over the last couple of generations, Native Americans trail the rest of the country in economic development, educational levels, and access to quality healthcare.

7. Diversity of American Indian cultures is reflected in religious and spiritual expression.

8. Despite the loss of so much of their historical settlement areas, Native Americans struggle to achieve environmental justice

Key Terms

environmental justice p. 163

fish-ins p. 151

kickout or pushout p. 159

panethnicity p. 150

pan-Indianism p. 150

powwows p. 153

sovereignty p. 153

world systems theory p. 143

Review Questions

1. How have land rights been a continuing theme in White–Native American relations?

2. What was the motivation behind the Removal and Allotment Acts?

3. How have federal government policies influenced reservation life?

4. What steps in the last 50 years have tribal people collectively taken to improve their social situation?

5. How is American Indian identity determined?

6. Do casinos and other gaming outlets represent a positive force for Native American tribes today?

7. How would you describe Native American spirituality today?

8. What is the relationship between Native Americans and the physical environment?

Critical Thinking

1. Consider Independence Day and Thanksgiving Day. How do these national holidays remind Native Americans today of their marginal status?

2. Chronicle how aspects of leisure time, from schoolyard games to Halloween costumes to team mascots, trivialize Native Americans. What experience have you had with such episodes, or what have you seen in the mass media?

3. Why do you think that many people in the United States hold more benevolent attitudes toward Native Americans than they do toward other subordinate groups such as African Americans and Latinos?

7 African Americans

7-1 Explain how slavery influences life today.

7-2 Address the challenge of Black leadership in the early twentieth century.

7-3 Discuss the reemergence of Black protest.

7-4 Summarize the outcome of the Civil Rights Movement.

7-5 Identify how urban areas in the 1960s and 1970s refocused Black–White relations.

7-6 Describe the special role religion has within the African American community.

7-7 Examine how recent immigration is adding to the Black community.

The past is always reflected in the present. Back in 1816, Joseph Gee, a large landowner from North Carolina, settled along with his 18 slaves in a bend of the Alabama River to establish a cotton plantation. After slaves were freed, the Black workers largely remained as sharecroppers and tenant farmers up through the 1930s. People in the Alabama community, now called Gee's Bend, became so impoverished, the Red Cross arrived to prevent starvation.

Across the river from overwhelmingly Black Gee's Bend sits the Wilcox county seat, virtually all-White Camden. In 1962, Camden, like several communities in the South, was the site of civil rights protests. Camden was just one example of a sundown town. **Sundown towns** are communities from which non-Whites were systematically excluded from living.

The protesters came from Gee's Bend. They came by ferry, about a ten-minute trip. The people of predominantly White Camden did not like the marchers, so the county closed down the ferry. For over three decades, the ferry remained closed, requiring the 400 residents of all-Black Gee's Bend to drive more than 80 miles each way to get to their jobs, schools, or the hospital. Finally, in 1996, the isolation ended when ferry service was reinstated.

Two residents noted the significance of this event. "This is the first time there has been a concerted effort on the part of Blacks and Whites to do something positive," said Perry Hale, a Black high school teacher. Newspaper publisher Hollis Curl, who is White, remarked, "It's hard for people in other parts of the country to realize what a coming together this has been" (Tyson 1996:4). Relationships between Whites and Blacks in the United States have been marked by many episodes like those along the Alabama River—sometimes those relationships take a step backward and occasionally a step forward.

The United States, with more than 42 million Blacks (or African Americans), has the eighth-largest Black population in the world; only Brazil and six countries in Africa have larger Black populations. Despite their large numbers, Blacks in this country have had virtually no role in major national and political decisions and, therefore, captured the world's attention when Barack Obama was elected the first Black President in 2008 (Rastogi et al. 2011).

To a significant degree, the history of African Americans is the history of the United States. Black people accompanied the first explorers, and a Black man was among the first to die in the American Revolution. The enslavement of Africans was responsible for the South's wealth in the nineteenth century and led to the country's most violent domestic strife. After Blacks were freed from slavery, their continued subordination led to sporadic outbreaks of violence in the rural South and throughout urban America. This chapter begins with a brief history of African Americans into the beginning of the twenty-first century and brings us to contemporary times.

The Black experience in what came to be the United States began with them having something less than citizenship, but their experience was only slightly better than slavery. In 1619, twenty Africans arrived in Jamestown as indentured servants. Their children were born free people. Blacks in the British colonies were not the first in the New World, however; some Blacks had accompanied European explorers, perhaps even Columbus. But this information is a historical footnote only. By the 1660s, the British colonies passed laws making Africans slaves for life, forbidding interracial marriages, and making children of slaves bear the status of their mother regardless of their father's race. Slavery had begun in North America. More than three and a half centuries later, we still live with its legacy.

Slavery

Explain how slavery influences life today.

Slavery seems far removed from the debates over issues that divide Whites and Blacks today. However, contemporary institutional and individual racism, which is central to today's conflicts, has its origins in the institution of slavery. Slavery was not merely a lone aspect of American society for three centuries; it has been an essential part of our country's life. For nearly half of this country's history, slavery was not only tolerated but also legally protected by the U.S. Constitution as interpreted by the U.S. Supreme Court.

In sharp contrast to the basic rights and privileges enjoyed by White Americans, Black people in bondage lived under a system of repression and terror. For several decades, nearly one out five people was Black and enslaved in the United States. Because the institution of slavery was so fundamental to our culture, it continues to influence Black–White relations in the twenty-first century.

7-1

Slave Codes

Slavery in the United States rested on five central conditions: slavery was for life, the status was inherited, slaves were considered mere property, slaves were denied rights, and coercion was used to maintain the system (Noel 1972). As slavery developed in colonial America and the United States, so did **slave codes**—laws that defined the low position of slaves in the United States. Although the rules varied from state to state and from time to time and were not always enforced, the more common features demonstrate how completely subjugated the Africans were:

1. A slave could not marry or even meet with a free Black.
2. Marriage between slaves was not legally recognized.
3. A slave could not legally buy or sell anything except by special arrangement.
4. A slave could not possess weapons or liquor.
5. A slave could not quarrel with or use abusive language toward Whites.
6. A slave could not possess property (including money) except as allowed by his or her owner.
7. A slave could neither make a will nor inherit anything.
8. A slave could not make a contract or hire him- or herself out.
9. A slave could not leave a plantation without a pass noting his or her destination and time of return.
10. No one, including Whites, was to teach a slave (in some areas, even a free Black) to read or write or to give a slave a book, including the Bible.
11. A slave could not gamble.
12. A slave had to obey established curfews.
13. A slave could not testify in court except against another slave.

Violations of these rules were dealt with in a variety of ways. Mutilation and branding were not unknown. Imprisonment was rare; most violators were whipped. An owner was largely immune from prosecution for any physical abuse of slaves. Because slaves could not testify in court, a White's actions toward enslaved African Americans were practically above the law (ACLU 1996; Elkins 1959; Franklin and Higginbotham 2011; Stampp 1956).

Slavery, as enforced through the slave codes, controlled and determined all facets of the lives of enslaved Africans. No exceptions were made for organization of family life and religious worship. Naturally, the Africans had brought their own cultural traditions to America. In Africa, they were accustomed to a closely regulated family life and a rigidly enforced moral code. Slavery rendered it impossible for them to retain family ties in the New World as kinfolk including their children were scattered among plantations.

Through the research of W. E. B. Du Bois and many others, we know that slave families had no standing in law. Marriages between slaves were not legally recognized, and masters rarely respected those unions when they sold adults or children. Slave breeding—a

7-1

For many generations, Africans were treated by their White slave owners as property, yet they tried to maintain a sense of family life. This 1862 image shows five generations of a family whose members were all born on a plantation in Beaufort, South Carolina.

deliberate effort to maximize the number of offspring—was practiced with little attention to the emotional needs of the slaves. The slaveholder, not the parents, decided at what age children would begin working in the fields. The slave family could not offer its children shelter or security, rewards or punishments. The man's only recognized family role was to sire offspring—be the sex partner of a woman. In fact, slave men often were identified as a slave woman's possession, for example, "Nancy's Tom." Southern law consistently ruled that "the father of a slave is unknown to our law." However, the male slave did occupy an important economic role: Men held almost all managerial positions open to slaves (Du Bois 1970; Dunaway 2003).

Equating Black Africans with slavery reinforced blackness as a race, an inferior race. This process of **racial formation** was introduced in Chapter 1. Racial formation is a sociohistorical process by which racial categories are created, inhabited, transformed, and destroyed. The stigmatization of Black Africans during slavery and continuing after its end underscores how people socially construct race. So deeply constructed was this racial formation that it took generations before White people even began to question it.

The Attack on Slavery

Although the slave was vulnerable to his or her owner's wishes, slavery as an institution was vulnerable to outside opinion. For a generation after the American Revolution, restrictions on slaves increased even as Southerners accepted slavery as permanent. Slave revolts and antislavery propaganda only accelerated the intensity of oppression the slaves endured. This increase in restrictions led to the ironic situation that as slavery was attacked from within and without, conditions for the slaves became harsher and its defenders became more outspoken in asserting what they saw as its benefits.

Antislavery advocates, or **abolitionists**, included Whites and free Blacks. Many Whites who opposed slavery, such as Abraham Lincoln, did not believe in racial equality. In their minds, even though slavery was a moral evil, racial equality was unimaginable. This inconsistency did not lessen the emotional fervor of the efforts to end slavery. Antislavery societies had been founded even before the American Revolution, but the Constitution dealt the antislavery movement a blow. To appease the South, the framers of the Constitution recognized and legitimized slavery's existence. The Constitution even allowed slavery to increase Southern political power. A slave was counted as three-fifths of a person in determining population representation in the House of Representatives.

Abolitionists, both Black and White, continued to speak out against slavery and the harm it was doing not only to the slaves but also to the entire nation, which had become economically dependent on bondage. Frederick Douglass and Sojourner Truth, both freed slaves, became very visible in the fight against slavery through their eloquent speeches and publications. Harriet Tubman, along with other Blacks and sympathetic Whites, developed the Underground Railroad to transport escaping slaves to freedom in the North and Canada (Franklin and Higginbotham 2011).

Another aspect of Black enslavement was the slaves' own resistance to servitude. Slaves did revolt, and between 40,000 and 100,000 escaped from the South and slavery. Yet fugitive slave acts provided for the return of slaves even though they had reached free states. Enslaved Blacks who did not attempt escape, in part because failure often led to death, resisted slavery through such means as passive resistance. Slaves feigned clumsiness or illness; pretended not to understand, see, or hear; slaves ridiculed Whites with a mocking, subtle humor that their owners did not comprehend; and slaves destroyed farm implements and committed similar acts of sabotage. The most dramatic form of resistance was to flee enforced servitude by escaping through the Underground Railroad that linked safe houses and paths to freedom in the North and Canada (Kimmons 2008; V. Williams 2008).

Slavery's Aftermath

On January 1, 1863, President Lincoln issued the Emancipation Proclamation. The document created hope in slaves in the South, but many Union soldiers resigned rather than participate in a struggle to free slaves. The proclamation freed slaves only in the Confederacy, over which the president had no control. Six months after the surrender of the Confederacy in 1865, abolition became law when the Thirteenth Amendment abolished slavery throughout the nation.

From 1867 to 1877, during the period called Reconstruction, Black–White relations in the South were unlike anything they had ever been. The Reconstruction Act of 1867 put each Southern state under a military governor until a new state constitution could be written, with Blacks participating fully in the process. Whites and Blacks married each other, went to public schools and state universities together, and rode side by side on trains and streetcars. The most conspicuous evidence of the new position of Blacks was their presence in elected office (Du Bois 1969b; Foner 2006).

Discrimination based on racism developed deep roots in the period following the Civil War, as Southern states enacted laws meant to keep former slaves and their descendants in a subordinate status. Through these laws, referred to colloquially as **Jim Crow**, segregation became entrenched in the South. The term Jim Crow appears to have originated in a dance tune; by the 1890s it was synonymous with segregation and the statutes that kept African Americans in an inferior position. There was nothing musical about Jim Crow as people took law in to their own hands lynching Black people who they suspected to doing some indiscretion or in some instances just to show others to "stay in their place." Jim Crow laws gave White people their ultimate authority. In 1896, the U.S. Supreme Court ruled in *Plessy v. Ferguson* that state laws requiring "separate but equal" accommodations for Blacks were a "reasonable" use of state governments' power. Although Jim Crow statutes were eventually overturned, new laws may have a similar impact in the twenty-first century, as we will see in the next section on institutional discrimination.

It was in the political sphere that Jim Crow exacted its price soonest. In 1898, the Court's decision in *Williams v. Mississippi* declared constitutional the use of poll taxes, literacy tests, and residential requirements to discourage Blacks from voting. In Louisiana that year, 130,000 Blacks were registered to vote. Eight years later, the number dropped to only 1,342. When all these measures failed to deprive every African American of the right to vote, White supremacists erected a final obstacle: the **White primary**, which forbade Black voting in election primaries. By the turn of the century, the South had a one-party system, making the primary the significant contest and the general election a mere rubber stamp. Beginning with South Carolina in 1896 and spreading to 12 other states within 20 years, statewide Democratic Party primaries were adopted. The party explicitly excluded Blacks from voting, an exclusion that was constitutional because the party was defined as a private organization that was free to define its own membership qualifications. The White primary brought an end to the political gains of Reconstruction (Lacy 1972; Lewinson 1965; Woodward 1974).

The United States is not the only country with White people as the socially dominant group and a significant Black population. In the United States, of course, this population grows out of the history of slavery, while as we see in A Global View, it arises out of colonialism in France.

7-1 🌐 A Global View

France Noire: Black France

Among the ways that subordinate-group status is created as we introduced in Chapter 1 are migration and colonialism. Both played a role in France's contemporary Black population, estimated at 2 to 5 million out of a population of over 60 million.

Historically, like most European nations, France maintained slavery in its colonies. In the spirit of the French Revolution, slavery was abolished in 1794. Napoleon briefly reintroduced it but it was definitively abolished in 1834. Given the traditions of liberty, equality, and fraternity, racial inequality was seen as incompatible. Until recently race was rarely mentioned publically and still it is illegal for the government to collect data about race.

For Black Americans, France has had special appeal as such notables as James Baldwin, Josephine Baker, Nina Simone, and Richard Wright found a welcoming atmosphere in the artistic neighborhoods of Paris. The contemporary Black population has its roots in post–World War II immigration from former colonies such as Algeria, Haiti, and elsewhere in Africa and the Caribbean. Despite the tradition of race not being a formal political issue, the French could not ignore injustices and began passing anti-discrimination and anti-racism laws in 1972. A 2007 national survey found that 56 percent of French Blacks had reported discrimination and over a third felt it was getting worse.

The fall of 2005 was a turning point as France, and much of the world, was shocked at extended rioting in neighborhoods throughout the country populated by youth of African descent, leading to a national state of emergency. Pre-existing tensions were ignited when two Black youth of Tunisian and Malian descent, thinking they were being chased by police, hid in a power station in suburban Paris only to be accidentally electrocuted. French-born young people burned thousands of cars, angry about discrimination, poverty, and unemployment. The events still simmer as in 2012 courts reopened an investigation into whether police failed to come to the aid of the youth.

Given the high cost of central Paris housing, most immigrants live in high-rise apartment complexes in the outer Paris suburbs or *banlieues*. However, so stigmatized have these suburban, isolated Black neighborhoods become as "lawless zones" or "outlaw estates" that *banlieues* have evolved into a meaning more of "ghettos." However, the advanced marginality of the French Blacks is a product of very different racial formation than that of the United States. People of color in France are a new form of exclusion linked to the modern-day degradation of unskilled labor. The *banlieue* population is not nearly as segregated as is typical of urban Black and Latino neighborhoods in the United States. Also, since housing in the *banlieues* is largely government controlled, the state plays a much more active role, good and bad, in the lives of Black French people than is typical in the United States.

Today much of the French Black population feels marginalized. French celebrations of Obama's election in 2008 evolved in the *banlieues* into more car burnings as young people saw the election of a Black president in America as underscoring their lack of mobility in France. However, in the national conversation, talk is less about promoting multiculturalism and more about restricting immigration. Underscoring this trend has been the success of the National Front (*Front national*) political party in its cries to deport unemployed immigrants and halting any immigration from former Black colonies of Africa. In spite of and in response to such developments, a more cohesive Black community is merging in France with spokespeople, organizations, conferences, and even an annual Black History month being promoted in February with special emphasis on the colonial roots of its Black citizens.

Sources: Browne 2013; Chrisafis 2012; *International Herald Tribune* 2007; Keaton, Sharpley-Whiting, and Stoval 2012; Kimmelman 2008; Mann 2008; Wacquant, 2007; Winant 2001.

Reflecting on Slavery Today

The legacy of slavery continues more than 150 years after its end in the United States. We can see it in the nation's Capitol and the White House, which were built with slave labor, but we can also see it in the enduring poverty that grips a large proportion of the descendants of slavery.

Insights into slavery emerge. For example, historian Craig Steven Wilder (2013) in his book *Ebony and Ivory* documents the role that the most elite universities played in contributing to slavery. While it also has been documented that private colleges readily accepted donations from those who profited from the slave trade or their own plantations, slaves were used on northern universities and owned by college presidents. Whatever may have been the abolitionist sentiment at the time, colleges frequently tolerated or even encouraged pro-slavery research and lectures. Episodes of antislavery faculty being released by institutions such as Harvard are not hard to document. Even as the Civil War drew near, Wilder grimly observes that the leading American colleges seemed caught in the past.

Serious discussions have taken place for more than 30 years about granting reparations for slavery. **Slavery reparation** refers to the act of making amends for the injustice of slavery. Few people would argue that slavery was wrong and continues to be wrong where it is still practiced in parts of the world. However, what form should reparations take? Since 1989, Congressman John Conyers, a Black Democrat from Detroit, has annually introduced in Congress a bill to acknowledge the "fundamental injustice and inhumanity of slavery" and that calls for the creation of a commission to examine the institution and to make recommendations on appropriate remedies. This bill has never made it out of committee, but the discussion continues outside the federal government. In 2009, Congress issued a joint resolution apologizing for slavery but it contained the specific "disclaimer" that nothing in the resolution authorized or supported any claim against the United States (Conyers 2013).

7-2

The year 2011 marked the sesquicentennial of the start of the Civil War. The United States still finds it difficult to come to terms with the power of slavery. Here, we see Confederate soldiers in a mock battle at a Civil War reenactment at a state park in Oregon.

From every direction, the historical and social significance of slavery has been marginalized. Just prior to the 150th anniversary of the Civil War, various southern organizations and political leaders spoke of the need to *not* forget the Civil War and the bravery of the soldiers. However, many of the statements created a measure of controversy because they make no mention of slavery and suggested that the Confederacy was formed primarily because those states wanted the right to have more control over their affairs and not be subject to federal laws. In 2010, Virginia Governor Bob McDonnell designated April as Confederate History Month without mention of slavery. A 2011 national survey showed 25 percent of White people sympathize more with the Southern states than the Northern states looking back on the Civil War. Given the unease with which most people think of our nation's history of slavery, it is no surprise that national recognition of the Sesquicentennial (150th anniversary) of the Civil War was limited to the issuance of commemorative postage stamps (Blow 2013, Seelye 2010).

The Challenge of Black Leadership

The institutionalization of White supremacy precipitated different responses from African Americans, just as slavery had. In the late 1800s and early 1900s, several articulate Blacks attempted to lead the first generation of freeborn Black Americans. Most prominent were Booker T. Washington and W. E. B. Du Bois. The personalities and ideas of these two men contrasted. Washington was born a slave in 1856 on a Virginia plantation. He worked in coal mines after emancipation and attended elementary school. Through hard work and driving ambition, Washington became the head of an educational institute for Blacks in Tuskegee, Alabama. Within 15 years, his leadership brought national recognition to the Tuskegee Institute and he became a national figure. Du Bois, on the other hand, was born in 1868 to a free family in Massachusetts. He attended Fisk University and the University of Berlin and became the first Black to receive a doctorate from Harvard. Washington died in 1915, and Du Bois died in self-imposed exile in Africa in 1963.

7-2 Address the challenge of Black leadership in the early twentieth century.

The Politics of Accommodation

Booker T. Washington's approach to White supremacy is called the *politics of accommodation*. He was willing to forgo social equality until White people saw Blacks as deserving of it. Perhaps his most famous speech was made in Atlanta on September 18, 1895, to an audience that was mostly White and mostly wealthy. Introduced by the governor of

Georgia as "a representative of Negro enterprise and Negro civilization," Washington (1900) gave a five-minute speech in which he pledged the continued dedication of Blacks to Whites:

As we have proved our loyalty to you in the past, in nursing your children, watching by the sick-bed of your mothers and fathers, and often following them with tear-dimmed eyes to their graves, so in the future, in our humble way, we shall stand by you with a devotion that no foreigner can approach, ready to lay down our lives, if need be, in defense of yours. **(p. 221)**

The speech catapulted Washington into the public forum, and he became the anointed spokesperson for Blacks for the next 20 years. President Grover Cleveland congratulated Washington for the "new hope" he gave Blacks. Washington's essential theme was compromise. Unlike Frederick Douglass, who had demanded the same rights for Blacks as for Whites, Washington asked that Blacks be educated because it would be a wise investment for Whites. He called racial hatred "the great and intricate problem which God has laid at the doors of the South." The Blacks' goal should be economic respectability. Washington's accommodating attitude ensured his popularity with Whites. His recognition by Whites contributed to his large following of Blacks, who were not used to seeing their leaders achieve fame among Whites.

It is easy in retrospect to be critical of Washington and to write him off as simply a product of his times. Booker T. Washington entered the public arena when the more militant proposals of Douglass had been buried. Black politicians were losing political contests and influence. To become influential as a Black, Washington reasoned, required White acceptance. His image as an accommodator allowed him to fight discrimination covertly. He assisted Presidents Roosevelt and Taft in appointing Blacks to patronage positions. Washington's goal was for African Americans eventually to have the same rights and opportunities as Whites. Just as people disagree with leaders today, some Blacks disagreed with the means Washington chose to reach that goal. No African American was more outspoken in his criticism of the politics of accommodation than W. E. B. Du Bois (Norrell 2009).

The Niagara Movement

The rivalry between Washington and Du Bois has been exaggerated. They enjoyed fairly cordial relations for some time. In 1900, Washington recommended Du Bois, at his request, for superintendent of Black schools in Washington, DC. By 1905, however, relations between the two had cooled. Du Bois spoke critically of Washington's influence, arguing that his power was being used to stifle African Americans who spoke out against the politics of accommodation. He also charged that Washington had caused the transfer of funds from academic programs to vocational education. Du Bois's greatest objection to Washington's statements was that they encouraged Whites to place the burden of the Blacks' problems on the Blacks themselves (Du Bois 1903).

As an alternative to Washington's program, Du Bois (1903) advocated the theory of the *talented tenth*, which reflected his atypical educational background. Unlike Washington, Du Bois was not at home with both intellectuals and sharecroppers. Although the very phrase *talented tenth* has an elitist ring, Du Bois argued that these privileged Blacks must serve the other nine-tenths. This argument was also Du Bois's way of criticizing Washington's emphasis on vocational education. Although he did not completely oppose the vocational approach, Du Bois thought education for African Americans should emphasize academics, which would be more likely to improve their position. Drawing on the talented tenth, Du Bois invited 29 Blacks to participate in a strategy session near Niagara Falls in 1905. Out of a series of meetings came several demands that unmistakably placed the responsibility for the problems facing African Americans on the shoulders of Whites.

The Niagara Movement, as it came to be called, was closely monitored by Booker T. Washington. Du Bois encountered difficulty gaining financial support and recruiting prominent people, and Du Bois (1968) himself wrote, "My leadership was solely of ideas. I never was, nor ever will be, personally popular" (p. 303). The movement's legacy was educating a new generation of African Americans in the politics of protest. After 1910, the Niagara Movement ceased to hold annual conventions. In 1909, however, the Niagara Movement leaders founded the National Association for the Advancement of Colored People (NAACP), with White and Black members. It was through the work of the NAACP that the Niagara Movement accomplished most of the goals set forth in 1905. The NAACP also marked the merging of White liberalism and Black militancy, a coalition unknown since the end of the abolition movement and Reconstruction (Rudwick 1957; Wortham 2008).

Remarkably, as Du Bois agitated for social change, he continued to conduct ground-breaking research into race relations. He oversaw the Atlanta Sociological Laboratory; its work at the time was generally ignored by the White-dominated academic institutions but is now gradually being rediscovered (Wright 2006).

In 1900, 90 percent of African Americans lived in the South. Blacks moved out of the South and into the West and North, especially the urban areas in those regions, during the post–Civil War period and continued to migrate through the 1950s and 1960s. By the 1980s and 1990s, a return to the South began as job opportunities grew in that part of the country and most vestiges of Jim Crow vanished in what had been the Confederacy states. By 2010, 55 percent of African Americans lived in the South, compared to 33 percent of the rest of the population (see Figure 7.1).

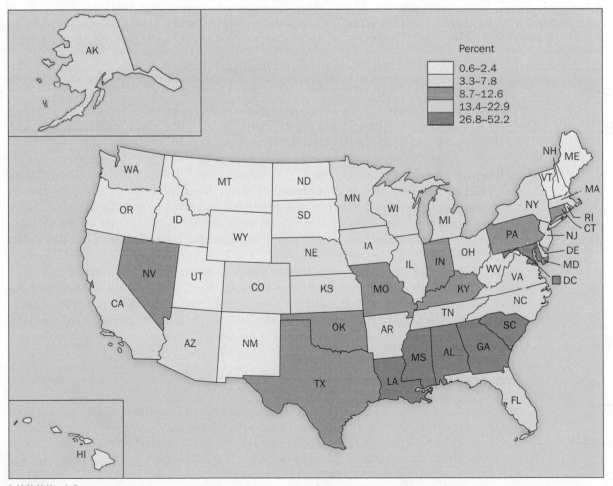

FIGURE 7.1
Black Population, 2010

Source: Rastogi et al. 2011: Table 5 on p. 8.

7-3 **Research Focus**

Sundown Towns, USA

Sundown towns are communities from which non-Whites were systematically excluded from living. They emerged in the late nineteenth century and persisted for a hundred years into the late twentieth century. Sundown towns existed throughout the nation, but more often they were located in northern states that were not pre–Civil War slave states. Although the precise number of sundown towns in the United States is unknown, it is estimated that there were several thousand such towns throughout the nation.

The term *sundown town* comes from signs once posted at the city limits reading "Nigger, Don't Let the Sun Set on YOU." In addition to excluding African Americans from many small towns, Chinese Americans, Japanese Americans, Mexican Americans, Jews, and Native Americans—citizens and noncitizens alike—were also subject to such exclusions. Sundown towns emerged in the late nineteenth century and persisted for a hundred years into the late twentieth century. In some cases, the exclusion was official town policy. In other cases, the racism policy was enforced through intimidation. This intimidation could occur in a number of ways, including harassment by law enforcement officers with the blessing of the local citizens.

Although the thought of sundown towns may seem a relic of the past to many of us today, sociologist James Loewen estimates that by 1970, still *more than half* of all incorporated communities outside the traditional South probably excluded African Americans. Many of these communities had no history of Blacks in residence. Such laws persisted even throughout the era of the civil rights movement. The city council of New Market, Iowa, for example, suspended its sundown ordinance for one night in the mid-1980s to allow an interracial band to play at a town festival, but it went back into effect the next day.

So what is it like today in these communities? Few sundown towns today have significant populations of excluded people. Some towns where colleges are located have benefited from efforts to desegregate their hometown. Such has been the case with initiatives by Lawrence University in Appleton, Wisconsin. What Loewen calls "recovering" sundown towns face continuing challenges to developing good race relations to attract African American families, including biased school curricula and overwhelmingly White teaching staffs. Practices that discourage desegregation persist across the country.

Sources: Loewen 2005, 2012; Loewen and Schaefer 2008.

A pattern of violence, with Blacks usually the victims, started in the South during Reconstruction and continued into the twentieth century, when it also spread northward. In 1917, a riot in East St. Louis, Illinois, claimed the lives of 39 Blacks and nine Whites. The several days of violence resulted from White fear of social and economic gains made by Blacks. So much violence occurred in the summer of 1919 that it is commonly called the "red summer." Twenty-six riots broke out throughout the country as White soldiers who returned from World War I feared the new competition that Blacks represented. This period of violence against African Americans also saw a resurgence of the Ku Klux Klan, which at its height had nearly 9 million members (Berlin 2010; Grinspan 2013; Schaefer 1971, 1980).

By no stretch of the imagination, and certainly as documented by historians and sociologists, the South had no monopoly on racism. In the Research Focus we consider the evidence of communities called sundown towns considered at the beginning of this chapter that kept Blacks out at night and were found throughout the North beginning in 1890 and continuing well into the last quarter of the twentieth century.

Reemergence of Black Protest

7-3 Discuss the reemergence of Black protest.

American involvement in World War II signaled improved economic conditions for both Whites and Blacks. Nearly a million African Americans served in the military in rigidly segregated units. Generally, more Blacks participated in the armed services in World War II than in previous military engagements, but efforts by Blacks to contribute to the war effort at home were hampered by discriminatory practices in defense plants.

A. Philip Randolph, president of the Brotherhood of Sleeping Car Porters, threatened to lead 100,000 Blacks in a march on Washington in 1941 to ensure their employment and not have Black workers targeted for dismissal. Randolph's proposed tactic was nonviolent

direct action, which he modeled on Mahatma Gandhi's practices in India. Randolph made it clear that he intended the march to be an all-Black event because he saw it as neither necessary nor desirable for Whites to lead Blacks to their own liberation. President Franklin Roosevelt responded to the pressure and agreed to issue an executive order prohibiting discrimination if Randolph would call off the march. The order and the Fair Employment Practices Commission it set up did not fulfill the original promises, but a precedent had been established for federal intervention in job discrimination (Garfinkel 1959).

Racial turmoil during World War II was not limited to threatened marches. Racial disturbances occurred in cities throughout the country, the worst riot occurring in Detroit in June 1943. In that case, President Roosevelt sent in 6,000 soldiers to quell the violence, which left 25 Blacks and 9 Whites dead. The racial disorders were paralleled by a growth in civil disobedience as a means to achieve equality for Blacks. The Congress of Racial Equality (CORE) was founded in 1942 to fight discrimination with nonviolent direct action. This interracial group used sit-ins to open restaurants to Black patrons in Chicago, Baltimore, and Los Angeles (Grimshaw 1969).

The war years and the postwar period saw several U.S. Supreme Court decisions that suggested the Court was moving away from tolerating racial inequities. The White primary elections endorsed in Jim Crow's formative period were finally challenged in the 1944 *Smith v. Allwright* decision. The effectiveness of the victory was limited; many states simply passed statutes that used new devices to frustrate African American voters.

A particularly repugnant legal device for relegating African Americans to second-class status was the **restrictive covenant**, a

Despite their second-class status until well after World War II, African Americans have contributed to every war effort. Notable were the Tuskegee Airmen, an all-Black unit of pilots who flew during World War II and received numerous decorations for valor. Surviving members continue to gather in celebratory reunions.

private contract entered into by neighborhood property owners stipulating that property could not be sold or rented to certain minority groups, thus ensuring that they could not live in the area. In 1948, the Supreme Court finally declared in *Shelley v. Kramer* that restrictive covenants were not constitutional, although it did not actually attack their discriminatory nature. The victory was in many ways less substantial than it was symbolic of the new willingness by the Supreme Court to uphold the rights of Black citizens.

The Democratic administrations of the late 1940s and early 1950s made a number of promises to Black Americans. The party adopted a strong civil rights platform in 1948, but its provisions were not enacted. Once again, union president Randolph threatened Washington, DC, with a march. This time, he insisted that as long as Blacks were subjected to a peacetime draft, the military must be desegregated. President Truman responded by issuing an executive order on July 26, 1948, that desegregated the armed forces. The U.S. Army abolished its quota system in 1950, and training camps for the Korean War were integrated. Desegregation was not complete; however, especially in the reserves and the National Guard, and even today the armed forces face charges of racial favoritism. Whatever its shortcomings, the desegregation order offered African Americans an alternative to segregated civilian life (Moskos and Butler 1996).

The Civil Rights Movement

It is difficult to say exactly when a social movement begins or ends. Usually, a movement's ideas or tactics precede the actual mobilization of people and continue long after the movement's driving force has been replaced by new ideals and techniques. This description applies to the civil rights movement and its successor: the continuing struggle for African American freedom. Before 1954, there were some confrontations of White supremacy: the CORE sit-ins of 1942 and efforts to desegregate buses in Baton Rouge, Louisiana, in 1953.

7-4 Summarize the outcome of the Civil Rights Movement.

The civil rights movement gained momentum with a Supreme Court decision in 1954 that eventually desegregated the public schools, and it ended as a major force in Black America with the civil disorders of 1965 through 1968. However, beginning in 1954, toppling the traditional barriers to full rights for Blacks was the rule, not the exception.

Struggle to Desegregate the Schools

For the majority of Black children, public school education meant attending segregated schools. Southern school districts assigned children to school by race rather than by neighborhood, a practice that constituted **de jure segregation**, or segregation that results from children being assigned to schools specifically to maintain racially separate schools. It was this form of legal humiliation that was attacked in the landmark decree of *Linda Brown et al. v. Board of Education of Topeka, Kansas.*

Seven-year-old Linda Brown was not permitted to enroll in the grade school four blocks from her home in Topeka, Kansas. Rather, school board policy dictated that she attend the Black school almost two miles away. This denial led the NAACP Legal Defense and Educational Fund to bring suit on behalf of Linda Brown and 12 other Black children. The NAACP argued that the Fourteenth Amendment was intended to rule out segregation in public schools. Chief Justice Earl Warren of the Supreme Court wrote the unanimous opinion that "in the field of public education the doctrine of 'separate but equal' has no place. Separate educational facilities are inherently unequal."

The freedom that African Americans saw in their grasp at the time of the *Brown* decision amounted to a reaffirmation of American values. What Blacks sought was assimilation into White American society. The motivation for the *Brown* suit did not come merely because Black schools were inferior, although they were. Blacks were assigned to poorly ventilated and dilapidated buildings, with overcrowded classrooms and unqualified teachers. Less money was spent on Black schools than on White schools throughout the South in both rural and metropolitan areas. The issue was not such tangible factors, however, but the intangible effect of not being allowed to go to school with Whites. All-Black schools could not be equal to all-White schools. Even in this victory, Blacks reaffirmed White society and the importance of an integrated educational experience (Supreme Court of the United States 347 U.S. 483, August 17, 1954).

Although *Brown* marked the beginning of the civil rights movement, the reaction to it showed how deeply prejudice was rooted in the South. Resistance to court-ordered desegregation took many forms: Some people called for impeachment of all the Supreme Court justices. Others petitioned Congress to declare the Fourteenth Amendment unconstitutional. Cities closed schools rather than comply. The governor of Arkansas used the state's National Guard to block Black students from entering a previously all-White high school in Little Rock (see Figure 7.2).

The issue of school desegregation was extended to higher education, and Mississippi state troopers and the state's National Guard confronted each other over the 1962 admission of James Meredith, the first African American accepted by the University of Mississippi. Scores of people were injured and two were killed in this clash between segregationists and the law. A similar defiant stand was taken a year later by Governor George Wallace, who "stood in the schoolhouse door" to block two Blacks from enrolling in the University of Alabama. President Kennedy federalized the Alabama National Guard to guarantee admission of the students. *Brown* did not resolve the school controversy, and many questions remain unanswered. More recently, the issue of school segregation resulting from neighborhood segregation has been debated. Later, another form of segregation—*de facto segregation*—is examined more closely (Bell 2004, 2007; Pettigrew 2011).

Civil Disobedience

The success of a yearlong boycott of city buses in Montgomery, Alabama, dealt Jim Crow another setback. On December 1, 1955, Rosa Parks defied the law and refused to give her seat on a crowded bus to a White man. Her defiance led to the organization of the

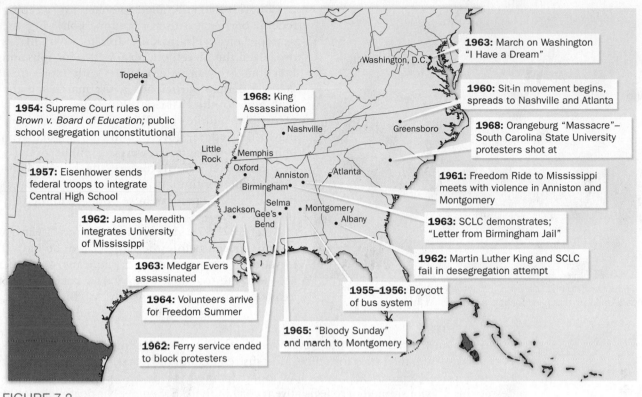

FIGURE 7.2
Major Events of the Civil Rights Movement

Montgomery Improvement Association, headed by 26-year-old Martin Luther King, Jr., a Baptist minister with a PhD from Boston University. The bus boycott was the first of many situations in which Blacks used nonviolent direct action to obtain the rights that Whites already enjoyed. The boycott eventually demanded the end of segregated seating. The *Brown* decision woke up all of America to racial injustice, but the Montgomery boycott marked a significant shift away from the historical reliance on NAACP court battles (Killian 1975).

Civil disobedience is based on the belief that people have the right to disobey the law under certain circumstances. This tactic was not new; Blacks in the United States had used it before and Gandhi also had urged its use in India. Under King's leadership, however, civil disobedience became a widely used technique and even gained a measure of acceptability among some prominent Whites. King distinguished between man-made laws that were unjust and should not be obeyed because they were not right, not in accordance with God's higher moral code (1963:82).

In disobeying unjust laws, King (1958:101–107) developed this strategy:

- actively but nonviolently resisting evil,
- not seeking to defeat or humiliate opponents but to win their friendship and understanding,
- attacking the forces of evil rather than the people who happen to be doing the evil,
- being willing to accept suffering without retaliating,
- refusing to hate the opponent, and
- acting with the conviction that the universe is on the side of justice.

King, like other Blacks before him and since, made it clear that passive acceptance of injustice was intolerable. He hoped that by emphasizing nonviolence, Southern Blacks would display their hostility to racism in a way that would undercut violent reaction by Whites.

7-5

Martin Luther King and Malcolm X, Jr. were the defining figures of the African American struggle for rights and dignity in the 1960s.

Congress had still failed to enact any sweeping federal barrier to discrimination. Following the example of A. Philip Randolph in 1941, Blacks organized the March on Washington for Jobs and Freedom on August 28, 1963. With more than 200,000 people participating, the march was the high point of the civil rights movement. The mass of people, middle-class Whites and Blacks looking to the federal government for support, symbolized the struggle. However, a public opinion poll conducted shortly before the march documented the continuing resentment of the majority of Whites: 63 percent were opposed to the rally (Gallup 1972).

King (1971:351) delivered his famous "I Have a Dream" speech before the large crowd; he looked forward to a time when all Americans would be able to unite together. Just 18 days later, a bomb exploded in a Black church in Birmingham, Alabama, killing four little girls and injuring 20 other people.

Despair only increased as the November 1963 election results meant segregationists were successful in their bids for office. Most distressing was the assassination of President Kennedy on November 22. Blacks had found Kennedy to be an appealing president despite his previously mediocre legislative record in the U.S. Senate. His death left doubt as to the direction and pace of future actions on civil rights by the executive branch under President Lyndon Baines Johnson. Two months later, however, the Twenty-Fourth Amendment was ratified, outlawing the poll tax that had long prevented Blacks from voting. The enactment of the Civil Rights Act on July 2, 1964, was hailed as a major victory and provided, at least for a while, what historian John Hope Franklin called "the illusion of equality" (Franklin and Higginbotham 2011).

In the months that followed passage of the act, the pace of the movement to end racial injustice slowed. The violence continued, however, from the Bedford–Stuyvesant section of Brooklyn to Selma, Alabama. Southern state courts still found White murderers of Blacks innocent, and they had to be tried and convicted in federal civil, rather than criminal, court on the charge that by killing a person one violates that person's civil rights. Government records, which did not become public until 1973, revealed a systematic campaign by the FBI to infiltrate civil rights groups in an effort to discredit them in the belief that such activist groups were subversive. It was in such an atmosphere that the Voting Rights Act was passed in August 1965, but this significant, positive event was somewhat overshadowed by violence in the Watts section of Los Angeles that same week (Blackstock 1976).

The Urban Stage

7-5 Identify how urban areas in the 1960s and 1970s refocused Black–White relations.

Just as the Civil Rights Movement was reaching what seemed at the time the ever-growing attention of the entire nation, the focus and rhetoric shifted very quickly from small town Dixie to the urban industrial North.

Urban Violence and Oppression

Riots involving Whites and Blacks did not begin in the 1960s. As noted earlier in this chapter, urban violence occurred after World War I and even during World War II, and violence against Blacks in the United States is nearly 350 years old. But the urban riots of the 1960s affected Blacks and Whites in the United States and throughout the world so extensively that they deserve special attention. However, it is important to remember that most violence between Whites and Blacks has not been large-scale collective action but has involved only a small number of people.

The summers of 1963 and 1964 were a prelude to the riots that gripped the country's attention. Although most people knew of the civil rights efforts in the South and legislative victories in Washington, everyone realized that the racial problem was national after several cities outside the South experienced violent disorder. In April 1968, after the assassination of Martin Luther King, Jr., more cities exploded than had in all of 1967. Even before the summer of 1968 began, there were 369 civil disorders. Communities of all sizes were hit (Oberschall 1968).

As the violence continued and embraced many ghettos, a popular explanation was that riot participants were mostly unemployed youths who had criminal records, often involving narcotics, and who were vastly outnumbered by the African Americans who repudiated the looting and arson. This explanation was called the **riff-raff theory** or the rotten-apple theory because it discredited the rioters and left the barrel of apples, White society, untouched. On the contrary, research shows that the Black community expressed sympathetic understanding toward the rioters and that the rioters were not merely the poor and uneducated but included middle-class, working-class, and educated residents (Sears and McConahay 1969, 1973; Tomlinson 1969; Turner 1994).

Several alternatives to the riff-raff theory explain why Black violent protest increased in the United States at a time when the nation was seemingly committed to civil rights for all. Two explanations stand out. One ascribes the problem to Black frustration with rising expectations in the face of continued deprivation relative to Whites.

The standard of living of African Americans improved remarkably after World War II, and it continued to do so during the civil rights movement. However, White income and occupation levels also improved, so the gap between the groups remained. Chapter 3 showed that feelings of relative deprivation often are the basis for perceived discrimination. **Relative deprivation** is the conscious feeling of a negative discrepancy between legitimate expectations and current actualities (Wilson 1973).

At the same time that African Americans were feeling relative deprivation, they also were experiencing growing discontent. **Rising expectations** refers to the increasing sense of frustration that legitimate needs are being blocked. Blacks felt that they had legitimate aspirations to equality, and the civil rights movement reaffirmed that discrimination had blocked upward mobility. As the horizons of African Americans broadened, they were more likely to make comparisons with Whites and feel discontented. The civil rights movement resulted in higher aspirations for Black America, yet for the majority, life remained unchanged. Not only were their lives unchanged but they also had a widespread feeling that the existing social structure held no prospect for improvement (Garner 1996; Sears and McConahay 1970; Thomas and Thomas 1984).

Black Power

The riots in the Northern ghettos captured the attention of Whites, and Black Power was what they heard. But Black Power was born *not* of Black but of White violence. On June 6, 1966, James Meredith was carrying out a one-person march from Memphis to Jackson, Mississippi, to encourage fellow African Americans to overcome their own fears and vote after the passage of the Voting Rights Act. During that march, an unidentified assailant shot and wounded Meredith. Blacks from throughout the country immediately continued the march. During the march, Stokely Carmichael of the Student Nonviolent Coordinating Committee proclaimed to a cheering Black crowd, "What we need is Black Power." King and others later urged "Freedom Now" as the slogan for the march. A compromise dictated that no slogan would be used, but the mood of Black America said otherwise (King 1967; Lomax 1971).

In retrospect, it may be puzzling that the phrase *Black Power* frightened Whites and offended so many Blacks. It was not really new. The National Advisory Commission on Civil Disorders (1968) correctly identified it as old wine in new bottles: Black consciousness was not new, even if the phrase was.

7-5

By advocating Black Power, Carmichael distanced himself from the assimilationism of King. Carmichael rejected the goal of assimilation into White middle-class society. Instead, he said, Blacks must create new institutions. To succeed in this endeavor, Carmichael argued that Blacks must follow the same path as the Italians, Irish, and other White ethnic groups. "Before a group can enter the open society, it must first close ranks.... Group solidarity is necessary before a group can operate effectively from a bargaining position of strength in a pluralistic society" (Ture and Hamilton 1992:44). Prominent Black leaders opposed the concept; many feared that Whites would retaliate even more violently. King (1967) saw Black Power as a "cry of disappointment" but acknowledged that it had a "positive meaning."

Eventually, Black Power gained wide acceptance among Blacks and even many Whites. Although it came to be defined differently by nearly every new proponent, support of Black Power generally implied endorsing Black control of the political, economic, and social institutions in Black communities. One reason for its popularity among African Americans was that it gave them a viable option for surviving in a segregated society. The civil rights movement strove to end segregation, but the White response showed how committed White society was to maintaining it. Black Power presented restructuring society as the priority item on the Black agenda (Carmichael and Thelwell 2003).

In the wake of generations of struggle by African Americans allied with sympathetic Whites and members of other minority groups, it is both remarkable and discouraging how much remains to be done.

(🎙) Speaking Out

The New Jim Crow

Jarvious Cotton cannot vote. Like his father, his grandfather, great-grandfather, and great-great-grandfather, he has been denied the right to participate in our electoral democracy. Cotton's family tree tells the story of several generations of black men who were born in the United States but who were denied the most basic freedom that democracy promises—the freedom to vote for those who will make the rules and laws that govern one's life. Cotton's great-great-grandfather could not vote as a slave. His great-grandfather was beaten to death by the Ku Klux Klan for attempting to vote. His grandfather was prevented from voting by Klan intimidation. His father was barred from voting by poll taxes and literacy tests. Today, Jarvious Cotton cannot vote because he, like many black men in the United States, has been labeled a felon and is currently on parole.

Michelle Alexander

Cotton's story illustrates, in many respects, the adage, "The more things change, the more they remain the same." In each generation, new tactics have been used to achieve the same goals—goals shared by the Founding Fathers. Denying African Americans citizenship was deemed essential to the formation of the original union. Hundreds of years later, America is still not an egalitarian democracy. The arguments and rationalizations that have been trotted out in support of racial exclusion and discrimination in its various forms have changed and evolved, but the outcome has remained largely the same. An extraordinary percentage of black men in the United States are legally barred from voting today, just as they have been throughout most of American history. They are also subject to legalized discrimination in employment, housing, education, public benefits, and jury service, just as their parents, grandparents, and great-grandparents once were.

Since the collapse of Jim Crow, what has changed has less to do with the basic structure of society than with the language we use to justify it. In the era of colorblindness, it is no longer socially permissible to use race, explicitly, as a justification for discrimination, exclusion, and social contempt. So we don't. Rather than rely on race, we use our criminal justice system to label people of color "criminals" and then engage in all the practices we supposedly left behind. Today, it is perfectly legal to discriminate against criminals in nearly all the ways that it was once legal to discriminate against African Americans. Once you're labeled a felon, the old forms of discrimination—employment discrimination, housing discrimination, denial of the right to vote, denial of educational opportunity, denial of food stamps and other public benefits, and exclusion from jury service—are suddenly legal. As a criminal, you have scarcely more rights, and arguably less respect, than a Black man living in Alabama at the height of Jim Crow. We have not ended racial caste in America: We have merely redesigned it.

Source: Alexander 2012:1–3.

7-6

In the Speaking Out box, legal scholar Michelle Alexander considers how African Americans, especially males, are much more likely to be imprisoned and face lifetime consequences even after they have served their time. While Whites and Blacks equally engage in drug crimes (if anything, White youth more), Black men have been admitted to prison on drug offenses 20 to 50 times more often than White men.

The Religious Force

It is not possible to overstate the role religion has played, good and bad, in the social history of African Americans. Historically, Black leaders have emerged from the pulpits to seek out rights on behalf of all Blacks. Churches have served as the basis for community organization in neighborhoods abandoned by businesses and even government. Religion may be a source of antagonism as well.

7-6 Describe the special role religion has within the African American community.

The Africans who were brought involuntarily to the Western hemisphere were non-Christian, and therefore were seen as heathens and barbarians. To "civilize" the slaves in the period before the Civil War, Southern slaveholders encouraged and often required their slaves to attend church and embrace Christianity. The Christian churches to which Blacks were introduced in the United States encouraged them to accept the inferior status enforced by Whites, and the religious teaching that the slaves received equated Whiteness with salvation, presenting Whiteness as an acceptable, if not preferred, object of reverence.

Despite being imposed in the past by Whites, the Christian faiths are embraced by most African Americans today. As shown in Figure 7.3, African Americans are overwhelmingly Protestant, with the majority belonging to historically Black churches. Du Bois (1996, 2003) wrote of the importance of the church in the Black community but was also critical that the church failed at times to be more than a social organization often stratified by class boundaries.

Black churches continue to be socially involved in their communities. About 12 percent of Black Americans, compared to 16 percent of Whites, indicated in a 2007 survey that they were religiously unaffiliated, atheistic, or agnostic. Even when upwardly mobile African Americans move out of the central city, many travel long distances to return to their congregations to support them financially and spiritually (Pew Forum on Religion and Public Life 2008a, 2008b; Watson 2004).

However, a variety of non-Christian groups have exerted a much greater influence on African Americans than the reported numbers of their followers suggest. The Nation of Islam, for example, which became known as the Black Muslims, has attracted a large number of followers and received the most attention. We look at this group in greater detail in Chapter 11 when we consider the large Muslim community in the United States.

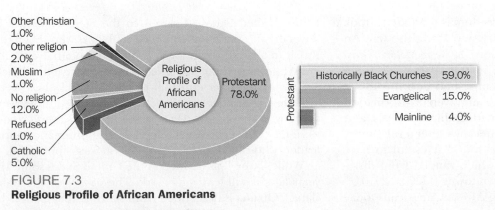

FIGURE 7.3
Religious Profile of African Americans

Source: Pew Forum on Religion and Public Life 2008a.

7-7

Improved living conditions for Black people made the United States an attractive destination for Black people, as it had been for generations for people from Europe. The increase is dramatic with over 2 million in the 2010 Census having been born in Africa and the Caribbean and the majority of them having arrived in the previous ten years. Here, some Somali women are selling clothes in Minneapolis.

7-7 Examine how recent immigration is adding to the Black community.

The New Immigration

When they think of the upsurge of arrivals in the United States seeking permanent residency, most people imagine immigrants from Latin America and Asia. Yet another dramatic flow has come from Africa and the Caribbean. This is all the more dramatic because there had been little immigration of Black people to the United States for the first 100 years after the Civil War. Obviously, the world's Black population was acutely aware of how people of color had been treated in the United States. Furthermore, restrictive legislation made it difficult for people to emigrate from Africa.

Improved living conditions for Black people made the United States an attractive destination for Black people, as it had been for generations for people from Europe. The increase is startling: from 125,000 foreign-born Blacks in 1960 to 816,000 in 1980 and to 3.1 million in 2008. About half were born in the Caribbean, with Jamaica and Haiti representing the majority. About one million of foreign-born Blacks are from Africa, with 30 percent born in either Nigeria or Ethiopia.

This new addition to the African American community is a diverse group, including newcomers who first came to study, others to join relatives, and some who came as refugees. They and their descendants are often not taking long to make their presence felt, as witnessed by Colin Powell, the son of Jamaican immigrants, and President Barack Obama, whose father was a Kenyan immigrant.

To many people in the United States, the sheer size of this group has gone unnoticed. This is probably because of the relative concentration of the immigrants in certain urban areas. Nearly two-thirds of Caribbean Blacks live in either the New York City or Miami–Fort Lauderdale metropolitan areas. African-born Blacks are more dispersed; local efforts to make refugees feel welcome have led to selected settlement patterns in cities such as Minneapolis, where one out of five Blacks are African-born.

These new immigrants experience all the problems of transitioning into a new society experienced by other immigrants. Similarly, many foster ties to home and to fellow countrymen. Yet these Black immigrants are confronted by a society still deeply divided by race. Although they typically were aware of divisions before immigrating, trying to navigate racial formation as it has emerged often presents daily challenges to these newcomers (Berlin 2010; Kent 2007; Traoré 2008).

Conclusion

While moving from slavery to freedom is dramatic, it took centuries and was opposed every step along the way. An example is the popular publication *The Negro Motorist Green Book*, which began publication in the 1930s by Harlem civic leader Victor Green and continued into the 1960s. The book offered African American travelers information on where they could be welcomed in diners, hotels, and even private residences. Even decades after end slavery ended, Blacks taking road trips found it useful to have guidance to avoid indignities, which ranged from disrespectful service to actual sundown towns (McGee 2010).

The dramatic events affecting African Americans today have their roots in the forcible bringing of their ancestors to the United States as slaves. In the South, whether as slaves or later as victims of Jim Crow, Blacks were not a real threat to any but the poorest Whites, although even affluent Whites feared the perceived potential threat that Blacks posed. During their entire history here, Blacks have been criticized when they rebelled and praised when they went along with the system. During the time of slavery, revolts were met with increased suppression; after emancipation, leaders who called for accommodation were applauded.

While slavery was banned in the United States some 150 years ago, it still leaves its mark. The news that President Barack Obama is descended from slaves at first glance did not seem newsworthy. But remember, his African heritage

SPECTRUM OF INTERGROUP RELATIONS

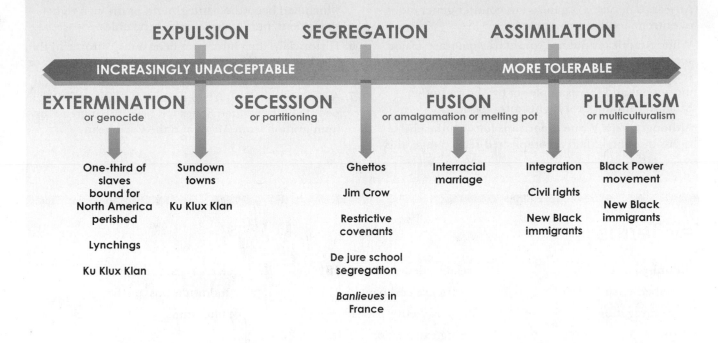

is through his father, who came to the United States in the twentieth century. Actually his roots are from John Punch, a native of Cameroon in Africa. Held in bondage on a plantation near Jamestown in the 1600s, he fathered children with a White woman, among whose descendants are Ann Durham, Obama's White mother (Nicholson 2013:70).

Blacks, in their efforts to bring about change, have understandably differed in their willingness to form coalitions with Whites. African Americans who resisted in the days of either slavery or the civil rights movement (see the Spectrum of Intergroup relations continuum) would have concurred with Du Bois's (1903) comment that a Black person "simply wishes to make it possible to be both a Negro and an American, without being cursed and spit upon by his fellows, without having the door of opportunity closed roughly in his face" (pp. 3–4). The object of Black protest seems simple enough, but for many people, including presidents, the point was lost.

How much progress has been made? When that progress covers several hundred years, beginning with slavery and ending with rights recognized constitutionally, it is easy to be impressed. However, let us consider Topeka, Kansas, the site of the 1954 *Brown v. Board of Education* case. Linda Brown, one of the original plaintiffs, also was touched by another segregation case. In 1992, the courts held that Oliver Brown, her grandchild, was victimized because the Topeka schools were still segregated, now for reasons of residential segregation. The remedy to separate schools in this Kansas city is still unresolved (Hays 1994).

Chapter 8 assesses the status of African Americans today. Recall the events chronicled in this chapter as you consider the advances that have been made. These events are a reminder that any progress has followed years—indeed, generations—of struggle by African Americans, enlisting the support of Whites seeking to end second-class status for African Americans in the United States.

Summary

1. Slavery was a system that defined the people forcibly brought from Africa, and their descendants, as property of their masters having no rights, yet governed by a series of slave codes. Despite the total restrictiveness of slavery as an institution, slaves often tried to resist the system while abolitionists worked for their freedom.

2. Throughout history, many individuals have emerged as leaders within the African American community. Particularly noteworthy were Booker T. Washington and W. E. B. Du Bois, both of who, although they took different approaches, expressed dissatisfaction with the second-class status of being Black in America.

3. An often overlooked period in Black–White relations historically is the period around World War II when African Americans organized to counter generations of entrenched Jim Crow practices.

4. White Americans did not voluntarily embrace major social change. It was achieved only in response to years of civil disobedience through the civil rights movement and the example set by Martin Luther King, Jr. with the Civil Rights movement.

5. Although many White Americans felt that the civil rights movement had accomplished real change, this illusion was dramatically shattered as urban violence and growing militancy occurred not in the South, which had been the battleground of the civil rights movement, but in Northern central cities.

6. Historically, the church has been a major force in the Black community and continues to be a major part of the social culture.

7. A significant recent trend in the long history of Black people in the United States has been the increase in immigration from Africa and the Caribbean.

Key Terms

abolitionists, p. 170

civil disobedience, p. 179

de jure segregation, p. 178

Jim Crow, p. 171

racial formation, p. 170

relative deprivation, p. 181

restrictive covenant, p. 177

riff-raff theory, p. 181

rising expectations, p. 181

slave codes, p. 169

slavery reparations, p. 173

sundown towns, p. 168

White primary, p. 171

Review Questions

1. In what ways were slaves defined as property?

2. How are William E. Du Bois and Booker T. Washington both similar and different in what they sought to accomplish?

3. How did Black Americans respond to injustices during World War II?

4. If civil disobedience is nonviolent, then why has so much violence been associated with it?

5. How did observers of the urban riots tend to dismiss any social importance to the outbreaks?

6. Why has religion proved to be a force for both unity and disunity among African Americans?

7. How has the African American community in the United States been enhanced recently by immigration?

Critical Thinking

1. How much time do you recall spending in school thus far learning about the history of Europe? How about Africa? What do you think this says about the way education is delivered or what we choose to learn?

2. What would you consider the three most important achievements in civil rights for African Americans since 1950? What roles did Whites and Blacks play in making these events happen?

3. Growing numbers of Blacks are immigrating to the United States (especially to the eastern United States) from the Caribbean. What impact might this have on what it means to be Black or African American in the United States? What would the social construction of race say about this development?

8

African Americans Today

8-1 Describe the major educational issues facing African Americans.

8-2 Understand the economic situation of Black Americans.

8-3 Identify the strengths of and challenges facing family life.

8-4 Articulate the housing situation in the African American community.

8-5 Identify the present concerns about the criminal justice system.

8-6 Explain the healthcare dilemma.

8-7 Address the current role of African Americans in politics.

8-1

African Americans have made significant progress in many areas, but they have not kept pace with White Americans in many sectors. African Americans have advanced in formal schooling to a remarkable degree, although in most areas residential patterns have left many public schools predominantly Black or White. Higher education also reflects the legacy of a nation that has operated two schooling systems: one for Blacks and another for Whites. Gains in earning power have barely kept pace with inflation, and the gap between Whites and Blacks has remained largely unchanged. African American families are susceptible to the problems associated with a low-income group that also faces discrimination and prejudice. Housing in many areas remains segregated, despite growing numbers of Blacks in suburban areas. African Americans are more likely to be victims of crimes and to be arrested for violent crimes. The subordination of Blacks is also apparent in healthcare delivery. African Americans have made substantial gains in elective office but still are underrepresented compared with their numbers in the general population.

Congressman Charles Rangel is the currently the third longest-serving Congressman, having represented since 1971. Obviously he has witnessed a lot of history, whether as a serviceman in the Korean War or as a founding member of the Black Congressional Caucus. As a thirty-something attorney and community activist in Harlem, he was at the 1963 March on Washington. Before we turn to all the scholarly studies and data on African Americans today, let's consider his thoughts in the Speaking Out box on where Black America has been and where it needs to go.

As you read this chapter, try to keep in perspective the profile of African Americans in the United States today. This chapter assesses education, the economy, family life, housing, criminal justice, healthcare, and politics among the nation's African Americans. Progress has occurred, and some of the advances are nothing short of remarkable. The

🎙 Speaking Out

On the 50th Anniversary of the March on Washington

Fifty years ago today, I participated in the March on Washington for Jobs and Freedom, and I heard Dr. Martin Luther King give his historic "I Have A Dream" speech that inspired not only me but also a nation. More than 200,000 people—of all races and backgrounds—came from all over the country to participate in the March, calling for fundamental social and economic justice for all Americans, at a time when many public facilities in regions of the country were still segregated.

The energy created by that March on Washington has changed America. It helped to awaken the country and less than one year after the March, on July 2, 1964, President Lyndon Johnson signed the 1964 Civil Rights Act, the most sweeping civil rights bill since Reconstruction, into law. Then, a year later, on August 6, 1965, President Johnson signed the landmark 1965 Voting Rights Act, which has helped secure the right to vote for millions of Americans, into law.

We can all be proud of the progress that has been made in moving forward the vision of America that Dr. King laid

Charles Rangel

out in his "I Have A Dream" speech, but more needs to be done. The work of our nation is far from complete and it requires constant vigilance to protect our rights. With the Supreme Court's recent decision to strike down a key section of the Voting Rights Act, we have much work ahead to restore the promise of our democracy to every eligible voter. When millions remain out of work or facing discrimination in employment, with one in five children going to bed hungry, when many feel that our justice system remains unfairly stacked against them, and when there are major achievement gaps in our education system, we must remember that we have a long way to go and we must work together.

With thousands gathered here today in Washington, I hope that the energy created 50 years ago will be recreated today, so that we can all continue to strive until Dr. King's vision is finally realized and America fully lives up to its true promise and ideals.

Source: Rangel 2013.

deprivation of the African American people relative to Whites remains, however, even if absolute deprivation has been softened. A significant gap remains between African Americans and the dominant group, and to this gap a price is assigned: the price of being African American in the United States.

Education

The African American population in the United States has placed special importance on acquiring education, beginning with its emphasis in the home of the slave family even when the formal institution of marriage was prohibited and continuing through the creation of separate schools for Black children because public schools were closed to them by custom or law. Today, long after the civil rights coalition has disbanded, education remains a controversial issue. Because racial and ethnic groups realize that formal schooling is the key to social mobility, they want to maximize this opportunity for upward mobility and, therefore, want better schooling. White Americans also appreciate the value of formal schooling and do not want to do anything that they perceive will jeopardize their own position.

Several measures document the inadequate education received by African Americans, starting with the quantity of formal education. Blacks as a group have always attained less education than Whites as a group. Despite programs such as Head Start, which are directed at all poor children, White children are still more likely to have formal prekindergarten education than are African American children. Later, Black children generally drop out of school sooner and, therefore, are less likely to receive high school diplomas, let alone college degrees. The gap in receiving college degrees has not been reduced in recent years, as shown in Figure 8.1. Presently, about 31 percent of non-Hispanic Whites 25 years and over have a bachelor's degree or higher compared to less than 18 percent of African Americans, who have fewer degrees than Ecuadorian Americans or Nicaraguan Americans. Despite this progress, however, the gap remains substantial, with the proportion of Blacks holding a college degree in 2010 about what it was for Whites in the early 1980s (Ogunwole, Drewery, and Rios-Vargas 2012).

Proposals to improve educational opportunities often argue for more adequate funding. Yet there are disagreements over what changes would lead to the best outcome. For example, educators and African Americans in general have significant debates over the content of curriculum that is best for minority students. Some schools have developed academic

8-1 Describe the major educational issues facing African Americans.

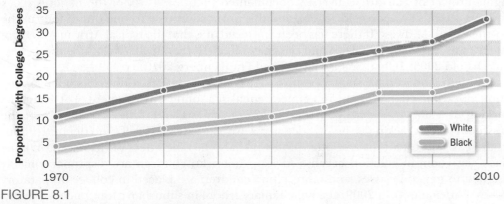

FIGURE 8.1
Percentage of Adults Receiving College Degrees

Blacks have made tremendous progress in terms of receiving college degrees but so have Whites. Today's level of college completion among adult African Americans is about the level White Americans reached in the mid-1980s.

Note: Date since 2000 for non-Hispanic Whites. Proportion of population over age 25.

Source: Bureau of the Census 2010a:Table 146; 2011d.

8-1

programs that take an Afrocentric perspective and immerse students in African American history and culture. However, a few of these programs have been targeted as ignoring fundamentals. On other occasions, the Afrocentric curriculum has even been viewed as racist against Whites. The debates over a few controversial programs attract a lot of attention, clouding the widespread need to reassess the curriculum for racial and ethnic minorities.

Middle- and upper-class children occasionally face barriers to a high-quality education, but they are more likely than the poor to have a home environment that is favorable to learning. Even African American schoolchildren who stay in school are not guaranteed equal opportunities in life. Many high schools do not prepare students who are interested in college for advanced schooling. The problem is that schools are failing to meet the needs of students, not that students are failing in school. Therefore, the problems with schooling were properly noted as a part of the past discrimination component of total discrimination illustrated in Figure 3.1 on page 61.

School Segregation

It has been more than 50 years since the U.S. Supreme Court issued its unanimous ruling in *Brown v. Board of Education of Topeka, Kansas* that separate educational facilities are inherently unequal. What has been the legacy of that decision? Initially, the courts, with the support of the federal government, ordered Southern school districts to end racial separation. But as attention turned to larger school districts, especially in the North, the challenge was to have integrated schools even though the neighborhoods were segregated. In addition, some city school districts were predominantly African American and Hispanic and were surrounded by suburban school districts that were predominantly White. This type of school segregation, which results from residential patterns, is called **de facto segregation.**

Initially, courts sought to overcome de facto segregation just as they had de jure school segregation in the *Brown* case. Typically, students were bused within a school district to achieve racial balance, but in a few cases, Black students were bused to predominantly White suburban schools and White children were bused into the city. In 1974, however, the Supreme Court ruled in *Millikin v. Bradley* that it was improper to order Detroit and the suburbs to have a joint metropolitan busing solution. These and other Supreme Court decisions effectively ended initiatives to overcome residential segregation, once again creating racial isolation in the schools. Indeed, even in Topeka, one-third of the schools are segregated (Orfield et al. 1996).

School segregation has been so enduring that the term *apartheid schools* has been coined to refer to schools that are all Black. An analysis released in 2003 by the Civil Rights Project of Harvard University documented that one in six of the nation's Black students attends an **apartheid school,** and this proportion rose to one out of four in the Northeast and Midwest. If there has been any trend, it is that the typical African American student was less likely to have White classmates in 2010 than in 1970 (Frankenberg, Lee, and Orfield 2003; Tefera, Seigel-Hawley, and Frankenberg 2010).

Although studies have shown positive effects of integration, a diverse student population does not guarantee an integrated, equal schooling environment. For example, **tracking** in schools, especially middle and high schools, intensifies segregation at the classroom level. Tracking is the practice of placing students in specific curriculum groups on the basis of test scores and other criteria. It also has the effect of decreasing White–Black classroom interaction because African American children are disproportionately assigned to general classes, and more White children are placed in college-preparatory classes. For example, in 2009, at an elementary school in suburban Montgomery County, Maryland, the school's faculty, which is nearly 75 percent White, identified the percentage of the student body, which is about 64 percent White, likely to be considered "gifted and talented": Forty-nine percent of White students and 67 percent of Asian students were so identified, compared to less than 8 percent of Latino students and less than 4 percent of African American children. Studies indicate that African American students are more likely than White students to be classified as learning disabled or emotionally disturbed. Although there are successes in public education, integration is not one of them (Ellison 2008; Thompson 2010).

Acting White, Acting Black, or Neither

A common view advanced by some educators is that African Americans, especially males, do not succeed in school because they do not want to be caught acting White. That is, they avoid at all costs taking school seriously and do not accept the authority of teachers and administrators. Whatever the accuracy of such a generalization, acting White clearly shifts the responsibility of low school attainment from the school to the individual and, therefore, can be seen as yet another example of blaming the victim. **Acting White** is also associated with speaking proper English or with cultural preferences like listening to rock music rather than hip-hop. This characterization is also sometimes referred to as *oppositional culture* (Fordham and Ogbu 1986; Lewis 2013; Ogbu 2004; Ogbu with Davis 2003).

In the context of high achievers, to what extent do Blacks *not* want to act White? Many scholars have noted that individuals' efforts to avoid looking like they want an education has a long history and is hardly exclusive to any one race. Students of all colors may hold back for fear of being accused of being "too hardworking."

Back in the 1950s, one heard disparaging references to "teacher's pet" and "brown nosing." Does popularity come to high school debaters and National Honor Society students or to cheerleaders and athletes? Academic-oriented classmates are often viewed as social misfits, nerds, and geeks and are seen as socially inept even if their skill building will later make them more economically independent and often more socially desirable. For minority children, including African Americans, to take school seriously means they must overcome their White classmates' same desire to be cool and not a nerd. In addition, Black youth must also come to embrace a curriculum and respect teachers who are much less likely to look or sound like them (Tyson, Darity, and Castellino 2005).

The acting-White thesis overemphasizes personal responsibility rather than structural features such as quality of schools, curriculum, and teachers. Therefore, it locates the source of Black miseducation—and by implication, the remedy—in the African American household. As scholar Michael Dyson (1995) observes, "When you think the problems are personal, you think the solutions are the same." Often one may hear the comment, If we could only get African American parents to encourage their children to work a little harder and act better (i.e., White), everything would be fine. As Dyson notes, "It's hard to argue against any of these things in the abstract; in principle such suggestions sound just fine."

Of course, not all Whites act White. To equate acting White with high academic achievement has little empirical or cultural support. Although more Whites between ages 18 and 19 are in school, the differences are relatively small—69 percent of Whites compared to 65 percent of Blacks. Studies comparing attitudes and performance show that Black students have the same attitudes—good and bad—about achievement as their White counterparts. Too often, we tend to view White slackers who give a hard time to the advanced placement kids as "normal," but when low-performing African Americans do the same thing, it becomes a systemic pathology undermining everything good about schools. The primary stumbling block is not acting White or acting Black but being presented with similar educational opportunities (Buck 2011; Bureau of the Census 2011a: Table 224; Downey 2008; Lewis 2013; Tyson 2011; Tyson, Darity, and Castellino 2005).

So if the notion of the difficulty that some Black students face in school is not due to their opposition to act White, why are so many people still advancing this as fact? It allows us to blame the student and "Black culture" whatever one may wish that to mean, and not confront how our educational institutions

Is there a difference between Black and White schoolchildren in achievement orientation? Although some people feel that African American youth avoid acting White, research points to no difference in this respect. Members of high school science clubs, whether Black or White, are equally likely to overcome being regarded as "geeks" or "nerds."

8-1

are underperforming. This is another example of **color-blind racism** first present in Chapter 2 when we use race-neutral principles to defend the racial unequal status quo. Majority-minority schools today persist with far fewer educational resources. Where African Americas attend more integrated schools they are often relegated to less demanding curricular programs and face increased disciplinary actions compared to their fellow students (Lewis 2013).

Higher Education

Higher education for Blacks reflects the same pattern: The overall picture of African American higher education is not promising. Although strides were made in the period after the civil rights movement, a plateau was reached in the mid-1970s. African Americans are more likely than Whites to be part-time students and to need financial aid, which began to be severely cut in the 1980s. They are also finding the social climate on predominantly White campuses less than positive. As a result, the historically Black colleges and universities (HBCUs) are once again playing a significant role in educating African Americans. For a century, they were the only real source of college degrees for Blacks. Then, in the 1970s, predominantly White colleges began to recruit African Americans. As of 2010, however, the 105 HBCUs still accounted for about one-fifth of all Black college graduates (National Center for Education Statistics 2011: Tables 250, 297).

As shown in Figure 8.1, although African Americans are more likely today to be college graduates, the upward trend in the 1970s and 1980s has moderated. Several factors account for this reversal in progress:

1. Reductions in financial aid and more reliance on loans than on grants-in-aid, coupled with rising costs, have discouraged students who would be the first members of their families to attend college.

2. Pushing for higher standards in educational achievement without providing remedial courses has locked out many minority students.

3. Employment opportunities, though slight for African Americans without some college, have continued to lure young people who must contribute to their family's income and who otherwise might have gone to college.

4. Negative publicity about affirmative action may have discouraged some African Americans from even considering college.

5. Attention to what appears to be a growing number of racial incidents on predominantly White college campuses has also been a discouraging factor.

Colleges and universities seem uneasy about these problems; publicly, the schools appear committed to addressing them.

There is little question that special challenges face the African American student at a college with overwhelmingly White faculty, advisors, coaches, administrators, and student body. The campus culture may be neutral at best, and it is often hostile to members of racial minorities. The high attrition rate of African American students on predominantly White college campuses confirms the need for a positive environment.

The disparity in schooling becomes even more pronounced at the highest levels, and the gap is not closing. Only 6.5 percent of all doctorates awarded in 2009 were to native-born African Americans, reflecting twice the proportion of 3.0 percent in 1990. However foreign students received three times the number of doctorates of U.S.-born Black Americans (Bureau of the Census 2011a: Table 300).

Thus far, few but now growing in numbers, African Americans are entering positions that few people of any color reach. Don Thompson was named CEO of McDonalds in 2012 having begun his career with the corporation in 1990 as an electrical engineer with a degree from Purdue University. In 2012, just five other African Americans were heads of Fortune 500 corporations.

In summary, the picture of education for Black Americans is uneven—marked progress in absolute terms (much better educated than a generation ago), but relative to Whites the gap in educational attainment remains at all levels. Sixty years ago, the major issue appeared to be school desegregation, but the goal was to improve the quality of education received by Black schoolchildren. Today, the concerns of African American parents and most educators are similar—quality education. W. E. B. Du Bois advanced the same point in 1935—what a Black student needs "is neither segregated schools nor mixed schools. What he needs is Education" (p. 335).

The Economic Picture

The general economic picture for African Americans has gradually improved over the last 50 years, but this improvement is modest compared with that of Whites, whose standard of living also has increased. Therefore, in terms of absolute deprivation, African Americans are much better off today but have not experienced significant improvement with respect to their relative deprivation to Whites on almost all economic indicators. To better understand today's economic reality, we first focus on the middle class and then turn to a broader overview of the occupations that African Americans fill.

8-2 Understand the economic situation of Black Americans.

The Middle Class

Many characterizations of the African American community have been attacked because they overemphasize the poorest segment of that community. Also overemphasized and exaggerated is how much success African Americans have achieved. Social scientists face the challenge of avoiding a selective, one-sided picture of Black society. The problem is similar to viewing a partially filled glass of water. Does one describe it as half empty and emphasize the need for assistance? Or does one describe the glass as half full to give attention to what has been accomplished? The most complete description acknowledges both perspectives.

A clearly defined African American middle class has emerged. In 2012, about 31 percent of African American households earned more than the median income for White non-Hispanic households. Nearly one-third of Blacks, then, are middle class or higher. Although, as noted in Chapter 3, Black income has increased, their wealth relative to Whites has lagged significantly. Many observers have debated the character of this middle class. E. Franklin Frazier (1957), a Black sociologist, wrote an often-critical study of the African American middle class in which he identified its overriding goal as achieving petty social values and becoming acceptable to white society (DeNavas-Walt, Proctor, and Smith 2013: Table HINC-03; Desilver 2013a).

Directing attention to the Black middle class also requires that we consider the relative importance of race and social class. The degree to which affluent Blacks identify themselves in class terms or racial terms is an important ideological question. W. E. B. Du Bois (1952) argued that when racism decreases, class issues become more important. As Du Bois saw it, exploitation would remain, and many of the same people would continue to be subordinate. Black elites might become economically successful, either as entrepreneurs (Black capitalists) or professionals (Black white-collar workers), but they would continue to identify with and serve the dominant group's interest.

Social scientists have long recognized the importance of class. **Class** is a term used by sociologist Max Weber to refer to people who share a similar level of wealth and income. The significance of class in people's lives is apparent to all. This is not just in terms of the type of cars one drives or where one goes on vacation but also in the quality of public schools available and the healthcare one receives.

Besides class, two measures are useful to determine the overall economic situation of an individual or household: income and wealth. **Income** refers to salaries, wages, and other money received; **wealth** is a more inclusive term that encompasses all of a person's material assets, including land and other types of property. The Research Focus box, "Moving on Up, or Not," considers how African Americans are doing in terms of income and wealth.

Research Focus

Moving on Up, or Not

Harvard political scientist Jennifer Hochschild (1995:44) observed that, "One has not really succeeded in America unless one can pass on the chance for success to one's children." By this standard, how well is the Black American community doing?

To begin with, relative to White Americans, Blacks have much less income and wealth. According to a report released in 2012, the proportion of Blacks and Whites rising to the top and falling to (or starting from) the bottom of the income and wealth ladders differs dramatically. Just over two-thirds (65 percent) of Blacks grew up at the bottom of the income ladder compared with only 11 percent of Whites. In Table 8-1, we look at income and wealth spread across quartiles or fifths of the entire population. Clearly Blacks are clustered toward the bottom quartile, while almost half of the Whites are in the top two-fifths. The same pattern exists for family wealth: 57 percent of blacks grew up at the bottom but only 14 percent of Whites. At the other end of the income and wealth pyramids, almost one-quarter (23 percent) of Whites were raised at the top versus only 2 percent of Blacks.

How do African Americans fare on matching or even enjoying greater economic success than their parents?

Admittedly, the current economic times are tough for *all* households, but even considering that, Blacks are less likely to rise above their parents' typically modest circumstances.

Black children are much less likely to end up in the middle class than White children. Not only is this true for the ones who grow up in poverty but also for those whose parents have made it to the middle class.

Only 23 percent of Blacks raised in the middle class exceed their parents' wealth, compared with 56 percent of Whites. Only at the very bottom do a majority of Blacks surpass their parents' wealth, but even there, White people below the poverty level do much better.

The American dream of upward mobility, while not being carried out as successfully by Black Americans, is certainly embraced by them. While only 52 percent of Whites believe their economic circumstances will be better in ten years, 73 percent of Blacks foresee improved personal finances ahead.

Sources: Economic Mobility Project 2012; Landry and Marsh 2011, Pew Charitable Trust 2011, 2012; Sawhill, Winship, and Grannis 2012.

TABLE 8.1
Percentage of Americans Raised in Each Quintile, by Race

	Family Income		Family Wealth	
	Black	White	Black	White
Raised in Top Quintile	2%	23%	2%	23%
Raised in Fourth Quintile	7%	23%	6%	22%
Raised in Middle Quintile	8%	22%	7%	23%
Raised in Second Quintile	18%	21%	28%	19%
Raised in Bottom Quintile	65%	11%	57%	14%

Notes: Numbers in each column may not sum to 100 percent due to rounding.
Source: Economic Mobility Project 2012:18.

The complexity of the relative influence of race, income, and wealth was apparent in the controversy surrounding the publication of sociologist William J. Wilson's *The Declining Significance of Race* (1980 [2012]). Pointing to the increasing affluence of African Americans, Wilson concluded, "class has become more important than race in determining black life-chances in the modern industrial period" (p. 150). The policy implications of his conclusion are that programs must be developed to confront class subordination rather than ethnic and racial discrimination. Wilson did not deny the legacy of discrimination reflected in the disproportionate number of African Americans who are poor, less educated, and living in inadequate and overcrowded housing. However, he pointed to "compelling evidence" that young Blacks were competing successfully with young Whites.

Early critics of Wilson commented that focusing attention on this small, educated elite ignores vast numbers of African Americans relegated to the lower class (Pinkney 1984; Willie 1978, 1979). Wilson himself was not guilty of such an oversimplification and indeed expressed concern over the plight of lower-class, inner-city African Americans as they seemingly fall even further behind. He pointed out that the poor are socially isolated and have shrinking economic opportunities (2012). However, it is easy for many people to conclude superficially that because educated Blacks are entering the middle class, race has ceased to be of concern.

Employment

This precarious situation for African Americans—the lack of dependable assets—is particularly relevant as we consider their employment picture. Higher unemployment rates for Blacks have persisted since the 1940s, when they were first documented. Even in the best economic times, the Black unemployment rate is still significantly higher than it is for Whites. In 2012, as the United States tried to emerge from a long recession, the Black unemployment rate stood at 14.4 percent compared to 7.0 percent for Whites. Considerable evidence exists that Blacks are the first fired as the business cycle weakens.

The employment picture is especially grim for African American workers aged 16 to 24. During the height of the recent recession, for Black youth aged 16–19, unemployment in 2012 hit just over 39 percent—equivalent to the national unemployment rate during the darkest period of the Great Depression (Bureau of Labor Statistics 2012b; Couch and Fairlic 2010).

Social scientists have cited many factors to explain why official unemployment rates for young African Americans are so high:

- Many African Americans live in the depressed economy of the central cities.
- Immigrants and illegal aliens present increased competition.
- White middle-class women have entered the labor force.
- Illegal activities whereby youths can make more money are increasingly prevalent.

None of these factors is likely to change soon, so depression-like levels of unemployment probably will persist (Haynes 2009).

The picture grows even more somber because we are considering only official unemployment. The federal government's Bureau of Labor Statistics counts as unemployed people only those who are actively seeking employment. Therefore, to be officially unemployed, a person must not hold a full-time job, must be registered with a government employment agency, and must be engaged in submitting job applications and seeking interviews. The official unemployment rate leaves out millions of Americans, Black and White, who are effectively unemployed. It does not count people who are so discouraged they have temporarily given up looking for employment. The problem of unemployment is further compounded by **underemployment,** or working at a job for which one is overqualified, involuntarily working part-time instead of full-time, or being employed only intermittently.

Although a few African Americans have crashed through the glass ceiling and made it into the top echelons of business or government, more have entered a wider variety of jobs. As shown in Table 8.2, African Americans, who constitute 12.4 percent of the population, are underrepresented in high-status, high-paying occupations. The taboo against putting Blacks in jobs in which they would supervise Whites has weakened, and the percentage of African Americans in professional and managerial occupations has shown remarkable improvement. However, much improvement can still be made.

TABLE 8.2
Percentages of African American Employees in Selected Occupations, 1982–2010

Occupation	1982	1995	2012
Lawyers and judges	7.2	7.6	4.4
Physicians	2.3	3.6	7.2
Registered nurses	8.2	8.4	11.5
College professors	4.8	6.2	7.9
Librarians	7.2	7.6	7.9
Social workers	16.1	23.7	23.0
Managers	3.9	7.5	6.9
Sales workers	3.8	7.8	10.5
Cashiers	10.0	15.8	17.2
Police and detectives	9.3	11.2	12.8

Sources: Bureau of the Census 1984: Table 616 on pp. 419–420; 1996: Table 637 on pp. 405–407; and Bureau of Labor Statistics 2013b: Table 10.

8-3

8-3 Identify the strengths of and challenges facing family life.

Family Life

The family in its role as a social institution providing for the socialization of children is crucial to its members' life satisfaction. The family also reflects the influence, positive or negative, of income, housing, education, and other social factors. For African Americans, the family reflects both amazing stability and the legacy of racism and low income across many generations.

Challenges to Family Stability

More than one-third of African American children had both a father and a mother present in 2009 (see Figure 8.2). Although single-parent African American families are common, they are not universal. In comparison, such single-parent arrangements were also present in about one in five White families. Regardless of race, there has been a remarkable retreat from marriage (Acs 2013).

It is just as inaccurate to assume that a single-parent family is necessarily deprived as it is to assume that a two-parent family is always secure and happy. Nevertheless, life in a single-parent family can be extremely stressful for all single parents and their children, not just those who are members of subordinate groups. Because the absent parent is more often the father, the lack of a male presence almost always means the lack of a male income. This monetary impact on a single-parent household cannot be overstated.

For many single African American women living in poverty, having a child is an added burden. However, the tradition of extended family among African Americans eases this burden somewhat. The absence of a husband does not mean that no one shares in childcare: out-of-wedlock children born to Black teenage mothers often live with their grandparents and form three-generation households.

No single explanation accounts for the rise in single-parent households. Sociologists attribute the rapid expansion in the number of such households primarily to shifts in the economy that have kept Black men, especially in urban areas, out of work. The phenomenon certainly is not limited to African Americans. Increasingly, both White and Black unmarried women bear children. More and more parents, both White and Black, divorce, so even children born into a two-parent family might end up living with only one parent.

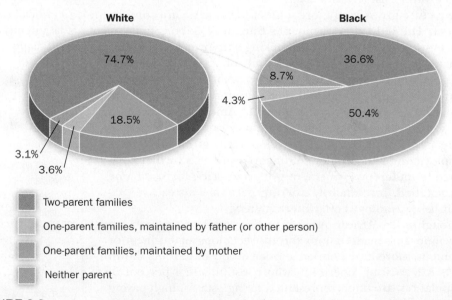

White

74.7%

18.5%

3.1%

3.6%

Black

36.6%

8.7%

4.3%

50.4%

■ Two-parent families

■ One-parent families, maintained by father (or other person)

■ One-parent families, maintained by mother

■ Neither parent

FIGURE 8.2
Living Arrangements for Children Younger Than 18

Note: Data reported in 2011 for 2009. White data are for White non-Hispanic and do not total to 100 percent due to rounding error.

Source: Kreider and Ellis 2011: 4–5.

Strengths of African American Families

In the midst of ever-increasing single parenting, another picture of African American family life becomes visible: success despite discrimination and economic hardship. Robert Hill (1999), of the National Urban League and Morgan State University, listed the following five strengths of African American families that allow them to function effectively in a hostile (racist) society.

1. *Strong kinship bonds:* Blacks are more likely than Whites to care for children and the elderly in an extended family network.

2. *A strong work orientation:* Poor Blacks are more likely to be working, and poor Black families often include more than one wage earner.

3. *Adaptability of family roles:* In two-parent families, an egalitarian pattern of decision making is the most common. The self-reliance of Black women who are the primary wage earners best illustrates this adaptability.

4. *Strong achievement orientation:* Working-class Blacks indicate a greater desire for their children to attend college than do working-class Whites. A majority of low-income African American children want to attend college.

5. *A strong religious orientation:* Since the time of slavery, Black churches have been the impetus behind many significant grassroots organizations.

Social workers and sociologists have confirmed through social research the strengths that Hill noted first in 1972. In the African American community, these are the sources of family strength (Hudgins 1992).

Increasingly, social scientists are looking at both the weaknesses and the strengths of African American family life. Expressions of alarm about instability date back to 1965, when the Department of Labor issued the report *The Negro Family: The Case for National Action.* The document, commonly known as the Moynihan Report, after its principal author, sociologist Daniel Patrick Moynihan, outlined a "tangle of pathology" with the Black family at its core. More recently, two studies—the Stable Black Families Project and the National Survey of Black Americans—sought to learn how Black families encounter problems and resolve them successfully with internal resources such as those that Hill outlined in his highly regarded work (Department of Labor 1965; Massey and Sampson 2009).

The most consistently documented strength of African American families is the presence of an extended family household. The most common feature is having grandparents residing in the home. Extended living arrangements are much more common among Black households than among White ones. These arrangements are recognized as having the important economic benefit of pooling limited economic resources. Because of the generally lower earnings of African American heads of household, income from second, third, and even fourth wage earners is needed to achieve a desired standard of living or, in all too many cases, simply to meet daily needs (Haxton and Harknett 2009).

Housing

Housing plays a major role in determining the quality of a person's life. For African Americans, as for Whites, housing is the result of personal preferences and income. However, African Americans differ from Whites because their housing has been restricted through discrimination, which has not been the case for Whites. We devote significant attention to housing because, for most people, housing is critical to their quality of life and often represents their largest single asset.

Although Black housing has improved—as indicated by statistics on home ownership, new construction, density of living units, and quality as measured by plumbing facilities—African Americans remain behind Whites on all these standards. The quality of Black housing is inferior to that of Whites at all income levels, yet Blacks pay a larger proportion of their income for shelter.

8-4 Articulate the housing situation in the African American community.

8-5

Typically in the United States, as noted, White children attend predominantly White schools, Black children attend predominantly Black schools, and Hispanic children attend predominantly Hispanic schools. This school segregation is not only the result of the failure to accept busing but also the effect of residential segregation. In their studies on segregation, Douglas Massey and Nancy Denton (1993) concluded that racial separation "continues to exist because white America has not had the political will or desire to dismantle it" (p. 8). In Chapter 1, we noted the pervasiveness of residential segregation as reflected in the most recent analysis of housing patterns (refer back to Table 1.2). Racial isolation in neighborhoods has only improved modestly over the last two generations.

What factors create residential segregation in the United States? Among the primary factors are the following:

- Because of private prejudice and discrimination, people refuse to sell or rent to people of the "wrong" race, ethnicity, or religion.
- The prejudicial policies of real estate companies steer people to the "correct" neighborhoods.
- Government policies do not effectively enforce anti-bias legislation.
- Public housing policies today, as well as past construction patterns, reinforce locating housing for the poor in inner-city neighborhoods.
- Policies of banks and other lenders create barriers based on race to financing home purchasing.

The issue of racial-based financing deserves further explanation. In the 1990s, new attention was focused on the persistence of **redlining,** the practice of discriminating against people trying to buy homes in minority and racially changing neighborhoods.

It is important to recall the implications of this discrimination in home financing for the African American community. Earlier in the chapter, we noted the great disparity between Black and White family wealth and the implications of this for the present and future generations. The key factor in this inequality was the failure of African Americans to accumulate wealth through home buying.

A dual housing market is part of today's reality, although attacks continue against the remaining legal barriers to fair housing. In theory, **zoning laws** are enacted to ensure that specific standards of housing construction will be satisfied. These regulations can also separate industrial and commercial enterprises from residential areas. However, some zoning laws in suburbs have curbed the development of low- and moderate-income housing that would attract African Americans who want to move out of the central cities.

8-5 Identify the present concerns about the criminal justice system.

Zoning laws that may stipulate expensive building materials help keep out the less affluent, who are more likely to be African American homebuyers.

For years, constructing low-income public housing in the ghetto has furthered racial segregation. The courts have not ruled consistently in this matter in recent years so, as with affirmative action, public officials lack clear guidance. Even if court decisions continue to dismantle exclusionary housing practices, the rapid growth of integrated neighborhoods is unlikely. In the future, African American housing probably will continue to improve and remain primarily in all-Black neighborhoods. This gap is greater than can be explained by differences in social class.

Criminal Justice

A complex, sensitive topic affecting African Americans is their role in criminal justice. It was reported for 2012 that Blacks constitute 4.4 percent of all lawyers, 9.2 percent of police officers and detectives, and 26.6 percent of security guards but 39 percent of jail and prison inmates.

Data collected annually in the FBI's Uniform Crime Report show that Blacks account for 28 percent of arrests, even though they represent only about 12 percent of the nation's population. Conflict

8-5

While the number of African American judges is growing, they still are too few in number. For example, In Cook County, which includes Chicago, Black criminal court judges account for 21 percent of the total, which seems impressive, but Blacks are the defendants in 72 percent of the cases (Chaney 2009).

theorists point out that the higher arrest rate is not surprising for a group that is disproportionately poor and, therefore, much less able to afford private attorneys, who might be able to prevent formal arrests from taking place. Even more significantly, the Uniform Crime Report focuses on index crimes (mainly property crimes), which are the type of crimes most often committed by low-income people.

These numbers are staggering but, as dramatic as they are, it is not unusual to hear exaggerations presented as facts, such as "more Black men are in prison than in college." The reality is sobering enough—581,000 in prison compared to 2,584,000 in college. About one in 16 White males can expect to go to a state or federal prison during his lifetime, yet for Black males this lifetime probability is one out of three (Carson and Sabol 2012: Table 7; National Center for Education Statistics 2011: Table a-39-1).

Most (actually 70 percent) of all the violent crimes against Whites are perpetrated by Whites, according to the FBI. In contrast to popular misconceptions about crime, African Americans and the poor are especially likely to be the victims of serious crimes. This fact is documented in **victimization surveys,** which are systematic interviews of ordinary people carried out annually to reveal how much crime occurs. These Department of Justice statistics show that African Americans are 35 percent more likely to be victims of violent crimes than are Whites (Truman 2011).

Central to the concerns of minorities regarding the criminal justice system is **differential justice**—that is, Whites are dealt with more leniently than are Blacks, whether at the time of investigation, arrest, indictment, conviction, sentencing, incarceration, or parole. Studies demonstrate that police often deal with African American youths more harshly than with White youngsters. Law is a public social institution and in many ways reproduces the inequality experienced in life (Peterson 2012).

It has also been accepted, albeit reluctantly, that the government cannot be counted on to address inner-city problems. In crimes involving African Americans, legal system scholars have observed **victim discounting,** or the tendency to view crime as less socially significant if the victim is viewed as less worthy. For example, the numerous killings of Black youth going to and from school attract much less attention than, for example, a shooting spree that takes five lives in a suburban school. When a schoolchild walks into a cafeteria or schoolyard with automatic weapons and kills a dozen children and teachers, it is a case of national alarm, as with Columbine. When children kill each other in drive-by shootings, it is viewed as a local concern, reflecting the need to clean up a dysfunctional neighborhood. Many African Americans note that the main difference between these two situations is not the death toll but who is being killed: middle-class Whites in the schoolyard shootings and Black ghetto youth in the drive-by shootings.

It is most important to remember that crime and victimization cannot be viewed in isolation but must be seen as interconnected with everything from education to employment, the quality of healthcare, to the homes to which one returns at the end of the day. W. E. B. Du Bois noted over a century ago that crime was difficult to address precisely because, "It is phenomenon that stands not alone, but rather as a symptom of countless wrong social conditions" (1996:242).

Healthcare

The price of being an African American took on new importance when a shocking study published in a prestigious medical journal revealed that two-thirds of boys in Harlem, a predominantly Black neighborhood in New York City, can expect to die young or in mid-adulthood—that is, before they reach age 65. In fact, they have less chance of surviving even to age 45 than their White counterparts nationwide have of reaching age 65. The medical researchers noted that it is not the stereotyped images of AIDS and violence that explain the staggering difference. Black men are much more likely to fall victim to unrelenting stress, heart disease, and cancer (Fing, Madhavan, and Alderman 1996).

Morbidity and mortality rates for African Americans as a group, and not just Harlem men, are equally distressing. Compared with Whites, Blacks have higher death rates from diseases of the heart, pneumonia, diabetes, and cancer. Significant differences exist among segments of the population with Whites living longer than Blacks. So, for example, among those born in 1994, at one extreme a White female could anticipate living to 79.6 years, while a Black male could expect a lifespan of 64.9 years—that is, equivalent to what White females could reasonably expect who were born in 1935 (Arias 2010: Table 12; Bureau of the Census 2010a: Table 102).

Drawing on the conflict perspective, sociologist Howard Waitzkin (1986) suggests that racial tensions contribute to the medical problems of African Americans. In his view, the stress resulting from racial prejudice and discrimination helps explain the higher rates of hypertension found among African Americans (and Hispanics) than among Whites. Death resulting from hypertension is twice as common in Blacks as in Whites; it is believed to be a critical factor in Blacks' high mortality rates from heart disease, kidney disease, and strokes. Although medical experts disagree, some argue that the stress resulting from racism and suppressed hostility exacerbates hypertension among African Americans (Cooper, Rotimi, and Ward 1999; Green et al. 2007).

Even when medical care is accessible, numerous studies have documented the reluctance of African Americans to trust the medical establishment. Whether it's seeking medical care or even donating blood or signing up for organ donation programs, Black Americans are underrepresented.

A NATIONAL ACADEMY OF SCIENCE'S INSTITUTE OF MEDICINE REPORT FINDS MINORITIES ARE LESS LIKELY TO RECEIVE PROPER MEDICAL CARE THAN WHITES.

www.cagle.com

8-6

There is good reason—a long history of mistreatment up to the present. Some is the result of explicit discrimination—banned from medical schools, denied access to "White blood" as soldiers in the military until after World War II, and even, until the 1960s, prohibited from joining the American Medical Association. But it has more to do with the way Black Americans have been looked upon.

Many people, White as well as Black, are familiar with the notorious Tuskegee syphilis study. In this federal government study, which began in 1932, Black men in Alabama were left untreated with syphilis so that researchers could observe the progression of the disease. Despite the discovery of effective treatments in 1945, the men were not given any medical assistance until the press uncovered the program in 1972. Such events caused contemporary African Americans to be particularly leery of the medical establishment.

Regrettably, this was neither an isolated incident nor the first or last abuse of African Americans with respect to health care. For generations, the role of medical practitioners with respect to people of color was either to verify their worth as slaves or to determine for their masters whether their property was really sick or just trying to get out of doing slave labor. Professor of Ethics at Harvard Medical School Harriet Washington (2007) coined the term **medical apartheid** to refer to the separate and unequal healthcare system in the United States that often has and continues to characterize healthcare for African Americans as well as Latinos.

A 1991 experiment implanted the now-defunct birth control device Norplant into African American teenagers in Baltimore in a program that was applauded by some observers as a way to "reduce the underclass." From 1992 to 1997, Columbia University undertook a study that sought to determine whether there is a biological or genetic basis that might cause violent behavior to run in families—and all the boys recruited for the study were Black. Researchers had misled the parents, claiming their children were simply coming in for a series of tests and questions when, in fact, they were given potentially risky doses of the same drug found in the controversial Fen-phen weight loss pill, which was later banned when it was found to have caused heart irregularities.

All of these episodes make the Black community's suspicions of medicine fairly understandable—but perhaps most telling has been the actual avoidance of the community when it should have been considered. Only 1 percent of the nearly 20 million Americans enrolled in biomedical studies or clinical trials are Black. This means that African Americans have often missed out on the latest breakthroughs. For example, virtually no Blacks were included in the original studies of the HIV inhibitor AZT, so when the drug came into widespread use in 1991, the Food and Drug Administration had little evidence of its impact on Blacks and erroneously reported that it was not effective for Black patients (Centers for Disease Control and Prevention 2007; Head 2007; Jecker 2000; Reverby 2000; Washington 2007).

Related to the healthcare dilemma is the problem of environmental justice, which was introduced in Chapter 3 and again in Chapter 6 with reference to Native Americans. Problems associated with toxic pollution and hazardous garbage dumps are more likely to be faced by low-income Black communities than by their affluent counterparts. This disproportionate exposure to environmental hazards can be viewed as part of the complex cycle of discrimination faced by African Americans and other subordinate groups in the United States.

Just how significant is the impact of poorer health on the lives of the nation's less-educated people, less-affluent classes, and subordinate groups? Drawing on a variety of research studies, population specialist Evelyn Kitagawa (1972) estimated the "excess mortality rate" to be 20 percent. In other words, 20 percent more people were

The Black Congressional Caucus gathered outside the White House. Now numbering 33 members, collectively they present an important political force and individually represent areas in Alabama, California, District of Columbia, Florida, Georgia, Illinois, Indiana, Louisiana, Maryland, Michigan, Minnesota, Mississippi, Missouri, Nevada, New York, North Carolina, Ohio, Pennsylvania, South Carolina, Texas, Virgin Islands, Virginia, and Wisconsin.

8-7

dying than otherwise might have because of poor health linked to race and class. Using Kitagawa's model, we can calculate that if every African American in the United States were White and had at least one year of college education, some 57,000 fewer Blacks would have died in 2012 and in each succeeding year (author's estimate based on Bureau of the Census 2011a: Table 1).

Politics

8-7 Address the current role of African Americans in politics.

Despite Barack Obama entering the White House as president in 2009, African Americans have not received an equal share of the political pie. After Reconstruction, it was not until 1928 that a Black was again elected to Congress. With Obama's election to the presidency, once again, no African American serves in the U.S. Senate at the time of this writing. Recent years brought some improvement at local levels; the number of Black elected officials increased from fewer than 1,500 in 1970 to over 10,500 in 2011 (Joint Center for Political and Economic Studies 2011).

Obama's 2008 electoral victory was impressive and, while not a landslide victory, his winning margin indicated widespread support. Expectedly, at least 93 percent of Blacks backed Obama in 2008 and again in 2012, but he also had 66 percent of all voters under 30, and 69 percent of first-time voters were prepared to vote for the first African American president (Connelly 2008; Edison Research 2012).

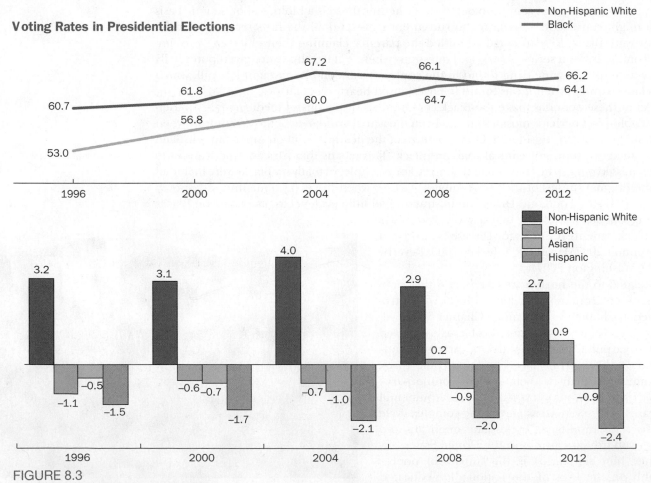

Voting Rates in Presidential Elections

FIGURE 8.3
Voting Races in Presidential Elections

In the space of two generations, African Americans emerged blocked from voting booths in many parts of the nation where they lived to exceeding Whites in the proportion turning out to vote in the 2012 Presidential election. This was achieved through a combination of hard work on the part of Black Americans themselves, many facets of the civil rights movement, favorable federal and court actions, and finally, in 2008 and 2012, the lure to vote for a Black man for president of the United States.

Source: File 2013:3.

One major landmark came in 2012, when the proportion of Blacks voting exceeded that of White non-Hispanics for the first time. As shown in Figure 8.3, over 66 percent of African Americans eligible voted compared to 64 percent of White non-Hispanics. Scholars and others will be watching to see if this is some sort of "Obama effect" or a lasting pattern. In any event, it represents a dramatic change from a half century ago of Jim Crow practices preventing millions of Black people from reaching the polls.

Yet major problems confront the continued success of African American politicians. Locally elected Black officials find it difficult to make the jump to statewide office. Voters, particularly non-Black voters, have difficulty seeing Black politicians as anything other than representatives of the Black community and express concern that the views of Whites and other non-Blacks will not be represented by an African American. Another big hurdle is acquiring the money necessary to seek a major office. Current Black Congressman Keith Ellison observes that, "As long as minority congressional members represent districts that tend to be lower income, then your funding base is going to be smaller, which will put you at a dollar disadvantage when you want to run for statewide office" (Nicholas and King 2013: A4).

The political gains by African Americans, as well as Hispanics, have been placed in jeopardy by legal actions that questioned race-based districts. Boundaries for elective office, ranging from city council positions to the U.S. House of Representatives, have been drawn in such a way so as to concentrate enough members of a racial or ethnic group to create a "safe majority" to make it likely that a member of that group will get elected. In Chapter 3, we noted how the push to require photo ID, regarded by many as a modern-day example of institutional discrimination, by a growing number of states would have a greater negative impact on potential Black voters than the general electorate.

The changing racial and ethnic landscape can be expected to have an impact on future strategies to elect African Americans to office, especially in urban areas. However, now that the number of Hispanics exceeds the number of Blacks nationwide, observers wonder how this might play out in the political world. A growing number of major cities, including Los Angeles and Chicago, are witnessing dramatic growth in the Hispanic population. Latinos often settle near Black neighborhoods or even displace Blacks who move into the suburbs, making it more difficult to develop African American districts. For example, South Central Los Angeles, the site of rioting in 1992 described earlier, is now two-thirds Latino. The full impact has not been felt yet because the Latino population tends to be younger, with many not yet reaching voting age. Nearly all elected officials who represent the area are Black. Yet resident concerns are nearly the same as they were a generation earlier—quality schools, public safety, and economic development (Medina 2012a).

Conclusion

The major new story of the early twenty-first century was the growth of the Hispanic population to the point where collectively Latino people overtook African Americans in size. To some degree this event and accompanying coverage began to move attention away from the African American experience in the United States. This less attention is not warranted. As shown in Figure 8.4, the African American population continues to grow except in some rural counties in the South. In 1998, for every African American there were six White non-Hispanics; by 2020 that will drop to less than five.

Maintaining the African American agenda a part of the larger American agenda is warranted again. Twice before in this nation's history, African Americans have received significant attention from the federal government and, to some degree, from the larger White society. The first period extended from the Civil War to the end of Reconstruction. The second period was during the civil rights movement of the 1960s. In both periods, the government acknowledged that race was a major issue, and society made commitments to eliminate inequality. As noted in Chapter 7, Reconstruction was followed by decades of neglect, and on several measures the position of Blacks deteriorated in the United States. A similar situation reoccurred after the gains of the civil right movement. Although the 1980s and 1990s were not without their successes, race was clearly not a major social issue on the national agenda. Even inner-city violence only diverted much of the nation's attention for a few fleeting moments, whereas color-blind attacks on school integration and affirmative action persisted.

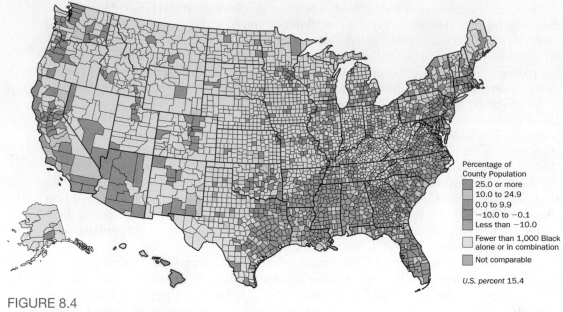

FIGURE 8.4
Percent Change of Black Population by County: 2000–2010

Source: Jones 2012:Slide 10.

With the election and re-election of Barack Obama, many people summed up his *individual* achievement as "mission accomplished" for the equality of opportunity for *all* Black Americans with the rest of society. So is it really necessary to keep talking "race" or the need to address any legacy of slavery, an institution now behind us by about 150 years?

Now in the 21ˢᵗ Century, the issues confronting Black Americans are still ones that serve to highlight concerns of the entire population. For example, affordable

SPECTRUM OF INTERGROUP RELATIONS

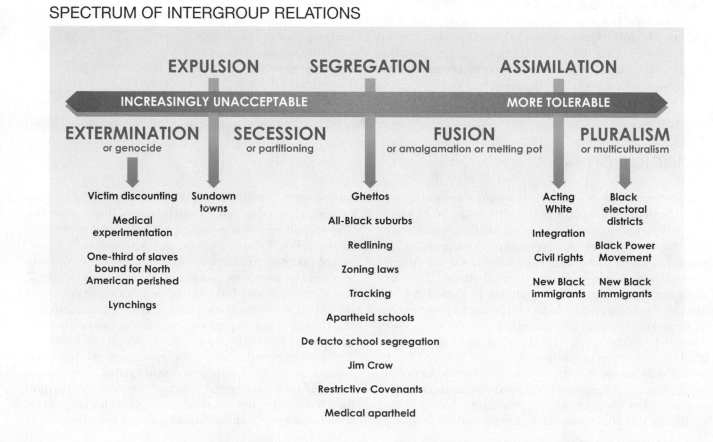

housing continues to reappear in the headlines especially in the wake of so many people unable to pay their mortgages the last few years. While Black renters and house owners face the additional burden of the legacy of housing discrimination, any significant effort to address poor housing conditions and the high costs of decent family housing would benefit the nation as a whole.

Furthermore, in the last few years, people of all colors and national origins expressed concern for public safety. So as a nation if we were to address the issues of racial profiling and unsafe inner city neighborhoods, all people would benefit. If stagnating gains in the life expectancy of African Americans and medical apartheid were seriously addressed, the general health of the entire nation would improve. Similarly, and perhaps most dramatically, if the quality of education that Black students receive from pre-school through college were to improve so too would the schooling of all young people.

Black and White Americans have dealt with the continued disparity between the two groups by endorsing several ideologies, as shown in the representation of the Spectrum of Intergroup Relations. Assimilation was the driving force behind the civil rights movement, which sought to integrate Whites and Blacks into one society. People who rejected contact with the other group endorsed separatism. As Chapter 2 showed, both Whites and Blacks generally lent little support to separatism. In the late 1960s, the government and various Black organizations began to recognize cultural pluralism as a goal, at least paying lip service to the desire of many African Americans to exercise cultural and economic autonomy. Perhaps on no other issue is this desire for control more evident than in the schools.

Substantial gains have been made, but will the momentum continue? Improvement has occurred in a generation inspired and spurred on to bring about change. If the resolve to continue toward that goal lessens in the United States, then the picture may become bleaker, and the rate of positive change may decline further.

Summary

1. African Americans have made gains in all levels of formal schooling but still fall behind the gains made by others. Debate continues over the appropriateness of the notion that Black youths avoid appearances of acting White.

2. Typically, Black Americans are underrepresented in high-wage, high-status occupations and overrepresented in low-wage, low-status occupations. Income and wealth disparities persist between Black and White Americans, with African Americans facing the challenge of accumulating assets.

3. Family life among Black Americans has many identifiable strengths. A particular challenge faces the growing proportion of households that are moving into the middle class.

4. While de jure segregation has faded, residential de facto segregation persists.

5. Blacks are more likely to be victims of crime as well as more likely to be arrested and imprisoned. Critics question whether minorities are subjected to differential justice.

6. Healthcare statistics reveal significantly higher morbidity and mortality rates for African Americans built upon a pattern of healthcare that has been termed medical apartheid.

7. Black Americans have made strides in being elected to office and increased their voter turnout in recent decades.

Key Terms

acting White, p. 191

apartheid schools, p. 190

class, p. 193

color-bind racism, p. 192

de facto segregation, p. 190

differential justice, p. 199

income, p. 193

medical apartheid, p. 201

redlining, p. 198

tracking, p. 190

underemployment, p. 195

victim discounting, p. 199

victimization surveys, p. 199

wealth, p. 193

zoning laws, p. 198

Review Questions

1. To what degree have the civil rights movement initiatives in education been realized, or do they remain unmet?

2. What challenges face the African American middle class?

3. What are the biggest assets and challenges facing African American families?

4. Describe the impact that residential segregation has on the quality of housing for Black Americans.

5. How would you characterize the experiences of African Americans in the criminal justice system?

6. What is meant by "medical apartheid"?

7. How is race-based gerrymandering related to affirmative action?

Critical Thinking

1. Now more than 50 years after he made his famous "I Have a Dream" speech, how would Martin Luther King, Jr. view the state of Black progress today?

2. Specifically review the three paragraphs in King's 1963 speech where he speaks of his "dream." (Available at http://www.archives.gov/press/exhibits/dream-speech.pdf.) He speaks of children in Alabama, working together, and freedom. What dreams might he hold today for the nation's future?

3. What has been the ethnic and racial composition of the neighborhoods you have lived in and the schools you have attended? Consider how the composition of one may have influenced the other. What steps would have been necessary to ensure more diversity?

4. How are the problems in crime, housing, and health interrelated?

 **Latinos: The Largest Minority**

9-1 Discuss the characteristics of Latinos and explain panethnicity.

9-2 Describe the current economic picture.

9-3 Understand the patterns of education and English language attainment.

9-4 Address the present role of Latinos in politics.

9-5 Summarize the role of religion for Latinos.

9-6 Examine and understand the culture of Cuban Americans.

9-7 Restate the diversity among Central and South Americans.

One would not be surprised to hear fellow citizens in Miami or El Paso speaking Spanish, but what about in a small town in Illinois, Kansas, or Alabama? Change can be unsettling in a small town, and when it comes to diversity in the United States, the pattern can vary from one community to the next.

Beardstown is an Illinois river town of about 6,000 people that serves the surrounding rich agriculture land. The major employer for over two decades is a meat-processing plant that offers decent wages for hard, often dangerous work. Immigrants directly from Mexico as well as Mexican Americans from elsewhere were lured to Beardstown by the low cost of living and the jobs that locals passed on. Today, the town founded by Germans is over a third Hispanic and its public schools are 44 percent Hispanic. While townspeople say the influx of Hispanic people has kept the local economy alive and culturally vibrant, the area was slow to mount bilingual programs not just for the schools but also for local businesses and public services from the hospital to the city hall.

The outlook for rural America is even more economically stressful in the Plains. In Ulysses, Kansas, which is similar in size and ethnic composition to Beardstown, Luz Gonzalez opened The Down-Town Restaurant to serve the growing area Hispanic population. Initially, she mainly served Mexican food but found a clientele among long-term residents for diner food. So Gonzalez learned to prepare potato salad and other dishes that were exotic to her.

As noted at the outset, change is not easy. In Slocomb, Alabama, a town of 2,000 people that bills itself "Home of the Tomato," many of the local Latino workers who pick green beans, peaches, and strawberries fear seeking healthcare at the local clinic. The staff is friendly enough and speaks Spanish, but on the way there, the workers may face roadblocks as part of immigration crackdowns. Even if the laborers are citizens, they fear exposing relatives and friends who are illegal immigrants. The quest for healthcare becomes an exercise in overcoming moral issues that most Americans would rarely consider.

In many rural areas, the population has declined steadily. Latinos are often filling in the void whether it be in Alabama, Illinois, Kansas, or, as we saw in Chapter 4, America's Dairyland in Wisconsin. By one estimate, more than a third of the counties have lost population, but in 86 percent of these, the Hispanic population has increased, which serves to minimize overall population lost. While increases in the number of Spanish-speaking children is a challenge for schools, without their growing presence, districts would face an almost certain dramatic loss of school funding and massive spending cuts (Beardstown CUSD 15 2012; Costantini 2011; Galewitz 2012; Jordan 2012; Mather and Pollard 2007; Sulzberger 2011; Wisniewski 2012).

According to Census Bureau projections, just over 57 million Americans will be of Spanish or Latin American origin by 2015. This will be more than one in six people in the United States. Collectively, this group is called *Hispanics* or *Latinos,* two terms that we use interchangeably in this book. Latinos accounted for over half the entire nation's population growth between 2000 and 2010. Just considering the public schools in larger cities, Latinos account for over 40 percent of first-graders in Chicago, New York City, San Diego, and Phoenix; over 60 percent in Dallas and Houston; over 70 percent in Los Angeles; and over 85 percent in San Antonio (Bureau of the Census 2012e; Passel, Cohn, and Lopez 2011; Thomás Rivera Policy Institute 2009).

As of 2010, nearly 32 million Hispanics in the United States (two-thirds) are Mexican Americans, or Chicanos. The diversity of Latinos and their national distribution in the United States are shown in Figures 9.1 and 9.2. Except for Puerto Ricans, who are citizens by birth, legal status is a major issue within the Latino community. The specter of people questioning Latinos about their legal

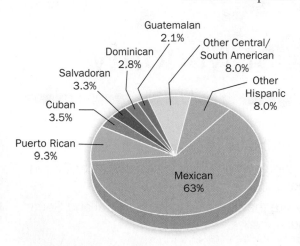

FIGURE 9.1

Hispanic Population of the United States by Origin

Note: "Other Hispanic" includes Spanish Americans and Latinos identified as mixed ancestry as well as other Central and South Americans not otherwise indicated by specific country. All nationalities with more than one million are indicated.

Source: 2010 census data in Ennis, Rios-Vargas, and Albert 2011: 3.

9-1

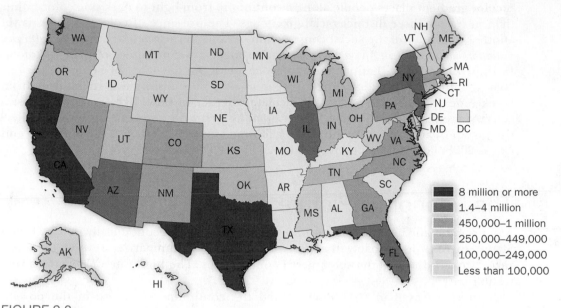

FIGURE 9.2
Where Most Hispanic Americans Live

55 percent of the nation's Hispanics live in just three states—California, Florida, and Texas.

Source: Ennis, Rios-Vargas, and Albert 2011.

status even looms over legal residents. According to a national survey, the majority of Hispanic adults in the United States worry that they, a family member, or a close friend could be deported (Lopez et al. 2010).

Latino Identity

Is there a common identity among Latinos? Is a panethnic identity emerging? **Panethnicity** is the development of solidarity between ethnic subgroups. Hispanics do not share a common historical or cultural identity. We noted in Chapter 1 that ethnic identity is not self-evident in the United States and may lead to heated debates even among those who share the same ethnic heritage. Non-Hispanics often give a single label to the diverse group of native-born Latino Americans and immigrants. This labeling by the outgroup is similar to how the dominant group views American Indians or Asian Americans as one collective group. The treating of all Hispanics alike is an unfortunate lack of attention to their history and the history of the United States (Rodriquez 1994: 32).

> **9-1** Discuss the characteristics of Latinos and explain panethnicity.

Are Hispanics or Latinos themselves developing a common identity? While generally two-thirds of Latinos and Hispanics in the United State agree that they share a common culture that does not mean they feel they share a common name. Overall, about half would prefer to use country of origin to identify themselves, such as *Mexican American*; the balance is split between *Hispanic* or *Latino* and *American*.

Among Hispanic youth aged 16–25, only a minority, about 20 percent, prefers to use panethnic names such as *Hispanic* or *Latino*. In Miami, Florida, bumper stickers proclaim "No soy Hispano, soy Cubano": "I am not Hispanic, I am Cuban." As might be expected, identity preferences vary according to whether one is an immigrant or is U.S.-born of U.S.-born Hispanics. About 72 percent of immigrant youth prefer country of origin compared to 32 percent of grandchildren (Pew Hispanic Center 2009, 2012a).

An even trickier issue is how Latinos identify themselves in racial terms now and how they will in the future. Typically, the sharp White–Black divide is absent in their home countries, where race, if socially constructed, tends to be along a color gradient.

9-2

A **color gradient** places people along a continuum from light to dark skin color rather than in two or three distinct racial groupings. The presence of color gradients is yet another reminder of the social construction of race. Terms such as *mestizo Hondurans*, *mulatto Colombians*, or *African Panamanians* reflect this continuum of color gradient. In the United States, Latinos tend to avoid taking on the label of being "White" or "Black," although lighter-skinned Hispanics generally distinguish themselves from Black Americans. Social scientists speculate whether in time, like the Irish almost a century ago, Latinos will come to be viewed as "White" rather than as a third collective group in addition to White and Black Americans (Bonilla-Silva 2004; Feagin and Cobas 2008; Pew Hispanic Center 2012a).

The Economic Picture

9-2 Describe the current economic picture.

Among the many indicators of how well a group is doing economically in the United States, income is probably the best one. Table 9.1 summarizes several key measures broken down by the six largest Latino groups. The high rate of poverty is very troubling.

A study released in 2011 documented the continuing high rise in the poverty rate from 1977 through 2010 except for some decline during the relative prosperity the nation experienced in the late 1990s. The government has measured poverty for generations and while Blacks have a higher rate, the largest group of children below the poverty level had always been Whites. In the last two years, however, Hispanics as a group have far overreached the number of White children in poverty. By 2010, 6.1 million Latino children were in poverty compared to 5 million White and 4.4 million Black children. Reflecting the low wages that Latinos often receive in the United States, poor Hispanic children are much more likely to have a working parent than either poor children in the White or Black communities (Lopez and Velasco 2011).

In Figure 9.3, we can see a side-by-side picture of income of Hispanic vs. White non-Hispanic workers as tabulated in the census. The picture is very stark, with the Latino incomes appearing to be just the reverse of the White earnings. These data are limited to only full-time year-round workers, so they significantly understate the difference. Many more Latino workers are unemployed or work only seasonally and/or part-time.

Income is just part of the picture. Low levels of wealth—total assets minus debt—are characteristic of Hispanic households. Although they appear to have slightly higher levels of median wealth than African American households, Hispanic households average less than 12 cents for every dollar in wealth owned by White non-Hispanic households. Also, the trend is not encouraging, with the Hispanic–non-Hispanic gap growing. Latinos not

TABLE 9.1
Hispanic Origin Groups

Group	Foreign Born	Bachelor's Degree	Proficient in English	Poverty Rate
Mexican Americans	36%	9%	64%	27%
Puerto Ricans	1	16	82	27
Cubans	59	24	58	18
Salvadorans	62	7	46	20
Dominicans	57	15	55	26
Guatemalans	67	8	41	26

Note: Includes the six largest groups; all reporting one million in 2010.
Source: Motel and Patten 2012.

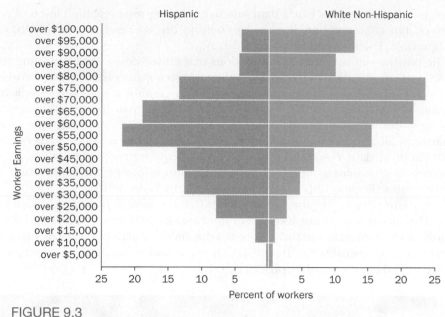

FIGURE 9.3
Hispanic vs. White Earnings

Note: Data for 2010 as tabulated in the Annual Social and Economic Supplement, 2011. Only for full-time, year-round workers 15 years and over; earnings are the sum of wage and salary income and self-employment income.

Source: Bureau of the Census 2011e: Table 21.

only are likely to continue to earn much less annually but also to have fewer financial resources to fall back on (Kent 2010).

By studying the income and poverty trends of Latino households, we can see how much—but also how little—has been accomplished to reduce social inequality among ethnic and racial groups. Although the income of Latinos has gradually increased over the last 30 years, so has White income. The gap between the two groups in both income and poverty level has remained relatively constant. Indeed, the $39,005 income of the typical Latino household in 2012 was *less than half of the typical 2002* White non-Hispanic household (DeNavas-Walt, Proctor, and Smith 2013: Tables H-12WANH and HINC-01).

Chapter 8 noted the growing proportion of poor African Americans who find it increasingly difficult to obtain meaningful work. Once employed, studies suggest they hit a "blue-collar ceiling," finding it difficult to move into better paying jobs with benefits such as insurance and pension. This also has been said of today's poor Latinos, but their situation is much more difficult to predict. On the one hand, as a group, poor Latinos are more geographically mobile than poor African Americans, which increases their prospects of a brighter future. On the other hand, 54 percent of foreign-born Latinos and 17 percent of native-born Latinos send money abroad to help relatives, which puts a greater strain on supporting themselves in the United States (Fuller, McElmurry, and Koval 2011; Lopez, Livingston, and Kochhar 2009).

Education

Looking at education among contemporary Latinos is a study of contrasts. Progress has been significant but they are often stigmatized as being more academically challenged than their White and Asian American peers. Yet Latinos are *more* likely to aspire to continue their education with 49 percent of high-school graduates enrolled in college compared to 47 percent of Whites.

The level of attainment as measured by years of schooling completed beyond high school remains modest. As a group, 13 percent of Latinos 25 years and over have a bachelor's degree compared to over 29 percent of Whites. As we saw in Table 9.1, there is a

9-3 Understand the patterns of education and English language attainment.

9-3

wide range with some groups like Cuban Americans having relatively high levels of college completion, but collectively attainment lags behind the Whites (Desilver 2013b; Ochoa 2013; Ogunwole, Drewery, and Rios-Vargas 2012).

On the positive side are the high aspirations that Latinos show for continuing school. About 88 percent of Latinos agree that a college degree is necessary to get ahead in life compared to 74 percent of the general population. As shown in Figure 9.4, a higher percentage of Hispanics leave high school to start college than the general population, and are now the largest minority group on four-year college campuses, and comprise one-quarter of all 18- to 24-year-old students enrolled in two-year colleges. As one might expect from these data, more and more Latino students are receiving their degrees but their success in completing college in a timely fashion is lower than that of their fellow White classmates (Fry and Lopez 2012; Fry, Lopez, and Taylor 2013).

Clearly a complicating factor in educational attainment is becoming proficient in English. The importance is not lost on Latinos, who in 2007 cited language skills more frequently than immigration status, income, education, or skin color as an explanation for discrimination against them. In 2007, 46 percent said it was the biggest cause of discrimination (Hakimzadeh and Cohn 2007).

Research Focus

English-Language Acquisition

Few issues swirling around the everyday life of Latinos in the United States are more heated than fluency in English. As we saw in Chapter 3, political efforts to declare English the official language continue, and the funding of bilingual programs is constantly in jeopardy, Native English speakers often resent hearing even accented English in the workplace or in public. Ironically, people who proudly see themselves as Latino but do not speak Spanish experience resentment from some Hispanics who feel they are too assimilated. Arizona Diamondbacks pitcher David Hernandez, a third-generation Mexican American raised in Sacramento, told reporters that when he first broke in to professional baseball, his many Latin American teammates kept trying to speak Spanish and could not understand why he would not engage them in conversations.

Yet these tensions occur against a backdrop where English language acquisition is not an issue among immigrants themselves. A 2007 survey showed that 59 percent of Latinos support the notion that immigrants should be required to be proficient in English to remain in the country. They see this as vital to advancement because other surveys have documented that those who lack fluency have greater problems in the job market and even have more limited exposure to newer technologies such as the Internet. Significantly, they also know that speaking with a Spanish accent, much less not speaking English very well, is devalued and stigmatized throughout the United States outside of Latino communities.

The reality is that most immigrants and their offspring quickly become fluent in English and abandon their mother tongue. By the second generation after the immigrants, that is, the grandchildren of the immigrants, use of the "mother tongue" has virtually disappeared.

In surveying 5,703 adults using both English and Spanish-speaking interviewers in southern metropolitan Los Angeles and San Diego, scholars looked at language retention across a variety of immigrant nationalities. This area is the nation's largest receiver of immigrants, accounting for one out of five of immigrants to the United States, and has the largest concentration of Spanish-speaking individuals. In such metropolitan areas one might anticipate significant language retention and slow acceptance of use of English. Given all the outlets to hear and read Spanish, for instance, one might expect there to be little motivation to learn English.

Instead, the researchers found in Southern California a move away from speaking the mother tongue and a move to use English. With each succeeding generation, the proportion speaking the mother tongue drops. Retention of Spanish is higher than is the survival of mother tongue by Asian and European immigrants. But even among the grandchildren of immigrants from Mexico and other Spanish-speaking countries, at most one in three speak fluent Spanish. Among their children, that is, the great-grandchildren of the immigrants, only 5 percent can speak Spanish. "Fluency" in speaking is not a very high standard, since many people who may be fluent could not write or read even a simple document in Spanish.

The apparent move toward the use of English in preference to the mother tongue persists even though they continue to live in the presence of the nation's large Latino population. These findings confirm other studies that show immigrants' acquisition of the English language in a couple of generations. Researchers given these data stress the limits of language retention and speak of the United States being aptly described as a "graveyard" for languages. The ability to sustain bilingualism across several generations is very limited. In summary, language continues to be a hot issue, but largely by the second generation, and certainly by the third generation, proficiency in the language of the host society becomes dominant.

Sources: The Arizona Republic 2013; Carroll 2007; Feagin and Cobas 2014; Fox and Livingston 2007; Hakimzadeh and Cohn 2007; Rumbaut, Massey, and Bean 2006.

Therefore, language acquisition is key to both education and the future economic development of Hispanics, as it is for immigrants from most countries. In the Research Focus, we consider the latest data on immigrants and their descendants' fluency in English.

The Political Presence

Until the late twentieth century, Latinos' political activity has been primarily outside conventional electoral activities. In the 1960s, urban Hispanics, especially Mexican Americans, developed activist groups aimed at what were regarded as especially unsympathetic policies of school administrators. About the same time, labor organizer César Chávez crusaded to organize migrant farmworkers. Efforts to organize agricultural laborers date back to the turn of the twentieth century, but Chávez was the first to enjoy any success. These laborers had never won collective bargaining rights, partly because their mobility and extreme poverty made it difficult for them to organize into a unified group.

Both major political parties have begun to acknowledge that Latinos form a force in the election process. Admittedly, for Puerto Ricans and Cuban Americans, as is discussed later, their central political issue has been the political future of their respective island homelands. Nonetheless, Republicans and Democrats have sought to gain support among Latinos. This recognition by establishment political parties has finally come primarily through the growth of the Hispanic population and also through policies that have facilitated non-English voters.

In 1975, Congress moved toward recognizing the multilingual background of the U.S. population. Federal law now requires bilingual or even multilingual ballots in voting districts where at least 5 percent of the voting-age population or 10,000 people do not speak English. The growing Latino presence documented in the 2010 Census has led Hispanic communities to anticipate that, following reapportionment, they will have even greater political representation, ranging from local council members to representatives and senators in Congress. As we can see in Figure 9.5, eligible Latino voters are very visible in many parts of the nation.

For a generation, political scholars spoke of the Latino power at the ballot box, but the Hispanic presence at the polls did not always live up to expectations. The turnout often has been poor because although Hispanics were interested in voting, many were ineligible to vote under the U.S. Constitution. They were noncitizens or, despite bilingual voting information, getting properly registered was a challenge.

This began to change with the 2010 Congressional elections and especially the 2012 presidential election. In the Obama–Romney race, Latinos nationwide constituted one out of every ten voters and their numbers were almost double that or even more in the key swing or battleground states of Colorado, Florida, Nevada, and Virginia. The potential for an even greater Latino political presence is strong.

Anticipating greater turnout, political parties are advancing more Hispanic candidates. Democrats have been decidedly more successful in garnering the Hispanic vote with ultimately 71 percent of Latinos backing Democrat candidate Obama in 2012. Even Cuban Americans, who have tended the favor the Republicans and their strong anti-Castro position, split their vote between Obama and Romney. While not all Latinos necessarily support easing immigration regulations, much of the tone in arguments for strict immigration

9-4 Address the present role of Latinos in politics.

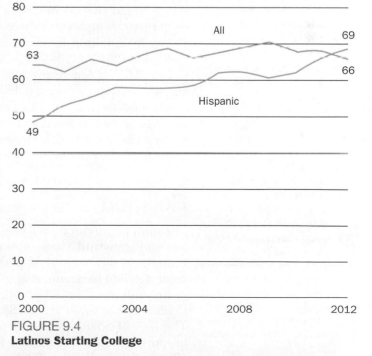

FIGURE 9.4
Latinos Starting College

Note: Data are for 18- to 24-year-olds having completed public high school or its equivalency.

Source: National Center for Educational Statistics 2013; Indicator 34.

9-5

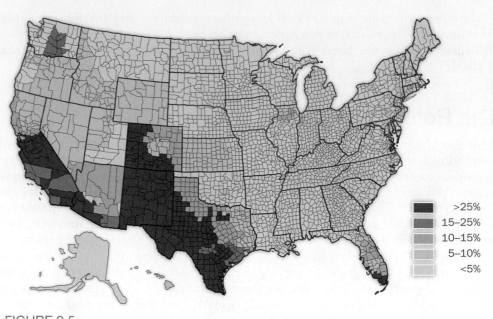

FIGURE 9.5
Latinos as a Percent of Eligible Voters

Source: Pew Hispanic Center 2011a, data based on 2008 Census Bureau sample.

laws alienates most Latinos. The Democrats promoted policies that allowed those who immigrated illegally as children or even infants with their parents a path to permanent residency following successful completion of their schooling. However, the Republicans officially opposed such steps and encouraged self-deportation for illegal immigrants and, if they do not comply with that, immediate deportation upon detection.

The Hispanic community's rapidly growing population, higher proportions of voter registration, and higher participation in elections guarantee future efforts by politicians to gain their support. The Democrats have clearly garnered the allegiance of Hispanics, and the Republicans face a difficult challenge to sway them to their candidates. A 2013 survey found that six in ten Latinos felt closer to the Democratic Party than they had in the past, compared to three in ten who felt closer to the Republican Party (Campo-Flores 2012; Edison Research 2012; Goodstein 2013; Lopez and Velasco 2011; Preston and Santos 2012).

Like African Americans, many Latinos resent that every four years the political movers and shakers rediscover that they exist. Latino community leaders derisively label candidates' fascination with Latino concerns near election time as either *fiesta politics* or *Hispandering*. Between major elections, modest efforts have been made to court their interest except by Latino elected officials; however, this may change as Latino presence at the ballot box is felt.

Religion

9-5 Summarize the role of religion for Latinos.

The most important formal organization in the Hispanic community is the Church. Most Puerto Ricans and Mexican Americans express a religious preference for the Catholic Church. In 2011, about 62 percent of Hispanics were Catholic. Figure 9.6 examines a more detailed background of specific religious affiliations indicated by Latinos.

Recently, the Roman Catholic Church has become more community oriented, seeking to identify Latino, or at least Spanish-speaking, clergy and staff to serve Latino parishes. The lack of Spanish-speaking priests has been complicated further because a smaller proportion of men are training for the priesthood, and even fewer of them speak Spanish (Ramirez 2000; Rosales 1996).

Not only is the Catholic Church important to Hispanics but Hispanics also play a significant role for the Church. The selection of Pope Frances from Argentina in 2013 was

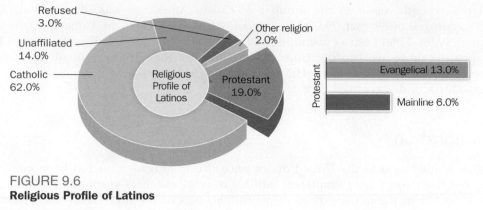

FIGURE 9.6
Religious Profile of Latinos

Source: Pew Hispanic Center 2012a.

interpreted by many as an acknowledgment of the Latin American role in the global Roman Catholic Church. The population growth of Mexican Americans and other Hispanics has been responsible for the Catholic Church's continued growth in recent years, whereas mainstream Protestant faiths have declined in size. Hispanics account for more than a third of Roman Catholics in the United States. The Church is trying to adjust to Hispanics' more expressive manifestation of religious faith, which is reflected by frequent reliance on their own patron saints and the presence of special altars in their homes. Catholic churches in some parts of the United States are even starting to accommodate observances of the Mexican Día de los Muertos, or Day of the Dead. Such practices are a tradition from rural Mexico, where religion was followed without trained clergy. Yet in the United States today, Hispanics continue to be underrepresented among priests: only 4.4 percent nationwide are Hispanic (O'Connor 1998).

Although Latinos are predominantly Catholic, their membership in Protestant and other Christian faiths is growing. According to a national survey, first-generation Latinos (that is, the immigrant generation) are 69 percent Catholic, but by the third generation (that is, grandchildren of immigrants) only 40 percent are Catholic. As one pastor of the New Life Covenant Church in Chicago observed, when the young Latino parishioners leave his church saying thank you for the Mass today, it is not hard to identify them as converts from Catholicism (Pew Hispanic Center 2012a: 35).

Available data show religious Latinos who are not Catholic are more likely to attend services, feel religion is very important in their daily lives, and tend to be younger. Typically these non-Catholics attend independent and sometimes literally storefront churches. But this is quickly evolving as witnessed by the 17,000 attending services at one of the four campuses of New Life Covenant Church in Chicago (Dias 2013).

Pentecostalism, a type of evangelical Christianity, is growing in Latin America and is clearly making a significant impact on Latinos in the United States. Adherents to Pentecostal faiths hold beliefs similar to those of evangelicals but also believe in the infusion of the Holy Spirit into services and in religious experiences such as faith healing. Pentecostalism and similar faiths are attractive to many Latinos because they offer followers the opportunity to express their religious fervor openly. Furthermore, many of the churches are small and, therefore, offer a sense of community, often with Spanish-speaking leadership. Gradually, the more established faiths are recognizing the desirability of offering Latino parishioners a greater sense of belonging (Hunt 1999).

Cuban Americans

Third in numbers only to Mexican Americans and Puerto Ricans, Cuban Americans are a significant ethnic Hispanic minority in the United States. Their presence in this country has a long history, with Cuban settlements in Florida dating back to as early as 1831. These settlements tended to be small, close-knit communities organized around a single enterprise such as a cigar-manufacturing firm.

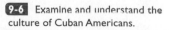
9-6 Examine and understand the culture of Cuban Americans.

Until recently, however, the number of Cuban Americans was very modest. The 1960 census showed that 79,000 people who had been born in Cuba lived in the United States. Fidel Castro's assumption of power after the 1959 Cuban Revolution led to sporadic movements to the United States and for generations defined the Cuban American political agenda in the United States. By 2010, more than 1.7 million people of Cuban birth or descent lived here.

Immigration

Cuban immigration to the United States since the 1959 revolution has been continuous, but there were three significant influxes of large numbers of immigrants through the 1980s. First, the initial exodus of about 200,000 Cubans after Castro's assumption of power lasted about three years. Regular commercial air traffic continued despite the United States' severing of diplomatic relations with Cuba. This first wave stopped with the missile crisis of October 1962, when all legal movement between the two nations was halted.

An agreement between the United States and Cuba in 1965 produced the second wave through a program of freedom flights—specially arranged charter flights from Havana to Miami. Through this program, more than 340,000 refugees arrived between 1965 and 1973. Despite efforts to encourage these arrivals to disperse into other parts of the United States, most settled in the Miami area (Abrahamson 1996).

The third major migration, the 1980 Mariel boatlift, has been the most controversial. In 1980, more than 124,000 refugees fled Cuba in the "freedom flotilla." In May of that year, a few boats from Cuba began to arrive in Key West, Florida, with people seeking asylum in the United States. President Carter (1978:1623), reflecting the nation's hostility toward Cuba's communist government, told the new arrivals and anyone else who might be listening in Cuba that they were welcome "with open arms and an open heart." As the number of arrivals escalated, it became apparent that Castro had used the invitation as an opportunity to send prison inmates, patients from mental hospitals, and drug addicts. However, the majority of the refugees were neither marginal to the Cuban economy nor social deviants.

Now a Chicago real estate broker, Alfredo Jimenez tells in the Speaking Out box of the experience he had as a young child being taken by his family and leaving everything behind in Cuba to go to the United States.

Other Cubans soon began to call the refugees of this migration **Marielitos**. The word, which implies that these refugees were undesirable, refers to Mariel, the fishing port west of Havana from which the boats departed and where Cuban authorities herded people into boats. The term *Marielitos* remains a stigma in the media and in Florida. Because of their negative reception by longer-established Cuban immigrants and the group's modest skills and lack of formal education, these immigrants had a great deal of difficulty in adjusting to their new lives in the United States (Masud-Piloto 2008b).

There are some interesting parallels between the freedom flotilla and Irish immigration of more than a century earlier discussed in Chapter 5. Both represent immigration based on difficult economic conditions, reliance on family ties to make it successful, and were greeted in the United States with an often hostile reaction. Both were exploited but in different ways. The Irish were taken advantage by people who used them for cheap labor and the Cuban refugees were exploited by both the United States and Cuba for political reasons One important difference is that dissatisfied Irish immigrants could return if they wished, whereas for the Cubans there was no turning back (Miller 2014).

The difficult transition for many members of this freedom flotilla also has other reasons. Unlike the earlier waves of immigrants, they grew up in a country bombarded with anti-American images. Despite these problems, their eventual acceptance by the Hispanic community has been impressive, and many members of this third significant wave have found employment. Most have applied for permanent resident status. Government assistance to these immigrants was limited, but help from some groups of Cuban Americans in the Miami area was substantial. However, for a small core group,

(◉) Speaking Out

9-6

Leaving Cuba

At the age of eight I first realized my family was planning on leaving Cuba when my mother went to my second grade school in Havana to inform the principal that my brother and I would not be returning. I remember my teacher was not surprised that we were leaving but was surprised that we were *gusanos*, literally meaning worms or political dissidents. I returned home as my family waited to receive word that we were allowed to leave.

We waited about a week when a policeman knocked at our door in the middle of the night on May 17, 1980, and handed my father a document granting permission to leave Cuba. Within hours we had to get to the processing center, so my parents woke us up and prepared my grandmother who was in a wheelchair. At the center, the Cuban government confiscated our passports and searched us, keeping all valuables including my parents' wedding rings. From there it was to Mariel Port three hours away by a special bus.

The trip on the bus was tough for an eight-year-old as people along the entire route beat on our bus with bats, sticks, stones, eggs, and tomatoes. Once at the Port, my brother and

J. Alfredo Jimenez

I managed to get away from the adults to play with other children at the beach, where I remember playing with small crabs in the sand. My parents got very upset when our pant legs got wet. They had written on the inside of our pant legs the names, addresses, and phone numbers of friends and family in the United States and Spain.

After days of waiting we were finally able to board an overcrowded boat headed for Florida. Already filled to the brim, the boat in the middle of the night rescued 12 people from another boat that was sinking. After 12 hours, we arrived in Key West to be greeted by waving American flags. Soon we headed on to Tampa to live with an aunt and her family—she had come to America soon after Fidel Castro assumed power.

The entire trip was an experience that my family values very much to this day. As young as my brother and I were, we didn't appreciate how difficult it was for my parents to leave everything behind.

Source: Jiminez 2005.

adjustment was impossible. The legal status of a few of these detainees (for example, arrivals who were held by the government pending clarification of their refugee or immigrant status) was ambiguous because of alleged offenses committed in Cuba or in the United States (Peréz 2001).

Since 1994, the United States has had a **dry foot, wet foot** policy with respect to arrivals from Cuba. Government policy generally allows Cuban nationals who manage to actually reach the United States (dry foot) to remain, whereas those who are picked up at sea (wet foot) are sent back to Cuba. Furthermore, 20,000 visas are issued annually to immigrants who are seeking economic freedom and, for the most part, are not strongly anti-Castro. Unfortunately, other Cubans have taken great risks in crossing the Florida Straits, and an unknown number have perished before reaching the mainland or being intercepted by the Coast Guard. Through all these means, about 300,000 Cubans have come to the United States since 1964 (*Economist* 2009).

The Current Picture

Compared with other recent immigrant groups and with Latinos as a whole, Cuban Americans are doing well. As shown in Table 9.1, Cuban Americans have college completion rates that are significantly higher than other Latino groups. In this and all other social measures, the pattern is similar. Cuban Americans today compare favorably with other Hispanics, although recent arrivals as a group trail behind White Americans.

The presence of Cubans has been felt in urban centers throughout the United States but most notably in the Miami area. Throughout their various immigration phases, Cubans have been encouraged to move out of southern Florida, but many have returned to Dade County (metropolitan Miami), with its warm climate and proximity to other Cubans and Cuba itself. As of 2010, 48 percent of all Cuban Americans lived in the Miami area; another 20 percent lived elsewhere in Florida. Metropolitan Miami itself now has a Hispanic majority of 62 percent of the total population, compared with a Hispanic

9-6

Like all other immigrant groups, ethnic enclaves of shopping, restaurants, and just a place to converse emerge wherever people of the same nationality are concentrated. Pictured here is Little Havana in Miami.

presence of only 4 percent in 1950 (American Community Survey 2009: Table B03001; Logan and Turner 2013).

Probably no ethnic group has had more influence on the fortunes of a city in a short period of time than have the Cubans on Miami. Most people consider the Cubans' economic influence to be positive. With other Latin American immigrants, Cubans have transformed Miami from a quiet resort to a boomtown. To a large degree, they have re-created the Cuba they left behind. Today, the population of Miami is more than 59 percent foreign born—more than any other city. Residents like to joke that one of the reasons they like living in Miami is that it is close to the United States (Malone et al. 2003).

The relations between Miami's Cuban Americans and other groups have not been perfect. For example, other Hispanics—including Venezuelans, Ecuadorians, and Colombians—resent being mistaken for Cubans and feel that their own distinctive nationalities are being submerged. Cubans now find that storefronts in Miami's Little Havana area advertise Salvadoran corn pancakes and that waitresses hail from El Salvador. Cuban Miamians are also slowly adjusting to sharing their influence with the growing diversity of Hispanics. One obvious symbol is the investment of the park district in building more and more soccer fields—Cubans traditionally play baseball (Dahlburg 2004).

All Cuban immigrants have had much to adjust to, and they have not been able to immediately establish the kind of life they sought. Although some of those who fled Cuba were forced to give up their life's savings, the early immigrants of the first wave were generally well educated, had professional or managerial backgrounds, and therefore met with greater economic success than later immigrants. However, regardless of the occupations the immigrants were able to enter, their families had to make tremendous adjustments. Women who typically did not work outside the home often had to seek employment. Immigrant parents found their children being exposed to a foreign culture. All the challenges typically faced by immigrant households were complicated by the uncertain fates of those they left behind in Cuba.

The primary adjustment among South Florida's Cuban Americans has been more to each other than to Whites, African Americans, or other Latinos. The prolonged immigration now stretching across two generations has led to differences between Cuban Americans in terms of ties to Cuba, social class, and age. There is no single Cuban American lifestyle.

The long-range prospects for Cubans in the United States depend on several factors. Of obvious importance are events in Cuba; many exiles have publicly proclaimed their desire to return to Cuba if the communist government is overturned. A powerful force in politics in Miami is the Cuban American National Foundation, which takes a strong anti-Castro position. The organization has actively opposed any proposals that the United States develop a more flexible policy toward Cuba. More moderate voices in the Cuban exile community have not been encouraged to speak out. Indeed, sporadic violence has even occurred within the community over U.S.–Cuban relations. In addition, artists or speakers who come from Cuba receive a cold reception in Miami unless they are outspoken critics of Fidel Castro.

Cuban Americans have selectively accepted Anglo culture. Cuban culture itself has been tenacious; the Cuban immigrants do not feel they need to forget Spanish while establishing fluency in English, the way other immigrant children have shunned their linguistic past. Still, a split between the original exiles and their children is evident. Young people are more concerned about the Miami Dolphins football team than they are about what is happening in Havana. They are more open to reestablishing relations with a Castro-led Cuba. However, the more recent wave of immigrants, the *recién llegados* (recently arrived), have again introduced more openly anti-Castro feelings even as the presidency transferred from Fidel Castro to his brother Raúl in 2008 (Masud-Piloto 2008a).

Central and South Americans

Immigrants who have come from Central and South America are a diverse population that has not been closely studied. Indeed, most government statistics treat its members collectively as "other" and rarely differentiate among them by nationality. As we can see in Figure 9.7, there are 20 nations, each with own identity in Latin America.

9-7 Restate the diversity among Central and South Americans.

People from Chile and Costa Rica have little in common other than their hemisphere of origin and the Spanish language, if that. Still others may come from indigenous populations, especially in Guatemala and Belize, and have a social identity apart from any national allegiance. Also, not all Central and South Americans even have Spanish as their native tongue; for example, immigrants from Brazil speak Portuguese, immigrants from French Guyana speak French, and those from Suriname speak Dutch.

One fact that is clear is that immigration from Central and Latin America has increased dramatically. For example in the 20 years through 2010, Cuban and Puerto Rican population in the United States increased about 70 percent, compared to 137 percent for Mexican Americans. During the same time Salvadorans increased by 192 percent, Guatemalans 289 percent, and Hondurans 383 percent (Logan and Turner 2013).

Many of the nations of Central and South America have a complex system of placing people into myriad racial groups. Their experience with a color gradient necessitates an adjustment when they experience the Black–White racial formation of the United States.

Added to language diversity and the color gradient are social class distinctions, religious differences, urban-versus-rural backgrounds, and differences in dialect, even among those who speak the same language. Social relations among Central and South American groups with each other, Latinos, and non-Latinos defy generalization. Central and South Americans do not form, nor should they be expected to form, a cohesive group, nor do they naturally form coalitions with Cuban Americans, Mexican Americans, or Puerto Ricans (Orlov and Ueda 1980).

Immigration

Immigration from the various Central and South American nations has been sporadic, influenced by our immigration laws and social forces operating in the home countries. Perceived economic opportunities escalated the northward movement in the 1960s. By 1970, Panamanians and Hondurans represented the largest national groupings, most of them being identified in the census as "nonwhite." By 2010, El Salvador, Guatemala, and Columbia were the top countries of origin, each with at least a million present. Immigration often comes through Mexico, which may serve as a brief stop along the way or represent a point of settlement for six months to three years or even longer.

Since the mid-1970s, increasing numbers of Central and South Americans have fled unrest. Although Latinos as a whole are a fast-growing minority, the numbers of Central and South Americans increased even faster than the numbers of Mexicans or any other group in the 1980s. In particular, from about 1978, war and economic chaos in El Salvador, Nicaragua, and Guatemala prompted many to seek refuge in the United States.

9-7

FIGURE 9.7
Latin America

Diversity is the name of the game when it comes to Latin America. Central America includes 6 nations, and South America another 13. Mexico is typically considered part of North America.

The impact of the turmoil cannot be exaggerated. Regarding the total populations of each country, it is estimated that anywhere from 13 percent in Guatemala to 32 percent in El Salvador left their respective countries. Not at all a homogeneous group, they range from Guatemalan Indian peasants to wealthy Nicaraguan exiles. These latest arrivals probably had some economic motivation for migration, but this concern was overshadowed or at least matched by their fear of being killed or hurt if they remained in their home country (Camarillo 1993; López 2004).

In the A Global View box, we look at the close relationship between the people of El Salvador and the United States.

A Global View

The Salvadoran Connection

El Salvador is a Central American country with over 6 million people. Like many other Latin American countries, most Salvadorans are mestizo (mixed Native American and Spanish origin), with maybe one in ten of Spanish ancestry viewing themselves as "White." An even smaller group is indigenous native people who have held on to their native cultures, including distinctive languages.

Political unrest, hurricanes, and volcanic eruptions have propelled people to emigrate in search of better opportunities. Salvadorans immigrated to the United States not so much out of a desire to be a citizen of another country but largely out of fear of remaining in their home country. Reliance on coffee as an export, which was controlled by a small elite, also limited upward mobility by those who sought to improve their lives. Early in the twentieth century, emigration to neighboring countries such as Honduras was the goal, but by the 1980s, immigration patterns had expanded to include not only the region but also Canada, Australia, and, in particular, the United States. A 2013 survey in El Salvador showed 79 percent had a positive view of the United States compared to only 17 percent who had a negative view. Fully two-thirds report having acquaintances who have moved to the better life in the United States and six in ten say they would migrate if they had the means and opportunity to do so.

As of 2010, about 1.7 million Salvadorans were in the United States. About two-thirds were born in El Salvador; the balance was born in the United States of Salvadoran immigrants. Economically, they are doing much better than their counterparts back home, but their income is approximately 14 percent less than that of the general U.S. population. Poverty rates run about 50 percent higher than the general population.

Most people think of assimilation in positive or neutral terms. An immigrant acquires the language of the host society or adjusts their attire to "fit in" a bit more. Assimilation means taking on the characteristics of the dominant culture, even though some of those behaviors and traits may actually be negative.

Media coverage in both the United States and El Salvador has drawn attention to some young Salvadorans who have returned to the Central American nation and reestablished gang organizations to which they belonged in the United States. At the other extreme are those who returned and resisted gang membership, only to be killed. The Immigration and Customs Enforcement (ICE), part of the U.S. Department of Homeland Security, has cracked down on foreign-born residents involved in criminal activities and quickly deported them. This get-tough policy has led to a deportation-and-return cycle as Salvadoran police report that 90 percent of the gang members return to the United States. Critics of the ICE policy argue that most arrests are for immigration offenses and not criminal actions and that many suspected "associates" are often lumped in with hardcore gang members, which only reinforces gang ties.

In contrast and perhaps more typical of the Salvadoran–U.S. connection is the hamlet of Brentwood on Long Island. The Salvadoran presence is unmistakable in Brentwood's fish stores, markets, and 40 restaurants whose culinary offerings range from Salvadoran *pupusas* to Italian dishes such as chicken francese. In the 1980s, as Salvadorans fled civil war in their home country, they were attracted to the wooded landscape of Long Island and the presence of Spanish-speaking Puerto Ricans.

Like Mexican Americans, the Salvadorans have created hometown clubs or associations that relate to a specific village that receives remittances. **Remittances** are monies that immigrants send to their countries of origin. Salvadorans have the highest level among Hispanics in sending money back home— 70 percent of Salvadoran Americans make remittances, compared to 48 percent of Mexican Americans and 39 percent of Cuban Americans. In some cases, these immigrant-created organizations have specific objectives of improving the quality of life back home so that people are less likely to want or need to leave El Salvador. The process of movement between the United States and El Salvador is very complex indeed.

Sources: American Community Survey 2009; Berger 2008; Cordova 2005; Hernández-Arias 2008; Pew Research Global Attitudes Project 2013; Preston 2010; Quirk 2008; Waldinger 2007.

The Current Picture

Two issues have clouded the recent settlement of Central and South Americans. First, many of the arrivals are illegal immigrants. Among those uncovered as undocumented workers, citizens from El Salvador, Guatemala, and Colombia are outnumbered only by Mexican nationals. Second, significant numbers of highly trained and skilled people have left these countries, which are in great need of professional workers. We noted in Chapter 4 how immigration often produces a **brain drain**: immigration to the United States of skilled workers, professionals, and technicians.

The challenges to immigrants from Latin America are reflected in the experience of Colombians, who number more than a half million in the United States. The initial arrivals from this South American nation after World War I were educated middle-class people who quickly assimilated to life in the United States. Rural unrest in Colombia in the

9-7

1980s, however, triggered large-scale movement to the United States, where these newer Colombian immigrants had to adapt to a new culture and to urban life. The adaptation of this later group has been much more difficult. Some have found success by catering to other Colombians. For example, enterprising immigrants have opened bodegas (grocery stores) to supply traditional, familiar foodstuffs. Similarly, Colombians have established restaurants, travel agencies, and real estate firms that serve other Colombians. However, many immigrants are obliged to take menial jobs and to combine the income of several family members to meet the high cost of urban life. Colombians of mixed African descent face racial as well as ethnic and language barriers (Guzmán 2001).

What is likely to be the future of Central and South Americans in the United States? Although much will depend on future immigration, they could assimilate over the course of generations. One less-positive alternative is that they will become trapped with Mexican Americans as a segment of the dual labor market for the urban areas where they live. A more encouraging possibility is that they will retain an independent identity, like the Cubans, while also establishing an economic base. For example, nearly 720,000 Dominicans (from the Dominican Republic) settled in the New York City area, where they make up a significant 6 percent of the population. In some neighborhoods, such as Washington Heights, one can easily engage in business, converse, and eat just as if one were in the Dominican Republic. People continue to remain attentive to events in Dominican politics, which often command greater attention than events in the United States. However, within their local neighborhoods, Dominicans are focused on improving employment opportunities and public safety (American Community Survey 2009: Table B03001).

Conclusion

The signals are mixed today as they have been for the last two hundred years. Progress alternates with setbacks. Moves forward in one Latino group coincide with steps back among other groups. Social processes are highlighted in the Spectrum of Intergroup Relations that summarizes the experience of Latinos in the United States described throughout this chapter.

Latinos' role in the United States typically began with warfare resulting in the United States annexing territory or as a result of revolutions pushing refugees or immigrants here. In recent times, the Latino role in warfare has been to serve in uniform for the United States. "In World War II, more Latinos won Medals of Honor than any other ethnic group," said Democratic Representative

SPECTRUM OF INTERGROUP RELATIONS

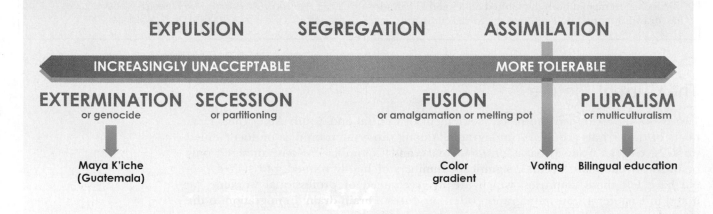

Matthew Martinez, a former U.S. Marine who represented part of Los Angeles. "How much blood do you have to spill before you prove you are a part of something?" (Whitman 1987:49). Many veterans of Iraq and Afghanistan are Latinos who, even though legal residents of the United States, were not in a status that would make citizenship easy. Typically, Congress had to pass a resolution making fallen soldiers citizens after their death and on rare occasion would facilitate citizenship for a living veteran. Under a new rule, the families can now use their deceased as a sponsor for their own residency papers.

In the 20 years from 1990 to 2010, the proportion of Latino ready reserve military personnel rose from 5 to 9.3 percent (Bureau of the Census 2011a: Table 514 on p. 337; Jonsson 2005; McKinley 2005).

While considering Latinos in an examination of American society, we constantly must also consider the impact of events in home countries, whether that be Cuba, El Salvador, or any of the many nations represented. Still, a contrasting image is offered by the refrain "Si usted no habla inglés puede quedarse rezagado": "If you don't speak English, you might be left behind."

Summary

1. Latinos do not share a common cultural or single historical identity, yet a panethnic identity emerges in many aspects of life in the United States.

2. Economically, life for Latinos continues to improve—but relative to non-Hispanics, the gap has hardly changed over the last two generations.

3. Latinos aspire to further education but completion of college remains a challenge despite a commitment to becoming fluent in English.

4. A part of the assimilation as well as pluralism among Latinos has been growing involvement in electoral politics, which has been recognized by both the Democratic and Republican parties.

5. Religion is a central focus in the lives of Latinos but is increasingly being defined by denominations outside of Roman Catholicism.

6. Cuban Americans are the third largest Hispanic group and continue to be defined by the political relationship between the USA and Cuba.

7. Many of the nations of Central and South America have been major sources of immigrants to the United States in recent years, with each group having distinctive cultural traditions.

Key Terms

brain drain, p. 221

color gradient, p. 210

dry foot, wet foot, p. 217

Marielitos, p. 216

panethnicity, p. 209

Pentecostalism, p. 215

remittances, p. 221

Review Questions

1. What different factors seem to unite and divide the Latino community in the United States?

2. How would you summarize the economic status of Latinos as a group?

3. What are the aspirations and the accomplishments of Latinos in education?

4. Identify the factors that contribute to and limit the political power of Latinos as a group in the United States.

5. What are the major patterns that religion serves for the Hispanic community?

6. To what extent has the Cuban migration been positive, and to what degree do significant challenges remain?

7. How have Central and South Americans contributed to the diversity of the Hispanic peoples in the United States?

Critical Thinking

1. Language and culture are almost inseparable. How do you imagine your life would change if you were not permitted to speak your native language? How has it been affected if you have been expected to speak some other language?

2. Is a single Latino identity good or counterproductive?

3. What do see as the social forces propelling Latinos to a single ethnic identity and what served to maintain individual nationality groups?

10 Mexican Americans and Puerto Ricans

10-1 Understand the expansive story of Mexican Americans.

10-2 Clarify the special role that Puerto Ricans have.

10-1

Citizenship is the basic requirement for receiving one's legal rights and privileges in the United States. However, for Mexican Americans, citizenship has been an ambiguous concept at best. Mexican Americans (or Chicanos) have a long history in the United States that stretches back before the nation was even formed to the early days of European exploration. Santa Fe, New Mexico, was founded more than a decade before the Pilgrims landed at Plymouth. Mexican American people trace their ancestry to the merging of Spanish settlers with the Native Americans of Central America and Mexico. This ancestry dates to the brilliant Mayan and Aztec civilizations, which attained their height about 700 and 1500 CE, respectively. However, roots in the land do not guarantee a group any dominance over it. Over several centuries, the Spaniards conquered the land and merged with the Native Americans to form the Mexican people. In 1821, Mexico obtained its independence, but this independence was short-lived: Domination from the north began less than a generation later.

Today, Mexican Americans are creating their own destiny in the United States while functioning in a society that is often concerned about immigration, both legal and illegal. In the eyes of some, including a few in positions of authority, to be Mexican American is to be suspected of being in the country illegally or, at least, of knowingly harboring illegal aliens. Two-thirds of legal Mexican immigrants have yet to take that step. Yet annually about 100,000 take that step—the largest of any country of origin and twice that of the next largest sources of citizens, India and the Philippines (Gonzalez-Barrera et al. 2013; Office of Immigration Statistics 2013: Table 21).

As opposed to other Latinos, it seems that United States citizenship should be clear for Puerto Ricans. Since a federal act in 1917 clarifying any ambiguities, Puerto Ricans born on the island are as much a citizen as someone born in Kansas. However, it continues to be ambiguous. Even Native Americans, who are subject to some unique laws and are exempt from others because of past treaties, have a future firmly dominated by the United States. This description does not necessarily fit Puerto Ricans. Their island home is the last major U.S. colonial territory and, for that matter, one of the few colonial areas remaining in the world. Besides assessing the situation of Puerto Ricans on the mainland, we also need to consider the relationship of the United States to Puerto Rico.

Mexican Americans

10-1 Understand the expansive story of Mexican Americans.

Wars play a prominent part in any nation's history. The United States was created as a result of the colonies' war with England to win their independence. In the 1800s, the United States acquired significant neighboring territory in two different wars. The legacy of these wars and the annexation that resulted were to create the two largest Hispanic minorities in the United States: Mexican Americans and Puerto Ricans.

A large number of Mexicans became aliens in the United States without ever crossing a border. These people first became Mexican Americans at the conclusion of the Mexican–American War. This two-year war culminated with a U.S. occupation of 11 months. Today, Mexicans visit the Museum of Interventions in Mexico City, which outlines the war and how Mexico permanently gave up half its country. The war is still spoken of today as "the Mutilation" (Weiner 2004).

In the war-ending Treaty of Guadalupe Hidalgo, signed February 2, 1848, Mexico acknowledged the annexation of Texas by the United States and ceded California and most of Arizona and New Mexico to the United States for $15 million. In exchange, the United States granted citizenship to the 75,000 Mexican nationals who remained on the annexed land after one year. With citizenship, the United States was to

The Roman Catholic Church has a long history among Mexicans and Mexican Americans. The Mission San Xavier del Bac in Arizona was founded in 1700.

guarantee religious freedom, property rights, and cultural integrity—that is, the right to continue Mexican and Spanish cultural traditions and to use the Spanish language.

The beginnings of the Mexican experience in the United States were as varied as the people themselves. Some Mexican Americans were affluent, with large land holdings. Others were poor peasants barely able to survive. Along such rivers as the Rio Grande, commercial towns grew up around the increasing river traffic. In New Mexico and Arizona, many Mexican American people welcomed the protection that the U.S. government offered against several Native American tribes. In California, the gold miners quickly dominated life, and Anglos controlled the newfound wealth. One generalization can be made about the many segments of the Mexican American population in the nineteenth century: They were regarded as a conquered people. In fact, even before the war, many Whites who traveled into the West were already prejudiced against people of mixed blood (in this instance, against Mexicans). Whenever Mexican American and Anglo interests conflicted, Anglo interests won.

A pattern of second-class treatment for Mexican Americans emerged well before the twentieth century. Gradually, the Anglo system of property ownership replaced the Hispanic and Native American systems. Mexican Americans who inherited land proved no match for Anglo lawyers. Court battles provided no protection for poor Spanish-speaking landowners. Unscrupulous lawyers occasionally defended Mexican Americans successfully, only to demand half the land as their fee. Anglo cattle ranchers gradually pushed out Mexican American ranchers. By 1892, the federal government was granting grazing privileges on public grasslands and forests to anyone except Mexican Americans. Effectively, the people who became Mexican *Americans* had also become outsiders in their own homeland. The ground was laid for the twentieth century social structure of the Southwest, an area of growing productivity in which minority groups increased in size but remained largely subordinate.

The Immigrant Experience

Nowhere else in the world do two countries with such different standards of living and wage scales share such an open border. Immigration from Mexico is unique in several respects. First, it has been a continuous large-scale movement for most of the last hundred years. The United States did not restrict immigration from Mexico through legislation until 1965. Second, the proximity of Mexico encourages past immigrants to maintain strong cultural and language ties with their homeland through friends and relatives. Return visits to the old country are only one- or two-day bus rides for Mexican Americans, not once-in-a-lifetime voyages, as they were for most European immigrants. The third point of uniqueness is the aura of illegality that has surrounded Mexican migrants. Throughout the twentieth century, the suspicion in which Anglos have held Mexican Americans has contributed to mutual distrust between the two groups.

The years before World War I brought large numbers of Mexicans into the expanding agricultural industry of the Southwest. The Mexican revolution of 1909–1922 thrust refugees into the United States, and World War I curtailed the flow of people from Europe, leaving the labor market open to Mexican Americans. After the war, continued political turmoil in Mexico and more prosperity in the Southwest brought still more Mexicans across the border.

Simultaneously, corporations in the United States, led by agribusiness, invested in Mexico in such a way as to maximize their profits but minimize the amount of money remaining in Mexico to provide needed employment. Conflict theorists view this investment as part of the continuing process in which American businesses, with the support and cooperation of affluent Mexicans, have used Mexican people when it has been in corporate leaders' best interests. Their fellow Mexicans use Mexican workers as cheap laborers in their own country, and Americans use them here as cheap labor or as undocumented workers and then dismiss them when they are no longer useful (Guerin-Gonzales 1994).

Beginning in the 1930s, the United States embarked on a series of measures aimed specifically at Mexicans. The Great Depression brought pressure on local governments to care for the growing number of unemployed and impoverished. Government officials

10-1

developed a quick way to reduce welfare rolls and eliminate people seeking jobs: Ship Mexicans back to Mexico. This program of deporting Mexicans in the 1930s was called **repatriation**. As officially stated, the program was constitutional because only illegal aliens were to be repatriated. In reality, Mexicans and even people born in the United States of Mexican background were deported to relieve the economic pressure of the depression. The legal process of fighting a deportation order was overwhelming, however, especially for a poor Spanish-speaking family. The Anglo community largely ignored this outrage against the civil rights of those deported and showed no interest in helping repatriates ease the transition (Balderrama and Rodriguez 2006).

When the depression ended, Mexican laborers again became attractive to industry. In 1942, when World War II depleted the labor pool, the United States and Mexico agreed to a program allowing migration across the border by contracted laborers, or **braceros**. Within a year of the initiation of the bracero program, more than 80,000 Mexican nationals had been brought in; they made up one-eleventh of the farmworkers on the Pacific Coast. The program continued with some interruptions until 1964. It was devised to recruit labor from poor Mexican areas for U.S. farms. In the program, which was supposed to be supervised jointly by Mexico and the United States, minimum standards were to be maintained for transportation, housing, wages, and healthcare of the braceros. Ironically, these safeguards placed the braceros in a better economic situation than Mexican Americans, who often worked alongside the protected Mexican nationals. Mexicans were still regarded as a positive presence by Anglos only when useful, and the Mexican American people were merely tolerated.

Like many policies of the past relating to disadvantaged racial and ethnic groups, the bracero program lives on. After decades of protests, the Mexican government finally issued checks of $3,500 to former braceros and their descendants. The payments were to resolve disputes over what happened to the money the U.S. government gave to the Mexican government to assist in resettlement. To say this has been regarded as too little, much too late, is an understatement.

Latinos rarely appear in the mass media in central roles, much less on successful television programs. Although animated, Dora the Explorer on Nickelodeon is an exception to this rule as she makes her appearance here in the annual Macy's Thanksgiving Day Parade.

Another crackdown on illegal aliens was to be the third step in dealing with the perceived Mexican problem. Alternately called Operation Wetback and Special Force Operation, it was fully inaugurated by 1954. The term *wetbacks*, or **mojados**—derisive slang for Mexicans who enter illegally—refers to those who secretly swim across the Rio Grande. Like other roundups, this effort failed to stop the illegal flow of workers. For several years, some Mexicans were brought in under the bracero program while other Mexicans were being deported. With the end of the bracero program in 1964 and stricter immigration quotas for Mexicans, illegal border crossings increased because legal crossings became more difficult (J. Kim 2008).

More dramatic than the negative influence that continued immigration has had on employment conditions in the Southwest is the effect on the Mexican and Mexican American people themselves. Routinely, the rights of Mexicans, even the rights to which they are entitled as illegal aliens, are ignored. Of the illegal immigrants deported, few have been expelled through formal proceedings. The Mexican American Legal Defense and Education Fund (MALDEF) has repeatedly expressed concern over how the government handles illegal aliens.

Against this backdrop of legal maneuvers is the tie that the Mexican people have to the land both in today's Mexico and in the parts of the United States that formerly belonged to Mexico. *Assimilation* may be the key word in the history of many immigrant groups, but for Mexican Americans the key term is **La Raza**, literally *the people* or *the race*. Among contemporary Mexican Americans, however, the term connotes pride in a pluralistic Spanish, Native American, and Mexican heritage. Mexican Americans cherish their legacy and, as we shall see, strive to regain some of the economic and social glory that once was theirs (Delgado 2008).

Despite the passage of various measures designed to prevent illegal immigration, neither the immigration nor the apprehension of illegal aliens is likely to end. Economic conditions are the major factor. For example, the prolonged recession beginning in 2008 leading to a weakened U.S. job market led to a significant decline in individuals seeking to enter the United States from Mexico either legally or illegally. Increased deportations might have contributed to a decline in the number of Mexican Americans in the United States if it were not for U.S.-born children of Mexican ancestry. Whether Mexican immigration returns to its historical levels of the 1990s remains to be seen (Pew Hispanic Center 2012b).

Mexican Americans will continue to be more closely scrutinized by law enforcement officials because their Mexican descent makes them more suspect as potential illegal aliens. The Mexican American community is another group subject to racial profiling that renders their presence in the United States suspect in the eyes of many Anglos.

In the United States, Mexican Americans have mixed feelings toward the illegal Mexican immigrants. Many are their kin, and Mexican Americans realize that entry into the United States brings Mexicans better economic opportunities. However, numerous deportations only perpetuate the Anglo stereotype of Mexican and Mexican American alike as surplus labor. Mexican Americans, largely the product of past immigration, find that the continued controversy over illegal immigration places them in the conflicting role of citizen and relative. Mexican American organizations opposing illegal immigration must confront people to whom they are closely linked by culture and kinship, and they must cooperate with government agencies they deeply distrust.

Chavez and the Farm Laborers

The best known Hispanic labor leader for economic empowerment was César Chávez, the Mexican American who crusaded to organize migrant farm workers. Efforts to organize agricultural laborers date back to the turn of the twentieth century, but Chávez was the first to enjoy any success. These laborers had never won collective bargaining rights, partly because their mobility made it difficult for them to organize into a unified group.

In 1962, Chávez, then 35 years old, formed the National Farm Workers Association, later to become the United Farm Workers (UFW). Organizing migrant farm workers was not easy because they had no savings to pay for organizing or to live on while striking. Growers could rely on an almost limitless supply of Mexican laborers to replace the Mexican Americans and Filipinos who struck for higher wages and better working conditions.

Despite initial success, Chávez and the UFW were plagued with continual opposition by agribusiness and many lawmakers. This was about the time the UFW was also trying to heighten public consciousness about the pesticides used in the fields. Chávez had difficulty fulfilling his objectives. By 2011, union membership had dwindled from a high of 80,000 in 1970 to a reported 5,000. Nevertheless, what he and the UFW accomplished was significant. First, they succeeded in making federal and state governments more aware of the exploitation of migrant laborers. Second, the migrant workers, or at least those organized in California, developed a sense of their own power and worth that will make it extremely difficult for growers to abuse them in the future as they had in the past. Third, working conditions improved. California agricultural workers were paid an average of less than $2 an hour in the mid-1960s. Still, given the lack of regular harvesting, by 2011 a migrant farm worker's wages for a year rarely topped $12,000 doing labor few people would consider at three times that wage.

César Chávez died in 1993. Although his legacy is clear, many young people, when they hear mention of Chávez, are more likely to think of professional boxer Julio César Chávez. By the beginning of the twenty-first century, the primary challenge came from efforts to permit more foreign workers, primarily

Labor leader Cesar Chávez advocating a boycott of grapes until workers receive better wages and improved working conditions.

10-1

Today, farm workers protest their working conditions and the pesticide use that may threaten their lives as well as low wages.

FARM WORKERS' SANITATION FACILITIES...

from Mexico and Central America, to enter the United States temporarily at even lower wages. About three-quarters of all farm workers are Mexican or Mexican American. The problems of migrant farm workers are inextricably tied to the lives of both Latinos and Latin Americans (Ríos 2011; Sanchez 1998; Triplett 2004; Wozniacka 2011).

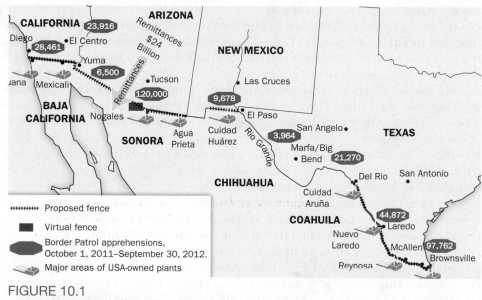

FIGURE 10.1
The Borderlands

In search of higher wages, undocumented Mexicans often attempt to cross the border illegally, risking their lives in the process. Maquiladoras located just south of the U.S.–Mexican border employ Mexican workers at wages far lower than those earned by U.S. workers. The Mexican workers and Mexican Americans send large amounts of money, called remittances, to assist kinfolk and communities in Mexico. Simultaneously the U.S. government continues to harden the border, even experimenting with a "virtual fence" where a system of radar towers and ground sensors have been set along a 28-mile stretch of the Arizona–New Mexico desert.

Sources: Prepared by the author based on Archibold and Preston 2008; Marosi 2007; Migration News 2012a; United States Border Patrol 2012.

The Borderlands

"The border is not where the U.S. stops and Mexico begins," said Mayor Betty Flores of Laredo, Texas. "It's where the U.S. blends into Mexico" (Gibbs 2001:42). The term **borderlands** in this book refers to the area of a common culture along the border between Mexico and the United States. Though particularly relevant to Mexicans and Mexican Americans, the growing Mexican influence is relevant to the other Latino groups that we discuss. A representation and pertinent information about the borderlands is presented in the map in Figure 10.1.

Legal and illegal emigration from Mexico to the United States, day laborers crossing the border regularly to go to jobs in the United States, the implementation of the North American Free Trade Agreement (NAFTA), and the exchange of media across the border all make the notion of separate Mexican and U.S. cultures obsolete in the borderlands.

The economic position of the borderlands is complex in terms of both businesses and workers. Very visible on the Mexican side are **maquiladoras**. These foreign-owned operations are exempt from paying Mexican taxes and are not required to provide insurance or benefits for their workers. Mexican labor costs (wages plus benefits) are typically $8 to $16 per hour, which is considered very good by prevailing wage standards in Mexico. However, this one example of international trade soon was trumped by another aspect of globalization. As low as these hourly wages seem to people in industrial countries, multinational corporations soon found even lower wages in China. More than 75 percent of the *new* 700,000 maquiladora jobs created by NAFTA were eliminated between 2000 and 2011 (Archibold 2011; Cañas, Coronado, and Gilmer 2006; Rabinovitch 2011).

Maquiladoras are foreign-owned manufacturers located in Mexico along the United States border. Workers assemble components for export to the United States at a plant in Nuevo Laredo, Mexico.

Immigrant workers have a significant economic impact on their home country while employed in the United States. Many Mexicans, as well as other Hispanic groups we discuss in this chapter, send some part of their earnings back to family members remaining in their native countries. This substantial flow of money, sometimes called remittances, totals an estimated $24 billion annually. Most of the money is spent to pay for food, clothing, and housing, but increasingly a growing proportion is being invested to create small businesses (Migration News 2012a).

The close cultural and economic ties to the home country that are found in the borderlands also can be found with other Latino groups. Such economic and political events continue to have a prominent role in the lives of immigrants and their children, and even grandchildren, in the United States. In recent years, Mexicans have also turned their attention to their other borders as migrants from other Latin American countries enter Mexico, sometimes illegally, to either settle there or move north to the United States.

Inland from the borders, **hometown clubs** (or associations) have sprung up in northern cities with large settlements of Mexicans. Hometown clubs typically are nonprofit organizations that maintain close ties to immigrants' hometowns in Mexico and other Latin American countries. Hometown clubs collect money for improvements in hospitals and schools that are beyond the means of the local people back home. The impact of hometown clubs has become so noticeable that some states in Mexico have begun programs whereby they will match funds from hometown clubs to encourage such public-spirited efforts. The work of more than 3,000 hometown clubs in the United States and Mexican communities alone reflects the blurring of border distinctions within the Latino community.

These links between the United States and the home countries are a visible presence of transnationals. As introduced in Chapter 4, **transnationals** are immigrants who sustain multiple social relationships that link their societies of origin and settlement. These clubs or associations began as informal, volunteer-driven social organizations and many still are. In increasing numbers of communities, they have used salaried staff and even formed federations with other hometown clubs (Portes, Escobar, and Radford 2007; Somerville, Durama, and Terrazas 2008).

10-1

Healthcare

Life chances are people's opportunities to provide themselves with material goods, positive living conditions, and favorable life experiences. We have consistently seen that Mexican Americans and other minority group members have more limited life chances. Perhaps in no other area does this apply so much as in the healthcare system.

Hispanics as a group are locked out of the healthcare system more often than any other racial or ethnic group. Although federal law requires that emergency medical treatment be available to all people, even illegal immigrants, many Hispanics—even those with legal residency but who have relatives here illegally—are wary of seeking medical treatment. About a third (29.1 percent) had no health insurance (or other coverage such as Medicaid) for all of 2012, compared with 11.1 percent of White non-Hispanics and 19 percent of Blacks. Predictably, the uninsured are less likely to have a regular source of medical care. This means that they wait for a crisis before seeking care. Fewer are immunized, and rates of preventable diseases such as lead poisoning are higher. Those without coverage are increasing in number, a circumstance that may reflect a further breakdown in healthcare delivery or may be a result of continuing immigration (DeNavas-Walt, Proctor, and Smith 2013: 23).

The healthcare problem facing Mexican Americans and other Hispanic groups is complicated by the lack of Hispanic or Spanish-speaking health professionals. Hispanics accounted for 2.5 percent of dentists and 5.2 percent of physicians. One does not need to be administered healthcare by someone in one's own ethnic group, but the paucity of Hispanic professionals increases the likelihood that the group will be underserved (Bureau of Labor Statistics 2013b).

Some Mexican Americans and many other Latinos have cultural beliefs that make them less likely to use the medical system. They may interpret their illnesses according to folk practices or **curanderismo**: Latino folk medicine, a form of holistic healthcare and healing. This orientation influences how one approaches healthcare and even how one defines illness. Most Hispanics probably use folk healers, or *curanderos*, infrequently, but perhaps 20 percent rely on home remedies. Although these are not necessarily without value, especially if a dual system of folk and establishment medicine is followed, reliance on natural beliefs may be counterproductive. Another aspect of folk beliefs is the identification of folk-defined illnesses such as *susto* (or fright sickness) and *atague* (or fighting attack). Although these complaints, alien by these names to Anglos, often have biological bases, they must be dealt with carefully by sensitive medical professionals who can diagnose and treat illnesses accurately (Belliard and Ramirez-Johnson 2005; Dansie 2004; Lara et al. 2005).

Family Life

The most important organization or social institution among Mexican Americans, or for that matter any group, is the family. The structure of the Mexican American family differs little from that of all families in the United States, a statement remarkable in itself, given the impoverished status of a significant number of Mexican Americans.

Latino households are described as laudably more familistic than others in the United States. **Familism** means pride and closeness in the family, which results in family obligation and loyalty coming before individual needs. The family is the primary source of both social interaction and caregiving. In the Research Focus, we look at familism more closely.

Familism has been viewed as both a positive and a negative influence on individual Mexican Americans and Puerto Ricans. It has been argued that familism has had the negative effect of discouraging youths with a bright future from taking advantage of opportunities that would separate them from their family. Familism is generally regarded as good, however, because an extended family provides emotional strength in times of crisis. Close family ties maintain the mental and social well-being of the elderly. Most Latinos, therefore, see the intact, extended family as a norm and as a nurturing unit that provides support throughout a person's lifetime. The many significant aspects of familism include

Research Focus

10-2

The Latino Family Circle: Familism

Familism within the Mexican American and the entire Latino community is associated with a sense of obligation to fellow family members, the placement of family interests over individual desires, and exclusiveness of the family even over friends and work. Familism has been likened to a thick social network where one's family defines everyday social interaction.

Familism for the U.S.-born Latino is also associated with familiarity with Spanish so that one can truly relate to the older relatives for whom English may remain very much a foreign language. Being nominally Roman Catholic is another means of maintaining strong extended family ties.

U.S. Hispanic families are undergoing transition with the simultaneous growth of more multigenerational families born in the United States as well as family members from the homeland. This is all complicated by the mixed status present in so many Latino extended families (with the obvious exception of Puerto Ricans, for whom citizenship is automatic). As explained in Chapter 4, **mixed status** refers to families in which one or more is a citizen and one or more is a noncitizen. This especially becomes problematic when the noncitizens are illegal or undocumented immigrants. All the usual pressures within a family become magnified when there is mixed status.

Although immigration makes generalizing about Latinos as a group very difficult at any one point in time, analysis of available data indicates that Hispanic households are taking on more of the characteristics of larger society. For example, cohabiting couples with or without children were relatively uncommon among Hispanic groups but now are coming to resemble the pattern of non-Hispanics. Similarly, Mexican-born women now living in the United States are more likely to enter marriage earlier, but later generations of women born in the United States are more likely to start marriage later. The same was true for Puerto Rican women born on the island, compared with those born on the mainland.

In the future, the greatest factor that may lead to a decline in familism is marriage across ethnic lines. Continuing immigration from Mexico has tended to slow outgroup marriage, but during periods of lessened migration, immigrants have been more likely to form unions with different Latino groups or with non-Hispanics.

Today, we begin to see a more individualistic orientation than a collective orientation or familism that is more likely to encourage family members to move away from their relatives or, more dramatically, lead to desertion or divorce. Studies with other established, longer-term immigrant groups suggest that family members become more individualistic in their values and behavior. People both within and outside the Latino community are interested to see if Hispanics will follow this pattern and whether the familism that has been so characteristic of much of the Latino community will fade.

Sources: Comeau 2012; Jacobson, England, and Barrus 2008; Landale and Oropesa 2002, 2007; Landale, Oropesa, and Bradatan 2006; Lichter et al. 2007; Sarkistan, Gerena, and Gerstel 2007; Zambrana 2011.

the importance of *campadrazgo* (the godparent–godchild relationship), the benefits of the financial dependency of kin, the availability of relatives as a source of advice, and the active involvement of the elderly in the family.

Puerto Ricans

Puerto Ricans' current association with the United States, like that of the Mexican people, began as the result of the outcome of a war. The island of Borinquén, subsequently called Puerto Rico, was claimed by Spain in 1493. The native inhabitants, the Taíno Indians, were significantly reduced in number by conquest, slavery, and genocide. Although for generations the legacy of the Taíno was largely thought to be archaeological in nature, recent DNA tests revealed that more than 60 percent of Puerto Ricans today have a Taíno ancestor. About 20,000 identified themselves as Taíno in the 2010 census (Cockburn 2003:41; Kearns 2011).

10-2 Clarify the special role that Puerto Ricans have.

After Spain ruled Puerto Rico for four centuries, the United States seized the island in 1898 during the Spanish–American War. Spain relinquished control of it in the Treaty of Paris. Puerto Rico's value for the United States, as it had been for Spain, was mainly its strategic location, which was advantageous for maritime trade.

10-2

The beginnings of rule by the United States quickly destroyed any hope that Puerto Ricans—or Boricua, as Puerto Ricans call themselves—had for self-rule. All power was given to officials appointed by the president, and Congress could overrule any act of the island's legislature. Even the spelling was changed briefly to Porto Rico to suit North American pronunciation. English, previously unknown on the island, became the only language permitted in the school systems. The people were colonized—first politically, then culturally, and finally economically (Aran et al. 1973; Christopulos 1974).

The Jones Act of 1917 extended citizenship to Puerto Ricans, but Puerto Rico remained a colony. This political dependence altered in 1948, when Puerto Rico elected its own governor and became a commonwealth. This status, officially Estado Libre Asociado, or Associated Free State, extends to Puerto Rico and its people privileges and rights different from those of people on the mainland. Although Puerto Ricans are U.S. citizens and elect their own governor, they may not vote in presidential elections and have no voting representation in Congress. They are subject to military service, Selective Service registration, and all federal laws. Puerto Ricans have a homeland that is and at the same time is not a part of the United States.

The Bridge Between the Island and the Mainland

Despite their citizenship, immigration officials occasionally challenge Puerto Ricans. Because other Latin Americans attempt to enter the country posing as Puerto Ricans, Puerto Ricans find their papers scrutinized more closely than do other U.S. citizens.

Puerto Ricans came to the mainland in small numbers in the first half of the twentieth century, often encouraged by farm labor contracts similar to those extended to Mexican braceros. During World War II, the government recruited hundreds of Puerto Ricans to work on the railroads, in food-manufacturing plants, and in copper mines on the mainland. But migration has been largely a post–World War II phenomenon. The 1940 census showed fewer than 70,000 Puerto Ricans on the mainland. By 2010, more than 4.6 million Puerto Ricans lived on the mainland and 3.7 million residents lived on the island (Lopez and Velasco 2011).

Among the factors that have contributed to migration are the economic pull away from the underdeveloped and overpopulated island, the absence of legal restrictions against travel, and the increasingly cheap air transportation. As the migration continues, the mainland offers the added attraction of a large Puerto Rican community in New York City, which makes adjustment easier for new arrivals.

New York City still has a formidable population of Puerto Ricans (786,000), but significant changes have taken place. First, Puerto Ricans no longer dominate the Latino scene in New York City, making up only a little more than a third of the city's Hispanic population. Second, Puerto Ricans are now more dispersed throughout the mainland's cities.

As the U.S. economy underwent recessions in the 1970s and 1980s, unemployment among mainland Puerto Ricans, always high, increased dramatically. This increase is evident in migration. In the 1950s, half of the Latino arrivals were Puerto Rican. By the 1970s, they accounted for only 3 percent. Indeed, in some years of the 1980s, more Puerto Ricans went from the mainland to the island than the other way around.

Puerto Ricans returning to the island have become a significant force. Indeed, they now are given the name **Neoricans**, or *Nuyoricans*, a term the islanders also use for Puerto Ricans in New York. Longtime islanders direct a modest amount of hostility toward these Neoricans, numbering near 100,000, or about 2 percent of the population. They usually return from the mainland with more formal schooling, more money, and a better command of English than

native Puerto Ricans. It is no surprise that Neoricans compete very well with islanders for jobs and land (Lopez and Velasco 2011).

The ethnic mix of the nation's largest city has gotten even more complex over the last ten years as Mexican and Mexican American arrivals in New York City have far outpaced any growth among Puerto Ricans. New York City is now following the pattern of other cities such as Miami, where a single group no longer defines the Latino identity.

The Island of Puerto Rico

Puerto Rico, located about a thousand miles from Miami (see Figure 10.2), has never been the same since Columbus discovered it in 1493. The original inhabitants of the island succumbed in large proportions to death by disease, tribal warfare, hard labor, unsuccessful rebellions against the Spanish, and fusion with their conquerors.

Among the institutions Spain imported to Puerto Rico was slavery. Although slavery in Puerto Rico was not as harsh as in the southern United States, the legacy of the transfer of Africans is present in the appearance of Puerto Ricans today, many of whom are seen by people on the mainland as Black.

The commonwealth period that began in 1948 has been significant for Puerto Rico. Change has been dramatic, although it is debatable whether it has all been progress. On the positive side, Spanish was reintroduced as the language of classroom instruction, but the study of English also is required. The popularity in the 1980s of music groups such as Menudo shows that Puerto Rican young people want to maintain ties with their ethnicity. Such success is a challenge because Puerto Rican music is almost never aired on non-Hispanic radio stations. The Puerto Rican people have had a vibrant and distinctive cultural tradition, as seen clearly in their folk heroes, holidays, sports, and contemporary literature and drama. Dominance by the culture of the United States makes it difficult to maintain their culture on the mainland and even on the island itself.

Puerto Rico and its people reflect a phenomenon called **neocolonialism**, which refers to continuing dependence of former colonies on foreign countries. Initially, this term

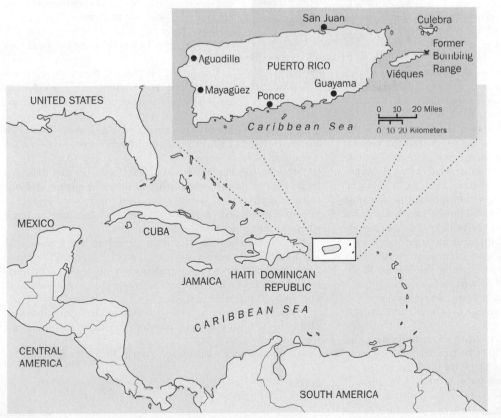

FIGURE 10.2
Puerto Rico

10-2

was introduced to refer to African nations that, even after gaining their political independence from Great Britain, France, and other European nations, continued to find their destiny in the hands of the former colonial powers. Although most Puerto Ricans today are staunchly proud of their American citizenship, they also want to have their own national identity independent of the United States. This has not been easy to achieve and likely will continue to be a challenge.

From 1902, English was the official language of the island, but Spanish was the language of the people, reaffirming the island's cultural identity independent of the United States. In 1992, however, Puerto Rico also established Spanish as an additional official language.

In reality, the language issue is related more to ideology than to substance. Although English is once again required in primary and secondary schools and textbooks might be written in English, classes are conducted in Spanish. Indeed, Spanish remains the language of the island; 8 percent of the islanders speak only English, and among Spanish-speaking adults, only about 15 percent speak English "very well" (Bureau of the Census 2007c).

In Speaking Out, in his remarks to the House of Representatives, Congressman Luis Gutierrez speaks about what he regards as abuse of authority by the Puerto Rican government against its residents. It is interesting that the U.S.-born representative of Puerto Rican parents defends himself against charges that he is an island "outsider" and thus should not comment on events in Puerto Rico.

(🎙) Speaking Out

Puerto Ricans Cannot Be Silenced

Two weeks ago, I spoke about a serious problem in Puerto Rico.

The problem is a systemic effort by the ruling party to deny the right of the people to speak freely, to criticize their government openly, and to make their voices heard.

I talked about student protests that had been met with violent resistance by Puerto Rican police. I talked about closed meetings of the legislature, and about efforts to silence the local Bar Association.... [A recent report] details the complaints of students, legislators, the press, and the general public who were beaten and pepper sprayed by police. Female students who were treated with gross disrespect by the police.

This was the government's overreaction to demonstrations at the University over budget cuts and layoffs of at least 17,000 and maybe as many as 34,000 public employees. And demonstrations at the Capitol over budget cuts and layoffs were also met by riot police, clubs, and more pepper spray.

The images of police tactics and behavior explain why the Department of Justice is investigating the Puerto Rican police for "excessive force" and "unconstitutional searches."

How could you see these images and not speak out?

And I was hardly the first to speak out about these matters and will not be the last....

And what was the response to my speech defending the right of the Puerto Rican people to be heard?

It was to challenge my right to be heard.... A leading member of the [Puerto Rican] ruling party even said, "Gutierrez was not born in Puerto Rico. His kids weren't born in Puerto

Luis Gutierrez

Rico. Gutierrez doesn't plan on being buried in Puerto Rico.... So Gutierrez doesn't have the right to speak about Puerto Rico...."

If you see injustice anywhere, it is not only your right but your duty to speak out about it....

I may not be Puerto Rican enough for some people, but I know this: Nowhere on earth will you find a people harder to silence than Puerto Ricans.

You won't locate my love for Puerto Rico on my birth certificate or a driver's license, my children's birth certificate, or any other piece of paper.

My love for Puerto Rico is right here—in my heart—a heart that beats with our history and our language and our heroes. A place where—when I moved there as a teenager—people talked and argued and debated because we care deeply about our island and our future.

That's still true today—and that freedom is still beating in the hearts of university students, workingmen and women, labor leaders, lawyers, and environmentalists and every person who believes in free speech. You will not silence them, and you will not silence me.

Abraham Lincoln, a leader who valued freedom above all else, said: "Those who deny freedom to others deserve it not for themselves."

It's good advice, and I hope Puerto Rican leaders take it.

Source: Spoken by Gutierrez in the House of Representatives, March 2, 2011. Gutierrez 2011.

Issues of Statehood and Self-Rule   Puerto Ricans have consistently argued and fought for independence for most of the 500 years since Columbus landed. They continue to do so, even in the twenty-first century. The contemporary hybrid commonwealth arrangement is popular with many Puerto Ricans, but others prefer statehood, whereas some call for complete independence from the United States. In Table 10.1, we summarize the advantages and the disadvantages of the current status as a territory or commonwealth and the alternatives of statehood and independence.

The arguments for continued commonwealth status include a perception of special protection from the United States. Among some island residents, the idea of statehood invokes the fear of higher taxes and an erosion of their cultural heritage. Commonwealth supporters argue that independence includes too many unknown costs, so they embrace the status quo. Others view statehood as a key to increased economic development and expansion for tourism.

Proponents of independence have a long, vocal history of insisting on the need for Puerto Rico to regain its cultural and political autonomy. Some supporters of independence have even been militant. In 1950, nationalists attempted to assassinate President Harry Truman, killing a White House guard in the process. Four years later, another

TABLE 10.1
Puerto Rico's Future

Continuing Territorial Status (Status Quo)	
Pros	**Cons**
<ul><li>Island is under U.S. protection.</li><li>Islanders enjoy U.S. citizenship with a distinct national identity.</li><li>Residents don't pay federal income taxes (they do pay into Social Security, Medicare, and 32 percent to island tax collectors).</li><li>United States provides federal funds in the sum of $22 billion annually and offers other tax advantages.</li><li>Island retains representation in the Miss Universe pageant and Olympic Games.</li></ul>	<ul><li>United States has ultimate authority over Island matters.</li><li>Residents cannot vote for president.</li><li>Residents who work for any company or organization that is funded by the United States must pay federal income taxes.</li><li>Although Puerto Rico has a higher standard of living compared to other Caribbean islands, it has half the per capita income of the poorest U.S. states.</li><li>Island cannot enter into free-trade agreements.</li></ul>

Statehood	
Pros	**Cons**
<ul><li>Permanent and guaranteed U.S. citizenship and an end to U.S. colonial rule over the island.</li><li>The island would receive federal money to build the infrastructure.</li><li>The island would be able to enjoy open-market trade with U.S. allies.</li><li>The island would acquire six seats in the House of Representatives and two seats in the Senate, enabling the island to have more political clout and the right to vote in presidential elections.</li></ul>	<ul><li>Possibility of English-only requirements (loss of cultural or national identity).</li><li>An increased standard of living could result in greater economic deterioration because of the current muddled economic situation.</li><li>Businesses that take advantage of certain tax benefits could leave the island, and future businesses might not consider working there.</li><li>Island would lose representation in the Miss Universe pageant and Olympic Games.</li></ul>

Independence	
Pros	**Cons**
<ul><li>Island would retain language and culture.</li><li>Island would be able to participate in the global economy.</li><li>End of U.S. colonial rule over the island.</li></ul>	<ul><li>Lose U.S. citizenship.</li><li>Lose U.S. protection.</li><li>Lose federal funds.</li></ul>

Sources: Author, based on Let Puerto Rico Decide 2005; President's Task Force on Puerto Rico's Status 2005; C. J. Williams 2006, 2007.

band of nationalists opened fire in the gallery of the U.S. House of Representatives, wounding five members of Congress. Beginning in 1974, a group calling itself the Armed Forces of National Liberation (FALN, for Fuerzas Armadas de Liberación Nacional) took responsibility for more than 100 explosions that continued through 1987. The FALN is not alone; at least four other militant groups advocating independence were identified as having been at work in the 1980s. The island itself is occasionally beset by violent demonstrations, often reacting to U.S. military installations there—a symbol of U.S. control (Santos-Hernández 2008).

The issue of Puerto Rico's political destiny is, in part, ideological. Independence is the easiest way for the island to retain and strengthen its cultural and political identity. Some nationalists express the desire that an autonomous Puerto Rico develop close political ties with communist Cuba. The crucial arguments for and against independence probably are economic. An independent Puerto Rico would no longer be required to use U.S. shipping lines, which are more expensive than those of foreign competitors. However, an independent Puerto Rico might be faced with a tariff wall when trading with its largest current customer, the mainland United States. Also, Puerto Rican migration to the mainland could be restricted.

Puerto Rico's future status most recently faced a vote in 2012. The latest nonbinding referendum had confusing wording in its two-part question. Observers of the results saw the voters split between statehood and continuation but with very few favoring independence. As it has for over a century, the political future of Puerto Rico remains in doubt (Patterson 2012).

The Social Construction of Race   The most significant difference between the meaning of race in Puerto Rico and on the mainland is that Puerto Rico, like so many other Caribbean societies, has a **color gradient**, a term that describes distinctions based on skin color made on a continuum rather than by sharp categorical separations. The presence of a color gradient reflects past fusion between different groups. Rather than seeing people as either black or white in skin color, Puerto Ricans perceive people as ranging from pale white to very black. Puerto Ricans are more sensitive to degrees of difference and make less effort to pigeonhole a person into one of two categories.

The presence of a color gradient rather than two or three racial categories does not necessarily mean less prejudice. Generally, however, societies with a color gradient permit more flexibility, and therefore are less likely to impose specific sanctions against a group of people based on skin color alone. Puerto Rico has not suffered interracial conflict or violence; its people are conscious of different racial heritages. Studies disagree on the amount of prejudice in Puerto Rico, but all concur that race is not as clear-cut an issue on the island as it is on the mainland.

Racial identification in Puerto Rico depends a great deal on the attitude of the individual making the judgment. If one thinks highly of a person, then he or she may be seen as a member of a more acceptable racial group. Several terms are used in the color gradient to describe people racially: *blanco* (white), *trigueño* (bronze- or wheat-colored), *moreno* (dark-skinned), and *negro* (black) are a few. Factors such as social class and social position determine race, but on the mainland race is more likely to determine social class. This situation may puzzle people from the mainland, but racial etiquette on the mainland may be just as difficult for Puerto Ricans to comprehend and accept. Puerto Ricans arriving in the United States may find a new identity thrust on them by the dominant society (Denton and Villarrubia 2007; Landale and Oropesa 2002; Loveman and Muniz 2007; Roth 2012).

The Island Economy   The United States' role in Puerto Rico has produced an overall economy that, though strong by Caribbean standards, remains well below that of the poorest areas of the United States. For many years, the federal government exempted U.S. industries locating in Puerto Rico from taxes on profits for at least ten years but that tax advantage suddenly ended in 2006 leading to a recession that has not ended yet. Unquestionably, Puerto Rico had become attractive to mainland-based corporations and the island's agriculture has been largely ignored. Furthermore, the economic benefits that did exist up to a few years ago to the island were limited. Businesses spent the profits gained on Puerto Rico back on the mainland.

Puerto Rico's economy is now in severe trouble, even when compared with that of the mainland in a recession. Its unemployment rate in 2013 was 13.9 percent, compared with 7.3 percent for the mainland. In addition, the median household income is one-third of what it is in the United States. In 2011, 46 percent of the population was below the poverty rate, compared with 16 percent in the nation as a whole at the time. Efforts to raise the wages of Puerto Rican workers only make the island less attractive to labor-intensive businesses—that is, those that employ larger numbers of unskilled people. A growing problem is that Puerto Rico has emerged as a major gateway to the United States for illegal drugs from South America. This, in turn, has led the island to experience waves of violence and the social ills associated with the drug trade. Between 2000 and 2013, 144 residents have left the Island eroding the labor and tax base (Bureau of the Census 2012e: Table S1701; Bureau of Labor Statistics 2013a; Gomez 2013:1B,) 6B.

Puerto Rico is an example of the world systems theory initially presented in Chapter 1. **World systems theory** is the view of the global economic system as divided between certain industrialized nations that control wealth and developing countries that are controlled and exploited. Although Puerto Rico may be well off compared with many other Caribbean nations, it clearly is at the mercy of economic forces in the United States and, to a much lesser extent, other industrial nations. Puerto Rico continues to struggle with the advantages of citizenship and the detriment of playing a peripheral role in the economy of the United States.

New challenges continue to face Puerto Rico. First, with congressional approval in 1994 of the North American Free Trade Agreement, Mexico, Canada, and the United States became integrated into a single economic market. The reduction of trade barriers with Mexico, coupled with that nation's lower wages, combined to undercut Puerto Rico's commonwealth advantage. Second, many more island nations now offer sun-seeking tourists from the mainland alternative destinations to Puerto Rico. In addition, cruise ships present another attractive option for tourists. Given the economic problems of the island, it is not surprising that many Puerto Ricans migrate to the mainland.

For years, circular migration between the mainland and island has served as a safety valve for Puerto Rico's population, which has grown annually at a rate 50 percent faster than that of the rest of the United States. Typically, migrants from Puerto Rico represent a broad range of occupations. There are seasonal fluctuations as Puerto Rican farm workers leave the island in search of employment (Collado-Schwarz 2012; Meléndez 1994; Torres 2008).

Conclusion

David Gomez (1971) described Mexican Americans as "strangers in their own land." Puerto Ricans, on the other hand, are still debating what should be the political destiny of their island nation. All of this makes nationality a very real part of the destiny of Mexican Americans and Puerto Ricans. Can they also preserve their cultures along with a sense of national fervor, or will these be a casualty of assimilation?

As we have seen, even when we concentrate on just Mexican Americans or Puerto Ricans out of the larger collective group of Hispanics or Latinos, diversity remains. Mexican Americans are divided among the Hispanos and the descendants of earlier Mexican immigrants and the more recent arrivals from Mexico. Puerto Ricans can be divided by virtue of residency and the extent to which they identify with the island culture. For many Puerto Ricans, the identity dilemma is never truly resolved: "No soy de aquí ni de allá"–"I am not from here nor from there" (Comas-Díaz et al. 1998).

Economic change is also apparent. Poverty and unemployment rates are high, and new arrivals from Mexico and Puerto Rico are particularly likely to enter the lower class, or working class at best, upon arrival. However, there is a growing middle class within the Hispanic community.

Mexican culture is alive and well in the Mexican American community. Some cultural practices that have

SPECTRUM OF INTERGROUP RELATIONS

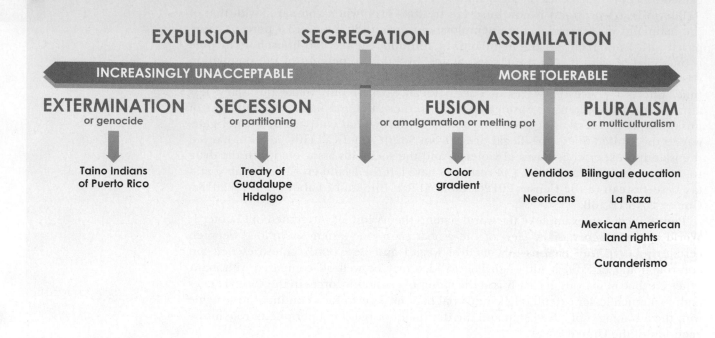

become more popular here than in Mexico are being imported back to Mexico, with their distinctive Mexican American flavor. All this is occurring in the midst of a reluctance to expand bilingual education and a popular move to make English the official language. In 1998, Puerto Rico observed its 500th anniversary as a colony: four centuries under Spain and another century under the United States. Its dual status as a colony and as a developing nation has been the defining issue for Puerto Ricans, even those who have migrated to the mainland.

Summary

1. As a result of the 1848 Treaty of Guadalupe Hidalgo, which ended the Mexican–American War, the United States acquired a significant amount of Mexican territory, starting the long history of Latinos in the United States.

2. Federal policies such as repatriation, the bracero program, Operation Wetback, and Special Force Operation reflect that the United States regards Mexico and its people as a low-wage labor supply to be encouraged or shut off as dictated by U.S. economic needs.

3. Puerto Ricans have enjoyed citizenship by birth since 1917 but have commonwealth status on the island. The future status of Puerto Rico remains the key political issue within the Puerto Rican community.

4. Like much of the rest of the Caribbean and Latin America, Puerto Rico has more of a color gradient in terms of race than the sharp Black–White dichotomy of the mainland.

Key Terms

borderlands, p. 231

bracero, p. 228

color gradient, p. 238

curanderismo, p. 232

familism, p. 232

hometown clubs, p. 231

La Raza, p. 228

life chances, p. 232

maquiladoras, p. 231

mixed status, p. 233

mojados, p. 228

neocolonialism, p. 235

Neoricans, p. 234

repatriation, p. 228

transnationals, p. 231

world systems theory, p. 239

Review Questions

1. In what respects has Mexico been viewed as both a source of workers and as a place to leave unwanted laborers?

2. In what respects are Hispanic families similar to and different from Anglo households?

3. How does the case of Puerto Rico support the notion of race as a social concept?

Critical Thinking

1. What role do the Borderlands have in defining Mexican Americans to themselves and to the nation as a whole?

2. Are Mexican Americans assimilated, and are recent Mexican immigrants likely to assimilate over time?

3. Observers often regard the family as a real strength in the Latino community. How can this strength be harnessed to address some of the challenges that Mexican Americans and Puerto Ricans face in the United States?

4. Consider what it means to be patriotic and loyal in terms of being a citizen of the United States. How do the concerns that Puerto Ricans have for the island's future and the Mexican concept of dual nationality affect those notions of patriotism and loyalty?

11 Muslim and Arab Americans: Diverse Minorities

11-1 Describe the Arab American community.

11-2 Describe the Muslim American community.

11-3 Summarize the Muslim and Arab immigration to the United States.

11-4 Put into your own words Islamophobia.

11-5 Discuss the contemporary experiences of Arab Americans.

Muslim and Arab Americans are different groups in the United States. Although the two groups overlap, with some Muslim Americans being of Arab ancestry, they are distinct from each other. Most Arab Americans are not Muslim, and most Muslim Americans are not of Arab background. Within each group is significant diversity that can be seen by differences in forms of religious expression, ancestral background, and how recently they arrived in the United States. Both groups have been seen and stereotyped in the West through the lens of orientalism. This stigmatizing of people grew more all-encompassing with the outbreak of terrorism and, specifically, the events of September 11, 2001. Even without these violent events, it is a challenge for Muslim and Arab Americans to sort out their identities, but nonetheless both function in strong and growing communities in the United States.

While stationed in Joint Base Balad, Iraq, Naveed Ali Shah was concerned when he decided to call his wife Angela stateside where she lived with their son Yusuf at Fort Hood, Texas. For too long he could not get through, only to learn that a fellow Muslim American soldier had inexplicably taken the lives of 12 on the base. While reassured his family was safe, he could not understand how someone raised in a Muslim household such as his could commit such evil. When asked what he would do next, the Army specialist responded that he would focus on teaching his son the alphabet via Webcam while he finished his deployment.

Planet Hollywood Resort in Las Vegas may seem an unlikely place to see the range within the Arab Muslim community, but in May 2010 Rima Fakih, an Arab American born in a Muslim Lebanese family, was crowned Miss USA as a part of the Miss Universe pageant. She recalls how her father's Manhattan restaurant lost business after 9/11 and how she moved with her family as a teenager to the larger, more supportive Arab American community found in Dearborn, Michigan. While many Muslims and Arabs applauded her victory, some Muslims questioned just how good a follower of Islam she could be to parade on stage in a bikini. Ironically, her victory came almost 20 years to the day that another Miss Michigan, Carole Gust, became the first African American to win the pageant.

Certainly, these are two different achievements—a soldier in the battlefield and a woman winning a pageant crown—but they underscore the diverse way Arab and Muslim Americans carry out their lives. Also, they show that these life choices may be very different from those that come to mind when most people in the United States think of "Muslim" or "Arab." Both Naveed and Rima, while pursuing a very American tradition, found their lives caught up with what it means to be Muslim or Arab in America (Pilkington 2010; Shah 2009).

We are considering Arab and Muslim Americans together in this chapter first to clarify the distinctions between two groups that are often incorrectly referred to as a single population. Second, we seek to overcome the prism of orientalism through which many contemporary Americans view the Arab and Muslim world. **Orientalism** is the simplistic view of the people and history of the Orient (generally, the region of the Middle East to East Asia), with no recognition of change over time or the diversity within its many cultures. Palestinian American literary scholar Edward Said (1978) stressed how so many people in North America and Europe came to define, categorize, and study the Orient and therefore created a static stereotype of hundreds of millions of people stretched around the globe.

The diversity of Arabs and Muslims is thereby discounted, which allows the outsider to come up with simplistic descriptions and often simplistic policies. Orientalism has led people to see a sweeping unity in both Arab and Muslim societies. It is an unchanging and a clearly non-modern image. One must focus on smaller, culturally consistent groups or countries rather than surrender to the temptation of a single broad generalization.

The Arab American and Muslim American communities are among the most rapidly growing subordinate groups in the United States. Westerners often confuse the two groups. Actually, Arabs are an ethnic group, and Muslims are a religious group. Typically, Islam is the faith (like Christianity), and a Muslim is a believer of that religion (like a Christian). Worldwide, many Arabs (12 million) are not Muslims, and most Muslims (85 percent) are not Arabs (David and Ayouby 2004).

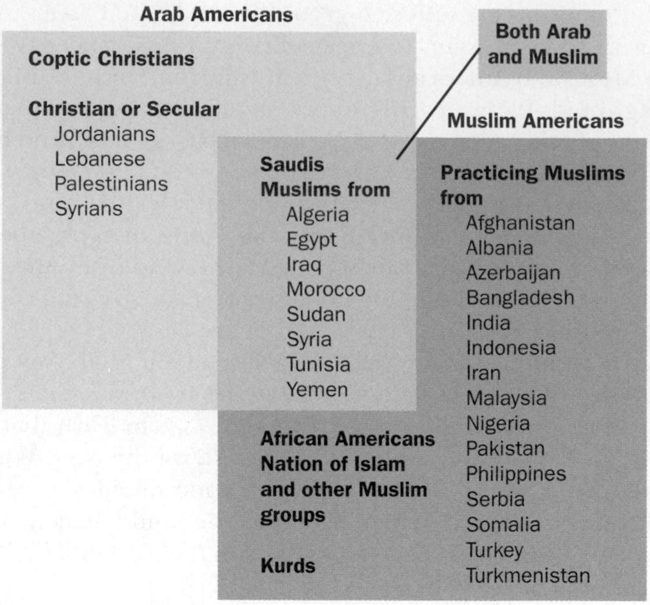

Arab Americans

Coptic Christians

Christian or Secular
Jordanians
Lebanese
Palestinians
Syrians

Both Arab and Muslim

Saudis
Muslims from
Algeria
Egypt
Iraq
Morocco
Sudan
Syria
Tunisia
Yemen

African Americans Nation of Islam and other Muslim groups

Kurds

Muslim Americans

Practicing Muslims from
Afghanistan
Albania
Azerbaijan
Bangladesh
India
Indonesia
Iran
Malaysia
Nigeria
Pakistan
Philippines
Serbia
Somalia
Turkey
Turkmenistan

FIGURE 11.1
Relationship between Muslim and Arab Americans
Many Arab Americans are not Muslims, and most Muslim Americans are not Arabs.

This relationship between religion and an ethnic group that crosses many nationalities is illustrated in Figure 11.1. As we can see, one cannot accurately identify the Muslim faithful by nationality alone, and clearly being Arab does not define one as being a follower of Islam.

Arab Americans

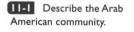
11-1 Describe the Arab American community.

The name *Arab Americans* refers to the immigrants and their descendants from the countries that now make up the Arab world (see Figure 11.2). As defined by the membership of the League of Arab States, these are the 22 nations of North Africa and what is popularly called the Middle East, including Morocco, Syria, Iraq, Saudi Arabia, and Somalia. Not all people living in these countries are necessarily Arab (e.g., the Kurds of Iraq), and some Arab Americans may have emigrated from non-Arab countries such as Great Britain or France, where their families have lived for generations.

Further complicating the use of collective terms of identity such as *Arab* and *Muslim* is evoking the term *Middle Eastern* (Middle Eastern American). Although it is frequently used, the *Middle East* is an ambiguous geographic designation that includes large numbers of people who are neither Muslim nor Arab (such as Israeli Jews). Collectively, in the view of orientalism, Middle Easterners are lumped together and collectively subjected to prejudice and discrimination but are not eligible for supportive efforts such as affirmative action (Marvasti 2005; Wald 2008).

The Arabic language is the single most unifying force among Arabs, although not all Arabs and certainly not all Arab Americans can read and speak Arabic. As the language has evolved over the centuries, people in different parts of the Arab world speak with a different dialect, using their own choices of vocabulary and pronunciation. Although most Arab Americans are not Muslim, the fact that the Qur'an was originally in Arabic 1,400 years ago gives the knowledge of Arabic special importance. This is similar to many Jews' reading of the Torah in Hebrew; and it is unlike Christians, who almost always read the Bible in a translation that is in their native tongue.

Estimates of the size of the Arab American community differ widely. Despite efforts of the Census Bureau to enlist the assistance of experts, census results are widely thought to severely undercount the Arab American community. The government counts only those individuals who have identified their ancestry from the countries of the Arab world and, therefore, would not include those descended from other large overseas Arab communities.

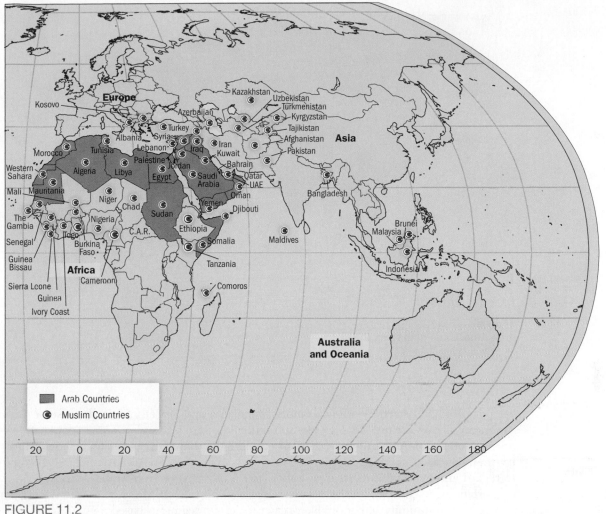

FIGURE 11.2
Arab and Muslim Countries

Source: Author, based on *Chambers Book of Facts* 2005; Coogan 2003; Pew Forum on Religion and Public Life 2011.

By some estimates, there are as many as 3 million people with Arab ancestry in the United States. Among those who identify themselves as Arab American, the largest single source of ancestry was Lebanon, followed by Syria, Egypt, and Palestine. These four groups accounted for two-thirds of Arab Americans in 2000. As with other racial and ethnic groups, Arab Americans, as shown in Figure 11.3, are not uniformly distributed throughout the United States. This rising population has led to the development of Arab retail centers in several cities, including Los Angeles, Chicago, New York City, Washington, DC, and Dearborn and Detroit, Michigan (Brittingham and de la Cruz 2005).

Diversity underlies virtually everything about Arab Americans, which is yet another example of *panethnicity* like Hispanics or Asian Americans. First, there are variations in time of arrival. Many Arab Americans have lived for several generations in the United States, whereas others are foreign-born. A second aspect of diversity is point of origin, which ranges from urban Cairo, Egypt, to rural Morocco. Third, there is a rich variety of religious tradition that can include Christian or Muslim, practicing or nonpracticing, and so forth. It becomes impossible to characterize Arab Americans having a family type or a gender role or an occupational pattern (Dallo, Ajrouch, and Al-Snih 2008; David 2008).

As with any ethnic or immigrant community, divisions arise over who can truly be counted as a member of the community. Sociologist Gary David (2003, 2007) developed the concept of the **deficit model of ethnic identity**. This states that others view one's identity as a factor of subtracting away characteristics corresponding to some ideal ethnic type. Each factor encompassing a perfect ethnic identity missing from a person's background or identity leads

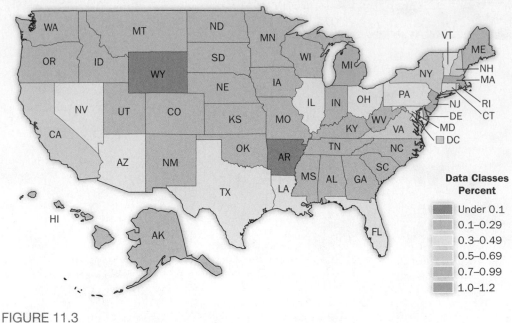

**Data Classes
Percent**

Under 0.1
0.1–0.29
0.3–0.49
0.5–0.69
0.7–0.99
1.0–1.2

FIGURE 11.3
Arab American Population, 2000

Source: U.S. Bureau of the Census data reported in Brittingham and de la Cruz 2005.

the person to be viewed by others as more assimilated and less ethnic. In the case of Arab Americans, if they are unable to speak Arabic, then they are less Arab to some people; if they are married to non-Arabs, then they are less ethnic; if they have never been to the home country, then they are less ethnic. Depending on one's perspective, an Arab American can come to regard another Arab American as either "too American" or "too Arab." Arab American organizations, magazines, and associations may seek to cater to the entire Arab American community, but, more likely, cater to certain segments based on nationality, religion, and degree of assimilation. Organization may also be found by groups that gravitated to one another because they share the same sense of what it means to be Arab American. As noted in the Research Focus, younger Arab Americans seem more willing to self-identify as Arab American even though they actually may be more assimilated to U.S. culture than their parents.

11-2 Describe the Muslim American community.

Although the Muslim presence in the United States has only very recently been recognized by the general public, it has a long history. Yarrow Marmout, an African Muslim and former slave, was painted in this portrait by famed artist Charles Wilson Peele in 1819.

Source: Courtesy of the Historical Society of Pennsylvania Collection, Atwater Kent Museum of Philadelphia.

Muslim Americans

Islam, with approximately 1.6 billion followers worldwide, is second to Christianity among the world's religions. Put another way, globally Muslims make up about 23 percent of the world's population compared with 30 to 33 percent Christian.

Although news events and a worldview of orientalism suggest an inherent conflict between Christians and Muslims, the two faiths are similar in many ways. Both are monotheistic (i.e., based on a single deity) and indeed worship the same God. *Allah* is the Arabic word for God and refers to the God of Moses, Jesus, and Muhammad. Both Christianity and Islam include a belief in prophets, an afterlife, and a judgment day. In fact, Islam recognizes Jesus as a prophet, though not the Son of God. Islam reveres both the Old and New Testaments as integral parts of its tradition. Both faiths impose a moral code on believers, which varies from fairly rigid proscriptions for fundamentalists to relatively relaxed guidelines for liberals (Goodstein 2011).

Although it has some beliefs in common with Christianity, Islam is guided by the teachings of the Qur'an (or Koran), which Muslims believe was

Research Focus

Self-Identifying as "Arab American"

Racial and ethnic identity are important aspects of the immigrant experience. We have already considered how *blended identity* functions, but how might this change over time? An immigrant does not necessarily go through a process of shedding one identity for another, or what is often described as assimilation. Immigrants and even their children and future generations may hold on to multiple identities. **Blended identity** is a self-image and worldview that combines religious faith, a cultural background based on nationality, and the status of being a resident of the United States.

Consider the example of a Pakistani American. As shown in Figure 11.4, Muslims often find their daily activities defined by their faith, their nationality, and their status as Americans. Younger Muslims especially can move freely among the different identities. In Chicago, Muslim college students perform hip-hop in Arabic with lyrics like "La ilaha ila Allah" ("There is no God but Allah"). In Fremont, California, high school Muslim girls and some of their non-Muslim girlfriends hold an alternative prom, decked out in silken gowns, dancing to both 50 Cent and Arabic music, and dining on lasagna but pausing at sunset to face toward Mecca and pray.

Sociologist Kristine Ajrouch and political scientist Amaney Jamal conducted a survey of Arab Americans in the Detroit metropolitan area. Overall in the United States, 80 percent of Arab Americans select "White" since the government does not offer "Arab" as an option for race. Yet when given that choice, Ajrouch and Jamal found many chose Arab American as a self-identifier but also considered themselves "White."

Being Arab American does not mean that you do not also see yourself as "American." Indeed, 94 percent of Arab Americans who are citizens describe themselves as very or quite proud to be American, compared to 98 percent of the general population.

Interestingly, younger Arab Americans seem more willing to use the label of "Arab American." Researchers wonder if the post–9/11 world has given being Arab and/or Muslim American new meaning. Will younger people as they become adults embrace "Arab American" in a sense of unity or seek to distance themselves from it in a fear of being marginalized by society?

Sources: Abdulrahim 2009; Ajrouch 2011; Ajrouch and Jamal 2007; de la Cruz and Brittingham 2003.

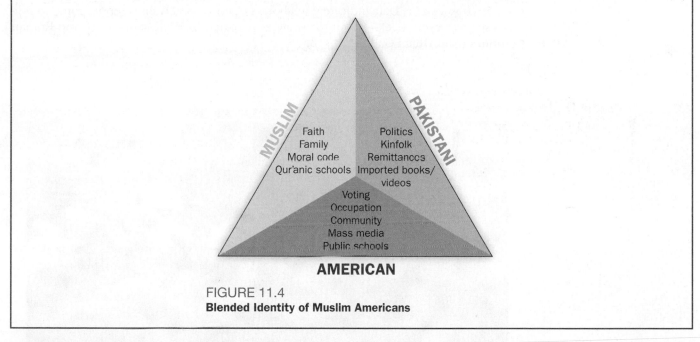

FIGURE 11.4
Blended Identity of Muslim Americans

revealed to the seventh-century Prophet Muhammad. The Qur'an includes the collected sayings, or *hadeeth*, and the deeds of Muhammad, which are called *Sunnah*, or the way of the prophet. Muhammad grew up an orphan and became a respected businessman who rejected the widespread polytheism of his day and turned to the one god (Allah) as worshipped by the region's Christians and Jews. Islam says that he was visited by the angel Gabriel, who began reciting the word of Allah, the Qur'an. Muslims see Muhammad as the last in a long line of prophets; he was preceded by Abraham, Moses, and Jesus. Islam is communal, encompassing all aspects of one's life. Consequently, in countries that are predominantly Muslim, the separation of religion and state is not considered necessary or even desirable. In fact, governments in Muslim countries often reinforce Islamic practices through their laws. Muslims do vary in their interpretation of several traditions, some of which—such as the requirement for women to wear face veils—are disputed.

Like other religious systems, certain rituals referred to as the "pillars of wisdom" characterize Islam. Muslims fast during the month of Ramadan, which marks the revelation of the Qur'an to the Prophet Muhammad; they pray to Allah, facing Mecca, five times a day; they make charitable donations; and they say, where possible, Friday afternoon prayers within their community. They also undertake the **hajj**, the pilgrimage to Mecca, at least once in their lifetime. This city in contemporary Saudi Arabia is home of the House of Allah, or Ka'aba, which was built by Abraham and his son Ishmael. Muslims perform the hajj in accordance with the Qur'an and in the manner prescribed by the Prophet Muhammad in his Sunnah.

Islamic believers are divided into a variety of faiths and sects such as Sunnis and Shi'is (or Shiites). These divisions sometimes result in antagonisms between the members, just as there are religious rivalries between Christian denominations. The large majority of Muslims in the United States are Sunni Muslims—literally, those who follow the Sunnah, the way of the prophet. Compared to other Muslims, they tend to be more moderate in their religious orthodoxy. The Shi'is (primarily from Iraq, Iran, and southern Lebanon) are the second-largest group. The two groups differ on who should have been the *caliph*, or ruler, after the death of the Prophet Muhammad. This disagreement resulted in different understandings of beliefs and practices, concluding in the Sunni and Shi'is worshipping separately from each other. They worship separately even if it means crossing national and linguistic lines to do so—provided there are sufficient numbers of Shi'is to support their own mosque, or *masjid*.

As a part of a larger national study of all religious congregations, regular surveys of mosques are conducted. The latest report placed the number at over 2,100 with a quarter founded since 2000. A mosque typically counts about 1,200 people participating in some religious observance. Data indicate that about 44 percent of Muslims report going to religious services every week—about the same as reported by Protestants, Jews, and Roman Catholics (Abu Dhabi Gallup 2011; Bagby 2012).

Another sign that Muslim Americans are being recognized in the mainstream: in 2013 Marvel Comics introduced a new Superhero Kamala Khan who lives in New Jersey and whose family came from Pakistan. The young Muslim American comes to realize she has superhuman strength and is a polymorph—that is, she can change her shape. All this as she experiences the usual angst of being in high school and dealing with her conservative parents and brother.

There are many other expressions of Islamic faith and even divisions among Sunnis and Shi'is, so to speak of Muslims as Sunni or Shi'i would be akin to speaking of Christians as Roman Catholic or Baptist, forgetting that there are other denominations as well as sharp divisions within the Roman Catholic and Baptist faiths. Furthermore, there are Muslim groups unique to the United States; later we focus on the largest one—Islam among African Americans.

Verses in the Qur'an prescribe to Muslims **jihad**, or struggle against the enemies of Allah. Typically, jihad is taken by Muslims to refer to their internal struggle for spiritual purity. Today, a very visible minority of Muslims in the world sees this as a pretext to carry out an armed struggle against what they view as the enemies of the Palestinians, such as Israel and the United States. Such interpretations, even if held by a few, cannot be dismissed because Islam is a faith without an established hierarchy; there is no Muslim pope to deliver the one true interpretation, and there is no provision for excommunication. Individual *imams*, leaders or spiritual guides of a mosque, can offer guidance and scholarship, but Islam's authority rests with the scripture and the teachings of the prophet (Belt 2002).

Based on the most recent studies, there are at least 2.6 million and perhaps as many as 3 million Muslims in the United States. About two-thirds are U.S.-born citizens. In terms of ethnic and racial background, the more-acceptable estimates still vary widely. Estimates range as follows:

- 20–42 percent African American
- 24–33 percent South Asian (Afghan, Bangladeshi, Indian, and Pakistani)
- 12–32 percent Arab
- 15–22 percent "other" (Bosnian, Iranian, Turk, and White and Hispanic converts)

There appears to be total agreement that the Muslim population in the United States is growing rapidly through immigration and conversion (Bagby 2012; Grossman 2008; Pew Forum on Religion and Public Life 2011).

A majority of U.S. Muslims (56 percent) believe that many religions can lead to eternal life. Most Americans (65 percent), including nearly two-thirds of American Christians (64 percent), share this view. American Muslims seem to be closer to their fellow citizens than compared to their global counterparts. This attitude is far less common among Muslims: a median of just 18 percent of Muslims worldwide think religions other than Islam can lead to eternal life (Lugo et al. 2013).

Black Muslims

African Americans who embrace Islam form a significant segment within the Muslim American community. Islam is also a significant expression of religious beliefs among Black Americans. They number around 1.6 to 1.7 million, or about 5 percent of all African Americans, yet they are estimated to account for 90 percent of all converts to Islam in the United States.

The history of Black American Islam begins in the seventeenth century, when members of some Muslim tribes were forcibly brought to the American colonies. It is estimated that 10 percent of African slaves were Muslim. Slave owners discouraged anything that linked them culturally to Africa, including their spiritual beliefs. Furthermore, many in the South saw making slaves Christians as part of their mission in civilizing the enslaved people. Enslaved Muslims in the colonies and elsewhere often resisted the pressure to assimilate to the dominant group's faith and maintained their dedication to Islam (Ba-Yunus and Kone 2004; Leonard 2003; McCloud 1995).

It was exceedingly difficult, if not impossible, for a collective Muslim community to survive slavery. Organized Muslim groups within the African American community grew and dispersed in the late nineteenth century and the first half of the twentieth

Malcolm X, reflecting his conversion to Islam, made a pilgrimage to the Muslim holy city of Mecca. On this trip in 1964, the year before his assassination in New York City, he also met with area leaders such as Prince Faisal al-Saud of Saudi Arabia.

11-2

century. Resurgence of Islam among Black Americans often centered around the leadership of charismatic people such as West Indian–born Edward Wilmot Blyden and North Carolinian Noble Drew Ali, who founded the Moorish Science Temple. Typically, followers of the movements dispersed at the death of the central leader; but with each movement, the core of converts to Islam grew within the African American community (R. Turner 2003).

Like other Muslims, generally African Americans who follow Islam are not tightly organized into a single religious fellowship. However, most today trace their roots either to the teachings of W. Fard Muhammad or, just as significantly, to those who responded against his version of the faith. Little is known of the early years of the immigrant W. Fard Muhammad, who arrived in Detroit around 1930, introducing the teaching of Islam to poor African Americans. He spoke strongly against adultery and alcohol consumption (which are forbidden by Islamic tradition) and smoking and dancing (which are prohibited among some Muslims). However, he also spoke of the natural superiority of Black people, which would cause them to win out in the inevitable struggle between Blacks and Whites—but only if they adopted their "natural religion" and reclaimed their identities as Muslims (Lincoln 1994; R. Turner 2003).

Malcolm X, originally a member of the Nation of Islam, became the most powerful and brilliant voice of Black self-determination in the 1960s. He was an authentic folk hero to his sympathizers then and remains so to many people today, more than a generation after his death. Besides his own followers, he commanded an international audience and is still referred to in a manner befitting a prophet. Indeed, Spike Lee's 1993 movie, based on the *Autobiography of Malcolm X,* reintroduced him to another generation. Malcolm X was highly critical of the civil rights movement in general and of Martin Luther King, Jr., in particular.

Malcolm X is remembered for his sharp attacks on other Black leaders, for his break with the Nation of Islam, and for his apparent shift to support the formation of coalitions with progressive Whites. He is especially remembered for taking the position that Blacks must resist violence "by any means necessary," which greatly concerned supporters of nonviolence. By the last year of his life, Malcolm X (by then known as Malik El-Shabazz) had taken on a very different orientation. He created the secular Organization of Afro-American Unity, which was meant to internationalize the civil rights movement. Three assassins ended Malcolm X's life in 1964. "His philosophy can be summarized as pride in Blackness, the necessity of knowing Black history, Black autonomy, Black unity, and self-determination for the Black community" (Pinkney 1975: 213; see also Dyson 1995; Kieh 1995).

In recent years, Minister Louis Farrakhan, despite leading a small proportion of Black Muslims, has been the most visible spokesperson among the various Muslim groups in the African American community. Farrakhan broke with the successors of Elijah Muhammad and named his group Nation of Islam, adopting, along with the name used by the earlier group, the more unorthodox-to-Islam ideas of Elijah Muhammad, such as Black moral superiority. Farrakhan jumped into the limelight, although his public statements about Jews and Israel have given his teachings an anti-Semitic taint (Abdo 2004b; Henry 1994; Lincoln 1994).

Although Farrakhan's statements against Whites—Jews in particular—and his anti-Israeli foreign policy have attracted the media's attention, many of his speeches and writings reflect the basic early tenets of the Nation of Islam. Abortion, drugs, and homosexuality are condemned. Self-help, bootstrap capitalism, and strict punishment are endorsed. Farrakhan is not pessimistic about the future of race relations in the United States. As leader of the 1995 Million Man March, he encouraged both marchers and African Americans nationwide to register to vote and work for positive change (Bositis 1996; Loury 1996).

Traditionally, there has been little contact at best and actually some friction between the African American Muslim community, particularly those who adhere to the Nation of Islam, and immigrant Muslims and their descendants. Black Muslims may feel that the larger Islamic community does not speak to what they feel is the unique oppression faced by people who are Black and Muslim in the United States. Meanwhile, other Muslims often assume incorrectly that all African American Muslims embrace the Black superiority view and do not follow orthodox Muslim traditions. It is likely that a single dominating voice of Islam will not emerge among African Americans. That is not surprising because a pluralistic interpretation of faith is common to Muslims worldwide just as it is to Christians and Jews (Abdo 2004b; McCloud 2004).

Immigration to the United States

The history of both Muslims and Arabs in the United States is a long one, but their visibility as a true immigrant presence is more of a twentieth-century phenomenon. As has already been noted, a significant proportion of African slaves were followers of Islam. Even earlier, Spanish Muslims accompanied explorers and conquistadores to the Americas. In the nineteenth century, contingents of Arabs made dramatic impressions at a series of world's fairs held in Philadelphia, St. Louis, and Chicago, where millions of fairgoers had certainly their first contact and probably their first awareness of Arab culture. Although often viewed through the lens of orientalism, fairgoers came away with an awareness of cultures previously unknown to them. Positive reports of the reception of these delegations began to encourage Arabs, particularly those from Syria and Lebanon, to immigrate to the United States. At about the same time, other Arabs immigrated as the result of encouragement from U.S.-funded missionary programs in the Middle East.

Just as immigration of Arabs and, to a lesser extent, practicing Muslims began to annually number in the thousands in the early twentieth century, World War I intervened; and then the restrictive national origin system (see Chapter 4), with its pro-Western and Northern Europe bias, slowed the movement to the United States. As with so many other immigrant groups, the pattern was for immigration to be disproportionately male and the destination to be cities of the East Coast. Pressure to assimilate caused many newcomers to try to reduce the differences between themselves and the host country. So, for example, many women ceased to cover their heads—a practice common to both Christian Arab and Muslim women.

The immediate aftermath of 9/11 led to a decline of about 30 percent of Arabs and Muslims immigrating to the United States because of apprehension over the reception they would receive and increased scrutiny of their entry documents by the federal government. For example, the numbers of tourists and students declined nearly by half. However, recently numbers have begun to rebound. In 2005, more than 40,000 arrivals from Muslim countries sought permanent residency, resulting in the highest annual numbers of Muslim immigrants since 2000. Some new residents even argue they are better off in post–9/11 America because Islamic centers are more organized and free legal help is more accessible (Elliott 2006).

The growth and continuing vibrancy of an Arab presence in the Dearborn, Michigan, area is a unique development in the history of Arab immigration. A few Lebanese immigrants in the late nineteenth century were joined by fellow countrymen and women. Immigrants also came from Lebanon and were largely Christian, as well as from Yemen, who were typically Sunni Muslims. With the expansion of the automobile industry during the 1910s, Arabs came to work in the area's many factories. These immigrants were pleased by their treatment and wages, so more immigrants joined them. By 1919, the first mosque was established, and a variety of service agencies began to serve the needs of the immigrant community.

The mosques in the metropolitan Detroit area serve an estimate of at least 200,000 Arabs. With about 5,000 Arab American-owned businesses, it is hard for a visitor not to see the evidence of this century-long immigration. Business establishments often feature greetings for Christmas, Ramadan, New Year's, and the two Islamic holidays (called Eids) in both English and Arabic. Today, metropolitan Detroit has by far the largest concentration of Arab Americans as well as Muslims. Indeed, this is probably the largest Arab community outside of the Arab world (Detroit Arab American Study Team 2009).

11-3

11-3 Summarize the Muslim and Arab immigration to the United States.

11-4

11-4 Put into your own words Islamophobia.

Islamophobia

In what ways do prejudice and discrimination manifest themselves with respect to Muslim and Arab Americans? In form and magnitude, they are much like that shown to other subordinate groups. Regrettably, this situation has gone beyond orientalism, in which one sees a group of people as "the other" and as somewhat frightening. **Islamophobia** refers to a range of negative feelings toward Muslims and their religion. Those feelings range from generalized intolerance to hatred. These current expressions of hostility are strikingly different because, in the twenty-first century, they have taken on a decidedly patriotic fervor; that is, many people who overtly express anti-Muslim or anti-Arab feelings also believe themselves to be pro-American (Halstead 2008).

Few normalizing or positive images are available. Rarely are Arab and Muslim Americans exhibiting normal behavior such as shopping, attending a sporting event, or even eating without the subtext of terrorism literally lurking in the shadows. Furthermore, the interests of the United States are depicted either as leaning against the Arabs and Muslims, as in the Israeli–Palestinian violence, or presented as hopelessly dependent on them, as in the case of our reliance on foreign oil production.

Evidence of hate crimes and harassment toward Arab and Muslim Americans rose sharply after 9/11, compared to studies done in the mid-1990s. Hate crimes and harassment remained high through 2008, according to more recent studies. Incidents have ranged from beatings to vandalism of mosques to organized resistance to Arabic school openings. Muslim Americans also have received unwarranted eviction notices. Surveys show that a complex view of Arab and Muslim Americans exists in the United States. Surveys since 2001 show that one in four people believe several anti-Muslim stereotypes, for example, that Islam teaches violence and hatred. It is curious that even as they harbor such views, people do not recognize that Arab Americans are poorly treated. Still by 2012, only 40 percent of people had a favorable image of Islam compared to 41 percent who viewed it unfavorably. Yet efforts to tap into college students' opinions find greater hostility toward Arabs and Muslims than any other racial or ethnic group (Parrillo and Donoghue 2013).

A major flashpoint has been the proposed: the "Ground Zero Mosque." A mosque that has operated since 1985, twelve blocks from the World Trade Center (WTC) site, planned to move into some empty retail area to accommodate its growing congregation and out of a desire to create an interfaith outreach center. However, the new site, initially approved by the local community, brought it within two blocks of the WTC site. By 2009, the plan became a national controversy and many people saw Muslims, in general, as being insensitive to the significance of Ground Zero. National surveys showed 61 percent opposed a mosque near Ground Zero and barely 25 percent favoring the location. Plans were set aside as advocates tried to explain they intended to reach out to the nation, not try to divide it (Mohamed and O'Brien 2011).

In the Speaking Out box, Moustafa Bayoumi (2009, 2010), a Brooklyn College, City University of New York, literature professor draws upon DuBois's work to frame how Arab Americans are viewed.

Arab Americans and Muslim Americans, like other subordinate groups, have not responded passively to their treatment. Their communities have created organizations to counter negative stereotypes and to offer schools material responding to the labeling that has occurred. Even before 2001, Arab Americans and Muslim Americans were becoming active in both major political parties in the United States. Given the presence

(🎙) Speaking Out

Arab Problem

Sade and four of his 20-something friends are at a hookah café almost underneath the Verrazano-Narrows Bridge in Brooklyn. It's late, but the summer heat is strong and hangs in the air. They sit on the sidewalk in a circle, water pipes bubbling between their white plastic chairs.

Sade is upset. He recently found out that his close friend of almost four years was an undercover police detective sent to spy on him, his friends, and his community. Even the guy's name, Kamil Pasha, was fake, which particularly irked the 24-year-old Palestinian American. After appearing as a surprise witness at a recent terrorism trial in Brooklyn, Pasha vanished. That's when Sade discovered the truth.

Moustafa Bayoumi

"I was very hurt," he says. "Was it friendship, or was he doing his job?" He takes a puff from his water pipe. "I felt betrayed." The smoke comes out thick and smells like apples. "How could I not have seen this? The guy had four bank accounts! He was always asking for a receipt wherever we went. He had an empty apartment: a treadmill, a TV, and a mattress. No food, no wardrobe." He shakes his head. "We were stupid not to figure it out."

"You have to know the family," Sade says. He points to those around the circle. "His mother is my aunt. I've known him since I was in second grade. I know where his family lives, and he's also my cousin," he says, ticking off each person in turn. He gets to me. "You I'm not so sure about!" he says, and all the young men laugh loudly.

Informants and spies are regular conversation topics in the age of terror, a time when friendships are tested, trust disappears, and tragedy becomes comedy. If questioning friendship isn't enough, Sade has also had other problems to deal with. Sacked from his Wall Street job, he is convinced that the termination stemmed from his Jerusalem birthplace. Anti-Arab and anti-Muslim invectives were routinely slung at him there, and he's happier now in a technology firm owned and staffed by other hyphenated Americans. But the last several years have taken their toll. I ask him about life after September 11 for Arab Americans. "We're the new blacks," he says. "You know that, right?"

How does it feel to be a problem? Just over a century ago, W.E.B. Du Bois asked that very question in his American classic *The Souls of Black Folk*, and he offered an answer. "Being a problem is a strange experience," he wrote, "peculiar even," no doubt evoking the "peculiar institution" of slavery. Du Bois composed his text during Jim Crow, a time of official racial segregation that deliberately obscured to the wider world the human details of African American life. Determined to pull back "the veil" separating populations, he showed his readers a fuller picture of the black experience, including "the meaning of its religion, the passion of its human sorrow, and the struggle of its greater souls."

It seems barely an exaggeration to say that Arab and Muslim Americans are constantly talked about but almost never heard from. The problem is not that they lack representations but that they have too many. And these are all abstractions. Arabs and Muslims have become a foreign-policy issue, an argument on the domestic agenda, a law-enforcement priority, and a point of well-meaning concern. They appear as shadowy characters on terror television shows, have become objects of sociological inquiry, and get paraded around as puppets from public diplomacy. Pop culture is awash with their images. Hookah cafés entice East Village socialites, fashionistas appropriate the checkered kaffiyah scarf, and Prince sings an ode to a young Arab American girl. They are floating everywhere in the virtual landscape of the national imagination, as either villains of Islam or victims of Arab culture. Yet as in the postmodern world in which we live, sometimes when you are everywhere, you are really nowhere.

Frankly, it's beleaguering; like living on a treadmill, an exhausting condition. University of Michigan anthropologists Sally Howell and Andrew Shryock succinctly describe the situation when they write that "in the aftermath of 9/11, Arab and Muslim Americans have been compelled, time and again, to apologize for acts they did not commit, to condemn acts they never condoned and to openly profess loyalties that, for most U.S. citizens, are merely assumed." Yet despite the apologies, condemnations, and professions, their voices still aren't heard. And while so many terrible things have happened in the past years, plenty of good things have also occurred, from Japanese American groups speaking out against today's wartime policies, to prominent civil-rights activists fighting for due process for Muslim and Arab clients, to ordinary people reaching out to one another in everyday encounters. Much of this happens quietly in church basements, in mosques holding open houses, in Jewish centers, or in university or community halls, but such events too are often obscured, drowned out by the ideology of our age. Yet what most remains in the shadows today are the human dimensions to how Arabs and Muslims live their lives, the rhythms of their work and days, the varieties of their religious experiences, the obstacles they face, and the efforts they shoulder to overcome them. In other words, what is absent is how they understand the meanings of their religion, the passions of their sorrow, and the struggle of their souls. But in today's landscape, none of that seems to matter. One could say that in the dawning years of the twenty-first century, when Arabs are the new chic and Islam is all the rage, Muslims and Arabs have become essentially a nagging problem to solve, one way or another.

And being a problem is a strange experience—frustrating, even.

Source: Bayoumi 2009:1–2, 5–6.

of Islamophobia, the position of being Arab or Muslim in the United States grew more complex and contentious in the wake of the events of September 11, 2001, despite the public efforts of many Arabs and Muslims to proclaim their loyalty to the United States (David and Jalbert 2008; Pew Forum on Religion and Public Life 2011; Selod and Embrick 2013).

Pulitzer Prize–winning journalist Andrea Elliott (2011) used the term "Generation 9/11" to refer to American Muslims who have come of an age since the attack on the World Trade Center. "Will we ever belong?" Young Muslim and Arab Americans are not the first ethnic or racial group to wonder this in light of a defining moment that causes a large group to be harshly stigmatized (Goodstein 2010).

Contemporary Life in the United States

11-5 Discuss the contemporary experiences of Arab Americans.

As has already been noted, Arab Americans tended to immigrate to urban areas. There they have filled a variety of occupational roles, and immigrants, since the 1965 Immigration and Naturalization Act, have been filling skilled and professional roles in the United States. Another area in which Arab Americans often find opportunities for upward mobility is to become self-employed merchants or entrepreneurs. They typically are financially unable to buy into prosperous businesses or high-end retail stores. Rather, they have tended to become involved in precisely those businesses that privileged Whites have long since left behind or avoided altogether. To some degree, Arabs follow a pattern of Jewish and Korean immigrant entrepreneurs, operating stores in low-income areas of central cities that major retailers ignore. Opportunities for success are great, but it also means that the Arab American merchant faces the challenges of serving a low-income population with few consumer choices and a history of being exploited by outsiders (Cainkar 2006).

In 2013, the Census Bureau released an analysis of the income of Arab American households. As we can see Figure 11.5, people reporting Arab ancestry show as a group a higher income than the general population. As is apparent, there is a dramatic range among Arab ancestry groups ranging from Lebanese Americans who report incomes over a quarter higher than the general population to those of Yemeni and Iraqi Americans with household incomes a third lower.

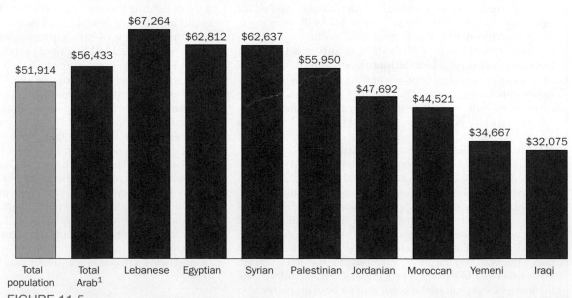

FIGURE 11.5
Median Household Income of Arab Americans

Note: Based on American Community Survey 2007–2010.

Source: Asi and Beaulieu 2013: Figure 2.

Family Life and Gender

11-5

As with any people, the family plays a central role in the lives of both Muslim and Arab Americans. Given the diversity within both groups, it is impossible to generalize about typical patterns. Traditionally, Islam permitted men to have multiple wives—a maximum of four. The Qur'an admonished Muslim men to do justice economically and emotionally to their wives, and if they could not, then they should have only one wife. In some non-Islamic countries, this practice of multiple marriages is legal, but it is exceedingly rare for Muslim households in countries where the law is not supportive.

In the United States, for those who are recent immigrants or the children of immigrants, family patterns are more likely to be affected by the traditions of their homeland than by the fact that they are Muslim or Arab. Certainly, the role of women receives a great deal of attention because their outer clothing is a conspicuous symbol that to some non-Muslims and non-Arabs seems to represent repression of women in society. There is a full range of views of women among Muslims and Arabs, just as there is among Christians and other ethnicities. However, Islam does stress that women need to be protected and should present themselves modestly in public. This code is operationalized very differently among countries where Muslims dominate, and it varies within Muslim populations in the United States (Haeri 2004).

Sexism and sexist behavior are universal. However, the perception of gender practices in Muslim societies has received special attention in the Western media. Individually, all Muslims, men and women alike, must cover themselves and avoid revealing clothes that are designed to accentuate contours of the body and to emphasize its physical beauty. According to the Qur'an, more revealing garments can be worn in private with one's family or before members of the same sex, so in some Muslim countries some beaches and public pools are designated for use by men only or by women only.

The Prophet Muhammad indicated in his Sunnah that the female body should be covered except for the face, hands, and feet. Hence, traditional Muslim women should wear head coverings. The **hijab** refers to a variety of garments that allow women to follow the guidelines of modest dress. It may include head coverings or a face veil and can take the form of a rather than something that actually covers the face; the latter would be dictated by a cultural tradition, not Islam. U.S. Muslims select from an array of traditional garments from Muslim countries. These garments include long, loosely tailored coats or a loose black overgarment along with a scarf and perhaps a face veil. U.S. Muslim women are just as apt to wear long skirts or loose pants and overblouses that they may

buy at any local retail outlet. While there is general tolerance of wearing a hijab in the United States, this perspective is not universal. In 2013, a federal court ruled that Abercrombie & Fitch wrongly fired a Muslim employee for wearing a headscarf. The retailer claimed her garment hurt sales but could offer no evidence of it (Haeri 2004; Lipka 2013).

When it comes to the hijab, or outer garments, research has identified three perspectives among Muslim women in the United States and other settlements outside Islamic countries. Younger, better-educated women who support wearing the hijab in public draw on Western ideas of individual rights, arguing in favor of veiling as a form of personal expression. In contrast, older, less-educated women who support the wearing of hijab tend to make their arguments without any reference to Western ideology. They cannot

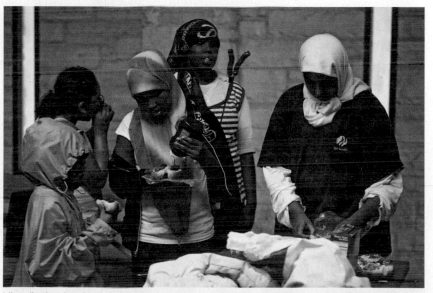

Like all other immigrants, Muslim Americans incorporate U.S. traditions into their daily lives. Here Girl Scout troop leader Farheen Hakeem (right) prepares hot dogs that are hallal—that is, dietary acceptable—during a Girl Scout outing in Minneapolis. Most of these troop members are Somali immigrants or their children.

11-5

see why veiling should be an issue in the first place. A third group of women, of all ages and educational backgrounds, oppose the hijab (Read 2007).

Education

Muslim and Arab Americans recognize the importance of education, and many of the recent immigrants have high levels of formal education and have benefited by the immigration policy that gave preference to those having job skills needed to enter the United States. Muslims also value formal instruction in their faith, and there are several hundred elementary and secondary schools, the majority attached to mosques, that offer what has been referred to in other religious contexts as a parochial school education. Increasing numbers of Muslims are turning to home schooling either out of a desire to adhere to their customs in a way that is difficult to do in public schools or out of a concern over the prejudice their children may experience (Brittingham and de la Cruz 2005).

Schools are specific to particular expressions of Islam and specific nationalities, and some schools serve principally Black Muslims. Qur'anic or Sunday schools also coexist, offering specifically religious instruction either to those attending mosque schools or as a supplement for children enrolled in public schools. A major growth industry has emerged in North America that provides curriculum materials and software to serve these schools, which range from preschool and continue through college, including graduate education (Leonard 2003; MacFarquhar 2008).

Children attending public schools encounter the type of adjustment experienced by those of a religious faith different from the dominant one of society. Although public schools are intended to be secular, it is difficult to escape the orientation of many activities to Christmas and Easter or dietary practices that may not conform to the cultural tradition of the children's families. In some school districts with larger Muslim student populations, strides have been made to recognize the religious diversity. A few have granted Eid-al-Fitr, the day marking the end of Ramadan, as an official school holiday for all students (Avila 2003; Sataline 2009).

Politics

Muslim and Arab Americans are politically aware and often active. For those who identify with their homeland, politics may take the form of closely monitoring international events as they affect their home country and perhaps their kinfolk who still live there. Admittedly, because U.S. foreign policy often is tilted against some areas such as Palestine, the concerns that Arab Americans may have about events abroad may not be relieved by statements and actions taken by U.S. government officials. On a different level, Muslims and Arab Americans are increasingly involved in politics in the United States. Certainly the most visible Arab American in politics has been consumer advocate Ralph Nader, who has tried to open up presidential politics to consider a true alternative to the two-party system.

Within the traditional two-party system, Arab and Muslim Americans tend to be socially conservative, favoring school vouchers, are anti-abortion, and are opposed to gay marriage and civil unions. Yet they tend to vote Democrat, who they perceive as being more sensitive to the problems facing Arab and Muslim countries. By 2011, a national survey indicated 70 percent of Muslims leaning toward the Democrats compared to only 13 percent toward the Republicans. A 2012 survey showed 75 percent of Arab Americans supporting President Obama for reelection. In 2012, Keith Ellison, an African

Congressman Keith Ellison, first elected in 2006, is the only Muslim to have served in Congress. Here Rep. Ellison is shown speaking with constituents in Minneapolis.

American Democrat from Minneapolis, was reelected to his fourth term to the House of Representatives, the first and only Muslim American to serve—and marking a new age (Arab American Institute 2012b; Pew Research Center 2011).

Muslims in the United States often express the view that their faith encourages political participation. They note that as the Prophet Muhammad lay on his deathbed, he explicitly refused to name a successor to his rule, preferring that the people choose their own leaders. Individual Arabs and Muslims have sought elective office and have been appointed to high-level positions.

There is a clear distancing that one can observe between the major parties and Muslims and Arab Americans. Although there are frequent official welcoming statements of support, close identification as might be shown in routine dinners and convention appearances are rare. This represents a contrast to how politicians cater to African Americans and Latinos to gain votes and more closely resembles the arm's-length relationship with gay and lesbian voters. As charges have escalated in the last decade that some organizations and charities in the Arab and Muslim community were financially assisting overseas groups unfriendly to Israel or even supportive of terrorist objectives, U.S. politicians began to take the safe position of refusing campaign money from virtually any group linked to the Muslim or Arab community. Some Muslims were also annoyed about how vociferous the Barack Obama campaign was to deny charges he was a Muslim, as his late Kenyan-born father had been, as if to be a Muslim was akin to being a Communist or, even worse, a terrorist.

Being a part of a Muslim minority in some place other than the United States can create challenges, as we consider in A Global View, "Muslims in France."

News events have fueled anti-Arab, anti-Muslim feeling. Activities carried out by Arabs or Muslims, including the 1972 terrorist raid at the Munich Olympics and the 1998 bombings of the U.S. embassies in Kenya and Tanzania, contributed to the negative image. The attack of September 11, 2001, engineered by Arab Muslim terrorists, caused many Americans to associate Arab and Muslim Americans with America's enemy in the war against terrorism. As the economy softened and taxpayers paid for increased security,

A Global View

Muslims in France

Historically, France has not been a destination of immigrants, especially from outside Europe. In the efforts to rebuild France following World War II, workers came to France from its colonies in North Africa; many of them were Muslim. As countries such as Algeria, Morocco, and Tunisia (refer back to Figure 11.2) gained their independence in the 1950s and 1960s, immigration grew. In 2010, the Muslim population totaled 7.5 percent of the general population and comprises both continuing immigration and the children and grandchildren of immigrants. It is projected to go over 10 percent by 2030.

For Muslims born in France, a growing proportion see their status in comparison to other French men and women rather than to the people in North Africa, as more likely did their immigrant parents.

In 1989, the French government banned Muslim girls in public school from wearing headscarves, taking the position that religious symbols have no place being displayed in schools. Critics argued that Muslims were being targeted while Christian children continued to wear crosses. Although the enforcement of the headscarf ban has been problematic, many Muslims saw it as an act of bigotry rather than an act promoting secular freedom.

In 2011, the wearing of the face veil became illegal in all public places. While such more complete covering is uncommon among Muslims in France, this latest prohibition was seen as a further stigmatization to the Muslim community. In the first year, 425 women wearing full-face veils were fined ($188 each) and another 66 received warnings. While for national figures these numbers are small, police admit they rarely enforce the law, having no desire to increase tensions. Government officials said it was merely a security measure to keep people from hiding their faces but the law also calls for a prison sentence for anyone forcing another to wear the full-face veil—clearly a measure aimed at Muslims.

Whatever may be the challenges of being Muslim in the United States, many observers in Europe contrast the sense of alienation that Muslims feel there with the perception of most Muslims in the United States that they at least fit in and that some may be enjoying success.

Sources: Chrisafis 2011; Erlanger and Camus 2012; Mann 2008; Pew Forum on Religion and Public Life 2011; Woesthoff 2008.

11-5

Arab and Muslim Americans became scapegoats. Vandalism of mosques, attacks on Arab-speaking people, and calls for widespread dragnets based on ethnicity or religion were common (Disha, Cavendish, and King 2011).

The events of September 11, 2001, catapulted the United States to focus on segments of the population with a scrutiny that had not been witnessed since the attack on Pearl Harbor 60 years earlier. Speaking from the Washington, DC, Islamic Center within days of the hijacking of four airliners, President George W. Bush (2001) assured the nation that "the face of terror is not the true faith of Islam.... Islam is peace" and that "Muslims make an incredibly valuable contribution to our country." However, much harm had already been done. Follow-up remarks in the days to come were made by the president and other administrative officials in front of mosques or in the presence of representatives of the Muslim and Arab American communities. Even the USA PATRIOT Act passed in October 2001, which has been sharply criticized for contributing to fear within the Arab and Muslim communities, has specific provisions condemning discrimination against Arab and Muslim Americans. Although these were positive symbols of reaching out, the further stigmatization of Muslim and Arab Americans was unstoppable. In addition, Muslims and Arabs became one indistinguishable and homogenous group (Winter and Watanabe 2007).

In light of these suspicions, some citizens have found themselves under special surveillance because of racial profiling at airports and border checkpoints. As noted earlier, in Chapter 2, **racial profiling** is any police-initiated action based on race, ethnicity, or national origin rather than a person's behavior. Profiling of Arabs and Muslims became especially intense after September 11, 2001.

In those weeks after 9/11, surveys showed that both Muslim and Arab Americans supported the president's policy of going after terrorists. At the same time, they were fearful that continued military action would hurt how the United States is viewed. In the wake of 9/11, expressions and proof of loyalty were forced on Arab and Muslim Americans.

In an effort to locate domestic terrorists, the U.S. Department of Justice required that all foreign-born Muslim men report to the Bureau of Citizenship and Immigration Services to be photographed, fingerprinted, and interviewed. Some questions were mundane: Where did they work? Were they married? Did they have children? Some were more pointed: Had they been asked by any Arabs or Muslims to teach them to fly airplanes? With very little public notice, 144,513 Muslim men from 25 countries reported during a five-month period ending in 2003. Of those who reported, about 13,000 faced deportation because of visa violations such as overstaying their visas, and 11 remained in custody because they were suspected terrorists.

The registration deepened fear and disillusionment among the many law-abiding Muslims in the United States. Many of the more than 144,000 men interviewed were embarrassed to even be questioned because their code of behavior (no drinking or illegal drugs) meant they were less likely to have faced routine encounters with law enforcement officials. Immigration advocates argued that the government was selectively enforcing immigration laws, but the courts have upheld the process and the right of the government to keep secret the names of those deported or detained (King 2004; Lewis 2003).

Conclusion

We have seen the diversity within the Native American tribal community and among Latinos. Prejudice, discrimination, and responses of resistance have typified these groups and African Americans' long history in the United States. Now we can see in a special way that Arab Americans and Muslim Americans share this experience. Not very numerous in absolute terms until the latter part of the twentieth century, both Arabs and Muslims have built on a fragmented history that in the United States literally goes back 200 years. When Muslims were less numerous, it was difficult to maintain any sense of communal identity, but as their numbers increased, identifiable groups emerged.

Diversity has marked both Arab Americans and Muslim Americans in the United States. For the descendants of earlier Arab settlers, their identity as Arabs may

SPECTRUM OF INTERGROUP RELATIONS

EXPULSION	SEGREGATION	ASSIMILATION	

INCREASINGLY UNACCEPTABLE ← → **MORE TOLERABLE**

EXTERMINATION
or genocide

SECESSION
or partitioning

FUSION
or amalgamation or melting pot

PLURALISM
or multiculturalism

Muslim African slaves bound for America

Deficit model

Blended identity

Arabic language retention

be discounted by recent Arab immigrants through a process of the deficit model of ethnic identity. For the Muslim community, the divisions within the faith overseas are reproduced in the United States, with the added significant presence of African Americans who have embraced Islam.

The world and domestic events of recent years, and especially in the early years of the twenty-first century, have created some new challenges. In some respects, the continuing conflict in Israel and Palestine has served to create an Arab identity that was largely missing a few generations ago when more strictly nationalistic agendas prevailed. Similarly, the agenda of fundamentalist and militant Muslims has created an us–them mentality found both in international organizations and on street corners of the United States. This lack of true understanding of one another is not totally new but is built on the orientalism that has its roots in the initial contacts between Europeans and the people of the Middle East and South Asia.

For many Arab and Muslim Americans, this is all ancient history. They, like other U.S. citizens, are seeking to define themselves and move ahead in their society. The challenges for them to do this seem measurably greater than they were just a few years ago, but their efforts to create bridges are also significant.

Summary

1. Arab Americans (an ethnic group) are a diverse group representing nationalities from Africa, Europe, and Asia who may or may not be Muslim.

2. Muslims (a religious group) include converts to the faith as well as immigrants and their descendants and they may or may not be Arab.

3. Many of the early Muslims in the Americas came as slaves, whereas most Arab Americans have come during the last half-century.

4. Given the presence of Islamophobia, the position of being Arab or Muslim in the United States grew more complex and contentious in the wake of the events of September 11, 2001, despite the public efforts of many Arabs and Muslims to proclaim their loyalty to the United States.

5. Muslims and Arab Americans are both diverse groups among whom there are differing patterns for approaching the family and gender roles while embracing education. Politics is becoming a growing aspect of both the Arab and the Muslim community and is expanding beyond issues specific to the Middle East.

Key Terms

blended identity, p. 247

deficit model of ethnic
identity, p. 245

hajj, p. 248

hijab, p. 255

Islamophobia, p. 252

jihad, p. 249

orientalism, p. 243

racial profiling, p. 258

Review Questions

1. What are the dimensions of diversity among Arab Americans?

2. How would you characterize the Muslim faith in the United States?

3. How has the immigration of Muslims and Arabs been influenced by the governmental policies of the United States?

4. What is the extent of Islamophobia?

5. Summarize the institutions of family, education, and politics.

Critical Thinking

1. Apply the deficit model of ethnic identity to another group besides Arab Americans.

2. How are the Arab and Muslim communities composed of differences by language, social class, citizenship status, nationality, and religion?

3. Identify groups other than Arab Americans and Muslim Americans that have recently been subjected to prejudice, perhaps in your own community.

4. What are some characteristics associated with Muslim and Arab Americans that have come to be viewed as negatives but when practiced by Christian Whites are seen as positives?

12 Asian Americans: Growth and Diversity

12-1 Explain the model minority image.

12-2 Characterize the political activity and level of pan-Asian identity.

12-3 Describe the Asian Indians.

12-4 Describe the Filipino Americans.

12-5 Discuss the Southeast Asian American communities in the United States.

12-6 Describe the Korean Americans.

12-7 Clarify how Hawai'i and its people embody cultural diversity.

12-1

If the diversity of racial and ethnic groups is not yet apparent in this book, one need only look at the diversity among those collectively labeled *Asian Americans.* Consider Priscilla Chan, who at the age of 27 in May 2012 was married and had sushi and Mexican food served at the reception. Both her parents, ethnic Chinese from Vietnam who arrived in the United States via refugee camps in the 1970s, worked such long hours in Boston restaurants that her grandmothers, who spoke no English, raised her. Born in the United States, Priscilla graduated from Harvard majoring in biology and later taught grade school while attending medical school. Of special interest is that she married a non-Asian (Facebook founder Mark Zuckerberg) and thus is an example of the 29 percent of recent Asian American newlyweds who marry non-Asians.

Then, one could look at football in Texas. Friday night lights are synonymous with Texas high school football, but at one school, many of the players were born in the Pacific island of Tonga. As 6-foot-2, 297-pound Trinity High offensive tackle Uatakini Cocker takes the line, he screams, "Mate ma'a Tonga," which means "I will die for Tonga." He is one of 16 Tongan Americans playing for the school. The school has won the state football championship three of the last six years and was runner-up in another year. Trinity is located in Euless, which adjoins the Dallas-Fort Worth Airport, where Tongans in the early 1970s first started working. The success among some of these first immigrants initiated a pattern of **chain immigration**, whereby Tongan immigrants sponsor later immigrants. Euless boasts about 4,000 people who were either born in Tonga or are their descendants.

Los Angeles's Little Tokyo is a happening place. Debbie Hazama, 35, a homemaker with three children, drove with her husband from the suburbs because not many Japanese Americans live where she does and she wants her children "to stay connected." Little Tokyo threw a day-long party of Asian hip-hop along with traditional martial arts demonstrations to gather Japanese Americans scattered across Southern California. During one festival, a 24-year-old South Pasadena woman grabbed a heavy mallet and took a swing at a drum, just as she had practiced for months. Nicole Miyako Cherry, the daughter of a Japanese American mother and a White American father, previously had little interest in her Japanese roots except for wearing a kimono for Halloween as a youngster. Yet in the last couple of years, she became interested in all things Japanese, including visiting Japan. Looking to her future as a social work therapist, she says she would like her own children to learn Japanese, go to Japanese festivals, play in Japanese sports leagues, and have Japanese first names.

Consider "The 100 Years Living Club," a group of elderly immigrants from India who gather at a mall in Fremont, California. These elders may talk about the latest community news, cheap flights to Delhi, or their latest run-in with their daughter-in-law.

Then there is Vietnamese American Tuan Nguyren, age 54, who tends to 80 areas in rural South Carolina overseeing 160,000 chickens. His wife lives 50 miles away where she operates a nail salon. They get together about once a week, and the main topic of conversation is how they are putting their four daughters through college. Making a poultry farm succeed is hard work and Nguyren has mentored other Vietnamese Americans who have struggled with the effort.

Finally we could venture to Minot, North Dakota, and dine at Charlie's Main Street Café on chicken fried steak and mashed potatoes. The proprietor is Korean-born Geewon Anderson who came here via Anchorage and Minneapolis. Ranch dressing and sunny-side ups were all new to her but she is already seen as a fixture in a city of 40,000 that is 94 percent White. At night, she relaxes by watching Korean soap operas on satellite television (Brown 2009; Copeland 2011; Eligon 2013; Euless Historical Preservation Committee 2011; Holson and Bilton 2012; Longman 2008; Small 2011; Watanabe 2007).

Immigration to the United States is more than quaint turn-of-the-century black-and-white photos taken at Ellis Island. Immigration, race, and ethnicity are being lived out among people of all ages, and for no collective group is this truer than for Asian Americans who live throughout the United States yet are not evenly distributed across the states (see Figure 12.1).

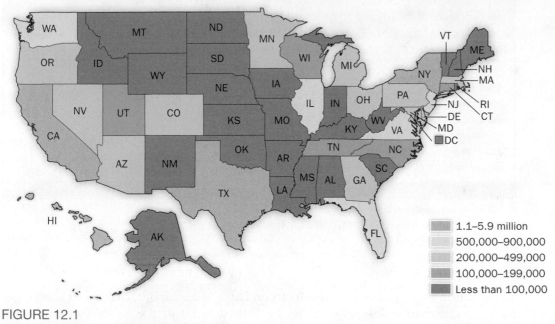

FIGURE 12.1
Where Most Asian Pacific Islanders Live

Sources: Census 2010 data in Hixson, Hepler, and Kim 2012: Tables 2.5; Hoeffel et al. 2012: Tables 2, 3.

The successive waves of immigrants to the United States from the continent of Asia comprise a large number of nationalities and cultures. In addition to the seven groups listed in Figure 12.2, the U.S. Bureau of the Census enumerates 47 groups, including Iwo Jimian, Native Hawaiian, Pakistani, and Samoan. Asian Americans and Pacific Islanders, like other racial and ethnic groups, are not evenly distributed across the United States. Asian Americans also include ethnic groups, such as the Hmong, that do not correspond to any one nation. Collectively, Asian Americans in 2010 numbered about 15 million—a 43 percent increase over 2000, compared with an overall population increase of only 9.7 percent. This is a larger increase than Latinos experienced during the first decade of the twenty-first century (Hixson, Hepler, and Kim 2012; Hoeffel et al. 2012).

Given this diversity among Asian Americans and Pacific Islanders, several generalizations made earlier about Native Americans also can apply to Asian Americans. Both groups are a collection of diverse peoples with distinct linguistic, social, and geographic backgrounds. As reflected in Table 12.1, even limiting the analysis to the six largest groups shows quite a range in the proportion of foreign born, attainment of a college degree, proficiency in English, and poverty rate.

Despite the large Asian American community—which is equivalent to the total African American population after World War II—Asian Americans feel ignored. They see "race and ethnicity" in America framed as a Black White issue or, more recently, as a "triracial" issue that includes Hispanics. But where are the Asian Americans in these pictures of the United States? For example, tens of thousands of Asian Americans, especially Vietnamese Americans, were displaced by Hurricane Katrina in 2005, but they received little media notice.

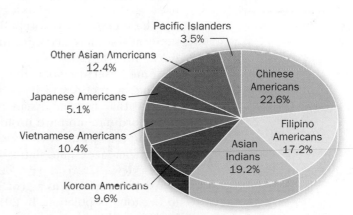

FIGURE 12.2
Asian Americans and Pacific Islanders

Source: See Figure 12.1.

Note: Lists all specific groups with more than 750,000.

TABLE 12.1
Asian Origin Groups

Group	Foreign Born	Bachelor's Degree	Proficient in English	Poverty Rate
Chinese Americans	76	51	52	14
Asian Indians	87	70	76	9
Filipino Americans	69	47	48	6
Vietnamese Americans	84	26	41	15
Korean Americans	78	53	64	15
Japanese Americans	32	46	82	8
General US Population	16	28	90	13

Note: Based on 2012 national survey except for poverty rate, which is based on 2010 income.
Source: Pew Social and Demographic Trends 2012: 13, 30, 33, 37, 41, 44, 47, 50.

Immigration issues understandably focus on Latin America, but what about challenges facing Asians who seek legal entry to the United States or the Asian Americans who are already here?

To better comprehend the collective picture of Asian Americans, we first consider the powerful image that many people have of Asian Americans constituting some kind of perfect, model minority. We then turn our attention to the role they play politically in the United States and the degree to which a pan-Asian identity is emerging.

We then consider four of the larger groups—Filipinos, Asian Indians, Filipinos, Koreans, and Southeast Asians—in greater depth. The chapter concludes by examining the coexistence of a uniquely mixed group of peoples—Hawaiians—among whom Asian Americans form the numerical majority. Chapter 13 concentrates on the Chinese and the Japanese, the two Asian groups with the longest historical tradition in the United States.

Is There a Model Minority?

12-1 Explain the model minority image.

"Asian Americans are a success! They achieve! They succeed! They have no protests, no demands. They just do it!" This is the general image people in the United States often hold of Asian Americans as a group. They constitute a **model minority** because, although they have experienced prejudice and discrimination, they seem to have succeeded economically, socially, and educationally without resorting to political or violent confrontations with Whites.

Some observers point to the existence of a model minority as a reaffirmation that anyone can get ahead in the United States. Proponents of the model-minority view declare that because Asian Americans have achieved success, they have ceased to be subordinate and are no longer disadvantaged. This labeling is only a variation of **blaming the victim**: With Asian Americans, it is praising the victim. Examining aspects of the socioeconomic status of Asian Americans allows a more thorough exploration of this view.

Asian Americans, as a group, have impressive school enrollment rates in comparison to the total population. In 2010, half of Asian Americans 25 years of age or older held bachelor's degrees, compared with 28 percent of the White population. These rates vary among Asian American groups: Asian Indians, Filipino Americans, Korean Americans, Chinese Americans, and Japanese Americans have higher levels of educational achievement than other Asian American groups. Yet other groups such as Vietnamese Americans and Pacific Islanders, including Native Hawaiians, fare much worse than White Americans (Bureau of the Census 2007b, 2011a).

This encouraging picture regarding some Asian Americans does have some qualifications, however, that question the optimistic model-minority view. According to a study of California's state university system, although Asian Americans often are viewed as successful overachievers, they have unrecognized and overlooked needs and experience discomfort and harassment on campus. As a group, they also lack Asian faculty and staff members to whom they can turn for support. They confront many identity issues and must do a "cultural balancing act" along with all the usual pressures faced by college students. The report noted that an "alarming number" of Asian American students appear to be experiencing intense stress and alienation, problems that have often been "exacerbated by racial harassment" (Ohnuma 1991; Teranishi 2010).

12-1

Despite the widespread belief that they constitute a model minority, Asian Americans are victims of both prejudice and violence. After the terrorist attacks of September 11, 2001, anti-Asian violence increased dramatically for several months in the United States. The first fatality was an Asian Indian American who was shot and killed by a gunman in Mesa, Arizona, shouting, "I stand for America all the way" (National Asian Pacific American Legal Consortium 2002).

This anti–Asian American feeling is built on a long cultural tradition. The term *yellow peril* dates back to the view of Asian immigration, particularly from China, as unwelcome. **Yellow peril** came to refer to the generalized prejudice toward Asian people and their customs. The immigrants were characterized as heathen, morally inferior, drug addicted, savage, or lustful. Although the term was first used around the turn of the twentieth century, this anti-Asian sentiment is very much alive today. Many contemporary Asian Americans find this intolerance very unsettling given their conscientious efforts to extend their education, seek employment, and conform to the norms of society. Hate crimes against Asian Americans persist and have even risen in recent years (Hurh 1994; Lee et al. 2007).

The resentment against Asian Americans is not limited to overt expressions of violence. Like other subordinate groups, Asian Americans are subject to institutional discrimination. For example, some Asian American groups have large families and find themselves subject to zoning laws stipulating the number of people per room, which make it difficult for family members to live together. Kinfolk are unable to take in family members legally. Whereas we may regard these family members as distant relatives, many Asian cultures view cousins, uncles, and aunts as relatives to whom they have a great deal of familial responsibility.

The marginal status of Asian Pacific Islanders leaves them vulnerable to both selective and collective oppression. In 1999, news stories implicated Wen Ho Lee, a nuclear physicist at Los Alamos National Laboratory in New Mexico, as a spy for China. Subsequent investigation, during which Lee was imprisoned under very harsh conditions, concluded that the naturalized citizen scientist had indeed downloaded secret files to an unsecured computer, but there was no evidence that the information ever went further.

In the aftermath of the Wen Ho Lee incident, a new form of racial profiling emerged. We introduced **racial profiling** in Chapter 2 as any police-initiated action that relies on race, ethnicity, or national origin rather than a person's behavior. Despite Lee's being found not guilty, Asian Americans were viewed as security risks. A survey found that 32 percent of the people in the United States felt that Chinese Americans are more loyal to China than to the United States. In fact, the same survey showed that 46 percent were concerned about Chinese Americans passing secrets to China. Subsequent studies found that Asian Americans were avoiding top-secret science labs for employment because they became subject to racial profiling at higher security levels (Committee of 100 2001; Department of Energy 2000; Lee with Zia 2006; Wu 2002).

12-1

Another misleading sign of the apparent success of Asian Americans is their high incomes as a group. Like other elements of the image, however, this deserves closer inspection. Asian American family income approaches parity with that of Whites because of their greater achievement than Whites in formal schooling. If we look at specific educational levels, however, Whites earn more than their Asian counterparts of the same age. Asian Americans' average earnings increased by at least $2,300 for each additional year of schooling, whereas Whites gained almost $3,000. Asian Americans as a group have significantly more formal schooling but have lower household family income. We should note that to some degree, some Asian Americans' education is from overseas and, therefore, may be devalued by U.S. employers. Yet in the end, educational attainment does not pay off as much if one is of Asian descent as it does for White non-Hispanics (Kim and Sakamoto 2010; Zeng and Xie 2004).

So even with all the "tools" to succeed—supportive family, high achievement, and often attending prestigious schools—Asian Americans often hit what has been termed a bamboo ceiling. The **bamboo ceiling** refers to the barrier that talented Asian Americans face because of resentment and intolerance directed toward Asian Americans. The bamboo ceiling is clearly a nod to the term *glass ceiling*, a term that has historically been used to address barriers that women and minority group men have faced in the workplace. The presence of the bamboo ceiling reflects the cultural values and social norms that impact Asian professionals' interactions with others and cause others to make negative judgments about them (Hyun 2006, 2009).

Asian Americans are just over 5 percent of the U.S. population, but they account for 15 to 25 percent of Ivy League college enrollment. At the same time, as of 2011, they represented fewer than 2 percent of Fortune 500 CEOs and corporate officers. A national survey showed that Asian Americans who are successful in the corporate world must manage themselves so they don't seem too ambitious or have too many ideas. Only 28 percent of Asian Americans feel very comfortable "being themselves" at the workplace, compared to 45 percent of African Americans, 41 percent of Latinos, and 42 percent of White workers (Center for Work-Life Policy 2011).

Even the positive stereotype of Asian American students as academic stars or whiz kids can be burdensome to the people so labeled. Asian Americans who do only modestly well in school may face criticism from their parents or teachers for their failure to conform to the whiz kid image. Some Asian American youths disengage from school when faced with these expectations or receive little support for their interest in vocational pursuits or athletics (Kibria 2002; Maddux et al. 2008; Ochoa 2013).

Striking contrasts are evident among Asian Americans. For every Asian American household in 2012 with an annual combined income of $200,000 or more, another earns fewer than $17,000 a year. Collectively, 11.7 percent of Asian Americans were below the poverty level in 2012 compared to 9.7 percent of White non-Hispanics. Almost every Asian American group has a higher poverty rate than non-Hispanic Whites. The lone exception is Filipinos, who tend to live in the relatively high-income states of Hawai'i and California (DeNavas-Walt, Proctor, and Smith 2013: Tables HINC-02 and POV01; National CAPACD 2012).

At first, one might be puzzled to see criticism of a positive generalization such as "model minority." Why should the stereotype of adjusting without problems be a disservice to Asian Americans? The answer is that this incorrect view helps exclude Asian Americans from social programs and conceals unemployment and other social ills. When representatives of Asian groups seek assistance for those in need, people who have accepted the model-minority stereotype resent them. This is especially troubling given that problems of substance abuse and juvenile delinquency need to be addressed within the Asian American community.

If a minority group becomes viewed as successful, its members no longer will be included in any program designed to alleviate any problems they encounter as minorities. The positive stereotype reaffirms the U.S. system of mobility: New immigrants as well as established subordinate groups ought to achieve more merely by working within the system. At the same time, viewed from the conflict perspective outlined in Chapter 1, this is yet another instance of blaming the victim: If Asian Americans have succeeded, then Blacks and Latinos must be responsible for their own low status rather than recognizing society's responsibility (Bascara 2008; Chen 2012; Chou and Feagin 2008; Ryan 1976; Xu and Lee 2013).

For young Asian Americans, life in the United States often is a struggle for identity when their heritage is so devalued by those in positions of influence. Sometimes identity means finding a role in White America; other times, it involves finding a place among Asian Americans collectively and then locating oneself within one's own racial or ethnic community.

Political Activity and Pan-Asian Identity

Against this backdrop of prejudice, discrimination, and a search for identity, it is no surprise to see Asian Americans seeking recognition for themselves. Historically, Asian Americans have followed the pattern of other immigrant groups: They bring social organizations, associations, and clubs from the homeland and later develop groups to respond to the special needs identified in the United States.

12-2 Characterize the political activity and level of pan-Asian identity.

Rather than being docile, as Asian Americans are often labeled, they have organized in labor unions, played a significant role in campus protests, and been active in immigration rights issues. Recently, given a boost by anti-alien feelings after 9/11, Asian Americans staged demonstrations in several cities in an effort to persuade people to become citizens and register to vote (Chang 2007).

For newly arrived Asians, grassroots organizations and political parties are a new concept. With the exception of Asian Indians, the immigrants come from nations where political participation was unheard of or looked on with skepticism and sometimes fear. Using the sizable Chinese American community as an example, we can see why Asian Americans have been slow to achieve political mobilization. At least six factors have been identified that explain why Chinese Americans— and, to a large extent, Asian Americans in general—have not been more active in politics:

1. To become a candidate means to take risks, invite criticism, be assertive, and be willing to extol one's virtues. These traits are alien to Chinese culture.

2. Older people remember when discrimination was blatant, and they tell others to be quiet and not attract attention.

3. Many recent immigrants have no experience with democracy and arrive with a general distrust of government.

4. Like many new immigrant groups, Chinese Americans have concentrated on getting ahead economically and educating their children rather than thinking in terms of the larger community.

5. The brightest students tend to pursue careers in business and science rather than law or public administration and, therefore, are not prepared to enter politics.

6. Chinatowns notwithstanding, Chinese and other Asian American groups are dispersed and cannot control the election of even local candidates.

The Voting Rights Act requires Asian language materials in cities and counties where either 5 percent or 10,000 voting-age citizens speak the same native Asian language and have limited English proficiency. Following the

Senator Daniel Inouye was the senior Asian American politician until his death in 2012. He continuously represented Hawai'i since it achieved statehood in 1959. Son of Japanese immigrants, he was a medical volunteer at Pearl Harbor at the time of the attack and went on to be decorated hero serving in Europe.

12-4   **Q** Research Focus

Arranged Marriages in America

The question becomes not does he or she love me, but whom do my parents want me to marry? An **arranged marriage** is when others choose the marital partners not based on any preexisting mutual attraction. Indeed, typically in arranged marriages, the couple does not even know one another.

The idea of arranged marriages seems strange to most youth growing up in the U.S. culture that romanticizes finding Mr. or Ms. Right. In an arranged marriage, the bride and groom start off on neutral ground, with no expectations of each other. Then understanding develops between them as the relationship matures. The couple selected is assumed to be compatible because they are chosen from very similar social, economic, and cultural backgrounds.

Historically, arranged marriages are not unusual and even today are common in many parts of Asia and Africa. In cultures where arranged marriage is common, young people tend to be socialized to expect and look forward to such unions.

Even among young people who theoretically accepted parental mate selection, the rise of new technology has altered the playing field. Texting and Skype facilitate getting to know a potential mate even before being formally introduced. New Internet sites allow parents to create a profile for their child by drawing upon large databases to facilitate narrowing of potential brides or grooms.

But what happens in cultures that send very different messages? For example, immigrants from India, Pakistan, Bangladesh, and Nigeria may desire that their children enter an arranged union, but their children are growing up in a culture where most of their schoolmates are obsessed with dating as a prelude to marriage and endlessly discuss the latest episodes of *The Bachelor* and *The Bachelorette.*

Studies of young people, in countries such as Canada and the United States, whose parents still cling to the tradition of arranging their children's marriages, document the challenges this represents. Many young people do still embrace the tradition of their parents. As one first-year female Princeton student of Asian Indian ancestry puts it, "In a lot of ways, it's easier. I don't have pressure to look for a boyfriend" (Herschthal 2004). Young people like her will look to their parents and other relatives to finalize a mate or even accept a match with a partner who has been selected in the country of their parents. Change has brought with it some variations because the expectation for formally arranged marriages has been modified to *assisted marriages* in which parents identify a limited number of possible mates based on what is referred to as "bio-data"—screening for caste, family background, and geography. Children get final veto power but rarely head out on their own when seeking a mate. Young men and women may date on their own, but when it comes to marrying, they limit themselves to a very narrow field of eligibles brought to them by their parents. The combination of arranged and assisted marriages has meant that Asian Indian immigrants have the highest rates of ethnic endogamy of any major immigrant group in the United States—about 90 percent in-group marriage.

Sources: Bellafante 2005; Herschthal 2004; Voo 2008; Zaidi and Shuraydi 2002.

Filipino Americans

12-4 Describe the Filipino Americans.

Little has been written about the Filipinos, although they are the third-largest Asian American group in the United States, with 2.5 million people living here. Social science literature considers them Asians for geographic reasons, but physically and culturally, they also reflect centuries of Spanish colonial rule and the more recent U.S. colonial and occupation governments.

Immigration Patterns

Immigration from the Philippines has been documented since the eighteenth century; it was relatively small but significant enough to create a "Manila Village" along the Louisiana coast around 1750. Increasing numbers of Filipino immigrants came as American nationals when, in 1899, the United States gained possession of the Philippine Islands at the conclusion of the Spanish–American War. In 1934, the islands gained commonwealth status. The Philippines gained their independence in 1948 and with it lost their unrestricted immigration rights. Despite the close ties that remained, immigration was sharply restricted to only 50–100 people annually until the 1965 Immigration Act lifted these quotas. Before the restrictions were removed, pineapple growers in Hawai'i lobbied successfully to import Filipino workers to the islands.

Besides serving as colonial subjects of the United States, Filipinos played another role in this country. The U.S. military accepted Filipinos in selected positions. In particular, the Navy put Filipino citizens to work in kitchens. Filipino veterans of World War II believed that their U.S. citizenship would be expedited. This proved untrue; the problem was only partially resolved by a 1994 federal court ruling. However, it was not until a special presidential action in 2009 that Filipino American veterans received compensation to partially acknowledge their service in World War II (Padilla 2008a; Perry and Simon 2009).

12-4

Filipino immigration can be divided into four distinct periods:

1. The first generation, which immigrated in the 1920s, was mostly male and employed in agricultural labor.

2. A second group, which also arrived in the early twentieth century, immigrated to Hawai'i to serve as contract workers on Hawai'i's sugar plantations.

3. The post–World War II arrivals included many war veterans and wives of U.S. soldiers.

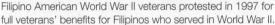

Filipino American World War II veterans protested in 1997 for full veterans' benefits for Filipinos who served in World War II.

4. The newest immigrants, who include many professionals (physicians, nurses, and others), arrived under the 1965 Immigration Act. More than 40 percent of Filipino Americans have immigrated since 1990 (Bureau of the Census 2007a; Min 2006; Posadas 1999).

As in other Asian groups, the people are diverse. Besides these stages of immigration, the Filipinos can also be defined by various states of immigration (different languages, regions of origin, and religions), distinctions that sharply separate people in their homeland as well. In the Philippines and among Filipino immigrants to the United States, eight distinct languages with an estimated 200 dialects are spoken. Yet assimilation is under way; a 1995 survey showed that 47 percent of younger Filipino Americans speak only English and do not speak Tagalog, the primary language of the Philippine people (Bonus 2000; Kang 1996; Pido 1986).

The Current Picture

The Filipino population increased dramatically when restrictions on immigration were eased in 1965. More than two-thirds of the new arrivals qualified for entry as professional and technical workers, but like Koreans, they have often worked at jobs ranked below those they left in the Philippines. Surprisingly, U.S.-born Filipinos often have less formal schooling and lower job status than the newer arrivals. They come from poorer families that are unable to afford higher education, and they have been relegated to unskilled work, including migrant farmwork. Their poor economic background means that they have little start-up capital for businesses. Therefore, unlike other Asian American groups, Filipinos have not developed small business bases such as retail or service outlets that capitalize on their ethnic culture.

A significant segment of the immigration from the Philippines, however, constitutes a more professional educated class in the area of health professionals. Although a positive human resource for the United States, it has long been a brain drain on the medical establishment of the Philippines. This is apparent when we consider areas in the United States that reflect Filipino settlement in the last 40 years. For example, in metropolitan Chicago, Filipino Americans have household incomes 30 percent higher than the general population and higher than that of Asian Indians. When the United States ceased giving preference to physicians from abroad, doctors in the Philippines began to enter the United States retrained as nurses, which dramatically illustrates the incredible income differences between the United States and the Philippines. They also send significant money back as remittances to help members of the extended family (DeParle 2007; Espiritu and Wolf 2001; Lau 2006; Zarembro 2004).

12-5

Despite their numbers, no significant single national Filipino social organization has formed for several reasons. First, Filipinos' strong loyalty to family (*sa pamilya*) and church, particularly Roman Catholicism, works against time-consuming efforts to create organizations that include a broad spectrum of the Filipino community. Second, their diversity makes forming ties here problematic. Divisions along regional, religious, and linguistic lines present in the Philippines persist in the United States. Third, although Filipinos have organized many groups, they tend to be club-like or fraternal. They do not seek to represent the general Filipino population and, therefore, remain largely invisible to Anglos. Fourth, although Filipinos initially stayed close to events in their homeland, they show every sign of seeking involvement in broader non-Filipino organizations and avoiding group exclusiveness. Three-quarters of Filipino Americans are citizens, which is a larger proportion than most Asian American groups. The two political terms of Filipino American Benjamin Cayetano as governor of Hawai'i from 1994 to 2002 are an example of such involvement in mainstream political organizations (Bonus 2000; Kang 1996; Lau 2006; Padilla 2008a; Posadas 1999).

Korean Americans

12-5 Discuss the Southeast Asian American communities in the United States.

The population of Korean Americans, with more than 1.4 million (see Figure 12.2), is now the fifth-largest Asian American group, yet Korean Americans often are overlooked in studies in favor of groups such as Chinese Americans and Japanese Americans, who have a longer historical tradition in the United States.

Historical Background

Today's Korean American community is the result of three waves of immigration. The initial wave of a little more than 7,000 immigrants came to the United States between 1903 and 1910, when laborers migrated to Hawai'i. Under Japanese colonial rule (1910–1945), Korean migration was halted except for a few hundred "picture brides" allowed to join their prospective husbands.

The second wave took place during and after the Korean War, accounting for about 14,000 immigrants from 1951 through 1964. Most of these immigrants were war orphans and wives of American servicemen. Little research has been done on these first two periods of immigration.

The third wave was initiated by the passage of the 1965 Immigration Act, which made it much easier for Koreans to immigrate. In the four years before the passage of the act, Koreans accounted for only 7 of every 1,000 immigrants. In the first four years after the act's passage, 38 of every 1,000 immigrants to the United States were Korean. This third wave, which continues today, reflects the admission priorities set up in the 1965 immigration law. These immigrants have been well educated and have arrived in the United States with professional skills. More than 40 percent of Korean Americans have arrived in the United States since 1990, but by 2011 immigration had slowed to a trickle of fewer than 5,000 annually (Bureau of the Census 2007b; Dolnick 2011; Kim and Yoo 2008; Min 2013).

However, many of the most recent immigrants must at least initially settle for positions of lower responsibility than those they held in Korea and must pass through a period of economic adjustment and even disenchantment for several years. These problems documented the pain of adjustment: stress, loneliness, alcoholism, family strife, and mental disorders. Korean American immigrants who accompanied their parents to the United States when young now occupy a middle, marginal position between the cultures of Korea and the United States. They have also been called the **ilchomose**, or "1.5 generation." Today, they are middle-aged, remain bilingual and bicultural, and tend to form the professional class in the Korean American community (Hurh 1998; Kim 2006).

In 1948, Sammy Lee, born of Korean immigrants, became the first Asian American to win a gold medal at the Olympics. It was not an easy path to victory because he faced prejudice and discrimination in Southern California. He was able to practice in the public pool only one day a week—the day on which the water was immediately drained and refilled. The rest of the time he was forced to dive into a pile of sand.

The Current Picture

Today's young Korean Americans face many of the cultural conflicts common to any initial generation born in a new country. The parents may speak the native tongue, but the signs on the road to opportunity are in the English language, and the road itself runs through U.S. culture. It is very difficult to maintain a sense of Korean culture in the United States; the host society is not particularly helpful. Although the United States fought a war there and U.S. troops remain in South Korea, Korean culture is foreign to contemporary Americans. In the few studies of attitudes toward Koreans, White Americans respond with vague, negative attitudes or simply lump Korean Americans with other Asian groups.

Korean Americans have established many Christian churches in the United States with 61 percent affiliated with Protestant denominations such as the Presbyterians and Methodists (Pew Forum on Religion and Public Life 2008a, 2008b.)

Studies by social scientists indicate that Korean Americans face many problems typical for immigrants, such as difficulties with language—79 percent of Korean Americans over age 5 do not speak English at home. In Los Angeles, home to the largest concentration, more than 100 churches have only Korean-language services, and local television stations feature several hours of Korean programs. The Korean immigrants' high level of education should help them cope with the challenge. Although Korean Americans stress conventional Western schooling as a means to success, Korean schools have also been established in major cities. Typically operated on Saturday afternoons, they offer classes in Korean history, customs, music, and language to help students maintain their cultural identity (Bureau of the Census 2007a; Hurh and Kim 1984; Johnson et al. 2010).

Korean American women commonly participate in the labor force, as do many other Asian American women. About 60 percent of U.S.-born Korean American women and half the women born abroad work in the labor force. These figures may not seem striking compared with the data for White women, but the cultural differences make the figures more significant. Korean women come here from a family system with established, well-defined marital roles: the woman is expected to serve as homemaker and mother only. Although these roles are carried over to the United States, because of their husbands' struggles to establish themselves, women are pressed to help support their families financially as well.

Many Korean American men begin small service or retail businesses and gradually involve their wives in the business. Wages do not matter because the household mobilizes to make a profitable enterprise out of a marginal business. Under economic pressure, Korean American women must move away from traditional cultural roles. However, the move is only partial; studies show that despite the high rate of participation in the labor force by Korean immigrant wives, first-generation immigrant couples continue in sharply divided gender roles in other aspects of daily living.

Korean American businesses are seldom major operations; most are small. They do benefit from a special form of development capital (or cash) used to subsidize businesses called a **kye** (pronounced "kay"). Korean Americans pool their money through the kye, an association that grants members money on a rotating basis to allow them to gain access to additional capital. Kyes depend on trust and are not protected by laws or insurance, as bank loans are. Kyes work as follows: Say, for example, that 12 people agree to contribute $500 a year. Then, once a year, one of these individuals receives $6,000. Few records are kept, because the entire system is built on trust and friendship. Rotating credit associations are not unique to Korean Americans; West Indians and Ethiopians have used them in the United States, for example. Not all Korean business entrepreneurs use the kye, but it does represent a significant source of capital. Ironically, these so-called mom-and-pop entrepreneurs, as they encounter success,

Asian Americans, like members of other racial and ethnic minorities, suffer daily indignities ranging from slights to outright hostility. Here, a Japanese American cartoonist portrays such an event in his comic strip that he calls Secret Asian Man.

feel competitive pressure from national chains that come into their areas after Korean American businesses have created a consumer market (Reckard 2007; Watanabe 2007).

In the early 1990s, nationwide attention was given to the friction between Korean Americans and other subordinate groups, primarily African Americans but also Hispanics. In New York City, Los Angeles, and Chicago, Korean American merchants confronted African Americans who were allegedly robbing them. The African American neighborhood groups sometimes responded with hostility to what they perceived as the disrespect and arrogance of the Korean American entrepreneurs toward their Black customers. Such friction is not new; earlier generations of Jewish, Italian, and Arab merchants encountered similar hostility from what to outsiders seems an unlikely source—another oppressed subordinate group. The contemporary conflict was dramatized in Spike Lee's 1989 movie *Do the Right Thing*, in which African Americans and Korean Americans clashed. The situation arose because Korean Americans are the latest immigrant group prepared to cater to the needs of the inner city and, as of 2011, own 70 percent of small grocery stores in New York City, which has been abandoned by business owners who have moved up the economic ladder (Dolnick 2011; Hurh 1998; N. Kim 2008; New American Media 2007).

Among Korean Americans, the church is the most visible organization holding the group together. Half of the immigrants were affiliated with Christian churches before immigrating. One study of Koreans in Chicago and Los Angeles found that 70 percent were affiliated with Korean ethnic churches, mostly Presbyterian, with small numbers of Catholics and Methodists. Korean ethnic churches are the fastest-growing segment of the Presbyterian and Methodist faiths. The church performs an important function, apart from its religious one, in giving Korean Americans a sense of attachment and a practical way to meet other Korean Americans. The churches are much more than simply sites for religious services; they assume multiple secular roles for the Korean community. As the second generation seeks a church with which to affiliate as adults, they may find the ethnic church and its Korean-language services less attractive, but for now, the fellowship in which Korean Americans participate is both spiritual and ethnic (Min 2013).

Southeast Asian Americans

12-6 Describe the Korean Americans.

The people of Southeast Asia—Vietnamese, Cambodians, and Laotians—were part of the former French Indochinese Union. Southeast Asian is an umbrella term used for convenience; the peoples of these areas are ethnically and linguistically diverse. Ethnic Laotians constitute only half of the Laotian people, for example; a significant number of Mon-Khmer, Yao, and Hmong form minorities. Numbering more than 2.2 million in 2010, Vietnamese Americans are the largest group, with more than 1.5 million members, or about 15 percent of the total Asian American population (Hoeffel et al. 2012).

The Refugees

The problem of U.S. involvement in Indochina did not end when all U.S. personnel were withdrawn from South Vietnam in 1975. The final tragedy was the reluctant welcome Americans and people of other nations gave to the refugees from Vietnam, Cambodia, and Laos. One week after the evacuation of Vietnam in April 1975, a Gallup poll reported that 54 percent of Americans were against giving sanctuary to the Asian refugees, with 36 percent in favor and 11 percent undecided. The primary objection to Vietnamese immigration was that it would further increase unemployment (Schaefer and Schaefer 1975).

Many Americans offered to house refugees in their homes, but others declared that the United States had too many Asians already and was in danger of losing its "national character." This attitude toward the Indochinese has been characteristic of the feeling that Harvard sociologist David Riesman called the **gook syndrome**. *Gook* is a derogatory term for an Asian, and the syndrome refers to the tendency to stereotype these people in the worst possible light. Riesman believed that the American news media created an unflattering image of the South Vietnamese and their government, leading the American people to believe they were not worth saving (Luce 1975).

The initial 135,000 Vietnamese refugees who fled in 1975 were joined by more than a million running from the later fighting and religious persecution that plagued Indochina. The United States accepted about half of the refugees, some of them the so-called boat people, primarily Vietnamese of ethnic Chinese background, who took to the ocean in overcrowded vessels, hoping that some ship would pick them up and offer sanctuary. Hundreds of thousands were placed in other nations or remain in overcrowded refugee camps administered by the United Nations.

The Current Picture

Like other immigrants, the refugees from Vietnam, Laos, and Cambodia face a difficult adjustment. Few expect to return to their homelands for visits, and fewer expect to return permanently. Therefore, many look to the United States as their permanent home and the home of their children. However, the adult immigrants still accept jobs well below their former occupational positions in Southeast Asia; geographic mobility has been accompanied by downward social mobility. For example, only a small fraction of refugees employed as managers in Vietnam have been employed in similar positions in the United States.

Language also is a factor in adjustment by the refugees; a person trained as a manager cannot hold that position in the United States until he or she is fairly fluent in English. The available data indicate that refugees from Vietnam have increased their earnings rapidly, often by working long hours. Partly because Southeast Asians comprise significantly different subgroups, assimilation and acceptance are not likely to occur at the same rate for all.

Although most refugee children spoke no English upon their arrival here, they have done extremely well in school. Studies indicate that immigrant parents place great emphasis on education and are pleased by the prospect of their children going to college—something rare in their homelands. The children do very well with this encouragement. It remains to be seen whether this motivation will decline as members of the next young generation look more to their American peers as role models.

The picture for young Southeast Asians in the United States is not completely pleasant. Crime is present in almost all ethnic groups, but some observers fear that in this group it has two very ugly aspects. Some of the crime may represent reprisals for the war: anti-Communists and Communist sympathizers who continue their conflicts here. At the same time, gangs are emerging as young people seek the support of close-knit groups even if they engage in illegal and violent activities. Of course, this pattern is similar to that followed by all groups in the United States. Indeed, defiance of authority can be regarded as a sign of assimilation. Another unpleasant but well-documented aspect of the current picture is the series of violent episodes directed at Southeast Asians by Whites and others expressing resentment over their employment or even their mere presence (Alvord 2000; Chu 2010; Zhou and Bankston 1998).

In 1995, the United States initiated normal diplomatic relations with Vietnam, which has led to more movement between the nations. Gradually, Vietnamese Americans are returning to visit but generally not to take up permanent residence. **Viet Kieu**, Vietnamese living abroad, are making the return—some 500,000 in 2010 compared to 270,000 in 1996. Generational issues are also emerging as time passes. In Vietnamese communities from California to Virginia, splits emerge over a powerful symbol—under what flag to unite a nationality. Merchants, home residents, and college Vietnamese student organizations take a stand by whether they decide to display the yellow-with-red-bars flag of the now-defunct South Vietnam, sometimes called the "heritage flag," or the red-with-yellow-star flag of the current (and Communist) Vietnam (Tran 2008).

Meanwhile, for the more than 1.5 million Vietnamese Americans who remain, settlement patterns here vary. Little Saigons can be found in major cities in the United States long after the former South Vietnam capital of Saigon became Ho Chi Min City. Like many other immigrant groups in the second generation, some Vietnamese have moved into suburbs where residential patterns tend to be rather dispersed, but one can still spot mini-malls with Vietnamese restaurants and grocery stores—some even sporting a sloping red-tiled roof. Other Vietnamese Americans remain in rural areas—for example, the Gulf Coast fishermen who were rendered homeless by Hurricane Katrina in 2005. Perhaps one sign of how settled Vietnamese Americans have become is that some of the same organizations that helped the refugees learn English are now helping younger Vietnamese Americans learn Vietnamese (Anguilar-SanJuan 2009; Pfeifer 2008b; Triev 2009).

Case Study: A Hmong Community

Wausau (population 38,000) is a community in rural Wisconsin that is best known, perhaps, for the insurance company bearing its name. To sociologists, it is distinctive for its sizable Hmong (pronounced "Mong") population. The Hmong come from rural areas of Laos and Vietnam, where they were recruited to work for the CIA during the Vietnam War. This association made life very difficult for them after the United States pulled out. Hence, many immigrated, and the United States has maintained a relatively open policy to their becoming permanent residents. Wausau finds itself with the greatest percentage of Hmong of any city in Wisconsin. Hmong and a few other Southeast Asians account for 11 percent of the city's population and about 18 percent of its public school students (Christensen 2012).

The Hmong, who numbered 248,000 as of 2010, immigrated to the United States from Laos and Vietnam after the end of the U.S. involvement in Vietnam in April 1975. The transition for the Hmong was difficult because they were typically farmers with little formal education. Poverty levels have been high and home ownership has been uncommon. Hmong have tended to form tight-knit groups organized around community leaders. Nationwide divisions exist along generational lines as well as dialect spoken and whether they are veterans of military service. Typically, cultural traditions surrounding marriage and funerals remain strong Hmong Americans. Some are giving up Hmong traditional worship of spirits for Christian faiths. Perhaps reflecting their entry into mainstream culture, Hmong culture and the challenges faced by the Hmong in the United States were explored in Clint Eastwood's 2008 fictional film *Gran Torino* (Pfeifer 2008a).

Like other refugees from South Asia at the time, the first Hmong came to Wausau at the invitation

In the 2008 motion picture *Gran Torino*, Clint Eastwood portrays a bitter retired autoworker who is suspicious of his Hmong neighbors in Detroit but comes to appreciate their willingness to help and their strong family values.

of religious groups. Others followed as they found the surrounding agricultural lands were places they could find work. This created a pipeline of chain immigration to communities like Wausau. As introduced earlier, chain immigration refers to an immigrant who sponsors several other immigrants who, on their arrival, may sponsor still more. Even with sponsors or relatives, coming from a very rural peasant society, the immigrants faced dramatic adjustment upon arrival in the industrialized United States (Vang 2010).

Wausau school officials believed that progress in teaching the Hmong English was stymied because the newcomers continued to associate with each other and spoke only their native tongue. In the fall of 1993, the Wausau school board decided to distribute the Hmong and other poor students more evenly by restructuring its elementary schools in a scheme that required two-way busing.

Recalls of elected officials are rare in the United States, but in December 1993, opponents of the busing plan organized a special election that led to the removal of the five board members. This left the Wausau board with a majority who opposed the busing plan that had integrated Asian American youngsters into mostly White elementary schools. By 2011, neighborhood schools continued to play an important role in Wausau so that among elementary schools, the proportion of Hmong children ranged from less than 1 percent to 38 percent (School Digger 2011; Seibert 2002).

How events will unfold in Wausau is unclear. However, positive signs are identifiable in Wausau and other centers of Hmong life in the United States. Immigrants and their children are moving into nonagricultural occupations. Enrollment in citizenship classes is growing. Public healthcare programs directed at the Hmong community are widely publicized. The Wausau Area Hmong Mutual Association, funded by a federal grant and the local United Way, offers housing assistance. Although many of these immigrants struggle to make a go of it economically, large numbers have been able to move off public assistance. Language barriers and lack of formal schooling still are barriers encountered by older Hmong residents, but the younger generation is emerging to face some of the same identity and assimilation questions experienced by other Asian American groups. To help facilitate the adjustment, some Wausau residents are learning Hmong through a special program at a local college (Dally 2011; Menchaca 2008; Peckham 2002).

Hawai'i and Its People

The entire state of Hawai'i appears to be the complete embodiment of cultural diversity. Nevertheless, despite a dramatic blending of different races living together, prejudice, discrimination, and pressure to assimilate are very much present in Hawai'i. As we will see, life on the island is much closer to that in the rest of the country than to the ideal of a pluralistic society. Hawai'i's population is unquestionably diverse, as shown in Figure 12.3.

12-7 Clarify how Hawai'i and its people embody cultural diversity.

To grasp contemporary social relationships, we must first understand the historical circumstances that brought the following races together on the islands: the native Hawaiians, the **kanaka maoli** (meaning "real or true people"), the various Asian peoples, and the **Haoles** (pronounced "hah-oh-lehs"), the term often used to refer to Whites in Hawai'i (Ledward 2008, Okamura 2008).

Historical Background

Geographically remote, Hawai'i was initially populated by Polynesian people who had their first contact with Europeans in 1778, when English explorer Captain James Cook arrived. The Hawaiians (who killed Cook) tolerated the subsequent arrival of plantation operators and missionaries. Fortunately, the Hawaiian people were united under a monarchy and received respect from the European immigrants, a respect that developed into a spirit

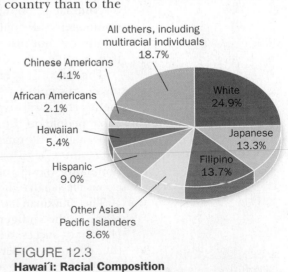

All others, including
multiracial individuals
18.7%

Chinese Americans
4.1%

African Americans
2.1%

Hawaiian
5.4%

Hispanic
9.0%

White
24.9%

Japanese
13.3%

Filipino
13.7%

Other Asian
Pacific Islanders
8.6%

FIGURE 12.3
Hawai'i: Racial Composition

Source: American Community Survey 2011b: Tables B02006, B03002, Cc02007.

of goodwill. Slavery was never introduced, even during the colonial period, as it was in so many areas of the Western hemisphere. Nevertheless, the effect of the White arrival on the Hawaiians themselves was disastrous. Civil warfare and disease reduced the number of full-blooded natives to fewer than 30,000 by 1900, and the number is probably well under 10,000 now. Meanwhile, large sugarcane plantations imported laborers from China, Portugal, Japan, and, in the early 1900s, the Philippines, Korea, and Puerto Rico.

In 1893, a revolution encouraged by foreign commercial interests overthrew the monarchy. During the revolution, the United States landed troops, and five years later, Hawai'i was annexed as a territory to the United States. The 1900 Organic Act guaranteed racial equality, but foreign rule dealt a devastating psychological blow to the proud Hawaiian people. American rule had mixed effects on relations between the races. Citizenship laws granted civil rights to all those born on the islands, not just the wealthy Haoles. However, the anti-Asian laws still applied, excluding the Chinese and Japanese from political participation.

The twentieth century witnessed Hawai'i's transition from a plantation frontier to the fiftieth state and an integral part of the national economy. During that transition, Hawai'i became a strategic military outpost, although that role has had only a limited effect on race relations. Even the attack on Pearl Harbor had little influence on Japanese Americans in Hawai'i.

The Sovereignty Movement

Hawai'i has achieved some fame for its good race relations. Tourists, who are predominantly White, have come from the mainland and have seen and generally accepted the racial harmony. Admittedly, Waikiki Beach, where large numbers of tourists congregate, is atypical of the islands, but even there tourists cannot ignore the differences in intergroup relations. If they look closely, they will see that the low-wage workers in the resorts and tourist industry tend to be disproportionately of Asian descent (Adler, Kess, and Adler 2004).

One clear indication of the multicultural nature of the islands is the degree of exogamy: marrying outside one's own group. The out-group marriage rate varies annually but seems to be stabilizing; about 40 percent of all marriages performed in the state involving residents are exogamous. The rate varies by group, from a low of 32 percent among Haoles to 66 percent among Chinese Americans with about half of Native Hawaiians outmarrying (Office of Hawaiian Affairs 2012).

Prejudice and discrimination are not alien to Hawai'i. Attitudinal surveys show definite racial preferences and sensitivity to color differences. Housing surveys taken before the passage of civil rights legislation showed that many people were committed to nondiscrimination, but racial preferences were still present. Certain groups sometimes dominate residential neighborhoods, but there are no racial ghettos. The various racial groups are not distributed uniformly among the islands, but they are clustered rather than sharply segregated.

The **sovereignty movement** is the effort by the indigenous people of Hawai'i, the kanala maoli, to secure a measure of self-government and restoration of their lands. The movement's roots and significance to the people are very similar to the sovereignty efforts by tribal people on the continental United States. The growing sovereignty movement has also sought restoration of the Native Hawaiian land that has been lost to Anglos over the last century, or at least compensation for it. Reaction to the movement has ranged from non-native Hawaiians seeing this as a big land grab and racist to those among the indigenous Hawaiians who see it as just not enough.

The Hawaiian term *kanaka maoli* meaning "real or true people" is gaining use to reaffirm the indigenous people's special ties to the islands. Sometimes, the Native Hawaiians successfully form alliances with environmental groups that want to halt further commercial development on the islands. In 1996, a Native Hawaiian vote was held, seeking a response to the question, "Shall the Hawaiian people elect delegates to propose a Native Hawaiian government?" The results indicated that 73 percent voting were in favor of such a government structure. Since then, the state Office of Hawaiian Affairs has sought to create a registry of Hawaiians that is only about halfway to having all the estimated 200,000 people of significant Hawaiian descent on the islands come forward. In 2008, a Native Hawaiian independence group seized the historic royal palace in Honolulu to protest the U.S.-backed overthrow of the Hawaiian government more than a century ago. Although the occupation lasted barely a day, the political discontentment felt by many Native Hawaiians persists (Halualani 2002; Magin 2008; Okamura 2008; Staton 2004).

Much of the present discussion about sovereignty has focused over Hawai'i's congressional delegation seeking passage of the Native Hawaiian Government Reorganization Act, or the Akaka Bill, after U.S. Senator Daniel Akaka. It would give people of Hawaiian ancestry more say over resources, provide affordable housing, take steps to preserve culture, and create a means by which they could better express their grievances. As of 2011, the measure had passed the House but was never discussed on the floor of the Senate (Akaka 2011). In the Speaking Out box, Senator Akaka tries to set aside some of the criticism of the bill while calling for Congress to take the same step for the kanaka maoli as it has for American Indian tribes on the mainland.

Regardless of the outcome of the sovereignty movement, the multiracial character of the islands will not change quickly, but the identity of the Native Hawaiians has already been overwhelmed. Although they have a rich cultural heritage, they tend to be very

(🎙) Speaking Out

Recognizing Native Hawaiians

(The Native Hawaiian Government Reorganization Act) … allows us to take the necessary next step in the reconciliation process. The bill does three things. First, it authorizes an office in the Department of the Interior to serve as a liaison between Native Hawaiians and the United States. Second, it forms an interagency task force chaired by the Departments of Justice and Interior, and composed of officials from federal agencies that administer programs and services impacting Native Hawaiians. Third, it authorizes a process for the reorganization of the Native Hawaiian government for the purposes of a federally recognized government-to-government relationship. Once the Native Hawaiian government is recognized, an inclusive democratic negotiations process representing both Native Hawaiians and non-Native Hawaiians would be established. There are many checks and balances in this process. Any agreements reached would still require the legislative approval of the State and Federal governments.

Opponents have spread misinformation about the bill. Let me be clear on some things that this bill does not do. My bill will not allow for gaming. It does not allow for Hawai'i to secede from the United States. It does not allow for private land to be taken. It does not create a reservation in Hawai'i.

What this bill does do is allow the people of Hawai'i to come together and address issues arising from the overthrow of the Kingdom of Hawai'i more than 118 years ago.

Daniel Akaka

It is time to move forward with this legislation. To date, there have been a total of twelve Congressional hearings, including five joint hearings in Hawai'i held by the Senate Committee on Indian Affairs and the House Natural Resources Committee. Our colleagues in the House have passed versions of this bill three times. We, however, have never had the opportunity to openly debate this bill on its merits in the Senate. We have a strong bill that is supported by Native communities across the United States, by the State of Hawai'i, and by the Obama Administration.

Last week, I met with officials and community leaders in the state of Hawai'i to share my intention to reintroduce this legislation. I received widespread support. This support was not surprising. A poll conducted by the *Honolulu Advertiser* in May of last year reported that 66 percent of the people of Hawai'i support federal recognition for Native Hawaiians. And 82 percent of Native Hawaiians polled support federal recognition.…

I encourage all of my colleagues to stand with me and support this legislation. I welcome any of my colleagues with concerns to speak with me so I can explain how important this bill is for the people of Hawai'i. The people of Hawai'i have waited for far too long. America has a history of righting past wrongs. The United States has federally recognized government-to-government relationships with 565 tribes across our country. It is time to extend this policy to the Native Hawaiians.

Source: Akaka 2011.

12-7

poor and often view the U.S. occupation as the beginning of their cultural and economic downfall. For centuries, they traditionally placed the earthly remains of their loved ones in isolated caves. However, as these archaeological sites were found by Haoles, the funeral remains made their way to the Bishop Museum, which is the national historical museum located in Honolulu. Now Native Hawaiians are using the Native American Graves and Protection Act to get the remains back and rebury them appropriately (LaDuke 2006).

"E Heluuelu Kaqkou," Nako'hlani Warrington tells her third graders ("Let's read together"). She has no need to translate because she is teaching at the public immersion school where all instruction is in the Hawaiian language. Not too long ago, it was assumed that only linguistic scholars would speak Hawaiian, but efforts to revive it in general conversation have resulted in its use well beyond "aloha." In 1983, only 1,500 people were considered native speakers; now native speakers number 68,000. This goes well beyond symbolic ethnicity. Language perpetuity is being combined with a solid grade school education, and a supportive doctoral program in the Hawaiian language was introduced in 2007 (Kana'iaupuni 2008).

Conclusion

Asian Americans are a rapidly growing group. Despite striking differences between them, they are often viewed as if they arrived all at once and from one culture. Also, they are often characterized as a successful or model minority. However, individual cases of success and some impressive group data suggest that the diverse group of peoples who make up the Asian American community are not uniformly successful. Indeed, despite high levels of formal schooling, Asian Americans earn far less than Whites with comparable education and continue to be victims of discriminatory employment practices.

The diversity within the Asian American community belies the similarity suggested by the panethnic label *Asian American*. Chinese and Japanese Americans share a history of several generations in the United States. Filipinos are veterans of a half century of direct U.S. colonization and a cooperative role with the military. In contrast, Vietnamese, Koreans, and Japanese are associated

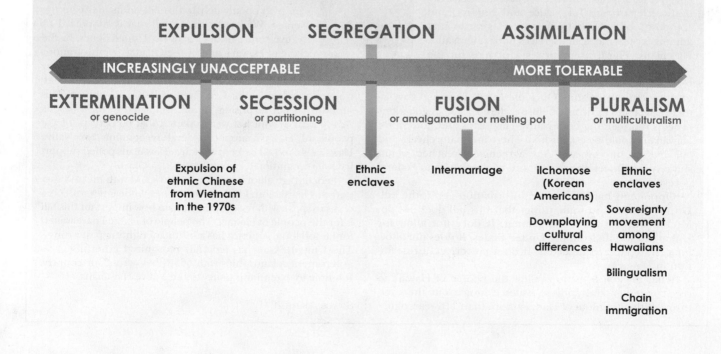

SPECTRUM OF INTERGROUP RELATIONS

in a negative way with three wars. Korean Americans come from a nation that still has a major U.S. military presence and a persisting "cold war" mentality. Korean Americans and Chinese Americans have taken on middleman roles, whereas Filipinos, Asian Indians, and Japanese Americans tend to avoid the ethnic enclave pattern.

Who are the Asian Americans? This chapter has begun to answer that question by focusing on four of the larger groups: Asian Indians, Filipino Americans, Southeast Asian Americans, and Korean Americans. Attention comes to Asian Americans in unusual ways. For example, 24-year-old Nina Davuluri of New York was crowned Miss America in 2013. Her parents immigrated from India 30 years ago. While many saw this

accomplishment of the acceptance of Asian Americans by the mainstream, the announcement was followed by a barrage of tweets disparaging the beauty queen's ethnic heritage and wondering if she was American enough (Sahgal 2013).

Hawai'i is a useful model because its harmonious social relationships cross racial lines. Although it is not an interracial paradise, Hawai'i does illustrate that, given proper historical and economic conditions, continuing conflict is not inevitable. Chinese and Japanese Americans, the subjects of Chapter 13, have experienced problems in American society despite striving to achieve economic and social equality with the dominant culture.

Summary

1. Often Asian Americans are labeled as a model minority, which overlooks the many problems they face and serves to minimize the challenges of succeeding despite prejudice and discrimination.

2. Asian Americans have been active politically through collective action and recently through seeking elected office. They embrace their unique identity but acknowledge their broader pan-Asian identity.

3. Asian Indians are a diverse group culturally and, although most are Hindu, embrace a number of faiths.

4. Filipino Americans have a long historical connection to the United States, with today's immigrants

including both professionals as well as the descendants of those who have served in the U.S. military.

5. Korean Americans have settled largely in urban areas, where many have become successful entrepreneurs.

6. Southeast Asians' presence in the United States has typically resulted from waves of refugees. They have created significant settlements throughout the United States and often have dispersed throughout the larger population.

7. Hawai'i and its Native Hawaiians present a different multiracial pattern from that of the mainland but not one without both prejudice and discrimination.

Key Terms

arranged marriage, p. 270

bamboo ceiling, p. 266

blaming the victim, p. 264

chain immigration, p. 262

desi, p. 269

gook syndrome, p. 275

Haoles, p. 277

ilchomose, p. 272

kanaka maoli, p. 277

kye, p. 273

model minority, p. 264

panethnicity, p. 268

racial profiling, p. 265

sovereignty movement, p. 278

symbolic ethnicity, p. 269

Viet Kieu, p. 276

yellow peril, p. 265

Review Questions

1. How is the model-minority image a disservice to both Asian Americans and other subordinate racial and ethnic groups?

2. How successful have Asian Americans been in organizing themselves politically?

3. How would you describe the Asian Indian community in the United States?

4. What are some of the defining moments in the Filipino American experience?

5. What generational differences can you identify among Korean Americans?

6. Distinguish among the different Southeast Asian groups in the United States.

7. To what degree do race relations in Hawai'i offer both promise and a chilling dose of reality to the future of race and ethnicity on the mainland?

Critical Thinking

1. What stereotypical images of Asian Americans can you identify in the contemporary media?

2. Coming of age is difficult for anyone, given the ambiguities of adolescence in the United States. How is it doubly difficult for the children of immigrants? How do you think the immigrants themselves, such as those from Asia, view this process?

3. *American Indians, Hispanics,* and *Asian Americans* are all convenient terms to refer to diverse groups of people. Do you see these umbrella terms as being more appropriate for one group than for the others?

13 Chinese Americans and Japanese Americans

13-1 Understand the history and present-day circumstances of the Chinese Americans.

13-2 Be able to summarize the Japanese American experience.

13-3 Identify how prejudice and discrimination persist.

13-1

As years and generations pass, how is identity maintained—or is it? And what if you throw a party and few come? In 2007, Japanese Americans in Los Angeles's Little Tokyo threw a day-long party of Asian hip-hop along with traditional martial arts demonstrations to bring Japanese Americans scattered across Southern California back for a day. Debbie Hazama, 35, a homemaker with three children, drove with her husband from the suburbs because she recognizes there are not many Japanese Americans where she lives, so she wants her children "to stay connected."

Three years earlier, the Los Angeles Japanese American festival was in full swing in mid-July 2004 when, during the opening ceremonies, a 24-year-old South Pasadena woman grabbed a heavy mallet and took a swing at a drum just as she had practiced doing for months. Nicole Miyako Cherry, the daughter of a Japanese American mother and a White American father, had not had much interest in her Japanese roots except for wearing a kimono for Halloween as a youngster. Yet in the last couple of years, she had begun to take interest in all things Japanese, including visiting Japan. Looking to her future as a social work therapist, she says she would like her own children to learn Japanese, go to Japanese festivals, play in Japanese sports leagues, and have Japanese first names (M. Navarro 2004; Watanabe 2007: B13).

Debbie's children and Nicole's experience are examples of the *principle of third-generation interest*—which ethnic awareness may increase among the grandchildren. But Nicole is of mixed ancestral background, so she is obviously making a choice to maintain her Japanese American identity as an important part of her future. But for many other Asian Americans, particularly recent immigrants, they are just trying to survive and accumulate savings for their family here and kinfolk in the old country.

Many people in the United States find it difficult to distinguish between Japanese Americans and Chinese Americans physically, culturally, and historically. As we will see in this chapter, the two groups differ in some ways but also share similar patterns in their experiences in the United States.

Chinese Americans

13-1 Understand the history and present-day circumstances of the Chinese Americans.

China, the most populous country in the world, has been a source of immigrants for centuries. Many nations have a sizable Chinese population whose history can be traced back more than five generations. The United States is such a nation. Even before the great migration from Europe began in the 1880s, more than 100,000 Chinese already lived in the United States. Today, Chinese Americans number more than 3.3 million, as noted in Table 13.1.

TABLE 13.1

Chinese American and Japanese American Population, 1860–2010

Year	Chinese Americans	Japanese Americans
1860	34,933	—
1880	105,465	148
1900	89,863	24,326
1930	74,954	138,834
1950	117,629	141,768
1960	237,292	464,332
1970	435,062	591,290
1980	806,027	700,747
1990	1,640,000	847,562
2000	2,314,533	796,700
2010	3,347,000	763,000

Note: Data beginning with 1960 include Alaska and Hawai'i.

Source: Barnes and Bennett 2002; Hixson, Hepler, and Kim 2012; Lee 1998:15.

Early Settlement Patterns

From its beginning, Chinese immigration has aroused conflicting views among Americans. In one sense, Chinese immigration was welcome because it brought needed hardworking laborers to these shores. At the same time, it was unwelcome because the Chinese also brought an alien culture that the European settlers were unwilling to tolerate. People in the western United States also had a perception of economic competition, and the Chinese newcomers proved to be convenient and powerless scapegoats. As detailed in Chapter 4, the anti-Chinese mood led to the passage of the Chinese Exclusion Act in 1882, which was not repealed until 1943. Even then, the group that lobbied for repeal, the Citizens' Committee to Repeal Chinese Exclusion, encountered the old racist arguments against Chinese immigration (Pfaelzer 2007).

Gradually, the Chinese were permitted to enter the United States after 1943. In the beginning, the annual limit was 105. Then several thousand wives of servicemen were admitted, and college students were later allowed to remain after finishing their education. Not until after the 1965 Immigration Act did Chinese immigrants arrive again in large numbers, almost doubling the Chinese American community. Immigration continues to exert a major influence on the growth of the Chinese American population. It has approached 100,000 annually. The influx was so great in the 1990s that the number of new arrivals in that decade exceeded the total number of Chinese Americans present in 1980.

As the underside of immigration, illegal immigration is also functioning in the Chinese American community. The lure of perceived better jobs and a better life leads overseas Chinese to seek alternative routes to immigration if legal procedures are unavailable. The impact of illegal entry in some areas of the country can be significant. For example, every month in 2002, 340 illegal Chinese immigrants were apprehended at Chicago's O'Hare Airport and taken to a rural jail (Starks 2002).

13-1

Before and after the Chinese Exclusion Act, settlers attacked Chinese enclaves throughout the West on 183 separate occasions, driving the immigrants eastward, where they created Chinatowns, some of which still are thriving today. This engraving depicts the Denver riot of 1880, which culminated in one Chinese man being hanged. The lynchers were identified but released the next year. There was no restoration for the damage done by the estimated mob of 3,000 men (Ellis 2004; Pfaelzer 2007).

A small but socially significant component of Chinese in the United States are those who have been adopted by American non-Chinese couples. Beginning in 1991, China loosened its adoption laws to address the growing number of children, particularly girls, who were abandoned under the country's one-child policy. This policy strongly encourages couples to have only one child; having more children can impede promotions and even force a household to accept a less-roomy dwelling. The numbers of adopted Chinese were small, but in recent years, about 7,000 have been adopted annually. This policy was tightened significantly in 2008 by the Chinese government, reducing the number of annual adoptions. Although most adoptees are still young, they and their adopting parents face the complex issues of cultural and social identity. Organized efforts now exist to reconnect these children with their roots in China, but for most of their lives, they are adjusting to being Chinese American in a non-Chinese American family (Department of State 2008; Olemetson 2005).

It is also important to appreciate that even *Chinese American* is a collective term. There is diversity within this group represented by nationality (China versus Taiwan, for example), language, and region of origin. It is not unusual for a church serving a Chinese American community to have five separate services, each in a different dialect. These divisions can be quite sharply expressed. For example, near the traditional Chinatown of New York City, a small neighborhood has emerged of Chinese from China's Fujian Province. In this area, job postings include annotations in Chinese that translate as "no north," meaning people from the provinces north of Fujian are not welcome. Throughout the United States, some Chinese Americans also divide along pro-China and pro-Taiwan allegiances (Guest 2003; Lau 2008; Louie 2004; Sachs 2001).

13-1

Occupational Profile of Chinese Americans

By many benchmarks, Chinese Americans are doing well. As a group they have higher levels of formal schooling and household income compared to all Asian Americans and even to White non-Hispanics. Note, however, that the Chinese American poverty rate is high—an issue we return to later.

As we might expect, given the high income levels, half of all Chinese Americans serve in management, professional, and related occupations, compared to only a third of the general population. This reflects two patterns: first, entrepreneurial development by Chinese Americans who start their own businesses and, second, the immigration of skilled overseas Chinese as well as Chinese students who chose to remain in the United States following the completion of their advanced degrees (Bureau of the Census 2007a).

The background of the contemporary Chinese American labor force lies in Chinatown. For generations, Chinese Americans were largely barred from working elsewhere. The Chinese Exclusion Act was only one example of discriminatory legislation. Many laws were passed that made it difficult or more expensive for Chinese Americans to enter certain occupations. Whites did not object to Chinese in domestic service occupations or in the laundry trade because most White men were uninterested in such menial, low-paying work. When given the chance to enter better jobs, as they were in wartime, Chinese Americans jumped at the opportunities. Where such opportunities were absent, however, many Chinese Americans sought the relative safety of Chinatown. The tourist industry and the restaurants dependent on it grew out of the need to employ the growing numbers of idle workers in Chinatown.

Chinatowns Today

Chinatowns represent a paradox. The casual observer or tourist sees them as thriving areas of business and amusement, bright in color and lights, exotic in sounds and sights. Behind this facade, however, they have large poor populations and face the problems associated with all slums. Older Chinatowns were often located in deteriorating sections of cities, but increasingly they are springing up in new neighborhoods and even in the suburbs such as Monterey Park outside Los Angeles. In the older enclaves, the problems of Chinatowns include the entire range of social ills that affect low-income areas but some have even greater difficulties because the glitter sometimes conceals the problems from outsiders and even social planners. A unique characteristic of Chinatowns, one that distinguishes them from other ethnic enclaves, is the variety of social organizations they encompass (Liu and Geron 2008).

Organizational Life   The Chinese in this country have a rich history of organizational membership, much of it carried over from China. Chief among such associations are the clans, or *tsu*; the benevolent associations, or *hui kuan*; and the secret societies, or *tongs*.

The clans, or **tsu**, that operate in Chinatown have their origins in the Chinese practice in which families with common ancestors unite. At first, immigrant Chinese continued to affiliate themselves with those sharing a family name, even if a blood relationship was absent. Social scientists agree that the influence of clans is declining as young Chinese become increasingly acculturated. The clans in the past provided mutual assistance, a function increasingly taken on by government agencies. The strength of the clans, although diminished today, still points to the extended family's important role for Chinese Americans. Social scientists have found parent–child relationships stronger and more harmonious than those among non–Chinese Americans. Just as the clans have become less significant, however, so has the family structure changed. The differences between family life in Chinese and non-Chinese homes are narrowing with each new generation.

The benevolent associations, or **hui kuan** (or *hui guan*), help their members adjust to a new life. Rather than being organized along kinship ties like the clans, hui kuan membership is based on the person's district of origin in China. Besides extending help with adjustment, the *hui kuan* lend money to and settle disputes between their members. They have thereby exercised wide control over their members. The various *hui kuan* are traditionally, in turn, part of an unofficial government in each city called the Chinese Six Companies, a name later changed to the Chinese Consolidated Benevolent Association (CCBA). The president of the CCBA is sometimes called the mayor of a Chinatown. The CCBA often protects newly arrived immigrants from the effects of racism. The organization works actively to promote political involvement among Chinese Americans and to support the democracy movement within the People's Republic of China. Some members of the Chinese community have resented, and still resent, the CCBA's authoritarian ways and its attempt to speak as the sole voice of Chinatown.

The Chinese have also organized in **tongs**, or secret societies. The secret societies' membership is determined not by family or locale but by interest. Some have been political, attempting to resolve the dispute over which China (the People's Republic of China or Taiwan) is the legitimate government, and others have protested the exploitation of Chinese workers. Other *tongs* provide illegal goods and services, such as drugs, gambling, and prostitution. Because they are secret, it is difficult to determine accurately the power of *tongs* today. Most observers concur that their influence has dwindled over the last 60 years and that their functions, even the illegal ones, have been taken over by elements less closely tied to Chinatown.

Some conclusions can be reached about these various social organizations. They serve as pillars of the Chinese American community but are less visible outside the traditional older Chinatowns. Metropolitan Chinese American communities see the increasing significance of nonprofit organizations that work between the ethnic community and the larger society, including the local, state, and federal government (Adams 2006; Soo 1999; Tong 2000; Zhao 2002; Zhou 2009).

Social Problems It is a myth that Chinese Americans and Chinatowns have no problems. We saw some indication of that in the data in Table 8.1. Although overall household income levels ran 20 percent ahead of White non-Hispanics, the poverty of Chinese Americans as a group was 14 percent, compared to only 8.8 percent of Whites. Obviously, many Chinese Americans are doing very well, but a significant group is doing very poorly.

The false impression of Chinese American success grows out of our tendency to stereotype groups as being all one way or the other, as well as the Chinese people's tendency to keep their problems within their community. The false image is also reinforced by the desire to maintain tourism. The tourist industry is a double-edged sword. It provides needed jobs, even if some of them pay substandard wages. But it also forces Chinatown to keep its problems quiet and not seek outside assistance, lest tourists hear of social problems and stop coming. Slums do not attract tourists. This parallel between Chinese Americans and Native Americans finds both groups depending on the tourist industry even at the cost of hiding problems (Light et al. 1994).

In the late 1960s, White society became aware that all was not right in the Chinatowns. This awareness grew not because living conditions suddenly deteriorated in Chinese American settlements but because the various community organizations could no longer maintain the facade that hid Chinatowns' social ills. Despite Chinese Americans' remarkable achievements as a group, the inhabitants were suffering by most socioeconomic measures. Poor health, high suicide rates, run-down housing, rising crime rates, poor working conditions, inadequate care for the elderly, and the weak union representation of laborers were a few of the documented problems (Liu and Geron 2008).

Life in Chinatown may seem lively to an outsider, but beyond the neon signs, the picture can be quite different. Chinatown in New York City remained a prime site of sweatshops well into the 1990s. Dozens of women labor over sewing machines, often above restaurants. These small businesses, often in the garment industry, consist of workers sewing twelve hours a day, six or seven days a week, and earning about $200 weekly—well below minimum wage. The workers, most of whom are women, can be victimized because they are either illegal immigrants who may owe labor to the smugglers who brought them into the United States, or they are legal residents yet unable to find better employment (Finder 1994; Kwong 1994).

13-1

Festivals and events serve to focus the members of the Chinese American community, who now live often far apart from one another. Shown here is a dragon boat race in Seattle, Washington.

The attacks on the World Trade Center in 2001 made the marginal economy of New York's Chinatown even shakier. Although not located near the World Trade Center, the economy was close enough to the devastation to feel the drop in customary tourism and a significant decline in shipments to the garment industry. Initially, emergency relief groups ruled out assistance to Chinatown, but within a couple of months, agencies opened up offices in Chinatown. Within two months, 42,000 people had received relief because 60 percent of businesses had cut staff. Like many other minority neighborhoods, New York City's Chinatown may be economically viable, but it always is susceptible to severe economic setbacks that most other areas could withstand much more easily. From 2000 to 2010, Chinatown's population in Manhattan dropped by 9 percent—the first decline ever. Notably, the proportion of foreign born also declined (Asian American Federation 2008; Lee 2001; Tsui 2011).

Increasingly, Chinese neither live nor work in Chinatowns; most have escaped them or have never experienced their social ills. Chinatown remains important for many of those who now live outside its borders, although less so than in the past. For many Chinese, movement out of Chinatown is a sign of success. Upon moving out, however, they soon encounter discriminatory real estate practices and White parents' fears about their children playing with Chinese American youths.

The movement of Chinese Americans out of Chinatowns parallels the movement of White ethnics out of similar enclaves. It signals the upward mobility of Chinese Americans, coupled with their growing acceptance by the rest of the population. This mobility and acceptance are especially evident in the presence of Chinese Americans in managerial and professional occupations.

Even with their problems and constant influx of new arrivals, we should not forget that first and foremost, Chinatowns are communities of people. Originally, in the nineteenth century, they emerged because the Chinese arriving in the United States had no other area in which they were allowed to settle. Today, Chinatowns represent cultural decompression chambers for new arrivals and an important symbolic focus for long-term residents. Even among many younger Chinese Americans, these ethnic enclaves serve as a source of identity.

Family Life

Family life is the major force that shapes all immigrant groups' experience in the United States. Generally, with assimilation, cultural behavior becomes less distinctive. Family life and religious practices are no exceptions. For Chinese Americans, the latest immigration wave has helped preserve some of the old ways, but traditional cultural patterns have undergone change even in the People's Republic of China, so the situation is very fluid.

The contemporary Chinese American family often is indistinguishable from its White counterpart except that it is victimized by prejudice and discrimination. Older Chinese Americans and new arrivals often are dismayed by the more American behavior patterns of Chinese American youths. Change in family life is one of the most difficult cultural changes to accept. Children questioning parental authority, which Americans grudgingly accept, are a painful experience for the tradition-oriented Chinese. The 2011 bestseller *Battle Hymn of the Tiger Mother* by legal scholar Amy Chu touched off heated discussions in her indictment of parents indulging their children and holding up as a model strong parental guidance in children's activities and interests. In Research Focus we look more closely at this controversy.

Research Focus

Tiger Mothers

It is not often a memoir sparks a national debate about parenting that extends around the world but such was the case with a Yale law professor. In 2011, Amy Chua authored *Battle Hymn of Tiger Mother*, which, in large part, is about how she raised her two American girls, now teenagers. Her parenting followed the childrearing she experienced from her Chinese parents who had immigrated from the Philippines had raised her in Illinois.

The quick takeaway readers came away with, or even those who never opened the book, was the "Tiger moms," or Chinese American, maybe all Asian American mothers, raise their children in a stern, but loving fashion that was highly competitive. **Tiger mother** has come to refer to a demanding mother who pushes her children to high levels of achievement following practices common in China and other parts of Asia.

Days are filled with music lessons and practice, and handmaking greeting cards with no sleepovers, no television or video games and no accepting any grade but A. Married to a fellow law professor, Chua agreed to raise the children in his Jewish faith (Chua is Roman Catholic) but only if she could be a "Chinese mother." The book came to be seen as an indictment of the more permissive US child-rearing practices. It was also seen by some as better too—the Wall Street Journal (2011) entitled its excerpt from the book, "Why Chinese Mothers are Superior."

Chua does not claim to be ac child development specialist and contends this was her story of one mother who came to be frustrated with when her second daughter became more rebellious at age thirteen then her sister because she chose tennis over piano and violin. Since the ensuing firestorm about the book, Chua has admitted she has some regrets but would still basically raise her children strictly and continues to defend her approach as taking the best from "Asian cultures."

Studies of Chinese parenting, much less parenting in all of Asia, stress that there is no one way that most parents rear their children. In addition Chua's relatively affluent life-style allowed her to hire many helpers and access experts while still being a fulltime professional. All of this is well beyond the financial means of most parents. The book also serves to reinforce the model minority stereotype discussed earlier in Chapter 12. There is more emphasis in Asia and among the immigrant households on stressing respect for authority and self-discipline. This approach has its roots in the ethnical and philosophical system developed from the teachings of the Chinese philosopher Confucius from the fifth century BC. Confucian parental goals do stress the importance of perseverance, working hard in school, being obedient, and being sensitive to parents' wishes.

Yet even if more common in Asia, this approach is not uniquely Chinese as Chua admits. The author said that NBC journalist Tom Brokaw told her that his working class South Dakotan father was a "Chinese mom." There is also evidence that in China today, especially urban China, parents are becoming more relaxed with their children and growing critical of schools emphasis on rote memorization.

Perhaps most telling about the notion of "tiger mother" and the ensuing debate is that it is set directly into viewing Asia and particularly China as a "threat" to America's superpower status. Chua makes explicit reference to how US children are being outperformed in standardized tests by children in other countries and especially in China. So while tiger mother offers some insight into the caregiving culture in Asia, it also highlights how Americans see Asia and Asian America.

Sources: Chua 2011, 2013; Miller 2011; Paul 2011; Pitt 2013; Russell, Crockett, and Chao 2010; Shah 2012; Wall Street Journal 2011.

The characterization of *Tiger Mother* should resonate in many immigrant communities. It is similar to the notion of familism that we considered in Chapter 10 with respect to Latino households. Familism means pride and closeness in the family, which results in family obligations and loyalty coming before individual needs. A Bureau of the Census (2009a: D7) confirmed the similarities finding, for example that children under 12 in Asian and Hispanic households in the United States were more likely to eat dinner with a parent every day than they were in White or Black households.

Where acculturation has taken hold less strongly among Chinese Americans, the legacy of China remains. Parental authority, especially the father's, is more absolute, and the extended family is more important than is typical in White middle-class families. Divorce is rare, and attitudes about sexual behavior tend to be strict because the Chinese generally frown on public expressions of emotion. We noted earlier that Chinese immigrant women in Chinatown endure a harsh existence. A related problem beginning to surface is domestic violence. Although the available data do not indicate that Asian American men are any more abusive than men in other groups, their wives, as a rule, are less willing to talk about their plight and to seek help. The nation's first shelter for Asian women was established in Los Angeles in 1981, but the problem is increasingly being recognized in more cities (Banerjee 2000; Tong 2000).

13-2

Another problem for Chinese Americans is the rise in gang activity since the mid-1970s. Battles between opposing gangs have taken their toll, including the lives of some innocent bystanders. Some trace the gangs to the tongs and, thus, consider them an aspect, admittedly destructive, of the cultural traditions some groups are trying to maintain. However, a more realistic interpretation is that Chinese American youths from the lower classes are not part of the model minority. Upward mobility is not in their future. Alienated, angry, and with prospects of low-wage work in restaurants and laundries, they turn to gangs such as the Ghost Shadows and Flying Dragons and force Chinese American shopkeepers to give them extortion money (Chin 1996; Takaki 1998).

Japanese Americans

13-2 Be able to summarize the Japanese American experience.

The nineteenth century was a period of sweeping social change for Japan: it brought the end of feudalism and the beginning of rapid urbanization and industrialization. Only a few pioneering Japanese came to the United States before 1885 because Japan prohibited emigration. After 1885, the numbers remained small relative to the great immigration from Europe at the time.

Early Japanese Immigration

With little consideration of the specific situation, the American government began to apply to Japan the same prohibitions it applied to China. The early feelings of anti-Asian prejudice were directed at the Japanese as well. The Japanese who immigrated into the United States in the 1890s took jobs as laborers at low wages under poor working conditions. Their industriousness in such circumstances made them popular with employers but unpopular with unions and other employees.

Japanese Americans distinguish sharply between themselves according to the number of generations a person's family has been in the United States. Generally, each succeeding generation is more acculturated, and each is successively less likely to know Japanese. The **Issue** (pronounced "EE-say") are the first generation, the immigrants born in Japan. Their children, the **Nisei** ("NEE-say"), are American-born. The third generation, the **Sansei** ("SAHN-say"), must go back to their grandparents to reach their roots in Japan. The **Yonsei** ("YOHN-say") are the fourth generation. Because Japanese immigration is recent, these four terms describe almost the entire contemporary Japanese American population. Some Nisei are sent by their parents to Japan for schooling and to have marriages arranged, after which they return to the United States. Japanese Americans expect such people, called **Kibei** ("keep-bay"), to be less acculturated than other Nisei. These terms sometimes are used loosely, and occasionally Nisei is used to describe all Japanese Americans. However, we use them here as they were intended to differentiate the four generational groups (Yamashiro 2008).

The Japanese arrived just as bigotry toward the Chinese had been legislated in the harsh Chinese Exclusion Act of 1882. For a time after the act, powerful business interests on the West Coast welcomed the Issei. They replaced the dwindling number of Chinese laborers in some industries, especially agriculture. In time, however, anti-Japanese feelings grew out of the anti-Chinese movement. The same Whites who disliked the Chinese made the same charges about Japanese Americans. Eventually, a stereotype developed of Japanese Americans as lazy, dishonest, and untrustworthy.

The attack on Japanese Americans concentrated on limiting their ability to earn a living. In 1913, California enacted the Alien Land Act; amendments to the act in 1920 made it still stricter. The act prohibited anyone who was ineligible for citizenship from owning land and limited leases to three years. The anti-Japanese laws permanently influenced the form that Japanese American business enterprise was to take. In California, the land laws drove the Issei into cities. In the cities, however, government and union restrictions prevented large numbers from obtaining the available jobs, leaving self-employment as the only option. Japanese, more than other groups, ran hotels, grocery stores, and other medium-sized businesses. Although this specialty limited their opportunities to advance, it did give urban Japanese Americans a marginal position in the expanding economy of the cities (Robinson 2001).

The Wartime Evacuation

Japan's attack on Pearl Harbor on December 7, 1941, brought the United States into World War II and marked a painful tragedy for the Issei and Nisei. Almost immediately, public pressure mounted to "do something" about the Japanese Americans living on the West Coast. Many White Americans feared that if Japan attacked the mainland, Japanese Americans would fight on behalf of Japan, making a successful invasion a real possibility. Pearl Harbor was followed by successful Japanese invasions of one Pacific island after another, and a Japanese submarine actually attacked a California oil tank complex early in 1943.

Rumors mixed with racism rather than facts explain the events that followed. Japanese Americans in Hawai'i were alleged to have cooperated in the attack on Pearl Harbor by using signaling devices to assist the pilots from Japan. Front-page attention was given to pronouncements by the Navy secretary that Japanese Americans had the greatest responsibility for Pearl Harbor. Newspapers covered in detail FBI arrests of Japanese Americans allegedly engaging in sabotage to assist the attackers. They were accused of poisoning drinking water, cutting patterns in sugarcane fields to form arrows directing enemy pilots to targets, and blocking traffic along highways to the harbor. None of these charges was substantiated, despite thorough investigations. It made no difference. In the 1940s, the treachery of the Japanese Americans was a foregone conclusion regardless of evidence to the contrary (Kashima 2003; Kimura 1988; Lind 1946; ten Brock, Barnhart, and Matson 1954).

Executive Order 9066 On February 13, 1942, President Franklin Roosevelt signed Executive Order 9066. It defined strategic military areas in the United States and authorized the removal from those areas of any people considered threats to national security. The events that followed were tragically simple. All people on the West Coast of at least one-eighth Japanese ancestry were taken to assembly centers for transfer to evacuation camps. These camps are identified in Figure 13.1. This order covered 90 percent of the 126,000 Japanese Americans on the mainland. Of those evacuated, two-thirds were citizens, and three-fourths were under age 25. Ultimately, 120,000 Japanese Americans were in the

13-2

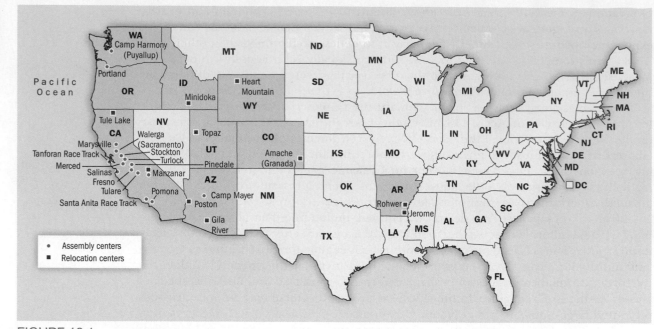

FIGURE 13.1

Japanese American Internment Camps

Japanese Americans were first ordered to report to assembly centers, from which, after a few weeks or months, they were resettled in internment camps or relocation centers.

Source: National Park Service 2012.

camps. Of mainland Japanese Americans, 113,000 were evacuated, but to those were added 1,118 evacuated from Hawai'i, 219 voluntary residents (White spouses, typically), and, most poignantly of all, the 5,981 who were born in the camps (Robinson 2001; Takaki 1998).

The evacuation order did not arise from any court action. No trials took place. No indictments were issued. Merely having a Japanese great-grandparent was enough to mark a person for involuntary confinement. The evacuation was carried out with little difficulty. For Japanese Americans to have fled or militantly defied the order would only have confirmed the suspicions of their fellow Americans. There was little visible objection initially from the Japanese Americans. The Japanese American Citizens League (JACL), which had been founded by the Nisei as a self-help organization in 1924, even decided not to arrange a court test of the evacuation order. The JACL felt that cooperating with the military might lead to sympathetic consideration later when tensions subsided (Iwamasa 2008b).

Even before reaching the camps, the **evacuees**, as Japanese Americans being forced to resettle came to be called officially, paid a price for their ancestry. They were instructed to carry only personal items. No provision was made for shipping their household goods. The federal government took a few steps to safeguard the belongings they left behind, but the evacuees assumed all risks and agreed to turn over their property for an indeterminate length of time. These Japanese Americans were destroyed economically. Merchants, farmers, and business owners had to sell all their property at any price they could get. Precise figures of the loss in dollars are difficult to obtain, but after the war the Federal Reserve Bank estimated it to be $400 million. To place this amount in perspective, in 2010 dollars, the economic damages sustained, excluding personal income, would be more than $3.6 billion (Bureau of the Census 2011a: 473; Commission on Wartime Relocation and Internment of Civilians 1982a, 1982b; Hosokawa 1969; Thomas and Nishimoto 1946).

The Camps   Ten camps were established in seven states. Were they actually concentration camps? Obviously, they were not concentration camps constructed for the murderous purposes of those in Nazi Germany, but such a positive comparison is no compliment to the United States. To refer to them by their official designation as *relocation centers* ignores these facts: The Japanese Americans did not go there voluntarily; they had been charged with no crime; and they could not leave without official approval.

Japanese Americans were able to work at wage labor in the camps. The maximum wage was set at $19 a month, which meant that camp work could not possibly recoup the losses incurred by evacuation. The evacuees had to depend on the government for food and shelter, a situation they had not experienced in prewar civilian life. More devastating than the economic damage of camp life was the psychological damage. Guilty of no crime, the Japanese Americans moved through a monotonous daily routine with no chance of changing the situation. Forced community life, with such shared activities as eating in mess halls, weakened the strong family ties that Japanese Americans, especially the Issei, took so seriously (Kitsuse and Broom 1956).

Amid the economic and psychological devastation, the camps began to take on some resemblance to U.S. cities of a similar size. High schools were established, complete with cheerleaders and yearbooks. Ironically, Fourth of July parades were held, with camp-organized Boy Scout and Girl Scout troops marching past proud parents. But the barbed wire remained, and the Japanese Americans were asked to prove their loyalty.

A loyalty test was administered in 1943 on a form all had to fill out: the Application for Leave Clearance. Many of the Japanese Americans were undecided on how to respond to two questions:

> No. 27. *Are you willing to serve in the armed forces of the United States on combat duty, wherever ordered?*

> No. 28. *Will you swear to abide by the laws of the United States and to take no action, which would in any way interfere with the war effort of the United States? (Daniels 1972:113)*

The ambiguity of the questions left many internees confused about how to respond. For example, if Issei said yes to the second question, would they then lose their Japanese citizenship and be left stateless? The Issei would be ending allegiance to Japan but were unable, at the time, to gain U.S. citizenship. Similarly, would Nisei who responded yes be suggesting that they had been supporters of Japan? For these reasons and out of protesting their illegal captivity, 6,700 Issei and Nisei answered "no" to the questions and were transferred to the high-security camp at Tule Lake for the duration of the war (Bigelow 1992; Onishi 2012).

Overwhelmingly, Japanese Americans showed loyalty to the government that had created the camps. In general, security in the camps was not a problem. The U.S. Army, which had overseen the removal of the Japanese Americans, recognized the value of the Japanese Americans as translators in the war ahead. About 6,000 Nisei were recruited to work as interpreters and translators, and by 1943, a special combat unit of 23,000 Nisei volunteers had been created to fight in Europe. The predominantly Nisei unit was unmatched, and it concluded the war as the most decorated of all American units.

Japanese American behavior in the concentration camps can be seen only as reaffirming their loyalty. True, some internees refused to sign an oath, but that was hardly a treasonous act. More typical were the tens of thousands of evacuees who contributed to the U.S. war effort.

A few Japanese Americans resisted the evacuation and internment. Several cases arising out of the evacuation and detention reached the U.S. Supreme Court during the war. Amazingly, the Court upheld lower court decisions on Japanese Americans without even raising the constitutionality of the whole plan. Essentially, the Court upheld the idea of an entire race's collective guilt. Finally, after hearing *Mitsuye Endo v. United States*, the Supreme Court ruled, on December 18, 1944, that the detainment was unconstitutional and consequently the defendant (and presumably all evacuees) must be granted freedom. Two weeks later, Japanese Americans were allowed to return to their homes for the first time in three years, and the camps were finally closed in 1946. Each internee was handed $25 and a train ticket (Orenstein 2011).

13-2

Japanese Americans gather in an annual "Lest We Forget" ceremony at the Manzanar internment camp in northern California.

The immediate postwar climate was not pro–Japanese American. Whites terrorized returning evacuees in attacks similar to those against Blacks a generation earlier. Labor unions called for work stoppages when Japanese Americans reported for work. Fortunately, the most blatant expression of anti-Japanese feeling disappeared rather quickly. Japan stopped being a threat as the atomic bomb blasts destroyed Nagasaki and Hiroshima. For the many evacuees who lost relatives and friends in the bombings, however, it must have been a high price to pay for marginal acceptance (Iwamasa 2008a; Robinson 2001, 2009).

The Evacuation: What Does It Mean?

The social significance of the wartime evacuation has often been treated as a historical exercise, but in the wake of the stigmatizing of Arab and Muslim Americans after 9/11, singling out people of Japanese descent almost 70 years ago takes on new meaning. Japanese American playwright Chay Yew reflected recently, "You think you can walk away from history and it taps you on the back" (Boehm 2004:E2). We do not know yet the consequences of the current focus on identifying potential disloyal Americans, but we do have some perspective on stigmatizing Japanese Americans during and after World War II.

The evacuation policy cost the U.S. taxpayers a quarter of a billion dollars in construction, transportation, and military expenses. Japanese Americans, as already noted, effectively lost at least several billion dollars. These are only the tangible costs to the nation. The relocation was not justifiable on any security grounds. No verified act of espionage or sabotage by a Japanese American was recorded. How could it happen?

Racism cannot be ignored as an explanation. Japanese Americans were placed in camps, but German Americans and Italian Americans were largely ignored. Many of those whose decisions brought about the evacuation were of German and Italian ancestry. The fact was that the Japanese were expendable. Placing them in camps posed no hardship for the rest of society, and, in fact, other Americans profited by their misfortune. That Japanese Americans were evacuated because they were seen as expendable is evident from the decision not to evacuate Hawai'i's Japanese. In Hawai'i, the Japanese were an integral part of the society; removing them would have destroyed the islands economically (Kimura 1988; Robinson 2009).

Documents recently unearthed show that government officials saw the Japanese Americans collectively as enemy aliens and that it would not be possible to determine loyalty of individual people. Why not? According to the thinking at the time, government leaders felt the "cultural traits" of the Japanese prevented outsiders from telling who was loyal and disloyal (Herzig-Yoshinaga and Lee 2011; Linthicum 2011) .

Some people argue that the Japanese lack of resistance made internment possible. This seems a weak effort to transfer guilt—*to blame the victim*. In the 1960s, some Sansei and Yonsei were concerned about the alleged timidity of their parents and grandparents when faced with evacuation orders. However, many evacuees, if not most, probably did not really believe what was happening. "It just cannot be that bad," they may have thought. At worst, the evacuees can be accused of being naive. But even if they did see clearly how devastating the order would be, what alternatives were open to them? None.

The Commission on Wartime Relocation and Internment of Civilians in 1981 held hearings on whether additional reparations should be paid to evacuees or their heirs. The final commission recommendation in 1983 was that the government formally apologize and give $20,000 tax-free to each of the approximately 82,000 surviving internees. Congress began hearings in 1986 on the bill authorizing these steps, and President Ronald Reagan signed the Civil Liberties Act of 1988, which authorized the payments. The payments, however, were slow in coming because other federal expenditures had higher priority. Meanwhile, the aging internees were dying at a rate of 200 a month. In 1990, the first checks were finally issued, accompanied by President Bush's letter of apology. Many Japanese Americans were disappointed by and critical of the begrudging nature of the compensation and the length of time it had taken to receive it (Commission on Wartime Relocation and Internment of Civilians 1982a, 1982b; Department of Justice 2000; Haak 1970; Kitano 1976; Robinson 2012; Takezawa 1991).

For over twelve years Mike Honda has represented in the U. S. House of Representatives the area of California including San Jose and the technology corridor dubbed "Silicon Valley." Between the ages of one and almost five, he lived at Camp Amache, a Japanese American internment camp in southeast Colorado during World War II. This was especially ironic for Honda given his father's service in the U.S. Military Intelligence Service.

Congressman Honda (2014) has observed, "One of the first lessons I learned was that being Japanese carried a negative connotation in America. My parents raised me talking about the injustices of camp, how it was a violation of the Constitution, and how Japanese Americans had been mistreated. I've since followed in their footsteps by advocating for social justice and publically serving communities that do not have a voice."

In Speaking Out, Congressman Honda draws upon this early experience to lead the drive to take steps to end, or at least, reduce bullying of young people in the United States.

Perhaps actor George Takei, of *Star Trek* fame in the role of Lieutenant Sulu, sums up best the wartime legacy of the evacuation of Japanese Americans. As a child, he had lived with his parents in the Tule Lake, California, camp. In 1996, on the fiftieth anniversary of the camp's closing and five years before 9/11 would turn the nation's attention elsewhere, he reflected on his arrival at the camp. "America betrayed American ideals at this camp. We must not have national amnesia; we must remember this" (Lin 1996:10).

🎙 Speaking Out

Anti-Bullying

Thank you for supporting the Congressional Anti-Bullying Caucus. Every year, millions of Americans are physically or psychologically attacked on the basis of their skin color, ethnicity, physical or mental abilities, sexual orientation, sex, gender identity, religion, or age. Addressing the bullying epidemic–in our schools, in the workplace, in assisted-living facilities–is a concern very close to my heart. It is our responsibility as human beings to empower the individuals who are discriminated against, scapegoated, and silenced by society.

Mike Honda

I know, firsthand, the pains of being bullied. As a Japanese American born at the height of World War II, I was placed in an internment camp before I could walk or talk. For many years after the war, I endured confrontations and insults from my peers solely because of my appearance. I had a few courageous friends, however, who transcended the discriminatory norms of the time. Their support, together with the wisdom and guidance from my parents, helped me realize some powerful and liberating truth; Japanese Americans had been treated unjustly—bullied by the U.S. government—because of "war hysteria, racial prejudice and a failure of political leadership" at the highest levels of leadership. I came to understand that our nation's founding principles support a more inclusive America, respectful of sex, gender, ethnicity, ability, sexual orientation, race, political philosophy, and age.

In the seventy years since internment, our nation has made leaps and bounds in reparations for the internment and ostracizing of individuals of Japanese descent. Today, however, America is threatened by an epidemic where more than thirteen million children are teased, taunted, and physically assaulted by their peers each year—embodied in racism, xenophobia, homophobia, sexism, or simply means of letting go of aggression and bottled emotions. This bullying is not confined to classroom walls; the fear and hurt that so many people feel in America today is an urgent call to action. As an educator of more than thirty years and a member of Congress who was bullied as a child, I am inspired to do my part. That's why I founded the Congressional Anti-Bullying Caucus. The Congressional Anti-Bullying Caucus will be a premier forum for individuals and advocates from private sector organizations and non-profit agencies, educators, students, and everyday individuals, along with Members of Congress, to proactively address issues of bullying.

As Chair of the Congressional Anti-Bullying Caucus, I appreciate your attention and support for holistically understanding and addressing the different aspects of bullying. On behalf of the Anti-Bullying Caucus, we thank you for your commitment and look forward to fostering a more inclusive and vibrant society.

Source: Honda 2013.

13-2

The Economic Picture

The socioeconomic status of Japanese Americans as a group is different from that of other Asian Americans. Japanese Americans as a group are even more educated and enjoy even higher incomes than Chinese Americans as well as White Americans (refer to Table 12.1). In contrast to other Asian Americans, the Japanese American community is more settled and less affected by new arrivals from the home country.

The camps left a legacy with economic implications; the Japanese American community of the 1950s was very different from that of the 1930s. Japanese Americans were more widely scattered. In 1940, 89 percent lived on the West Coast. By 1950, only 58 percent of the population had returned to the West Coast. Another difference was that a smaller proportion than before was Issei. The Nisei and even later generations accounted for 63 percent of the Japanese population. By moving beyond the West Coast, Japanese Americans seemed less of a threat than if they had remained concentrated. Furthermore, by dispersing, Japanese American businesspeople had to develop ties to the larger economy rather than do business mostly with other Japanese Americans. Although ethnic businesses can be valuable initially, those who limit their dealings to those from the same country may limit their economic potential (Oliver and Shapiro 1996: 46).

After the war, some Japanese Americans continued to experience hardship. Some remained on the West Coast and farmed as sharecroppers in a role similar to that of the freed slaves after the Civil War. Sharecropping involved working the land of others, who provided shelter, seeds, and equipment and who also shared any profits at the time of harvest. The Japanese Americans used the practice to gradually get back into farming after being stripped of their land during World War II (Parrish 1995).

However, perhaps the most dramatic development has been the upward mobility that Japanese Americans collectively and individually have accomplished. By occupational and academic standards, two indicators of success, Japanese Americans are doing very well. The educational attainment of Japanese Americans as a group, as well as their family earnings, is higher than that of Whites, but caution should be used in interpreting such group data. Obviously, large numbers of Asian Americans, as well as Whites, have little formal schooling and are employed in poor jobs. Furthermore, Japanese Americans are concentrated in areas of the United States such as Hawai'i, California, Washington, New York, and Illinois, where wages and the cost of living are far above the national average. Also, the proportion of Japanese American families with multiple wage earners is higher than that of White families. Nevertheless, the overall picture for Japanese Americans is remarkable, especially for a racial minority that had been discriminated against so openly and so recently (Inoue 1989; Kitano 1980; Nishi 1995).

The Japanese American story does not end with another account of oppression and hardship. Today, Japanese Americans have achieved success by almost any standard. However, we must qualify the progress that Newsweek (1971) once billed as their "Success Story: Outwhiting the Whites." First, it is easy to forget that several generations of Japanese Americans achieved what they did by overcoming barriers that U.S. society had created, not because they had been welcomed. However, many, if not most, have become acculturated. Nevertheless, successful Japanese Americans still are not wholeheartedly accepted into the dominant group's inner circle of social clubs and fraternal organizations. Second, Japanese Americans today may represent a stronger indictment of society than economically oppressed African Americans, Native Americans, and Hispanics. Whites can use few excuses apart from racism to explain why they continue to look on Japanese Americans as different—as "them."

Family Life

The contradictory pulls of tradition and rapid change that are characteristic of Chinese Americans are very strong among Japanese Americans today. Surviving Issei see their grandchildren as very nontraditional. Change in family life is one of the most difficult cultural changes for any immigrant to accept in the younger generations.

As cultural traditions fade, the contemporary Japanese American family seems to continue the success story. The divorce rate has been low, although it is probably rising. Similar conclusions apply to crime, delinquency, and reported mental illness. Data on all types of social disorganization show that Japanese Americans have a lower incidence of such behavior than all other minorities; it is also lower than that of Whites. Japanese Americans find it possible to be good Japanese and good Americans simultaneously. Japanese culture demands high ingroup unity, politeness, and respect for authority, and duty to community—all traits that are highly acceptable to middle-class Americans. Basically, psychological research has concluded that Japanese Americans share the high-achievement orientation held by many middle-class White Americans. However, one might expect that as Japanese Americans continue to acculturate, the breakdown in traditional Japanese behavior will be accompanied by a rise in social deviance (Nishi 1995).

In the last 40 years, a somewhat different family pattern has emerged in what can almost be regarded as a second Japanese community forming. As Japan's economic engine took off in the latter part of the twentieth century, corporate Japan sought opportunities abroad. Because of its large automobile market, the United States economy became one destination. Top-level executives and their families were relocated to look after these enterprises. This has created a small but significant community of Japanese in the United States. Although they are unlikely to stay, they are creating a presence that is difficult to miss. Several private schools have been established since 1966 in the United States, in which children follow Japanese curriculum and retain their native language and culture. Saturday school is maintained for Japanese American parents whose children attend public school during the week. Although these private academies are removed from the broader culture, they help facilitate the nearby creation of authentic markets and Japanese bookstores. Researchers are interested to see what might be the lasting social implications of these households from Japan (Dolnick and Semple 2011; Lewis 2008; Twohey 2007).

Remnants of Prejudice and Discrimination

Today, young Japanese Americans and Chinese Americans are very ambivalent about their cultural heritage. The pull to be American is intense, but so are the reminders that in the eyes of many others, Asian Americans are "they," not "we." Congressman David Wu emigrated from Taiwan in 1961 at the age of six and became the first person of Chinese descent elected to Congress. In this role, he was invited to a celebration of Asian American accomplishments at the Department of Energy building but was denied entry. Profiling was not involved was the official response, which stated that congressional ID is insufficient to clear security The next day an Italian American congressman gained entry using the same type of credential (Zhou 2009).

13-3 Identify how prejudice and discrimination persist.

Why does intolerance continue toward Chinese, Japanese and other Asian Americans? An analysis by the Japanese American Citizens League (2013) noted for its efforts to gain redress for the internment camp survivors, they offered four causes:

1. Xenophobia and the visibility of Asian and Pacific Americans. **Xenophobia**, the fear or hatred of strangers or outsiders, is certainly present in contemporary society.

2. Economic and international relations which often find the USA at a competitive disadvantage.

3. Media portrayals and public perceptions that continue the perpetuate stereotypes be they negative or more neutral like the "model minority" myth.

4. The "Asian Monolith" view which despite the diversity as we have seen in the Asian American community is still rampant among many Americans.

This serves to remind us that prejudice is not a historical phenomenon of the last century.

13-3

Seattle-born Edwin Mah Lee became in 2011 the first Asian American elected mayor of San Francisco. His parents immigrated from China in the 1930s.

Chinese Americans and Japanese Americans believe that prejudice and discrimination have decreased in the United States, but subtle reminders remain. Third-generation Japanese Americans, for example, feel insulted when they are told, "You speak English so well." Adopting new tactics, Asian Americans are now trying to fight racist and exclusionary practices (Lem 1976).

Marriage statistics also illustrate the effects of assimilation. At one time, 29 states prohibited or severely regulated marriages between Asians and non-Asians. Today, intermarriage, though not typical, is legal and certainly much more common. The increased intermarriage indicates that Whites are increasingly accepting of Chinese Americans and Japanese Americans. It also suggests that Chinese and Japanese ties to their native cultures are weakening. As happened with the ways of life of European immigrants, the traditional norms are being cast aside for those of the host society. In one sense, these changes make Chinese Americans and Japanese Americans more acceptable and less alien to Whites. But this points to all the changes in Asian Americans rather than any recognition of diversity in the United States. As illustrated in the Spectrum of Intergroup Relations, intermarriage patterns reflect the fusion of different racial groups; however, compared with examples of assimilation and pluralism, they are a limited social process at present

The Japanese American community struggles to maintain its cultural identity while also paying homage to those who were interned during World War II. Paradoxically, as many people see parallels between the collective guilt forced on people of Japanese ancestry during the 1940s and profiling of Arab and Muslim Americans, a few are seeking to justify the internment. Books and even a public middle school named after an internee in Washington state have been criticized; critics feel that when the subject of Japanese American internment was taught it was too biased and that arguments for internment being the correct action should be included. For many Japanese Americans, the more things change, the more they stay the same (Malkin 2004; Tizon 2004).

It would be incorrect to interpret assimilation as an absence of protest. Because a sizable segment of the college youth of the 1960s and early 1970s held militant attitudes, and because the Sansei are more heterogeneous than their Nisei and Issei relatives, it was to be expected that some Japanese Americans, especially the Sansei, would be politically active. For example, Japanese and other Asian Americans have emerged as activists for environmental concerns ranging from contaminated fish to toxic working conditions, and the targets of Japanese Americans' anger have included the apparent rise in hate crimes in the United States against Asian Americans in the 1990s. They also lobbied for

SPECTRUM OF INTERGROUP RELATIONS

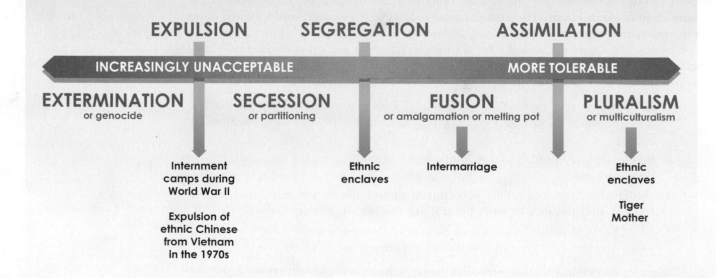

EXPULSION	SEGREGATION		ASSIMILATION
INCREASINGLY UNACCEPTABLE		MORE TOLERABLE	
EXTERMINATION or genocide	**SECESSION** or partitioning	**FUSION** or amalgamation or melting pot	**PLURALISM** or multiculturalism
Internment camps during World War II	Ethnic enclaves	Intermarriage	Ethnic enclaves
Expulsion of ethnic Chinese from Vietnam in the 1970s			Tiger Mother

passage of the Civil Rights Restoration Act, which extended reparations to the evacuees. They have expressed further activism through Hiroshima Day ceremonies that mark the anniversary of the detonation in World War II of the first atomic bomb over a major Japanese city. Also, each February, a group of Japanese American youths makes a pilgrimage to the site of the Tule Lake evacuation camp in a "lest we forget" observance. Such protests are modest, but they are a militant departure from the silent role played by the Nisei in the years immediately following the closing of the camps (Cart 2006).

Is pluralism developing? Japanese Americans show little evidence of wanting to maintain a distinctive way of life. The Japanese values that have endured are attitudes, beliefs, and goals shared by and rewarded by the White middle class in America. All Asian Americans, not only Japanese Americans, are caught in the middle. Any Asian American is culturally a part of a society that is dominated by a group that excludes him or her because of racial distinctions.

13-3

Conclusion

Most White adults are confident that they can distinguish Asians from Europeans. Unfortunately, though, White Americans often cannot tell Asians apart from their physical appearance and are not disturbed about their confusion.

However, as we have seen, there are definite differences in the experience of the Chinese and the Japanese in the United States. One obvious difference is in the degree of assimilation. The Chinese Americans have maintained their ethnic enclaves more than the Japanese Americans have. Chinatowns live on, both as welcomed halfway points for new arrivals and as enclaves where many residents make very low wages. But as we saw at the beginning of Chapter 5, New York City's Chinatown is expanding and has more than occupied the space formerly referred to as Little Italy. However, Little Tokyos are few because of the differences in the cultures of China and Japan. China was almost untouched by European influence, but even by the early 1900s, Japan had already been influenced by the West. Therefore, the Japanese arrived somewhat more assimilated than their Chinese counterparts. The continued migration of Chinese in recent years has also meant that Chinese Americans as a group have been less assimilated than Japanese Americans.

Both groups have achieved some success, but this success has not extended to all members. For Chinese Americans, a notable exception to success can be found in Chinatowns, which, behind the tourist front, are much like other poverty-stricken areas in American cities. Neither Chinese Americans nor Japanese Americans have figured prominently in the executive offices of the nation's large corporations and financial institutions. Compared with other racial and ethnic groups, Asian Americans have shown little interest in political activity on their own behalf.

However, the success of Asian Americans, especially that of the Japanese Americans, belongs to them, not to U.S. society. First, Asian Americans have been considered successful only because they conform to the dominant society's expectations. Their acceptance as a group does not indicate growing pluralism in the United States.

Second, the ability of the Nisei, in particular, to recover from the camp experience cannot be taken as a precedent for other racial minorities. The Japanese Americans left the camps a skilled group, ambitious to overcome their adversity and placing a cultural emphasis on formal education. They entered a booming economy in which Whites and others could not afford to discriminate even if they wanted to. African Americans after slavery and Hispanic immigrants have entered the economy without skills at a time when the demand for manual labor was limited. Many of them were forced to remain in a marginal economy, whether that of the ghetto, the barrio, or subsistence agriculture. For Japanese Americans, the post–World War II period marked the fortunate coincidence of their having assets and ambition when they could be used to full advantage.

Third, some Whites use the success of the Asian Americans to prop up their own prejudice. Bigoted people twist Asian American success to show that racism cannot possibly play a part in another group's subordination. If the Japanese or Chinese can do it, why cannot African Americans, the illogical reasoning goes? More directly, Japanese Americans' success may serve as a scapegoat for another's failure ("They advanced at my expense") or as a sign that they are clannish or too ambitious. Regardless of what a group does, a prejudiced eye will always view it as wrong.

As for other racial and ethnic minorities, assimilation seems to be the path most likely to lead to tolerance but not necessarily to acceptance. However, assimilation has a price that is well captured in the Chinese phrase "Zhancao zhugen": "To eliminate the weeds, one must pull out their roots." To work for acceptance means to uproot all traces of one's cultural heritage and former identity (Wang 1991).

Summary

1. Although welcomed for their labor in the nineteenth century, Chinese immigrants were shortly viewed as responsible for economic setbacks experienced by the nation, which culminated in the passage of the Chinese Exclusion Act. Chinatowns are very visible signs of continued growth of the Chinese American population and represent both promise and problems for the immigrants. The family is a central focus in the Chinese community and is critical to the successful adaptation of immigrants to the United States.

2. Immigrants from Japan, like so many others, were permitted to come when they fulfilled an economic niche but were quickly marginalized socially and legally. The internment of people of Japanese ancestry during World War II is a clear instance of guilt by virtue of race. The prosperity of Japanese Americans as a group reflects the willingness to endure post–World War II marginalization and continued investment in formal schooling for their children.

3. Despite competing effectively in the labor market, or perhaps because of it, Chinese and Japanese Americans continue to experience prejudice and discrimination in the twenty-first century.

Key Terms

evacuees, p. 292

hui kuan, p. 286

Issei, p. 290

Kibei, p. 291

Nisei, p. 290

Sansei, p. 290

tiger mother, p. 289

tongs, p. 287

tsu, p. 286

xenophobia, p. 297

Yonsei, p. 290

Review Questions

1. What has been the legacy of the "yellow peril"?

2. What made the placement of Japanese Americans in internment camps unique?

3. In what respects does diversity characterize Chinatowns?

4. How has Japanese American assimilation been blocked in the United States?

5. What are the most significant similarities between the Chinese American and Japanese American experiences? What are the differences?

Critical Thinking

1. Considering the past as well as the present, are the moves made to restrict or exclude Chinese and Japanese Americans based on economic or racist motives?

2. What events can you imagine that could cause the United States to again identify an ethnic group for confinement in some type of internment camps?

3. What stereotypical images of Chinese Americans and Japanese Americans can you identify in the contemporary media?

14 Jewish Americans: Quest to Maintain Identity

14-1 Examine whether the Jewish people are considered a race, religion, or ethnic group.

14-2 Restate the history of immigration of Jews to the United States.

14-3 Articulate the extent of anti-Semitism historically and in the present.

14-4 Explain the economic, educational, and political situation.

14-5 Describe the role of religion.

14-6 Explain Jewish Identity.

14-1

Critical to the Jewish faith is the ability to have a congregation of sufficient size to undertake religious obligations such as public prayer and to have a rabbi. For the many rural congregations and even for cities outside the Northeast, this can be a challenge. In response, Dotham, Mississippi, with the number of families belonging to Temple Emanu-El having fallen from 110 in the 1970s to 43 in 2010, has started to recruit families. Called the "Jewish stimulus package," the offer was as much as $50,000. Even in New Orleans, Jewish organizations offer a $15,000 loan to lure Jews back after Hurricane Katrina.

Swastikas scrawled on classroom walls, desks, lockers, textbooks and the playground slide. A social studies classroom displayed the country's leader with a swastika drawn on his forehead. Students exchange Nazi salutes. Germany perhaps in the 1930s? No, this was a middle and high school in New York State in 2013. For two years, Jewish students in Pine Bush, New York, had complained with the superintendent responding to parents that there were so many in the school exhibiting anti-Semitic behavior that "your expectations for changing inbred prejudice may be a bit unrealistic" their worship (Weiser 2013a:A29). As news of this hostile environment spread, the governor of New York directed the State Police and the State Division of Human Rights to investigate the situation (Austen 2010; Fishkoff 2008; Institute of Southern Jewish Life 2011; Weiser 2013a, 2013b).

The United States has the second-largest Jewish population in the world. This nation's approximately 5.4 million Jews account for 40 percent of the world's Jewish population. Jewish Americans not only represent a significant group in the United States but also play a prominent role in the worldwide Jewish community. The nation with the largest Jewish population, Israel, is the only one in which Jews are in the majority, accounting for 74 percent of the population, compared with 2 percent in the United States. Figure 14.1 depicts the worldwide distribution of Jews (DellaPergola 2012).

The Jewish people form a contrast to the other subordinate groups we have studied. At least 1,500 years had passed since Jews were the dominant group in any nation until Israel was created in 1948. Even there, Jews are in competition for power. American Jews superficially resemble Asian Americans in that both are largely free from poverty, compared to Chicanos or Puerto Ricans. Unlike those groups, however, the Jewish cultural heritage is not nationalistic in origin. Perhaps the most striking difference is that the history of anti-Jewish prejudice and discrimination (usually called **anti-Semitism**) is nearly as old as relations between Jews and Gentiles (non-Jews).

Without question, people in North America and Europe give the countries of the Southern hemisphere little attention unless they are directly impacted. To partially correct this pattern, we consider in this chapter's A Global View the Jewish community in Argentina whose Jewish community was the scene of a deadly attack in 1992.

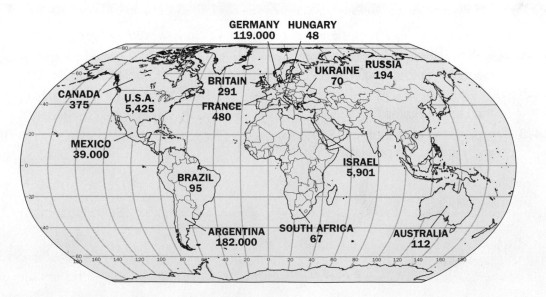

FIGURE 14.1
Worldwide Distribution of Jews, 2012

Note: Data include all nations with at least 35,000 Jews. Rounded to nearest thousand.

Source: DellaPergola 2012.

A Global View

14-1

Argentina's Jewish Community

Jewish settlements are found throughout the world as a result of the dispersal, or *Diaspora,* from Palestine. Efforts to resettle in Europe often led to local and national actions over several centuries to expel the Jews, so sizable settlements eventually developed not only in North America but also in Argentina, especially after it obtained its independence from Spain. Argentina currently has the largest Jewish population in Latin America, which is estimated at 181,800.

The first Jews settled in Argentina shortly after their expulsion from Spain in 1492. Stigmatized, these early settlers often hid their faith from others and soon assimilated with other immigrants from Europe. By the nineteenth century, public vestiges of Jewish worship began to emerge in Argentina. One significant group of Jews from Russia settled in the frontier of Argentina, becoming cowboys or, as they are called there, *gauchos.*

The years after World War II were mixed times for Jews in Argentina because the country's leader, Juan Peron, had been sympathetic to the Nazis and welcomed Hitler's followers to the country. Yet Peron also established early on diplomatic relations with Israel, smoothing the way for Israeli Jews who wished to settle in Argentina. Later, human rights abuses during the dictatorship of 1976–1983 were anti-Semitic in character because certain abuses were coded that way (carving swastikas in people's bodies, for example) and Jews were targeted.

Even more violent was the 1992 bombing of the Israeli embassy (29 dead) and the Jewish center of Asociación Mutual Israelita Argentina (85 dead). The government blamed these events on outside forces, perhaps Iran, but no convictions have occurred.

In the last three decades, Argentina has taken on a consistent pro-Israeli position and cooperated with efforts to locate Nazi war criminals who may still be hiding out. Argentine Jews have achieved some success in industry but are largely absent in the higher ranks of military, foreign affairs, and the court system. Visible Jewish buildings have been the targets of attacks, and many synagogues remain tightly guarded. Jewish immigration is now largely a factor of economic conditions. Downturns in the Argentine economy are associated with a migration to Israel and elsewhere while upswings lead to an influx of immigrants, including Jews. Evidence suggests that the Argentine Jewish population is aging and is not encountering growth.

The Jewish community resembles that of many other countries. Day schools provide instruction in Judaism and Hebrew and are attended by the majority of Jewish youth. McDonald's has even established its first kosher restaurant outside of Israel that, besides offering a menu conforming to dietary restrictions, closes for the Sabbath. Buenos Aires, with the largest urban Jewish population outside of Israel, North America, and Europe, is the center of Jewish life in today's Argentina and boasts numerous organizations and one of the world's four remaining daily Yiddish newspapers.

Sources: DellaPergola 2012; Jewish Agency for Israel 2011; Schwartz 2008; Schweimler 2007; Timerman 2002; Weiner 2008.

The Jewish People: Race, Religion, or Ethnic Group?

Jews are a subordinate group. They fulfill the criteria set forth in Chapter 1:

14-1 Examine whether the Jewish people are considered a race, religion, or ethnic group.

- Jewish Americans experience unequal treatment from non-Jews in the form of prejudice, discrimination, and segregation.
- Jews share a cultural history that distinguishes them from the dominant group.
- Jews do not choose to be Jewish, in the same way that Whites do not choose to be White or Mexican Americans to be Mexican American.
- Jews have a strong sense of group solidarity.
- Jewish men and women tend to marry one another rather than marry outside the group.

What are the distinguishing traits for Jewish Americans? Are they physical features, thus making Jews a racial group? Are these characteristics matters of faith, suggesting that Jews are best regarded as a religious minority? Or are they cultural and social, making Jews an ethnic group? To answer these questions, we must address the ancient and perennial question, What is a Jew?

The issue of what makes a Jew is not only a scholarly question; in Israel, it figures in policy matters. The Israel Law of Return defines who is a Jew and extends Israeli citizenship to all Jews. Currently, the law recognizes all converts to the faith, but pressure has grown recently to limit citizenship to those whose conversions were performed by Orthodox rabbis. Although the change would have little practical impact, symbolically this pressure shows the tension and lack of consensus even among Jews over who is a Jew.

The definition of race used here is fairly explicit. The Jewish people are not physically differentiated from non-Jews. True, many people believe they can tell a Jew from a non-Jew, but actual distinguishing physical traits are absent. Jews today come from all areas of the world and carry a variety of physical features. Most Jewish Americans are descended from northern and eastern Europeans and have the appearance of Nordic and Alpine people. Many others carry Mediterranean traits that make them indistinguishable from Spanish or Italian Catholics. Many Jews reside in North Africa, and although they are not significantly represented in the United States, many people would view them only as a racial minority, Black. The wide range of variation among Jews makes it inaccurate to speak of a Jewish race in a physical sense (Gittler 1981; Montagu 1972).

To define Jews by religion seems the obvious answer because there are Judaic religious beliefs, holidays, and rituals. But these beliefs and practices do not distinguish all Jews from non-Jews. To be a Jewish American does not mean that one is affiliated with one of the three religious groups: the Orthodox, the Reform, and the Conservative. A large segment of adult Jewish Americans, more than a third, do not participate in religious services or even belong, however tenuously, to a temple or synagogue. They have neither converted to Christianity nor ceased to think of themselves as Jews. Nevertheless, Jewish religious beliefs and the history of religious practices remain significant legacies for all Jews today, however secularized their everyday behavior. In a 2013 national survey, 62 percent of all Jews felt that an "ancestry or culture," much more so than religion, defined what it means to be Jewish (Lugo et al. 2013a).

The trend for some time, especially in the United States, has been toward a condition called **Judaization**, the lessening importance of Judaism as a religion and the substitution of cultural traditions as the ties that bind Jews. Depending on one's definition, Judaization has caused some Jews to become so assimilated in the United States that very traditional Jews no longer consider them acceptable spouses (Gans 1956).

Jewish identity is ethnic. Jews share cultural traits, not physical features or uniform religious beliefs. The level of this cultural identity differs for the individual Jew. Just as some Apaches may be more acculturated than others, the degree of assimilation varies among Jewish people. Judaization may base identity on such things as eating traditional Jewish foods, telling Jewish jokes, and wearing the Star of David. For others, this cultural identity may be the sense of a common history of centuries of persecution. For still others, it may be an unimportant identification. They say, "I am a Jew," just as they say, "I am a resident of California."

The question of what constitutes Jewish identity is not easily resolved. The most appropriate explanation of Jewish identity may be the simplest. A Jew in contemporary America is a person who thinks of himself or herself as a Jew. That also means that being a Jew is a choice and, as we return to later in the chapter, many Jews may not be making that choice (Abrahamson and Pasternak 1998; Himmelfarb 1982).

Immigration of Jews to the United States

14-2 Restate the history of immigration of Jews to the United States.

As every schoolchild knows, 1492 was the year in which Christopher Columbus reached the Western hemisphere, exploring on behalf of Spain. That year also marked the expulsion of all Jews from Spain. The resulting exodus was not the first migration of Jews, nor was it the last. This is but one illustration of several of the social processes in the Spectrum of Intergroup Relations illustrated in the figure on page 000. Other examples are presented throughout this chapter.

One of the most significant movements among Jews is the one that created history's largest concentration of Jews: the immigration to the United States. The first Jews arrived in 1654 and were of Sephardic origin, meaning that they were originally from Spain and Portugal. These immigrants sought refuge in America after they had been expelled from other European countries as well as from Brazil.

When the United States gained its independence from Great Britain, only 2,500 Jews lived here. By 1870 the Jewish population had climbed to about 200,000, supplemented mostly by Jews of German origin. They did not immediately merge into the older Jewish American settlements any more than the German Catholics fused immediately with native Catholics. Years passed before the two groups' common identity as Jews overcame nationality differences (Dinnerstein 1994; Jaher 1994).

The greatest migration of Jews to the

Jewish shoppers, many of them immigrants, crowd Orchard Street in New York City in 1923.

14-2

United States occurred around the end of the nineteenth century and was simultaneous with the great European migration described in Chapter 4. Because they arrived at the same time does not mean that the movements of Gentiles and Jews were identical in all respects. One significant difference was that Jews were much more likely to stay in the United States; few returned to Europe. Although between 1908 and 1937, one-third of all European immigrants returned, only 5 percent of Jewish immigrants did. The legal status of Jews in Europe at the turn of the century had improved since medieval times, but their rights were still revoked from time to time (Sherman 1974).

The immigration acts of the 1920s sharply reduced the influx of Jews, as they did for other European groups. Beginning in about 1933, the Jews arriving in the United States were not merely immigrants; they were also refugees. The tyranny of the Third Reich began to take its toll well before World War II. German and Austrian Jews fled Europe as the impending doom became more evident. Many of the refugees from Nazism in Poland, Hungary, and Ukraine tended to be more religiously orthodox and adapted slowly to the ways of the earlier Jewish immigrants, if they adapted at all. As Hitler's decline and fall came to pass, the concentration camps, the speeches of Hitler, the atrocities, the war trials, and the capture of Nazi leaders undoubtedly made all American Jews—natives and refugees, the secular and the orthodox—acutely aware of their Jewishness and the price one may be required to pay for ethnicity alone.

Because the U.S. Citizenship and Immigration Services do not identify an immigrant's religion, precise data are lacking for the number of people of Jewish background migrating recently to the United States. Estimates of 500,000 have been given for the number of Jews who made the United States their home in the 1960s and 1970s. The majority came from Israel, but 75,000 came from the Soviet Union and another 20,000 from Iran, escaping persecution in those two nations. As the treatment of Jews in the Soviet Union improved in the late 1980s, U.S. immigration officials began to scrutinize requests for entry to see whether refugee status was still merited. Although some Soviet Jews had difficulty demonstrating that they had a "well-founded fear of persecution," the United States admitted more than 13,600 in 1988 (through the processing center in Rome alone). The situation grew more complicated with the collapse of the Soviet Union in 1991. Throughout the period, the immigrants' arrival increased the size of the Jewish community in the United States.

The most distinctive aspect of the Jewish population in the United States today is its concentration in urban areas and in the Northeast. The most recent estimates place more than 44 percent of the Jewish population in the Northeast compared to 18 percent for the population as a whole (see Figure 14.2). Jews are concentrated especially in the metropolitan areas of New York City, Los Angeles, and South Florida, where altogether they account for 60 percent of the nation's Jewish population.

14-3

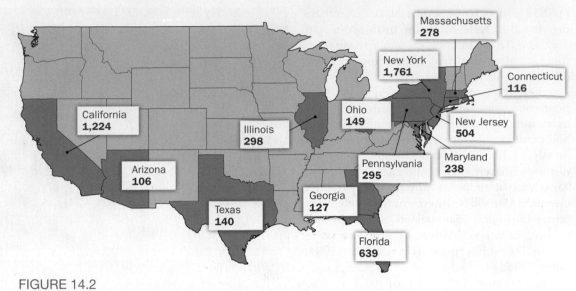

FIGURE 14.2
Jewish Population Distribution in the United States, 2012

Note: The highlighted states have Jewish populations estimated at more than 100,000 and are rounded off to the nearest thousand.

Source: Sheskin and Dashefsky 2012.

Anti-Semitism: Past and Present

14-3 Articulate the extent of anti-Semitism historically and in the present.

The history of the Jewish people is a history of struggle to overcome centuries of hatred. Several religious observances, such as Passover, Hanukkah, and Purim, commemorate the past sacrifices or conflicts Jews have experienced. Anti-Jewish hostility, or anti-Semitism, has followed the struggle of the Jewish people since before the beginning of the Christian faith to the present. Scholars have a long history in studying the nature of anti-Semitic thought and action. For example, as long ago as 1899, sociologist Emilé Durkheim wrote an essay during what he termed a period of "violent passions" of anti-Semitism sweeping Europe per political decisions (Durkheim 2008 [1899]).

Origins

Many anti-Semites justify their beliefs by pointing to the role of some Jews in the crucifixion of Jesus Christ, although he was also a Jew. For nearly 2,000 years, various Christians have argued that all Jews share in the responsibility of the Jewish elders who condemned Jesus Christ to death. Much anti-Semitism over the ages bears little direct relationship to the crucifixion, however, and has more to do with the persisting stereotype that Jews behave treacherously with members of the larger society in which they live.

A 2004 survey found that 26 percent of Americans felt Jews were "responsible for Christ's death"—a significant increase over a similar survey nine years earlier. At the time of the survey, many Jews felt that Mel Gibson's *The Passion of the Christ* reinforced such a view. Indeed, the same survey shows that among those who had seen the film, 36 percent held Jews responsible for the crucifixion (Pew Research Center 2004).

What truth is there in such stereotypes? Even prominent celebrities and political leaders have publicly expressed stereotyped opinions about Jews. In 2006, Gibson, a Hollywood director and actor, was stopped for drunk driving; he told the arresting officer, who happened to be Jewish, "The Jews are responsible for all wars in the world" (Cohen 2006). In 2009, a British bishop denied the existence of the Nazi gas chambers and the magnitude of the Holocaust. While the Roman Catholic Church denounced his remarks, his excommunication for earlier actions was actually lifted (Donadio 2009; Getlin 1998; Slavin and Pradt 1979, 1982).

14-3

If the stereotype that Jews are obsessed with money is false, how did it originate? Social psychologist Gordon Allport (1979), among others, advanced the **fringe-of-values theory**. Throughout history, Jews have occupied positions economically different from those of Gentiles, often because laws forbade them to farm or practice trades. For centuries, the Christian church prohibited the taking of interest in the repayment of loans, calling it the sin of usury. Consequently, in the minds of Europeans, the sinful practice of money lending was equated with the Jew. In reality, most Jews were not moneylenders, and most of those who were did not charge interest. In fact, many usurers were Christians, but because they worked in secret, it was only the reputation of the Jews that was damaged. To make matters worse, the nobles of some European countries used Jews to collect taxes, which only increased the ill feeling. To the Gentile, such business practices by the Jews constituted behavior on the fringes of proper conduct. Therefore, this theory about the perpetuation of anti-Semitism is called the *fringe-of-values theory* (American Jewish Committee 1965, 1966a, 1966b; *Time* 1974).

Another relevant approach is **scapegoating theory**, which says that prejudiced people believe they are society's victims. As introduced in Chapter 2, the theory of scapegoating suggests that, rather than accepting guilt for some failure, a person transfers the responsibility for failure to some vulnerable group. In the major tragic twentieth-century example, Adolf Hitler used the Jews as the scapegoat for all German social and economic ills in the 1930s. This premise led to the passage of laws restricting Jewish life in pre–World War II Germany and eventually escalated into the mass extermination of Europe's Jews. Yet scapegoating of Jews persists. A national survey in 2009 showed that one out of four people in the United States blame "the Jews" for the financial crisis that rocked the world starting in 2008 (Malhotra and Margalit 2009).

Fringe-of-values theory is given as an explanation for other stereotypes, such as the assertion that Jews are clannish, staying among themselves and not associating with others. In the ancient world, neighboring peoples often attacked Jews in the Near East area. Throughout history, Jews have also at times been required to live in closed areas, or ghettos. This experience naturally led them to unify and rely on themselves rather than others. More recently, the stereotype of clannishness has gained support because Jews have been more likely to interact with Jews than with Gentiles. But this behavior is reciprocal because Gentiles have tended to stay among their own kind too.

Being critical of others for traits for which you praise members of your own group is an example of **ingroup virtues** becoming **outgroup vices**. Sociologist Robert Merton (1968) described how proper behavior by one's own group becomes unacceptable when practiced by outsiders. For Christians to take their faith seriously is commendable; for Jews to withstand secularization is a sign of backwardness. For Gentiles to prefer Gentiles as friends is understandable; for Jews to choose other Jews as friends suggests clannishness. The assertion that Jews are clannish is an exaggeration and also ignores the fact that the dominant group shares the same tendency. It also fails to consider to what extent anti-Semitism has logically encouraged—and indeed, forced—Jews to seek out other Jews as friends and fellow workers (Allport 1979).

This only begins to explore the alleged Jewish traits, their origin, and the limited value of such stereotypes in accurately describing several million Jewish people. Stereotypes are only one aspect of anti-Semitism; another has been discrimination against Jews. In 313 C.E., Christianity became the official religion of Rome. Within another two centuries, Jews were forbidden to marry Christians or to try to convert them. Because Christians shared with Jews both the Old Testament and the origin of Jesus, they felt ambivalent toward the Jewish people. Gentiles attempted to purge themselves of their doubts about the Jews by projecting exaggerated hostility onto the Jews. The expulsion of the Jews from Spain in 1492 is only one example. Spain was merely one of many countries, including England and France, from which the Jews were expelled. In the mid-fourteenth century, the bubonic plague wiped out a third of Europe's population. Because of their social conditions and some of their religious prohibitions, Jews were less likely to die from the plague. Anti-Semites pointed to this as evidence that the Jews were in league with the devil and had poisoned the wells of non-Jews. Consequently, from 1348 to 1349, 350 Jewish communities were exterminated, not by the plague but by Gentiles.

14-3

The Holocaust

The injustices to the Jewish people continued for centuries. However, it would be a mistake to say that all Gentiles were anti-Semitic. History, drama, and other literature record daily presumably friendly interaction between Jews and Gentiles. At particular times and places, anti-Semitism was an official government policy. In other situations, it was the product of a few bigoted individuals and sporadically became very widespread. Regardless of the scope, anti-Semitism was a part of Jewish life, something that Jews were forced to contend with. By 1870, most legal restrictions aimed at Jews had been abolished in Western Europe. Since then, however, Jews have again been used as scapegoats by opportunists who blame them for a nation's problems.

The most tragic example of such an opportunist was Adolf Hitler, whose "final solution" represented a dramatic example; his scapegoating of German Jews for Germany's problems led directly to the Holocaust. The **Holocaust** was the state-sponsored systematic persecution and annihilation of European Jewry by Nazi Germany and its collaborators. The move to eliminate Jews from the European continent started slowly, with Germany gradually restricting the rights of Jews: preventing them from voting, living outside the Jewish ghetto, and owning businesses. Much of the anti-Semitic cruelty was evident before the beginning of the war. If there was any doubt, *Kristallnacht,* or the "Night of Broken Glass," in Berlin on November 9, 1938, ended any doubt. Ninety Berlin Jews were murdered, hundreds of homes and synagogues were set on fire or ransacked, and thousands of Jewish store windows were broken.

Despite the obvious intolerance, Jews desiring to immigrate were turned back by government officials in the United States and elsewhere. Just a few months after Kristallnacht, 903 Jewish refugees aboard the liner *St. Louis* were denied entry to Cuba. Efforts to gain entry in the United States, including special appeals to Congress and President Roosevelt, were useless. Ultimately the ship returned, and many of the Jews later died in the death camps. Between 1933 and 1945, two-thirds of Europe's total Jewish population was killed; in Poland, Germany, and Austria, 90 percent were murdered. Even today, there is still only 12 percent of the number of Jews who were present in 1938 (Berger 2010; DellaPergola 2007; Institute for Jewish and Community Research 2008).

Many eyewitnesses to the events of the Holocaust remind us of the human tragedy involved. Among the most eloquent are the writings and speeches of Nobel Peace Prize winner, Romanian-born Elie Wiesel (pronounced "EL-ee Vee-SELL"). In the Speaking Out, he recalls the moments before he, aged 16 at the time, and other Jews were freed from the Buchenwald concentration camp.

Despite the enormity of the tragedy, a small but vocal proportion of the world community are **Holocaust revisionists** who claim that the Holocaust did not happen. A controversial conference was held in 2006 in Iran that brought together revisionists from throughout the world. Debates also continue between those who contend that this part of modern history must be remembered and others, in the United States and Europe, who feel that it is time to put the Holocaust behind us and go on (Fathi 2006).

Despite these attacks on historical reality, the poignant statements by Holocaust survivors such as Wiesel, *The Diary of Ann Frank*, and the release of such films as *Schindler's List* (1993), *Life Is Beautiful* (1998), *The Pianist* (2002), *Munich* (2005), *The Reader* (2008), and *Inglorious Bastards* (2009) keep the tragedy of the Holocaust and its legacy in our minds.

Anti-Semitism is definitely not just a historical social phenomenon in Europe. A 2013 survey of Jewish Europeans found that 66 percent believed that anti-Semitism is "a problem" where they live and 76 percent felt that anti-Jewish bigotry had increased over the past five

The United States Holocaust Memorial Museum, Washington DC. This picture shows the exhibit entitled the Tower of Faces which brings visitors face to face the story of a single small town near the border of Poland and Lithuania, known in Polish as Ejszyszki. In two days in September 1941, the Nazis eradicated almost all of the town's Jews and 900 years of Jewish life in the town. Today, no Jews live there. The hundreds of photographs in Tower of Faces represent the once thriving Jewish life that existed before the Holocaust

Speaking Out

14-3

Night

On April 10, [1945], there were still some twenty thousand prisoners in the camp, among them a few hundred children. It was decided to evacuate all of us at once. By evening. Afterward, they would blow up the camp.

And so we were herded into the huge *Appelplatz* [assembly square], in ranks of five, waiting for the gate to open. Suddenly, the sirens began to scream. Alert! We went back to the blocks. It was too late to evacuate us that evening. The evacuation was postponed to the next day.

Elie Wiesel

Hunger was tormenting us; we had not eaten for nearly six days except for a few stalks of grass and some potato peels found on the grounds of the kitchens.

At ten o'clock in the morning, the SS took positions throughout the camp and began to herd the last of us toward the *Appelplatz*.

The resistance movement decided at that point to act. Armed men appeared from everywhere. Bursts of gunshots. Grenades exploding. We, the children stayed, remained flat on the floor of the block.

The battle did not last long. Around noon, everything was calm again. The SS had fled and the resistance had taken charge of the camp.

At six o'clock that afternoon, the first American tank stood at the gates of Buchenwald.

Our first act as free men was to throw ourselves onto the provisions. That's all we thought about. No thought of revenge, or of our parents. Only of bread.

And then when we were no longer hungry, not one of us thought of revenge. The next day, a few of the young men ran into Weimar to bring back some potatoes and clothes—and to sleep with the girls. But still no trace of revenge.

Three days after the liberation of Buchenwald, I became very ill: some form of [food] poisoning. I was transferred to a hospital and spent two weeks between life and death.

One day when I was able to get up, I decided to look at myself in the mirror on the opposite wall. I had not seen myself since the ghetto.

From the depths of the mirror, a corpse was contemplating me.

The look in his eyes as he gazed at me has never left me.

Source: Wiesel 2006:114–115. Originally published in 1958. Reprinted by permission of Hill & Wang, a division of Farrar, Straus & Giroux, LLC.

years. An amazing 40 percent or more of Jews in Belgium, France, and Hungary said they had been considering emigrating for safety reasons. Troubling to many observers is that the recent rise in such perceptions and the rise in accusations against Jews worldwide have excited the anger or disbelief of the non-Jewish masses and non-Jewish elites alike (European Union Agency for Fundamental Rights. 2013; Goldberg 2013; Goldhagen 2013).

U.S. Anti-Semitism: Past

Compared with the brutalities of Europe from the time of the early Christian church to the rule of Hitler, the United States cannot be described as a nation with a history of severe anti-Semitism. Nevertheless, the United States has also had its outbreaks of anti-Semitism, though none have begun to approach the scope or level of that seen in Western Europe. An examination of the status of Jewish Americans today indicates the extent of remaining discrimination against Jews. However, contemporary anti-Semitism must be seen in relation to past injustices.

In 1654, the year Jews arrived in colonial America, Peter Stuyvesant, governor of New Amsterdam (the Dutch city later named New York), attempted to expel them from the city. Stuyvesant's efforts failed, but they were the beginning of an unending effort to separate Jews from the rest of the population. Because the pre-1880 immigration of Jews was small, anti-Semitism was little noticed except, of course, by Jews. Most nineteenth-century movements against minorities were targeted at Catholics and Blacks and ignored Jews. In fact, Jews occasionally joined in such movements. By the 1870s, however, signs of a pattern of social discrimination against Jews had appeared. Colleges limited the number of Jewish students or excluded Jews altogether. The first Jewish fraternity was founded in 1898 to compensate for the barring of Jews from campus social organizations. As Jews

14-3

began to compete for white-collar jobs early in the twentieth century, job discrimination became the rule rather than the exception (Higham 1966; Selzer 1972).

The 1920s and the 1930s were periods of the most virulent and overt anti-Semitism. In these decades, the myth of an internationally organized Jewry took shape. According to a forged document titled *Protocols of the Learned Elders of Zion*, Jews throughout the world planned to conquer all governments, and the major vehicle for this rise to power was Communism, said by anti-Semites to be a Jewish movement. Absurd though this argument was, some respected Americans accepted the thesis of an international Jewish conspiracy and believed in the authenticity of the Protocols.

Henry Ford, founder of the automobile company that bears his name, was responsible for the publication of the *Protocols*. In his later years, Ford expressed regret for his espousal of anti-Semitic causes, but the damage had been done; he had lent an air of respectability to the most exaggerated charges against Jewish people.

It is not clear why Henry Ford, even for a short period of his life, so willingly accepted anti-Semitism. But Ford was not alone. Groups such as the Ku Klux Klan and the German American Bund, as well as radio personalities, preached about the Jewish conspiracy as if it were fact. By the 1930s, these sentiments expressed a fondness for Hitler. Even famed aviator Charles Lindbergh made speeches to gatherings claiming that Jews were forcing the United States into a war so that Jewish people could profit by wartime production. When the barbarous treatment of the Jews by Nazi Germany was exposed, most Americans were horrified by such events, and people such as Lindbergh were as puzzled as anyone about how some Americans could have been so swept up by the pre–World War II wave of anti-Semitism (Baldwin 2001; Meyers 1943; Selzer 1972).

Historical anti-Semitism is never far below the surface. The discredited *Protocols* was sold online by Wal-Mart through 2004 and described as "genuine" until protests made the large retailer rethink its sale. In 2006, a Spanish-language version published in Mexico City enjoyed wide distribution. A 40-part television series based on the Protocols produced in 2002 was shown as recently as March 2012 in Egypt (Goldhagen 2012; *Intelligence Report* 2004; Rothstein 2006).

The next section examines anti-Semitic feelings in contemporary America. Several crucial differences between anti-Semitism in Europe and in the United States must be considered. First, and most important, the U.S. government has never promoted anti-Semitism. Unlike its European counterparts, the U.S. government has never embarked on an anti-Semitic program of expulsion or extermination. Second, because anti-Semitism was never institutionalized in the United States as it sometimes has been in Europe, American Jews have not needed to develop a defensive ideology to ensure the survival of their people. A Jewish American can make a largely personal decision about how much to assimilate or how secular to become.

Contemporary Anti-Semitism

Next to social research on anti-Black attitudes and behavior of Whites, anti-Semitism has been the major focus of studies of prejudice by sociologists and psychologists. Most of the conclusions described in Chapter 2 apply equally to the data collected on anti-Semitism. Jews in the United States expressed little concern about anti-Semitism immediately after World War II. From the late 1960s through the 1990s, however, anti-Semitism has again appeared to be a threat in many parts of the world. A 2010 national survey found that 25 percent of Jews felt anti-Semitism was a "very serious problem" and 66 percent "somewhat of a problem" in the United States. Looking at the statistical data, there is good reason to see this strong concern. More than two-thirds of reported religious hate crimes are against Jews. A 2012 multi-nation study of acceptance of anti-Semitic stereotypes found much less acceptance of such images in the United States than in European nations surveyed (American Jewish Committee 2010a; Chanes 2007; Landau 2012:9).

Incidents of Anti-Semitism The Anti-Defamation League (ADL) of B'nai B'rith, founded in 1913, makes an annual survey of reported anti-Semitic incidents. Although the number has fluctuated, the 1994 tabulation reached the highest level in the more than 30 years the ADL has been recording such incidents. Figure 14.3 shows the fluctuating reported numbers of harassment, threats, and assaults, which, adding episodes of vandalism, brings the total to 927 incidents for 2012. Some incidents were inspired and carried out by neo-Nazis or skinheads, groups of young people who champion racist and anti-Semitic ideologies.

In recent years, fewer anti-Semitic incidents have been reported from organized hate groups, but disturbing has been the growing number of reported anti-Semitic incidents on college campuses. Incidents continue to be reported. Anti-Jewish graffiti, anti-Semitic speakers, and swastikas affixed to predominantly Jewish fraternities were among the documented incidents. Another manifestation of it appears in editorial-style advertisements in college newspapers that argue that the Holocaust never occurred. A chilling development is the growing use of the Internet as a vehicle for anti-Semitism, either delivering such messages or serving as a means of reaching Web sites that spread intolerance (Anti-Defamation League 2008; Chanes 2007).

American Jews and Israel When the Middle East became a major hot spot in international affairs in the 1960s, a revival of 1930s levels of anti-Semitism occurred. Many Jewish Americans expressed concern that because Jews are freer in the United States than they have been in perhaps any other country in their history, they would ignore the struggle of other Jews. Israel's precarious status has proven to be a strong source of identity for Jewish Americans. Major wars in the Middle East in 1967, 1973, and 1991 reminded the world of Israel's vulnerability. Palestinian uprisings in the occupied territories and international recognition of the Palestine Liberation Organization (PLO) in 1988 and 2002 eroded the strong pro-Israeli front among the Western powers. Some Jewish Americans have shown their commitment to the Israeli cause by immigrating to Israel.

The majority of Jewish Americans feel the United States should remain active in world affairs, compared to 36 percent of the total U.S. population. However, even among Jews, support of Israel is not uniform. Although not all American Jews agree with Israel's actions, many Jews express support for Israel's struggles by contributing money and trying to influence American opinion and policy to be more favorable to Israel. A survey taken in 2013 showed that 30 percent of Jewish Americans feel "very attached" to Israel

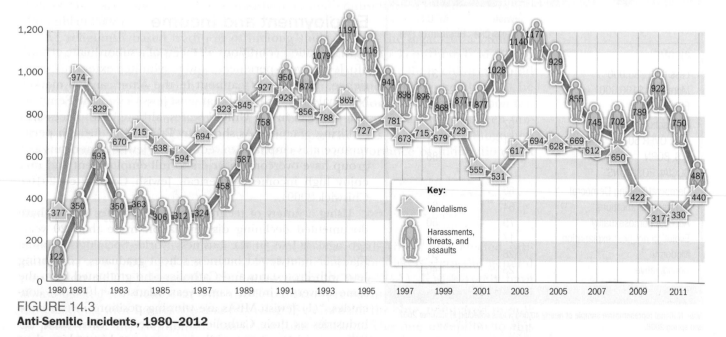

FIGURE 14.3
Anti-Semitic Incidents, 1980–2012

Source: ADL 2013. Reprinted with permission of the Anti-Defamation League, *www.adl.org*.

14-5

among ultraorthodox Jews, whom we consider later. Other Jewish religious traditions tend to be very open to egalitarian participation in most aspects of religious ritual, especially when compared to many Christian faiths (Connelly 2008; Fishman and Parmer 2008).

Jews have long been successful in being elected to office, but it was not until 1988 that an Orthodox Jew from Connecticut was elected to the U.S. Senate. Joseph Lieberman refrained from campaigning on the Sabbath (Shabbat) each week; his religious views were not an issue. He went on to be named as the vice presidential running mate of Al Gore. Even during the campaign, he honored the Sabbath and did not actively campaign, even avoiding dialing a telephone to potential supporters. Many view the positive response to his campaign as a sign of openness to devout Jews as political candidates (Issacson and Foltin 2001; Pew Charitable Trust 2000).

As in all subordinate groups, the political activity of Jewish Americans has not been limited to conventional electoral politics. The Jewish community has encompassed a variety of organizations since its beginnings. These groups serve many purposes: some are religious, and others are charitable, political, or educational. No organization, secular or religious, represents all American Jews, but there are more than 300 nationwide organizations (Chanes 2008).

Religious Life

14-5 Describe the role of religion.

Jewish identity and participation in the Jewish religion are not the same. Many Americans consider themselves Jewish and are considered Jewish by others even though they have never participated in Jewish religious life. The available data indicate that about half of American Jews are affiliated with a synagogue or temple, but only a small proportion consider participation in religious worship as extremely important. Even in Israel, only 30 percent of Jews are religiously observant. Nevertheless, the presence of a religious tradition is an important tie among Jews, even secular Jews (American Jewish Committee 2007; Cohen 1991).

The Judaic faith embraces several factions or denominations that are similar in their roots but marked by sharp distinctions. No precise data reveal the relative numbers of the three major groups. Part of the problem is the difficulty of placing individuals in the proper group. For example, it is common for a Jew to be a member of an Orthodox congregation but consider him- or herself Conservative. The following levels of affiliation are based on a 2013 national survey of Jewish Americans:

- Orthodox—10 percent
- Conservative—18 percent
- Reform—35 percent
- Reconstructionist (and others)—6 percent
- Just Jewish—27 percent
- Don't know/Atheist/ Other—4 percent

Large Orthodox families, conversion to orthodoxy by other Jews, and immigration of traditional Jews to the United States lead to more conservative patterns of religion. Yet many Jewish households are attracted to the moderation of Reform Jews (Lugo et al. 2013a).

We focus on two forms of Judaism at either end of the continuum: the Orthodox faith, which attempts to uphold a very traditional practice of Judaism; and the Reform faith, which accommodates itself to the secular world.

The Orthodox Tradition

The unitary Jewish tradition developed in the United States into three sects beginning in the mid-nineteenth century. The differences between Orthodox, Conservative, and Reform Judaism are based on their varying acceptance of traditional rituals. All three sects embrace a philosophy based on the Torah, the first five books of the Old Testament. The differences developed because some Jews wanted to be less distinguishable from other Americans. Another significant factor in explaining the development of different groups is the absence of a religious elite and bureaucratic hierarchy. This facilitated the breakdown in traditional practices.

Orthodox Jewish life is very demanding, especially in a basically Christian society such as the United States. Almost all conduct is defined by rituals that require an Orthodox Jew to constantly reaffirm his or her religious conviction. Most Americans are familiar with **kashrut**, the laws pertaining to permissible and forbidden foods. When strictly adhered to, kashrut governs not only what foods may be eaten (kosher) but also how the food is prepared, served, and eaten. Besides day-to-day practices, Orthodox Jews have weekly and annual observances. Women may not be rabbis among the Orthodox, although beginning in 2006, women were named to head a congregation in one faction of the faith, but only male members of the congregation could read publicly from the Torah (Goldstein 2010; Luo 2006a).

Even Orthodox Jews differ in their level of adherence to traditional practices. Among the ultraorthodox are the Hasidic Jews, or Hasidim, who number some 200,000, with half residing chiefly in several neighborhoods in Brooklyn. To the Hasidim, following the multitude of *mitzvahs,* or commandments of behavior, is as important today as it was in the time of Moses. Their spiritual commitment extends well beyond customary Jewish law even as interpreted by Orthodox Jews.

Hasidic Jews wear no garments that mix linen and wool. Men wear a *yarmulke,* or skullcap, constantly, even while sleeping. Attending a secular college is frowned upon. Instead, the men undertake a lifetime of study of the Torah and the accompanying rabbinical literature of the Talmud. Women's education consists of instruction on how to run the home in keeping with Orthodox tradition. Hasidic Jews, who themselves are organized in separate communities, have courts with jurisdiction recognized by the faithful in many matters, especially as they relate to family life.

Orthodox children attend special schools in order to meet minimal New York State educational requirements. The devotion to religious study is reflected in this comment by a Hasidic Jew: "Look at Freud, Marx, Einstein—all Jews who made their mark on the non-Jewish world. To me, however, they would have been much better off studying in a yeshiva [a Jewish school]. What a waste of three fine Talmudic minds" (Arden 1975:294). Although devoted to their religion, the Hasidim participate in local elections and politics and are employed in outside occupations. All such activities are influenced by their orthodoxy and a self-reliance rarely duplicated elsewhere in the United States.

The Reform Tradition

Reform Jews, although deeply committed to the religious faith, have altered many of the rituals. Women and men sit together in Reform congregations, and both sexes participate in the reading of the Torah at services. Women have been ordained as rabbis since 1985. A few Reform congregations have even experimented with observing the Sabbath on Sunday and freely allow its members to drive to attend (thus violating an Orthodox prohibition against operating

Among those Jews in the United States who follow a more Orthodox religious tradition are the Hasidic Jews. Among these Hasidic men in the Williamsburg neighborhood of Brooklyn, one man is wearing a round fur hat called a shtreimel worn on the Shabbat (day of Sabbath) or Jewish holidays.

14-5

A rabbi blesses a young girl at her Bat Mitzvah in the temple. Jewish children often celebrate a coming-of-age ceremony. According to Jewish law, when Jewish children reach the age of maturity (12 years for girls, 13 years for boys), they become responsible for their actions. At this point a boy is said to become Bar Mitzvah; a girl is said to become Bat Mitzvah.

machinery on the Sabbath). Circumcision for males is not mandatory. Civil divorce decrees are sufficient and recognized so that a divorce granted by a three-man rabbinical court is not required before remarriage. Reform Jews recognize the children of Jewish men and non-Jewish women as Jews with no need to convert. All these practices would be unacceptable to the Orthodox Jew.

Conservative Judaism is a compromise between the rigidity of the Orthodox and the extreme modification of the Reform. Because of the middle position, the national organization of Conservatives, the United Synagogue of America, strives to create its own identity and seeks to view its traditions as an appropriate, authentic approach to the faith.

Table 14.2 displays some results of a 2013 national survey on Jewish identification. The three sects here include both members and nonmembers of local congregations. Reform Jews are the least likely of the three religious groups to participate in religious events, to be involved in the Jewish community, or to participate in predominantly Jewish organizations. Yet in Reform temples, there has been an effort to observe religious occasions such as Rosh Hashanah.

Like Protestant denominations, Jewish denominations are associated with class, nationality, and other social differences. The Reform Jews are the wealthiest and have the best formal education of the group, the Orthodox are the poorest and least educated in years of formal secular schooling, and the Conservatives occupy a position between the two. A fourth branch of American Judaism, Reconstructionism, an offshoot of the Conservative movement, has only recently developed an autonomous institutional structure with ritual practices similar to those of Reform Jews. Religious identification is associated with particular generations: immigrants and older Jews are more likely to be Orthodox, and their grandchildren are more likely to be Reform (*Los Angeles Times* Poll 1998).

Concerned about the number of followers, some Jewish leaders are trying new tactics to attract or at least not to lose observant Jews. For example, Jews historically have not embarked on recruitment or evangelistic programs to attract new members. Beginning in the late 1970s, Jews, especially Reform Jews, debated the

TABLE 14.2
Jewish Identification by Group

Indices	Orthodox (%)	Conservative (%)	Reform (%)	No Denomination (%)
Very Important Being Jewish	87	69	43	22
Eating Jewish foods	51	18	9	6
Observance of Jewish law	79	24	11	8
Observance of Christian holidays	6	6	17	28
Involvement with Jewish organizations	39	27	20	4
Caring about Israel	55			

Source: Lugo et al. 2013a: 51, 57, 60.

possibility of outreach programs. Least objectionable to Jewish congregations were efforts begun in 1978 aimed at non-Jewish partners and children in mixed marriages. In 1981, the program was broadened to invite conversions by Americans who had no religious connection, but these very modest recruitment drives are still far from resembling those that have been carried out by Protestant denominations for decades (Luo 2006b).

Some Reform leaders are rethinking the requirement that one has to attend three or four years of religious school as a prerequisite to bar or bat mitzvahs. Others are considering dispensing with the youth reading from the Torah in Hebrew—once regarded as a central point of the ceremony. Embracing change is not limited to the more liberal end of the spectrum. Dwindling Orthodox parishes in some parts of the country are offering relocation bonuses to Orthodox families to come join in worship. Many faithful Jews oppose such efforts and argue that practices need to become stricter and less adaptable (Goldstein 2010; Goodstein 2013; Hu 2012; Luo 2006b).

Jewish Identity

Ethnic and racial identification can be positive or negative. Awareness of ethnic identity can contribute to a person's self-esteem and give that person a sense of group solidarity with similar people. When a person experiences an identity only as a basis for discrimination or insults, he or she may want to shed that identity in favor of one more acceptable to society. Unfavorable differential treatment can also encourage closer ties between members of the community being discriminated against, as it has for Jews.

14-6 Explain Jewish Identity.

Most would judge the diminishing of outgroup hostility and the ability of Jews to leave the ghetto as a positive development (Friedman 1967). However, the improvement in Jewish–Gentile relations also creates a new problem in Jewish social identity. It has become possible for Jews to shed their "Jewishness," or **Yiddishkait**. Many retain their Yiddishkait even in suburbia, but it is more difficult there than in the ghetto. In the end, however, Jews cannot lose their identity entirely. Jews are still denied total assimilation in the United States no matter how much the individual ceases to think of him- or herself as Jewish. Social clubs may still refuse membership, and prospective non-Jewish in-laws may try to interfere with plans to marry.

Events in the world also remind the most assimilated Jew of the heritage left behind. A few such reminders in the past generation include Nazi Germany, the founding of Israel in 1948, the Six-Day War of 1967, Soviet interference with Jewish life and migration, the terrorist attack at the 1972 Munich Olympics, the Yom Kippur War of 1973, the 1973 oil embargo, the United Nations' 1974 anti-Zionism vote, and the Scud missile attacks during the 1991 Gulf War.

A unique identity issue presents itself to Jewish women, whose religious tradition has placed them in a subordinate position. For example, it was not until 1972 that the first female rabbi was ordained. Jewish feminism has its roots in the women's movement of the 1960s and 1970s, several of whose leaders were Jewish. There have been some changes in **halakha** (Jewish law covering obligations and duties), but it is still difficult for a woman to get a divorce recognized by the Orthodox Jewish tradition. Sima Rabinowicz of upstate New York has been hailed as the Jewish Rosa Parks for her recent bus battle. Rabinowicz refused to give up her seat in the women's section of a Hasidic-owned, publicly subsidized bus to Orthodox men who wanted to pray in private, segregated from women as required by halakha. The courts defended her right to ride as she wished, just as an earlier court had ruled with Rosa Parks in the Birmingham bus boycott. Jewish women contend that they should not be forced to make a choice between their identities as women and as Jews (Baum 1998; Frankel 1995).

We now examine three factors that influence the ethnic identity of Jews in the United States: family, religion, and cultural heritage.

14-6

Many Gentiles mistakenly suppose that a measure of Jewishness is the ability to speak Yiddish. Few people have spoken as many languages as the Jews have through their long history. Yiddish is only one, and it developed in Jewish communities in eastern Europe between the tenth and twelfth centuries. Fluency in Yiddish in the United States has been associated with the immigrant generation and the Orthodox. Sidney Goldstein and Calvin Goldscheider (1968) reported that evidence overwhelmingly supports the conclusion that linguistic assimilation among Jews is almost complete by the third generation. However, in the last generation or two there has been a slight increase in the use of Hebrew. This change probably resulted from increased pride in Israel and a greater interaction between that nation and the United States. Other contributing factors are the increase in the use of Hebrew texts in Jewish day schools and in college Jewish studies programs.

Overall, the differences between Jews and Gentiles have declined in the United States. To a large extent, this reduction is a product of generational changes typical of all ethnic groups. The first-generation Mexican American in Los Angeles contrasts sharply with the middle-class White living in suburban Boston. The convergence in culture and identity is much greater between the fourth-generation Mexican American and his or her White counterpart. A similar convergence is occurring among Jews. This change does not signal the eventual demise of the Jewish identity. Moreover, Jewish identity is not a single identity, as we can see from the heterogeneity in religious observance, dedication to Jewish and Israeli causes, and participation in Jewish organizations.

Being Jewish comes from the family, the faith, and the culture, but it does not require any one criterion. Jewishness transcends nation, religion, or culture. A sense of peoplehood is present that neither anti-Semitic bigotry nor even an ideal state of fellowship among all religions would destroy. American life may have drastically modified Jewish life in the direction of dominant society values, but it has not eliminated it. Milton Gordon (1964) refers to **peoplehood** as a group with a shared feeling. For Jews, this sense of identity originates from a variety of sources, past and present, both within and without (Goldscheider 2003).

Conclusion

Jewish Americans are the product of three waves of immigration originating from three different Jewish communities: the Sephardic, the western European, and the eastern European. They brought different languages and, to some extent, different levels of religious orthodoxy. Today, they have assimilated to form an ethnic group that transcends the initial differences in nationality.

Jews are not a homogeneous group. Among them are the Reform, Conservative, and Orthodox denominations, listed in ascending order of adherence to traditional rituals. Nonreligious Jews make up another group, probably as large as any one segment, and they still see themselves as Jewish.

Jewish identity is reaffirmed from within and outside the Jewish community; however, both sources of affirmation are weaker today. Identity is strengthened by the family, religion, and the vast network of national and community-based organizations. Anti-Semitism outside the Jewish community strengthens the ingroup feeling and the perception that survival as a people is threatened.

Today, American Jews face a new challenge: they must maintain their identity in an overwhelmingly Christian society in which discrimination is fading and outbreaks of prejudice are sporadic. Yiddishkait may not so much have decreased as changed. Elements of the Jewish tradition have been shed in part because of modernization and social change. Some of this social change—a decline in anti-Semitic violence and restrictions—is certainly welcome. Although kashrut observance has declined, most Jews care deeply about Israel, and many engage in pro-Israel activities. Commitment has changed with the times, but it has not disappeared (Cohen 1988).

Some members of the Jewish community view the apparent assimilation with alarm and warn against the grave likelihood of the total disappearance of a sizable and identifiable Jewish community in the United States. Others see the changes not as erosion but as an accommodation to a pluralistic, multicultural environment. We

SPECTRUM OF INTERGROUP RELATIONS

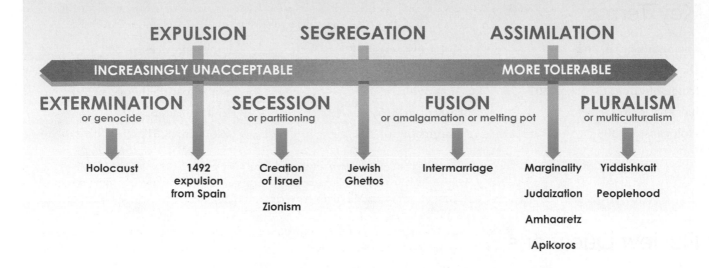

are witness to a progressive change in the substance and style of Jewish life. According to this view, Jewish identity, the Orthodox and Conservative traditions notwithstanding, has shed some of its traditional characteristics and has acquired others. The strength of this view comes with the knowledge that doomsayers have been present in the American Jewish community for at least two generations. Only the passage of time will reveal the future of Jewish life in the United States (Finestein 1988; Glazer 1990).

Although discrimination against Jews has gone on for centuries, far more ancient than anti-Semitism and the experience of the Diaspora is the subordinate role of women. Women were perhaps the first to be relegated to an inferior role and may be the last to work collectively to struggle for equal rights. Studying women as a subordinate group in Chapter 15 reaffirms the themes in our study of racial and ethnic groups.

Summary

1. Jews as a group are best considered an ethnic group whose members may or may not be obedient to a Jewish religious tradition.

2. Jewish immigration began in the earliest colonial times and has reflected the ebb and flow of immigration from Europe.

3. Anti-Semitism has a long history worldwide, having been institutionalized in many European countries. Although not absent in the United States, it has never been endorsed by government action. The Holocaust is a turning point in modern history and was followed by an influx of Jewish immigrants to the United States. Contemporary anti-Semitism in the United States is frequently documented but

is as likely to be punctuated by spirited discussions about U.S.–Israeli relations.

4. Jewish Americans demonstrate high levels of occupational success built on extensive formal schooling. As a group they are very politically active.

5. Religious life is varied among Jews in the United States and split between nonobservant and observant; among the latter, a variety of expressions range from very conservative to very liberal expressions of ritual.

6. The very acceptance of Jews in the United States has led to high levels of intermarriage, leading many in the Jewish community to lament that Jews are assimilating too quickly and losing their identity.

Key Terms

anti-Semitism, p. 302

Diaspora, p. 312

fringe-of-values theory, p. 307

halakha, p. 317

Holocaust, p. 308

Holocaust revisionists, p. 308

ingroup virtues, p. 307

Judaization, p. 304

kashrut, p. 315

marginality, p. 319

outgroup vices, p. 307

peoplehood, p. 320

scapegoating theory, p. 307

Yiddishkait, p. 317

Zionism, p. 312

Review Questions

1. Why are the Jewish people most accurately characterized as an ethnic group?

2. What are major patterns of immigration of Jews to the United States?

3. How have the patterns of anti-Semitism changed or remained the same?

4. What are the positive and negative aspects of the status of Jewish Americans as a group today?

5. What are the major aspects of Jewish religious life?

6. Why is maintaining Jewish identity so difficult in the United States?

Critical Thinking

1. Most minority groups regard acceptance as a positive outcome. Why do some Jewish Americans seem threatened by being accepted in contemporary Gentile society?

2. How different and similar have the experiences of women in organized religion been compared with those of women in the Jewish faith?

3. Using the Jewish experience as a basis for comparison, how has fusion functioned or not functioned for any other subordinate group when compared with Jews in the United States?

4. Reviewing the Spectrum of Intergroup Relations on p. 000, how do the different entries define and affect Jewish Americans today?

15 Women: The Oppressed Majority

15-1 Understand gender roles.

15-2 Contrast sociological perspectives on gender.

15-3 Summarize the feminist movement.

15-4 Discuss the women's economic situation.

15-5 Describe the experience of women in education.

15-6 Explain gender as it relates to the family.

15-7 Describe women's role in politics.

15-8 Define the matrix of domination.

15-1

Many high tech corporations have not a single female board member despite having so many female consumers and clients

Women are an oppressed group even though they form the numerical majority. They are a social minority in the United States and throughout Western society. Men dominate in influence, prestige, and wealth. Women do occupy positions of power, but those who do are the exceptions, as evidenced by newspaper accounts that declare "she is the first woman" or "the only woman" to be in a particular position.

Yet many were still taken aback when Twitter became a publicly held company in 2013 and had to reveal its board—it had not a single woman member. In some ways that should not come as a surprise, as 49 percent of publicly traded information technology businesses have no women on their boards—not even a token member (that compares to 36 percent of public companies having at least one board member) (Klinkenborg 2013).

Many people, men and women, find it difficult to conceptualize women as a subordinate group even when hearing news like that of Twitter's all-male board. Why is it hard to think of women as a subordinate group? After all, not all women live in ghettos. They no longer have to attend inferior schools. They freely interact and live with their alleged oppressors, men. How, then, are they a subordinate group? Let us reexamine the five properties of a subordinate or minority group introduced in Chapter 1:

1. Women do experience unequal treatment. Although they are not segregated by residence, they are victims of prejudice and discrimination.

2. Women have physical and cultural characteristics that distinguish them from the dominant group (men).

3. Membership in the subordinate group is involuntary.

4. Through the rise of contemporary feminism, women have become increasingly aware of their subordinate status and have developed a greater sense of group solidarity.

5. Women are not forced to marry, yet many women feel that their subordinate status is most irrevocably defined within marriage.

In this chapter, the similarities between women and racial and ethnic groups will become apparent.

The most common analogy about minorities used in the social sciences is the similarity between the status of African Americans and that of women. Blacks are considered a minority group, but, one asks, how can women of all groups be so similar in condition? We recognize some similarities in recent history; for example, an entire generation has observed and participated in both the civil rights movement and the women's movement. A background of suffrage campaigns, demonstrations, sit-ins, lengthy court battles, and self-help groups is common to the movements for equal rights for both women and African Americans. But similarities were recognized long before the recent protests against inequality. In *An American Dilemma* (1944), the famous study of race, Gunnar Myrdal observed that a parallel to the Blacks' role in society was found among women. Other observers, such as Helen Mayer Hacker (1951, 1974), later elaborated on the similarities.

What do these groups have in common besides recent protest movements? The negative stereotypes directed at the two groups are quite similar: Both groups have been considered emotional, irresponsible, weak, or inferior. Both are thought to fight subtly against the system: women allegedly try to outwit men by feminine wiles, as historically Blacks allegedly outwitted Whites by pretending to be deferential or respectful. To these stereotypes must be added another similarity: Neither women nor African Americans are accepting a subordinate role in society any longer.

Nearly all Whites give lip service, even if they do not wholeheartedly believe it, to the contention that African Americans are innately equal to Whites. They are inherently the same. But men and women are not the same, and they vary most dramatically in their roles in reproduction. Biological differences have contributed to sexism. **Sexism** is the ideology that one sex is superior to the other. Quite different is the view that there are few differences between the sexes. Such an idea is expressed in the concept of **androgyny**. An androgynous model of behavior permits people to see that humans can be both aggressive and expressive, depending on the requirements of the situation. People do not have to be locked into the behavior that accompanies the labels *masculine* and *feminine*. In the United States, people disagree widely as to what implications, if any, the biological differences between the sexes have for social roles. We begin our discussion of women as a subordinate group with this topic.

Gender Roles

A college man, done with afternoon classes, heads off to get a pedicure and, while the nail polish is drying, sits on a nearby park bench finishing some needlepoint he started. Meanwhile, a college woman walks through the park chewing tobacco and spitting along the path. What is wrong with this picture? We are witnessing the open violation of how men and women are expected to act. So unlikely are these episodes that I have taken them from sociology teachers who specifically ask their students to go out, violate gender expectations, and record how they feel and how people react to their behavior (Nielsen, Walden, and Kunkel 2000:287).

15-1   Understand gender roles.

Gender roles are society's expectations of the proper behavior, attitudes, and activities of males and females. Toughness has traditionally been seen in the United States as masculine, desirable only in men, whereas tenderness has been viewed as feminine. A society may require that one sex or the other take the primary responsibility for the socialization of the children, economic support of the family, or religious leadership.

Without question, socialization has a powerful impact on the development of females and males in the United States. Indeed, the gender roles first encountered in early childhood often are a factor in defining a child's popularity. Sociologists Patricia Adler and her colleagues (1992) observed elementary school children and found that boys typically achieved high status on the basis of their athletic ability, coolness, toughness, social skills, and success in relationships with girls. By contrast, girls gained popularity based on their parents' economic background and their own physical appearance, social skills, and academic success.

It may be obvious that males and females are conditioned to assume certain roles, but the origin of gender roles as we know them is less clear. Many studies have been done on laboratory animals, such as injecting monkeys and rats with male and female hormones. Primates in their natural surroundings have been closely observed for the presence and nature of gender roles. Animal studies do not point to instinctual gender differences similar to what humans are familiar with as masculinity and femininity. Historically, women's work came to be defined as a consequence of the birth process. Men, free of childcare responsibilities, generally became the hunters and foragers for food. Even though women must bear children, men could have cared for the young. Exactly why women were assigned that role in societies is not known.

Women's and men's roles vary across different cultures. Furthermore, we know that acceptable behavior for men and women changes over time in a society. For example, the men in the royal courts of Europe in the late 1700s fulfilled present-day stereotypes of feminine appearance in their display of ornamental dress and personal vanity rather than resembling the men of a century later, although they still engaged in duels and other forms of aggression. The social roles of the sexes have no constants in time or space (Lorber 2005; Taylor, Rupp, and Whittier 2009).

Sociological Perspectives

15-2 Contrast sociological perspectives on gender.

Gender differences are maintained in our culture through the systematic socialization of babies and infants, children, adolescents, and adults. Even though different subcultures and even different families vary in childrearing, we teach our children to be boys and girls, even though men and women are more alike than they are different.

We are bombarded with expectations for behavior as men and women from many sources simultaneously. Many individual women hold positions involving high levels of responsibility and competence but may not be accorded the same respect as men. Similarly, individual men find the time to get involved with their children's lives only to meet with disbelief and occasional surprise from healthcare and educational systems accustomed to dealing only with mothers. Even when individuals are motivated to stretch the social boundaries of gender, social structure and institutions often impede them. Gender differentiation in our culture is embedded in social institutions: the family, of course, but also education, religion, politics, the economy, medicine, and the mass media.

Functionalists maintain that sex differentiation has contributed to overall social stability. Sociologists Talcott Parsons and Robert Bales (1955) argued that to function most efficiently, the family needs adults who will specialize in particular roles. They believed that the arrangement of gender roles with which they were familiar had arisen because marital partners needed a division of labor.

The functionalist view is initially persuasive in explaining the way in which women and men are typically brought up in U.S. society. However, it would lead us to expect even girls and women with no interest in children to still become babysitters and mothers. Similarly, males with a caring feeling for children may be "programmed" into careers in the business world. Clearly, such a differentiation between the sexes can have harmful consequences for the person who does not fit into specific roles, while depriving society of the optimal use of many talented people who are confined by sexual labeling. Consequently, the conflict perspective is increasingly convincing in its analysis of the development of gender roles (Taylor, Rupp, and Whittier 2009).

Conflict theorists do not deny the presence of a differentiation by sex. In fact, they contend that the relationship between females and males has been one of unequal power, with men being dominant over women. Men may have become powerful in preindustrial times because their size, physical strength, and freedom from childbearing duties allowed them to dominate women physically. In contemporary societies, such considerations are not as important, yet cultural beliefs about the sexes are now long established.

Three women on the Supreme Court looks impressive but is less so when one realizes only four have ever served in the history of the United States among the 112 justices that have served.

Both functionalists and conflict theorists acknowledge that it is not possible to change gender roles drastically without dramatic revisions in a culture's social structure. Functionalists see potential social disorder, or at least unknown social consequences, if all aspects of traditional sex differentiation are disturbed. Yet for conflict theorists, no social structure is ultimately desirable if it has to be maintained through the oppression of its citizens.

15-3

The Feminist Movement

Women's struggle for equality, like the struggles of other subordinate groups, has been long and multifaceted. From the very beginning, women activists and sympathetic men who spoke of equal rights were ridiculed and scorned.

15-3 Summarize the feminist movement.

In a formal sense, the American feminist movement was born in upstate New York in a town called Seneca Falls in the summer of 1848. On July 19, the first women's rights convention began, attended by Elizabeth Cady Stanton, Lucretia Mott, and other pioneers in the struggle for women's rights. This first wave of feminists, as they are currently known, battled ridicule and scorn as they fought for legal and political equality for women, but they were not afraid to risk controversy on behalf of their cause. In 1872, for example, Susan B. Anthony was arrested for attempting to vote in that year's presidential election.

The Suffrage Movement

The **suffragists** worked for years to get women the right to vote. From the beginning, this reform was judged to be crucial. If women voted, it was felt, other reforms would quickly follow. The struggle took so long that many of the initial advocates of women's suffrage died before victory was reached. In 1879, an amendment to the Constitution was introduced that would have given women the right to vote. Not until 1919 was it finally passed, and not until the next year was it ratified as the Nineteenth Amendment to the Constitution.

The opposition to giving women the vote came from all directions. Liquor interests and brewers correctly feared that women would assist in passing laws restricting or prohibiting the sale of their products. The South feared the influence that more Black voters (i.e., Black women) might have. Southerners had also not forgotten the pivotal role women had played in the abolitionist movement. Despite the opposition, the suffrage movement succeeded in gaining women the right to vote, a truly remarkable achievement because it had to rely on male legislators to do so.

The Nineteenth Amendment did not automatically lead to other feminist reforms. Women did not vote as a bloc and have not been elected to office in proportion to their numbers. The feminist movement as an organized effort that gained national attention faded, regaining prominence only in the 1960s. Nevertheless, the women's movement did not die out completely in the first half of the century. Many women carried on the struggle in new areas, such as the effort to lift restrictions on birth control devices (Freeman 1975; Stansell 2010).

The Women's Liberation Movement

Ideologically, the women's movement of the 1960s had its roots in the continuing informal feminist movement that began with the first subordination of women in Western society. Psychologically, it

Suffragists struggled for many years to convince Congress and the states to pass the Nineteenth Amendment to the Constitution, which they finally did, extending to women the right to vote beginning in 1920.

15-3

grew in America's kitchens, as women felt unfulfilled and did not know why, and in the labor force, as women were made to feel guilty because they were not at home with their families. Demographically, by the 1960s, women had attained greater control about when and whether to become pregnant if they used contraception.

Sociologically, several events delayed progress in the mid-1960s. The civil rights movement and the antiwar movement were slow to embrace women's rights. The New Left seemed as sexist as the rest of society in practice, despite its talk of equality. Groups protesting the draft and demonstrating on college campuses generally rejected women as leaders and assigned them traditional duties such as preparing refreshments and publishing organization newsletters. The core of early feminists often knew each other from participating in other protest or reform groups that had initially been unwilling to accept women's rights as a legitimate goal. Beginning in about 1967, as Chapter 7 showed, the movement for Black equality was no longer as willing to accept help from sympathetic Whites. White men moved on to protest the draft, a cause not as crucial to women's lives. Although somewhat involved in the antiwar movement, many White women began to struggle for their own rights, although at first they had to fight alone. Eventually, civil rights groups, the New Left, and most established women's groups endorsed the feminist movement with the zeal of new converts, but initially they resisted the concerns of feminists (Freeman 1973, 1983).

The movement has also brought about a reexamination of men's roles. Supporters of "male liberation" wanted to free men from the constraints of the masculine value system. The masculine mystique is as real as the feminine one. Boys are socialized to think that they should be invulnerable, fearless, decisive, and even emotionless in some situations. Men are expected to achieve physically and occupationally at some risk to their own values, not to mention those of others. Failure to take up these roles and attitudes can mean that a man will be considered less than a man. Male liberation is the logical counterpart of female liberation. If women are to redefine their gender role successfully, men must redefine theirs as workers, husbands, and fathers (Messner 1997; National Organization for Men Against Sexism 2011).

Amid the many changing concerns since the mid-1960s, the feminist movement too has undergone significant change. Betty Friedan, a founder of the National Organization for Women (NOW), argued in the early 1960s that women had to understand the **feminine mystique**, recognizing that society saw them only as their children's mother and their husband's wife. Later, in the 1980s, though not denying that women deserved to have the same options in life as men, she called for restructuring the "institution of home and wife." Friedan and others now recognize that many young women are frustrated when time does not permit them to do it all: career, marriage, and motherhood. Difficult issues remain, and feminists continue to discuss and debate concerns such as the limits businesses put on careers of women with children, domestic violence, and male bias in medical research (Coontz 2010; Friedan 1963, 1981, 1991).

Feminism Today

Feminism is an ideology establishing equal rights for women. In its long history, writers spoke of "wanes" as feminism stressed entry into the public life of politics and jobs, then added equality at home, respect for the body, the environment, and finally a 1998 cover of *Time* proclaimed "Is Feminism Dead?" articulating the public perspective that young women seem to take their improved status for granted and saw their mother's struggles no longer relevant.

Well, is feminism dead? Many feminists resent that question since it may imply that all the concerns facing women have been resolved. A national survey in 2013 show that about 23 percent of women (and 12 percent of men) accept the label "feminists." There is little evidence to indicate that younger women are less willing to self-label themselves as feminists. Perhaps more telling is that 32 percent of women and 42 percent of men think "feminist" has a negative connotation.

Today's feminists argue that they have moved well beyond the early charges that the movement was too obsessed with the concerns of the white middle-class and that African American feminists and others were marginalized. Indeed current polling shows African Americans and Latinos more likely to be self-proclaimed feminists. While recognizing legal and economic victories over the last 40 years, feminists today look to further advance equality in women' rights in non-industrial countries where discussions focus on malnutrition, starvation, extreme poverty, and violence (Breines 2007; Schnittker, Freese, and Powell 2003; Robison 2002; Swanson 2013).

The Economic Picture

The labor force has changed in terms of gender over the last 40 years in industrial nations. As shown dramatically in Figure 15.1, more and more women are participating in the labor force—that is, either seeking work or already employed.

He works. She works. They work in the same fields in the twenty-first century so they earn the same. Right? Wrong. As shown in Figure 15.2, in almost every major occupational classification, men earn more.

What about specific job titles? The U.S. Bureau of the Census looked at the earnings of 821 occupations ranging from chief executives to dishwashers, considering individuals' age, education, and work experience. The unmistakable conclusion was there is a substantial gap in median earnings between full-time male and female workers in the same occupation. He's an air traffic controller and makes $67,000. She earns $56,000. He's a housekeeper and makes $19,000. She earns $15,000. He's a teacher's assistant and makes $20,000. She earns $15,000. Men do not always earn more. The Census Bureau found two occupations out of 821 in which women typically earn about 1 percent more: hazardous materials recovery workers and telecommunications line installers (Weinberg 2004).

But it's different with high-status occupations, isn't it? No, concluded a 2011 study of the incomes of female and male physicians. Typically female physicians' starting salaries were

15-4 Discuss the women's economic situation.

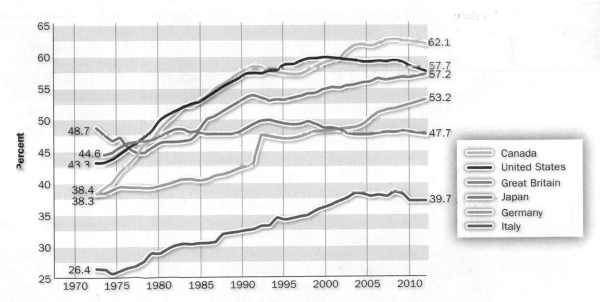

FIGURE 15.1

Women's Labor Force Participation: International Comparisons

In the United States, as with many other industrial nations, women are increasingly participating in the labor force by either working or seeking employment.

Source: Developed by author based on data in Department of Labor 2011, 2013c.

15-4

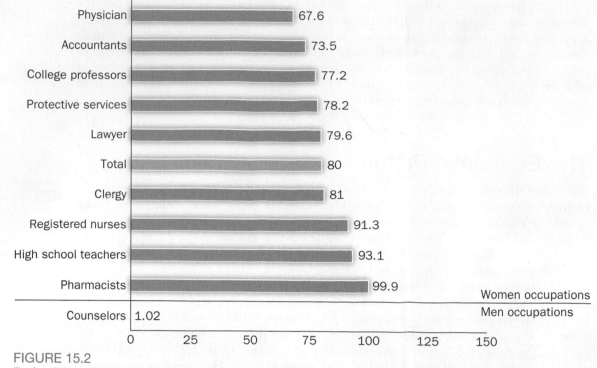

FIGURE 15.2
Ratio of Women's to Men's Earnings by Occupation

Note: Wage data for full-time workers in 2012. Protective services includes police, detectives, firefighters, correctional officers, and security guards.

Source: Developed by author based on data in Department of Labor 2013d: Table 39.

$17,000 a year *lower* than their male counterparts. This annual discrepancy keeps growing with each new survey. And this is not because women tend to go into lower-paying specialties. First, they are not more likely to go into pediatrics than heart surgery than their male counterparts. Second, even controlling for field, women make less. Well-compensated cardiologists make $228,000 if male, $205,000 if female. Even controlling for practice setting, work hours, or other possible factors, the salary gap persists (LoSasso et al. 2011).

Another aspect of women's subordinate status is that more than any other group, they are confined to certain occupations. **Occupational segregation** by gender is the tendency for men and women to be employed in different occupations from each other. Some gender-typed jobs for women pay well above the minimum wage and carry moderate prestige, such as nursing and teaching. Nevertheless, they are far lower in pay and prestige than such stereotyped male positions as physician, college president, and university professor. When they do enter nontraditional positions, as we have seen, women as a group receive lower wages or salaries.

The data in Table 15.1 present an overall view of the male dominance of high-paying occupations. Among the representative occupations chosen, men unquestionably dominate in those that pay well. Women dominate as receptionists, seamstresses, healthcare workers, and domestic workers.

Trends show the proportions of women increasing slightly in the professions, indicating that some women have advanced into better-paying positions, but these gains have not significantly changed the overall picture. Evidence indicates that professions are developing more of a gender balance but women continue to be at a disadvantage (Wallace and Kay 2012). The gains made by women in management, limited as they are relative to men, have placed more females in leadership positions. However as indicated in the Research Focus, this development is not necessarily welcomed by other women workers.

Women's earnings have increased significantly over the last quarter century. However, so have the earnings of men. The female–male wage gap has narrowed from women's

TABLE 15.1
Women as a Percentage of All Workers in Selected Occupations, 1950–2012

Occupation	1950	1980	2012
PROFESSIONAL WORKERS (%)			
Accountants	14.9	36.2	60.9
Engineers	1.2	4.0	13.7
Lawyers	4.1	12.8	31.1
Physicians	6.5	12.9	34.3
Registered nurses	97.8	96.5	90.6
College professors	22.8	33.9	48.2
OTHER OCCUPATIONS (%)			
Carpenters	0.4	1.5	1.6
Protective services (firefighters, police officers, guards)	2.0	9.5	20.1
Retail salespersons	48.9	45.3	50.2
Cashiers	81.7	86.6	71.8
Bookkeepers	77.7	90.5	89.1
Food preparation workers	61.6	66.9	58.0
Private household workers	94.9	97.5	88.1

Source: Developed by author based on data in Bureau of the Census 1951: table 218, 1981: Table 675, Bureau of Labor Statistics 2013b: Table 10.

weekly earnings being just over 59 cents on the dollar earned by men in the 1970s to about 80 cents in 2012. One cannot assume that the trend will continue at the same rate, because much of the narrowing of the gap actually has to do with men's wages leveling off so that women's very modest increases have come closer to matching their male counterparts, while still remaining 20 percent behind (Department of Labor 2013d; Stone 2009).

Inequality between women and men is a worldwide social phenomenon. In the Global View we look at the gender divide in Japan.

Research Focus

Give Me a Male Boss

As women more than doubled their presence in the managerial ranks from 19.7 percent in 1972 to 43.6 percent in 2012 the desirability of having a male supervisor became a topic of casual conversation. Numerous studies suggest that compared to all the other social factors present in the workplace, the boss's gender has little effect on the nature and quality of the manger–employee relationship. However, that fact does not prevent potential workers—male or female—from preferring a male boss. National opinion polls consistently show that in general—that is, without reference to particular people—workers prefer to take orders from a man by a two-to one margin. If anything, women are more likely than men to prefer a male supervisor.

This preference is so strong that many people are willing to accept less pay to get a male boss. Researchers at the University of Chicago's business school asked college students who were about to graduate to consider hypothetical job opportunities at consulting firms. The positions varied in terms of their starting salary, location, paid holidays, and the boss's sex. The results showed that students' choices matched their stated preferences for salary, location, and holidays. Surprisingly, the boss's sex turned out to be a far more important variable than the other three, whether students were male or female. In a variety of scenarios describing both salary and the boss's characteristics, students chose to take a 22 percent reduction in starting salary to get a male boss.

Many had hoped that the rise of women to management would be accompanied by a surge in mentoring the next generation. But instead, it has led some to talk of a "queen bee syndrome" where women who have struggled up the corporate ladder see their female subordinates as just not good enough. Some observers note that male managers do the same and it is wrong to expect women in management to act differently.

Sources: Bureau of the Census 2009a; Bureau of Labor Statistics 2003, 2013b; Caruso, Rahnev, and Banaji 2009; Gibbs 2009:31; Whittaker 2006.

15-4

🌐 A Global View

Gender Inequality in Japan

Gender inequality is not difficult to document in Japan. With the world's highest literacy rate and high school enrollment rate for women, half of Japanese quit their jobs upon getting married. Women who do work earn only about 70 percent of men's wages. Only about 9 percent of Japanese managers are female—a ratio that is one of the lowest in the world. Even in developing countries, women are twice as likely to be managers as women in Japan.

It is not hard to understand since until after World War II, women could not vote, and had little say on where to live compared to their husbands. Women were given the right to vote but in the workforce the assumption persisted that they would leave the labor force upon getting married to apply themselves to maintaining the home and preparing for the inevitable arrival of children.

In 1985, Japan's parliament—at the time, 97 percent male—passed an Equal Employment bill that encourages employers to end sex discrimination in hiring, assignment, and promotion policies. However, feminist organizations were dissatisfied because the law lacked strong sanctions. In a landmark ruling issued in late 1996, a Japanese court for the first time held an employer liable for denying promotions due to sex discrimination.

Has this made a difference? Labor force participation has increased but it has largely been in part-time positions where women account for 70 percent of such workers. Women in full-time positions have moved up the occupational hierarchy a bit but mainly through delaying marriage or not marrying at all. Once married, college-educated Japanese women, whether they are mothers or not, follow previous generations, leaving the labor force except perhaps for part-time employment.

Recent recessions and the 2011 tsunami and nuclear power plant disasters notwithstanding, Japanese corporations admit they need a skilled labor force including women. Of the total number of managers heading larger departments, women made up 2.5 percent. In contrast, around 4 percent of corporate managers are women in other advanced countries, such as the United States and Germany. Research shows that employers typically exclude women in advance from jobs that provide higher wages.

Progress has also been made in terms of public opinion. In 1987, 43 percent of Japanese adults agree that married women should stay home, but by 2000 the proportion had dropped to 25 percent. On the political front, Japanese women have made progress but remain vastly underrepresented. In a 2013 study of women in government around the world, Japan ranked 159th of 189 of the countries studied, with only 8.1 percent of its national legislators female.

Given the situation, even if it improving a bit, women in Japan have increasingly begun to start their own businesses. This is a tactic similar to minorities in the United States who when blocked at the usual entry points to economic success literally create their own new entry points. While start-up money is important, aspiring businesswomen are finding training and mentoring by female entrepreneurs as invaluable.

Sources: Abe 2011; Aguirre et al. 2012:52–53, Ehara 2005; French 2003; Fujimoto 2004; Goodman and Kashiwagi 2002; Inter-Parliamentary Union 2013; Kambayashi 2013; *Kyodo News* 2010; Mun 2010, Raymo and Lim 2011.

Sources of Discrimination

If we return to the definition of discrimination cited earlier, are not men better able to perform some tasks than women, and vice versa? If ability means performance, there certainly are differences. The typical woman can sew better than the typical man, but the latter can toss a ball farther than the former. These are group differences. Certainly, many women out throw many men, and many men out sew many women, but society expects women to excel at sewing and men to excel at throwing. The differences in those abilities result from cultural conditioning. Women usually are taught to sew, and men are less likely to learn such a skill. Men are encouraged to participate in sports that require the ability to throw a ball much more than are women. True, as a group, males have greater potential for the muscular development needed to throw a ball, but U.S. society encourages men to realize their potential in this area more than it encourages women to pursue athletic skills.

Today's labor market involves much more than throwing a ball and using a needle and thread, but the analogy to these two skills is repeated time and again. Such examples are used to support sexist practices in all aspects of the workplace. Just as African Americans can suffer from both individual acts of racism and institutional discrimination, women are vulnerable to both sexism and institutional discrimination. Women are subject to direct sexism, such as sexist remarks, and also to differential treatment because of institutional policies.

Removing barriers to equal opportunity would eventually eliminate institutional discrimination. Theoretically, men and women would sew and throw a ball equally well. We say "theoretically" because cultural conditioning would take generations to change. In some formerly male jobs, such as gas station clerk and attendant, society seems quite willing to accept women. In other occupations, such as President of the United States, it will take longer; many years may pass before full acceptance can be expected in other fields such as professional contact sports.

Many efforts have been made to eliminate institutional discrimination as it applies to women. The 1964 Civil Rights Act and its enforcement arm, the Equal Employment Opportunity Commission, address cases of sex discrimination. As we saw in Chapter 3, the inclusion of sex bias along with prejudice based on race, color, creed, and national origin was an unexpected last-minute change in the provisions of the landmark 1964 act. Federal legislation has not removed all discrimination against women in employment. The same explanations presented in Chapter 3 for the lag between the laws and reality in race discrimination apply to sex discrimination: lack of money, weak enforcement powers, occasionally weak commitment to using the laws available, and, most importantly, institutional and structural forces that perpetuate inequality.

What should be done to close the gap between the earnings of women and men? As shown in Figure 15.3, women earn more annually with more formal schooling, just like their male counterparts. However, as women continue their education, the wage gap does not narrow and even shows signs of growing.

In the 1980s, **pay equity**, or comparable worth, was a controversial solution presented to alleviate the second-class status of working women. It directly attempted to secure equal pay when occupational segregation by gender was particularly pervasive. Pay equity calls for equal pay for different types of work that are judged to be comparable by measuring such factors as employee knowledge, skills, effort, and responsibility.

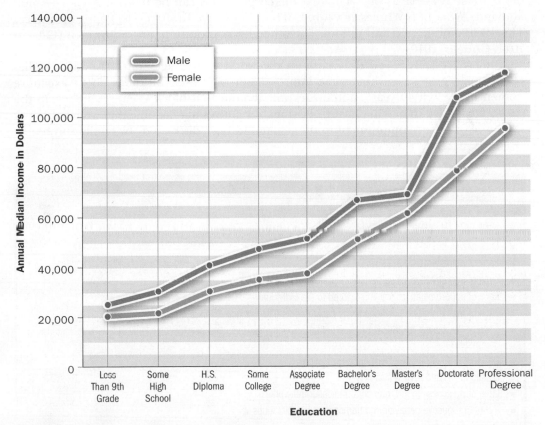

FIGURE 15.3

Financial Return on Education for Women and Men, 2012

Note: See Table 3.1.

Source: Developed by author based on data in DeNavas-Walt, Proctor, and Smith 2013:PINC-03.

15-4

This doctrine sounds straightforward, but it is not so simple to put into operation. How exactly does one determine the comparability of jobs to identify comparable worth? Should a zookeeper be paid more than a childcare worker? Does our society pay zookeepers more because we value caregiving for children less than for animals? Or do zookeepers earn more than childcare workers because the former tend to be male and the latter are generally female?

Despite some local initiatives, pay equity has not received much support in the United States except from the feminist movement. From a policy perspective, pay equity would have to broaden the 50-year-old Equal Pay Act and be initiated at the federal level. The Lily Ledbetter Fair Pay Act (see Chapter 3) still requires an individual or a group to initiate action alleging discrimination to mobilize much support. Also, employers can keep salary information secret and even prevent employees from sharing their own wage records. With the government backing away from affirmative action, it is unlikely to launch an initiative on pay equity conditions (National Committee on Pay Equity 2013; National Women's Law Center 2012).

What about women aspiring to crack the glass ceiling? The phrase **glass ceiling**, as noted in Chapter 3 and illustrated in Figure 3.7, refers to the invisible barrier blocking the promotion of a qualified worker because of gender or minority membership. Despite continuing debate over affirmative action, the consensus is that there is little room at the top for women and minorities. The glass ceiling operates so that all applicants may be welcomed by a firm, but when it comes to the powerful or more visible positions, there are limits—generally unstated—on the number of women and non-Whites welcomed or even tolerated (Table 15.2).

Women are doing better in top-management positions than minorities, but they still lag well behind men, according to a study that showed that women held only 15 percent of the director seats of the largest corporations. As for CEOs of the Fortune 500, there are so few—12 as of 2011—that the corporations can be named: Archer Daniels Midland, Avon, BJ'S Wholesale Club, DuPont, Key Corp, Kraft Foods, PepsiCo, Sunoco, TJX, WellPoint, Xerox, and Yahoo!. The other 488 corporations are led by men (Catalyst 2011; Crumley 2010).

Women are still viewed differently in the world of management. Although studies of top male executives show some improvement over their attitudes about executive women in the last 40 years, stereotypes still abound that block women's ascent up the corporate ladder. In making hiring decisions, executives may assume that women are not serious about their commitment to the job and will be "distracted" by family and home.

TABLE 15.2
Major Barriers to Women's Executive Advancement

- Initial placement and clustering in dead-end staff jobs or highly technical professional jobs
- Lack of mentoring
- Lack of management training
- Lack of opportunities for career development
- Lack of opportunities for training tailored to the individual
- Lack of rotation to line positions or job assignments that produce revenue
- Little or no access to critical developmental assignments, including service on highly visible task forces and committees
- Different standards for performance evaluation
- Biased rating and testing systems
- Little or no access to informal communication networks
- Counterproductive behavior and harassment by colleagues

Source: Glass Ceiling Commission, cited in Department of Labor 1995:7–8.

They assume that women are on a **mommy track**, an unofficial career track that firms use for women who want to divide their attention between work and family. This assumption would be false if applied to all women. It also implies that corporate men are not interested in maintaining a balance between work and family. Even competitive, upwardly mobile women are not always taken seriously in the workplace (Carlson, Kacmar, and Whitten 2006; Heilman 2001; Schwartz and Zimmerman 1992).

Sexual Harassment

Under evolving legal standards, **sexual harassment** is recognized as any unwanted and unwelcome sexual advances that interfere with a person's ability to perform a job and enjoy the benefits of a job. Increased national attention was given to harassment in the 1990s and into the present through allegations made against elected officials and high-ranking military officers.

The most obvious example of sexual harassment is the boss who tells an employee, "Put out or get out!" However, the unwelcome advances that constitute sexual harassment may take the form of subtle pressures regarding sexual activity, inappropriate touching, attempted kissing, or sexual assault. Indeed, in the computer age, there is growing concern that sexually harassing messages are being sent anonymously over computer networks through e-mail and picture phones.

In 1986, in a unanimous decision (*Meritor Savings Bank v. Vinson*), the Supreme Court declared that sexual harassment by a supervisor violates the federal law against sex discrimination in the workplace as outlined in the 1964 Civil Rights Act. If sufficiently severe, harassment is a violation even if the unwelcome sexual demands are not linked to concrete employment benefits such as a raise or promotion. Women's groups hailed the court's decisiveness in identifying harassment as a form of discrimination. A federal judge subsequently ruled that the public display of photographs of nude and partly nude women at a workplace constitutes sexual harassment. Despite these rulings, it is very difficult legally and emotionally for a person to bring forward a case of sexual harassment (Domino 1995; Roscigno and Schmidt 2007).

Feminization of Poverty

Since World War II, an increasing proportion of the poor in the United States has been female; many of these poor Americans are divorced or never-married mothers. This alarming trend has come to be known as the **feminization of poverty**. In 2012, 11.8 percent of all families in the United States lived in poverty, but 30.9 percent of families headed by single mothers did so. Not only are female-headed families much more likely to be poor but also their income deficit relative to being non-poor is much greater than other types of poor families (DeNavas-Walt, Proctor, and Smith 2013:17).

Poor women share many social characteristics with poor men: low educational attainment, lack of market-relevant job skills, and residence in economically deteriorating areas. However, conflict theorists believe that the higher rates of poverty among women can be traced to two distinct causes: Sex discrimination and sexual harassment on the job place women at a clear disadvantage when seeking vertical social mobility.

The burden of supporting a family is especially difficult for single mothers, not only because of low salaries but also because of inadequate child support. The average child-support payment reported in 2011 (for money collected in 2007) for the 40 percent who received the *full* award was a mere $110 per week. This level of support is clearly insufficient for rearing a child in the early twenty-first century. In light of these data, federal and state officials have intensified efforts to track down delinquent spouses and ensure the payment of child support: nearly 16 million cases were under investigation in 2006 (Bureau of the Census 2010c:Table 566).

15-5

According to a study based on census data by the advocacy group Women Work, families headed by single mothers and displaced homemakers are four times as likely to live in poverty as other households in the United States. **Displaced homemakers** are defined as women whose primary occupation had been homemaking but who did not find full-time employment after being divorced, separated, or widowed. Single mothers and displaced homemakers tend to work in service jobs, which offer low wages, few benefits, part-time work, and little job security. Moreover, single mothers and displaced homemakers are also more likely to have an unstable housing situation, including frequent changes of residence (Women Work 2011).

Many feminists feel that the continuing dominance of the political system by men contributes to government indifference to the problem of poor women. As more and more women fall below the official poverty line, policymakers will face growing pressure to combat the feminization of poverty.

Education

15-5 Describe the experience of women in education.

The experience of women in education has been similar to their experience in the labor force: a long history of contribution but in traditionally defined terms. In 1833, Oberlin College became the first institution of higher learning to admit women, two centuries after the first men's college began in this country. In 1837, Wellesley became the first women's college. But it would be a mistake to believe that these early experiments brought about equality for women in education: at Oberlin, the women were forbidden to speak in public. Furthermore,

> *Washing the men's clothes, caring for their rooms, serving them at table, listening to their orations, but themselves remaining respectfully silent in public assemblages, the Oberlin "coeds" were being prepared for intelligent motherhood and a properly subservient wifehood. (Flexner 1959:30)*

The early graduates of these schools, despite the emphasis in the curriculum on traditional roles, became the founders of the feminist movement.

Today, research confirms that boys and girls are treated differently in school: teachers give boys more attention. In teaching students the values and customs of the larger society, schools in the United States have treated children as if men's education were more important than that of women. Professors of education Myra and David Sadker (2003) documented this persistence of classroom sexism: the researchers noted that boys receive more teacher attention than girls, mainly because they call out in class eight times more often. Teachers praise boys more than girls and offer boys more academic assistance.

Interestingly, they found that this differential treatment was present in both male and female teachers.

Despite these challenges, in many communities across the nation, girls seem to outdo boys in high school, grabbing a disproportionate share of the leadership positions, from valedictorian to class president to yearbook editor—everything, in short, except captain of the boys' athletic teams. Their advantage numerically seems to be continuing after high school. In the 1980s, girls in the United States became more likely than boys to go to college. Women accounted for more than 56 percent of college students nationwide. And in 2002, for the first time, more women than men in the United States earned doctoral degrees.

At all levels of schooling, significant changes also occurred with congressional amendments to the Education Act of 1972 and the Department of Health,

Education, and Welfare guidelines developed in 1974 and 1975. Collectively called Title IX provisions, the regulations are designed to eliminate sexist practices from almost all school systems. Schools must make these changes or risk the loss of all federal assistance:

1. Schools must eliminate all sex-segregated classes and extracurricular activities.

2. Schools cannot discriminate by sex in admissions or financial aid and cannot inquire into whether an applicant is married, pregnant, or a parent. Single-sex schools are exempted.

3. Schools must end sexist hiring and promotion practices among faculty members.

4. Although women do not have to be permitted to play on all-men's athletic teams, schools must provide more opportunities for women's sports, intramural and extramural.

Title IX became one of the more controversial steps ever taken by the federal government to promote and ensure equality.

Efforts to bring gender equity to sports have been attacked as excessive. The consequences have not fully been intended: for example, colleges have often cut men's sports rather than build up women's sports. Also, most of the sports with generous college scholarships added for women are in athletic fields that have not been traditionally attractive to minority women. Yet the number of girls participating in high school athletics has jumped from 300,000 in 1972 at the time of the passage of Title IX to over 3.2 million in 2013 (Suggs 2002; *Economist* 2013b).

Family Life

Our society generally equates work with wages and holds unpaid work in low esteem. Women who do household chores and volunteer work are given little status in our society. Typically, this unrecognized labor is done on top of wage labor in the formal economy. These demands traditionally placed on a mother and homemaker are so extensive that simultaneously pursuing a career is extremely difficult. For women, the family is, according to sociologists Lewis Coser and Rose Laub Coser (1974), a "greedy institution." More recently, other social scientists have also observed the overwhelming burden of the multiple social roles associated with being a mother and working outside the home.

15-6 Explain gender as it relates to the family.

15-6

Childcare and Housework

A man can act as a homemaker and caregiver for children, but in the United States, women customarily perform these roles. Studies indicate that men do not even think about their children as much as women do. Sociologist Susan Walzer (1996) was interested in whether there are gender differences in the amount of time that parents spend thinking about the care of their children. Drawing on interviews, Walzer found that mothers are much more involved than fathers in the invisible mental labor associated with taking care of a baby. For example, while involved in work outside the home, mothers are more likely to think about their babies and to feel guilty later if they become so consumed with the demands of their jobs that they fail to think about their babies.

Juggling work and home is an equal opportunity challenge. The majority of both working mothers and working fathers report that it is somewhat or very difficult to balance the responsibilities of their job and their family. This is not surprising since only 16 percent of mothers and fathers in 2012 felt that the ideal situation for young children is to have a mother who works full time (Parker and Wang 2013).

Sociologist Arlie Hochschild has used the term **second shift** to describe the double burden—work outside the home followed by childcare and housework—that many women face and that few men share equitably. As shown in Figure 15.4, this issue has become increasingly important as greater proportions of mothers work outside the home. On the basis of interviews with and observations of 52 couples over an eight-year period, Hochschild reports that the wives (and not their husbands) planned domestic schedules and play dates for children while driving home from the office and then began their second shift (Hochschild 1990; Hochschild and Machung 1989).

Hochschild found that the married couples she studied were fraying at the edges psychologically and so were their careers and their marriages. The women she spoke with hardly resembled the beautiful young businesswomen pictured in magazine advertisements, dressed in power suits but with frilled blouses, holding briefcases in one hand and happy young children in the other. Instead, many of Hochschild's female subjects talked about being overtired and emotionally drained by the demands of their multiple roles. They were much more intensely torn by the conflicting demands of work outside the home and family life than were their husbands. Hochschild (1990:73) concludes that "if we as a culture come to see the urgent need of meeting the new problems posed by the second shift, and if society and government begin to shape new policies that allow working parents more flexibility, then we will be making some progress toward happier times at home and at work." Many feminists share this view.

There is an economic cost to this second shift. Households do benefit from the free labor of women, but women pay what has been called the **mommy tax**: the lower salaries women receive over their lifetime because they have children. Mothers earn less than men and other women over their lifetime because having children causes them to lose job experience, trade higher wages for following the mommy track, and are discriminated against by employers. How high is this mommy tax? Estimates range from 5 to 13 percent of lifetime wages for the first child alone. Having two children lowers earnings 10–19 percent. There is no denying that motherhood and the labor market are intertwined. While the mommy tax is not unique to the USA, cross-national comparisons show the mommy tax to be greater in the United States compared with what women face in countries that have expansive publicly financed child care systems (Budig and Misra 2010; Coontz 2013).

Family and work continue to present challenges to women and men in the twenty-first century. Sociologist Kathleen Gerson contends in the Speaking Out that the workplace is still not adequately meeting the needs of parents.

15-6

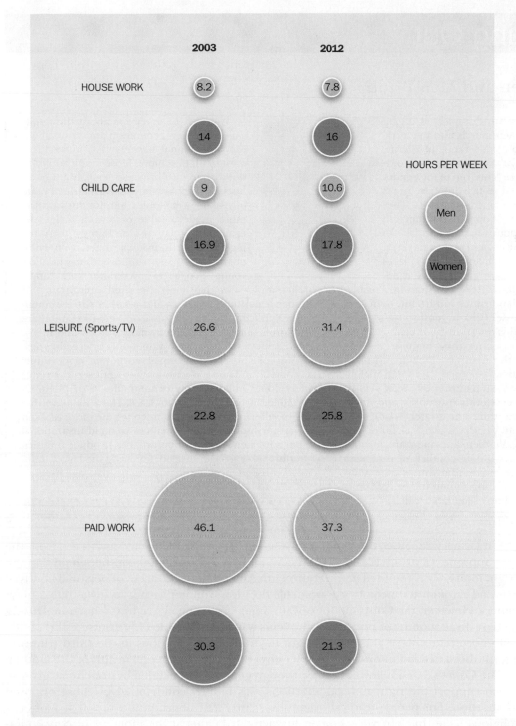

FIGURE 15.4
Chore Wars

Note: Data from American Time Use Survey based on primary activities.

Source: Developed by author based on data in Bureau of Labor Statistics 2004: Table 6, 2013c: Table 8.

Abortion

A particularly controversial subject affecting family life in the United States has been the call for women to have greater control over their bodies, especially their reproductive lives, through contraceptive devices and the increased availability of abortions. Abortion law reform was one of the demands NOW made in 1967, and the controversy continues despite many court rulings and the passage of laws at every level of government.

15-6

(🎙) Speaking Out

What Do Women and Men Want?

Young workers today grew up in rapidly changing times: They watched women march into the workplace and adults develop a wide range of alternatives to traditional marriage. Now making their own passage to adulthood, these "children of the gender revolution" have inherited a far different world from that of their parents or grandparents. They may enjoy an expanded set of options, but they also face rising uncertainty about whether and how to craft a marriage, rear children, and build a career....

If the realities of time-demanding workplaces and missing supports for care giving make it difficult for young adults to achieve the sharing, flexible, and more egalitarian relationships most want, then how can we get past this impasse? Clearly, most young women are not likely to answer this question by returning to patterns that fail to speak to either their highest ideals or their greatest fears. To the contrary, they are forming fallback strategies that stress personal autonomy, including the possibility of single parenthood. Men's most common responses to economic pressures and time-demanding jobs stress a different strategy—one that allows for two incomes but preserves men's claim on the most rewarding careers. Women and men are leaning in different directions, and their conflicting responses are fueling a new gender divide. But this schism stems from the intensification of long-simmering work/family dilemmas, not from a decline of laudable values.

Kathleen Gerson

We need to worry less about the family values of a new generation and more about the institutional barriers that make them so difficult to achieve. Most young adults do not wish to turn back the clock, but they do hope to combine the more traditional value of making a lifelong commitment with the more modern value of having a flexible, egalitarian relationship. Rather than trying to change individual values, we need to provide the social supports that will allow young people to overcome work/family conflicts and realize their most cherished aspirations.

Since a mother's earnings and a father's involvement are both integral to the economic and emotional welfare of children (and also desired by most women and men), we can achieve the best family values only by creating flexible workplaces, ensuring equal economic opportunity for women, outlawing discrimination against all parents, and building child-friendly communities with plentiful, affordable, and high-quality childcare. These long-overdue policies will help new generations create the more egalitarian partnerships they desire. Failure to build institutional supports for new social realities will not produce a return to traditional marriage. Instead, following the law of unintended consequences, it will undermine marriage itself.

Source: Gerson 2007: A8, A11.

On January 22, 1973, the feminist movement received unexpected assistance from the U.S. Supreme Court in its *Roe v. Wade* decision. By a 7–2 margin, the justices held that the "right to privacy... founded in the Fourteenth Amendment's concept of personal liberty... is broad enough to encompass a woman's decision whether or not to terminate a pregnancy." However, the Court did set certain limits on a woman's right to abortion. During the last three months of pregnancy, the fetus was ruled capable of life outside the womb. Therefore, states were granted the right to prohibit all abortions in the third trimester except those needed to preserve the life, physical health, or mental health of the mother.

The Court's decision in *Roe v. Wade*, though generally applauded by pro-choice groups, which support the right to legal abortions, was bitterly condemned by those opposed to abortion. For people who call themselves "pro-life," abortion is a moral and often a religious issue. In their view, human life actually begins at the moment of conception rather than when the fetus could stay alive outside the womb. On the basis of this belief, the fetus is a human, not merely a potential life. Termination of this human's life, even before it has left the womb, is viewed as an act of murder. Consequently, antiabortion activists are alarmed by the more than 1 million legal abortions carried out each year in the United States (Luker 1984).

The early 1990s brought an escalation of violent antiabortion protests. Finally, a 1994 federal law made it a crime to use force or threats or to obstruct, injure, or interfere with anyone providing or receiving abortions and other reproductive health services. In a 6–3 decision, the Supreme Court's majority upheld the constitutionality of a 36-foot buffer zone that keeps antiabortion protesters away from a clinic's entrance and parking lot. Abortion remains a disputed issue both in society and in the courts. The law has apparently had some impact, but acts of violence, including deaths of clinic workers and physicians, continue.

In terms of social class, the first major restriction on the legal right to terminate a pregnancy affected poor people. In 1976, Congress passed the Hyde Amendment, which banned the use of Medicaid and other federal funds for abortions. The Supreme Court upheld this legislation in 1980. State laws also restrict the use of public funds for abortions. Another obstacle facing the poor is access to abortion providers: in the face of vocal pro-life public sentiment, fewer and fewer hospitals throughout the world are allowing their physicians to perform abortions, except in extreme cases. Only about 13 percent of counties in the United States have even one provider who is able and willing to perform abortions (Blow 2010; Jones et al. 2008).

Political Activity

Women in the United States constitute 53 percent of the voting population and 49 percent of the labor force but only 8 percent of those who hold high government positions. As of the beginning of 2014, Congress included only 80 women (out of 435 members) in the House of Representatives and only 20 women (out of 100 members) in the Senate. The number of women serving in Congress has steadily increased. Only five states—Arizona, New Hampshire, New Mexico, Oklahoma, and South Carolina—had a woman governor at the beginning of 2014. In national elections women tend to vote less Republican than men. In 2008, 56 percent of women backed Barack Obama, the largest swing toward the Democrat presidential nominee during the last ten elections (Connelly 2008).

The low number of women officeholders until recently has not resulted from women's inactivity in politics. About the same proportion of eligible women and men vote in presidential elections. The League of Women Voters, founded in 1920, performs a valuable function in educating the electorate of both sexes, publishing newsletters describing candidates' positions, and holding debates among candidates. Perhaps women's most visible role in politics until recently has been as unpaid campaign workers for male candidates: doorbell ringers, telephone callers, newsletter printers, and petition carriers.

Runs for elective office in the 1990s showed women overcoming one of their last barriers to electoral office: attracting campaign funds. Running for office is very expensive, and women candidates have begun to convince backers to invest in their political future. Their success as fundraisers will also contribute to women's acceptance as serious candidates in the future.

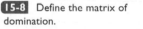
15-7 Describe women's role in politics.

15-8 Define the matrix of domination.

Matrix of Domination: Minority Women

Many women experience differential treatment not only because of their gender but also because of race and ethnicity. These citizens face a subordinate status twice defined. They are not separate, but coexist as intersecting identities. A disproportionate share of this low-status group also is poor. African American feminist Patricia Hill Collins (2000, 2013:232–234) has termed this the **matrix of domination** (Figure 15.5). Whites dominate non-Whites, men dominate women, and the affluent dominate the poor—race, class, and gender are interconnected.

Gender, race, and social class are not the only systems of oppression, but they do profoundly affect women and people of color in the United States. Other forms of categorization and stigmatization can also be included in this matrix, such as sexual identity, religion, disability status, and age. If we turn to a global stage, we can add citizenship status and being perceived as a "colonial subject" even after colonialism has ended (Winant 2006).

Feminists have addressed themselves to the needs of minority women, but the oppression of these women because of their sex is overshadowed by the subordinate status that both White men and White women impose on them because of their race or ethnicity. The question for the Latina (Hispanic woman), African American woman, Asian American woman, Native American woman, and so on appears to be whether she should unify with her brothers against racism or challenge them for their sexism.

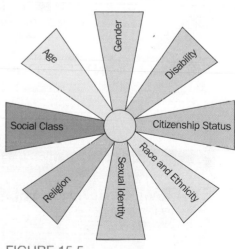

FIGURE 15.5
Matrix of Domination

The matrix of domination illustrates how several social factors—including gender, social class, and race and ethnicity—intersect to create a cumulative impact on a person's social standing.

15-8

Few women head a Fortune 500 corporation and almost no minority women reach those rarified heights. Xerox Corporation's Ursula Burns is the only African American woman to head such a corporation. She is also the first woman CEO of a top 500 to succeed another woman. Educated as a mechanical engineer, she began at Xerox as a summer intern in 1980 and rose to chief executive officer in 2009.

The answer is that society cannot afford to let up on the effort to eradicate sexism and racism as well as other forces that stigmatize and oppress (Beisel and Kay 2004; Breines 2007; Coontz 2010; Epstein 1999).

The discussion of gender roles among African Americans has always provoked controversy. Advocates of Black Nationalism contend that feminism only distracts women from full participation in the African American struggle. The existence of feminist groups among Blacks, in their view, simply divides the Black community and thereby serves the dominant White society. By contrast, Black feminists such as bell 0s (2004) argue that little is to be gained by accepting the gender-role divisions of the dominant society that place women in a separate, subservient position. African American journalist Patricia Raybon (1989) has noted that the media commonly portray Black women in a negative light: as illiterates, as welfare mothers, as prostitutes, and so forth. Black feminists emphasize that it is not solely Whites and White-dominated media that focus on these negative images; Black men (most recently, Black male rap artists) have also been criticized for the way they portray African American women (Threadcraft 2008; Wilkins 2012).

Native Americans stand out as a historical exception to the North American patriarchal tradition. At the time of the arrival of the European settlers, gender roles varied greatly from tribe to tribe. Southern tribes, for reasons unclear to today's scholars, usually were matriarchal and traced descent through the mother. European missionaries sought to make the native peoples more like the Europeans, and this aim included transforming women's role. Some Native American women, like members of other groups, have resisted gender stereotypes (Marubbio 2006).

The plight of Latinas usually is considered part of either the Hispanic or feminist movements, and the distinctive experience of Latinas is ignored. In the past, they have been excluded from decision making in the two social institutions that most affect their daily lives: the family and the Church. The Hispanic family, especially in the lower class, feels the

SPECTRUM OF INTERGROUP RELATIONS

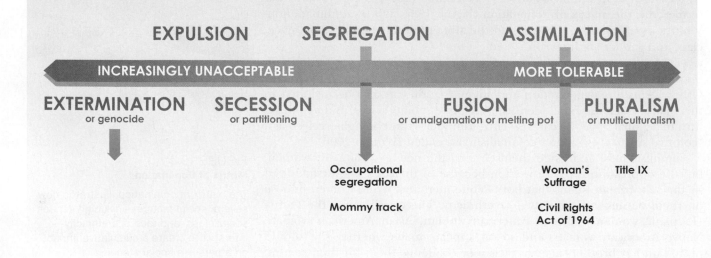

EXPULSION   SEGREGATION   ASSIMILATION

INCREASINGLY UNACCEPTABLE   MORE TOLERABLE

EXTERMINATION
or genocide

SECESSION
or partitioning

FUSION
or amalgamation or melting pot

PLURALISM
or multiculturalism

Occupational
segregation

Woman's
Suffrage

Title IX

Mommy track

Civil Rights
Act of 1964

pervasive tradition of male domination. The Catholic Church relegates women to support-ive roles while reserving for men the leadership positions (Browne 2001; De Anda 2004).

By considering the matrix of domination, we recognize how much of our discus-sion has focused on race and ethnicity coupled with data on poverty, low incomes, and meager wealth. Drawing upon this intersection of identities, we consider what Spectrum of Intergroup Relations would look for women and men. We recognize that issues of gender domination must be included to fully understand what women of color experience.

Conclusion

Women and men are expected to perform, or at least to prefer to perform, specific tasks in society. The appropri-ateness to one gender of all but a very few of these tasks cannot be justified by the biological differences between females and males any more than differential treatment based on race can be justified. Psychologists Sandra Bem and Daryl Bem (1970:99) made the following analogy a generation ago that still may have applicability today.

Suppose that a White male college student decided to room with a Black male friend. The typical White student would not blithely assume that his roommate was better suited to handle all domestic chores. Nor should his conscience allow him to do so even in the unlikely event that his room-mate said, "No, that's okay. I like doing housework. I'd be happy to do it." We would suspect that the White student would still feel uncomfortable about taking advantage of the fact that his roommate has simply been socialized to

be "happy with such an arrangement." But change this hypothetical Black roommate to a female marriage partner, and the student's conscience goes to sleep.

The feminist movement has awakened women and men to assumptions based on sex and gender. New oppor-tunities for the sexes require the same commitment from individuals and the government as those made to achieve equality between racial and ethnic groups.

Women are systematically disadvantaged in both employment and the family. Gender inequality is a seri-ous problem, just as racial inequality continues to be a sig-nificant social challenge. Separate, socially defined roles for men and women are not limited to the United States. Chapter 16 concentrates on the inequality of racial and ethnic groups in societies other than the United States. Just as sexism is not unique to this nation, neither is rac-ism nor religious intolerance.

Summary

1. Sociologists consider gender roles to be the expecta-tions of behavior.

2. Functionalists see role differences as contributing to carrying out family roles whereas conflict theorists argue they contribute to inequality between men and women.

3. The feminist movement has deep roots in the nine-teenth century, and although many younger people today may avoid the label of feminist, the movement continues to work for parity between men and women.

4. The labor force is characterized by occupation seg-regation by gender and significant differential in earnings for men and women working in the same occupations. A pattern of increasing poverty among single women has led to the feminization of poverty.

5. Women have encountered great success in formal schooling. Title IX is helping to eliminate inequities, especially in school athletic programs.

6. Men have increasingly accepted responsibilities for housework and childcare, but women continue to assume more responsibility, leading to a phenom-enon referred to as the *second shift*.

7. Despite highly public female politicians, the vast majority of elected officials in the United States, especially at the national level, are men.

8. Gender is only one basis for the unequal treatment that women experience; this leads to a formulation called the *matrix of domination* that considers a variety of social dimensions.

Key Terms

androgyny, p. 325

displaced homemakers, p. 336

feminine mystique, p. 328

feminism, p. 328

feminization of poverty, p. 335

gender roles, p. 325

glass ceiling, p. 334

matrix of domination, p. 341

mommy tax, p. 338

mommy track, p. 335

occupational segregation, p. 330

pay equity, p. 333

second shift, p. 338

sexism, p. 324

sexual harassment, p. 335

suffragists, p. 327

Review Questions

1. Explain how gender is socially constructed.

2. What are sociological approaches to studying women as a minority?

3. How has the focus of the feminist movement changed from the suffragist movement to the present?

4. How do the patterns of women in the workplace differ from those of men?

5. Clarify the role that women play in formal education.

6. How has the changing role of women in the United States affected the family?

7. What are the special challenges facing women of subordinate racial and ethnic groups?

8. Illustrate what the matrix of domination means.

Critical Thinking

1. Women have many characteristics similar to those of minority groups, but what are some differences? For example, they are not segregated from men residentially.

2. How is women's subordinate position different from that of oppressed racial and ethnic groups? How is it similar?

3. Earlier in the 1990s, the phrase *angry white men* was used by some men who viewed themselves as victims. In what respect may men now see themselves as victims of reverse discrimination? Do you think these views are justified?

4. How are men and women's roles defined differently when it comes to such concepts as the mommy track, the second shift, and the displaced homemaker?

16 Beyond the United States: The Comparative Perspective

16-1 Summarize the diversity in Mexico.

16-2 Understand what is meant by multiculturalism in Canada.

16-3 Analyze to what degree Brazil is a racial paradise.

16-4 Explain the historical and contemporary tensions between Israel and Palestine.

16-5 Explain inequality in the Republic of South Africa.

16-1

Confrontations between racial and ethnic groups have escalated in frequency and intensity in the twentieth century and continuing into the twenty-first century. In surveying these conflicts, we can see two themes emerge: the previously considered world systems theory and ethnonational conflict. **World systems theory** considers the global economic system as divided between nations that control wealth and those that provide natural resources and labor. Historically, the nations we are considering reflect this competition between the "haves" and "have-nots." Whether the laborers are poor Catholics in Ireland or Black Africans, their contribution to the prosperity of the dominant group created the social inequality that people are trying to address today (Wallerstein 1974, 2004).

Ethnonational conflict refers to conflicts among ethnic, racial, religious, and linguistic groups within nations. In some areas of the world, ethnonational conflicts are more significant than tension between nations as the source of refugees and even death. As we can see in Figure 16.1, countries in all parts of the world, including the most populous nations, have significant diversity within their borders. These conflicts remind us that the processes operating in the United States to deny racial and ethnic groups rights and opportunities are also at work throughout the world (Connor 1994; Olzak 1998).

The sociological perspective on relations between dominant and subordinate groups treats race and ethnicity as social categories. As social concepts, they can be understood only in the context of the shared meanings attached to them by societies and their members. Although relationships between dominant and subordinate groups vary greatly, there are similarities across societies. Racial and ethnic hostilities

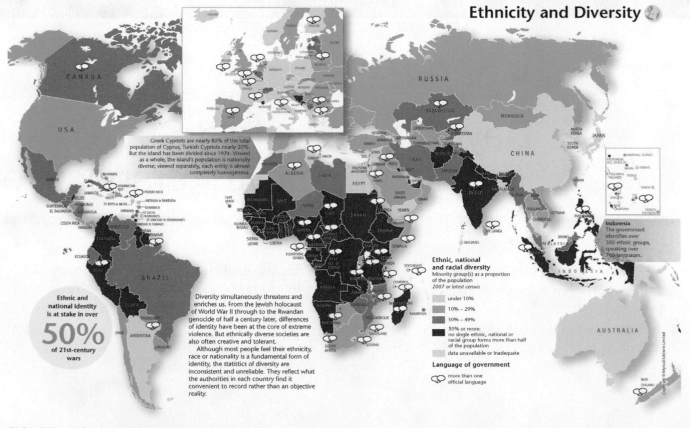

FIGURE 16.1
Ethnic Diversity Worldwide

Source: Smith 2008: 22–23.

arise out of economic needs and demands. These needs and demands may not always be realistic; that is, a group may seek out enemies where none exist or where victory will yield no rewards. Racial and ethnic conflicts are both the results and the precipitators of change in the economic and political sectors (Barclay, Kumar, and Simms 1976; Coser 1956).

Relations between dominant and subordinate groups differ from society to society, as this chapter shows. Intergroup relations in Mexico, Canada, Brazil, Israel, and South Africa are striking in their similarities and contrasts.

Mexico: Diversity South of the Border

Usually in the discussions of racial and ethnic relations, Mexico is considered only as a source of immigrants to the United States. In questions of economic development, Mexico again typically enters the discussion only as it affects our own economy. However, Mexico, a nation of 118 million people (in the Western hemisphere, only Brazil and the United States are larger) is an exceedingly complex nation (see Table 16.1). It is therefore appropriate that we understand Mexico and its issues of inequality better. This understanding will also shed light on the relationship of its people to the United States.

16-1 Summarize the diversity in Mexico.

TABLE 16.1
Five-Nation Comparison

Country	Population (in millions)	GNI per capita ($) (U.S. = $50,610)	Groups Represented	Current Nation's Formation
Mexico	117.6	16,630	Mexican Indians, 9%	1823: Republic of Mexico declared independence from Spain
Canada	35.3	42,690	French speaking, 13% Aboriginal peoples, 4% "Visible" minorities, 16%	1867: Unified as a colony of England 1948: Independence
Brazil	195.5	11,720	White, 48% Pardo (brown, moreno, mulatto), 39% Afro-Brazilians, 8% Asian and indigenous Indians, 1%	1889: Became independent of Portugal
Israel	8.1	28,070	Jews, 76% Arabs, 23%	1948: Independence from British mandate under United Nations
Palestinian Territories	4.0	4,247	Palestinians, 99% Others, 1% (Excluding Jewish settlements)	1999: Israel cedes authority under Oslo Accords
South Africa	53.0	11,190	Black Africans, 79% Whites, 9% Coloureds, 9% Asians, 3%	1948: Independence from Great Britain

Note: All data for 2010 or most resntly available.

Sources: Author estimates, based on Bourcier 2012; Canak and Swanson 1998; Central Intelligence Agency 2011; Haub and Kaneda 2013; Statistics Canada 2012; and sources in Table 16.2.

16-1

In the 1520s, Spain overthrew the Aztec Indian tribe that ruled Mexico. Mexico remained a Spanish colony until the 1820s. In 1836, Texas declared its independence from Mexico, and by 1846 Mexico was at war with the United States. As we described in Chapter 9, the Mexican–American War forced Mexico to surrender more than half of its territory. In the 1860s, France sought to turn Mexico into an empire under Austrian prince Maximilian but ultimately withdrew after bitter resistance led by a Mexican Indian, Benito Juárez, who later served as the nation's president.

The Mexican Indian People and the Color Gradient

In contemporary Mexico, a major need has been to reassess the relations between the indigenous peoples—the Mexican Indians, many descended from the Mayas, and the government of Mexico. In 1900, the majority of the Mexican population still spoke Indian languages and lived in closed, semi-isolated villages or tribal communities according to ancestral customs. Many of these people were not a part of the growing industrialization in Mexico and were not truly represented in the national legislature. Perhaps the major change for them in the twentieth century was that many intermarried with the descendants of the Europeans, forming a **mestizo** class of people of mixed ancestry. The term *mestizo* is used throughout the Americas to refer to people of mixed European (usually Spanish) and local indigenous ancestry. Mestizos have become increasingly identified with Mexico's growing middle class. They have developed their own distinct culture and, as the descendants of the European settlers are reduced in number and influence, have become the true bearers of the national Mexican sentiment.

Meanwhile, however, these social changes have left the Mexican Indian people even further behind the rest of the population economically. Indian cultures have been stereotyped as backward and resistant to progress and modern ways of living. Indeed, the existence of the many Indian cultures was seen in much of the twentieth century as an impediment to the development of a national culture in Mexico.

As noted in Chapter 9, a **color gradient** is the placement of people on a continuum from light to dark skin color rather than in distinct racial groupings by skin color. This is another example of the social construction of race, in which social class is linked to the social reality (or at least the appearance) of racial purity. An interesting result of the color gradient and a mestizo class is the belief that racism cannot exist in a racially mixed society. This is not true (Sue 2013).

At the top of this gradient or hierarchy are the *criollos,* the 10 percent of the population who are typically White, well-educated members of the business and intellectual elites with familial roots in Spain. In the middle is the large impoverished mestizo majority, most of whom have brown skin and a mixed racial lineage as a result of intermarriage. At the bottom of the color gradient are the destitute Mexican Indians and a small number of Blacks, some of them the descendants of 200,000 African slaves brought to Mexico. The relatively small Black Mexican community received national attention in 2005 and 2006 following a series of racist events that received media attention. Ironically, although this color gradient is an important part of day-to-day life—enough so that some Mexicans use hair dyes, skin lighteners, and blue or green contact lenses to appear more European—nearly all Mexicans are considered part Mexican Indian because of centuries of intermarriage (Villarreal 2010).

On January 1, 1994, rebels from an armed insurgent group called the Zapatista National Liberation Army seized four towns in the state of Chiapas in southern Mexico. Two thousand lightly armed Mayan Indians and peasants backed the rebels—who had named their organization after Emiliano Zapata, a farmer and leader of the 1910 revolution against a corrupt dictatorship. Zapatista leaders declared that they had turned to armed insurrection to protest economic injustices and discrimination against the region's Indian population. The Mexican government

The poverty of Mexican Indians is well documented and in some instances has led to violent protests for social change.

mobilized the army to crush the revolt but was forced to retreat as news organizations broadcast pictures of the confrontation around the world. A ceasefire was declared after only 12 days of fighting, but 196 people had already died. Negotiations collapsed between the Mexican government and the Zapatista National Liberation Army, and there has been sporadic violence ever since.

In response to the crisis, the Mexican legislature enacted the Law on Indian Rights and Culture, which went into effect in 2001. The act allows 62 recognized Indian groups to apply their own customs in resolving conflicts and electing leaders. Unfortunately, state legislatures must give final approval to these arrangements, a requirement that severely limits the rights of large Indian groups whose territories span several states. Tired of waiting for state approval, many indigenous communities in Chiapas have declared self-rule without obtaining official recognition.

Although many factors contributed to the Zapatista revolt, the subordinate status of Mexico's Indian citizens, who account for an estimated 14 percent of the nation's population, was surely important. More than 90 percent of the indigenous population lives in houses without access to sewers, compared with 21 percent of the population as a whole. And whereas just 10 percent of Mexican adults are illiterate, the proportion for Mexican Indians is 44 percent (Stahler-Sholk 2008).

The Status of Women

Often in the United States we consider our own problems to be so significant that we fail to recognize that many of these social issues exist elsewhere. Gender stratification is an example of an issue we share with almost all other countries, and Mexico is no exception. In 1975, Mexico City was the site of the first United Nations conference on the status of women. Much of the focus was on the situation of women in developing countries; in that regard, Mexico remains typical.

Women in Mexico did not receive the right to vote until 1953. They have made significant progress in that short period in being elected into office, but they have a long way to go. As of 2013, women accounted for 37 percent of Mexico's national assembly—20th highest out of 189 countries—but lack the ultimate decision-making authority in the government and the economic leadership (Inter-Parliamentary Union 2013).

Even when Mexican women work outside the home, they are often denied recognition as active and productive household members, and men are typically viewed as heads of the household in every respect. As one consequence, women find it difficult to obtain credit and technical assistance in many parts of Mexico and to inherit land in rural areas.

Men are preferred over women in the more skilled jobs, and women lose out entirely as factories, even in developing nations such as Mexico, require more complex skills. In 2009, only 47 percent of women were in the paid labor force, compared with about 69 percent in Canada and 22 percent in the United States (Organisation for Economic Co-operation and Development 2013).

In recent decades, Mexican women have begun to address an array of economic, political, and health issues. Often this organizing occurs at the grassroots level and outside traditional government forums. Because women continue to serve as household managers for their families, even when they work outside the home, they have been aware of the consequences of the inadequate public services in low-income urban neighborhoods. As far back as 1973, women in Monterrey, the nation's sixth-largest city, began protesting the continuing disruptions of the city's water supply. At first, individual women made complaints to city officials and the water authority, but subsequently, groups of female activists emerged. They sent delegations to confront politicians, organized protest rallies, and blocked traffic as a means of getting media attention. As a result of their efforts, there have been improvements in Monterrey's water service, although the issue of reliable and safe water remains a concern in Mexico and many developing countries (Bennett 1995; Bennett and Rico 2005).

Mexico is beginning to recognize that the issue of social inequality extends beyond poverty. A national survey found that eight out of ten Mexicans felt it was as important to

16-2

eliminate discrimination as poverty, yet 40 percent said that they did not want to live next to an Indian community, and one-third considered it "normal" for women not to earn as much as men (Thompson 2005).

Canada: Multiculturalism Up North

16-2 Understand what is meant by multiculturalism in Canada.

Multiculturalism is a fairly recent term in the United States; it is used to refer to diversity. In Canada, it has been adopted as a state policy for more than two decades. Still, many people in the United States, when they think of Canada, see it as a homogeneous nation with a smattering of Arctic-type people—merely a cross between the northern mainland United States and Alaska. This is not the social reality.

One of the continuing discussions among Canadians is the need for a cohesive national identity or a sense of common peoplehood. The immense size of the country, much of which is sparsely populated, and the diversity of its people have complicated this need.

The First Nations

Canada, like the United States, has had an adversarial relationship with its native peoples. However, the Canadian experience has not been as violent. During all three stages of Canadian history—French colonialism, British colonialism, and Canadian nationhood—there has been, compared with the United States, little warfare between Canadian Whites and Canadian Native Americans. Yet the legacy today is similar. Prodded by settlers, colonial governments (and later Canadian governments) drove the Native Americans from their lands. Already by the 1830s, Indian reserves were being established that were similar to the reservations in the United States. Tribal members were encouraged to renounce their status and become Canadian citizens. Assimilation was the explicit policy until recently (Champagne 1994; Waldman 1985).

The 1.2 million native peoples of Canada are collectively referred to by the government as the *First Nations* or *Aboriginal Peoples* and represent about 4 percent of the population. This population is classified into the following groups:

Status Indians—The more than 600 tribes or bands officially recognized by the government, numbering about 680,000 in 2006, of whom 40 percent live on Indian reserves (or reservations).

Inuit—The 50,480 people living in the northern part of the country, who in the past were called Eskimos.

Métis (pronounced "may-TEE")—Canadians of mixed Aboriginal ancestry, officially numbering 390,000 and many of whom still speak French Métis, a mixed language combining Aboriginal and European words.

Another 35,000 Canadians of mixed native ancestry are counted by the government as First Nations people, but there are perhaps another 600,000 non-status Indians who self-identify themselves as having some Aboriginal ancestry but who are not so considered by the Canadian government (Huteson 2008; Statistics Canada 2012).

The Métis and non-status Indians have historically enjoyed no separate legal recognition, but efforts continue to secure them special rights under the law, such as designated health, education, and welfare programs. The general public does not understand these legal distinctions, so if a Métis or non-status Indian "looks like an Indian," she or he is subjected to the same treatment, discriminatory or otherwise (Indian and Northern Affairs Canada and Canadian Polar Commission 2000: 4).

Similar to the situation of indigenous people in the United States, Brazil, and Mexico, Canada has only recently begun to make amends for past injustices to its First Nations people. Pictured is a settlement of the Nunavut Territory, which has been given special autonomy from the central government of Ottawa.

The new Canadian federal constitution of 1982 included a charter of rights that "recognized and affirmed ... the existing aboriginal and treaty rights" of the Canadian Native American, Inuit, and Métis peoples. This recognition received the most visibility through the efforts of the Mohawk, one of the tribes of status Indians. At issue were land rights involving some property areas in Quebec that had spiritual significance for the Mohawk. Their protests and militant confrontations reawakened the Canadian people to the concerns of their diverse native peoples (Warry 2007).

Some of the contemporary issues facing the First Nations of Canada are very similar to those faced by Native Americans in the United States. Contemporary Canadians are shocked to learn of past mistreatment leading to belated remedies. Exposure of past sexual and physical abuse of tens of thousands in boarding schools led to compensation to former students and an official apology by the government in 2008. Earlier in 2006, as part of a legal settlement, the government set aside $2 billion for payments to surviving students and to document their experiences.

Another parallel with native peoples of the United States, the First Nations people are demanding control over natural resources. Tribal people also feel that **environmental justice** must be addressed because of the disproportionate pollution they experience. As noted in Chapter 6, environmental justice refers to efforts to ensure that hazardous substances are controlled so that all communities receive protection regardless of race or socioeconomic circumstances. Seeking better opportunities, First Nations people move to urban areas in Canada where social services are slowly meeting the needs.

The social and economic fate of contemporary Aboriginal Peoples reflects many challenges. Only 40 percent graduate from high school compared to more than 70 percent for the country as a whole. The native peoples of Canada have unemployment rates twice as high and an average income one-third lower (Farley 2008; Guly and Farley 2008; Statistics Canada 2012; Warry 2007).

In a positive step, in 1999 Canada created a new territory in response to a native land claim in which the resident Inuit (formerly called *Eskimos*) dominated. Nunavut ("NOO-nah-voot"), meaning "our land," recognizes the territorial rights of the Inuit. Admirable as this event is, observers noted it was easier to grant such economic rights and autonomy to 29,000 people in the isolated expanse of northern Canada than to the Aboriginal Peoples of the more populated southern provinces of Canada (Krauss 2006).

The Québécois

Assimilation and domination have been the plight of most minority groups. The French-speaking people of the province of Quebec—the **Québécois**, as they are known—represent a contrasting case. Since the mid-1960s, they have reasserted their identity and captured the attention of the entire nation.

Quebec accounts for about one-fourth of the nation's population and wealth. Reflecting its early settlement by the French, fully 95 percent of the province's population claims to speak French compared with only 13 percent in the nation as a whole (Statistics Canada 2012).

The Québécois have sought to put French Canadian culture on an equal footing with English Canadian culture in the country as a whole and to dominate in the province. At the very least, this effort has been seen as an irritant outside Quebec and has been viewed with great concern by the English-speaking minority in Quebec.

In the 1960s, the Québécois expressed the feeling that bilingual status was not enough. Even to have French recognized as one of two official languages in a nation dominated by the English-speaking population gave the Québécois second-class status in their view. With some leaders threatening to break completely with Canada and make Quebec an independent nation, Canada made French the official language of the province and the only acceptable language for commercial signs and public transactions. New residents are now required to send their children to French schools. The English-speaking residents felt as if they had been made aliens, even though many of them had roots extending back to the 1700s (Salée 1994).

16-2

In 1995, the people of Quebec were given a referendum that they would vote on alone: whether they wanted to separate from Canada and form a new nation. In a very close vote, 50.5 percent of the voters indicated a preference to remain united with Canada. The vote was particularly striking, given the confusion over how separation would be accomplished and its significance economically. Separatists vowed to keep working for secession and called for another referendum in the future, although surveys show the support for independence has dropped. Many French-speaking residents now seem to accept the steps that have been taken, but a minority still seeks full control of financial and political policies (Mason 2007).

Canada is characterized by the presence of two linguistic communities: the Anglophone and the Francophone, with the latter occurring largely in the one province of Quebec. Outside Quebec, Canadians are opposed to separatism; within Quebec, they are divided. Language and cultural issues, therefore, both unify and divide a nation of 32 million people.

Immigration and Race

Immigration has also been a significant social force contributing to Canadian multiculturalism. Toronto and Vancouver both have a higher proportion of foreign-born residents than either Los Angeles or New York City. In 2010, Canada admitted over 280,000 immigrants—the most in 50 years. Canada, proportionately to its population, receives consistently the most immigrants of any nation—twice the rate of the United States. About 20 percent of its population is foreign-born, with an increasing proportion being of Asian background rather than European (Migration News 2012c).

Canada also speaks of its **visible minorities**—persons other than Aboriginal or First Nation people who are non-White in racial background. This would include much of the immigrant population as well as the Black population. In the 2006 census, the visible minority population accounted for 16 percent, compared to less than 5 percent 25 years earlier. The largest visible minority are the Chinese, followed by South Asians collectively, Black Canadians, and Filipinos (Bélanger and Malenfant 2005; Statistics Canada 2012).

People in the United States tend to view Canada's race relations in favorable terms. In part, this view reflects Canada's role as the "promised land" for slaves escaping the U.S. South and crossing the free North to Canada, where they were unlikely to be recaptured. Canadians, themselves with the United States, also foster the view of Canada as a land of positive intergroup relations. They have long been willing to compare their best social institutions to the worst examples of racism in the United States and to pride themselves on being more virtuous and high-minded (McClain 1979).

The social reality, past and present, is quite different. Africans came in 1689 as involuntary immigrants to be enslaved by French colonists. Slavery officially continued until 1833. It never flourished because the Canadian economy did not need a large labor force, so most slaves worked as domestic servants. Blacks from the United States did flee to Canada before slavery ended, but some fugitive slaves returned after Lincoln's issuance of the Emancipation Proclamation in 1863. The early Black arrivals in Canada were greeted in a variety of ways. Often they were warmly received as fugitives from slavery, but as their numbers grew in some areas, Canadians became concerned that they would overwhelm the White population (Winks 1971).

The contemporary Black Canadian population, about 2.5 percent of the nation's population, consists of indigenous Afro-Canadians with several generations of roots in Canada, West Indian immigrants and their descendants, and a number of post–World War II immigrants from the United States. Slightly more than half of Canada's Blacks are foreign born.

Racial issues are barely below the surface. A 2011 study of Toronto's online rental market was done by sending 5,620 rental enquiries using names that were either typically White or Black or Asian or Muslim or Jewish. Evidence of less willingness to rent was found to be ten times greater among the visible minorities as compared to Whites. This was true throughout the city and regardless of the relative affluence of the neighborhood where the apartment was available. Interestingly, the same year that the study was published, the Ontario Human Rights Commission launched programs called "In the Zone" and "Room for Everyone" attempting to end discrimination in housing and encouraged looking to the United States for best practices to accomplish this end (Hogan and Berry 2011; Ontario Human Rights Commission 2013; Statistics Canada 2012).

In 1541, Frenchman Jacques Cartier established the first European settlement along the St. Lawrence River, but within a year he withdrew because of confrontations with the Iroquois. Almost 500 years later, the descendants of the Europeans and Aboriginal Peoples are still trying to resolve Canada's identity as issues of ethnicity, race, and language shape it.

Brazil: Not a Racial Paradise

To someone who is knowledgeable about race and ethnic relations in the United States, Brazil seems familiar in several respects. Like the United States, Europeans who overwhelmed the native people colonized Brazil. There continues to be a variety of issues, economic and cultural, facing the indigenous people of Brazil. Like the United States, Brazil imported Black Africans as slaves to meet the demand for laborers. Even today, Brazil is second only to the United States in the number of people of African descent, excluding nations on the African continent. Another similarity is the treatment of indigenous people. Although the focus here is on Black and White people in Brazil, another continuing concern is the treatment of Brazil's native peoples as this developing nation continues to industrialize.

The current nature of Brazilian race relations is influenced by the legacy of slavery, as is true of Black–White relations in the United States. It is not necessary to repeat here a discussion of the brutality of the slave trade and slavery itself or of the influence of slavery on the survival of African cultures and family life. Scholars agree that slavery was not the same in Brazil as it was in the United States, but they disagree on how different it was and how significant these differences were (Elkins 1959; Tannenbaum 1946).

Brazil depended much more than the United States on the slave trade. Estimates place the total number of slaves imported to Brazil at 4 million, eight times the number brought to the United States. At the height of slavery, however, both nations had approximately the same slave population: 4–4.5 million. Brazil's reliance on African-born slaves meant that typical Brazilian slaves had closer ties to Africa than did their U.S. counterparts. The most significant difference between slavery in the southern United States and in Brazil was the amount of *manumission*—the freeing of slaves. For every 1,000 slaves, 100 were freed annually in Brazil, compared to four per year in the U.S. South.

It would be hasty to assume, however, as some people have, that Brazilian slave masters were more benevolent. Quite the contrary. Brazil's slave economy was poorer than that of the U.S. South, and so slave owners in Brazil freed slaves into poverty whenever they became crippled, sick, or old. But this custom does not completely explain the presence of the many freed slaves in Brazil. Again unlike in the United States, the majority of Brazil's population was composed of Africans and their descendants throughout the nineteenth century. Africans were needed as craft workers, shopkeepers, and boatmen, not just as agricultural workers. Freed slaves filled these needs.

The "Racial Democracy" Illusion

For some time in the twentieth century, Brazil was seen by some as a "racial democracy" and even a "racial paradise." Indeed, historically the term *race* is rare in Brazil; the term *côr* or *color* is far more common. Historian Carl Degler (1971) identified the **mulatto escape hatch** as the key to the differences in Brazilian and American race relations. In Brazil, the mulatto or *moreno* (brown) is recognized as a group separate from either *brancos* (Whites) or *prêtos* (Blacks), whereas in the United States, mulattos are classed with Blacks. Yet this escape hatch is an illusion because mulattoes fare only marginally better economically than Black Brazilians or *Afro Brazilians* or *Afro-descendant,* the term used there to refer to

16-3

16-3 Analyze to what degree Brazil is a racial paradise.

Increasingly, people of Brazil are recognizing the significant social inequality evident along color lines.

the dark end of the Brazilian color gradient and increasingly used by college-educated persons and activists in Brazil. In addition, mulattoes do not escape through mobility into the income and status enjoyed by White Brazilians. Labor market analyses demonstrate that Blacks with the highest levels of education and occupation experience the most discrimination in terms of jobs, mobility, and income. In addition, they face a *glass ceiling* that limits their upward mobility (Fiola 1989, 2008; Silva and Reis 2012).

Today, the use of dozens of terms to describe oneself along the color gradient (as mentioned earlier with respect to Mexico) is obvious in Brazil because, unlike in the United States, people of mixed ancestry are viewed as an identifiable social group. The 2010 census in Brazil classified 48 percent White, 43 percent pardo (mestizo, brown, or mulatto), 8 percent Afro-Brazilian, and 1 percent Asian and indigenous Brazilian Indian (Bourcier 2012).

In Brazil, today as in the past, light skin color enhances status, but the impact is often exaggerated. When Degler advanced the idea of the mulatto escape hatch, he implied that it was a means to success. The most recent income data controlling for gender, education, and age indicate that people of mixed ancestry earn 12 percent more than Blacks. Yet Whites earn another 26 percent more than the pardo. Clearly, the major distinction is between Whites and all "people of color" rather than between people of mixed ancestry and Afro-Brazilians (IBGE 2006; Telles, 1992, 2004).

Brazilian Dilemma

Gradually in Brazil there has been the recognition that racial prejudice and discrimination do exist. A 2000 survey in Rio de Janeiro found that 93 percent of those surveyed believe that racism exists in Brazil and 74 percent said there was a lot of bias. Yet 87 percent of the respondents said they themselves were not racist (Bailey 2004, 2009b).

During the twentieth century, Brazil changed from a nation that prided itself on its freedom from racial intolerance to a country legally attacking discrimination against people of color. One of the first measures was in 1951 when the Afonso Arinos law was unanimously adopted, prohibiting racial discrimination in public places. Opinion is divided over the effectiveness of the law, which has been of no use in overturning subtle forms of discrimination. Even from the start, certain civilian careers, such as the diplomatic and military officer ranks, were virtually closed to Blacks. Curiously, the push for the law came from the United States, after a Black American dancer, Katherine Dunham, was denied a room at a São Paulo luxury hotel.

Today, the income disparity is significant in Brazil. As shown in Figure 16.2, people of color are disproportionately clustered in the lowest income levels of society. Although not as disadvantaged as Blacks in South Africa, which we take up later in this chapter, the degree of inequality between Whites and people of color is much greater in Brazil than in the United States.

There is a long history of activism among Afro-Americans overcoming the challenge of a society that thinks distinctions are based on social class. After all, if problems are based on poverty, they are easier to overcome than if problems are based on color. However, activism is also understandable because societal wealth is so unequal—the concentration of income and assets in the hands of a few is much greater than even in the United States. For Afro-Brazilians, even professional status can achieve only so much in one's social standing. An individual's blackness does not suddenly become invisible simply because

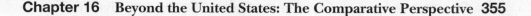

16-3

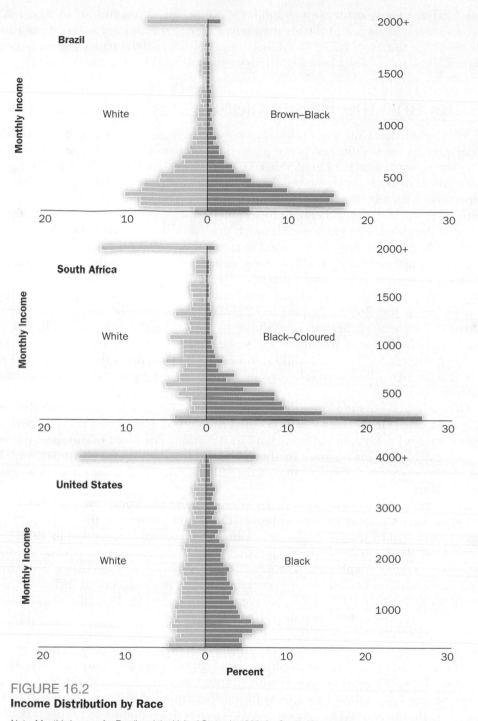

FIGURE 16.2
Income Distribution by Race

Note: Monthly income for Brazil and the United States in 1996; for South Africa, 1998.

Source: Government agencies as reported in Telles 2004: 108.

he or she has acquired some social standing. The fame achieved by the Black Brazilian soccer player Pelé is a token exception and does not mean that Blacks have it easy or even have a readily available "escape hatch" through professional sports.

A dramatic step was taken to explicitly acknowledge the role of race when affirmative action measures were introduced. Quotas were begun in 2007, by which students could indicate their race with their college-entrance applications. Reflecting the color gradient and the lack of clear-cut racial categories, committees were actually created to examine photographs of prospective students for the purpose of determining race. In its initial implementation, charges of reverse racism and specific cases of inexplicable

16-4

classifications being made were common. Coming up with solutions in Brazil will be just as intractable as the problems themselves even if the country seems more likely to acknowledge the existence of racial discrimination (Ash 2007; Bailey 2009a; Bailey and Péria 2010; Daniel 2006; Llana 2013; Telles and Bailey 2013).

Israel and the Palestinians

16-4 Explain the historical and contemporary tensions between Israel and Palestine.

In 1991, when the Gulf War ended, hopes were high in many parts of the world that a comprehensive Middle East peace plan could be hammered out. Just a decade later, after the terrorist attacks of September 11, 2001, and then the toppling of the Egyptian government in 2011, which was the first Arab state to diplomatically recognize Israel, the expectations for a lasting peace were much dimmer. The key elements in any peace plan were to resolve the conflict between Israel and its Arab neighbors and to resolve the challenge of the Palestinian refugees. Although the issues are debated in the political arena, the origins of the conflict can be found in race, ethnicity, and religion.

Nearly 2,000 years ago, the Jews were exiled from Palestine in the **Diaspora**. The exiled Jews settled throughout Europe and elsewhere in the Middle East, where they often encountered hostility and the anti-Semitism described in Chapter 14. With the conversion of the Roman Empire to Christianity, Palestine became the site of many Christian pilgrimages. Beginning in the seventh century, Palestine gradually fell under the Muslim influence of the Arabs. By the beginning of the twentieth century, tourism had become established. In addition, some Jews had migrated from Russia and established settlements that were tolerated by the Ottoman Empire, which then controlled Palestine.

Great Britain expanded its colonial control from Egypt into Palestine during World War I, driving out the Turks. Britain ruled the land but endorsed the eventual establishment of a Jewish national homeland in Palestine. The spirit of **Zionism**, the yearning to establish a Jewish state in the biblical homeland, was well under way. From the Arab perspective, Zionism meant the subjugation, if not the elimination, of the Palestinians.

Thousands of Jews came to settle from throughout the world; even so, in the 1920s, Palestine was only about 15 percent Jewish. Ethnic tension grew as the Arabs of Palestine were threatened by the Zionist fervor. Rioting grew to such a point that in 1939, Britain yielded to Palestinian demands that Jewish immigration be stopped. This occurred at the same time as large numbers of Jews were fleeing Nazism in Europe. After World War II, Jews resumed their demand for a homeland, despite Arab objections. Britain turned to the newly formed United Nations to settle the dispute. In May 1948, the British mandate over Palestine ended, and the state of Israel was founded.

The Palestinian people define themselves as the people who lived in this former British mandate, along with their descendants on their fathers' side. They are viewed as an ethnic group within the larger group of Arabs. They generally speak Arabic, and most of them (97 percent) are Muslim (mostly Sunni). With a rapid rate of natural increase, the Palestinians have grown in number from 1.4 million at the end of World War II to about 7 million worldwide: 700,000 in Israel, 2.6 million in the West Bank, and 1.7 million in the Gaza Strip (Central Intelligence Agency 2011; Third World Institute 2007: 419).

Arab–Israeli Conflicts

No sooner had Israel been created than the Arab nations—particularly Egypt, Jordan, Iraq, Syria, and Lebanon—announced their intention to restore control to the Palestinian Arabs, by force if necessary. As hostilities broke out, the Israeli military stepped in to preserve the borders, which no Arab nation agreed to recognize. Some 60 percent of the 1.4 million Arabs fled or were expelled from Israeli territory, becoming refugees in neighboring countries. An uneasy peace followed as Israel attempted to encourage new Jewish immigration. Israel also extended the same services that were available to the Jews, such as education and healthcare, to the non-Jewish Israelis. The new Jewish population continued to grow under the country's Law of Return, which gave every Jew in the world the right to settle permanently as a citizen. The question of Jerusalem remained unsettled, and the city was divided into two separate sections—Israeli Jewish and Jordanian Arab—a division both sides refused to regard as permanent.

In 1967, Egypt, followed by Syria, responded to Israel's military actions to take surrounding territory in what came to be called the Six-Day War. In the course of defeating the Arab states' military, Israel occupied the Gaza Strip and the West Bank (Figure 16.3). The defeat was all the more bitter for the Arabs as Israeli-held territory expanded.

Although our primary attention here is on the Palestinians and the Jews, another significant ethnic issue is present in Israel. Among Israel's Jews, about 67 percent are Israeli-born, 23 percent are European or American, 6 percent are African, and 6 percent are Asian. The Law of Return has brought to Israel Jews of varying cultural backgrounds. European Jews have been the dominant force, but a significant migration of the more religiously observant Jews from North Africa and other parts of the Middle East has created what sociologist Ernest Krausz (1973) called "the two nations." Not only are the various Jewish groups culturally diverse but also there are significant socioeconomic differences: the Europeans generally are more prosperous, better represented in the Knesset (Israel's parliament), and better educated. The secular Jews feel pressure from the more traditional and ultraorthodox Jews, who push for a nation more reflective of Jewish customs and law (Central Intelligence Agency 2011; Sela-Sheffy 2004; Third World Institute 2007: 291).

16-4

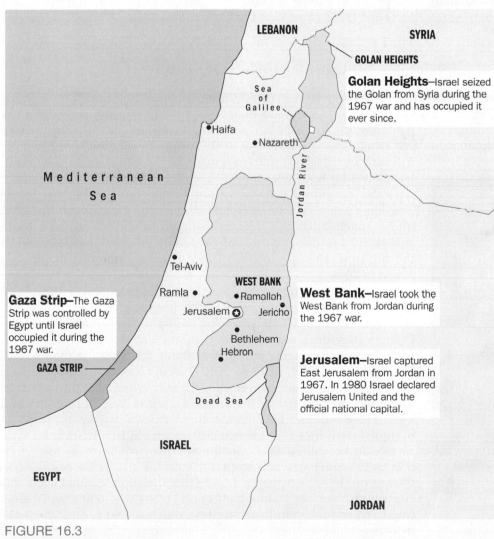

FIGURE 16.3
Israeli and Palestinian Lands

16-4

The Intifada

The occupied territories were regarded initially by Israel as a security zone between it and its belligerent neighbors. By the 1980s, however, it was clear that the territories were also serving as the location of new settlements for Jews migrating to Israel, especially from Russia. Palestinians, though enjoying some political and monetary support of Arab nations, saw little likelihood of a successful military effort to eliminate Israel. Therefore, in December 1987, they began the first **Intifada**, the uprising against Israel by the Palestinians in the occupied territories through attacks against soldiers, the boycott of Israeli goods, general strikes, resistance, and noncooperation with Israeli authorities. The target of this first Intifada, lasting five years, was the Israelis.

The Intifada was a popular grassroots movement whose growth in support was as much a surprise to the Palestine Liberation Organization (PLO) and the Arab nations as it was to Israel and its supporters. The broad range of participants in the Intifada—students, workers, union members, professionals, and business leaders—showed the unambiguous Palestinian opposition to occupation. The Intifada began out of the frustration of the Palestinians within Israel, but the confrontations were later encouraged by the PLO, an umbrella organization for several Palestinian factions of varying militancy.

With television news footage of Israel soldiers appearing to attack defenseless youths, the Intifada transformed world opinion, especially in the United States. Palestinians came to be viewed as people struggling for self-determination rather than as terrorists out to destroy Israel. Instead of Israel being viewed as the "David" and its Arab neighbors "Goliath," Israel came to take on the bully role and the Palestinians the sympathetic underdog role (Hubbard 1993; Third World Institute 2007).

The Search for Solutions amid Violence

The 1993 Oslo Accords between Israeli Prime Minister Yitzhak Rabin and PLO Chairman Yasser Arafat and subsequent agreements ended the state of war and appeared to set in motion the creation of the first-ever self-governing Palestinian territory in the Gaza Strip and the West Bank. This is referred to as the **two-state solution**—an Israel and Palestine living side-by-side recognized by the entire world community. Hardliners on both sides, however, grew resistant to the move toward separate recognized Palestinian and Israeli states. Rabin was assassinated at a peace rally by an Israeli who felt the government had given up too much. Succeeding governments in Israel took stronger stands against relinquishing control of the occupied territories. Meanwhile, the anti-Israel Hamas party was elected to power following the death of Arafat in 2004.

Despite the assurances at Oslo, Israel did not end its occupation of the Palestinian territories by 1999, justifying its actions as necessary to stop anti-Israel violence originating in Palestinian settlements. Complicating the picture was the continued growth of officially recognized Israeli settlements in the West Bank, bringing the total population to 550,000 by the end of 2012. Palestinians, assisted by Arabs in other countries, mounted a second Intifada from 2000 through 2004, which was precipitated by the Israeli killing of several Palestinians at a Jerusalem mosque. This time, militant Palestinians went outside the occupied territories and bombed civilian sites in Israel through a series of suicide bombings. Each violent episode brought calls for retaliation by the other side and desperate calls for a ceasefire from outside the region. Israel, despite worldwide denunciation, created a 430-mile "security barrier" of 30-foot-high concrete walls, ditches, and barbed wire to try to protect its Jewish settlers, which served to limit the mobility of peaceful Palestinians trying to access crops, schools, hospitals, and jobs (Clabaugh 2012).

Beginning in 2005, Israel started constructing a 30-foot-high 430-mile barrier for security purposes, but the wall also served to keep Palestinians from schools and jobs.

The immediate problem is to end the violence, but any lasting peace must face a series of difficult issues, including the following:

- The status of Jerusalem, Israel's capital, which is also viewed by Muslims as the third-most-holy city in the world.
- The future of the Jewish settlements in the West Bank of the Palestinian Authority territories.
- The future of Palestinians and other Arabs with Israeli citizenship.
- The creation of a truly independent Palestinian national state with strong leadership.
- Israel–Palestinian Authority relations, with the latter's government under control of Hamas, which is sworn to Israel's destruction.
- The future of Palestinian refugees elsewhere.

Added worries are the uneasy peace between Israel and its Arab neighbors and the sometimes interrelated events in Egypt, Lebanon, Iraq, Iran, and Syria. This has led some to question the likelihood of a two-state solution and shift discussion to a united country with equal rights for all citizens. But even the mere suggestion of a united state does not mean there is any enthusiasm anywhere politically for a united Israeli-Palestinian territory but points to how little progress has been made to a two-state reality (Lustick 2013).

The last 65 years have witnessed significant changes: Israel has gone from a land under siege to a nation whose borders are recognized by almost everyone. Israel has come to terms with the various factions of religious and secular Jews trying to coexist. The Palestinian people have gone from disfranchisement to having territory. The current solution is fragile and very temporary, as is any form of secession with a foundation for accommodation amid continuing violence.

Republic of South Africa

In every nation in the world, some racial, ethnic, or religious groups enjoy advantages denied to other groups. Nations differ in the extent of this denial and in whether it is supported by law or by custom. In no other industrial society has the denial been so entrenched in recent law as in the Republic of South Africa.

16-5 Explain inequality in the Republic of South Africa.

The Republic of South Africa is different from the rest of Africa because the original African peoples of the area are no longer present. Today, the country is multiracial, as shown in Table 16.2.

The largest group is the Black Africans who migrated from the north in the eighteenth century as well as more recent migrations from neighboring African countries over the last 20 years. The Coloured (or Cape Coloureds), the product of mixed race, and Asians (or Indians) make up the remaining non-Whites. The small White community

TABLE 16.2
Racial Groups in the Republic of South Africa

	Whites (%)	All Non-Whites (%)	Black Africans (%)	Coloureds (%)	Asian Indians (%)
1904	22	78	67	9	2
1936	21	79	69	8	2
1951	21	79	68	9	3
2010	9	91	79	9	3
2021 (projected)	8	90	80	9	2

Sources: Author's estimates, based on Statistics South Africa and Bureau of Market Research in MacFarlane 2006: 8–9; South African Institute of Race Relations 2007: 6, 12; MacFarlane 2008: 2; van den Berghe 1978: 102.

consists of the English and the Afrikaners, the latter descended from Dutch and other European settlers. As in all other multicultural nations we have considered, colonialism and immigration have left their mark.

The Legacy of Colonialism

The permanent settlement of South Africa by Europeans began in 1652, when the Dutch East India Company established a colony in Cape Town as a port of call for shipping vessels bound for India. The area was sparsely populated, and the original inhabitants of the Cape of Good Hope, the Hottentots and Bushmen, were pushed inland like the indigenous peoples of the New World. To fill the need for laborers, the Dutch imported slaves from areas of Africa farther north. Slavery was confined mostly to areas near towns and involved more limited numbers than in the United States. The Boers, semi-nomads descended from the Dutch, did not remain on the coast but trekked inland to establish vast sheep and cattle ranches. The trekkers, as they were known, regularly fought off the Black inhabitants of the interior regions. Sexual relations between Dutch men and slave and Hottentot women were quite common, giving rise to a mulatto group referred to today as Cape Coloureds.

The British entered the scene by acquiring part of South Africa in 1814, at the end of the Napoleonic Wars. The British introduced workers from India as indentured servants on sugar plantations. They had also freed the slaves by 1834, with little compensation to the Dutch slave owners, and had given Blacks almost all political and civil rights. The Boers were not happy with these developments and spent most of the nineteenth century in a violent struggle with the growing number of English colonists. In 1902, the British finally overwhelmed the Boers, leaving bitter memories on both sides. Once in control, however, they recognized that the superior numbers of the non-Whites were a potential threat to their power, as they had been to the power of the Afrikaners.

The growing non-White population consisted of the Coloureds, or mixed population, and the Black tribal groups, collectively called Bantus. The British gave both groups the vote but restricted the franchise to people who met certain property qualifications. **Pass laws** were introduced, placing curfews on the Bantus and limiting their geographic movement. These laws, enforced through "reference books" until 1986, were intended to prevent urban areas from becoming overcrowded with job-seeking Black Africans, a familiar occurrence in colonial Africa (Marx 1998; van den Berghe 1965).

Apartheid

In 1948, South Africa was granted its independence from the United Kingdom, and the National Party, dominated by the Afrikaners, assumed control of the government. Under the leadership of this party, the rule of White supremacy, already well under way in the colonial period as custom, became more and more formalized into law. To deal with the multiracial population, the Whites devised a policy called apartheid to ensure their dominance. **Apartheid** (in Afrikaans, the language of the Afrikaners, it means "separation" or "apartness") came to mean a policy of separate development, euphemistically called *multinational development* by the government. At the time, these changes were regarded as cosmetic outside South Africa and by most Black South Africans.

The White ruling class was not homogeneous. The English and Afrikaners belonged to different political parties, lived apart, spoke different languages, and worshipped separately, but they

South Africa employed an explicit system of de jure segregation under apartheid that included spatial separation as reflected in this entryway in Johannesburg. The top line is Afrikaans for "Whites Only".

16-5

shared the belief that some form of apartheid was necessary. Apartheid can perhaps be best understood as a twentieth-century effort to reestablish the master–slave relationship. Blacks could not vote. They could not move throughout the country freely. They were unable to hold jobs unless the government approved. To work at approved jobs, they were forced to live in temporary quarters at great distances from their real homes. Their access to education, healthcare, and social services was severely limited (Wilson 1973).

Events took a significant turn in 1990, when South African Prime Minister F. W. De Klerk legalized 60 banned Black organizations and freed Nelson Mandela (1918–2013), leader of the African National Congress (ANC), after 27 years of imprisonment. Mandela's triumphant remarks after his release appear in the Speaking Out.

The next year, de Klerk and Black leaders signed a National Peace Accord, pledging themselves to the establishment of a multiparty democracy and an end to violence. After a series of political defeats, de Klerk called for a referendum in 1992 to allow Whites to vote on ending apartheid. If he failed to receive popular support, he vowed to resign. A record high turnout gave a solid 68.6 percent vote that favored the continued dismantling of legal apartheid and the creation of a new constitution through negotiation. The process toward power sharing ended symbolically when de Klerk and Mandela were jointly awarded the 1993 Nobel Peace Prize (Marx 1998; Ottaway and Taylor 1992; Winant 2001).

(🎙️) Speaking Out

Africa, It Is Ours!

Amandla! Amandla! i-Afrika, mayibuye! [Power! Power! Africa, it is ours!]

My friends, comrades and fellow South Africans, I greet you all in the name of peace, democracy and freedom for all. I stand here before you not as a prophet but as a humble servant of you, the people.

Your tireless and heroic sacrifices have made it possible for me to be here today. I therefore place the remaining years of my life in your hands.

On this day of my release, I extend my sincere and warmest gratitude to the millions of my compatriots and those in every corner of the globe who have campaigned tirelessly for my release.

Negotiations on the dismantling of apartheid will have to address the overwhelming demand of our people for a democratic nonracial and unitary South Africa. There must be an end to white monopoly on political power.

And [there must be] a fundamental restructuring of our political and economic systems to ensure that the inequalities of apartheid are addressed and our society thoroughly democratized....

Our struggle has reached a decisive moment. We call on our people to seize this moment so that the process toward democracy is rapid and uninterrupted. We have waited too long for our freedom. We can no longer wait. Now is the time to intensify the struggle on all fronts.

To relax our efforts now would be a mistake which generations to come will not be able to forgive. The sight of

Nelson Mandela

freedom looming on the horizon should encourage us to redouble our efforts. It is only through disciplined mass action that our victory can be assured.

We call on our white compatriots to join us in the shaping of a new South Africa. The freedom movement is the political home for you, too. We call on the international community to continue the campaign to isolate the apartheid regime.

To lift sanctions now would be to run the risk of aborting the process toward the complete eradication of apartheid. Our march to freedom is irreversible. We must not allow fear to stand in our way.

Universal suffrage of a common voters' role in a united democratic and nonracial South Africa is the only way to peace and racial harmony.

In conclusion, I wish to go to my own words during my trial in 1964. They are as true today as they were then. I wrote: I have fought against white domination, and I have fought against black domination. I have cherished the idea of a democratic and free society in which all persons live together in harmony and with equal opportunities.

It is an ideal which I hope to live for and to achieve. But if needs be, it is an ideal for which I am prepared to die.

16-5

The Era of Reconciliation and Moving On

In April 1994, South Africa held its first universal election. Apartheid had ended. Nelson Mandela's ANC received 62 percent of the vote, giving him a five-year term as president. Mandela enjoyed the advantage of wide personal support throughout the nation. He retired in 1999 when his second term ended. His successors have faced a daunting agenda because of the legacy of apartheid.

A significant step to help South Africa move past apartheid was the creation of the Truth and Reconciliation Commission (TRC). People were allowed to come forward and confess to horrors they had committed under apartheid from 1961 through 1993. If they were judged by the TRC to be truly remorseful, and most were, they were not subject to prosecution. If they failed to confess to all crimes they had committed, they were prosecuted. The stories gripped the country as people learned that actions taken in the name of the Afrikaner government were often worse than anyone had anticipated (Gobodo-Madikizela 2003).

The immediate relief that came with the end of apartheid has given way to greater concerns about the future of all South Africans. In the Research Focus, we consider how intergroup contact may affect the views expressed by contemporary South Africans.

With the emergence of the new multiracial government in South Africa, we see a country with enormous promise but many challenges that are similar to those of our own multiracial society. Some of the controversial issues facing the ANC-led government are very familiar to citizens in the United States.

Desperate poverty: Despite the growth of a small but conspicuous middle class among Black South Africans, poverty rates stand at 40 percent, compared to 4–5 percent of White South Africans.

Research Focus

Intergroup Contact and South Africa

There is little question that the Republic of South Africa's recent history has been defined by racism. With less than two decades since the end of apartheid, every aspect of South African society from transportation to hospitals to sports reflects this legacy. So how do White and Black South Africans get along on a daily basis? They are certainly more likely to meet on an equal-status basis whether it is in schools or the workplace than they were under apartheid. This would seem to be an ideal opportunity to test the validity of **contact hypothesis**. First introduced in Chapter 2, the contact hypothesis draws upon the interactionist perspective stating that intergroup contact between people of equal status in noncompetitive circumstances will reduce prejudice. Can this hold true in a country with such a long history of intergroup discrimination and conflict supported by the central government?

Since the end of apartheid, surveys show that Black Africans are increasingly identifying themselves by the national social identity of "South African" while retaining their own tribal identity. Afrikaans- and English-speaking Whites seem to more increasingly identify with their ethnic group and are less likely to see themselves less as South Africans. This would not seem to suggest that intergroup contact in the new South Africa can lead to lessening of prejudice. Yet national surveys conducted in the twenty-first century find contact and especially more regular, intimate contact leads to more positive feelings among racial groups in South Africa. Successive studies show increased interaction especially by Whites,

as measured by self-reports of having non-White friends or dining with those friends. Contact across racial lines seems to have less positive impact on the attitudes held by Black South Africans. Tests of the contact hypothesis among South African college students showed relatively little contact across racial lines but when it does occur, more positive feelings follow, especially among Whites.

Why do White South Africans seem to be affected more positively by contact? Even if the contemporary contact is harmonious, it occurs within the social context of unequal power position in which "Whiteness" is privileged over "Blackness." Researchers note that given the racist backdrop of today's South Africa, Whites may be quicker to evaluate intergroup contact as equal whereas the long-oppressed Black South Africans may find equal status more difficult to accept. This is understandable since so often even today Black–White relationships are still occurring, with Whites in a distinctly more powerful position, while the reverse is much less likely. Furthermore, given the magnitude of structural change that South Africa must undergo, it may be especially difficult for Black South Africans to be quick to move beyond the Apartheid past. Intergroup contact is not a panacea anywhere, including South Africa, but, rather, one element moving from an exclusionary society to a more pluralistic one.

Sources: Bornman 2010, Gibson and Classen 2010; Pettigrew 2010; Tredoux and Finchilescu 2010; Vincent 2008.

Affirmative action: Race-based employment goals and other preference programs have been proposed, yet critics insist that such efforts constitute reverse apartheid.

Medical care: The nation is trying to confront the duality of private care for the affluent (usually Whites) and government-subsidized care (usually for people of color). AIDS has reached devastating levels, with 11 percent of the population having HIV or AIDS as of 2010.

Crime: Although the government-initiated violence under apartheid has ended, the generations of conflict and years of intertribal attacks have created a climate for crime, illegal gun ownership, and disrespect for law enforcement.

School integration: Multiracial schools are replacing the apartheid system, but for some, the change is occurring too fast or not fast enough.

These issues must be addressed with minimal increases in government spending as the government seeks to reverse deficit spending without an increase in taxes that would frighten away needed foreign investment. As difficult as all these challenges are, perhaps the most difficult is land reform (Dugger 2010; Geddes 2010; South African Institute of Race Relations 2010).

The government has pledged to address the issue of land ownership. Between 1960 and 1990, the government forced Black South Africans from their land and often allowed Whites to settle on it. Beginning in 1994, the government took steps to transfer 30 percent of agricultural land to Black South Africans. Where feasible, the government plans to restore the original inhabitants to their land; where this is not feasible, the government is to make "just and equitable compensation." The magnitude of this land reform issue cannot be minimized. Originally, the goal was to achieve the land transfer by 2004, but by 2012 780 percent of the farmland remained White-controlled. This has now been deferred to 2025. Certain critics say at the current rate it will take until 2060 to reach the 2004 objective (McGroarty and Chaykowski 2012; South Africa Institute of Race Relations 2010).

Conclusion

As shown in the figure below, each society, in its own way, illustrates the processes in the Spectrum of Intergroup Relations first introduced in Chapter 1. The examples range from the Holocaust, which precipitated the emergence of Israel, to the efforts to create a multiracial government in South Africa. A study of these five societies, coupled with knowledge of subordinate groups in the United States, provide the background from which to draw some conclusions about patterns of race and ethnic relations in the world today.

By looking beyond our borders, we gather new insights into the social processes that frame and define intergroup relationships. The colonial experience has played a role in all cases under consideration in this chapter but particularly in South Africa. In Mexico and South Africa, which have long histories of multiethnic societies, intergroup sexual relations have been widespread but with different results. Mestizos in Mexico occupy a middle racial group and experience less tension, whereas in South Africa, the Cape Coloureds had freedoms under apartheid almost as limited as those of the Black Africans. South Africa enforced de jure segregation, whereas Israeli communities seem to have de facto segregation. Israel's and South Africa's intergroup conflicts have involved the world community. Indigenous people figure in the social landscape of Canada, Brazil, and Mexico. Policies giving preference to previously devalued racial groups are in place in both Brazil and South Africa. Complete assimilation is absent in all five societies considered in this chapter and is unlikely to occur in the near future; the legal and informal barriers to assimilation and pluralism vary for subordinate people choosing either option. Looking at the status of women in Mexico reminds us of the worldwide nature of gender stratification and also offers insight into the patterns present in developing nations.

If we add the United States to these societies, the similarities become even more striking. The problems of racial and ethnic adjustment in the United States have dominated our attention, but they parallel past and present experiences in other societies with racial, ethnic, or religious heterogeneity. The U.S. government has been involved in providing educational, financial, and legal support for programs intended to help particular racial or ethnic groups, and it continues to avoid interfering with religious freedom. Bilingual, bicultural

SPECTRUM OF INTERGROUP RELATIONS

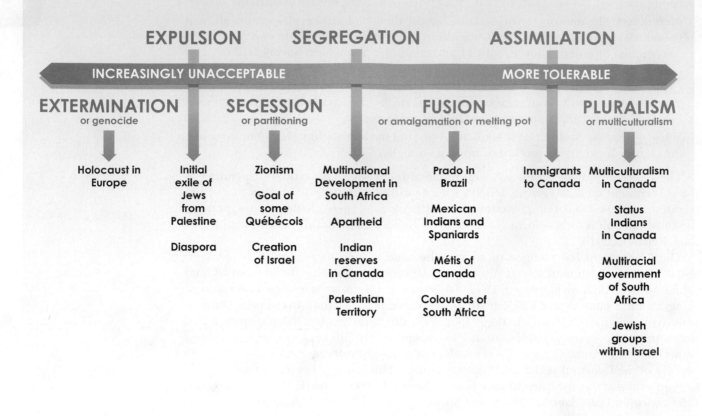

programs in schools, autonomy for Native Americans on reservations, and increased participation in decision making by residents of ghettoes and barrios are all viewed as acceptable goals, although they are not pursued to the extent that many subordinate-group people would like.

The analysis of this chapter has reminded us of the global nature of dominant–subordinate relations along dimensions of race, ethnicity, religion, and gender. In the next chapter, we provide an overview of racial and ethnic relations as well as explore social inequality along the dimensions of age, disability status, and sexual orientation.

Summary

1. Mexico's mosaic of mestizos and native indigenous people creates a diversified society, with segments of the population that definitely feel disadvantaged and ignored.

2. Canada, with one of the largest proportions of indigenous peoples, continues to develop strategies to promote economic development while preserving cultural traditions. A similar pattern has emerged among the growing immigrant community.

3. The sizable French-speaking population within Canada has asked and receives consideration for its special cultural heritage, which is not fully endorsed by others in the nation.

4. Brazil is not a racial paradise, as has sometimes been suggested, but continues to deal with significant disparity among people of color.

5. Israel has both a significant Arab population and a diverse Jewish community among whom there are sharp political and religious differences.

6. Palestinians in the occupied territories are in a desperate economic situation that has been aggravated by violent divisions within their ranks and by reprisals from Israel in response to attacks from those within the territories.

7. The apartheid era in South Africa underscores how race can be a tool for total subjugation of millions of people.

8. The South Africa of the post-apartheid era is marked by reconciliation of the different racial groups, which are facing significant issues involving land, education, health, and public safety.

Key Terms

apartheid p. 360

color gradient p. 348

contact hypothesis p. 362

Diaspora p. 356

environmental justice p. 351

ethnonational conflict p. 346

Intifada p. 358

mestizo p. 348

mulatto escape hatch p. 353

pass laws p. 360

Québécois p. 351

two-state solution p. 358

visible minorities p. 352

world systems theory p. 346

Zionism p. 356

Review Questions

1. How is color defined in Mexico and what are the social implications?

2. On what levels can one speak of an identity issue facing Canada as a nation?

3. What role does race play in Brazilian life?

4. What is the outlook for a two-state solution for Israel and Palestine?

5. To what extent are the problems facing South Africa today the legacy of racial divisions?

Critical Thinking

1. Identify whom the native peoples are and what their role has been in each of the societies discussed in this chapter.

2. Social construction of race emphasizes how we create arbitrary definitions of skin color that then have social consequences. Drawing on the societies discussed, select one nation and identify how social definitions work in other ways to define group boundaries.

2. Apply the functionalist and conflict approaches of sociology first introduced in Chapter 1 to each of the societies under study in this chapter.

3. The conflicts outlined in this chapter are examples of ethnonational conflicts, but how have the actions or inactions of the United States contributed to these problems?

17

Overcoming Exclusion

17-1 Explain how the aged are a social minority.

17-2 Summarize the experience of people with disabilities.

17-3 Identify the equality issues facing gays and lesbians.

What metaphor do we use to describe a nation whose racial, ethnic, and religious minorities are on the way to becoming numerical majorities in many cities and, now in the twenty-first century, in several states? For several generations, the image of the melting pot has been used as a convenient description of our culturally diverse nation. The analogy of an alchemist's cauldron was clever, even if a bit ethnocentric. It originated in the Middle Ages, when alchemists used a melting pot to attempt to change less-costly metals into gold and silver.

"The Melting Pot" was the title of a 1908 play by Israel Zangwill. In this play, a young Russian immigrant to the United States composes a symphony that portrays a nation that serves as a crucible (or pot) where all ethnic and racial groups melt together into a new, superior stock.

The vision of the United States as a melting pot became popular in the first part of the twentieth century, particularly because it suggested that the United States had an almost divinely inspired mission to destroy artificial divisions and create a single human-kind. However, the image did not mesh with reality, as the dominant group indicated its unwillingness to welcome Native Americans, African Americans, Hispanics or Latinos, Jews, and Asians, among many others, into the melting pot.

The image of the melting pot is not invoked as much today. Instead, people speak of a salad bowl to describe a country that is ethnically diverse. As we can distinguish the let-tuce from the tomatoes from the peppers in a tossed salad, we can see ethnic restaurants and the persistence of foreign languages in conversations on street corners. The dressing over the ingredients is akin to the shared value system and culture, covering but not hid-ing the different ingredients of the salad.

Yet even the notion of a salad is wilting. Like the melting pot that came before, the image of a salad is static, certainly not indicative of the dynamic changes we see in the United States. It also fails to conjure up the myriad cultural pieces that make up the fab-ric or mosaic of our diverse nation.

The kaleidoscope offers another familiar and more useful analogy. Patented in 1817 by Scottish scientist Sir David Brewster, the kaleidoscope was a toy and then became a table ornament in the parlors of the rich. Users of this optical device turn a set of mir-rors and observe the seemingly endless colors and patterns that are reflected off pieces of glass, tinsel, or beads. The growing popularity of the phrase "people of color" fits well with the idea of the United States as a kaleidoscope. The changing images correspond to the often bewildering array of groups found in our country (Schaefer 1992).

The images created by a kaleidoscope are hard to describe because they change dra-matically with little effort. Similarly, in the kaleidoscope of the United States, we find it a challenge to describe the dynamic multiracial nature of this republic. Yet even as we begin to understand the past, present, and future of all the many racial and ethnic groups, we recognize that there are still people other than racial and ethnic minorities who are stig-matized in society. There are many such groups, such as cancer survivors, ex-convicts, many marginalized religious groups, obese people, and transgendered individuals, to name a few.

We now consider the cases of the aged, people with disabilities, and the gay and lesbian community. This chapter in a large part continues the discussion begun in Chapter 15 about the intersection with each a variety of social factors besides race, class, and gender. The **matrix of domination** describes this cumulative impact of oppression with which many people come to live (refer back to Figure 15.5 on page 341). As we shall see, not to be elderly or people with disabilities, or to have a heterosexual sexual orientation privileges people in a way that they typically give little thought about as they go about their daily lives.

The Aged: A Social Minority

Older people in the United States are subject to a paradox. They are a significant segment of the population who, as we shall see, are often viewed with negative stereotypes and are subject to discrimination. Yet they also have successfully organized into a potent collec-tive force that wields significant political clout on certain social issues. Unlike other social groups subjected to differential treatment, this social category will include most of us some-day. So, in this one case, the notion of the elderly as "them" will eventually give way to "us."

17-1 Explain how the aged are a social minority.

17-1

Older adults share the characteristics of subordinate or minority groups that we introduced in Chapter 1. Specifically:

1. Older adults experience unequal treatment in employment and may face prejudice and discrimination.

2. Older adults share physical characteristics that distinguish them from younger people, and their cultural preferences and leisure-time activities often differ from those of the rest of society.

3. Membership in this disadvantaged group is involuntary.

4. Older people have a strong sense of group solidarity, as reflected in senior citizen centers, retirement communities, and advocacy organizations.

5. Older people generally are married to others of comparable age.

There is one crucial difference between older people and other subordinate groups, such as racial and ethnic minorities or women: All of us who live long will eventually assume the ascribed status of being an older person (Barron 1953; Wagley and Harris 1958).

Who Are the Elderly?

As shown in Figure 17.1, an increasing proportion of the population will be composed of older people. This trend is expected to continue well through the twenty-first century as mortality declines and the postwar baby boomers age. Looking over a period of a century, we see the proportion over age 65 increases from less than one in 10 in 1960 to almost one in four by 2050.

Compared with the rest of the population, older adults are more likely to be female, White, and living in certain states. Men generally have higher death rates than women at every age. As a result, elderly women outnumber men by a ratio of 3 to 2. The difference grows with advancing age, so that among the oldest old group (over 100 years), women outnumber men 4 to 1. About 80 percent of older adults are White and non-Hispanic. Although the aged population is growing more racially and ethnically diverse, the higher death rates of members of racial and ethnic minorities, coupled with immigration to the United States of younger Latinos and Asian Americans, are likely to keep the older population more White than the nation as a whole. Yet the overall pattern of a more diversified population will also be present among our oldest Americans. As seen in projections in Figure 17.2, the population aged 65 and over will become increasingly non-White and Latino.

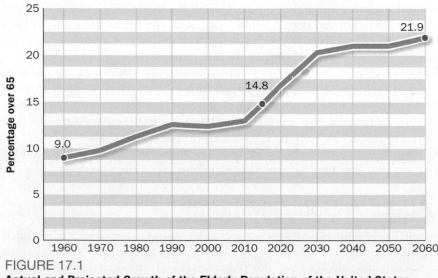

FIGURE 17.1

Actual and Projected Growth of the Elderly Population of the United States, 1960–2060

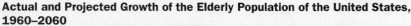

Sources: Bureau of the Census 2008: Table 2-c, 2012c: Table 3; Howden and Meyer 2011: Figure 4.

Ageism

Respected gerontologist Bernice Neugarten (1996) observed that negative stereotypes of old age are strongly entrenched in a society that prides itself on being oriented toward youth and the future. In 1968, physician Robert Butler (1990), the founding director of the National Institute on Aging, coined the term **ageism** to refer to prejudice and discrimination against the elderly. Ageism reflects a deep uneasiness among young and middle-aged people about growing old. For many, old age symbolizes disease and death; seeing older adults serve as a reminder that they too may someday become old and infirm. By contrast, society glorifies youth, seeing it as interchangeable with beauty and the future.

Ageism can be subtle and seen as well intentioned as when well-meaning people speak to older people slowly and using simple words. Yet even this behavior can be very offsetting to the older person and seen as patronizing and insincere.

When Neugarten first brought attention to age discrimination, she was thinking of attitudes toward old people age 55 to 75. With the greater health and expanding lifespan, this bracket needs to be extended into the 80s and beyond. Despite the widespread belief that ageing may be changing, does this mean that ageism is gone? In the 2008 presidential election, the age of 72-year-old John McCain served as a factor in some people's minds about his competency. Criticisms of him as "confused" and "losing his bearings" were used, according to some observers, as code words for him being "just too old" (North and Fiske 2013c).

In the Research Focus, we consider some innovative studies that try to pinpoint how young people view the elderly and if these views could have social implications for larger society.

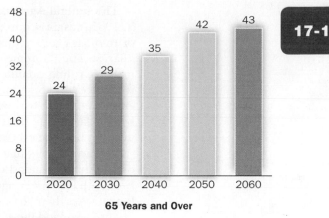

FIGURE 17.2
Minority Population Aged 65 and Older

Source: Bureau of the Census 2008, 2012c.

The Three Maxes

Three actors, neither ugly nor handsome, step before a video camera and play the same part, "Max." The man in the checked shirt identified himself as from New Jersey and working in a hardware store. And the three actors? One was 25, another 45, and the third 75. This was all a set-up to see if students reacted differently to Max based on his age.

Viewing these "interviews," people responded differently on whether they liked Max. In one series, the older Max indicates he enjoys the music of Rihanna and Justin Timberlake and sports a Black Eyed Peas t-shirt when he goes out. "Not good, less capable" said the younger evaluators; they liked it better if Max listened to Bing Crosby and wore a Frank Sinatra t-shirt. In another variation the young participants were told they would actually be interacting with Max in a community service project. Again they did not like the Max who was embracing a more youthful culture. Interestingly, evaluators who were in their thirties or older had no problem with the Rihanna-loving Max.

In another variation, undergraduates were asked by the researcher to offer their opinion of Max, thinking he was to become their partner in a trivia game. In this instance the video either showed Max as assertive or compliant. Students did not seem to care whether their prospective 25- or

45-year-old teammate was assertive, but the elder Max received a very negative rating if he was assertive. Male evaluators tend to be harsher raters than women in all the studies with racial and ethnic differences less significant than age or gender.

These studies point to the belief among younger people that older people should act their age and know their place. The kindly "grandfather" and "elder statesman" stereotypes persist. Researchers acknowledge that more work is needed. For example, would gender make a difference—a Maxine as well as a Max? That is, would young people be more accepting of a 75-year-old woman sporting a Justin Timberlake t-shirt? How about a more outspoken older woman? Also, the focus here overall is on the older person's plight. Future research should focus on anti-young prejudice and hence discrimination.

The conclusion from these studies is that stereotyping of older people is alive and well among young adults and that, perhaps, this has implications for the lives of senior citizens. As social psychologist Susan Fiske, a co-author of the studies, said, "If you want to be an aging gray panther, and speak your mind to your manager, that's fine, but expect consequences" (Winerip 2013: B1).

Sources: North and Fiske 2013a, 2013b; Winerip 2013.

17-1

The federal Age Discrimination in Employment Act (ADEA), which went into effect in 1968, was passed to protect workers 40 years of age or older from being fired because of their age and replaced with younger workers who presumably would receive lower salaries. The Supreme Court strengthened federal protection against age discrimination in 1996, ruling unanimously that such lawsuits can be successful even if an older worker is replaced by someone older than 40. Consequently, if a firm unfairly fires a 65-year-old employee to make way for a 45-year-old, this still can constitute age discrimination. Yet, by and large, age discrimination is not viewed as severe as racial or sex discrimination, perhaps because everyone will come to experience it (North and Fiske 2013c).

Research shows that before the enactment of the ADEA, there was evidence of hiring discrimination against older workers as well as discrimination in promotions and training. Even with the ADEA, age continues to work against many older people, as evidenced by how long it takes them to find employment, the wage loss they experience when they do become reemployed, and the size of court awards to victims of age discrimination (He et al. 2005).

Although firing workers simply because they are old violates federal law, courts have upheld the right to lay off older workers for economic reasons. Critics contend that later the same firms hire younger, cheaper workers to replace experienced older workers. When economic growth began to slow in 2001 and companies cut back on their workforces, complaints of age bias grew sharply as older workers began to suspect they were bearing a disproportionate share of the layoffs. According to the Equal Employment Opportunity Commission, between 1999 and 2004, complaints of age discrimination rose more than 41 percent. However, evidence of a countertrend has emerged. Some firms have been giving larger raises to older workers to encourage their retirement at the higher salary—a tactic that prompts younger workers to complain of age discrimination (Novelli 2004; Uchitelle 2003).

Yet in contradiction to these negative stereotypes present in an ageist society, researchers have found that an older worker can be an asset for employers. One study concluded that older workers can be retrained in new technologies, have lower rates of absenteeism than younger employees, and often are more effective salespeople. The study focused on two corporations based in the United States (the hotel chain Days Inns of America and the holding company Travelers Corporation of Hartford) and a British retail chain, all of which have long-term experience in hiring workers age 50 and over. Clearly, the findings pointed to older workers as good investments. Yet despite such studies, complaints of age bias grew during the economic slowdown beginning in 2001, when companies cut back on their workforces (Equal Employment Opportunity Commission 2001; Telsch 1991: A16).

The courts have made some significant decisions favoring older workers. In 2008, the Supreme Court ruled 7–1 in *Meachan v. Knolls Atomic Power Laboratory* that employers under ADEA had the burden to prove laying off older workers was based not on age but "some reasonable factor." In this instance, the employer had stated that the older workers were less "flexible" or "retrainable" but failed to present any convincing basis for their layoffs, which affected 31 employees—30 of whom were old enough to be covered by ADEA (Greenhouse 2008).

A degree of conflict is emerging along generational lines that resemble other types of intergroup tension. Although the conflict involves neither violence nor the degree of subjugation found with other dominant–subordinate relations in the United States, a feeling still prevails that jobs and benefits for the elderly are at the expense of younger generations. Younger people are increasingly unhappy about paying Social Security taxes and underwriting the Medicare program, especially because they speculate that they themselves will never receive benefits from these fiscally insecure programs.

The Economic Picture

The elderly, like the other groups we have considered, do not form a single economic profile. The perception of "elderly" and "poor" as practically synonymous has changed in recent years to a view that the noninstitutionalized elderly are economically better off than the population as a whole. Both views are too simplistic; income varies widely among the aged.

There is significant variation in wealth and poverty among the nation's older people. Some individuals and couples find themselves poor in part because of fixed pensions and skyrocketing healthcare costs. As shown in Figure 17.3, poverty has declined among the elderly of all racial groups.

As a group, older people in the United States are neither homogeneous nor poor. The typical older adult enjoys a standard of living that is much higher than at any point in the nation's past. Class differences among the elderly tend to narrow somewhat: Retirees who had middle-class incomes while younger tend to remain better off after retirement than those who had lower incomes, but the financial gap is declining (He et al. 2005).

The decline in poverty rates is welcome. However, advocates of the position that the elderly are receiving too much at the expense of the younger generations point to the rising affluence of the aged as evidence of an unfair economic burden placed on the young and future generations of workers.

As we can see in the previously mentioned data, the aged who are most likely to experience poverty are the same people more likely to be poor earlier in their lives: female-headed households and racial and ethnic minorities. Although overall the aged are doing well economically, poverty remains a particularly difficult problem for the thousands of older adults who are impoverished annually by paying for long-term medical care (Quadagno 2014).

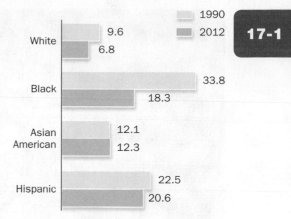

FIGURE 17.3
Poverty Rate among Older Adults

Note: Data for Whites are for White non-Hispanics as reported in 2012 for 2013.

Sources: DeNavas-Walt , Proctor, and Smith 2013: Table POV01.

Advocacy Efforts by the Elderly

As we have seen with racial, ethnic, and gender groups, efforts to bring about desired change often require the formation of political organizations and advocacy groups. This is true with older adults and, as we will see later, is also true for people with disabilities, gay men, and lesbian women. The growing collective consciousness among older people also contributed to the establishment of the Older Women's League (OWL) in 1980. OWL focuses on affordable healthcare, access to health insurance, Social Security benefits, and pension reform. OWL leaders and the group's 15,000 members hope that the organization will serve as a critical link between the feminist movements described in Chapter 15 and activists for "gray power" (Kening 2004; OWL 2013).

The largest organization representing the nation's elderly is the American Association of Retired Persons (AARP), which was founded in 1958 by a retired school principal who was having difficulty obtaining insurance because of age prejudice. Many of AARP's services involve discounts and insurance for its 40 million members (43 percent of Americans aged 50 and older). After recognizing that many elderly are still gainfully employed, the full name was dropped and the organization is now simply AARP.

The potential power of AARP is enormous; it represents one out of every four registered voters in the United States. AARP has endorsed voter-registration campaigns, nursing home reforms, and pension reforms. Acknowledging its difficulties in recruiting members of racial and ethnic minority groups, AARP began a Minority Affairs Initiative. The spokeswoman for this initiative, Margaret Dixon, became AARP's first African American president in 1996 (AARP 2003).

People grow old in many different ways. Not all the elderly face the same challenges or enjoy the same resources. Whereas AARP lobbies to protect older adults in general, other groups work in more specific ways. For example, the National Committee to Preserve Social Security and Medicare, founded in 1982, unsuccessfully lobbied Congress to keep Medicare benefits for the ailing poor elderly. Other large special-interest groups represent retired federal employees, retired teachers, and retired union workers (Quadagno 2014).

Older adults in the United States are better off today financially and physically than ever before. Many of them have strong financial assets and medical care packages that will take care of almost any need. But, as we have seen, a significant segment is impoverished and faces the prospect of declining health and mounting medical bills. Older

17-2

People with disabilities are often the first to identify an unmet need. Here 17-year-old student intern Bobby Harris has created for the Frederick, Maryland, police department a series of cards that serve as a visual communication to help first-responders interact with hearing-impaired people or, for that matter, non-English speakers. Brown, who was born deaf, found that the resource was more practical than trying to teach even basic sign language to the many people who may wish to help in times of emergency.

people of color may have to add being aged to a lifetime of discrimination. As in all other stages of the life course, the aged constitute a diverse group in the United States and around the world.

Although organizations such as the OWL and AARP are undoubtedly valuable, the diversity of the nation's older population necessitates many different responses to the problems of older adults. For example, older African Americans and Hispanics tend to rely more on family members, friends, and informal social networks than on organizational support systems. Because of their lower incomes and greater incapacity resulting from poor health, older Blacks and Hispanics are more likely to need substantial assistance from family members than are older Whites. In recent years, older people of color have emerged as a distinct political force, independent of the larger elderly population, in some urban centers and in the Southwest. Advocacy groups for the aged are still in their early stages, and low-income elderly are often the least represented.

People with Disabilities: Moving On

17-2 Summarize the experience of people with disabilities.

John Grant, 50 years old, has had a difficult time finding work after a career as a computer programmer and instructor came to a sudden end. He was let go when his position was eliminated and the response to his job seeking has been, to use his word, "ruthless." Brown has had a hearing impairment since birth and, like a lot of people with disabilities, the recession has been even harder to overcome. If a company calls to speak with Grant and he is having difficult hearing, he asks if he can call back using a third-party transcription service. The service provides real-time captions for what the caller is saying so people like Grant can more easily follow the conversation. Often his request to use this service causes the job search to end or, more decisively, the potential employer just hangs up (Murray 2010).

Throughout history, people have been socially disadvantaged, not because of the limits of their own skills and abilities but because assumptions are made about them based on some group characteristics. People with disabilities are such a group. The very term *disabilities* suggest lack of ability in some area, but as we shall see, society often assumes that a person with a disability is far less capable than she or he is. Furthermore, society limits the life chances of people with disabilities in ways that are unnecessary and unrelated to any physical infirmity.

Disability in Contemporary Society

Societies have always had members with disabilities. Historically, they have dealt differently with people who had physical or mental limitations, but rarely have they been treated as equals. According to the Bureau of the Census, an estimated 38 million people had a disability in 2011. **Disability** is considered a reduced ability to perform tasks one would normally do at a given stage in life. This includes everyone from those who have difficulty carrying 10 pounds to people who use wheelchairs, crutches, or walkers (Brault 2012).

We often marginalize people with disabilities, but many individuals have accomplished much in their lives. As we can see in Table 17.1, some people's disabilities are well known, whereas others' go largely unnoticed.

Disabilities are found in all segments of the population, but racial and ethnic minorities are disproportionately more likely to experience them and also to have less access to assistance. African Americans and Asian Latinos report higher rates of disability. Fewer African Americans and Hispanic people with disabilities are graduating from college

TABLE 17.1
Famous People with Disabilities

17-2

Can you match the person with the disability? All the famous people listed in this table have at least one disability. Match each person with one or more disabilities, then check your answers below.
Match the letters in Column A with the names in Column B.

Column A	Column B
A. Blind	_____ Stevie Wonder
B. Learning disability	_____ Michael J. Fox
C. Polio	_____ Beethoven
D. Epilepsy	_____ Tom Cruise
E. Dwarfism	_____ Patrick Dempsey
F. Parkinson's disease	_____ Napoleon Bonaparte
G. Quadriplegic	_____ Sting
H. Deaf	_____ Franklin Delano Roosevelt
I. Stuttering	_____ John Mellencamp
J. HIV–AIDS	_____ Christopher Reeve
K. Multiple sclerosis	_____ "Mini-me" Verne Troyer
L. Attention-deficit disorder	_____ Homer
M. Bipolar disorder	_____ James Earl Jones
N. Spina bifida	_____ Frida Kahlo
	_____ Montel Williams
	_____ Steven Spielberg
	_____ John Lennon
	_____ Jay Leno
	_____ Axl Rose
	_____ Charles Schwab
	_____ Robin Williams
	_____ Richard Pryor
	_____ Magic Johnson
	_____ Bruce Willis

Answers: Wonder A, Fox F, Beethoven H, Cruise B, Dempsey B, Napoleon B, Sting N, Roosevelt C, Mellencamp C, Reeve G, Mini-me E, Homer A, Jones I, Kahlo CN, Montel Williams K, Spielberg B, Lennon L, Leno I, Rose BL, Schwab B, Williams LM, Pryor K, Johnson J, Willis L.

Source: Author, based on Meyer 2011

compared with White people with disabilities. They also have incomes consistently lower than their White counterparts (Brault 2012; Steinmetz 2006).

Although disability knows no social class, about two-thirds of working-age people with a disability in the United States are unemployed. African Americans and Hispanics with disabilities are even more likely to be jobless. Most of them believe that they would be able to work if they were offered the opportunity or if some reasonable accommodation could be made to address the disability (Kirkpatrick 1994; Noble 1995; Shapiro 1993).

Labeling People with Disabilities

Labeling theorists, drawing on the work of sociologist Erving Goffman (1963), suggest that society attaches a stigma to many forms of disability and that this stigma leads to prejudicial treatment. Indeed, people with disabilities often observe that people without disabilities see them only as blind, deaf, wheelchair users, and so forth, rather than as complex human beings with individual strengths and weaknesses whose blindness or deafness is merely one aspect of their lives.

In the Speaking Out we hear sociologist Erik Olin Wright, the 2012 President of the American Sociological Association, describing his visit to Gallaudet University. The

17-2 (🎙) Speaking Out

My Journey Into the Deaf World

The first image of Gallaudet: Two students in animated conversation strolling along a walk next to classic liberal arts type buildings—an ordinary, everyday thing to see on campus, only they are talking with their hands. I have, of course, seen people signing before, and once, at a performance of a play in Madison {Wisconsin] by the National Theater of Deaf, I had been at an event with many people signing, but this was the first time I had visited a place in Deaf world and spoken, with the help of an interpreter, for an extended period with Deaf people. The day was extraordinary....

In preparation for the visit I decided to learn some ASL [American Sign Language] so I could give a greeting at the beginning of my talk....

Erik Olin Wright

At first doing this sequence of signs was really hard—I had to constantly look at my notes and everything was stilted and jerky. By my third lesson the ASL teacher said that I was making a lot of progress, but needed to pay a little attention to phrasing—otherwise it would be like speaking in a monotone with equal emphasis on every word. She also said not to worry about little mistakes. They would just seem like someone saying "wabbit" instead of "rabbit." ....

The lecture was in a beautiful space designed with the specific objective of being congenial to the Deaf. This meant having lots of light and good sight lines for visual communication. The room was a kind of atrium-like space with a circular balcony on the second floor overlooking the lecture space below and with clear glass panels perhaps four feet high instead of a guard rail. You could sit behind these panels and still communicate with people below—communicating through walls, I was told. The elevators that went up from the bottom of the atrium-space also had glass sides so people in the elevator could talk to people outside with ASL.

I was introduced at the talk by Thomas Horejes, a young, energetic, very appealing Deaf sociologist on the Gallaudet faculty. Then I did my signed greeting—quite smoothly, without hesitation, I thought. Later one person said that although everyone understood what I meant, my "thrilled" look a little like "pasta," so the greeting was: "Hello, I'm pasta and honored to be here...." Other people reassured me that my sign looked pretty close to "thrilled." Anyway, wabbit or pasta, everyone seemed very appreciative of my effort.

After I did my signed introduction, I added a few comments about my experience signing....

After I was finished speaking there was a lively question and answer discussion. A number of students and professors came up and asked me questions in ASL....

A young African-American woman: "I wanted to ask you about utopia. Do you think that this ignores individualism or individual expectations because it focuses so much on the group? Especially in such a highly individualistic society I think it would be hard in American to combine both a group and individuals goals as well." I responded by talking about the utopian aspiration being to create the conditions for individual persons to flourish. The issue is really about the relationship between institutions and individuals more than between groups and individuals. [I also realized when I was listening to this young woman's question that I was looking at the interpreter who was speaking rather than at the person who was signing the question. I guess this is a natural mistake by someone not used to interacting with Deaf people—making eye contact with the speaking interpreter rather than the silent signing person. But from then on I looked at the person asking the question.]

....

When the lecture was done, we went to lunch with a number of faculty members from the sociology department. At lunch there was a really interesting discussion of the complex issue of cochlear implants between one person who had been Deaf from birth and the other who became Deaf as an adult. Both had actually learned ASL as adults. The person who was Deaf since birth had been mainstreamed as a child, learning lip-reading, and only learned ASL as a young adult. Many issues were in play in the discussion:

- At what age was it appropriate to have cochlear implants? If a young child is to have this procedure done, then it means that the parents would have the power to impose it on a child. One position is that this should not be done until around age 9 when the child could decide. But, the contrary argument goes, the benefits of the procedure are greatest if done very early, since then the brain can adapt more easily to the cochlear implant signals. Also, if done earlier, this can have a bigger impact on language acquisition and cognitive development.

- A deaf child born to a deaf parent is a very different situation from a deaf child born to hearing parent.

- All this raised the issue of what is "normal" and what needs to be "fixed." The deaf/hearing spectrum is a natural form of variation, and so being deaf is not "abnormal," it is just one form in which human lives take place.

- There was also an interesting disagreement over whether a person could in fact be fully part of both worlds. Why can't a child with a cochlear implant which results in some hearing also become fully conversant in sign language and thus be in both worlds? The person who was opposed to early childhood implants felt that this is in practice very unlikely. This led to a very interesting discussion of ways in which the long-term trajectory of medical solutions to deafness is likely to undermine the support for signing and deaf culture. The disappearance of those supports would mean that in the future ASL would become less of an available option for parents. One of the hearing people at lunch who was fluent in ASL said that she would be happy with a deaf child, but if the supports disappeared she would definitely do an implant because the task of providing those supports would be overwhelming.

■ There was a time when most deafness was the result of medical conditions, not genes, but now medical interventions have greatly reduced deafness as a consequence of disease. Eventually most deafness will be because of genes, rather than disease, and since the genetic conditions are rare this means that being Deaf will become very rare. As Deafness becomes rarer it will be harder to become proficient in sign since there will be no one to sign with. There is also a decline in Deaf schools with more mainstreaming, which also results in decreased proficiency of signing.

■ The next controversy will be over aborting fetuses with the deaf gene, just like there is controversy over aborting fetuses with Down syndrome.

After lunch we had a brief tour of the campus. It is a lovely environment—some old, charming late 19th century buildings along with new, well designed modern ones. The University was chartered by Abraham Lincoln in 1864 and clearly has become an anchor for Deaf culture and education....

At 4 pm I met with a group of undergraduates for a freewheeling discussion. A few of the questions seemed a bit naïve to me, or at least not well informed. Later Margaret explained that many of the students at Gallaudet have large challenges to overcome because they haven't had access to the kind of diffuse general knowledge while growing up that most undergraduates have. Much of this knowledge is picked up serendipitously in overhearing conversations, casually watching the news and listening to the radio, all things which are much less likely for a Deaf child, especially if their parents are hearing. A child Deaf from birth also has a much bigger challenge learning to read, since the English words are all purely marks on a page with no sounds connected to them. This is more like learning to read Chinese or some other system of symbols that have no sounds connected to them. Each word has to be learned as a separate entity. As a result many students read at a pretty low level, but are still trying to do college work. These are really very stiff challenges.

The day ended with relaxing, laughter-filled dinner at a Sushi restaurant with a number of sociology faculty and two interpreters. The interpreters had to work really hard, and their professional code meant that they weren't supposed to eat while on the job. It really is a full translation issue, because the grammar of ASL and spoken English are not the same. As it was explained to me, ASL does not have a fixed word order the way spoken English does. And of course, there is not a direct sign for every word in English, so sometimes the interpreter has to spell out the word with hand spelling. They seemed to do a really good job, because the conversation flowed very smoothly and easily. In one way this was a bit easier than if they were translating from English to a foreign language: in ordinary translation, the translation needs to be sequential at a dinner table, because the interpreter cannot speak at the same time as one is talking. But in signed interpretation, they can do the signing as a simultaneous translation, since there are no sounds.

Source: Wright 2012: 12, 13.

college, founded in 1864 to serve deaf students, is located in Washington DC. Wright very clearly acknowledges that entering this campus of a school that was created to serve the deaf, he is entering a different culture that he seeks to understand and appreciate.

As with other subordinate statuses, the mass media have contributed to the stereotyping of people with disabilities. Too often, they are treated with a mixture of pity and fear. Nationwide charity telethons promote a negative image of people with disabilities as being childlike and nonproductive, suggesting that until they are "cured," they cannot contribute to society like other people. At the very least, the poster-child image proclaims that it is not okay to have a disability. By contrast, in literature and film, evil characters with disabilities—from Captain Hook to Dr. Strangelove to Freddy Krueger—reinforce the view that disability is a punishment for evil. Efforts to encourage sober driving or safety in the workplace use images of people with disabilities to frighten people into the appropriate behavior.

There has been some evidence of positive portrayal of people with disabilities on television series such as *Ironside* (1967–1975, again in 2013), *Life Goes On* (1989–1993), *Breaking Bad* (2008–2013), *Secret Life of the American Teenager* (2008–), *Lie to Me* (2009–2013), *Michael J. Fox Show* (2013), but there is a lot of ground to make up in the image department.

Negative attitudes are not the only challenge facing people with disabilities. Among men and women aged 16–64 with any kind of disability, 35 percent are employed, compared to 72 percent without a disability. People with disabilities are also 1.5 times more likely to be victims of both violent and nonviolent crimes. In about one in five incidents, the victim felt that their disability was why they were victimized (Brault 2012; Rand and Harrell 2009).

17-2

In Chapter 3, we introduced **institutional discrimination**, which describes the denial of opportunities and equal rights to individuals or groups, resulting from the normal operations of a society. This applies to people with disabilities. For example, society is sometimes organized in a way that limits people with disabilities. Architectural barriers and transportation difficulties often add to the problems of people with disabilities when they seek and obtain employment. Simply getting around city streets can be quite difficult for people with mobility challenges. Many streets are not properly equipped with curb cuts for wheelchair users. A genuinely barrier-free building needs more than a ramp; it should also include automatic doors, raised letters and Braille on signs, and toilets that are accessible to people with disabilities. Even if a person with disabilities finds a job, and even if the job is in a barrier-free building, he or she still faces the problem of getting to work in a society in which many rail stations and most buses remain inaccessible to wheelchair users and others with disabilities.

Advocacy for Disability Rights

Until recently, people with disabilities as a group have scarcely been thought of in any terms except perhaps pity. Often history has forgotten how deep the mistreatment has been. There has been a steadily growing effort to ensure not only the survival of people with disabilities but also the same rights enjoyed by others. In the early 1960s, Ed Roberts and some other young adults with disabilities wanted to attend the University of California at Berkeley. Reluctant at first, the university was eventually persuaded to admit them and agreed to reserve space in the university infirmary as living quarters for students with disabilities. These students and others established their own student center and became known as the Rolling Quads. They eventually turned their attention to the surrounding community and established the Berkeley Center for Independent Living, which became a model for hundreds of independent living centers (Brannon 1995).

By the early 1970s, following the example of the Rolling Quads, a strong social movement for disability rights had emerged across the United States, which drew on the experiences of the Black civil rights movement and the feminist movement. This movement now includes a variety of organizations; some work on behalf of people with a single disability (such as the National Federation of the Blind), and others represent people with any of many disabilities (such as New York City's Disabled in Action). The large number of Vietnam veterans with disabilities who joined the effort gave a boost to advocacy efforts and a growing legitimacy in larger society.

Many of these organizations worked for the 1990 passage of the Americans with Disabilities Act (ADA). In many respects, this law is the most sweeping antidiscrimination legislation since the 1964 Civil Rights Act. The ADA went into effect in 1992, covering people with a disability, defined as a condition that "substantially limits" a "major life activity" such as walking or seeing. It prohibits bias in employment, transportation, public accommodations, and telecommunication against people with disabilities. Businesses with more than 15 employees cannot refuse to hire a qualified applicant with a disability; these companies are expected to make a "reasonable accommodation" to permit such a worker to do the job. Commercial establishments such as office buildings, hotels, theaters, supermarkets, and dry cleaners are barred from denying service to people with disabilities (Burgdorf 2005).

The ADA represents a significant framing of the issues of people with disabilities. Basically, we can see it taking a civil-rights view of disabilities that seeks to humanize the way society sees and treats people with disabilities. The ADA does not take the perspective adopted in other nations, such as Great Britain, of seeing disability as totally an entitlement issue; that is, because you have a disability, you automatically receive certain benefits. Rather, its perspective is that people with disabilities are being denied certain rights. As disability rights activist Mark Johnson said, "Black people fought for the right to ride in the front of the bus. We're fighting for the right to get on the bus" (Shapiro 1993: 128; see also Albrecht 2005; Burgdorf 2005).

A more specific concern relevant to people with disabilities has arisen at Gallaudet University, an institution that Wright visited in the Speaking Out box. Gallaudet has been

17-3

the scene of unrest during the last 20 years concerning the selection of its president. For many students and sympathetic supporters, the president of this institution must not only be deaf but also embrace the primacy of American Sign Language (ASL). First in 1988 and then again in 2006, students mounted "Deaf President Now" campaigns after presidents were proposed who were not "deaf enough" because they relied too much on reading lips or spoke without using ASL. The disability rights movement has caused people both with and without disabilities to rethink what constitutes fairness and equity (Basken 2007).

There are examples of businesses that are pioneers in expanding opportunities to people with disabilities. The National Governors Association has worked with Walgreens in the large retailer's effort to expand its talent pool with those with disabilities, ranging from autism and mental retardation to those who are visually or hearing impaired. Their own research shows workers with disabilities are often more efficient, loyal, and have lower absenteeism. Any cost of accommodating such workers with new technologies and education has been shown to be minimal (National Governors Association 2013; Walgreens 2013).

Rethinking the rights of people with disabilities began with the ADA but has now come with the call for visitability. **Visitability** refers to making private homes built so that they are accessible for visitors with disabilities. In the mid-1990s, cities such as Atlanta and Austin, Texas, as well as Great Britain, passed ordinances encouraging new homes to have at least one no-step entrance, wider doorways, grab bars in bathrooms, and other accommodations. This new idea suggests that *all* environments should be accessible—not just public places, such as courtrooms or token handicapped-accessible accommodations in hotels, but *all* living spaces. Many people oppose such a move as unnecessary government interference; others see it as a long-overdue recognition that people with disabilities should be able to move freely throughout the country (Buchholz 2003; Visitability 2013).

A significant stigma is attached to having a major visible disability. Not wishing to present an image of a "disabled" president, Franklin Roosevelt enlisted the cooperation of the press corps to avoid being shown in a wheelchair or using crutches. This picture shows the president leaving a New York City townhouse in 1933 with a rare view of the president's leg braces.

Source: © New York Daily News, L. P. Reprinted with permission.

17-3 Identify the equality issues facing gays and lesbians.

Activists remain encouraged since the passage of the ADA. Those working on behalf of the veterans of the Iraq and Afghanistan wars who have returned with significant disabilities have joined long-time activists in their continuing efforts for disability rights. Although the ADA has been in effect for less than two decades, studies reveal that people with disabilities feel empowered and perceive increased access to employment opportunities. However, one must remember that civil rights activists felt a measure of optimism after passage of the major civil rights legislation more than 40 years ago (Albrecht 2005; Meyer 2008).

Gays and Lesbians: Coming Out for Equality

When and how did you first realize you were a heterosexual?

What do you think caused your heterosexuality?

Is it possible that your heterosexuality is just a phase you may grow out of?

Why are heterosexuals so promiscuous?

These are not questions heterosexuals are likely to hear being asked because these queries assume something is wrong with being attracted to members of the opposite sex. On the other hand, we are all accustomed to hearing homosexuals questioned about their orientation.

17-3

We live at a time when heterosexuality is taken for granted and healthy. Homosexuality is, therefore, seen as a social issue. Yet, at certain times in many societies, it was possible to acknowledge same-sex love and act on it without necessarily encountering open hostility.

In the United States, and to a varying degree in all contemporary societies, heterosexuality is privileged and labeled as "normal." Young children are often presented that romantic relationships are only between a man and a woman. Heterosexuality is taken for granted without need for explanation. Gay male and lesbian relationships are often invisible and, in some households, openly scorned. While presenting heterosexuality as the norm as the typical approach is not necessarily motivated by homophobia, it still serves to raise heterosexuality to the standard of what a child should expect of others and, most importantly, of themselves. Well before dating, much less mate selection, is a social reality, terms like "boyfriends" and "girlfriends" are used in a way to reinforce opposite-sex relationships (Fischer 2013; Martin 2009; Martin and Luke 2010).

Many preschool educators now talk of the value of such books as *Two Mommies, It's OK to Be Different, My Princess Boy, William's Doll,* and *Daddy, Papa and Me* to broaden toddlers' realization that there are a variety of household types. Yet even when used, they have to be set against a social environment where homosexuality is not the norm.

The focus in this chapter is on differential treatment because one is a homosexual—that is, gay or lesbian—but human sexuality is very diverse. Yet typically in the United States, sexual orientation is constructed as either homosexual or heterosexual and ignores people who are *bisexuals*—that is, individuals sexually attracted to both sexes. Sometimes included in discussions about gays, lesbians, and bisexuals are *transgendered persons*—people whose gender identity does not match their physical identity at birth; transgendered individuals, for example, may see themselves as both male and female. *Transsexuals* are people who see themselves as the sex opposite of their birth identity and may take surgical measures to bring their physical being closer to their gender identity. Sometimes confused with these issues of gender identity and sexual orientation are *transvestites*, which today usually refers to cross-dressers who wear clothing of the opposite sex. These are typically men choosing to wear women's clothing, who may be either gay or heterosexual in their orientation.

Being Gay and Lesbian in the United States

There are anecdotal accounts of public recognition of homosexuality throughout U.S. history, but it was not until the 1920s and 1930s that it became visible. By that time, clubs for gays and lesbians were growing in number, typically in urban areas. Plays, books, and organizations were created to meet the social needs of gays and lesbians. As homosexuality has become more visible, efforts to suppress it have been institutionalized. At about the same time, the U.S. Army hired psychiatrists to screen recruits for evidence of homosexuality and dismissed volunteers who were gay (Schwartz 1992).

Given that gay men and lesbians are severely stigmatized, accurate data are hard to obtain. Researchers for the National Health and Life Survey and the Voter News Service in their election exit polls estimate that 2 to 5 percent of U.S. adults identify themselves as gay or lesbian. An analysis of the 2010 Census shows the numbers of gay and lesbian adult population approaching 10 million (Laumann et al. 1994; Lofquist 2011).

In Figure 17-4, we see the national pattern of same-sex households. The highest proportion is found in the Northeast, parts of the Midwest, and the Far West. Typically relatively high levels are found in states that have laws that prohibit discrimination based on sexual orientation (Gates and Newport 2013).

Discussion and growing recognition of a sizable gay population did not lead to a consistent effort to promote understanding over the last 60 years. The general focus was to explore ways to prevent and control homosexuality as a disease, which is what psychiatrists thought it was. Well into the 1960s, discrimination against gays and lesbians was common and legal. Police raided bars frequented by people seeking same-sex partners and people were jailed, their names often published in local newspapers. Although not surprising, it was disappointing to hear that the county board in Rhea County, Tennessee,

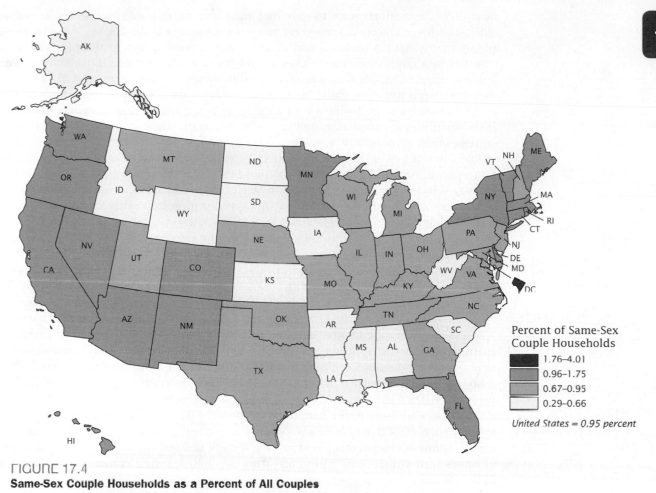

FIGURE 17.4

Same-Sex Couple Households as a Percent of All Couples

About 594,000 same-sex couples lived in the United States in 2010.

Source: 2010 American Community Survey data in Lofquist 2011; 4.

unanimously passed a measure in 2004 that allowed the county to prosecute someone for being gay or lesbian as a "crime against nature." A few days later, after recognizing the losing court battle they would face, the county commissioners rescinded the antigay motion, but clearly they did not take back their view of gays and lesbians. Little wonder then that public health officials have detected increased risk for a variety of risky behaviors as well as mental health disorders including depression among adolescent lesbian and gay youth (Barry 2004; Coker, Austin, and Shuster 2010).

Prejudice and Discrimination

Homophobia, the fear of and prejudice toward homosexuality, is present in every facet of life: the family, organized religion, the workplace, official policies, and the mass media. Like the myths and stereotypes of race and gender, those about homosexuality keep gay men and lesbian women oppressed as a group and may also keep sympathetic members of the dominant group, the heterosexual community, from joining in support.

Homophobia is considered a much more respectable form of bigotry than voicing negative feelings and ideas against any other oppressed groups. People still openly avoid homosexuals, and group members are stereotyped on television and in motion pictures. Although homophobia has decreased, many people still feel at ease in expressing their homophobic feelings that a homosexual lifestyle is unacceptable.

As we will see later, gays and lesbians have made extensive efforts to make their feelings known, to ask for respect and a variety of rights, and to have their sexual orientation

17-3

accepted. Their efforts seem to have had some impact on public opinion as we will consider shortly with national surveys on marriage of same-sex couples, yet about 39 percent of gay and lesbian Americans said in 2013 that at some point in their lives they were rejected by a family member or close friend because of their sexual orientation. Nearly a third report being physically attacked or threatened at some point and 21 percent felt they have been treated unfairly by an employer (Pew Research Center 2013).

The entertainment business is often seen as being welcoming to openly gay and lesbian performers. The reality appears to be different. Although openly gay actors and actresses find employment, starring roles are few and far between. Furthermore, highly visible roles of gay individuals are generally played by heterosexual actors, such as Sean Penn playing the title role in the 2008 motion picture *Milk,* which chronicles the life of Harvey Milk, the first openly gay man to be elected to office in California. And, ironically, openly gay actors are more likely to achieve recognition in playing straight roles such as Neil Patrick Harris in the *How I Met Your Mother* television series, which ran from 2005 through 2014. An analysis found a decrease in the percentage of lesbian, gay, bisexual, and transgender (LGBT) characters in 2013–2014 scripted broadcast television with only 3.3 percent of series regular roles from the year before. It also represented only a slight increase over 2009–2010 season with 3.0 percent LGBT characters (GLAAD 2013).

The stigmatization of gays and lesbians was seen as a major factor in the slow initial response to the presence of AIDS (acquired immunodeficiency syndrome), which, when it first appeared in the United States, overwhelmingly claimed gay men as its victims. The inattention and the reluctance to develop a national policy forced gay communities in major cities to establish self-help groups to care for the sick, educate the healthy, and lobby for more responsive public policies. The most outspoken AIDS activist group has been the AIDS Coalition to Unleash Power (ACT-UP), which has conducted controversial protests and sit-ins in the halls of government and at scientific conferences. Although initially such efforts may have siphoned away participants from the broader gay rights effort, ultimately, new constituencies of gay men and lesbians were created, along with alliances with sympathetic supporters from the heterosexual community (Adam 1995; Shilts 1982).

In 1998, the nation was shocked by the unprovoked, brutal murder of Matthew Shepard, a University of Wyoming student, by two men. Subsequent investigation showed that Shepard's being gay was the reason his attackers murdered him rather than leaving him alone after robbing the young man. This tragic event galvanized a move to include sexual orientation as a basis of hate crimes in many states. Gays and lesbians themselves began to actively resist their mistreatment, sometimes working with local law enforcement agencies and prosecutors to end antigay violence. Many activists bemoaned the fact that there is still no memorial and no antigay violence law in Wyoming. Yet in his name, Congress passed the Matthew Shepard Act, which did extend hate-crime protection to gay men and lesbians.

On a more everyday level, studies point to the price people pay for being gay and lesbian. While some entrepreneurial people may create successful gay-oriented businesses in entertainment or travel, most of society proceeds against a backdrop that normalizes heterosexuality. Finally beginning in 2013, gay couples no longer had to file separate tax forms, which generally deprives them of some significant savings experienced by heterosexual married people. Despite continuing differences, as noted in the Research Focus, efforts are being made to normalize homosexuality as heterosexuality has been for generations.

5.18.08 The PHILADELPHIA INQUIRER. UNIVERSAL PRESS SYNDICATE

MARRIAGE

CIVIL UNION

SEPARATE BUT EQUAL

A continuing social issue at the local, state, and national levels is whether same-sex couples should be recognized. And if recognized, should they be as civil unions or with the same privileges of married men and women?

Source: AUTH © 2008 The Philadelphia Inquirer. Reprinted with permission of UNIVERSAL UCLICK. All rights reserved.

Advocacy for Gay and Lesbian Rights

The first homosexual organization in the United States was founded in Chicago in 1924. Such groups grew steadily over the next 50 years, but they were primarily local and were more likely to be self-help and social rather than confrontational. The social movements of the 1950s and 1960s on behalf of African Americans and women caused lesbians and gay men also to reflect more directly on the oppression their sexual orientation caused.

The contemporary gay and lesbian movement marks its beginning in New York City on June 28, 1969. Police raided the Stonewall Inn, an after-hours gay bar, and forced patrons into the street. Instead of meekly dispersing and accepting the disruption, the patrons locked police inside the bar and rioted until police reinforcements arrived. For the next three nights, lesbians and gay men marched through the streets of New York, protesting police raids and other forms of discrimination. Within months, gay liberation groups appeared in cities and campuses throughout the United States (Armstrong and Crage 2006).

Despite the efforts of the lesbian and gay rights movement, in 1986 the Supreme Court in *Bowers v. Hardwick* ruled by a 5–4 vote that the Constitution does not protect homosexual relations between consenting adults, even in the privacy of their own homes. The decision sent the clear message endorsing the normality of heterosexuality. This position held until the Court reversed itself in 2003 by a 6–3 vote in *Lawrence v. Texas*. The divisiveness of the issue nationally was reflected among the justices. Justice Anthony Kennedy declared in *Lawrence* that gays are "entitled to respect for their private lives" while Justice Antonio Scalia complained that the decision indicated that the Court had "largely signed on to the so-called homosexual agenda" (Kane 2010).

In 2000, the Supreme Court hurt the gay rights movement when it ruled 5–4 that the Boy Scouts organization had a constitutional right to exclude gay members because opposition to homosexuality was part of the organization's message. The Court clearly stated in its ruling that it was not endorsing this view but supporting the right of the organization to hold this position and to limit participation based on it. Despite this and earlier Supreme Court decisions, gays and lesbians worked to establish the principle that sexual orientation should not be the basis for discrimination.

Issues involving gays and lesbians have always been present, but because of advocacy efforts, political leaders and the courts are advancing the concerns. In 1993, President Bill Clinton, under pressure from the gay community, reviewed the prohibition of homosexuals from the military. However, he encountered even greater pressure from opponents and eventually compromised in 1994 with the "Don't ask, don't tell" policy. The policy allows lesbians and gay men to continue to serve in the military as long as they keep their homosexuality secret, but commanders investigated and dismissed 14,000 military personnel. Finally, facing likely court action ending the policy action, the policy was officially ended in 2011 allowing openly gay and lesbians to serve in the military for the first time.

The most vocal debate is over whether gay and lesbian couples should be able to legally get married. Congress enacted the Defense of Marriage Act (DOMA) in 1996, which defined marriage as between one man and one woman and let states and the federal government deny recognition of same-sex marriages. Despite criticism from the gay community and those who are supportive of legal recognition of same-sex marriage, the measure was initially popular with the public. Then in 2013, by a 5–4 vote in *United States v. Windsor*, the Court struck down a key section in the act, in effect declaring that the federal government must recognize gay marriage in the 12 states where it was legal at the time.

The ruling keeps the move for legalizing gay marriage to continue at the state level. Among the general public, support for same-sex couples has gradually increased; by 2013, 55 percent supported and 40 percent opposed same-sex marriage. At the local love, opponents to gay marriage are finding new ways to show their views. There is growing evidence that some photographers, wedding cake bakers, and florists have refused to serve wedding and civil union ceremonies involving same-sex couples. The legality of such rejection of business raises a number of issues that are complex and await numerous court sessions (Dimrock, Doherty, and Suls 2013; Koppel and Jones 2013).

17-3

SPECTRUM OF INTERGROUP RELATIONS

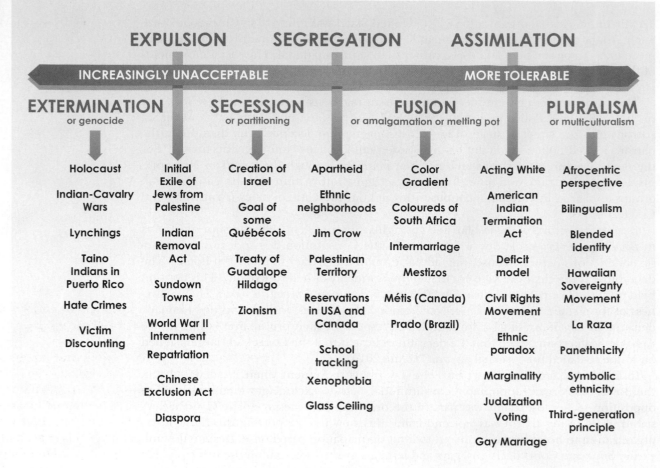

EXPULSION		SEGREGATION		ASSIMILATION		
INCREASINGLY UNACCEPTABLE					MORE TOLERABLE	
EXTERMINATION or genocide	**SECESSION** or partitioning		**FUSION** or amalgamation or melting pot		**PLURALISM** or multiculturalism	
Holocaust	Initial Exile of Jews from Palestine	Creation of Israel	Apartheid	Color Gradient	Acting White	Afrocentric perspective
Indian-Cavalry Wars		Goal of some Québécois	Ethnic neighborhoods	Coloureds of South Africa	American Indian Termination Act	Bilingualism
Lynchings	Indian Removal Act	Treaty of Guadalope Hildago	Jim Crow	Intermarriage	Deficit model	Blended identity
Taino Indians in Puerto Rico	Sundown Towns	Zionism	Palestinian Territory	Mestizos	Civil Rights Movement	Hawaiian Sovereignty Movement
Hate Crimes			Reservations in USA and Canada	Métis (Canada)		
Victim Discounting	World War II Internment			Prado (Brazil)	Ethnic paradox	La Raza
	Repatriation		School tracking		Marginality	Panethnicity
	Chinese Exclusion Act		Xenophobia		Judaization	Symbolic ethnicity
	Diaspora		Glass Ceiling		Voting	Third-generation principle
					Gay Marriage	

We have used assimilation throughout this book to describe the process by which individuals forsake their own heritage to become a part of a different culture. Assimilation has emerged as a hot issue in the gay community. Some argue that promoting marriage-equality is merely trying to assimilate or to become like the oppressor, adopting their social conventions. In addition, some argue these efforts are misguide energy away from helping those already marginalized among gays and lesbians such as people of color, transgender people, and those who prefer other forms of intimacy to marriage (Bernstein and Taylor 2013).

In our final Spectrum of Intergroup Relations we summarize how aspects of these relationships like assimilation have been utilized throughout this textbook. Efforts to downplay overt expression of homosexuality are yet another example of assimilation. Critics of assimilation argue that equal treatment is the real issue and should not be the result of conforming to the ways of the heterosexual-dominant society. The debate is unlikely to be resolved soon because full acceptance of gays and lesbians is far removed from today's social and political agenda. But this discussion repeats a pattern found with every subordinate group—how to maintain one's unique identity and become part of a multicultural society (Hartocullis 2006; Hequembourg and Arditi 1999).

Conclusion

As the United States promotes racial, ethnic, and religious diversity, it strives also to impose universal criteria on employers, educators, and realtors so that subordinate racial and ethnic groups can participate fully in the larger society. In some instances, to bring about equality of results—not just equality of opportunity—programs have been developed to give competitive advantages to women and minority men. Only more recently have

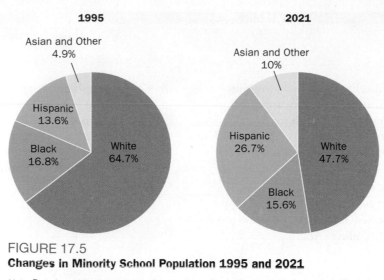

1995

Asian and Other
4.9%

Hispanic
13.6%

Black
16.8%

White
64.7%

2021

Asian and Other
10%

Hispanic
26.7%

White
47.7%

Black
15.6%

FIGURE 17.5

Changes in Minority School Population 1995 and 2021

Note: Data for public elementary and secondary schools. Race categories exclude Hispanics.

Source: National Center for Education Statistics 2013: Table 44.

similar strides been made on behalf of people with disabilities. These latest answers to social inequality have provoked much controversy over how to achieve the admirable goal of a multiracial, multiethnic society, undifferentiated in opportunity and rewards.

The huge outpouring of information for the census documents the racial and ethnic diversity of the entire nation. And as we see in Figure 17.5, driving the growth of the diverse population is the growing proportion of those under the age of 18 who are Latino, African American, Asian American, or Native American.

Relations between racial, ethnic, or religious groups take two broad forms, as situations characterized by either consensus or conflict. Consensus prevails where assimilation or fusion of groups has been completed. Consensus also prevails in a pluralistic society in the sense that members have agreed to respect differences between groups. By eliminating the contending group, extermination and expulsion also lead to a consensus society. In the study of intergroup relations, it is often easy to ignore conflict where there is a high degree of consensus because it is assumed that an orderly society has no problems. In some instances, however, this assumption is misleading. Through long periods of history, misery inflicted on a racial, ethnic, or religious group was judged to be appropriate, if not actually divinely inspired.

In recent history, harmonious relations between all racial, ethnic, and religious groups have been widely accepted as a worthy goal. The struggle against oppression and inequality is not new. It dates back at least to the revolutions in England, France, and the American colonies in the seventeenth and eighteenth centuries. The twentieth century was unique in the extension of equality to the less-privileged classes, many of whose members are racial and ethnic minorities. Conflict along racial and ethnic lines is especially bitter now because it evokes memories of slavery, colonial oppression, and overt discrimination. Today's African Americans are much more aware of slavery than contemporary poor people are of seventeenth-century debtors' prison.

Unquestionably, the struggle for justice among racial and ethnic groups has not completely met its goals. While the election of Barack Obama as president was historic and worthy of the global celebration it received, it does not reflect the broad movement of members of racial and ethnic groups into positions of power in the private and public sectors. Many people are still committed to repression, although they may see it only as the benign neglect of those less privileged. Such repression leads to the dehumanization of both the subordinated individual and the oppressor. Growth in equal rights movements and self-determination for third-world countries largely populated by non-White people has moved the world onto a course that seems irreversible. The old ethnic battle lines now renewed in Iran, the Darfur region of Sudan, Kenya, the Georgia Republic, and Chechnya in Russia have only added to the tensions.

Self-determination, whether for groups or individuals, often is impossible in societies as they are currently structured. Bringing about social equality, therefore, will entail significant changes in existing institutions. Because such changes are not likely to come about with everyone's willing cooperation, the social costs will be high. However, if there is a trend in racial and ethnic relations in the world today, it is the growing belief that the social costs, however high, must be paid to achieve self-determination.

It is naive to foresee a world of societies in which one person equals one vote and all are accepted without regard to race, ethnicity, religion, gender, age, disability status, or sexual orientation. It is equally unlikely to expect to see a society, let alone a world, that is without a privileged class or prestigious jobholders. Contact between different peoples, as we have seen numerous times, precedes conflict. Contact also may initiate mutual understanding, appreciation, and respect.

Summary

1. The elderly in the United States are growing in numbers and proportions, with a growing proportion being people of color. Although many gains have been made in ensuring the health and safety of older Americans, those who choose to continue to work often face ageism.

2. Advocacy efforts by people with disabilities and others on their behalf have a long history. A major milestone was achieved in 1990 with the passage of the Americans with Disabilities Act.

3. Gays and lesbians have been working to achieve equality but have yet to achieve the same kind of national recognition through either legislation or legal precedence. Issues such as gay marriage dominate newspaper coverage, but day-to-day concerns such as discrimination in employment often remain unaddressed.

Key Terms

ageism p. 369

disability p. 372

homophobia p. 379

institutional discrimination p. 376

matrix of domination p. 367

visitability p. 377

Review Questions

1. In what ways are the aged stereotyped, and how does it affect their quality of life?

2. What are common and differing challenges facing people with disabilities?

3. How would you describe the successes and limitations experienced by gay men and lesbians seeking to achieve equality?

Critical Thinking

1. Sociologists use the term *master status* to describe a status that dominates others and thereby determines a person's general position in society. To what degree can that term be applied to the three groups considered in this chapter?

2. The media—in advertisements, humor, dramas, and situation comedies—portray life in society. What are some examples, both positive and negative, of how older adults, people with disabilities, and gays and lesbians are presented in the media that you have seen? In what ways are these groups stereotyped?

3. How might advances in technology, including innovations for the home and computer chat rooms, have a unique effect on each of the groups trying to overcome exclusion discussed in this chapter?

4. How do policymakers trying to bring about change use the model of "half full" and "half empty"—either to argue for change on behalf of minorities or to use the same concepts to maintain that the status quo is adequate for addressing issues of social inequality?

Glossary

Parenthetical numbers refer to the pages on which the term is introduced.

abolitionists   Whites and free Blacks who favored the end of slavery. (170)

absolute deprivation   The minimum level of subsistence below which families or individuals should not be expected to exist. (60)

acting White   Taking school seriously and accepting the authority of teachers and administrators. (191)

affirmative action   Positive efforts to recruit subordinate group members, including women, for jobs, promotions, and educational opportunities. (72)

Afrocentric perspective   An emphasis on the customs of African cultures and how they have pervaded the history, culture, and behavior of Blacks in the United States and around the world. (27)

ageism   Prejudice and discrimination against the elderly. (368)

amalgamation   The process by which a dominant group and a subordinate group combine through intermarriage to form a new group. (24)

androgyny   The state of being both masculine and feminine, aggressive and passive. (325)

anti-Semitism   Anti-Jewish prejudice or discrimination. (37, 302)

apartheid   The policy of the South African government intended to maintain separation of Blacks, Coloureds, and Asians from the dominant Whites. (23, 360)

apartheid schools   All-Black schools. (190)

arranged marriage   When one's marital partner is chosen by others and the relationship is not based on any preexisting mutual attraction. (270)

assimilation   The process by which a subordinate individual or group takes on the characteristics of the dominant group. (24)

asylees   Foreigners who have already entered the United States and now seek protection because of persecution or a well-founded fear of persecution. (107)

authoritarian personality   A psychological construct of a personality type likely to be prejudiced and to use others as scapegoats. (37)

bamboo ceiling   The barrier that talented Asian Americans face because of resentment and intolerance directed toward Asian Americans. (266)

bilingual education   A program designed to allow students to learn academic concepts in their native language while they learn a second language. (96)

bilingualism   The use of two or more languages in places of work or education and the treatment of each language as legitimate. (96)

biological race   The mistaken notion of a genetically isolated human group. (9)

blaming the victim   Portraying the problems of racial and ethnic minorities as their fault rather than recognizing society's responsibilities. (15, 264)

blended identity   Self-image and worldview that is a combination of religious faith, cultural background based on nationality, and current residency. (247)

Bogardus scale   Technique to measure social distance toward different racial and ethnic groups. (51)

borderlands   The area of a common culture along the border between Mexico and the United States. (229)

bracero   Contracted Mexican laborers brought to the United States during World War II. (228)

brain drain   Immigration to the United States of skilled workers, professionals, and technicians who are desperately needed in their home countries. (93, 221)

chain immigration   Immigrants sponsor several other immigrants who, on their arrival, may sponsor still more. (84, 262)

civil disobedience   A tactic promoted by Martin Luther King, Jr., based on the belief that people have the right to disobey unjust laws under certain circumstances. (179)

civil religion   The religious dimension in American life that merges the state with sacred beliefs. (130)

class   As defined by Max Weber, people who share similar levels of wealth. (14, 193)

colonialism   A foreign power's maintenance of political, social, economic, and cultural dominance over people for an extended period. (19)

color-blind racism   Use of race-neutral principles to defend the racially unequal status quo. (42, 192)

color gradient   The placement of people on a continuum from light to dark skin color rather than in distinct racial groupings by skin color. (210, 238, 348)

conflict perspective   A sociological approach that assumes that the social structure is best understood in terms of conflict or tension between competing groups. (15)

contact hypothesis   An interactionist perspective stating that intergroup contact between people of equal status in noncompetitive circumstances will reduce prejudice. (51, 362)

creationists   People who support a literal interpretation of the biblical book of Genesis on the origins of the universe and argue that evolution should not be presented as established scientific thought. (136)

curanderismo   Hispanic folk medicine. (232)

de facto segregation   Segregation that is the result of residential patterns. (190)

deficit model of ethnic identity   One's ethnicity is viewed by others as a factor of subtracting away the characteristics corresponding to some ideal ethnic type. (245)

de jure segregation   Children assigned to schools specifically to maintain racially separated schools. (178)

denomination   A large, organized religion not officially linked with the state or government. (129)

desi   Colloquial name for people who trace their ancestry to South Asia, especially India and Pakistan. (269)

Diaspora   The exile of Jews from Palestine. (312, 356)

differential justice   Whites being dealt with more leniently than Blacks, whether at the time of arrest, indictment, conviction, sentencing, or parole. (199)

disability   Reduced ability to perform tasks one would normally do at a given stage in life. (372)

discrimination   The denial of opportunities and equal rights to individuals and groups because of prejudice or for other arbitrary reasons. (34, 59)

displaced homemakers   Women whose primary occupation had been homemaking but who did not find full-time employment after being divorced, separated, or widowed. (336)

dry foot, wet foot   Policy toward Cuban immigrants that allows those who manage to reach the United States (dry foot) to remain but sends those who are picked up at sea (wet foot) back to Cuba. (217)

dual or split labor market   Division of the economy into two areas of employment, the secondary one of which is populated primarily by minorities working at menial jobs.

dysfunction   An element of society that may disrupt a social system or decrease its stability. (15)

emigration   Leaving a country to settle in another. (18)

environmental justice   Efforts to ensure that hazardous substances are controlled so that all communities receive protection regardless of race or socioeconomic circumstances. (71, 163, 351)

environmental refugees   People forced to leave their communities because of natural disasters, or the effects of climate change and global warming. (106)

ethnic cleansing   Forced deportation of people accompanied by systematic violence. (20)

ethnic group   A group set apart from others because of its national origin or distinctive cultural patterns. (6)

ethnic paradox   The maintenance of one's ethnic ties in a way that can assist with assimilation in larger society. (115)

ethnocentrism   The tendency to assume that one's culture and way of life are superior to all others. (33)

ethnonational conflicts   Conflicts between ethnic, racial, religious, and linguistic groups within nations, which replace conflicts between nations. (346)

ethnophaulisms   Ethnic or racial slurs, including derisive nicknames. (33)

evacuees   Japanese Americans interned in camps for the duration of World War II. (292)

exploitation theory   A Marxist theory that views racial subordination in the United States as a manifestation of the class system inherent in capitalism. (38)

familism   Pride and closeness in the family that result in placing family obligation and loyalty before individual needs. (232)

feminine mystique   Society's view of a woman as only her children's mother and her husband's wife. (328)

feminism   An ideology establishing equal rights for women. (328)

feminization of poverty   The trend since 1970 in which women account for a growing proportion of those who live below the poverty line. (335)

fish-ins   Native American tribes' protests over government interference with their traditional rights to fish as they like. (151)

fringe-of-values theory   Behavior that is on the border of conduct that a society regards as proper and is often carried out by subordinate groups, subjecting those groups to negative sanctions. (307)

functionalist perspective   A sociological approach emphasizing how parts of a society are structured to maintain its stability. (14)

fusion   A minority and a majority group combining to form a new group. (23)

gender roles   Expectations regarding the proper behavior, attitudes, and activities of males and females. (325)

genocide   The deliberate, systematic killing of an entire people or nation. (20)

glass ceiling   The barrier that blocks the promotion of a qualified worker because of gender or minority membership. (77, 334)

glass escalator   The male advantage experienced in occupations dominated by women. (79)

glass wall   A barrier to moving laterally in a business to positions that are more likely to lead to upward mobility. (79)

globalization   Worldwide integration of government policies, cultures, social movements, and financial markets through trade, movements of people, and the exchange of ideas. (18, 104)

gook syndrome   David Riesman's phrase describing Americans' tendency to stereotype Asians and to regard them as all alike and undesirable. (275)

hajj   Pilgrimage to Mecca to be completed at least once in a Muslim's lifetime. (248)

halakha   Jewish laws covering obligations and duties. (317)

Haoles   Native Hawaiians' term for Caucasians. (277)

hate crime   Criminal offense committed because of the offender's bias against a race, religion, ethnic or national origin group, or sexual orientation group. (61)

hijab   A variety of garments that allow women to follow the guidelines of modest dress. (255)

Holocaust   The state-sponsored systematic persecution and annihilation of European Jewry by Nazi Germany and its collaborators. (20, 308)

Holocaust revisionists   People who deny the Nazi effort to exterminate the Jews or who minimize the numbers killed. (308)

hometown clubs   Nonprofit organizations that maintain close ties to immigrants' hometowns in Mexico and other Latin American countries. (231)

homophobia   The fear of and prejudice toward homosexuality. (40, 379)

hui kuan   Chinese American benevolent associations organized on the basis of the district of the immigrant's origin in China. (286)

ilchomose   The 1.5 generation of Korean Americans—those who immigrated into the United States as children. (272)

immigration Coming into a new country as a permanent resident. (18)

income Salaries, wages, and other money received. (65, 193)

ingroup virtues Proper behavior by one's own group; become unacceptable when practiced by outsiders (outgroup vices). (307)

institutional discrimination A denial of opportunities and equal rights to individuals or groups resulting from the normal operations of a society. (63, 375)

intelligence quotient (IQ) The ratio of a person's mental age (as computed by an IQ test) to his or her chronological age, multiplied by 100. (9)

intelligent design View that life is so complex that it must have been created by a higher intelligence. (136)

Intifada The Palestinian uprising against Israeli authorities in the occupied territories. (358)

Islamophobia A range of negative feelings toward Muslims and their religion that ranges from generalized intolerance to hatred. (252)

Issei First-generation immigrants from Japan to the United States. (291)

jihad Struggle against the enemies of Allah, usually taken to mean one's own internal struggle. (249)

Jim Crow Southern laws passed in the late nineteenth century that kept Blacks in their subordinate position. (171)

Judaization The lessening importance of Judaism as a religion and the substitution of cultural traditions as the tie that binds Jews. (304)

kanaka maoli The "real" or "true people" of Hawai'i, that is the Native Hawaiians. (277)

kashrut Laws pertaining to permissible (kosher) and forbidden foods and their preparation. (315)

Kibei Japanese Americans of the Nisei generation sent back to Japan for schooling and to have marriages arranged. (291)

kickout or pushout A Native American school dropout who leaves behind an unproductive academic environment. (159)

kye Rotating credit system used by Korean Americans to subsidize the start-up costs of businesses. (273)

labeling theory A sociological approach introduced by Howard Becker that attempts to explain why certain people are viewed as deviants and others engaging in the same behavior are not. (16)

La Raza Literally meaning "the people," the term refers to the rich heritage of Mexican Americans; it is therefore used to denote a sense of pride among Mexican Americans today. (228)

life chances People's opportunities to provide themselves with material goods, positive living conditions, and favorable life experiences. (231)

maquiladoras Foreign-owned companies on the Mexican side of the border with the United States. (231)

marginality The status of being between two cultures at the same time, such as the status of Jewish immigrants in the United States. (13, 319)

Marielitos People who arrived from Cuba in the third wave of Cuban immigration, most specifically those forcibly deported by way of Mariel Harbor. The term is generally reserved for refugees seen as especially undesirable. (216)

matrix of domination Cumulative impact of oppression because of race, gender, and class as well as sexual orientation, religion, disability status, and age. (341, 367)

medical apartheid The separate and unequal health care system in the United States that often has and continues to characterize health care for African Americans as well as Latinos. (201)

melting pot Diverse racial or ethnic groups or both, forming a new creation, a new cultural entity. (24)

mestizo People in the Americas of mixed European (usually Spanish) and local indigenous ancestry. (348)

migration A general term that describes any transfer of population. (18)

minority group A subordinate group whose members have significantly less control or power over their own lives than do the members of a dominant or majority group. (4)

mixed status Families in which one or more members are citizens and one or more are noncitizens. (94, 233)

model minority A group that, despite past prejudice and discrimination, succeeds economically, socially, and educationally without resorting to political or violent confrontations with Whites. (264)

mojados "Wetbacks"; derisive slang for Mexicans who enter illegally, supposedly by swimming the Rio Grande. (228)

mommy tax Lower salaries women receive over their lifetime because they have children. (338)

mommy track An unofficial corporate career track for women who want to divide their attention between work and family. (335)

mulatto escape hatch Notion that Brazilians of mixed ancestry can move into high-status positions. (353)

nativism Beliefs and policies favoring native-born citizens over immigrants. (87)

naturalization Conferring of citizenship on a person after birth. (102)

neocolonialism Continuing dependence of former colonies on foreign countries. (235)

Neoricans Puerto Ricans who return to the island to settle after living on the U.S. mainland (also called Nuyoricans). (234)

Nisei Children born of immigrants from Japan. (290)

normative approach The view that prejudice is influenced by societal norms and situations that encourage or discourage the tolerance of minorities. (38)

occupational segregation The tendency for a racial, ethnic, or gender group to be employed in different occupations from each other. (97, 330)

orientalism The simplistic view of the people and history of the Orient, with no recognition of change over time or the diversity within its many cultures. (243)

outgroup vices Ingroup virtues that become unacceptable when practiced by outsiders. (307)

panethnicity The development of solidarity between ethnic subgroups as reflected in the terms Hispanic and Asian American. (13, 150, 209, 268)

pan-Indianism Intertribal social movements in which several tribes, joined by political goals but not by kinship, unite in a common identity. (150)

pass laws Laws that controlled internal movement by non-Whites in South Africa. (360)

pay equity The same wages for different types of work that are judged to be comparable by such measures as employee knowledge, skills, effort, responsibility, and working conditions; also called comparable worth. (333)

Pentecostalism A religion similar in many respects to evangelical faiths that believes in the infusion of the Holy Spirit into services and in religious experiences such as faith healing. (215)

peoplehood Milton Gordon's term for a group with a shared feeling. (320)

pluralism Mutual respect for one another's culture, a respect that allows minorities to express their own culture without suffering prejudice or discrimination. (26)

powwows Native American gatherings of dancing, singing, music playing, and visiting, accompanied by competitions. (153)

prejudice A negative attitude toward an entire category of people such as a racial or ethnic minority. (33)

principle of third-generation interest Marcus Hansen's contention that ethnic interest and awareness increase in the third generation, among the grandchildren of immigrants. (115)

Québécois The French-speaking people of the province of Quebec in Canada. (351)

racial formation A sociohistorical process by which racial categories are created, inhibited, transformed, and destroyed. (11, 170)

racial group A group that is socially set apart because of obvious physical differences. (6)

racial profiling Any arbitrary police-initiated action based on race, ethnicity, or national origin rather than a person's behavior. (41, 258, 265)

racism A doctrine that one race is superior. (10)

redlining The pattern of discrimination against people trying to buy homes in minority and racially changing neighborhoods. (68, 198)

refugees People living outside their country of citizenship for fear of political or religious persecution. (106)

relative deprivation The conscious experience of a negative discrepancy between legitimate expectations and present actualities. (60, 181)

religion A unified system of sacred beliefs and practices that encompass elements beyond everyday life that inspire awe, respect, and even fear. (128)

remittances The monies that immigrants return to their countries of origin. (98, 221)

repatriation The 1930s program of deporting Mexicans. (227)

resegregation The physical separation of racial and ethnic groups reappearing after a period of relative integration. (23)

restrictive covenant A private contract or agreement that discourages or prevents minority-group members from purchasing housing in a neighborhood. (177)

reverse discrimination Actions that cause better-qualified White men to be passed over for women and minority men. (76)

riff-raff theory Also called the rotten-apple theory; the belief that the riots of the 1960s were caused by discontented youths rather than by social and economic problems facing all African Americans. (181)

rising expectations The increasing sense of frustration that legitimate needs are being blocked. (181)

Sansei The children of the Nisei—that is, the grandchildren of the original immigrants from Japan. (290)

scapegoating theory A person or group blamed irrationally for another person's or group's problems or difficulties. (37, 307)

secessionist minority Groups that reject assimilation and promote coexistence and pluralism. (135)

second shift The double burden—work outside the home followed by childcare and housework—that is faced by many women and that few men share equitably. (338)

segmented assimilation The outcome of immigrants and their descendants moving in to different classes of the host society. (25)

segregation The physical separation of two groups, often imposed on a subordinate group by the dominant group. (22)

self-fulfilling prophecy The tendency to respond to and act on the basis of stereotypes, a predisposition that can lead one to validate false definitions. (17)

sexism The ideology that one sex is superior to the other. (40, 324)

sexual harassment Any unwanted and unwelcome sexual advances that interfere with a person's ability to perform a job and enjoy the benefits of a job. (335)

sinophobes People with a fear of anything associated with China. (88)

slave codes Laws that defined the low position held by slaves in the United States. (169)

slavery reparations Act of making amends for the injustices of slavery. (173)

social distance Tendency to approach or withdraw from a racial group. (50)

sociology The systematic study of social behavior and human groups. (13)

sovereignty Tribal self-rule. (153)

sovereignty movement Effort by the indigenous peoples of Hawai'i to secure a measure of self-government and restoration of their lands. (278)

stereotypes Unreliable, exaggerated generalizations about all members of a group that do not take individual differences into account. (16, 39)

stratification A structured ranking of entire groups of people that perpetuates unequal rewards and power in a society. (14)

suffragists Women and men who worked successfully to gain women the right to vote. (327)

sundown towns Communities in which non-Whites were systematically excluded from living. (168)

symbolic ethnicity Herbert Gans's term that describes emphasis on ethnic food and ethnically associated political issues rather than deeper ties to one's heritage. (117, 269)

tiger mother A demanding mother who pushes her children to high levels of achievement following practices common in China and other parts of Asia. (289)

tongs Chinese American secret associations. (287)

tracking The practice of placing students in specific curriculum groups on the basis of test scores and other criteria. (190)

transnationals Immigrants who sustain multiple social relationships that link their societies of origin and settlement. (105, 231)

tsu Clans established along family lines and forming a basis for social organization by Chinese Americans. (286)

two-state solution An Israel and Palestine living side-by-side recognized by the entire world community. (358)

underemployment Working at a job for which the worker is overqualified, involuntary working part time instead of full time, or being intermittently employed. (195)

victim discounting Tendency to view crime as less socially significant if the victim is viewed as less worthy. (199)

victimization surveys Annual attempts to measure crime rates by interviewing ordinary citizens who may or may not have been crime victims. (199)

Viet Kieu Vietnamese living abroad, such as in the United States. (276)

visible minorities In Canada, persons other than Aboriginal or First Nation people who are non-White in racial background. (352)

visitability Building private homes to be accessible for visitors with disabilities. (377)

wealth An inclusive term encompassing all of a person's material assets, including land and other types of property. (65, 193)

White primary Legal provisions forbidding Black voting in election primaries; in one-party areas of the South, these laws effectively denied Blacks their right to select elected officials. (171)

White privilege Rights or immunities granted as a particular benefit or favor for being White. (36, 114)

world systems theory A view of the global economic system as divided between nations that control wealth and those that provide natural resources and labor. (19, 143, 239, 346)

xenophobia The fear or hatred of strangers or foreigners. (87, 297)

yellow peril A term denoting a generalized prejudice toward Asian people and their customs. (265)

Yiddishkait Jewishness. (317)

Yonsei The fourth generation of Japanese Americans in the United States; the children of the Sansei. (290)

Zionism Traditional Jewish religious yearning to return to the biblical homeland, now used to refer to support for the state of Israel. (312, 356)

zoning laws Legal provisions stipulating land use and the architectural design of housing, often used to keep racial minorities and low-income people out of suburban areas. (198)

References

Cyan color type denotes reference citations new to this fourteenth edition

AARP. 2003. *AARP Home.* Accessed May 12, 2003, at http://www.aarp.org.

Abbott, Andrew, and Ranier Egloff. 2008. The Polish Peasant in Oberlin and Chicago. The Intellectual Trajectory of W. I. Thomas. *American Sociologist,* 39: 217–258.

ABC Television. 2013. Arkansas Schools to Start Moment of Silence When Classes Begin. August 2. Accessed September 8, 2013, at http://www.4029tv.com.

Abdo, Geneive. 2004a. A Muslim Rap Finds Voice. *Chicago Tribune* (June 30): 1, 19.

——. 2004b. New Generation Lifting Muslims. *Chicago Tribune* (September 3): 1, 8.

Abdulrahim, Raja. 2009. UC urged to expand ethnic labels. *Los Angeles Times* (March 31): A4.

Abe, Yukiko. 2011. The Equal Employment Opportunity Law and Labor Force Behavior of Women in Japan. *Journal of the Japanese and International Economies* 25 (March): 39–55.

Abrahamson, Alan, and Judy Pasternak. 1998. For U.S. Jews, Era of Plenty Takes Many Far from Roots. *Los Angeles Times* (April 20): A1, A10–11.

Abrahamson, Mark. 1996. *Urban Enclaves: Identity and Place in America.* New York: St. Martin's Press. Accessible at http://www.msnbc.msn.com/id/23690567/print/1/displaymode/1098.

Abu Dhabi Gallup. 2011. *Muslim Americans: Faith, Freedom, and the Future.* Accessible at http://www.gallup.com.

ACLU. 1996. *Racial Justice.* New York: American Civil Liberties Union.

Acs, Gregory. 2013. *The Moynihan Report Revisited.* Washington DC: Urban Institute.

Adam, Barry D. 1995. *The Rise of a Gay and Lesbian Movement,* rev. ed. New York: Twayne.

Adams, Jane Meredith. 2006. Mystery Shrouds Slaying of Chinatown Businessman. *Washington Post* (March 31): 5.

ADL. 2013. *Anti-Semitic Incidents.* Accessed November 1, 2013, at http://www.adl.org/press-center/press-releases/anti-semitism-usa/adl-audit-us-anti-semitic-incidents-declined-14-percent.html.

Adler, Patricia A., Steven J. Kess, and Peter Adler. 1992. Socialization to Gender Role: Popularity among Elementary School Boys and Girls. *Sociology of Education* (July), 65: 169–187.

——. 2004. *Paradise Laborers: Hotel Work in the Global Economy.* Ithaca, NY: Cornell University.

Adorno, T. W., Else Frenkel-Brunswik, Daniel J. Levinson, and R. Nevitt Sanford. 1950. *The Authoritarian Personality.* New York: Wiley.

Aguirre, DeAnne, Leila Hoteit, Christine Rupp, and Karim Sabbagh. 2012. *Empowering the Third Billion: Women and the World of Work in 2012.* New York: Booz & Co.

Ajrouch, Kristine J. 2011. Correspondence with author. June 12.

Ajrouch, Kristine J., and Amancy Jamal. 2007. Assimilating to a White Identity: The Case of Arab Americans. *International Migration Review* (Winter): 860–879.

Akaka, Daniel. 2011. *Native Hawaiian Federal Recognition.* Accessed June 1, 2011, at http://Akaka.senate.gov/public/index.cfm?FuseAction=Issues.Home&issues=Akaka%20Bill&content_id=24#Akaka%20Bill.

Albrecht, Gary L. (ed.). 2005. *Encyclopedia of Disability.* Thousand Oaks, CA: Sage Publications.

Alexander, Michelle. 2012. *The New Jim Crow: Mass Incarceration in the Age of Colorblindness,* rev. ed. New York: The New Press.

Alliance for Board Diversity. 2009. *Women and Minorities on Fortune 100 Boards.* New York: Catalyst, the Executive Leadership Council, and the Hispanic Association on Corporate Responsibility.

Allport, Gordon W. 1979. *The Nature of Prejudice,* 25th anniversary ed. Reading, MA: Addison-Wesley.

Alvord, Valerie. 2000. Refugees' Success Breeds Pressure, Discrimination. *USA Today* (May 1): 74.

American Community Survey. 2009. *American Community Survey 2008.* Data released August 2009 and accessible at http://www.census.gov.

——. 2011a. *2008–2010 American Community Survey 3-Year Estimates.* Accessible at http://factfinder2.census.gov.

——. 2011b. *American Community Survey 2010.* Data released August 2011 and accessible at http://www.census.gov.

——. 2013a. *American Community Survey 2012.* Data released August 2013 and accessible at http://www.census.gov.

American Financial Resources, 2012. *Craigslist Has New Policy for Discriminatory Ads.* June 17. Accessed August 7, 2013, at http://www.afrmortgage.com.

American Indian Higher Education Consortium. 2012. Home Page. Accessed July 11, 2013, at http://www.aihec.org.

American-Jewish Committee. 1965. *Mutual Savings Banks of New York City.* New York: American Jewish Committee.

——. 1966a. *Mutual Savings Banks: A Follow-Up Report.* New York: American Jewish Committee.

——. 1966b. *Patterns of Exclusion from the Executive Suite: Corporate Banking.* New York: American Jewish Committee.

——. 2005. *2005 Annual Survey of American-Jewish Opinion.* New York: American Jewish Committee.

——. 2007. *2007 Annual Survey of American Jewish Opinion.* New York: American Jewish Committee.

——. 2010a. *2010 Annual Survey of American Jewish Opinion.* April 7. Accessible at http://www.ajc.org.

——. 2010b. *Fall 2010 Survey of American Jewish Opinion.* October 11. Accessible at http://www.ajc.org.

Anderson, Elijah. 2011. *The Cosmopolitan Canopy: Race and Civility in Everyday Life.* New York: W. W. Norton and Company.

Anderson, Warwick. 2003. *The Cultivation of Whiteness: Science, Health and Racial Destiny in Australia.* New York: Perseus Books.

Anguilar-San Juan, Karin. 2009. *Little Saigon: Staying Vietnamese in America.* Minneapolis: University of Minnesota Press.

Ansell, Amy E. 2008. Color Blindness. Pp. 320–322 in vol. 1, *Encyclopedia of Race, Ethnicity, and Society,* Richard T. Schaefer, ed. Thousand Oaks, CA: Sage.

Anti-Defamation League (ADL). 2008. *Audit of Anti-Semitic Incidents 2007.* New York: ADL.

——. 2013. *2012 Audit of Anti-Semitic Incidents.* Accessible at http://www.adl.org.

Applebome, Peter. 1996. 70 Years after Scopes Trial, Creation Debate Lives. *New York Times* (March 10): 1, 22.

——. 2010. Shinnecocks Hold Economic Cards, and Suitors Are Needy. *New York Times* (June 10).

Arab American Institute. 2012a. *Arabs (Really) Love Obama.* November 6. Accessed September 13, 2013, at http://www.aaiusa.org/index_ee.php/news/entry/arabs-really-love-obama/.

——. 2012b. *The Arab American Vote, 2012.* Accessible at http://www.aaiusa.org/reports/the-arab-american-vote-2012.

Aran, Kenneth, Herman Arthur, Ramon Colon, and Harvey Goldenberg. 1973. *Puerto Rican History and Culture: A Study Guide and Curriculum Outline.* New York: United Federation of Teachers.

Archibold, Randal C. 2007. A City's Violence Feeds on Black-Hispanic Rivalry. *New York Times* (January 17): A1, A15.

——. 2011. "Despite Violence, Mexico Plants Hum at Border. *New York Times* (July 11): A1, A3.

Archibold, Randal C., and Julia Preston. 2008. Homeland Security Stands by Its Fence. *New York Times* (May 21).

Arden, Harvey. 1975. The Pious Ones. *National Geographic* (August), 168: 276–298.

Arias, Elizabeth. 2010. U.S. Life Tables by Hispanic Origin, *Vital and Health Statistics*, series 2, no. 152.

Arizona Republic, The. 2013. Cultures Blend Over Time. (March 6): B6.

Armstrong, Elizabeth A., and Suzanna M. Crage. 2006. Movements and Memory: The Making of the Stonewall Myth. *American Sociological Review* (October), 71: 724–751.

Asante, Molefi Kete. 2007. *An Afrocentric Manifesto: Toward an African Renaissance.* Cambridge, UK: Polity.

———. 2008. Afrocentricity. Pp. 41–42 in vol. 1, *Encyclopedia of Race, Ethnicity, and Society*, Richard T. Schaefer, ed. Thousand Oaks, CA: Sage.

Ash, Timothy Garton. 2007. Welcome to a Mixed-Up World. *The Global Mail* (Toronto) (July 14): A19.

Asi, Maryam, and Daniel Beaulieu. 2013. *Arab Households in the United States 2006–2010.* ACSBR/10-20. Accessible at http://www.census.gov.

Asian American Federation. 2008. *Revitalizing Chinatown Businesses: Challenges and Opportunities.* New York: Asian American Federation.

Attwood, Bain. 2003. *Rights for Aborigines.* Crows Nest, Australia: Allen and Unwin.

Austen, Ben. 2010. A Promising Land. *The Atlantic* (July/August): 22, 24.

Australian Bureau of Statistics. 2012a. *The Health and Welfare of Australia's Aboriginal and Torres Strait Islander Peoples.* December 19. Accessed September 2013, at http://www.abs.gov.au/ausstats/abs@nsf/mf/4704.0.

———. 2012b. *Experimental Estimates and Projections, Aboriginal and Torres Strait Islander Australians.* Accessed September 2013, at http://www.abs.gov.au/ausstats.

Avila, Oscar. 2003. Muslim Holiday Testing Schools. *Chicago Tribune* (November 24): 1, 16.

Badgett, M. V. Lee, and Heidi I. Hartmann. 1995. The Effectiveness of Equal Employment Opportunity Policies. Pp. 55–83 in *Economic Perspectives in Affirmative Action*, Margaret C. Simms, ed. Washington, DC: Joint Center for Political and Economic Studies.

Bagby, Ihsan. 2012. *The American Mosque 2011.* Washington, DC: Council on American-Islamic Relations.

Bahr, Howard M. 1972. "An End to Invisibility." Pp. 404–412 in *Native Americans Today: Sociological Perspectives*, Howard M. Bahr, Bruce A. Chadwick, and Robert C. Day, eds. New York: Harper & Row.

Bailey, Stanley R. 2004. Group Dominance and the Myth of Racial Democracy: Antiracism Attitudes in Brazil. *American Sociological Review* 69 (October): 728–747.

———. 2009a. "Public Opinion on Nonwhite Underrepresentation and Racial Identity Politics in Brazil." *Latin American Politics and Society*, 51 (4): 69–99.

———. 2009b. *Legacies of Race: Identities, Attitudes, and Politics in Brazil.* Stanford, CA: Stanford University Press.

Bailey, Stanley R., and Michelle Péria. 2010. Racial Quotas and the Culture War in Brazilian Academia. *Sociology Compass* 4 (8): 592–604.

Baker, Bryan C. 2009. *Trends in Naturalization Rates: 2008 Update.* Washington, DC: Department of Homeland Security.

Balderrama, Francisco E., and Raymond Rodriguez. 2006. *Decade of Betrayal: Mexican Repatriation in the 1930s.* Revised. Albuquerque: University of New Mexico Press.

Baldwin, Neil. 2001. *Henry Ford and the Jews: The Mass Production of Hate.* New York: Public Affairs.

Baltzell, E. Digby. 1964. *The Protestant Establishment: Aristocracy and Caste in America.* New York: Vintage Books.

Bamshad, Michael J., and Steve E. Olson. 2003. Does Race Exist? *Scientific American* (December): 78–85.

Banton, Michael. 2008. The Sociology of Ethnic Relations. *Ethnic and Racial Studies* (May): 1–19.

Barclay, William, Krishna Kumar, and Ruth P. Simms. 1976. *Racial Conflict, Discrimination, and Power: Historical and Contemporary Studies.* New York: AMS Press.

Barnes, Jessica S., and Claudette L. Bennett. 2002. *The Asian Population: 2000.* Census Brief C2KBR/01-16. Washington, DC: U.S. Government Printing Office.

Barringer, Felicity. 2004. Bitter Division for Sierra Club on Immigration. *New York Times* (March 14): A1, A16.

Barron, Milton L. 1953. Minority Group Characteristics of the Aged in American Society. *Journal of Gerontology* (October), 8: 477–482.

Barry, Ellen. 2004. County Rescinds Vote. *Los Angeles Times* (March 19): A16.

Bartlett, Donald L., and James B. Steele. 2002. Casinos: Wheel of Misfortune. *Time* (December 10), 160: 44–53, 56–58.

Bascara, Victor. 2008. Model Minority. Pp. 910–912 in vol. 2, *Encyclopedia of Race, Ethnicity, and Society*, Richard T. Schaefer, ed. Thousand Oaks, CA: Sage.

Bash, Harry M. 2001. *If I'm So White, Why Ain't I Right? Some Methodological Misgivings on Taking Identity Ascriptions at Face Value.* Paper presented at the annual meeting of the Midwest Sociological Society, St. Louis.

Basken, Paul. 2007. A Year after Turmoil, Gallaudet Sees Progress and Problems. *Chronicle of Higher Education* (October 20), 54: A27.

Baum, Geraldine. 1998. New Power of Women Recasts Judaism. *Los Angeles Times* (April 21): A1, A14, A15.

Bayoumi, Moustafa. 2009. *How Does it Feel to be a Problem? Being Young and Arab in America.* New York: Penguin Books.

———. 2010. My Arab Problem. *Chronicle of Higher Education* (October 29): B13–B14.

Ba-Yunus, Ilyas, and Kassim Kone. 2004. Muslim Americans: A Demographic Report. Pp. 299–322 in *Muslims' Place in the American Public Square*, Zahid H. Bukhari et al., eds. Walnut Creek, CA: Altamira Press.

Bean, Frank D., and G. Stevens. 2003. *America's Newcomers and the Dynamics of Diversity.* New York: Russell Sage Foundation.

Beardsley, Eleanor. 2013. In France, Some Ask If Racism Is On The Rise. November 15. Accessible at http://www.wbur.org/npr/245295614/in-france-some-ask-if-racism-is-on-the-rise.

Beardstown CUSD 15. 2012. *2011 Illinois District Report Card.* Beardstown, IL.

Beisel, Nicola, and Tamara Kay. 2004. Abortion: Race and Gender in Nineteenth Century America. *American Sociological Review*, 69 (August): 498–518.

Bélanger, Alain, and Éric Caron Malenfant. 2005. Ethnocultural Diversity in Canada: Prospects for 2017. *Canadian Social Trends* (Winter).

Bell, Derrick. 1994. The Freedom of Employment Act. *The Nation* (May 23), 258: 708, 710–714.

———. 2004. *Silent Covenants: Brown v. Board of Education and the Unfulfilled Hopes for Racial Reform.* Cambridge, MA: Oxford University Press.

———. 2007. Desegregation's Demise. *Chronicle of Higher Education* (July 13), 53: B11.

Bell, Wendell. 1991. Colonialism and Internal Colonialism. Pp. 52–53 in *The Encyclopedic Dictionary of Sociology*, 4th ed., Richard Lachmann, ed. Guilford, CT: Dushkin Publishing Group.

Bellafante, Ginia. 2005. Young South Asians in America Embrace "Assisted" Marriages. *New York Times* (August 23): A1, A15.

Bellah, Robert. 1967. Civil Religion in America. *Daedalus* 96 (Winter): 1–21.

Belliard, Juan Carlos, and Johnny Ramirez-Johnson. 2005. Medical Pluralism in the Life of a Mexican Immigrant Woman. *Hispanic Journal of Behavioral Sciences* (August), 27: 267–285.

Belluck, Pam. 2009. New Hopes for Reform in Indian Health Care. *New York Times* (December 2): A1, A28.

Belson, Ken. 2013. Redskins' Name Change Remains Activist's Unfinished Business. *New York Times* (October 10): A1, B16.

Belt, Don. 2002. The World of Islam. *National Geographic* (January): 76–85.

Belton, Danielle C. 2009. Blacks in Space. *American Prospect* (June): 47–49.

Bem, Sandra L., and Daryl J. Bem. 1970. Case Study of a Nonconscious Ideology: Training the Woman to Know Her Place. Pp. 89–99 in *Beliefs, Attitudes, and Human Affairs*, Daryl J. Bem, ed. Belmont, CA: Brooks/Cole.

Bennett, Vivienne S. 1995. Gender, Class, and Water: Women and the Politics of Water Service in Monterrey, Mexico. *Latin American Perspective* (September), 22: 76–99.

Bennett, Vivienne S. Dávila-Poblete, and M. N. Rico, eds. 2005. *Opposing Currents: The Politics of Water and Gender in Latin America.* Pittsburg: University of Pittsburg Press.

Berger, Joseph. 2008. Salvadorans, Building Their Own Cultural Bridge. *New York Times* (May 4).

Berger, Ronald J. 2010 Jewish Americans and the Holocaust. *Contexts* (Winter): 40–45.

Bergman Institute. 2011. *FAQs on American Jews: Intermarriage Data.* May 11. Accessible at http://www.jewishdatabank.org.

Berlin, Ira. 2010. *The Making of African America: The Four Great Migrations.* New York: Viking Press.

Bernard, Tara Siegel. 2012. Blacks Face Bias in Bankruptcy, Study Suggests. *New York Times* (January 21), p. A1.

Bernstein, Mary, and Verta Taylor, eds. 2013. *The Marrying Kind?* Minneapolis: University of Minnesota Press.

Best, Joel. 2001. Social Progress and Social Problems: Toward a Sociology of Gloom. *Sociological Quarterly* 42 (1): 1–12.

Bigelow, Rebecca. 1992. Certain Inalienable Rights. *Friends Journal* (November), 38: 6–8.

Bjerk, David. 2008. Glass Ceilings or Sticky Floors? Statistical Discrimination in a Dynamic Model of Hiring and Promotion. *The Economic Journal*, 118 (530): 961–982.

Blackfeet Reservation Development Fund. 2006. *The Facts v. the Brochure.* Blackfeet Restoration.

Blackstock, Nelson. 1976. *COINTELPRO: The FBI's Secret War on Political Freedom.* New York: Vintage Press.

Blazak, Randy. 2011. Isn't Every Crime a Hate Crime? The Case for Hate Crime Laws. *Sociology Compass* 5 (4): 244–255.

Bloom, Leonard. 1971. *The Social Psychology of Race Relations.* Cambridge, MA: Schenkman Publishing.

Blow, Charles M. 2010. Abortion's New Battle Lines. *New York Times* (May 1), A19.

———. 2013. Escaping Slavery. *New York Times* (January 4): A15.

Bobo, Lawrence. 2013. The Antinomes of Racial Change. *DuBois Review* 10 (1): 1–5.

Bobo, Lawrence, and Mia Tuan. 2006. *Prejudices in Politics: Group Position, Public Opinion, and the Wisconsin Treaty Rights Dispute.* Cambridge, MA: Harvard University Press.

Bogardus, Emory. 1968. Comparing Racial Distance in Ethiopia, South Africa, and the United States. *Sociology and Social Research* 52 (January): 149–156.

Bohmer, Susanne, and Kayleen V. Oka. 2007. Teaching Affirmative Action: An Opportunity to Apply, Segregate, and Reinforce Sociological Concepts. *Teaching Sociology* (October), 35: 334–349.

Bonilla-Silva, Eduardo. 1996. Rethinking Racism: Toward a Structural Interpretation. *American Sociological Review* (June), 62: 465–480.

———. 2002. The Linguistics of Color Blind Racism: How to Talk Nasty about Blacks without Sounding Racist. *Critical Sociology* 28 (1–2): 41–64.

———. 2004. From Bi-Racial to Tri-Racial: Towards a New System of Racial Stratification in the USA. *Ethnic and Racial Studies* (November), 27: 931–950.

———. 2006. *Racism without Racists.* 2nd ed. Lanham, MD: Rowman & Littlefield.

———. 2012. The Invisible Weight of Whiteness: The Racial Grammar of Everyday Life in Contemporary America. *Ethnic and Racial Studies* (February), 35: 173–194.

Bonilla-Silva, Eduardo, and David Dietrich. 2011. The Sweet Enchantment of Color-Blind Racism in Obamerica. *The ANNALS of the American Academy of Political and Social Science* (March), 634: 190–206.

Bonilla-Silva, Eduardo, and David G. Embrick. 2007. "Every Place Has a Ghetto…" The Significance of Whites' Social and Residential Segregation. *Symbolic Interaction* 30 (3): 323–345.

Bonilla-Silva, Eduardo, and David G. Embrick, with Louise Seamster. 2011. The Sweet Enchantment of Color Blindness in Black Face: Explaining the "Miracle," Debating the Politics, and Suggesting a Way for Hope to be "For Real" in America. *Political Power and Social Theory* (22): 139–175.

Bonus, Rick. 2000. *Locating Filipino Americans: Ethnicity and the Cultural Politics of Space.* Philadelphia, PA: Temple University Press.

Borjas, George J., Jeffery Grogger, and Gordon H. Hanson. 2006. *Immigration and African-American Employment Opportunities: The Response of Wages, Employment, and Incarceration to Labor Supply Shocks.* Working Paper 12518. Cambridge, MA: National Bureau of Economic Research.

Bork, Robert H. 1995. What to Do About the First Amendment. *Commentary* (February), 99: 23–29.

Bornman, Eliréa. 2010. Emerging Patterns of Social Identification in Postapartheid South Africa. *Journal of Social Issues,* 66 (2): 237–254.

Bositis, David A. 1996. The Farrakhan Factor. *Washington Post National Weekly Edition* (December 16), 14: 24.

Bourcier, Nicolas. 2012. Brazil Tries To Face Its "Cordial" Racism. *The Guardian Weekly* (October 26): 28.

Bowles, Scott. 2000. Bans on Racial Profiling Gain Steam. *USA Today* (June), 2: 3A.

Bowman, Tom. 1998. Evangelicals Allege Bias in U.S. Navy, Marine Chaplain Corps. *Baltimore Sun* 23 (August): A12.

Bowser, Benjamin, and Raymond G. Hunt, eds. 1996. *Impacts of Racism on White Americans.* Beverly Hills, CA: Sage Publications.

Brannon, Ruth. 1995. The Use of the Concept of Disability Culture: A Historian's View. *Disability Studies Quarterly* (Fall), 15: 3–15.

Brault, Matthew W. 2012. Americans with Disaiblities: 2010. *Household Economic Studies* (July). Accessible at http://www.census.gov.

Braxton, Gregory. 2009. "Reality Television" in More Ways Than One. *Los Angeles Times* (February 17): A1, A15.

Breines, Winifred. 2007. Struggling to Connect: White and Black Feminism in the Movement Years. *Contexts* 6 (1): 18–24.

Brennan Center. 2006. *Citizens without Proof.* November. New York: Brennan Center for Justice at NYU School of Law.

———. 2013. *Election 2012 Laws Roundup.* Accessed January13, 2013, at http://www.brennancenter.org.

Brittingham, Angela, and G. Patricia de la Cruz. 2005. We the People of Arab Ancestry in the United States. CENSR-21. Washington, DC: U.S. Government Printing Office.

Brooks-Gunn, Jeanne, Pamela K. Klebanov, and Greg J. Duncan. 1996. Ethnic Differences in Children's Intelligence Test Scores: Role of Economic Deprivation, Home Environment, and Maternal Characteristics. *Child Development* (April), 67: 396–408.

Brown, Dee. 1971. *Bury My Heart at Wounded Knee.* New York: Holt, Rinehart & Winston.

Browne, Juliet. 2013. *Spirit of Black Paris.* Accessible at http://spiritofblackparis.blogspot.com.

Brown, Patricia Leigh. 2009. Invisible Immigrants, Old and Left with "Nobody to Talk To." *New York Times* (April 3): A1, A10.

———. 2011. Soup Without Fins? Some Californians Simmer. *New York Times* (March 5).

Browne, Irene, ed. 2001. *Latinas and African American Women at Work: Race, Gender, and Economic Inequality.* New York: Russell Sage Foundation.

Brulliard, Karin. 2006. A Proper Goodbye: Funeral Homes Learn Immigrants' Traditions. *Washington Post National Weekly Edition* (May 7): 31.

Buchanan, Angela B., Nora G. Albert, and Daniel Beaulieu. 2010. *The Population with Haitian Ancestry in the United States: 2009.* ACSR/09-18. Accessible at http://www.census.gov.

Buchholz, Barbara Ballinger. 2003. Expanded Access. *Chicago Tribune* (January 26): sect. 16, 1R, 5R.

Buck, Stuart. 2011. *Acting White: The Ironic Legacy of Desegregation.* New Haven: Yale University Press.

Budig, Michelle J. 2002. Male Advantage and the Gender Composition of Jobs: Who Rides the Glass Escalator? *Social Problems* 49 (2): 258–277.

Budig, Michelle J., and Joya Misra. 2010. How Care-Work Employment Shapes Earnings in Cross-National Perspective. *International Labour Review,* 149: 441–460.

Buetner, Russ. 2009. Shinnecock Indians See Prosperity Ahead. *New York Times* (December 28).

Bukowczyk, John J. 2007. *A History of Polish Americans.* New Brunswick, NJ: Transaction Books.

Bureau of the Census. 1951. *Statistical Abstract of the United States 1951.* Accessible at http://www2.census.gov/prod2/statcomp/documents/1951-01.pdf.

———. 1981. *Statistical Abstract of the United States 1981.* Accessible at http://www2.census.gov/prod2/statcomp/documents.

———. 1984. *Statistical Abstract of the United States 1984.* Accessible at http://www2.census.gov/prod2/statcomp/documents.

———. 1996. *Statistical Abstract of the United States 1996.* Accessible at http://www2.census.gov/prod2/statcomp/documents.

———. 2007a. *The American Community Survey—Asians: 2004.* ACS-05. Washington DC: U.S. Government Printing Office.

———. 2007b. *The American Community—Pacific Islanders: 2004.* ACS-06. Washington, DC: U.S. Government Printing Office.

———. 2007c. *2006 American Community Survey. Selected Economic Characteristics: Puerto Rico and the United States.* Accessed August 16, 2008, at http://www.census.gov.

———. 2008. *National Population Projections.* Accessible at http://www.census.gov/population/www/projections/summarytables.html.

———. 2009a. *Asian and Hispanic Children More Likely to Dine with Their Parents.* March 4. Accessed March 10, 2009, at http://www.census.gov/Press-Release/www/releases/archives/children/013383.html.

———. 2009b. *Irish-American Heritage Month (March) and St. Patrick's Day (March 17th): 2009.* Washington, DC: U.S. Census Bureau.

———. 2010a. *Statistical Abstract of the United States, 2011.* Washington, DC: U.S. Government Printing Office.

———. 2010b. U.S. Population Projections. Accessible at http://www.census.gov/population/www/projections/2009projections.html.

———. 2010c. *America's Families and Living Arrangements 2010.* Accessible at http://www.census.gov/population/www/socdemo/hh-fam/cps2010.html.

———. 2011a. *Statistical Abstract of the United States: 2012.* Accessible at http://www.census.gov.

———. 2011b. *Irish-American Heritage Month (March) and St. Patrick's Day (March 17): 2011.* Census Brief CB11-FF, 03, January 13.

———. 2011d. *Educational Attainment in the United States: 2010.* Accessible at http://www.census.gov/hhes/socdemo/education/data/cps/2010/tables.html.

———. 2011e. *2010 Center of Population.* Accessible at http://2010.census.gov/news/pdf/03242011_pressbrf_slides230pm.pdf.

———. 2012c. *U.S. Census Bureau Projections Show a Slower Growing, Older, More Diverse Nation a Half Century from Now.* News Release December 12. Accessible at http://www.census.gov.

———. 2012d. *Most Children Younger Than Age 1 are Minorities, Census Bureau Reports.* May 17. Accessible at http://www.census.gov/newsroom/releases/archives/population/cb12-90.html.

———. 2012e. *Annual Estimates of the Resident Population.* Accessible at http://www.census.gov/popest/data/national/asrh/2011/index.html.

———. 2012f. *New American Community Survey Data Sets Provide Detailed Look at Race, Tribal, Hispanic and Ancestry Groups.* (May 24.) Accessible at http://www.census.gov/newsroom/releases/archives/american_community_survey_acs/cb12-94.html.

———. 2013b. *2012 National Projections (Updated May 2013).* Accessible at http://www.census.gov/newsroom/releases/archives/population/cb13-211.html.

———. 2013d. *American Indian and Alaska Native Heritage Month: November 2013.* October 31. Accessible at http://www.census.gov/newsroom/releases/archives/facts_for_features_special_editions/cb13-ff26.html.

Bureau of Indian Affairs. 1986. *American Indians Today: Answers to Your Questions.* Washington, DC: U.S. Government Printing Office.

———. 2005. *American Indian Population and Labor Force Report.* Washington DC: BIA, Office of Indian Services.

Bureau of Labor Statistics. 2003. *Women at Work: A Visual Essay Monthly Labor Review* (October): 45–50.

———. 2004. *Time-Use Survey—First Results Announced By BLS.* News September 14. Accessible at http://www.bls.gov/tus/.

———. 2011. *Economy at a Glance: Puerto Rico.* Washington, DC: U.S. Department of Labor.

———. 2012b. *Databases, Tables and Calculators by Subject. White and Black Unemployment Rates From Current Population Survey 2002–2012.* Accessible at http://www.bls.gov.

———. 2013a. *Economy at a Glance: Puerto Rico.* Accessed November 12, 2013, at http://www.bls.gov/eag/eag.pr.htm.

———. 2013b. *Labor Force Statistics from the Current Population Survey. Table 11. Employed Persons by Detailed Occupation, Sex, Race, and Hispanic or Latino Ethnicity.* (February 6.) Accessible at http://www.bls.gov/cps/tables.htm.

———. 2013c. *American Time Use Survey—2012 Results Announced.* News June 20. Accessible at http://www.bls.gov/tus/.

Burgess, Melinda, Karen E. Dill, S. Paul Stermer, Stephen R. Burgess, and Brian P. Brown. 2011. Playing with Prejudice: The Prevalence and Consequences of Racial Stereotypes in Video Games. *Media Psychology,* 14: 289–311.

Burgdorf, Robert L., Jr. 2005. Americans with Disabilities Act of 1990 (United States). Pp. 93–101 in Gary Albrecht, ed., *Encyclopedia of Disability.* Thousand Oaks, CA: Sage.

Bush, George W. 2001. *Islam Is Peace.* Accessed October 16, 2004, at http://www.whitehouse.gov/news/releases.

Butler, Robert N. 1990. A Disease Called Ageism. *Journal of the American Geriatrics Society* (February), 38: 178–180.

Cafaro, Philip, and Winthrop Staples III. 2009. *The Environmental Argument for Reducing Immigration to the United States.* Washington, DC: Center for Immigration Studies.

Cainkar, Louise. 2006. Immigrants from the Arab World. Pp. 182–196 in *The New Chicago,* John P. Koval et al., eds. Philadelphia: Temple University Press.

Calavita, Kitty. 2007. Immigration Law, Race, and Identity. *Annual Reviews of Law and Social Sciences,* 3: 1–20.

Camarillo, Albert. 1993. Latin Americans: Mexican Americans and Central Americans. Pp. 855–872 in *Encyclopedia of American Social History,* Mary Koplec Coyton, Elliot J. Gorn, and Peter W. Williams, eds. New York: Charles Scribner.

Camarota, Steven A. 2007a. *Immigrants in the United States, 2007: A Profile of America's Foreign-Born Population.* Washington, DC: Center for Immigrant Statistics.

Camarota, Steven A., and Karen Jensenius. 2009. *A Shifting Tide: Recent Trends in the Illegal Immigrant Population.* Washington DC: Center for Immigration Studies.

Campbell, Gregory R. 2008. Sacred Sites, Native American. Pp. 1179–1182 in vol. 3, *Encyclopedia of Race, Ethnicity, and Society,* Richard T. Schaefer, ed. Thousand Oaks, CA: Sage.

Campion, Siah. 2013. Interview. September. Montello WI.

Campo-Flores, Arian. 2012. Cuban-Americans Move Left. *Wall Street Journal* (November 9): A6.

Canak, William, and Laura Swanson. 1998. *Modern Mexico.* New York: McGraw-Hill.

Cañas, Jesus, Roberto Coronado, and Robert W. Gilmer. 2006. U.S., Mexico Deepen Economic Ties. *Southwest Economy,* 1 (January/February). Accessible at http://www.dallasfed.org.

Canfield, Clarke. 2012. Maine Major: Somalis Should Leave Culture at Door. *Twin City Times* (Lewiston Auburn ME) October 4. Accessed November 12, 2012, at http://www.twincitytimes.com/columns/enough-is-enough-extremist-liberals-widen-the-divide-with-somalis.

Capps, Randy, Ku Leighton, and Michael Fix. 2002. *How Are Immigrants Faring after Welfare Reform? Preliminary Evidence from Los Angeles and New York City.* Washington, DC: Urban Institute.

Capriccioso, Rob. 2011a. Cobell's Final Toll. *Indian Country Today* (January 19): 16–19.

———. 2011b. The Donor Party. *Indian Country Today* (March 23): 43–49.

Carlson, Allan C. 2003. The Peculiar Legacy of German-Americans. *Society* (January/February): 77–88.

Carlson, Dawn S., K. Michele Kacmar, and Dwayne Whitten. 2006. What Men Think They Know About Executive Women. *Harvard Business Review* (September), 84: 28.

Carmichael, Stokely, with Ekwueme Michael Thelwell. 2003. *The Life and Struggles of Stokely Carmichael (Kwame Ture).* New York: Scribner.

Carr, James H., and Nandinee K. Kutty, eds. 2008. *Segregation: The Rising Costs for America.* New York: Routledge.

Carroll, Joseph. 2006. Public National Anthem Should Be Sung in English. *The Gallup Poll* (May): 3.

———. 2007. *Hispanics Support Requiring English Proficiency for Immigrants.* Accessed July 5, 2007, at http://www.gallup.com.

Carson, E. Ann, and William J. Sabol. 2012. *Prisoners in 2011.* December. Washington, DC: Bureau of Justice Statistics.

Carter, Jimmy. 1978. *Public Papers of the President of the United States. Book Two: June 30, to December 31, 1978.* Washington DC: National Archives and Records Service.

Caruso, Eugene M., Dobromir A. Rahnev, and Mahzarin R. Banaji. 2009. Using Conjoint Analysis to Detect Discrimination: Revealing Covert Preferences from Overt Choices. *Social Cognition* 27 (No. 1): 128–137.

Catalyst. 2001. *Women Satisfied with Current Job in Financial Industry but Barriers Still Exist.* Press release July 25, 2001. Accessed January 31, 2002, at http://www.catalystwomen.org.

———. 2011. *Women CEOs of the Fortune 1000.* May 2011. Accessed June 10, 2011, at http://www.catalyst.org/publication/322/women-ceos-of-the-fortune-1000.

Cave, Damien. 2011. Crossing Over, and Over. *New York Times* (October 3): A1, A6.

Center for Constitutional Rights. 2011. *Stop-and-Frisks of New Yorkers in 2010 Hit All-Time High at 600, 601; 87 percent of Those Stopped Black and Latino.* Accessed March 2, 2011, at http://ccrjustice.org.

Center for Work-Life Policy. 2011. *Asian-Americans Still Feel Like Outsiders in Corporate America, New Study from the Center for Work-Life Policy Finds.* July 20. New York: Center for Work-Life Policy.

Centers for Disease Control and Prevention. 2007. *U.S. Public Health Service Syphilis Study at Tuskegee.* Accessed April 25, 2007, at http://www.cdc.gov.

Central Intelligence Agency. 2011. *The World Factbook.* Accessed June 18, 2011, at http://www.cia.gov/library/publications/the-world-factbook/geos/is.html.

Chacko, Elizabeth, and Rajiv Menon. 2013. Longings and Belongings: Indian American Youth Identity, Folk Dance Competitions, and the Construction of "Tradition." *Ethnic and Racial Studies,* 36 (1): 97–116.

Chambers Book of Facts. 2005. Edinburgh: Chambers Harrap Publishers.

Champagne, Duane. 1994. *Native America. Portrait of the Peoples.* Detroit: Visible Ink.

Chanes, Jerome A. 2007. Anti-Semitism. Pp. 90–110 in *American Jewish Yearbook 2007,* David Singer and Lawrence Grossman, eds. New York: American Jewish Committee.

———. 2008. *A Primer in the American Jewish Community.* 3rd ed. New York: American Jewish Committee.

Chaney, Kathy. 2009. Are there too few Black criminal court judges? *Chicago Defender* (March 11). Accessible at http://www.chicagodefender.com/article3442-are-there-too-few-black-criminal-court-judges.html.

Chang, Cindy. 2007. Asians Flex Muscles in California Politics. *New York Times* (February 27): A11.

Chase-Dunn, Christopher, and Thomas D. Hall. 1998. World-Systems in North America: Networks, Rise and Fall and Pulsations of Trade in Stateless Systems. *American Indian Culture and Research Journal,* 22(1): 23–72.

Chazan, Guy, and Ainsley Thomson. 2011. Tough Irish Economy Turns Migration Influx to Exodus. *Wall Street Journal* (January 21): A8.

Chen, Carolyn. 2012. Asians: Too Smart for Their Own Good? *New York Times* (December 20): A35.

Chertok, Fern, Benjamin Phillips, and Leonard Saxe. 2008. *It's Not Just Who Stands Under the Chuppah: Intermarriage and Engagement.* Waltham, MA: Marilyn Cohen Center for Modern Jewish Studies, Brandeis University.

Chin, Ko-lin. 1996. *Chinatown Gangs: Extortion, Enterprise, and Ethnicity.* New York: Oxford University Press.

Chirot, Daniel, and Jennifer Edwards. 2003. Making Sense of the Senseless: Understanding Genocide. *Contexts* 2 (Spring): 12–19.

Chiswick, Carmel U. 2009. *Occupation and Gender: American Jews at the Millennium.* Accessed June 14, 2011, at http://www.thearda.com/workingpapers/.

Chou, Roslaind S., and Joe R. Feagin. 2008. *The Myth of the Model Minority: Asian Americans Facing Racism.* Boulder: Paradigm Publishers.

Chrisafis, Angelique. 2011. Muslim Women Protest on First Day of France's Face Veil Ban. *Guardian* (April 11). Accessible at http://www.guardian.co.uk.

———. 2012. Seven Years After the Riots, The Suburbs of Paris Still Simmer with Resentment. *The Guardian* (November 3). Accessible at ww.guardian.com.

Christensen, Kim. 2012. Interview. Wisconsin School District. November 8.

Christopher, Gail. 2013. The Conversation We're *Not* Having About Affirmative Action. *The Huffington Post.* (June 6). Accessible at http://www.huffingtonpost.com/dr-gail-christopher/the-conversation-were-not-having_b_3398540.html.

Christopulos, Diana. 1974. Puerto Rico in the Twentieth Century: A Historical Survey. Pp. 123–163 in *Puerto Rico and Puerto Ricans: Studies in History and Society,* Adalberto Lopez and James Petras, eds. New York: Wiley.

Chu, Judy. 2011. *Chinese Exclusion Act.* Congressional Record 157 (No. 77, June 1): H3809-H3810.

Chu, Kathy. 2010. Vietnam: A New Land of Opportunity. *USA Today* (August 18): A1, A2.

Chua, Amy. 2011. *Battle Hymn of the Tiger Mother.* New York: Penguin Press.

Citrin, Jack, Amy Lerman, Michael Murakami, and Kathryn Pearson. 2007. Testing Huntington: Is Hispanic Immigration a Threat to American Identity? *Perspectives on Politics* (March), 5: 31–48.

Clabaugh, Rich. 2012. Briefing: Why Settlements Issue Again Heats Up. *Christian Science Monitor* (December 17): 13.

Clemmitt, Marcia. 2005. Intelligent Design. *CQ Researcher* (July 29), 95: 637–660.

Cockburn, Andrew. 2003. True Colors: Divided Loyalty in Puerto Rico. *National Geographic Magazine* (March), 203: 34–55.

Cognard-Black, Andrew J. 2004. Will They Stay, or Will They Go? Sex—Atypical among Token Men Who Teach. *Sociological Quarterly,* 45 (1): 113–139.

Cohen, Patricia. 2010a. Discussing That Word That Prompts Either a Fist Pump or a Scowl. *New York Times* (January 23): C1, C5.

Cohen, Sandy. 2006. Gibson: "I Am Not an Anti-Semite." *Chicago Tribune* (August 2): 2.

Cohen, Steven M. 1988. *American Assimilation or Jewish Revival?* Bloomington: Indiana University Press.

———. 1991. *Content or Continuity? Alternative Bases for Commitment.* New York: American Jewish Committee.

Coker, Tumaini, et al. 2009. Perceived Racial/Ethnic Discrimination Among Fifth-Grade Students and Its Association with Mental Health. *American Journal of Public Health,* 99 (5): 878–884.

Coker, Tumaini., S. Bryan Austin, and Mark A. Shuster. 2010. The Health and Health Care of Lesbian, Gay, and Bisexual Adolescents. *Annual Review of Public Health,* 31: 456–477.

Collado-Schwarz, Ángel. 2012. *Decolonization Models for America's Last Colony: Puerto Rico.* Syracuse: Syracuse University Press.

Collins, Patricia Hill. 2000. *Black Feminist Thought: Knowledge, Consciousness, and the Politics of Empowerment,* 2nd ed. New York: Routledge.

———. 2013. *On Intellectual Activism.* Philadelphia: Temple University Press.

Comas-Díaz, Lillian, M. Brinton Lykes, and Renato D. Alarcón. 1998. Ethnic Conflict and the Psychology of Liberation in Guatemala, Peru, and Puerto Rico. *American Psychologist* (July) 53: 778–792.

Comeau, Joseph A. 2012. Race/Ethnicity and Family Contact: Toward a Behavioral Measure of Familism. *Hispanic Journal of Behavioral Sciences* 34 (2): 251–268.

Commission on Civil Rights. 1976. *Fulfilling the Letter and Spirit of the Law: Desegregation of the Nation's Public Schools.* Washington, DC: U.S. Government Printing Office.

———. 1981. *Affirmative Action in the 1980s: Dismantling the Process of Discrimination.* Washington, DC: U.S. Government Printing Office.

Commission on Wartime Relocation and Internment of Civilians. 1982a. *Recommendations.* Washington, DC: U.S. Government Printing Office.

———. 1982b. *Report.* Washington, DC: U.S. Government Printing Office.

Committee of 100. 2001. *American Attitudes Towards Chinese Americans and Asian Immigrants.* New York: Committee of 100.

Connelly, Marjorie. 2008. Dissecting the Changing Electorate. *New York Times* (November 8): sect. WK.

Connor, Walter. 1994. *Ethnonationalism: The Quest for Understanding.* Princeton, NJ: Princeton University Press.

Constantini, Cristina. 2011. Beardstown, Small Midwestern Meatpacking Town, Wrestles With Immigration Issue. *Huffington Post* (December). Accessible at http://www.huffingtonpost.com/2011/12/07/beardstown-illinois-small-town-wrestles-with-immigration-issues_n_1134797.html.

Conver, Bill. 1976. Group Chairman Lists Problems Endangering Jewish Family. *Peoria Journal Star* (December 4): A2.

Conyers, James L., Jr. 2004. The Evolution of Africology: An Afrocentric Appraisal. *Journal of Black Studies* (May), 34: 640–652.

Conyers, John. 2013. *Issues: Reparations.* Accessed September 20, 2013, http://conyers.house.gov/index.cfm/reparations.

Coogan, Michael D. 2003. *The Illustrated Guide to World Religions.* Oxford University Press.

Cook, Greg. 2012. *Bhangra in Boston: "It Makes The Move."* November 12. Accessible at http://www.wbur.org.

Coontz, Stephanie. 2010. *A Strange Stirring: "The Feminine Mystique" and American Women at the Dawn of the 1960s.* New York: Basic Books.

———. 2013. Progress at Work, But Mothers Still Pay a Price. *New York Times* (June 9): Week in Review section, p. 5.

Cooper, Richard S., Charles N. Rotimi, and Ryk Ward. 1999. The Puzzle of Hypertension in African Americans. *Scientific American* (February): 56–63.

Cooperman, Alan. 2005. One Way to Pray? *Washington Post National Weekly Edition* (September 5), 22: 10–11.

Copeland, Larry. 2011. Asian Farmers Crop Up in Southeast. *USA Today* (February 9): 3A.

Corbet, Sylvie. 2013. French Lawmaker on Defensive after Recorded Saying "Maybe Hitler Didn't Kill Enough." *Associated Press* (April 6). Accessible at http://www.neurope.eu.

Cordova, Carlos. 2005. *The Salvadoran Americans.* Westport, CT: Greenwood Press.

Cornacchia, Eugene J., and Dale C. Nelson. 1992. Historical Differences in the Political Experiences of American Blacks and White Ethnics: Revisiting an Unresolved Controversy. *Ethnic and Racial Studies* (January 15): 102–124.

Cornell, Stephen. 1984. Crisis and Response in Indian–White Relations: 1960–1984. *Social Problems* (October), 32: 44–59.

———. 1996. The Variable Ties that Bind: Content and Circumstance in Ethnic Processes. *Ethnic and Racial Studies* (April), 19: 265–289.

Correll, Joshua, Bernadette Park, Charles M. Judd, Bernd Wittenbrink, Melody S. Sadler, and Tracie Keesee. 2007a. Across the Thin Blue Line: Police Officers and Racial Bias in the Decision to Shoot. *Journal of Personality and Social Psychology,* 92 (6): 1006–1023.

———. 2007b. The Influence of Stereotypes and Decisions to Shoot. *European Journal of Social Psychology* 37: 1102–1117.

Cose, Ellis. 1993. *The Rage of a Privileged Class.* New York: HarperCollins.

———. 2008. So What if He Were Muslim? *Newsweek* (September 1): 37.

Coser, Lewis A. 1956. *The Functions of Social Conflict.* New York: Free Press.

Coser, Lewis A., and Rose Laub Coser. 1974. *Greedy Institutions.* New York: Free Press.

Couch, Kenneth A., and Robert Fairlie. 2010. Last Hired, Fast Fired? Black–White Unemployment and the Business Cycle. *Demography* 47 (February): 227–247.

Cox, Oliver C. 1942. The Modern Caste School of Social Relations. *Social Forces* (December), 21: 218–226.

Crumley, Bruce. 2010. Governance: Boardroom Revolution. *Time* (April 26): Global 1–2.

Cullen, Andrew. 2011. Struggle and Progress: 10 Years of Somalis in Lewiston. *Lewiston-Auburn Sun Journal* (December 18). Accessed April 16, 2012, at http://www.sunjournal.com/news/city/2011/12/18/struggle-and-progress-10-years-somalis-lewiston/1127846.

DaCosta, Kimberly McClain. 2007. *Making Multiracials: State, Family, and Market in the Redrawing of the Color Line.* Stanford, CA: Stanford University Press.

Dade, Corey. 2012a. *Census Bureau Rethinks The Best Way to Measure Race.* Accessed December 29, 2012, at http://www.wbur.org.

———. 2012b. *The Fight Over Voter ID Laws Goes to the United Nations.* March 9. Accessible at http://www.npr.org.

Dahlburg, John-Thor. 2004. The Spanish-Speaking Heritage of the State Now Reflects All of Latin America, Not Just Cuba" *Los Angeles Times,* June 28, A1, A12.

Dallo, Florence J., Kristine J. Ajrouch, and Soham Al-Snih. 2008. The Ancestry Question and Ethnic Heterogeneity: The Case of Arab Americans. *International Migration Review* (Summer): 505–517.

Dally, Chad. 2011. Hmong Heritage Month Refocuses on Health. *Wausau Daily Herald* (April 3): A3.

Daniel, G. Reginald. 2006. *Race Multiraciality in Brazil and the United States: Converging Paths?* University Park: Pennsylvania State University Press.

Dansie, Roberto. 2004. Curanderismo. *Indian Country Today* (December 8): C5.

David, Gary C. 2003. Rethinking Who's an Arab American: Arab-American Studies in the New Millennium. *Al-Jadid* (Fall): 9.

———. 2004. Scholarship on Arab Americans Post 9/11. *Al-Jadid* (Winter/Spring): 26–27.

———. 2007. The Creation of "Arab American": Political Activism and Ethnic (Dis)Unity. *Critical Sociology*, 32: 833–862.

———. 2008. Arab Americans. Pp. 84–87 in vol. 2, *Encyclopedia of Race, Ethnicity, and Society*, Richard T. Schaefer, ed. Thousand Oaks, CA: Sage.

David, Gary C., and Kenneth Kahtan Ayouby. 2004. Perpetual Suspects and Permanent Others: Arab Americans and the War and Terrorism. Pp. 30–71 in *Guerras e Imigracioes*, Marco Aurélio Machado de Oliveira, ed. Campo Grande, Brazil: Universidade Federal de Mato Grosso do Sul.

David, Gary C., and Paul L. Jalbert. 2008. Undoing Degradation: The Attempted "Rehumanization" of Arab and Muslim Americans. *Ethnographic Studies* 10: 23-47.

Davidson, James D., and Ralph E. Pyle. 2011. *Ranking Faiths: Religious Stratification in America.* Lanham MD: Rowman and Littlefield.

Davis, James A., Tom W. Smith, and Peter V. Marsden. 2007. *General Social Surveys, 1972–2006: Cumulative Codebook.* Chicago: NORC.

Davis, Michelle R. 2008. Checking Sources: Evaluating Web Sites Requires Careful Eye. (Released by *Education Week*, March 6.) Accessed June 20, 2008, at http://www.edweek.org.

De Anda, Roberto M. 2004. *Chicanas and Chicanos in Contemporary Society*, 2nd ed. Lanham, MD: Rowman & Littlefield & Bacon.

Degler, Carl N. 1971. *Neither Black nor White: Slavery and Race Relations in Brazil and the United States.* New York: Macmillan.

de la Garza, Rodolfo O., Louis DeSipio, F. Chris Garcia, John Garcia, and Angelo Falcon. 1992. *Latino Voices: Mexican, Puerto Rican, and Cuban Perspectives on American Politics.* Boulder, CO: Westview Press.

Delgado, Héctor L. 2008. La Raza. Pp. 830–831 in vol. 2, *Encyclopedia of Race, Ethnicity, and Society*, Richard T. Schaefer, ed. Thousand Oaks, CA: Sage.

Dell'Angela, Tracy. 2005. Dakota Indians Say Kids Trapped in "School-to-Prison" Pipeline. *Chicago Tribune* (November 29): 1, 19.

DellaPergola, Sergio. 2007. World Jewish Population, 2007. Pp. 551–600 in *American Jewish Yearbook 2007*, David Singer and Lawrence Grossman, eds. New York: American Jewish Committee.

———. 2012. *Jewish Population of the World*. Accessible at http://www.jewishvirtuallibrary.org

Del Olmo, Frank. 2003. Slow Motion Carnage at the Border. *Los Angeles Times* (May 18): M5.

Deloria, Vine, Jr. 1969. *Custer Died for Your Sins: An Indian Manifesto.* New York: Avon.

———. 1971. *Of Utmost Good Faith.* New York: Bantam.

———. 1992. Secularism, Civil Religion, and the Religious Freedom of American Indians. *American Indian Culture and Research Journal*, 16 (2): 9–20.

———. 1995. *Red Earth, White Lies.* New York: Scribner's.

———. 2004. Promises Made, Promises Broken. Pp. 143–159 in *Native Universe: Voices of Indian America*, Gerald McMaster and Clifford E. Trofzer, eds. Washington, DC: National Geographic.

Deloria, Vine, Jr. and Clifford M. Lytle. 1983. *American Indians, American Justice.* Austin: University of Texas Press.

DeNavas-Walt, Carman, Bernadette D. Proctor, and Jessica C. Smith. 2013. *Income, Poverty, and Health Insurance Coverage in the United States: 2012.* Washington, DC: U.S. Government Printing Office.

Denton, Nancy A., and Jacqueline Villarrubia. 2007. Residential Segregation on the Island: The Role of Race and Class in Puerto Rican Neighborhoods. *Sociological Forum* (March), 22: 1573–1586.

DeParle, Jason. 2007. A Good Provider Is One Who. *New York Times* (April 22): 50–57, 72, 122–123.

Department of Agriculture. 2010. *2007 Census Publications: Wisconsin.* Accessed August 13, 2010 at http://www.agcensus.usda.gov/Publications/2007/Full_Report/Census_by_State/Wisconsin.

Department of Dine' Education 2012. *Navaho Nation Department of Diné Education.* Accessed December 10, 2010 at http://www.navajonationode.org.

Department of Energy. 2000. *Final Report: Task Force against Racial Profiling.* Washington, DC: U.S. Government Printing Office.

Department of Homeland Security. 2013. *Naturalization Self Test.* Accessed August 7, 2013, at http://www.uscis.gov.

Department of Justice. 2000. *The Civil Liberties Act of 1988: Redress for Japanese Americans.* Accessed June 29, 2000, at http://www.usdoj.gov/crt/ora/main.html.

———. 2001. *Report to the Congress of the United States: A Review of Restrictions on Persons of Italian Ancestry During World War II.* Accessed February 1, 2002, at http://www.house.gov/judiciary/Italians.pdf.

———. 2011. *Hate Crime Statistics, 2010.* Accessible at http://www.fbi.gov.

Department of Labor. 1965. *The Negro Family: The Case for National Action.* Washington, DC: U.S. Government Printing Office.

———. 1995. *Good for Business: Making Full Use of the Nation's Capital.* Washington, DC: U.S. Government Printing Office.

———. 2011. *Women at Work.* March 2011. Accessible at http://www.bls.gov/spotlight/2011/women/.

———. 2013c. *International Comparisons of Annual Labor Force Statistics, 1970–2012.* June 7. Accessible at http://www.bls.gov.

———. 2013d. *Median Weekly Earnings of Full-Time Wage and Salary Workers by Detailed Occupation and Sex.* Accessible at http://www.bls.gov.

Department of State. 2008. *Immigrant Visas Issued to Orphans Coming to U.S.* Accessed September 3, 2008, at http://www.travel.state.gov/family/adoption/stats/stats_451.html.

———. 2013. *US State Department Services Dual Nationality.* Accessed August 7, 2013, at http://travel.state.gov/travel/cis_pa_tw/cis/cis_1753.html.

DeSante, Christopher D. 2013. Working Twice as Hard to Get Half as Far: Race, Work Ethnic, and America's Deserving Poor. *American Journal of Political Science* 57 (April): 342–356.

Desilver, Drew. 2013a. *Black Incomes Are Up, But Wealth Isn't.* August 30. Release by Pew Research Center at http://www.pewresearch.org.

———. 2013b. *5 Facts about Hispanics for Hispanic Heritage Month.* September 17. Release by Pew Research Center at http://www.pewresearch.org.

Desmond, Scott A., and Charise E. Kubrin. 2009. The Power of Place: Immigrant Communities and Adolescent Violence. *Sociological Quarterly*, 50: 581–607.

Detroit Arab American Study Team, Amaney Jamal, Ann Chih Lin, Andrew Shryock, Mark Tessler, Sally Howell, Ron Stockton. 2009. *Citizenship and Crisis: Arab Detroit After 9/11.* New York: Russell Sage Foundation.

Deutscher, Irwin, Fred P. Pestello, and H. Frances Pestello. 1993. *Sentiments and Acts.* New York: Aldine de Gruyter.

DeVoe, Jill Fleury, Kristen E. Darling-Church, and Thomas D. Snyde. 2008. *Status and Trends in the Education of American Indians and Alaska Natives: 2008.* Washington, DC: National Center for Education Statistics.

Dhingra, Pawan. 2012. *Life Behind the Lobby: Indian American Motel Owners and the American Dream.* Stanford CA: Stanford University Press.

Diamond, Jared. 2003. Globalization, Then. *Los Angeles Times* (September 14): M1, M3.

Dias, Elizabeth. 2013. Evangélicos! *Time* (April 15): 20–28.

Dickinson, Elizabeth. 2012. Addressing Environmental Racism Through Storytelling: Toward an Environmental Justice Narrative Framework. *Communication, Culture & Critique*, 5: 57–74.

Dickson, Lisa M. 2006. Book Review: Italians Then, Mexicans Now. *Industrial and Labor Relations Review* 60 (2): 293–295.

Dimrock, Michael, Carroll Doherty, and Rob Suls. 2013. Uncertainty Over Court's Voting Rights Decision, Public Divided Over Same-Sex Marriage Rulings. July 1. Accessible at http://www.peoplepress.org.

Dinnerstein, Leonard. 1994. *Anti-Semitism in America.* New York: Oxford University Press.

Disha, Ilir, James C. Cavendish, and Ryan D. King. 2011. Historical Events and Spaces of Hate. Hate Crimes Against Arabs and Muslims in Post-9/11 America. *Social Problems* 58 (1): 21–46.

DiTomaso, Nancy, Corinne Post, and Rochelle Parks-Yancy. 2007. Workforce Diversity and Inequality: Power, Status, and Numbers. *Annual Review of Sociology* 33: 473–501.

Dixon, Robyn. 2007. Running for Their Lives. *Los Angeles Times* (September 9): A1, A10.

Dobbin, Frank, and Alexandra Kalev. 2013. The Origins and Effects of Corporate Diversity Programs. Pp. 253–281 in *Oxford Handbook of Diversity and Work*, Quintetta M. Roberson, ed. New York: Oxford University Press.

Dobbin, Frank, Alexandra Kalev, and Erin Kelly. 2007. Diversity Management in Corporate America. *Contexts*, 6 (4): 21–27.

Dobbin, Frank, Soohan Kim, and Alexandra Kalev. 2011. You Can't Always Get What You Need: Organizational Determinants of Diversity Programs. *American Sociological Review*, 76 (3): 386.

Dolan, Sean, and Sandra Stotsky. 1997. *The Polish Americans.* New York: Chelsea House.

Dolan, Timothy. 2013. Immigration and the Welcome Church. *Wall Street Journal* (October 18): A11.

Dolnick, Sam. 2011. Many Korean Grocers, a New York Staple, Are Closing Down. *New York Times* (June 2): A19.

Dolnick, Sam, and Kirk Semple. 2011. Scattered Across New York, with Disaster at Home. *New York Times* (March 16): A25-26.

Domino, John C. 1995. *Sexual Harassment and the Courts.* New York: HarperCollins.

Donadio, Rachel. 2009. Bishop Offers Apology for Holocaust Remarks. *New York Times* (January 27): A6.

Dorris, Michael. 1988. For the Indians, No Thanksgiving. *New York Times* (November 24): A23.

Dorschner, Cheryl. 2013. *The New Face of Vermont Dairy Farming.* Accessed August 13, 2013, at http://www.uvm.edu/~cals/?Page=news&storyID=15296&category=calshome.

Downey, Douglas B. 2008. Black/White Differences in School Performance: The Oppositional Culture Explanation. *Annual Review of Sociology*, 34: 107–126.

Du Bois, W. E. B. 1903. *The Souls of Black Folks: Essays and Sketches* (reprint). New York: Facade Publications, 1961.

———. 1935. Does the Negro Need Separate Schools? *Journal of Negro Education* (July), 1: 328–335.

———. 1939. *Black Folk: Then and Now.* New York: Holt, Rinehart & Winston.

———. 1952. *Battle for Peace: The Story of My 83rd Birthday.* New York: Masses and Mainstream.

———. 1968. *Dusk of Dawn.* New York: Schocken.

———. 1969a. *An ABC of Color* [1900]. New York: International Publications.

———. 1969b. *The Suppression of the African Slave-Trade to the United States of America, 1638–1870.* New York: Schocken.

———. 1970. *The Negro American Family.* Cambridge, MA: MIT Press.

———. 1996. *The Philadelphia Negro: A Social Study* [1899]. Philadelphia: University of Pennsylvania Press.

———. 2003. *The Negro Church* [1903]. Walnut Creek: Alta Mira Press.

———. 2008. Anti-Semitism and Social Crisis [1899]. Translated by Chad Alan Goldberg. *Sociological Theory*, 26 (December): 321–323.

Dugger, Celia W. 2010. South Africa Redoubles Efforts Against AIDS. *New York Times* (April 26): A1, A3.

Dunaway, Wilma. 2003. *The African-American Family in Slavery and Emancipation.* New York: Cambridge University Press.

Durkheim, Émile. 2001. *The Elementary Forms of Religious Life* [1912]. New translation by Carol Cosman. New York: Oxford University Press.

———. 2008 [1899]. Anti-Semitism and Social Crisis. *Sociological Theory*, 26: 321–323.

Duszak, Thomas. 1997. Lattimer Massacre Centennial Commemoration. *Polish American Journal* (August). Accessed June 4, 2008, at http://www.polamjournal.com/Library/APHistory/Lattimer/lattimer.html.

Dyson, Michael Eric. 1995. *Making Malcolm: The Myth and Meaning of Malcolm X.* New York: Oxford University Press.

Dyson, Michael Eric. 2006. *Is Bill Cosby Right?: Or Has the Black Middle Class Lost Its Mind? New York:* Basic Civitas Books.

Eckholm, Erik. 2010. In Drug War, Tribe Feels Invaded by Both Sides. *New York Times* (January 25): A1, A10.

Eckstrom, Kevin. 2001. New, Diverse Take Spot on Catholic Altars. *Chicago Tribune* (August 31): 8.

Economic Mobility Project. 2012. *Pursuing the American Dream: Economic Mobility Across Generations.* Washington DC: Pew Charitable Trusts.

Economist. 2009. Cuba and America: Gently Does It. (May 9): 32–33.

———. Secure Enough. (June 22): 31–32.

———. 2013b. Game, Sex and Match. (September 7): 61–62.

Edison Research. 2012. Voters and Issues: National Election Poll. Reproduced in *New York Times* (November 7): 5 and (November 8): 1, 4.

Ehara, Yumiko. 2005. Feminism in the Grips of a Pincher Attack—Traditionalism, Liberalism, and Globalism. *International Journal of Japanese Sociology*, 14 (November): 6–14.

El-Haj, Nadia Abu. 2007. The Genetic Reinscription of Race. *Annual Review of Anthropology*, 16: 283–300.

Eligon, John. 2013. Down-Home American, Korean Style. *New York Times* (January 6): 17, 21.

Elkins, Stanley. 1959. *Slavery: A Problem in American Institutional and Intellectual Life.* Chicago: University of Chicago Press.

Elliott, Andrea. 2006. Muslim Voters Detect a Snub from Obama. *New York Times* (June 24): A1, A20.

———. 2011. Generation 9/11. *New York Times* (September 11): 25.

Ellis, Mark R. 2004. Denver's Anti-Chinese Riot. Pp. 142–143 in *Encyclopedia of the Great Plains*, David J. Wishart, ed. Lincoln: University of Nebraska Press.

Ellison, Brandy J. 2008. Tracking. Pp. 1316–1318 in vol. 3, *Encyclopedia of Race, Ethnicity, and Society*, Richard T. Schaefer, ed. Thousand Oaks, CA: Sage.

Ennis, Sharon R., Merarys Rios-Vargas, and Nora G. Albert. 2011. *The Hispanic Population: 2010.* C2010BR-404. Accessible at http://www.census.gov/prod/cen2010/briefs/c2010br-04.pdf.

Epstein, Cynthia Fuchs. 1999. The Major Myth of the Women's Movement. *Dissent* (Fall): 83–111.

Equal Employment Opportunity Commission. 2001. *Age Discrimination in Employment Act (ADEA), Changes FY 1992–FY 2000.* Accessed December 10, 2001, at http://www.eeoc.gov/stats/adea.html.

Erdmans, Mary Patrice. 1998. *Opposite Poles: Immigrants and Ethnics in Polish Chicago, 1976–1990.* University Park: Pennsylvania State University.

———. 2006. New Chicago Polonia: Urban and Suburban. Pp. 115–127 in *The New Chicago,* John Koval et al., eds. Philadelphia: Temple University Press.

Erlanger, Steven, and Elvire Camus. 2012. In a Ban, a Measure of European Tolerance. *New York Times* (September 2): 6, 8.

Eschbach, Karl, and Kalman Applebaum. 2000. Who Goes to Powwows? Evidence from the Survey of American Indians and Alaskan Natives. *American Indian Culture and Research Journal*, 24(2): 65–83.

Espiritu, Yen Le. 1992. *Asian American Panethnicity: Bridging Institutions and Identities.* Philadelphia: Temple University Press.

Espiritu, Yen Le, and Diane Wolf. 2001. Pp. 157–186 in *Ethnicities: Children of Immigrants in America,* Ruben G. Rumbaut and Alejandro Portes, eds. Berkeley: University of California Press.

Euless Historical Preservation Committee. 2011. Halatono Netane with Chris Jones. Accessible at http://www.eulesstx.gov/history/narratives/HalatonoNetane.htm.

European Union Agency for Fundamental Rights. 2013. *Discrimination and Hate Crime Against Jews in EU Member States: Experiences and Perceptions of Anti-Semitism.* Vienna: European Union.

European Roma Rights Centre. 2008. *Ostravis Case: D. H. and Others v. The Czech Republic.* Accessed June 29, 2008, at http://www.errc.org.

———. 2012. *Czech Republic: A Report by the European Roma Rights Centre.* Accessible at http://www.errc.org.

Fallows, Marjorie R. 1979. *Irish Americans: Identity and Assimilation.* Englewood Cliffs, NJ: Prentice Hall.

Farkas, Steve. 2003. *What Immigrants Say About Life in the United States.* Washington, DC: Migration Policy Institute.

Farley, Maggie. 2008. Canada to Apologize for Abuse of Native Students. *Los Angeles Times* (June 10): A4.

Fathi, Nazila. 2006. Iran Opens Conference on Holocaust. *New York Times* (December 12).

Feagin, Joe R., and José A. Cobas. 2008. Latinos/as and White Racial Frame: The Procrustean Bed of Assimilation. *Sociological Inquiry* (February), 78: 39–53.

———. 2014. *Latinos Facing Racism: Discrimination, Resistance and Endurance.* Boulder: Paradigm Books.

Feagin, Joe R., José A. Cobas, and Sean Elias. 2012. Rethinking Racial Formation Theory: A Systematic Racism Critique. *Ethnic and Racial Studies* (April): 1–30.

Feagin, Joe R., and Karyn D. McKinney. 2003. *The Many Costs of Racism.* Lanham, MD: Rowan and Littlefield.

Feagin, Joe R., and Eileen O'Brien. 2003. *White Men on Race, Power, Privilege, and the Shaping of Cultural Consciousness.* Boston: Beacon Press.

Feagin, Joe R., Hernán Vera, and Pinar Batur. 2000. *White Racism,* 2nd ed. New York: Routledge.

Federal Bureau of Investigation. 2012. *Hate Crime Statistics, 2011.* Accessible at http://www.fbi.gov.

Federal Register. 1975. HEW submitted Title IX regulations to Congress. 40 Fed. Reg. 24128. Summarized in *University of Pennsylvania Law Review* (124) and reproduced in Department of Justice. Accessed September 22, 2013, at http://www.justice.gov/crt/about/cor/coord/ixlegal.php.

Feldman, Marcus W. 2010. The Biology of Race. Pp. 136–159 in *Doing Race,* Hazel Rose Markus and Paula M. L. Moya, eds. New York: W. W. Norton.

Ferber, Abby L. 2008. Privilege. Pp. 1073–1074 in vol. 3, *Encyclopedia of Race, Ethnicity, and Society,* Richard T. Schaefer, ed. Thousand Oaks, CA: Sage.

Fernandez, Manny, and Kareem Fahim. 2006. Five on Plane Are Detained at Newark but Later Freed. *New York Times* (May 5): 29.

File, Thom. 2013. *The Diversifying Electorate-Voting Rates by Race and Hispanic Origin in 2012 (and Other Recent Elections).* Current Population Survey P20-568. Accessible at http://www.census.gov.

Finder, Alan. 1994. Muslim Gave Racist Speech, Jackson Says. *New York Times* (January 23): 21.

Fine, Gary. 2008. Robber's Cave. Pp. 1163–1164 in vol. 3, *Encyclopedia of Race, Ethnicity, and Society,* Richard T. Schaefer, ed. Thousand Oaks, CA: Sage.

Finestein, Israel. 1988. The Future of American Jewry. *The Jewish Journal of Sociology,* 30 (December): 121–125.

Fing, Jing, Shantha Madhavan, and Michael H. Alderman. 1996. The Association between Birthplace and Mortality from Cardiovascular Causes among Black and White Residents of New York City. *New England Journal of Medicine* (November 21), 335: 1545–1551.

Fiola, Jan. 2008. Brazil. Pp. 200–204 in vol. 2, *Encyclopedia of Race, Ethnicity, and Society,* Richard T. Schaefer, ed. Thousand Oaks, CA: Sage.

Fischer, Nancy L. 2013. Seeing "Straight," Contemporary Critical Heterosexuality Studies and Sociology: An Introduction. *Sociological Quarterly*, 54: 501–510.

Fishkoff, Sue. 2008. The Lights of Tolerance. *Jewish News of Greater Phoenix Online* (February 8). Accessed June 13, 2011, at http://www.jewishaz.com/issues/story.mv?080208+lights.

Fishman, Sylvia Barack, and Daniel Parmer. 2008. *Matrilineal Ascent/Patrilineal Descent: The Gender Imbalance in American Jewish Life.* Waltham, MA: Maurice and Marilyn Cohen Center for Modern Jewish Studies, Brandeis University.

Fitzgerald, Kathleen J. 2008. Native American Identity. Pp. 954–956 in vol. 2, *Encyclopedia of Race, Ethnicity, and Society,* Richard T. Schaefer, ed. Thousand Oaks, CA: Sage.

Flexner, Eleanor. 1959. *Century of Struggle: The Women's Rights Movement in the United States.* Cambridge, MA: Harvard University Press.

Foerstrer, Amy. 2004. Race, Identity, and Belonging: "Blackness" and the Struggle for Solidarity in a Multiethnic Labor Union. *Social Problems,* 51 (3): 386–409.

Foner, Eric. 2006. *Forever Free: The Story of Emancipation and Reconstruction.* New York: Knopf.

Foner, Eric., and Joanna Dreby. 2011. Relations Between the Generations In Immigrant Families. *Annual Reviews of Sociology,* 37: 545–564.

Forced Migration Studies Programme. 2009. *Regularising Zimbabwean Migration to South Africa.* Witwatersrand. South Africa: FMSP.

———. 2010. *Population Movements In and To South Africa.* Witwatersrand South Africa: FMSP.

Fordham, Signithia, and John U. Ogbu. 1986. Black Students' School Success: Coping with the Burden of "Acting White." *Urban Review,* 18 (3): 176–206.

Fox, Stephen. 1990. *The Unknown Internment.* Boston: Twayne.

Fox, Susannah, and Gretchen Livingston. 2007. *Hispanics with Lower Levels of Education and English Proficiency Remain Largely Disconnected from the Internet.* Washington, DC: Pew Hispanic Center.

Frank, Reanne, Ilana Redstone A Krech, and Bob Lu. 2010. Latino Immigrants and the U.S. Racial Order: How and Where Do They Fit In? *American Sociological Review,* 75(3): 378–401.

Frankel, Bruce. 1995. N.Y.'s "Jewish Rosa Parks" Wins Bus Battle. *USA Today* (March 17): 4A.

Frankenberg, Erica, Chungmei Lee, and Gary Orfield. 2003. A Multiracial Society with Segregated Schools: Are We Losing the Dream? Cambridge, MA: Civil Rights Project, Harvard University.

Franklin, John Hope, and Evelyn Brooks Higginbotham. 2011. *From Slavery to Freedom: A History of African Americans,* 9th ed. New York: McGraw-Hill.

Frazier, E. Franklin. 1957. *Black Bourgeois: The Rise of a New Middle Class.* New York: Free Press.

Freedman, Samuel G. 2003. *Sex and the City* Celebrates Judaism. *USA Today* (July 17): 13A.

Freeman, Jo. 1973. The Origins of the Women's Liberation Movement. *American Journal of Sociology* (January), 78: 792–811.

———. 1975. *The Politics of Women's Liberation.* New York: David McKay.

———. 1983. On the Origins of Social Movements. Pp. 1–30 in *Social Movements of the Sixties and Seventies,* Jo Freeman, ed. New York: Longman.

French, Howard W. 2003. Japan's Neglected Resource: Female Workers. *New York Times* (July 25).

Frey, William H. 2011. *Census Data: Blacks and Hispanics Take Different Segregation Paths.* (February 24.) Accessible at http://www.brookings.edu.

Friedan, Betty. 1963. *The Feminine Mystique.* New York: Dell.

———. 1981. *The Second Stage.* New York: Summit Books.

———. 1991. Back to *The Feminine Mystique? The Humanist* (January–February), 51: 26–27.

Frieden, Thomas R. 2011. CDC Health Disparities and Inequities Report—United States, 2011. *Morbidity and Mortality Weekly Report* (January 14).

Friedman, Georges. 1967. *The End of the Jewish People?* Garden City New York: Doubleday.

Frosch, Dan. 2008. Its Native Tongue Facing Extinction, Arapaho Tribe Teaches the Young. *New York Times* (October 17): A14.

Fry, Richard, and Mark Hugo Lopez. 2012. *Hispanic Student Enrollments Reach New Highs in 2011.* Washington DC : Pew Hispanic Center.

Fry, Richard, Mark Hugo Lopez, and Paul Taylor. 2013. *Hispanic High School Graduates Pass Whites in Rate of College Enrollments.* Washington DC : Pew Hispanic Center.

Fryer, Roland G. , Lisa Kahn, Steven D. Levitt, and Jörg L. Spenkuch. 2012. The Plight of Mixed Race Adolescents. *Review of Economics and Statistics* (August), 94: 6231–6234.

Fujimoto, Kayo. 2004. Feminine Capital: The Forms of Capital in the Female Labor Market in Japan. *Sociological Quarterly* 45 (1): 91–111.

Fuller, Bruce, Sara McElmurry, and John Koval. 2011. *Latino Workers Hitting a Blue-Collar Ceiling.* Berkeley CA: Institute of Human Development.

Fuller, Chevon. 1998. Service Redlining. *Civil Rights Journal,* 3 (Fall): 33–36.

Galewitz, Phil. 2012. Many Migrants Get Care in Field. *USA Today* (June 7): 3A.

Gallup, George H. 1972. *The Gallup Poll, Public Opinion, 1935–1971.* New York: Random House.

Gans, Herbert J. 1956. American Jewry: Present and Future. *Commentary* (May), 21: 424–425.

———. 1979. Symbolic Ethnicity: The Future of Ethnic Groups and Cultures in America. *Ethnic and Racial Studies* 2 (January): 1–20.

Garfinkel, Herbert. 1959. *When Negroes March.* New York: Atheneum.

Garner, Roberta. 1996. *Contemporary Movements and Ideologies.* New York: McGraw-Hill.

Garroutte, Era M. 2009. Religiosity and Spiritual Engagement in Two American Indian Populations. *Journal for the Scientific Study of Religion,* 48(3): 480–500.

Gates, Gary J., and Frank Newport. 2013. *Gallup Special Report: New Estimates of the LGBT Population in the United States.* February. Accessed September 23, 2013, at http:williansinstutute.law.ucla.edu/research/census-lgbt-demographics-studies/gallup-lgbt-pop-feb-2013/.

Geddes, Diana. 2010. The Price of Freedom: A Special Report on South Africa. *The Economist* (Junc 5): 1–16.

Gerson, Kathleen. 2007. What Do Women and Men Want? *The American Prospect* (March): A8–A11.

Gerth, H. H., and C. Wright Mills. 1958. *From Max Weber: Essays in Sociology.* New York: Galaxy Books.

Getlin, Josh. 1998. Leaving an Impact on American Culture. *Los Angeles Times* (April 22): A1, A26, A27.

Giago, Tim. 2013. Holocaust Museum of the Indigenous People Should Be Built at Wounded Knee. *Huffington Post* (April 29). Accessible at http://www.huffingtonpost.com.

Gibbs, Nancy. 2001. A Whole New World. *Time* (June 11): 36–45.

———. 2009. What Women Want Now. *Time,* 174 (No. 16): 24–33.

Gibson, Campbell, and Kay Jung. 2006. *Historical Census Statistics on the Foreign-Born Population of the United States: 1850 to 2000.* Working Paper No. 81. Washington, DC: Bureau of the Census.

Gibson, James L., and Christopher Classen. 2010. Racial Reconciliation in South Africa: Interracial Contact and Changes over Time. *Journal of Social Issues,* 66 (2): 255–272.

Girardelli, Davide. 2004. Commodified Identities: The Myth of Italian Food in the United States. *Journal of Communication Inquiry* (October), 28: 307–324.

Giroux, Henry A. 1997. Rewriting the Discourse of Racial Identity: Towards a Pedagogy and Politics of Whiteness. *Harvard Educational Review* (Summer) 67: 285–320.

Gittler, Joseph B., ed. 1981. *Jewish Life in the United States: Perspectives from the Social Sciences.* New York: New York University Press.

GLAAD. 2013. *Where We are On TV 2013.* Accessible at http://www.glaad.org/whereweareontv13.

Glazer, Nathan. 1990. American Jewry or American Judaism? *Society* (November–December), 28: 14–20.

Gleason, Philip. 1980. American Identity and Americanization. Pp. 31–58 in *Harvard Encyclopedia of American Ethnic Groups,* Stephen Therstromm, ed. Cambridge, MA: Belknap Press of Harvard University Press.

Gobodo-Madikizela, Pumla. 2003. *A Human Being Died That Night.* New York: Houghton Mifflin.

Goering, John M. 1971. The Emergence of Ethnic Interests: A Case of Serendipity. *Social Forces* (March), 48: 379–384.

Goffman, Erving. 1963. *Stigma: Notes on Management of Spoiled Identity.* Englewood Cliffs, NJ: Prentice Hall.

Gold, Matea, and Joseph Tanfani. 2012. Tribal Leaders Bet on Obama. *Chicago Tribune* (September 27): 19.

Gold, Michael. 1965. *Jews Without Money.* New York: Avon.

Goldberg, Jeffrey. 2013. New Chapter, Old Story. *New York Times* (October 13): Book Review section, p. 28.

Goldhagen, Daniel Jonah. 2013. *The Devil that Never Dies: The Rise and Threat of Global Anti-Semitism.* New York: Little, Brown.

Goldscheider, Calvin. 2003. Are American Jews Vanishing Again? *Contexts* (Winter): 18–24.

Goldstein, Evan R. 2010. Not Everybody Is Ready for an Orthodox Rabbi. *New York Times* (April 23): W11.

Goldstein, Joseph. 2013. Judge Rejects New York Stop-And-Frisk Policy. *New York Times* (August 12): A1, A16.

Goldstein, Sidney, and Calvin Goldscheider. 1968. *Jewish Americans: Three Generations in a Jewish Community.* Englewood Cliffs, NJ: Prentice Hall.

Gomez, Alan. 2010. Rise Seen in Births to Illegal Dwellers. *USA Today* (August 12): A1.

Gomez, David F. 1971. Chicanos: Strangers in Their Own Land. *America* 124 (June 26), 649–652.

———. 2013. Is Puerto Rico the Next Greece? Nest Eggs Could Suffer. *USA Today* (November 7): 1B, 6B.

Gonzales, Roberto G. 2011. Learning to Be Illegal: Undocumented Youth And Shifting Legal Contexts in the Transition to Adulthood. *American Sociological Review*, 76 (45): 602–619.

Gonzalez, David. 2009. A Family Divided by 2 Worlds, Legal and Illegal. *New York Times* (April 26): 1, 20–21.

González, Jennifer. 2012. Tribal Colleges Offer Basic Education to Students "Not Prepared for College." *Chronicle of Higher Education* (April 13): A25.

Gonzalez-Barrera, Ana, Mark Hugo Lopez, Jeffrey S. Passel, and Paul Taylor. 2013. *The Path Not Taken: Two-Thirds of Legal Mexican Immigrants Are Not U.S. Citizens.* (February 4.) Accessible at http://www.pewhispanic.org.

Goodman, Peter S. and Akiko Kashiwagi. 2002. In Japan: Housewives No More. *Washington Post National Weekly Edition* (November 4): 18–19.

Goodstein, Laurie. 2005. Issuing Rebuke: Judge Rejects Teaching of Intelligent Design. *New York Times* (December 21): A1, A21.

———. 2010. American Muslims Ask, Will We Ever Belong? *New York Times* (September 6): A1, A3.

———. 2011. Report Offers Surprises on Muslims' Growth. *New York Times* (January 27): A8.

———. 2013a. Bar Mitzvahs Get New Look to Build Faith. *New York Times* (September 4): A1, A13.

———. 2013b. Hispanics Grow Cool to G.O.P., Poll Finds. *New York Times* (September 28): A9.

Goodstein, Laurie, and Jennifer Steinhauer. 2010. Pope Picks Latino to Lead Los Angeles Archdiocese. *New York Times* (April 7): A17.

Gordon, Milton M. 1964. *Assimilation in American Life: The Role of Race, Religion, and National Origins.* New York: Oxford University Press.

Gorski, Phillip S. 2010. *Civil Religion Today* (ARDA Guiding Paper Series). State College: Association of Religion Data Archives at the Pennsylvania State University. Accessible at http://www.thearda.com/rrh/papers/guidingpapers.asp.

Gose, Ben. 2013. Diversity Offices Aren't What They Used to Be. *Chronicle of Higher Education* (June 14): A14–A15, A17.

Gray-Little, Bernadette, and Hafdahl, Adam R. 2000. Factors Influencing Racial Comparisons of Self-Esteem: A Qualitative Review. *Psychological Bulletin*, 126 (1): 26–54.

Greeley, Andrew M. 1981. *The Irish Americans: The Rise to Money and Power.* New York: Harper & Row.

Green, Alexander R., et al. 2007. Implicit Bias among Physicians and Its Prediction of Thrombolysis Decisions for Black and White Patients. *Journal of General Internal Medicine* (September), 22: 1231–1238.

Greenhouse, Linda. 1996. Court Accepts Case Tied to Separation Powers. *New York Times* (October 16). Accessed November 20, 2013, at http://www.nytimes.com/1996/10/16/us/court-accepts-case-tied-to-separation-of-powers.html?pagewanted=all&src=pm.

———. 2008. Justices, in Beas Case, Rule for Older Workers. *New York Times* (June 20): A15.

Greenhouse, Steven. 2012. Equal Opportunity Panel Updates Hiring Policy. *New York Times* (April 26): B3.

Grieco, Elizabeth M., Yesenia D. Acosta, G. Patricia de la Cruz, Christine Gambino, Thomas Gryn, Luke J. Larsen, Edward N. Trevelyan, and Nathan P. Watters. 2012. *The Foreign-Born Population in the United States: 2010.* May 2012 ACS-19. Accessible at http://www.census.gov.

Grieco, Elizabeth M. and Rachel C. Cassidy. 2001. Overview of Race and Hispanic Origin. *Current Population Reports.* Ser. CENBR/01-1. Washington, DC: U.S. Government Printing Office.

Grimshaw, Allen D. 1969. *Racial Violence in the United States.* Chicago: Aldine.

Grinspan, Jon. 2013. When the Civil War Came to New York. *New York Times* (July 14): Week in Review, p. 8.

Grossman, Cathy Lynn. 2008. Muslim Census a Difficult Count. *USA Today* (August 6): 5D.

———. 2010. Day of Prayer Divides Some. *USA Today* (May 5): 6D.

Guerin-Gonzales, Camille. 1994. *Mexican Workers and American Dreams.* New Brunswick, NJ: Rutgers University Press.

Guest, Kenneth J. 2003. *God in Chinatown: Religion and Survival in New York's Evolving Immigrant Community.* New York: University Press.

Guglielmo, Jennifer, and Salvatore Salerno, eds. 2003. *Are Italians White?* New York: Routledge.

Guly, Christopher, and Maggie Farley. 2008. Canada Natives Get Apology. *Los Angeles Times* (June 12): A3.

Gupta, Sanjay. 2012. Interview of Dr. Alfredo Quinones-Hinojosa. CNN Interview. (May 18.)

Gutierrez, Luis. 2011. *Rep. Gutierrez Returns To House Floor to Address Civil Rights Crisis in Puerto Rico Speech to House of Representatives Underscores Congressman's Commitment to Free Speech, Asserts Puerto Ricans Cannot Be Silenced.* Accessed September 10, 2011, at http://www.gutierrez.house.gov/index.php?option=com_content&task=view&id=647&Itemid=71.

Guzmán, Betsy. 2001. *The Hispanic Population.* Census 2000 Brief Series C2kBR/01-3. Washington, DC: U.S. Government Printing Office.

Haak, Gerald O. 1970. Co-Opting the Oppressors: The Case of the Japanese-Americans. *Society* (October), 7: 23–31.

Hacek, Miro. 2008. Roma. Pp. 1168–1170 in vol. 3, *Encyclopedia of Race, Ethnicity, and Society,* Richard T. Schaefer, ed. Thousand Oaks, CA: Sage.

Hacker, Helen Mayer. 1951. Women as a Minority Group. *Social Forces* (October), 30: 60–69.

———. 1974. Women as a Minority Group: Twenty Years Later. Pp. 124–134 in *Who Discriminates against Women,* Florence Denmark, ed., Beverly Hills, CA: Sage Publications.

Haeri, Shaykh Fadhilalla. 2004. *The Thoughtful Guide to Islam.* Alresford, UK: O Books.

Hakim, Danny. 2010. U.S. Recognizes an Indian Tribe on Long Island, Clearing the Way for a Casino. *New York Times* (June 15).

Hakimzadeh, Shirin, and D'Vera Cohn. 2007. *English Usage among Hispanics in the United States.* Washington, DC: Pew Hispanic Center.

Haller, William, Alejandro Portes, and Scott M. Lynch. 2011. Dreams Fulfilled, Dreams Shattered: Determinants of Segmented Assimilation in the Second Generation. *Social Forces*, 89 (3): 733–762.

Halstead, Mark L. 2008. Islamophobia. Pp. 762–764 in vol. 2, *Encyclopedia of Race, Ethnicity, and Society,* Richard T. Schaefer, ed. Thousand Oaks, CA: Sage.

Halualani, Rona Tamiko. 2002. *In the Name of Hawaiians: Native Identities and Cultural Politics.* Minneapolis: University of Minnesota Press.

Hammond, Laura. 2010. Obliged to Give: Remittances and the Maintenance of Transitional Networks Between Somalis at Home and Abroad. *Bildhaan: An International Journal of Somali Studies*, 10 (Article 11). Accessible at http://digitalcommons.macalester.edu/bildhaan/.

Handlin, Oscar. 1951. *The Uprooted: The Epic Story of the Great Migrations That Made the American People.* New York: Grossett and Dunlap.

Hansen, Marcus Lee. 1952. The Third Generation in America. *Commentary* (November 14): 493–500.

Harlow, Caroline Wolf. 2005. *Hate Crime Reported by Victims and Police.* Bureau of Justice Statistics Special Report (November). Accessed May 8, 2008, at http://www.ojp.usdoj.gov/bjs/pub/pdf/hcrvp.pdf.

Harrison, Jill Lindsay, and Sarah E. Lloyd. 2012. Illegality at Work: Deportability and the Productive New Era of Immigration Enforcements. *Antipode*, 44 (2): 365–385.

———. 2013. New Jobs, New Workers, and New Inequalities: Explaining Employers' Roles in Occupational Segregation by Nativity and Race. *Social Problems*, 60 (3): 281–301.

Harrison, Jill Lindsay, Sarah E. Lloyd, and Trish O'Kane. 2009. *Overview of Immigrant Workers on Wisconsin Dairy Farmers.* Briefing No. 1. Madison WI: Program on Agricultural Technology Studies.

Hartocullis, Anemona. 2006. For Some Gays, a Right They Can Forsake. *New York Times* (July 30): sect. ST, 2.

Harzig, Christine. 2008. German Americans. Pp. 540–544 in vol. 1, *Encyclopedia of Race, Ethnicity, and Society,* Richard T. Schaefer, ed. Thousand Oaks, CA: Sage.

Hassrick, Elizabeth McGhee. 2007. *The Transnational Production of White Ethnic Symbolic Identities.* Paper presented at the Annual Meeting of the American Sociological Association.

Haub, Carl, and Toshiko Kaneda. 2013. *2013 World Population Data Sheet.* Washington DC: Population Reference Bureau.

Haxton, Charrisse, and Kristen Harknett. 2009. Racial and Gender Differences in Kin Support. *Journal of Family Issues* (August), 30: 1019–1040.

Haynes, V. Dio. 2009. Blacks Hit Hard by Economy's Punch. *Washington Post* (November 24). Accessed July 27, 2011, at http://www.washingtonpost.com/wp-dyn/content/article/2009/11/23/AR2009112304092.html.

Hays, Kristen L. 1994. Topeka Comes Full Circle. *Modern Maturity* (April–May): 34.

He, Wan, Manisha Sengupta, Victoria A. Velkoff, and Kimberly A. DeBarros. 2005. 651 in the United States: 2005. *Current Population Reports.* Ser. P23. No. 209. Washington, DC: U.S. Government Printing Office.

Head, John F. 2007. Why, Even Today, Many Blacks Are Wary about American Medicine. *Crisis* (January): 48–49.

Heilman, Madeline E. 2001. Description and Prescription: How Gender Stereotypes Present Women's Ascent Up the Organizational Ladder. *Journal of Social Issues*, 57 (4): 657–674.

Helmore, Edward. 2013. Desert "Death Map" Aims to Save Lives of Mexican Migrants. *The Guardian* (May 7): 30–31.

Henry, William A., III. 1994. Pride and Prejudice. *Time* (February 28), 143: 21–27.

Hentoff, Nicholas. 1984. Dennis Banks and the Road Block to Indian Ground. *Village Voice* (October), 29: 19–23.

Hequembourg, Amy, and Jorge Arditi. 1999. Fractured Resistances: The Debate over Assimilationism among Gays and Lesbians in the United States. *Sociological Quarterly*, 40 (4): 663–680.

Herbert, Bob. 2010. Jim Crow Policy. *New York Times* (February 2): A27.

Hernández-Arias, P. Rafael. 2008. Salvadoran Americans. Pp. 1185–1187 in vol. 3, *Encyclopedia of Race, Ethnicity, and Society*, Richard T. Schaefer, ed. Thousand Oaks, CA: Sage.

Herrnstein, Richard J., and Charles Murray. 1994. *The Bell Curve: Intelligence and Class Structure in American Life*. New York: Free Press.

Herschthal, Eric. 2004. Indian Students Discuss Pros, Cons of Arranged Marriages. *Daily Princetonian* (October 20).

Herzig-Yoshinaga, Aiko, and Marjorie Lee (eds.). 2011. *Speaking Out for Personal Justice (Site Summaries of Testimonies and Witnesses Registry)*. Los Angeles, CA: UCLA Asian American Studies.

Hevesi, Dennis. 2011. Elouise Cobell, 65, Sued for Indian Funds. *New York Times* (October 18): A19.

Higham, John. 1966. American Anti-Semitism Historically Reconsidered. Pp. 237–258 in *Jews in the Mind of America*, Charles Herbert Stember, ed. New York: Basic Books.

Hilberg, Soleste, and Ronald G. Tharp. 2002. *Theoretical Perspectives, Research Findings, and Classroom Implications of the Learning Styles of American Indian and Alaska Native Students*. Washington, DC: Eric Digest.

Hill, Robert B. 1999. *The Strengths of African American Families: Twenty-Five Years Later*. Lanham, MD: University Press of America.

Himmelfarb, Harold S. 1982. Research on American Jewish Identity and Identification: Progress, Pitfalls, and Prospects. Pp. 56–95 in *Understanding American Jewry*, Marshall Sklare, ed. New Brunswick, NJ: Transaction Books.

Hirsch, Mark. 2009. Thomas Jefferson: Founding Father of Indian Removal. *Smithsonian Institution* (Summer): 54–58.

Hirsley, Michael. 1991. Religious Display Needs Firm Count. *Chicago Tribune* (December 20), section 2: 10.

Hisnanick, John J., and Katherine G. Giefer. 2011. *Dynamics of Economic Well-Being: Fluctuations in the U.S. Income Distribution 2004–2007*. Washington, DC: U.S. Government Printing Office.

Hixson, Lindsay, Bradford B. Hepler, and Myoung Ouk Kim. 2012. *Islander Population: 2010*. May 2012. C2010BR-12. Washington DC: U.S. Government Printing Office.

Hochschild, Arlie Russell. 1990. The Second Shift: Employed Women Are Putting in Another Day of Work at Home. *Utne Reader* (March–April), 38: 66–73.

Hochschild, Arlie Russell, and Anne Machung. 1989. *The Second Shift*. New York: Viking.

Hochschild, Jennifer L. 1995. *Facing Up to the American Dream: Race, Class, and the Soul of the Nation*. Princeton, NJ: Rutgers University Press.

Hoeffel, Elizabeth M., Sonya Rastogi, Myoung Ouk Kim, and Hasan Shahid. 2012. *The Asian Population: 2010*. C2010BR-11. Accessible at http://www.census.gov.

Hogan, Bernie, and Brent Berry. 2011. Racial and Ethnic Biases in Rental Housing: An Audit Study of Online Apartment Listings. *City and Community*, 10 (4): 351–372.

Holson, Laura M., and Nick Bilton. 2012. Facebook's Royal Wedding. *New York Times* (May 25).

Holzer, Harry J. 2008. The Effects of Immigration on the Employment Outcomes of Black Americans. Testimony before the U.S. Commission on Civil Rights.

Honda, Mike. 2013. "Chairman's Message to the Congressional Anti-Bullying Caucus (CABC)." Accessed May 31, 2014 at http://honda.house.gov/priorities/chairmans-message-to-the-congressional-anti-bullying-caucus-cabc.
———. 2014, "Who I Am." Accessed May 31, 2014 at http://honda.house.gov/meet-mike/who-i-am.

Hondagneu-Sotelo, Pierette, ed. 2003. *Gender and U.S. Immigration: Contemporary Trends*. Berkeley: University of California Press.

hooks, bell. 2000. *Feminist Theory: From Margin to Center*. 2nd edition. Boston: South End Press.

Hoover, Eric. 2013. Colleges Contemplate a "Race Neutral" Future. *Chronicle of Higher Education* (October 18): 30, 32–33.

Hosokawa, Bill. 1969. *Nisei: The Quiet Americans*. New York: Morrow.

Howden, Lindsay, and Julie A. Meyer. 2011. *Age and Sex Composition: 2010*. May. C2010BR-03. Accessible at http://www.census.gov.

Hu, Winnie. 2012. To Revive Communities in U.S., Jewish Groups Try Relocation Bonuses. *New York Times* (September 19): A23–A24.

Hubbard, Amy S. 1993. *U.S. Jewish Community Responses to the Changing Strategy of the Palestinian Nationalist Movement: A Pilot Study*. Paper presented at annual meeting of the Eastern Sociological Society, Boston.

Hudgins, John L. 1992. The Strengths of Black Families Revisited. *The Urban League Review* (Winter), 15: 9–20.

Hughley, Matthew W., and Jessie Daniels. 2013. Racist Comments at Online News Sites: A Methodological Dilemma for Discourse Analysis. *Media, Culture & Society*, 35 (3): 332–347.

Huhndorf, Roy M., and Shari M. Huhndorf. 2011. Alaska Native Policies Since the Alaska Native Claims Settlement Act. *The South Atlantic Quarterly*, 111 (2): 385–401.

Huisman, Kimberly A., Mazie Hough, Kristin M. Langellier, and Carol Nordstrom Toner. 2011. *Somalis in Maine: Crossing Cultural Currents*. Berkeley CA: North Atlantic Books.

Humes, Karen R., Nicholas A. Jones, and Roberto R. Ramirez. 2011. Overview of Race and Hispanic Organization. *2010 Census Briefs*. C2010 BR-02.

Hundley, Tom. 2009. Return Trip. *Chicago Tribune Magazine* (January 18): 8–14.

Hunt, Larry L. 1999. Hispanic Protestantism in the United States: Trends by Decade and Generation. *Social Forces*, 77 (4): 1601–1624.

Huntington, Samuel P. 1993. "The Clash of Civilizations?" *Foreign Affairs* 73 no. 3, (Summer): 22–49.
———. 1996. *The Clash of Civilizations and the Remaking of World Order*. New York: Simon & Schuster.

Hurh, Won Moo. 1994. Majority Americans' Perception of Koreans in the United States: Implications of Ethnic Images and Stereotypes. Pp. 3–21 in *Korean Americans: Conflict and Harmony*, H. Kwon, ed. Chicago: Center for Korean Studies.

Hurh, Won Moo. 1998. *The Korean Americans*. Westport, CT: Greenwood Press.

Hurh, Won Moo., and Kwang Chung Kim. 1984. *Korean Immigrants in America: A Structural Analysis of Ethnic Confinement and Adhesive Adaptation*. Cranbury, NJ: Farleigh Dickinson University Press.

Huteson, Pamela Rae. 2008. Canada, First Nations. Pp. 230–233 in vol. 1, *Encyclopedia of Race, Ethnicity, and Society*, Richard T. Schaefer, ed. Thousand Oaks, CA: Sage.

Hyun, Jane. 2006. *Breaking the Bamboo Ceiling: Career Strategies for Asians*. New York: Harper Business.
———. 2009. Better Luck Tomorrow: Breaking the Bamboo Ceiling. Interview with Peter Nguyen. (October 14.) Accessed July 30, 2012, at http://diversitymbamagazine.com.

IAAMS. 2009. *Italian-Americans Against Media Stereotypes*. Accessed January 4, 2011, at http://iaams.blogspot.com.

IBGE. 2006. *PME–Color and Race*. (November 17.) Instituto Brasiliro de Geografia e Estatistica. Accessed June 8, 2011, at http://www.ibge.gov.br/english/presidencia/noticias/noticia_impressao.php?id_noticia=737.

Iceland, John, Gregory Sharp, and Jeffrey M. Timberlake. 2013. Sun Belt Rising: Regional Population Change and the Decline in Residential Segregation, 1970–2009. *Demography*, 50 (1): 97–123.

Ignatiev, Noel. 1994. Treason to Whiteness Is Loyalty to Humanity. Interview with Noel Ignatiev. *Utne Reader* (November–December): 83–86.
———. 1995. *How the Irish Became White*. New York: Routledge.

Indian and Northern Affairs Canada and Canadian Polar Commission. 2000. *2000–2001 Estimates*. Ottawa: Canadian Government Publishing.

Indian Arts and Crafts Board. 2013. *Indian Arts and Crafts Act: Know the Law*. Accessed January 20, 2013, at http://www.iacb.doi.gov.

Inoue, Miyako. 1989. Japanese Americans in St. Louis: From Internees to Professionals. *City and Society* (December), 3: 142–152.

Institute for Jewish and Community Research. 2008. *How Many Jews Are in World Today*. Accessed September 7, 2008, at http://bechollashon.org/population/today.php.

Institute of Southern Jewish Life. 2011. *About Rabbinic Services*. Accessed June 13, 2011, at http://www.isjl.org/rabbinic/index.html.

Institute on Taxation and Economic Policy. 2013. *Undocumented Immigrants' Share and Local Tax Contributions*. (July.) Washington DC: ITEP.

Intelligence Report. 2004. Wal-Mart Drops Protocols, but Controversy Lives On (Winter): 3.

International Herald Tribune. 2007. Black Residents of France Say They Are Discriminated Against. *International Herald Tribune* (January 31). Accessible at http://www.nytimes.com.

International Organization for Migration. 2009. *Migration, Climate Change and the Environment*. Geneva, Switzerland: IOM.

Inter-Parliamentary Union. 2013. *Women in National Parliaments*. (July 1.) Accessed September 14, 2013, at http://www.ipu.org/wmn-e/classif.htm.

Issacson, Jason, and Richard Foltin. 2001. *Election 2000: Post Election*. New York: American Jewish Committee.

Iwamasa, Gayle Y. 2008a. Internment Camps. Pp. 745–747 in vol. 2, *Encyclopedia of Race, Ethnicity, and Society*, Richard T. Schaefer, ed. Thousand Oaks, CA: Sage.

———. 2008b. Japanese American Citizens League. Pp. 781–782 in vol. 2, *Encyclopedia of Race, Ethnicity, and Society*, Richard T. Schaefer, ed. Thousand Oaks, CA: Sage.

Jacobson, Cardell, J. Lynn England, and Robyn J. Barrus. 2008. Familism. Pp. 477–478 in vol. 1, *Encyclopedia of Race, Ethnicity, and Society*, Richard T. Schaefer, ed. Thousand Oaks, CA: Sage.

Jacoby, Susan. 2009. Keeping the Faith, Ignoring the History. *New York Times* (March 1): 11.

Jaher, Frederic Caple. 1994. *A Scapegoat in the New Wilderness*. Cambridge, MA: Harvard University Press.

Janisch, Roy F. 2008. Wounded Knee 1890 and 1973. Pp. 1415–1417 in vol. 3, *Encyclopedia of Race, Ethnicity, and Society*, Richard T. Schaefer, ed. Thousand Oaks, CA: Sage.

Japanese American Citizens League. 2013. *Goals of the JACL Anti-Hate Program*. Accessed September 13, 2013, at http://www.jacl.org/public_policy/goals.htm.

Jaroszyn'ska-Kirchmann. 2004. *The Exile Mission: The Polish Political Diaspora and Polish Americans, 1939–1956*. Athens: Ohio University Press.

Jecker, Nancy. 2000. Review of Medical Apartheid. *New England Journal of Medicine* (November 23).

Jefferies, Sierra M. 2007. Environmental Justice and the Skull Valley Goshute Indians' Proposal to Store Nuclear Waste. *Journal of Land, Resources, and Environmental Law*, 27 (2): 409–429.

Jewish Agency for Israel. 2011. *Argentina*. Accessed June 13, 2011, at http://www.jafi.org.is.

Jimenez, Alfredo. 2005. *Leaving Cuba*. Unpublished paper. DePaul University, Chicago.

Jiménez, Tomás R. 2007. The Next Americans. *Los Angeles Times* (May 27): M1, M7.

Johnson, David. 2005. Uncertain Progress 25 Years After Defying State. *News from Indian County* (June 27), 19: 1, 5.

Johnson, Greg. 2005. Narrative Remains: Articulating Indian Identities in the Repatriation Context. *Society for Comparative Study of Society and History* (July), 47: 480–506.

Johnson, Kevin. 2004. *Immigration and Civil Rights*. Philadelphia: Temple University Press.

Johnson, Tallese D., Merarys Rios, Malcolm P. Drewery, Sharon R. Ennis, and Myoung Ouk Kim. 2010. People Who Spoke a Language Other Than English at Home by Hispanic Origin and Race: 2009. *American Community Survey Brief* ACSBR/09-19. Accessible at http://www.census.gov.

Johnston, Tim. 2008. Australia to Apologize to Aborigines for Past Mistreatment. *New York Times* (January 31).

Joint Center for Political and Economic Studies. 2011. *National Roster of Black Elected Officials: Fact Sheet*. Washington DC: JCPES.

Jolivette, Andrew. 2008. Pan-Indianism. Pp. 1022–1028 in vol. 2, *Encyclopedia of Race, Ethnicity, and Society*, Richard T. Schaefer, ed. Thousand Oaks, CA: Sage.

Jones, Adele. 2008. A Silent but Mighty River: The Costs of Women's Economic Migration. *Signs: Journal of Women in Culture and Society*, 33 (4): 761–769.

Jones, Jeff, and Lydia Saad. 2013. *Gallup Poll Social Series: Minority Rights and Relations*. (July 5.) Accessible at http://www.gallup.com.

Jones, Nicholas. 2012. *Who is "Black" in America?* (July 6.) Accessible at http://www.census.gov/newsroom/cspan/black/.

Jones, Nicholas, and Amy Symens Smith. 2001. *The Two or More Races Population: 2000*. Series C2KBR/01-6. Washington, DC: U.S. Government Printing Office.

Jones, Rachel K., Mia R. S. Zolna, Stanley K. Henshaw, and Laurence B. Finer. 2008. Abortion in the United States: Incidence and Access to Services, 2005. *Perspectives on Sexual and Reproductive Health* (March), 40: 6–16.

Jones-Puthoff, Alexa. 2013. *Is the U.S. Population Getting Older and More Diverse?* (June 14.) Accessible at http://www.census.gov/newsroom/cspan/pop_diverse/.

Jonsson, Patrik. 2005. Noncitizen Soldiers: The Quandaries of Foreign-Born Troops. *Christian Science Monitor* (July 5): 1.

Jordan, Miriam. 2009. Got Workers? Dairy Farmers Run Low on Labor. *Wall Street Journal* (July 30). Accessible at http://online.wsj.com.

———. 2012. Heartland Draws Hispanics To Help Revive Small Towns. *New York Times* (November 9): A1, A8.

Joseph, Dan. 2010. *America's 10 Poorest Counties are in Gulf Coast States, Kentucky and on Indian Reservations*. (December 17.) Accessed April 27, 2011, at http://www.cnsnews.com.

Kagan, Jerome. 1971. The Magical Aura of the IQ. *Saturday Review of Literature* (December 4), 4: 92–93.

Kahlenberg, Richard D. 2010. 10 Myths About Legacy Preference in College Admissions. *Chronicle of Higher Education* (October 1): A23–A25.

Kalev, Alexandria, Frank Dobbin, and Erin Kelly. 2006. Best Practices or Best Guesses? Diversity Management and the Remediation of Inequality. *American Sociological Review*, 71: 589–617.

Kalita, S. Mitra. 2003. *Suburban Sahibs: Three Immigrant Families and Their Passage from India to America*. New Brunswick, NJ: Rutgers University Press.

Kambayashi, Takegiko. 2013. Kyoko Okutani Helps Women Start Their Own Businesses, So They Can Skirt Japan's Gender Gap In The Workplace. *Christian Science Monitor Weekly Edition* (September 9): 44–45.

Kana'iaupuni, Shawn Malia. 2008. Hawaiians. Pp. 599–602 in vol. 1, *Encyclopedia of Race, Ethnicity, and Society*, Richard T. Schaefer, ed. Thousand Oaks, CA: Sage.

Kane, Melinda D. 2010. You've Won, Now What? The Influence of Legal Change on Gay and Lesbian Mobilization, 1974–1999. *Sociological Quarterly*, 51: 255–272.

Kang, Jerry, and Kristen Lane. 2010. Seeing Through Colorblindness: Implicit Bias and the Law. *UCLA Law Review*, 58: 465–520.

Kang, K. Connie. 1996. Filipinos Happy with Life in U.S. but Lack United Voice. *Los Angeles Times* (January 26): A1, A20.

Kashima, Tetsuden. 2003. *Judgment Without Trial: Japanese Americans Imprisonment During World War II*. Seattle: University of Washington Press.

Katel, Peter. 2006. American Indians. *CQ Researcher* (April 28): 16.

Katz, Jeffrey. 2012. Google's Monopoly and Internet Freedom. *Wall Street Journal* (June 8): A15.

Katz, Michael B., Mark J. Stern, and Jamie J. Fader. 2007. The Mexican Immigration Debate. *Social Science History*, 3 (Summer): 157–189.

Kazal, Russell A. 2004. The Interwar Origins of the White Ethnic: Race, Residence, and German Philadelphia, 1917–1939. *Journal of American Ethnic History* (Summer): 78–131.

Kearns, Rick. 2011. On the Rise. *Indian County Today* (May 18): 10.

Keaton, Trica Danielle, T. Dean Sharpley-Whiting, and Tyler Stoval, eds. 2012. *Black France/France Noire: The History and Politics of Blackness*. Durham NC: Duke University Press.

Keen, Judy. 2011. Transmitting the Immigrant Life." *USA Today* (June 16): 3A.

Kening, Dan. 2004. OWL Keeps an Eye Out for Issues Affecting Women. *Chicago Tribune* (March 12), sec. 9: 1, 12.

Kenji America. 2013. *Cheerios Parody "Just Checking" Response to Haters*. Accessed August 5, 2013, at http://www.youtube.com/user/kenjiamerica.

Kent, Mary Mederios. 2007. Immigration and America's Black Population. *Population Bulletin* (December), 62.

———. 2010. *Large Wealth Gap Among U.S. Racial and Ethnic Groups*. Accessed September 9, 2010, at http://www.prb.org/Articles/2010/usnetworth.aspx?p=1.

Kibria, Nazli. 2002. *Becoming Asian American: Second-Generation Chinese and Korean American Identities*. Baltimore: Johns Hopkins Press.

Kieh, George Klay, Jr. 1995. Malcolm X and Pan-Africanism. *Western Journal of Black Studies*, 19 (4): 293–299.

Killian, Lewis M. 1975. *The Impossible Revolution, Phase 2: Black Power and the American Dream*. New York: Random House.

Kim, Barbara, and Grace J. Yoo. 2008. Korean Americans. Pp. 811–814 in vol. 2, *Encyclopedia of Race, Ethnicity, and Society*, Richard T. Schaefer, ed. Thousand Oaks, CA: Sage.

Kim, ChangHwan, and Arthur Sakamoto. 2010. Have Asian American Men Achieved Labor Market Parity with White Men? *American Sociological Review* 73 (6): 934–957.

Kim, Joon K. 2008. Wetbacks. Pp. 1393–1395 in vol. 3, *Encyclopedia of Race, Ethnicity, and Society*, Richard T. Schaefer, ed. Thousand Oaks, CA: Sage.

Kim, Kiljoong. 2006. The Korean Presence in Chicago. In *The New Chicago*, John Koval et al., eds. Philadelphia: Temple University Press.

Kim, Nadia U. 2008. *Imperial Citizens: Koreans and Race from Seoul to LA*. Stanford, CA: Stanford University Press.

Kimmelman, Michael. 2008. For Blacks in France, Obama's Rise is Reason to Rejoice, and to Hope. *New York Times* (June 17).

Kimmons, Leslie C. Baker. 2008. Abolitionism: The People. Pp. 3–5 in vol. 1, *Encyclopedia of Race, Ethnicity, and Society*, Richard T. Schaefer, ed. Thousand Oaks, CA: Sage.

Kimura, Yukiko. 1988. *Issei: Japanese Immigrants in Hawaii*. Honolulu: University of Hawaii Press.

King, Martin Luther, Jr. 1958. *Stride Towards Freedom: The Montgomery Story*. New York: Harper.

———. 1963. *Why We Can't Wait.* New York: Mentor.

———. 1967. *Where Do We Go from Here: Chaos or Community?* New York: Harper & Row.

———. 1971. I Have a Dream. Pp. 346–351 in *Black Protest Thought in the Twentieth Century,* August Meier, Elliott Rudwick, and Francis L. Broderick, eds. Indianapolis, IN: Bobbs-Merrill.

King, Peter. 2004. Private Moments in the Public Eye. *Los Angeles Times* (August 5): A1, A16, A17.

Kinloch, Graham C. 1974. *The Dynamics of Race Relations: A Sociological Analysis.* New York: McGraw-Hill.

Kinzer, Stephen. 2000. Museums and Tribes: A Tricky Truce. *New York Times* (December 24), sec. 2: 1, 39.

Kirkpatrick, P. 1994. Triple Jeopardy: Disability, Race and Poverty in America. *Poverty and Race,* 3: 1–8.

Kitagawa, Evelyn. 1972. Socioeconomic Differences in the United States and Some Implications for Population Policy. Pp. 87–110 in *Demographic and Social Aspects of Population Growth,* Charles F. Westoff and Robert Parke, Jr., eds. Washington, DC: U.S. Government Printing Office.

Kitano, Harry H. L. 1976. *Japanese Americans: The Evolution of a Subculture,* 2nd ed. Englewood Cliffs, NJ: Prentice Hall.

Kitano, Harry H. L. 1980. Japanese. In *Harvard Encyclopedia of American Ethnic Groups,* Stephen Thernstrom, ed. Cambridge, MA: Belknap Press of Harvard University Press.

Kivisto, Peter. 2008. Third Generation Principle. Pp. 1302–1304 in vol. 3, *Encyclopedia of Race, Ethnicity, and Society,* Richard T. Schaefer, ed. Thousand Oaks, CA: Sage.

Klausner, Samuel Z. 1988. Anti-Semitism in the Executive Suite: Yesterday, Today, and Tomorrow. *Moment* (September), 13: 32–39, 55.

Klinkenborg, Verlyn. 2013. Notebook: A Striking Absence of Women. *New York Times* (October 13): 10.

Koch, Wendy. 2006. Push for "Official" English Heats Up. *USA Today* (October 9): 1A.

Kochhar, Rakesh. 2006. *Growth in the Foreign-Born Workforce and Employment of the Native Born.* Washington, DC: Pew Hispanic Center.

Kochhar, Rakesh, Richard Fry, and Paul Taylor. 2011. *Twenty to One: Wealth Gaps Rise to Record Highs Between Whites, Blacks and Hispanics.* Washington DC: Pew Social and Demographic Trends.

Kohli, Martin. 2013. Correspondence with author. Chief Regional Economist, Bureau of Labor Statistics.

Kolpack, Dave. 2012. *ND Voters Dump Fighting Sioux Nickname.* Minnesota Public Radio (June 11). Accessible at http://minnesotat.publicradio.org.

Kopacz, Maria A., and Bessie Lee Lawton. 2013. Talking about the YouTube Indians: Images of Native Americans and Viewer Comments on a Viral Video Site. *Howard Journal of Communications,* 24: 17–37.

Koppel, Nathan, and Asjby Jones. 2013. Firms Balk at Gay Weddings. *Wall Street Journal* (October 2): A3.

Koser, Khalid. 2008. *Protecting Displaced Migrants in South Africa.* Brookings Institution (June 23). Accessible at http://www.brookings.edu.

Kosmin, Barry A. 2009. *The Changing Population Profile of American Jews 1990–2008.* Paper presented at the Fifteenth World Congress of Jewish Studies, Jerusalem, Israel, August.

Kotkin, Joel. 2010. Ready Set Grow. *Smithsonian* (July/August): 61–73.

Krammer, Arnold. 1997. *Undue Process: The Untold Story of America's German Alien Internees.* Lanham, MD: Rowman & Littlefield.

Krase, Jerome. 2006. Seeing Ethnic Succession in Little Italy: Change Despite Resistance. *Modern Italy,* 11 (February): 79–95.

Krauss, Clifford. 2006. Seven Years into Self-Rule, Inuit Are Struggling. *New York Times* (June 18): 4.

Krausz, Ernest. 1973. Israel's New Citizens. Pp. 385–387 in *1973 Britannica Book of the Year.* Chicago: Encyclopedia Britannica.

Kreider, Rose M., and Renee Ellis. 2011. *Living Arrangements of Children: 2009,* P70–126. Washington DC: U.S. Government Printing Office.

Kristof, Nicholas D. 2010. America's History of Fear. *New York Times* (September 5): A10.

Kroeger, Brooke. 2004. When a Dissertation Makes a Difference. *New York Times* (March 20). Accessed January 15, 2005, at http://www.racematters.org/devahpager.htm.

Krysan, Maria, Reynolds Farley, and Mick P. Couper. 2008. In the Eye of the Beholder. *DuBois Review* 5 (1): 5–26.

Kuebler, Meghan. 2013. Closing the Wealth Gap: A Review of Racial and Ethnic Inequalities in Homeownership. *Sociology Compass* 7/8: 670–685.

Kurien, Prena. 2004. Multiculturalism, Immigrant Religion, and Diasporic Nationalism: The Development of an American Hinduism. *Social Problems,* 51 (3): 362–385.

Kurien, Prena. 2007. Who Speaks for Indian Americans? Religion, Ethnicity, and Political Formation. *American Quarterly* 59 (September): 759–783.

Kwong, Peter. 1994. The Wages of Fear. *Village Voice* (April 26), 39: 25–29.

Kyodo News. 2010. *Japanese Women Stand Low on Corporate Ladder 25 Years After Law Change.* (August 30.) Accessed June 14, 2011, at http://www.japantoday.com.

Lacy, Dan. 1972. *The White Use of Blacks in America.* New York: McGraw-Hill.

LaDuke, Winona. 2006. Hui Na Iwa—The Bones Lives: Hawaiians and NAGPRA. News from Indian Country, April 3, 17.

Lal, Barbara Ballis. 1995. Symbolic Interaction Theories. *American Behavioral Scientist* (January), 38: 421–441.

Landale, Nancy S., and R. S. Oropesa. 2002. White, Black, or Puerto Rican? Racial Self-Identification among Mainland and Island Puerto Ricans. *Social Forces,* 81 (1): 231–254.

———. 2007. Hispanic Families: Stability and Change. *Annual Review of Sociology,* 33: 381–405.

Landale, Nancy S., R. S. Oropesa, and C. Bradatan. 2006. Hispanic Families in the United States: Family Structure and Process in an Era of Family Change. Pp. 138–178, in *Multiple Origins, Uncertain Destinies: Hispanics and the American Future.* Washington, DC: National Academic Press.

Landau, David. 2012. Judaism and the Jews. *The Economist* (July 28): 1–12.

Landry, Bart, and Kris Marsh. 2011. The Evolution of the New Black Middle Class. *Annual Review of Sociology,* 37: 373–394.

LaPiere, Richard T. 1934. Attitudes vs. Actions. *Social Forces* (October 13): 230–237.

———. 1969. Comment of Irwin Deutscher's Looking Backward. *American Sociologist* (February), 4: 41–42.

Lara, Marielena, Cristina Gamboa, M. Iya Kahramanian, Leo S. Morales, and David E. Hayes Bautista. 2005. Acculturation and Latino Health in the United States: A Review of the Literature and Its Sociopolitical Context. Pp. 367–397 in *Annual Review of Public Health 2005.* Palo Alto, CA: Annual Reviews.

Lau, Yvonne M. 2006. Re-Envisioning Filipino American Communities: Evolving Identities, Issues, and Organizations. Pp. 141–153 in *The New Chicago,* John Koval et al., eds. Philadelphia: Temple University Press.

Laumann, Edward O., John H. Gagnon, Robert T. Michael, and Stuart Michaels. 1994. *The Social Organization of Sexuality: Sexual Practices in the United States.* Chicago: University of Chicago Press.

Lavender, Abraham D., ed. 1977. *A Coat of Many Colors: Jewish Subcommunities in the United States.* Westport, CT: Greenwood Press.

Laxson, Joan D. 1991. "We" See "Them": Tourism and Native Americans. *Annals of Tourism Research,* 18(3): 365–391.

Lazar, Louie. 2013. Delivering News from the Homeland. *Wall Street Journal* (September 6): A16, A17.

Leavitt, Paul. 2002. Bush Calls Agent Kicked Off Flight "Honorable Fellow." *USA Today* (January 8).

Ledward, Brandon C. 2008. Haole. Pp. 579–581 in vol. 2, *Encyclopedia of Race, Ethnicity, and Society,* Richard T. Schaefer, ed. Thousand Oaks, CA: Sage.

Lee, J. J., and Marion R. Casey. 2006. *Making the Irish American.* New York: New York University Press.

Lee, James. 2011. *U.S. Naturalizations: 2010.* Washington, D.C: Office of Immigration Statistics.

Lee, Jennifer. 2001. Manhattan's Chinatown Reeling from the Effects of September 11. *New York Times* (November 21): B1, B9.

Lee, Jennifer, and Frank D. Bean. 2007. Redrawing the Color Line. *City and Community,* 6: 49–62.

Lee, Tanya. 2011. A Sign of Hope. *Indian County Today* (April 6): 25–27.

Lee, Wen Ho, with Helen Zia. 2006. *My Country Versus Me: The First-Hand Account by the Los Alamos Scientist Who Was Falsely Accused of Being a Spy.* New York: Hyperion.

Lee, Yueh-Ting, Sandy Vue, Richard Seklecki, and Yue Ma. 2007. How Did Asian Americans Respond to Negative Stereotypes and Hate Crimes? *American Behavioral Scientist* (October), 51: 271–293.

Leehotz, Robert. 1995. Is Concept of Race a Relic? *Los Angeles Times* (April 15): A1, A14.

Lem, Kim. 1976. Asian American Employment. *Civil Rights Digest* (Fall), 9: 12–21.

Leonard, Karen Isaksen. 2003. *Muslims in the United States: The State of Research.* New York: Russell Sage Foundation.

Let Puerto Rico Decide. 2005. *Status Choices.* Accessed October 7, 2006, at http://www.letpuertoricodecide.com (Citizens' Educated Foundation 2005).

Leung, Angela Ka-yee, William W. Maddux, Adam D. Galinsky, and Chi-yue Chiu. 2008. Multicultural Experience Enhances Creativity. *American Psychologist* 63 (April): 169–181.

Levin, Jack, and Jim Nolan. 2011. *The Violence of Hate: Confronting Racism, Anti-Semitism, and Other Forms of Bigotry.* 3rd ed. Upper Saddle River, NJ: Pearson.

Levine, Naomi, and Martin Hochbaum, eds. 1974. *Poor Jews: An American Awakening.* New Brunswick, NJ: Transaction Books.

Levitt, Peggy, and B. Nadya Jaworsky. 2007. Transnational Migration Studies: Past Developments and Future Trends. *Annual Review of Sociology,* 33: 129–156.

Lewin, Tamar. 2006. Campaign to End Race Preferences Splits Michigan. *New York Times* (October 31): A1, A19.

Lewinson, Paul. 1965. *Race, Class, and Party: A History of Negro Suffrage and White Politics in the South.* New York: Universal Library.

Lewis, Amanda E. 2004. "What Group?" Studying Whites and Whiteness in the Era of "Color-Blindness." *Sociological Theory* (December), 22: 623–646.

———. 2013. The "Nine Lives" of Oppositional Culture? *DuBois Review,* 10 (1): 279–289.

Lewis, Gregory. 2007. Love Sees No Color. *Sun Sentinel* (June 16): 1A, 17A.

Lewis, Neil A. 2003. Secrecy Is Backed on 9/11 Detainees. *New York Times* (June 18): A1, A16.

Lewis, Shawn D. 2008. Pressuring Culture: Japanese-Style Private School Thrives with U.S. Transplants. *Detroit News* (July 17).

Lichter, Daniel T., J. Brian Brown, Zhenchao Qian, and Julie H. Carmalt. 2007. Marital Assimilation among Hispanics: Evidence of Declining Cultural and Economic Incorporation? *Social Science Quarterly,* 88 (3): 745–765.

Liebman, Charles S. 1973. *The Ambivalent American Jew.* Philadelphia: Jewish Publication Society of America.

Light, Ivan H., Georges Sabagh, Mendi Bozorgmehr, and Claudia Der-Martirosian. 1994. Beyond the Ethnic Enclave Economy. *Social Problems* (February), 41: 65–80.

Light, Steven Andrew, and Kathryn R. L. Rand. 2007. *Indian Gaming and Tribal Sovereignty: The Casino Compromise.* Lawrence: University of Kansas Press.

Lin, Sam Chu. 1996. Painful Memories. *AsianWeek* (July 12), 17: 10.

Lincoln, C. Eric. 1994. *The Black Muslims in America,* 3rd ed. Grand Rapids, MI: William B. Eerdmans.

Lind, Andrew W. 1946. *Hawaii's Japanese: An Experiment in Democracy.* Princeton, NJ: Princeton University Press.

Lindner, Eileen. 2011. *Yearbook of American and Canadian Churches.* Nashville, TN: Abingdon Press.

Lipka, Michael. 2013. *Abercrombie Hijab Firing Highlights Muslim Concern about Discrimination.* (September 11.) Accessed September 24, 2013, at http://www.researchcenter.org.

Lipman, Francine J. 2008. *The Undocumented Immigrant Tax: Enriching Americans from Sea to Shining Sea.* Chapman University Law Research Paper No. 2008. Accessible at http://ssrn.com/abstract=1292960.

Linthicum, Kate. 2011. Pain Propels a Quest for the Truth. *Chicago Tribune* (July 26): 13.

Liu, Michael, and Kim Geron. 2008. Changing Neighborhood: Ethnic Enclaves and the Struggle for Social Justice. *Social Justice* 35 (2): 18–35.

Livingston, Gretchen, and D'Vera Cohn. 2012. *U.S. Birth Rate Falls to a Record Low; Decline Is Greatest Among Immigrants.* Washington DC: Pew Research Center.

Llana, Sara Miller. 2013. Brazil's Affirmative Action Law Offers a Huge Hand Up. *Christian Science Monitor* (February 13). Accessible at http://www.csmonitor.com.

Llosa, Alvaro Vargas. 2013. *Global Crossings: Immigration, Civilization, and America.* Oakland CA: The Independent Institute.

Loewen, James. 2005. *Sundown Towns: A Hidden Dimension of American Racism.* New York: Free Press.

Loewen, James. 2012. *Something Has Gone Very Wrong.* Accessible at http://sundown.afro.illinois.edu/index.php.

Loewen, James, and Richard Schaefer. 2008. Sundown Towns. Pp. 301–304 in vol. 2, *Encyclopedia of Race, Ethnicity, and Society,* Richard T. Schaefer, ed. Thousand Oaks, CA: Sage.

Lofquist, Daphne. 2011. Same-Sex Couple Households. *American Community Survey Briefs.* ACSBR/10-03. (September.) Accessible at http://www.censu.gov.

Lofquist, Daphne, Terry Lugaila, Martin O'Connell, and Sarah Feliz. 2012. *Households and Families: 2010.* C2012BR-14. Accessible at http://www.census.gov/newsroom/releases/archives/2012_census/cb12-68.html.

Logan, John R., and Brian J. Stults. 2011. *The Persistence of Segregation in the Metropolis: New Findings from the 2010 Census.* Providence RI: US 2010 Project.

Logan, John R., and Richard N. Turner. 2013. *Hispanics in the United States: Not Only Mexicans.* Brown University: US 2010 Project.

Lomax, Louis E. 1971. *The Negro Revolt,* rev. ed. New York: Harper & Row.

Longman, Jeré. 2008. Polynesian Pipeline Feeds a Football Titan. *New York Times* (October 8): A1, A20.

Lopata, Helena Znaniecki. 1994. *Polish Americans,* 2nd ed. New Brunswick, NJ: Transaction Books.

Lopez, Ana Alicia Peña. 2004. Central American Labor Migration, 1980–2000. *Diálgo* (Spring): 3–14.

Lopez, David, and Yen Espiritu. 1990. Panethnicity in the United States: A Theoretical Framework. *Ethnic and Racial Studies* (April 13): 198–224.

Lopez, Julie Amparano. 1992. Women Face Glass Walls as Well as Ceilings. *Wall Street Journal* (March 3).

Lopez, Mark Hugo, and Ana Gonzalez-Barrera. 2013. If They Could, How Many Unauthorized Immigrants Would Become U.S. Citizens? (June 27). Accessible at http://www.pewresearch.org.

Lopez, Mark Hugo, Gretchen Livingston, and Rakesh Kochhar. 2009. *Hispanics and the Economic Downturn: Housing Woes and Remittance Cuts.* Washington, DC: Pew Hispanic Center.

Lopez, Mark Hugo, Gretchen Livingston, Rich Moran, and Paul Taylor. 2010. *Illegal Immigration Backlash Worries, Divides Latinos.* Washington, DC: Pew Research Center.

Lopez, Mark Hugo, and Gabriel Velasco. 2011. *A Demographic of Puerto Ricans, 2009.* Washington DC: Pew Hispanic Center.

Lorber, Judith. 2005. *Breaking the Bounds: Degendering and Feminist Change.* New York: W. W. Norton.

Los Angeles Times Poll. 1998. American and Israeli Jews. Los Angeles: Los Angeles Times and Yedioth Ahronoth.

LoSasso, Anthony T., Michael R. Richards, Chiu-Fang Chou, and Susan E. Gerber. 2011. The $16,819 Pay Gap for Newly Trained Physicians: The Unexplained Trend of Men Earning More Than Women. *Health Affairs* 30 (2): 193–201.

Louie, Andrea. 2004. *Chineseness across Borders: Renegotiation Chinese Identities in China and the United States.* Durham, NC: Duke University Press.

Loury, Glenn C. 1996. Joy and Doubt on the Mall. *Utne Reader* (January–February), 73: 70–73.

Loveman, Mora, and Jeronimo O. Muniz. 2007. How Puerto Rico Became White: Boundary Dynamics and Intercensus Racial Reclassification. *American Sociological Review* (December), 72: 915–939.

Luce, Clare Boothe. 1975. Refugees and Guilt. *New York Times* (May 11): E19.

Luconi, Stefano. 2001. *From Peasant to White Ethnics: The Italian Experience in Philadelphia.* Albany: State University Press of New York.

Lugo, Luis, Alan Cooperman, James Bell, Erin O'Connell, and Sandra Stencel. 2013. *The World's Muslims: Religion, Politics and Society.* Washington DC: Pew Research Center.

Lugo, Luis, Alan Cooperman, Gregory A. Smith, Erin O'Connell, and Sandra Stencel. 2013a. *A Portrait of Jewish Americans: Findings from a Pew Research Center Survey of U.S. Jews.* (October 1.) Accessible at http://www.pewforum.org/files/2013/10/jewish-american-full-report-for-web.pdf

Luker, Kristin. 1984. *Abortion and the Politics of Motherhood.* Berkeley: University of California Press.

Luo, Michael. 2006a. Reform Jews Hope to Unmix Mixed Marriages. *New York Times* (February 12): 1, 30.

———. 2006b. An Orthodox Jewish Woman and Soon, a Spiritual Leader. *New York Times* (August 21): B1, B4.

Lustick, Ian S. 2013. Two-State Illusion. New York Times (September 6), Sunday Review section, pp. 1,6.

Macartney, Suzanne, Alemayehu Bishaw, and Kayla Fontenot. 2013. Poverty Rates for Selected Detailed Race and Hispanic Groups by State and Place: 2007–2011. (February.) *American Community Survey Briefs.* ACSBR/11-17. Accessible at http://www.census.gov.

MacFarlane, Marco. 2006. Demographics. Pp. 1–50 in *South African Survey 2004/2005.* Johannesburg: South African Institute of Race Relations.

———. 2008. South Africa in Brief. *Fast Facts,* 10 (October): 1–15.

MacFarquhar, Neil. 2008. Resolute or Fearful, Many Muslims Turn to Home Schooling. *New York Times* (March 26).

Mack, Raymond W. 1996. Whose Affirmative Action? *Society* 33 (March–April): 41–43.

Macmillian, Leslie. 2012. Uranium Mines Dot Navajo Land, Neglected and Still Perilous. *New York Times* (April 1): 16.

Maddux, William W., Adam D. Galinsky, Amy J. C. Cuddy, and Mark Polifroni. 2008. When Being a Model Minority Is Good ... and Bad: Realistic Threat Explains Negativity Toward Asian Americans. *Personality and Social Psychology Bulletin,* 34 (January): 74–89.

Madigan, Nick. 2013. In the Shadow of 'Old Smokey," A Toxic Legacy. *New York Times* (September 23): A10, A13.

Magin, Janis L. 2008. Occupation of Royal Palace Invigorates Native Hawaiian Movement. *New York Times* (May 3): A14.

Malhotra, Nei, and Yotam Margalit. 2009. State of the Nation: Anti-Semitism and the Economic Crisis. *Boston Review* (May/June). Accessible at http://bostonreview.net/BR34.3/malhotra_margalit.php.

Malkin, Michelle. 2004. *In Defense of the Internment: The Case for Racial Profiling in World War II and the War on Terror.* Regency Books.

Malone, Nolan, Kaari F. Baruja, Joseph M. Costanzo, and Cynthia J. Davis. 2003. *The Foreign-Born Population: 2000.* C2KBR-34. Accessible at http://www.census.gov/prod/2003pubs/c2kbr-34.pdf.

Mandela, Nelson. 1990. Africa, It Is Ours. *New York Times* (February 12): A10.

Mann, Keith A. 2008. France. Pp. 506–508 in vol. 1, *Encyclopedia of Race, Ethnicity, and Society,* Richard T. Schaefer, ed. Thousand Oaks, CA: Sage.

Manning, Robert D. 1995. Multiculturalism in the United States: Clashing Concepts, Changing Demographics, and Competing Cultures. *International Journal of Group Tensions* (Summer): 117–168.

Marosi, Richard. 2007. The Nation: A Once-Porous Border Is a Turning-Back Point. *Los Angeles Times* (March 21): A1, A20.

Marshall, Patrick. 2001. Religion in Schools. *CQ Research* (July 12), 11: 1–24.

Martin, Daniel C., and James E. Yankay. 2013. *Refugees and Asylees: 2012.* Washington DC: Office of Immigration Statistics.

Martin, Joel W. 2001. *The Land Looks After Us: A History of Native American Religion.* New York: Oxford University Press.

Martin, Karin A. 2009. Normalizing Heterosexuality: Mothers' Assumptions, Talk, and Strategies with Young Children. *American Sociological Review* 24 (April): 190–207.

Martin, Karin A., and Katherine P. Luke. 2010. Gender Differences in the ABC's of the Birds and the Bees: What Mothers Teach Young Children about Sexuality and Reproduction. *Sex Roles* 62 (3-4): 151–291.

Martin, Timothy W., Josh Dawsey, and Betsy McKay. 2012. The Gender Barrier Falls at Augusta. *Wall Street Journal* (August 21): B1.

Marubbio, M. Elise. 2006. *Killing the Indian Maiden: Images of Native American Women in Film.* Lexington: University Press of Kentucky.

Marvasti, Amir. 2005. Being Middle Eastern American: Identity Negotiation in the Context of the War on Terror. *Symbolic Interaction,* 28 (4): 525–547.

Marx, Anthony. 1998. *Making Race and Nation: A Companion of the United States, South Africa, and Brazil.* Cambridge, UK: Cambridge University Press.

Marx, Karl, and Frederick Engels. 1955. *Selected Works in Two Volumes.* Moscow: Foreign Languages Publishing House.

Masayesva, Vernon. 1994. The Problem of American Indian Religious Freedom: A Hopi Perspective. *American Indian Religions: An Interdisciplinary Journal,* 1 (Winter), pp. 93–96.

Mason, Christopher. 2007. Immigrants Reject Quebec's Separatists. *New York Times* (May 20): 6.

Massey, Douglas S. 2011. The Past and Future of American Civil Rights. *Daedalus,* 140 (Spring): 37–54.

———. 2012. Reflections on the Dimensions of Segregation. *Social Forces,* 91 (1): 39–43.

Massey, Douglas S., and Nancy A. Denton. 1993. *American Apartheid: Segregation and the Making of the Underclass.* Cambridge, MA: Harvard University Press.

Massey, Douglas S., Nancy A. Denton., Margarita Mooney, and Robert J. Sampson. 2009. The Moynihan Report Revisited: Lessons and Reflections after Four Decades. *Annuals,* 621 (January).

Massey, Douglas S., and Margarita Mooney. 2007. The Effects of America's Three Affirmative Action Programs on Academic Performance. *Social Problems* 54 (1): 99–117.

Massey, Douglas S., and Karen A. Pren. 2012. Unintended Consequences of US Immigration Policy: Explaining the Post-1965 Surge from Latin America. *Population and Development Review* 38 (1): 1–29.

Massey, Douglas S., and Robert J. Sampson. 2009. The Moynihan Report Revisited: Lessons and Reflections after Four Decades. *Annuals* 621 (January).

Mastony, Colleen. 2013. Poland Calling Them Home. *Chicago Tribune* (January 13): 1, 12.

Masud-Piloto, Felix. 2008a. Cuban Americans. Pp. 357–359 in vol. 1, *Encyclopedia of Race, Ethnicity, and Society,* Richard T. Schaefer, ed. Thousand Oaks, CA: Sage.

Masud-Piloto, Felix. 2008b. Marielitos. Pp. 872–874 in vol. 2, *Encyclopedia of Race, Ethnicity, and Society,* Richard T. Schaefer, ed. Thousand Oaks, CA: Sage.

Mather, Mark, and Kelvin Pollard. 2007. Hispanic Gains Minimize Population Losses in Rural and Small-Town America. *Population Reference Bureau.* Accessible at http://www.prb.org/Articles/2007/HispanicGains.aspx.

Matthiessen, Peter. 1991. *In the Spirit of Crazy Horse.* New York: Peking.

Mauro, Tony. 1995. Ruling Helps Communities Set Guidelines. *USA Today* (December 21): A1, A2.

Mazzocco, Philip J., Timothy C. Brock, Gregory J. Brock, Kristen R. Olson, and Mahzarin R. Banaji. 2006. The Cost of Being Black: White Americans' Perceptions and the Question of Reparations. *DuBois Review* 3 (2): 261–297.

McCabe, Kristen. 2012. *Foreign-Born Health Care Workers in the United States.* (June.) Accessible at http://www.migrationinformation.org/USfocus/display.cfm?id=898.

McClain, Paula Denice. 1979. *Alienation and Resistance: The Political Behavior of Afro-Canadians.* Palo Alto, CA: R&E Research Associates.

McCloud, Aminah Beverly. 1995. *African American Islam.* New York: Routledge.

———. 2004. Conceptual Discourse: Living as a Muslim in a Pluralistic Society. Pp. 73–83 in *Muslims Place in the American Public Square,* Zahid H. Bukhari et al., eds. Walnut Creek, CA: Altamira Press.

McCormack, Simon. 2011. *Census Can't Find a Single Italian-born Resident of Little Italy.* (February 22.) Accessible at http://www.huffingtonpost.com.

McGee, Celia. 2010. The Open Road Wasn't Quite Open to All. *New York Times* (August 23), pp. C1, C2.

McGroarty, Patrick, and Kathleen Craykowski. 2012. South Africa Reseeds Farm Debate. *Wall Street Journal* (June 29): A14.

McGurn, William. 2009. New Jersey's 'Italian' Problem. *Wall Street Journal* (July 28): A15.

McIntosh, Peggy. 1988. *White Privilege: Unpacking the Invisible Knapsack.* Wellesley, MA: Wellesley College Center for Research on Women.

McKernan, Signe-Mary, Caroline Radcliffe, Eugene Steuerle, and Sisi Zhang. 2013. *Less than Equal: Racial Disparities in Wealth Accumulation.* (April 2013.) Accessible at http://www.urban.org.

McKinley, James C., Jr. 2005. Mexican Pride and Death in U.S. Service. *New York Times* (March 22): A6.

McKinney, Karyn D. 2003. I Feel "Whiteness" When I Hear People Blaming Whites: Whiteness as Cultural Victimization. *Race and Society* 6: 39–55.

———. 2008. Confronting Young People's Perceptions of Whiteness: Privilege or Liability? *Social Compass* 2. Accessible at http://www.blackwell compass.com/subject/sociology.

McNickle, D'Arcy. 1973. *Native American Tribalism: Indian Survivals and Renewals.* New York: Oxford University Press.

Meagher, Timothy J. 2005. *The Columbia Guide to Irish American History.* New York: Columbia University Press.

Media Matters for America. 2013. *Diversity in Evening Cable News in 13 Charts.* (May 13.) Accessible at mediamatters.org.

Medina, Jennifer. 2012b. Rodney King Dies at 47. *New York Times* (June 17).

Meister, Alan. 2013. *Indian Gaming Industry Report 2013.* Newton, MA: Casino City Press.

Meléndez, Edwin. 1994. Puerto Rico Migration and Occupational Selectivity, 1982–1981. *International Migration Review* (Spring), 28: 49–67.

Menchaca, Charles. 2008. Scholars Learn Hmong Basics. *Wausau Daily Herald* (August 14).

Merton, Robert K. 1949. Discrimination and the American Creed. Pp. 99–126 in *Discrimination and National Welfare,* Robert M. MacIver, ed. New York: Harper & Row.

———. 1968. *Social Theory and Social Structure.* New York: Free Press.

———. 1976. *Sociological Ambivalence and Other Essays.* New York: Free Press.

Messner, Michael A. 1997. *Politics of Masculinities: Men in Movements.* Thousand Oaks, CA: Sage.

Meyer, Karen. 2008. Americans with Disabilities Act. In *Encyclopedia of Race, Ethnicity, and Society,* Richard T. Schaefer, ed. Thousand Oaks, CA: Sage.

———. 2011. *Match the Disability.* Unpublished paper (June 22). Chicago: DePaul University.

Meyers, Dowell. 2007. *Immigrants and Boomers: Forging a New Social Contract for the Future of America.* New York: Russell Sage.

Meyers, Gustavus. 1943. *History of Bigotry in the United States* (rev. by Henry M. Christman, 1960). New York: Capricorn Books.

Meyers, Norma. 2005. Environment Refugees: An Emergent Security Issue. Paper presented at the 13th Economic Forum, May 2005. Prague.

Migration News. 2012a. Remittance. *Migration News* (January). Accessible at migration.ucdavis.edu.mn.

———. 2012b. *DHS: Border, Interior, USCIS.* April 19 (2). Accessible at http://migration.ucdavis.edu/mn/comments.php?id-3745_0_2_0.

———. 2012c. *Canada, Latin America.* (January). Accessible at migration.ucdavis.edu.mn.

Mihesuah, Devon A., ed. 2000. *Reparation Reader: Who Owns American Indian Remains?* Lincoln: University of Nebraska Press.

Miller, David L. 2014. *Introduction to Collective Behavior and Collective Action.* 3rd. ed. Long Grove IL: Waveland Press.

Miller, Norman. 2002. Personalization and the Promise of Contact Theory. *Journal of Social Issues*, 58 (Summer): 387–410.

Min, Pyong Gap. 2006. *Asian Americans: Contemporary Trends and Issues*, 2nd ed. Thousand Oaks, CA: Sage.

———. (ed.). 2013. *Koreans in North America: Their Twenty-First Century Experiences*. Landam MD: Lexington Books.

Mitra, Diditi. 2008. Pan-Asian Identity. Pp. 1016–1019 in vol. 2, *Encyclopedia of Race, Ethnicity, and Society*, Richard T. Schaefer, ed. Thousand Oaks, CA: Sage.

Mocha, Frank, ed. 1998. *American "Polonia" and Poland*. New York: Columbia University Press.

Mohamed, Besheer and John O'Brien. 2011. Ground Zero of Misunderstanding. *Contexts* (Winter): 62–64.

Montagu, Ashley. 1972. *Statement on Race*. New York: Oxford University Press.

Mosisa, Abraham T. 2013. *Foreign-born workers in the U.S. Labor Force. Spotlight on Statistics*. (July.) Accessible at http://www.bls.gov.

Moskos, Charles C., and John Sibley Butler, eds. 1996. *All That We Can Be: Black Leadership and Racial Integration the Army Way*. New York: Basic Books.

Motel, Seth, and Eileen Patten. 2012. *The 10 Largest Hispanic Origin Groups: Characteristics, Rankings, Top Counties*. Washington DC: Pew Hispanic Center.

Moulder, Frances V. 1996. *Teaching about Race and Ethnicity: A Message of Despair or a Message of Hope?* Paper presented at annual meeting of the American Sociological Association, New York.

Mun, Eunmi. 2010. Sex Typing of Jobs in Hiring: Evidence from Japan. *Social Forces*, 88 (5): 1999–2026.

Murray, Sara. 2010. Disabled Face Sharply Higher Jobless Rate. *Wall Street Journal* (August 26): A5.

Muste, Christopher P. 2013. The Polls—Trends. The Dynamics of Immigration Opinion in the United States: 1992–2012. *Public Opinion Quarterly*, 77(Spring): 398–416.

Myers, Dowell, John Pitkin, and Julie Park. 2004. *California's Immigrants Turn the Corner. Urban Initiative Policy Relief*. Los Angeles: University of Southern California.

Myrdal, Gunnar. 1944. *An American Dilemma: The Negro Problem and Modern Democracy*. New York: Harper & Row.

NAACP. 2008. *Out of Focus—Out of Sync Take 4*. Baltimore MD: NAACP.

Nagel, Joane. 1988. *The Roots of Red Power: Demographic and Organizational Bases of American Indian Activism 1950–1990*. Paper presented at annual meeting of the American Sociological Association, Atlanta, GA.

———. 1996. *American Indian Ethnic Renewal: Red Power and the Resurgence of Identity and Culture*. New York: Oxford University Press.

Nahm, H. Y. 2012. 23 *Big Milestones in Asian American History*. Accessed November 9, 2013, at http://goldsea.com/AAD/Milestones/milestones.html.

Naimark, Norman M. 2004. Ethnic Cleaning, History of. Pp. 4799–4802 in *International Encyclopedia of Social and Behavioral Sciences*, N. J. Smelser and P. B. Baltes, eds. New York: Elsevier.

Nash, Manning. 1962. Race and the Ideology of Race. *Current Anthropology* (June), 3: 285–288.

National Advisory Commission on Civil Disorders. 1968. *Report*. New York: Bantam.

National Asian Pacific American Legal Consortium. 2002. *Backlash: When America Turned on its Own*. Washington, DC: NAPALC.

National CAPACD. 2012. *Data Points: Asian American and Pacific Islander Poverty*. (May 1, 2012.) Accessible at http://www.nationalcapacd.org/.

National Center for Education Statistics. 2011. *Digest of Education Statistics 2010*. Accessible at http://nces.ed.gov.

———. 2012. *Percentage of Degrees Conferred by Sex and Race*. Accessed July 11, 2012, at http://nces.ed.gov/fastfacts/display.asp?id=72.

———. 2013. *Digest of Education Statistics*. Accessible at http://nces.ed.gov/programs/digest/2012menu_tables.asp.

National Committee on Pay Equity. 2013. *Equal Pay Day 2013*. Accessed September 18, 2013, at http://www.pay-equity.org.

National Conference of State Legislatures. 2013. *Voter Identification Requirements*. Accessed August 6, 2013, at http://www.ncsl.org/legislatures-elections/elections/voter-id.aspx.

National Congress of American Indians. 2012. *Toward a New Era. Annual Report 2010–2011*. Washington DC: NCAI.

National Governors Association. 2013. A Better Bottom Line: Employing People with Disabilities. Accessed September 23, 2013, at http://ci.nga.org/cms/home/1213/index.

National Indian Gaming Association. 2006. *Indian Gaming Facts*. Accessed September 27, 2006, at http://www.indiangaming.org.

National Italian American Foundation. 2006. Stop Ethnic Bashing. *New York Times* (January). Accessed June 4, 2008, at http://www.niaf.org/news/index.asp?id=422.

National Organization for Men Against Sexism. 2011. *30 Years of NOMAS*. Accessed June 16, 2011, at http://www.nomas.org/.

National Park Service. 2009. *Chinatown and Little Italy Historic District*. Accessible at http://www.nps.gov.

———. 2012. *The War Relocation Camps of World War II: When Fear Was Stronger than Justice – Supplementary Resources*. Accessed July 16, 2012, at http://www.nps.gov/history/nr/twhp/wwwlps/lessons/89nanzanar/89lrnmore.htm.

———. 2014. Manzanar. Historic Resource Study/Special History Study. Accessed February 4, 2014 at http://www.nps.gov/history/history/online_books/manz/hrs14.htm.

National Public Radio. 2013. *Impossible Choice Faces America's First "Climate Refugees."* (May 18.) Accessible at http://wwww.wbur.org/npr/185068648/impossible-choice-faces-americas-first-climate-refugees.

National Women's Law Center. 2012. *How the Paycheck Fairness Act Will Strengthen the Equal Pay Act*. (May.) Accessed September 15, 2013, at http://www.nwic.org.

Native Federation. 2013. *Native Rights*. Accessed September 10, 2013, at http://www.natiefederation.org/publications/native-rights/.

Navarro, Mireya. 2004. Young Japanese-Americans Honor Ethnic Roots. *New York Times* (August 2): A1, A15.

Navarro-Rivera, Juhem, Marry A. Kosmin, and Ariela Keysar. 2010. *U.S. Latino Religious Identification 1990-2008 Growth, Diversity & Transformation*. Hartford, CT: American Religious Identification Project, Trinity College. Accessible at http://www.americanreligionsurvey-aris.org/latinos2008.pdf.

Nawa, Fariba. 2011. Struggling to Stay Bilingual. *Christian Science Monitor* (October 17): 38–39.

NCAA (National Collegiate Athletic Association). 2003a. *Executive Committee Reviews American Indian Mascot Input*. Press release (April 25).

———. 2003b. *NCAA Executive Committee Passes Recommendations Regarding American Indian Mascots, Confederate Flag and NCAA Budget*. Press release (August 11).

Nelsen, Frank C. 1973. The German-American Immigrants Struggle. *International Review of History and Political Science*, 10 (2): 37–49.

Neugarten, Bernice L. 1996. *The Meanings of Age. Selected Papers of Bernice L. Neugarten*. Ed. with a forward by Dail A. Neugarten. Chicago: University of Chicago Press.

Nevin, Tom. 2008. S Africa's "Open Door" Initiative Under Fire. *African Business* (July): 54.

New America Media. 2007. *Deep Divisions, Shared Destiny*. San Francisco: New America Media.

Newman, William M. 1973. *American Pluralism: A Study of Minority Groups and Social Theory*. New York: Harper & Row.

Newport, Frank. 2011. *Very Religious Have Higher Wellbeing Across All Faiths*. (January 6.) Accessible at http://www.gallup.com.

New York Times. 1991. For Two, an Answer to Years of Doubt on Use of Peyote in Religious Rite (July 9): A14.

New York Times. 2005. Warnings Raised About Exodus of Philippine Doctors and Nurses (November 27): 13.

Nicholas, Peter, and Neil King, Jr. 2013. Uneven Election Success for Black Politicians. *Wall Street Journal* (August 28): A4.

Nicholson, David. 2013. First Slaves First Hope. *American History* (June): 68–71.

Niebuhr, Gustav. 1998. Southern Baptists Declare Wife Should "Submit" to Her Husband. *New York Times*.

Nielsen, Joyce McCarl, Glenda Walden, and Charlotte A. Kunkel. 2000. Gendered Heteronormality: Empirical Illusions in Everyday Life. *Sociological Quarterly*, 41 (2): 283–296.

Nishi, Setsuko Matsunga. 1995. Japanese Americans. Pp. 95–133 in *Asian Americans: Contemporary Trends and Issues*, Pyong Gap Min, ed. Thousand Oaks, CA: Sage Publications.

Noble, Barbara Presley. 1995. A Level Playing Field, for Just $121. *New York Times* (March 5): F21.

Noel, Donald L. 1972. *The Origins of American Slavery and Racism*. Columbus, OH: Charles Merrill.

Norrell, Robert J. 2009. *Up From History: The Life of Booker T. Washington*. Cambridge, MA: Harvard University Press.

Norris, Tina, Paula L. Vines, and Elizabeth M. Hoeffel. 2012. *The American Indian and Alaska Native Population: 2010*. C2010BR-10. Accessible at http://www.census.gov.

North, Michael S., and Susan T. Fiske. 2012. An Inconvenient Youth? Ageism and Its Potential Intergenerational Roots. *Psychological Bulletin*, 138 (5): 982–997.

———. 2013a. Act Your (Old) Age: Prescriptive, Ageist Biases Over Succession, Consumption, and Identity. *Personality and Social Psychological Bulletin*, 39 (6): 720–734.

———. 2013b. A Prescriptive Intergenerational Tension: Ageism Scale: Succession, Identity, and Consumption. *Psychological Assessment Advance online publication.* Doi:10.1037/a0032367.

———. 2013c. Subtyping Ageism: Policy Issues in Succession and Consumption. *Social Issues and Policy Review*, 7(1): 36–57.

Norton, Michael I., and Samuel R. Sommers. 2011. Whites See Racism as a Zero-Sum Game That They are Now Losing. *Perspectives on Psychological Science*, 6 (3): 215.

Novelli, William D. 2004. Common Sense: The Case for Age Discrimination Law. Pp. 4, 7 in *Global Report on Aging*. Washington, DC: AARP.

Nudd, Tim. 2013. It's 2013, and People are Still Getting Worked Up about Interracial Couples in Ads. *Adweek* (May 30). Accessible at http://www.adweek.com.

Oberschall, Anthony. 1968. The Los Angeles Riot of August 1965. *Social Problems* (Winter), 15: 322–341.

Ochoa, Gilda L. 2013. *Academic Profiling: Latinos, Asian Americans, and the Achievement Gap*. Minneapolis: University of Minnesota Press.

O'Connor, Anne-Marie. 1998. Church's New Wave of Change. *Los Angeles Times* (March 25): A1, A16.

Office of Hawaiian Affairs. 2012. *Native Hawaiian Data Book 2011*. Accessible at http://www.ohadatabook.com/fr_statlinks.11.html.

Office of Immigration Statistics. 2009. *Yearbook of Immigration Statistics: 2008*. Accessible at www.dhs.gov.

———. 2012. *Yearbook of Immigration Statistics: 2011*. Accessible at http://www.dhs.gov/files/statistics/publications/LPR10.shtm.

———. 2013. *2012 Yearbook of Immigration Statistics*. Accessible at http://www.dhs.gov/yearbook-immigration-statistics.

Ogbu, John U. 2004. Collective Identity and the Burden of "Acting White" in Black History, Community, and Education. *Urban Review* (March), 36: 1–35.

Ogbu, John U., with Astrid Davis. 2003. *Black American Students in an Affluent Suburb: A Study of Academic Disengagement*. Mahwah, NJ: Lawrence Erlbaum Associates.

Ogunwole, Stella U., Malcolm P. Drewery, Jr., and Merarys Rios-Vargas. 2012. The Population with a Bachelor's Degree or Higher by Race and Hispanic Origin: 2006–2010. *American Community Survey Briefs*. ACSBR/10-19.

Ohnuma, Keiko. 1991. Study Finds Asians Unhappy at CSU. *AsianWeek* (August 8), 12: 5.

Okamoto, Dina, and Melanie Jones Gast. 2013. Racial Inclusion or Accommodation? Expanding Community Boundaries among Asian American Organizations. *DuBois Review*, 10 (1): 131–153.

Okamura, Jonathan Y. 2008. *Ethnicity and Inequality in Hawaii*. Philadelphia, PA: Temple University Press.

Olemetson, Lynette. 2005. Adopted in China, Seeking Identity in America. *New York Times* (March 23): A1.

Oliver, Melvin L., and Thomas M. Shapiro. 1996. *Black Wealth/White Wealth: New Perspective on Racial Inequality*. New York: Routledge.

———. 2006. *Black Wealth/White Wealth*. 10th anniversary ed. New York: Routledge.

Oliveri, Rigel C. 2009. Discriminatory Housing Advertisements On-Line: Lessons from Craigslist. *Indiana Law Review*, 43: 11225–1182.

Olzak, Susan. 1998. Ethnic Protest in Core and Periphery States. *Ethnic and Racial Studies* (March), 21: 187–217.

Omi, Michael, and Howard Winant. 1994. *Racial Formation in the United States*, 2nd ed. New York: Routledge.

Omniglot. 2013. *Links: Online Radio Stations*. Accessed November 3, 2013, at http://www.omniglot.com/links/radio.htm.

O'Neill, Maggie. 2008. Authoritarian Personality. Pp. 119–121 in vol. 1, *Encyclopedia of Race, Ethnicity, and Society*, Richard T. Schaefer, ed. Thousand Oaks, CA: Sage.

Onishi, Morimitsu. 2012. At Internment Camp, Pilgrims Explore Choices of the Past. *New York Times* (July 6): A8.

Ontario Human Rights Commission. 2013. *Room for Everyone: Human Rights and Rental Housing Licensing*. Accessed September 19, 2013, at http://www.ohrc.on.ca/en/.

Orenstein, Peggy. 2011. Did I Know You at Camp? *New York Times Sunday Magazine* (September 26): 18.

Orfield, Gary. 2007. The Supreme Court and the Resegregation of America's Schools. *Focus* (September–October): 1, 15–16.

Orfield, Gary, Susan E. Eaton, and the Harvard Project on School Segregation. 1996. *Dismantling Desegregation: The Quiet Reversal of Brown v. Board of Education*. New York: The New Press.

Orfield, Gary, John Kucsera, and Genevieve Siegel-Hawley. 2012. *E Pluribus ... Separation: Deepening Double Segregation for More Students*. Los Angeles: The Civil Rights Project. Accessible at http://civilrightsproject.ucla.edu/research/k-12-education/integration-and-diversity/mlk-national/e-pluribus...separation-deepening-double-segregation-for-more-students.

Orfield, Gary, and Chungmei Lee. 2005. *Why Segregation Matters: Poverty and Educational Inequality*. Cambridge, MA: Civil Rights Project.

Organisation for Economic Co-Operation and Development. 2013. *Employment Rate of Women—Employment and Labour Markets*. (July 16.) Accessed September 19, 2013, at http://oecd-ilibrary.org/employment-rate-of-women_20752342-table5.

Orlov, Ann, and Reed Ueda. 1980. Central and South Americans. Pp. 210–217 in *Harvard Encyclopedia of American Ethnic Groups*, Stephan Thernstrom, ed. Cambridge, MA: Belknap Press of Harvard University Press.

Ottaway, David S., and Paul Taylor. 1992. A Minority Decides to Stand Aside for Majority Rule. *Washington Post National Weekly Edition* (April 5), 9: 17.

OWL. 2013. *The Voice of Midlife and Older Women*. Accessed November 4, 2013, at http://www.owl-national.org.

Padget, Martin. 2004. *Indian Country: Travels in the American Southwest, 1840–1935*. Albuquerque: University of New Mexico Press.

Padilla, Efren N. 2008a. Filipino Americans. Pp. 493–497 in vol. 1, *Encyclopedia of Race, Ethnicity, and Society*, Richard T. Schaefer, ed. Thousand Oaks, CA: Sage.

Page, Scott E. 2007. *The Difference: How the Power of Diversity Creates Better Groups, Firms, Schools, and Societies*. Princeton, NJ: Princeton University Press.

Pager, Devah. 2003. The Mark of a Criminal. *American Journal of Sociology*, 108: 937–975.

Pager, Devah, and Bruce Western. 2012. Identifying Discrimination at Work: The Use of Field Experiments. *Journal of Social Issues*, 68 (2): 221–237.

Pager, Devah, Bruce Western, and Bart Bonikowski. 2009. Discrimination in a Low-Wage Labor Market: A Field Experiment. *American Sociological Review*, 74 (October): 777–799.

Paluck, Elizabeth Levy, and Donald P. Green. 2009. Prejudice Reduction: What Works? A Review and Assessment of Research and Practice. *Annual Review of Psychology* 60: 339–367.

Pariser, Eli. 2011a. The Filter Bubble: What the Internet Is Hiding from You. *New York: Penguin Press*.

———. 2011b. In Our Own Little Internet Bubbles. *The Guardian Weekly* (June 24): 32–33.

Park, Robert E. 1928. Human Migration and the Marginal Man. *American Journal of Sociology* (May), 33: 881–893.

———. 1950. Race and Culture: Essays in the Sociology of Contemporary Man. New York: Free Press.

Park, Robert E., and Ernest W. Burgess. 1921. *Introduction to the Science of Sociology*. Chicago: University of Chicago Press.

Parker, Kim, and Wendy Wang. 2013. *Modern Parenthood: Roles of Moms and Dads Converge as They Balance Work and Family*. (March 14.) Accessible at http://www.pewresearch.org.

Parrillo, Vincent. 2008. Italian Americans. Pp. 766–771 in vol. 2, *Encyclopedia of Race, Ethnicity, and Society*, Richard T. Schaefer, ed. Thousand Oaks, CA: Sage.

Parrillo, Vincent, and Christopher Donoghue. 2013. The National Social Distance Study: Ten Years Later. *Sociological Forum*, 28 (3): 597–614.

Parsons, Talcott, and Robert Bales. 1955. *Family, Socialization and Interaction Process*. Glencoe, IL: Free Press.

Passel, Jeffrey S., and D'Vera Cohn. 2009. *A Portrait of Unauthorized Immigrants in the United States*. Washington, DC: Pew Hispanic Center.

———. 2011. *Unauthorized Immigrant Population National and State Trends, 2010*. Washington DC: Pew Research Center.

Passel, Jeffrey S., D'Vera Cohn, and Mark Hugo Lopez. 2011. *Census 2010: 50 Million Latinos*. Washington, DC: Pew Hispanic Center.

Passel, Jeffrey S., D'Vera Cohn, and AnaGonzalez-Barrera. 2013. *Population Decline of Unauthorized Immigrants Stalls, May Have Reverse*. (September 23.) Accessible at http://www.pewresearch.org/hispanic.

Passel, Jeffrey S., Wendy Wang, and Paul S. Taylor. 2010. *Marrying Out: One-in-Seven New U.S. Marriages is Interracial or Interethnic*. Washington, DC: Pew Research Center. Accessible at http://www.pewsocialtrends.org/files/2010/10/755-marrying-out.pdf.

Pasternak, Judy. 2010. *Yellow Dirt: An American Story of a Poisoned Land a People Betrayed*. New York: Simon and Schuster.

Pastor, Jr., Manuel, Rachel Morello-Frosch, and James L. Saad. 2005. The Air Is Always Cleaner on the Other Side. Race, Space, and Ambient Air Toxics Exposure in California. *Journal of Urban Affairs*, 27 (2): 127–148.

Patterson, David Royston. 2012. Will Puerto Rico Be America's 51st State? *New York Times* (November 25), section SR BW: 4.

Paul, Annie Murphy. 2011. The Roar of the Tiger Mother. *Time* (January 31): 34–40.

Pearson, Bryan. 2006. Brain Drain Human Resource Crisis. *The Africa Report* (October): 95–98.

Peckham, Pat. 2002. Hmong's Resettlement Changes Agency's Focus. *Wausau Daily Herald* (February 10): 1A, 2A.

Pellow, David Naguib, and Hollie Nyseth Brehm. 2013. An Environmental Sociology for the Twenty-First Century. *Annual Review of Sociology,* 39: 229–250.

Pellow, David Naguib, and Robert J. Brulle. 2007. Poisoning the Planet: The Struggle for Environmental Justice. *Contexts,* 6 (Winter): 37–41.

Peréz, Linsandro. 2001. Growing Up in Cuban Miami: Immigrants, the Enclave, and New Generations. Pp. 91–125 in *Ethnicities,* Ruben G. Rumbaut and Alejandro Portes, eds. Berkeley: University of California Press.

Perlmann, Joel. 2005. *Italians Then, Mexicans Now: Immigrant Origins and Second-Generation Progress, 1890–2000.* New York: Russell Sage Foundation.

Perry, Barbara, ed. 2003. *Hate and Bias Crime: A Reader.* New York: Routledge.

Perry, Tony, and Richard Simon. 2009. Filipino Veterans of WWII to Get Long-Overdue Funds. *Los Angeles Times* (February 18): B1, B7.

Peterson, Ruth D. 2012. The Central Place of Race in Crime and Justice. *Criminology,* 50 (2): 303–327.

Pettigrew, Thomas F. 2010. Commentary: South African Contributions to the Study of Intergroup Relations. *Journal of Social Issues* 66 (2): 417–430.

———. 2011. Did Brown Fail. *Du Bois Review,* 8 (2): 511–516.

Pew Charitable Trust. 2000. *Jews and the American Public Square Data.* Accessed May 23, 2001, at http://www.pewtrusts.org.

———. 2011. *Downward Mobility from the Middle Class. Waking Up from the American Dream.* (September 6.) Accessible at http://www.pewstates.org/uploadedFiles/PCS_Assets/2011/MiddleClassReport.pdf.

———. 2012. *Weathering the Great Recession: Did High-Poverty Neighborhoods Fare Worse?* Accessible at http://www.pewstates.org/uploadedFiles/PCS_Assets/2012/Pew_urban_neighborhoods_report.pdf.

Pew Forum on Religion and Public Life. 2008a. *U.S. Religious Landscape Survey.* Washington, DC: Pew Forum. Accesible at http://religions.pewforum.org/pdf/report2-religious-landscape-study-full.pdf.

———. 2008b. *U.S. Religious Landscape Survey: Religious Beliefs and Practices: Diverse and Political Relevant.* Washington DC: Pew Forum on Religion and Public Life.

———. 2010. *Growing Number of Americans Say Obama Is a Muslim.* Washington, DC: Pew Forum.

———. 2011. *The Future of the Global Muslim Population.* Washington, DC: Pew Forum.

———. 2012. *Asian Americans: A Mosaic of Faiths.* (July 19.) Accessed November 1, 2013, at http://www.pewforum.org/2012/07/19/asian-americans-a-mosaic-of-faiths-overview/.

Pew Hispanic Center. 2009. *Between Two Worlds: How Young Latinos Come of Age in America.* Washington, DC: Pew Hispanic Center.

———. 2010. *National Survey of Latinos, Aug, 2010.* Accessed September 9, 2011, at http://pewhispanic.org/questions/?qid=1772973&pid=54&ccid=54#top.

———. 2011a. Mapping the Latino Electorate. Accessible at http://pewhispanic.org/docs/?DocID=26.

———. 2011b. *Unauthorized Immigrants: Length of Residency, Patterns of Parenthood.* (December 1.) Washington: Pew Hispanic Center.

———. 2012a *When Labels Don't Fit: Hispanics and Their Views of Identity.* (April 4.) Washington DC: Pew Hispanic Center.

———. 2012b. *Net Migration from Mexico Falls to Zero—and Perhaps Less.* Washington DC: Pew Hispanic Center.

Pew Research Center. 2004. *Beliefs That Jews Were Responsible for Christ's Death Increase.* Washington, DC: Pew Research Center.

———. 2010. *Blacks Upbeat about Black Progress, Prospects.* Accessible at http://pewsocialtrends.org/2010/01/12/blacks-upbeat-about-black-progress-prospects.

———. 2011. *Muslim Americans: No Signs of Growth in Alienation or Support for Extremism.* Washington DC: Pew Research Center.

———. 2013. *A Survey of LGBT Americans: Attitudes, Experiences and Values in Changing Times.* (June 13.) Accessible at http://www.pewresearch.org.

Pew Research Global Attitudes Project. 2013. *Mexicans and Salvadorans Have Positive Picture of Life in U.S.* (October 24.) Accessible at http://www.poewglobal.org.

Pew Social and Demographic Trends. 2012. *The Rise of Asian Americans.* Washington DC: Pew Social and Demographic Trends.

Pewewardy, Cornel. 1998. Our Children Can't Wait: Recapturing the Essence of Indigenous Schools in the United States. *Cultural Survival Quarterly* (Spring): 29–34.

Pfaelzer, Jean. 2007. *Driven Out: The Forgotten War Against Chinese Americans.* New York: Random House.

Pfeifer, Mark. 2008a. Hmong Americans. Pp. 633–636 in vol. 2, *Encyclopedia of Race, Ethnicity, and Society,* Richard T. Schaefer, ed. Thousand Oaks, CA: Sage.

———. 2008b. Vietnamese Americans. Pp. 1365–1368 in vol. 3, *Encyclopedia of Race, Ethnicity, and Society.* Richard T. Schaefer, ed. Thousand Oaks, CA: Sage.

Pido, Antonio J. A. 1986. *The Filipinos in America.* New York: Center for Migration Studies.

Pilkington, Ed. 2010. Rima Fakin is First Muslim Winner of Miss USA. *Guardian* (May 17). Accessible at http://www.guardian.co.uk.

Pincus, Fred L. 2003. *Reverse Discrimination: Dismantling the Myth.* Boulder, CO: Lynne Rienner.

———. 2008. *Reverse Discrimination.* Pp. 1159–1161 in vol. 3, *Encyclopedia of Race, Ethnicity, and Society,* Richard T. Schaefer, ed. Thousand Oaks, CA: Sage.

Pinkney, Alphonso. 1975. *Black Americans,* 2nd ed. Englewood Cliffs, NJ: Prentice Hall.

———. 1984. *The Myth of Black Progress.* New York: Cambridge University Press.

Pitt, Nicola Ann. 2013. *The Cultural and Political Significance of Tiger Mothering.* Doctorate. Monash University.

Polzin, Theresita. 1973. *The Polish Americans: Whence and Whither.* Pulaski, WI: Franciscan Publishers.

Porter, Eduardo. 2005. Illegal Immigrants Are Bolstering Social Security with Billions. *New York Times* (April 5): A1, C6.

Portes, Alejandro. 2006. Paths of Assimilation in the Second Generation. *Sociological Forum* (September), 21: 499–503.

Portes, Alejandro, Cristina Escobar, and Alexandria Walton Radford. 2007. Immigrant Transitional Organizations and Development: A Comparative Study. *International Migration Review* 41 (Spring): 242–281.

Portes, Alejandro, and Rubén G. Rumbaut. 2006. *Immigrant America,* 3rd ed. Berkeley: University of California Press.

Posadas, Barbara M. 1999. *The Filipino Americans.* Westport, CT: Greenwood Press.

Powell-Hopson, Darlene, and Derek Hopson. 1988. Implications of Doll Color Preferences Among Black Preschool Children and White Preschool Children. *Journal of Black Psychology* (February): 14: 57–63.

Pratt, Timothy. 2012. More Asian Immigrants Find Options on Ballots. *New York Times* (October 19): A14.

President's Task Force on Puerto Rico's Status. 2005. *Report by the President's Task Force on Puerto Rico's Status.* Washington, DC: U.S. Government Printing Office.

Preston, Julia. 2007. Polls Surveys Ethnic Views among Chief Minorities. *New York Times* (December 13).

———. 2010. On Gangs, Asylum Law Offers Little. *New York Times* (June 30): A15, A19.

Preston, Julia. 2013a. Huge Amounts Spent on Immigration, Study Finds. *New York Times* (January 8): A11.

———. 2013b. Legal Immigrants Seek Reward for Years of Following the Rules. *New York Times* (July 16): A1, A13.

Preston, Julia, and Fernanda Santos. 2012. A Record Latino Turnout, Solidly Backing Obama. *New York Times* (November 8): 13.

Pryor, John H., Kevin Egan, Laura Palucki Blake, Sylvia Hurtado, Jennifer Berdan, Matthew H. Case, and Linda DeAngelo, 2012. *The American Freshman: National Norms for Fall 2012.* Los Angeles, CA: Higher Education Research Institute, UCLA.

Purdy, Matthew. 2001. Ignoring and Then Embracing the Truth about Racial Profiling. *New York Times* (March 11).

Quadagno, Jill. 2014. *Aging and the Life Course: An Introduction to Social Gerontology,* 6th ed. New York: McGraw-Hill.

Quillian, Lincoln. 2006. New Approaches to Understanding Racial Prejudice and Discrimination. Pp. 299–328 in *Annual Reviews of Sociology 2006,* Karen S. Cook, ed. Palo Alto, CA: Annual Reviews Inc.

Quiñones-Hinojosa, Alfredo, with Mim Eichler Rivas. 2011. *Becoming Dr. Q: My Journey from Migrant Farm Worker to Brain Surgeon.* Berkeley: University of California Press.

Quirk, Matthew. 2008. How to Grow a Gang. *The Atlantic* (May), 301: 24–25.

Rabinovitch, Simon. 2011. China Labour Costs Soar as Wages Rise 22%. *Financial Times* (October 25). Accessed March 2, 2012, at http://www.ft.com/intl/cms/s/0/25f1c500-ff14-11e0-9b2f-00144feabdc0.html#axzz1nziV8URS.

Ramirez, Margaret. 2000. Study Finds Segregation of Latinos in Catholic Church. *Los Angeles Times* (March 1): A1, A24.

Ramos, Jorge. 2010. *A Country for All.* New York: Vintage Books.

Rand, Michael R., and Erika Harrell. 2009. Crime Against People with Disabilities. *2007 Bureau of Justice Statistics Special Report* (October).

Rangaswamy, Padma. 2005. Asian Indians in Chicago. In *The New Chicago,* John Koval et al., eds. Philadelphia: Temple University Press.

Rangel, Charles B. 2013. *Rangel Statement on the 50th Anniversary of the March on Washington*. (August 28.) Accessible at http://rangel.house.gov/press-release/rangel-statement-50th-anniversary-march-washington.

Rastogi, Sonya, Tallese D. Johnson, Elizabeth M. Hoeffel, and Malcolm P. Drewery, Jr. 2011. *The Black Population: 2010*. C2010BR-06. September 2011. Accessible at http://www.census.gov.

Ratledge, Ingela. 2012. Is the Bachelor Racist? *TV Guide* (May 6): 6.

Raybon, Patricia. 1989. A Case for "Severe Bias." *Newsweek* (October 2), 114: 11.

Raymo, James M., and So-jung Lim. 2011. A New look at Married Women's Labor Force Transitions in Japan. *Social Science Research*, 40: 460–472.

Read, Jen'nan Ghazal. 2007. More of a Bridge Than a Gap: Gender Differences in Arab-American Political Engagement. *Social Science Quarterly* (December), 88: 1072–1091.

Reckard, E. Scott. 2007. A Power Shift in Koreatown. *Los Angeles Times* (May 25): C1, C4.

Reskin, Barbara F. 2012. The Race Discrimination System. *Annual Review of Sociology*. 38.

Reverby, Susan M., ed. 2000. *Tuskegee's Truths: Rethinking the Tuskegee Syphilis Study*. Chapel Hill: University of North Carolina Press.

Rich, Meghan Ashlin. 2008. Resegregation. Pp. 1152–1153 in vol. 3, *Encyclopedia of Race, Ethnicity, and Society*, Richard T. Schaefer, ed. Thousand Oaks, CA: Sage.

Rich, Motoko. 2013. Creationists on Texas Panel for Biology Textbooks. *New York Times* (September 29): 16, 20.

Richmond, Anthony H. 2002. Globalization: Implications for Immigrants and Refugees. *Ethnic and Racial Studies* (September), 25: 707–727.

Richmond Hill Historical Society. 2013. *American Indians of Long Island, NY*. Accessed November 4, 2013, at http://www.richmondhillhistory.org/indians.html.

Ríos, Kristopher. 2011. After Long Fight, Farmworkers in Florida Win an Increase in Pay. *New York Times* (January 19): A11.

Roberts, Sam. 2011. Little Italy, Littler by the Year. *New York Times* (February 22): A19.

Robinson, Greg. 2001. *By Order of the President: FDR and the Internment of Japanese Americans*. Cambridge: Harvard University Press.

———. 2009. *A Tragedy of Democracy: Japanese Confinement in North America*. New York: Columbia University Press.

———. 2012. *After Camp: Portraits in Midcentury Japanese Americans Life and Politics*. Berkeley: University of California Press.

Robison, Jennifer. 2002. *Feminism—What's in a Name?* (September 3.) Accessible at http://www.gallup.com.

Robnett, Belinda, and Cynthia Feliciano. 2011. Patterns of Racial-Ethnic Exclusion by Internet Daters. *Social Forces*, 80 (No. 3, March): 807, 828.

Rodríquez, Robert. 1994. Immigrant Bashing: Latinos Besieged by Public Policy Bias. *Black Issues in Higher Education* (February 24), 10: 31–34.

Roediger, David R. 1994. *Towards the Abolition of Whiteness: Essays on Race, Politics, and Working Class History (Haymarket)*. New York: Verso Books.

Roediger, David R. 2006. Whiteness and Its Complications. *Chronicle of Higher Education* (July 14), 52: B6–B8.

———. 2009. To Be Continued? The "Problem of the Color-Line" in the Twenty-First Century. Pp 281-286 in *Twenty First Century Color Lines*, Andrew Grant-Thomas and Gary Orfield, eds. Philadelphia: Temple University Press.

Roodt, Marius. 2008. Xenophobic Violence: Simmering Volcano or Nasty Surprise? *Fast Facts* (August): 4–7.

Roof, Wade Clark. 2007. Introduction. *The Annals* (July), 612: 6–12.

Rosales, F. Arturo. 1996. *Chicano! The History of the Mexican American Civil Rights Movement*. Houston, TX: Arte Público Press.

Roscigno, Vincent J., and Theresa Schmidt. 2007. How Sexual Harassment Happens. Pp. 73–88 in *The Face of Discrimination*, Vincent J. Roscigno. Lanham, MD: Rowman & Littlefield.

Rose, Arnold. 1951. *The Roots of Prejudice*. Paris: UNESCO.

Rosenberg, Tom. 2000. Changing My Name After 60 Years. *Newsweek* (July 17), 136: 10.

Rosenblatt, Gary. 2008. What Do We Want from Hebrew Schools? *The Jewish Week* (August 13).

Roth, Wendy D. 2012. *Race Migrations: Latinos and the Cultural Transformation of Race*. Stanford: Stanford University Press.

Rothstein, Edward. 2006. The Anti-Semitic Hoax that Refuses to Die. *New York Times* (April 21): B27, B37.

Rudwick, Elliott. 1957. The Niagara Movement. *Journal of Negro History* (July), 42: 177–200.

Rumbaut, Ruben G., Douglas S. Massey, and Frank D. Bean. 2006. Linguistic Life Expectancies: Immigrant Language Retention in Southern California. *Population and Development Review* (September), 32: 447–460.

Rusk, David. 2001. *The "Segregation Tax": The Cost of Racial Segregation to Black Homeowners*. Washington, DC: Brookings Institution.

Russell, Stephen T., Lisa J. Crockett, and Ruth K. Chao. 2010. Asian American Parenting and Parent-Adolescent Relationships. *Journal of Youth and Adolescence*, 40: 245–247.

Russell, Steve. 2011. Of Blood and Citizenship. *Indian County Today* (July 27): 22–29.

Ryan, Camile. 2013. Language Use in the United States: 2011. *American Community Survey Report* (August 2013). Accessible at http://www.census.gov.

Ryan, William. 1976. *Blaming the Victim*, rev. ed. New York: Random House.

Ryo, Emily. 2013. Deciding to Cross: Norms and Economics of Unauthorized Migration. *American Sociological Review* 78 (4): 574–603.

Saad, Lydia. 2006. Anti-Muslim Sentiments Fairly Commonplace. *The Gallup Poll* (August 10).

Sachs, Susan. 2001. For Newcomers, a Homey New Chinatown. *New York Times* (July 22): A1, A44.

Sadker, Myra Pollack, and David Miller Sadker. 2003. *Teachers, Schools, and Sociology*, 6th ed. New York: McGraw-Hill.

Sahagun, Louis. 2004. Tribes Fear Backlash to Prosperity. *Los Angeles Times* (May 3): B1, B6.

Sahgal, Neha. 2013. *Miss America Pageant Puts Indian Americans in the Spotlight*. (September 16.) Accessible at http://www.pewresearch.org.

Said, Edward. 1978. *Orientalism*. New York: Viking.

Salée, Daniel. 1994. Identity Politics and Multiculturalism in Quebec. *Cultural Survival Quarterly* (Summer–Fall): 89–94.

Sanchez, Rene. 1998. The Winter of Their Discontent. *Washington Post National Weekly Edition* (December), 16: 20.

Sandage, Diane. 2008. Peltier, Leonard. Pp. 1033–1035 in vol. 2, *Encyclopedia of Race, Ethnicity, and Society*, Richard T. Schaefer, ed. Thousand Oaks, CA: Sage.

Santos-Hernández, Jennifer M. 2008. Puerto Rican Armed Forces of National Liberation. Pp. 1084–1085 in vol. 2, *Encyclopedia of Race, Ethnicity, and Society*, Richard T. Schaefer, ed. Thousand Oaks, CA: Sage.

Sanua, Marianne R. 2007. AJC and Intermarriage: The Complexities and Jewish Continuity, 1960–2006. Pp. 3–32 in *American Jewish Yearbook 2007*, David Singer and Lawrence Grossman, eds. New York: American Jewish Committee.

Saperstein, Aliya, and Andrew M. Penner. 2012. Racial Fluidity and Inequality in the United States. *American Journal of Sociology* 118 (3): 676–727.

Sarkisian, Natalia, Mariana Gerena, and Naomi Gerstel. 2007. Extended Family Integration among Euro and Mexican Americans: Ethnicity, Gender, and Class. *Journal of Marriage and Family* (February), 69: 40–54.

Sassler, Sharon L. 2006. School Participation among Immigrant Youths: The Case of Segmented Assimilation in the Early 20th Century. *Sociology of Education*, 79 (January): 1–24.

Sataline, Suzanne. 2009. Muslims Press for School Holidays in New York City. *Wall Street Journal* (September 15): H10.

Saulny, Susan. 2011. Black? White? Asian? More Young Americans Choose All of the Above. *New York Times* (January 29): A1, A17–A18.

Sawhill, Isabel V., Scott Winship, and Kerry Searle Grannis. 2012. *Pathways to the Middle Class: Balancing Personal and Public Responsibilities*. Washington DC: Brookings.

Schaefer, Richard T. 1971. The Ku Klux Klan: Continuity and Change. *Phylon* (Summer), 32: 143–157.

———. 1976. *The Extent and Content of Racial Prejudice in Great Britain*. San Francisco: R&E Research Associates.

———. 1980. The Management of Secrecy: The Ku Klux Klan's Successful Secret. Pp. 161–177 in *Secrecy: A Cross-Cultural Perspective*, Stanton K. Tefft, ed. New York: Human Sciences Press.

———. 1986. Racial Prejudice in a Capitalist State: What Has Happened to the American Creed? *Phylon* 47 (September): 192–198.

———. 1992. People of Color: The "Kaleidoscope" May Be a Better Way to Describe America than "the Melting Pot." *Peoria Journal Star* (January 19): A7.

———. 1996. Education and Prejudice: Unraveling the Relationship. *Sociological Quarterly* (January), 37: 1–16.

———. 2008a. Australia, Indigenous People. Pp. 115–119 in vol. 1, *Encyclopedia of Race, Ethnicity, and Society*, Richard T. Schaefer, ed. Thousand Oaks, CA: Sage.

———. 2008b. Nativism. Pp. 611–612 in vol. 1, *Encyclopedia of Social Problems*, Vincent N. Parrillo, ed. Thousand Oaks, CA: Sage.

Schaefer, Richard T., and Sandra L. Schaefer. 1975. Reluctant Welcome: U.S. Responses to the South Vietnamese Refugees. *New Community* (Autumn), 4: 366–370.

Schaefer, Richard T., and William Zellner. 2011. *Extraordinary Groups*, 9th ed. New York: Worth.

Schnittker, Jason, Jeremy Freese, and Brian Powell. 2003. Who Are Feminists and What Do They Believe? The Role of Generations. *American Sociologist Review* (August), 68: 607–622.

School Digger. 2011. *Wausau School District*. Accessed June 1, 2011, at http://www.schooldigger.com.

Schulz, Amy J. 1998. Navajo Women and the Politics of Identity. *Social Problems* (August), 45: 336–352.

Schwartz, Alex. 2001. *The State of Minority Access to Home Mortgage Lending: A Profile of the New York Metropolitan Area*. Washington, DC: Brooking Institution Center on Urban and Metropolitan Policy.

Schwartz, Felice, and Jean Zimmerman. 1992. *Breaking with Tradition: Women and Work, The New Facts of Life*. New York: Warner Books.

Schwartz, John. 1994. Preserving Endangered Speeches. *Washington Post National Weekly Edition* (March 21), 11: 38.

Schwartz, Margaret. 2006. A Question in the Shape of Your Body. Pp. 9–14 in *Half/Life: Jewish Tales from Interfaith Homes*, Laurel Synder, ed. Brooklyn, NY: Soft Skull Press.

———. 2008. Argentina. Pp. 87–89 in vol. 1, *Encyclopedia of Race, Ethnicity, and Society*, Richard T. Schaefer, ed. Thousand Oaks, CA: Sage.

Schwartz, Pepper. 1992. Sex as a Social Problem. Pp. 794–819 in *Social Problems*, Craig Calhoun and George Ritzer, eds. New York: McGraw-Hill.

Schweimler, Daniel. 2007. Argentina's Last Jewish Cowboys (February 12). Accessed September 5, 2008, at http://www.bbc.com.

Scott, Janny. 2003. Debating Which Private Clubs Are Acceptable and Private. *New York Times* (December 8), sec. 7: 5.

Scully, Marc. 2012. Whose Day Is It Anyway? St. Patrick's Day as a Contested Performance of National And Diasporic Irishness. *Studies in Ethnicity and Nationalism*, 12 (1): 118–135.

Sears, David O., and J. B. McConahay. 1969. Participation in the Los Angeles Riot. *Social Problems* (Summer), 17: 3–20.

———. 1970. Racial Socialization, Comparison Levels, and the Watts Riot. *Journal of Social Issues* (Winter), 26: 121–140.

———. 1973. *The Politics of Violence: The New Urban Blacks and the Watts Riots*. Boston: Houghton-Mifflin.

Seelye, Katharine A. 2010. Celebrating Secession Without the Slaves. *New York Times* (November 30): A19, A21.

Seibert, Deborah. 2002. Interview with Author. *Wausau Daily Herald*, Staff Member (March 27).

Sela-Sheffy, Rakefet. 2004. What Makes One an Israeli: Negotiating Identities in Everyday Representations of "Israeliness." *Nations and Nationalism*, 10 (40): 479–497.

Selod, Saher, and David G. Embrick. 2013. Racialization and Muslims: Situating the Muslim Experience in Race Scholarship. *Sociology Compass*, 7/8: 644–655.

Selzer, Michael. 1972. *"Kike": Anti-Semitism in America*. New York: Meridian.

Semple, Kirk. 2012. Many U.S. Immigrants' Children Seek American Dream Abroad. *New York Times* (April 16). Accessed April 21, 2013, at http://www.nytimes.com/2012/04/16/us/more-us-children-of-immigrants-are-leaving-us.html?ref=kirksemple.

Shah, Naveed Ali. 2009. Upside-Down World. *Washington Post National Weekly Edition* (November 16): 25–26.

Shah, Priyank G. 2012. *Asian Americans' Achievement Advantage: When and Why Does it Emerge*. Dissertation. The Ohio State University.

Shanklin, Eugenia. 1994. *Anthropology and Race*. Belmont, CA: Wadsworth.

Shapiro, Joseph P. 1993. *No Pity: People with Disabilities Forging a New Civil Rights Movement*. New York: Times Books.

Shapiro, Thomas M., Tatjana Meschede, and Laura Sullivan. 2010. *The Racial Wealth Gap Increases Fourfold*. Research and Policy Brief (May), Institute on Assets and Social Policy: University of Michigan.

Sherif, Musafer, and Carolyn Sherif. 1969. *Social Psychology*. New York: Harper & Row.

Sherman, C. Bezalel. 1974. Immigration and Emigration: The Jewish Case. Pp. 51–55 in *The Jew in American Society*, Marshall Sklare, ed. New York: Behrman House.

Sherwood, Jessica Holden. 2010. *Wealth, Whiteness, and the Matrix of Privilege: The View from the Country Clubs*. Lanham, MD: Rowman and Littlefield.

Sheskin, Ira M., and Arnold Dashefsky. 2012. *Vital Statistics: Jewish Population in the United States by State*. Accessible at http://www.jewishvirtuallibrary.org.

Shilts, Randy. 1982. *The Mayor of Castro Street: The Life and Times of Harvey Milk*. New York: St. Martin's.

Shin, Hyon B., and Robert A. Kominski. 2010. Language Use in the United States 2007. *Census Brief ACS-12*. Washington, DC: U.S. Government Printing Office.

Shinnecock Nation. 2013. *An Ancient History and Culture*. Accessed November 4, 2013, at http://www.shinnecocknation.org/history.

Siebens, Julie, and Tiffany Julian. 2011. *Native North American Languages Spoken at Home in the United States and Puerto Rico: 2006–2010*. ACSBF/10-10. Accessible at http://www.census.gov.

Siegal, Erin. 2013. Amnesty: Back to the Future. *Christian Science Monitor* (April 8): 26–31.

Sigelman, Lee, and Steven A. Tuch. 1997. Metastereotypes: Blacks' Perception of Whites' Stereotypes of Blacks. *Public Opinion Quarterly*, 61 (Spring): 87–101.

Silberman, Charles E. 1971. *Crisis in the Classroom: The Remaking of American Education*. New York: Random House.

Silva, Graziella Moraes D., and Elisa P. Reis. 2012. The Multiple Dimensions of Racial Mixture in Rio De Janeiro, Brazil: From Whitening to Brazilian Negritude. *Ethnic and Racial Studies*, 35 (March): 382–399.

Simon Wiesenthal Center. 2008. *iReport: Online Terror + Hate: The First Decade*. Los Angeles: Simon Wiesenthal Center.

Simpson, Jacqueline C. 1995. Pluralism: The Evolution of a Nebulous Concept. *American Behavioral Scientist* (January), 38: 459–477.

Skrentny, John D. 2008. Culture and Race/Ethnicity: Bolder, Deeper, and Broader. *Annals* 619 (September): 59–77.

Slavin, Robert E., and Alan Cheung. 2003. *Effective Reading Programs for English Language Learners*. Baltimore: Johns Hopkins University, Center for Research on the Education of Students Placed at Risk.

Slavin, Steven, and Mary Pradt. 1979. Anti-Semitism in Banking. *The Bankers Magazine* (July–August), 162: 19–21.

———. 1982. *The Einstein Syndrome: Corporate Anti-Semitism in America Today*. Washington, DC: University Press of America.

Small, Cathy A. 2011. *Voyages: From Tongan Villages to American Suburbs*. 2nd ed. Ithaca NY: Cornell University Press.

Smith, Dan. 2008. *The Penguin State of the World Atlas*. 8th ed. London: Penguin Books.

Smith, Julian. 2011. Insider: Who Owns the Dead? *Archaeology*, 64 (January/February).

Smith, Tom W. 2006. *Taking America's Pulse III. Intergroup Relations in Contemporary America*. Chicago: National Opinion Research Center, University of Chicago.

Snipp, C. Matthew. 1989. *American Indians: The First of This Land*. New York: Sage.

Society for Human Resource Management. 2010. *Workplace Diversity Practices: How Has Diversity and Inclusion Changed Over Time?* Alexandra VA: SHRM.

———. 2011. *SHRM Survey Findings: An Examination of Organizational Commitment to Diversity and Inclusion*. Alexandra VA: SHRM.

Soltero, Sonia White. 2008. Bilingual Education. Pp. 142–146 in vol. 1, *Encyclopedia of Race, Ethnicity, and Society*, Richard T. Schaefer, ed. Thousand Oaks, CA: Sage.

Somerville, Will, Jamie Durama, and Aaron Matteo Terrazas. 2008. Hometown Associations: An Untapped Resource for Immigrant Integration? *MPI Insight* (July).

Song, Tae-Hyon. 1991. *Social Contact and Ethnic Distance between Koreans and the U.S. Whites in the United States*. M.A. thesis, Western Illinois University, Macomb.

Soo, Julie D. 1999. Strained Relations: Why Chinatown's Venerable Associations Are Ending Up in Court. *AsianWeek* (January 14): 15–18.

South African Institute of Race Relations. 2007. *South Africa Survey 2006/2007*. Johannesburg: SAIRR.

———. 2010. *South Africa Survey 2009–2010*. Johannesburg: SAIRR.

———. 2011. *South Africa Survey 2010/2011*. Johannesburg: SAIRR.

———. 2013. *Racial Transformation Not "Complete Failure."* September 12 Press Release. Accessible at http://www.sairr.org.za.

Southern Poverty Law Center. 2010. *Ten Ways to Fight Hate: A Community Response Guide*. Montgomery, AL: SPLC.

Stahler-Sholk, Richard. 2008. Zapatista Rebellion. Pp. 301–304 in vol. 2, *Encyclopedia of Race, Ethnicity, and Society*, Richard T. Schaefer, ed. Thousand Oaks, CA: Sage.

Stampp, Kenneth M. 1956. *The Peculiar Institution: Slavery in the Ante-Bellum South*. New York: Random House.

Standen, Amy. 2010. *Tribal Lands Struggle to Bring Clean Power Online*. Accessible at http://www.wbur.org/npr.

Stansell, Christine. 2010. *The Feminist Promise: 1792 to the Present*. New York: The Modern Library.

Stark, Rodney, and Charles Glock. 1968. *American Piety: The Nature of Religious Commitment*. Berkeley: University of California Press.

Starks, Carolyn. 2002. Sitting Here in Limbo. *Chicago Tribune* (March 26).

Statistics Canada. 2012. *Aboriginal Peoples*. (Modified December 24.) Accessed September 19, 2013, at http://www.statcan.gc.ca/pub/11-402-x/2012000pdf-eng.htm.

Staton, Ron. 2004. Still Fighting for National Hawaiian Recognition. *AsianWeek* (January 22): 8.

Steinberg, Stephen. 2005. Immigration, African Americans, and Race Discourse. *New Politics* (Winter): 10.

———. 2007. *Race Relations: A Critique*. Stanford, CT: Stanford University Press.

Steinhauer, Jennifer. 2006. An Unwelcome Light on Club Where Legends Teed Off. *New York Times* (September 23): A8.

Steinmetz, Erica. 2006. Americans with Disabilities: 2002. *Current Population Reports*. Ser. P70, No. 107. Washington, DC: U.S. Government Printing Office.

Stern, Nicolas. 2007. *Review on the Economics of Climate Change*. London: HM Treasury.

Stone, Emily. 2006. Hearing the Call—In Polish. *Chicago Tribune* (October 13): 15.

Stone, Pamela. 2009. Getting to Equal: Progress, Pitfalls, and Policy Solutions on the Road to Gender Parity in the Workplace. *Pathways* (Spring): 3–7.

Stonequist, Everett V. 1937. *The Marginal Man: A Study in Personality and Culture Conflict*. New York: Scribner's.

Stout, David. 2000. At Indian Bureau, a Milestone and an Apology. *New York Times* (September 9): A47.

Stretesky, Paul, and Michael Lynch. 2002. Environmental Hazards and School Segregation in Hillsborough County, Florida, 1987–1999. *Sociological Quarterly*, 43: 553–573.

Strong, John A. 1998. *"We Are Still Here!" The Algonquian Peoples of Long Island Today*. 2nd ed. Interlaken NY: Empire State Books.

Sturtevant, William C., and Jessica R. Cattelino. 2004. Florida Seminole and Miccosukee. Pp. 429–449 in *Handbook of North American Indians (Southeast)*, Vol. 14, R. D. Fogelson, ed. Washington, DC: Smithsonian Institution Press.

Sue, Christina A. 2013. *Land of the Cosmic Race: Race Mixture, Racism, and Blackness in Mexico*. New York: Oxford University Press.

Suggs, Welch. 2002. Title IX at 30. *Chronicle of Higher Education* (June 21), 48: A38–A42.

Sulzberger, A. G. 2011. Hispanics Reviving Faded Towns on the Plains. *New York Times* (November 14): A1, A20.

Supreme Court. 1923. *United States v. Bhagat Singh Thind*. Decided February 19. *United States Reprints*, v. 261, October Term, 1922, 204–215.

Swagerty, William R. 1983. Native Peoples and Early European Contacts. Pp. 15–16 in *Encyclopedia of American Social History*, Mary Kupiec Clayton, Elliot J. Gorn, and Peter W. Williams, eds. New York: Scribner's.

Swanson, Emily. 2013. Poll: Few Identify as Feminists, But Most Believe in Equality of Sexes. *Huffington Post* (April 15). Accessible at http://www.huffingtonpost.com.

Takaki, Ronald. 1998. *Strangers from a Different Shore: A History of Asian Americans*. Updated and revised. Boston, MA: Little, Brown, Back Bay edition.

Takezawa, Yasuko I. 1991. Children of Inmates: The Effects of the Redress Movement among Third Generation Japanese Americans. *Qualitative Sociology* (Spring), 14: 39–56.

Tannenbaum, Frank. 1946. *Slave and Citizen*. New York: Random House.

Taylor, Jonathan B. and Joseph P. Kalt. 2005. *American Indians on Reservations: A Databook of Socioeconomic Change between the 1990 and 2000 Censuses*. Cambridge, MA: The Harvard Project on American Indian Development.

Taylor, Stuart, Jr. 1987. High Court Backs Basing Promotion on a Racial Quota. *New York Times* (February 26): 1, 14.

———. 1988. Justices Back New York Law Ending Sex Bias by Big Clubs. *New York Times* (June 21): A1, A18.

Taylor, Verta, Leila J. Rupp, and Nancy Whittier. 2009. *Feminist Frontiers*, 8th ed. New York: McGraw-Hill.

Tefera, Adai, Genevieve Seigel-Hawley, and Erica Frankenberg. 2010. *School Integration Efforts Three Years after Parents Involved*. Los Angeles: The Civil Rights Project, UCLA.

Telles, Edward E. 1992. Residential Segregation by Skin Color in Brazil. *American Sociological Review* (April), 57: 186–197.

———. 2004. *Race in Another America: The Significance of Skin Color in Brazil*. Princeton, NJ: Princeton University Press.

Telles, Edward, and Stanley Bailey. 2013. Understanding Latin American Beliefs about Racial Inequality. *American Journal of Sociology* (May): 1559–1595.

Telsch, Kathleen. 1991. New Study of Older Workers Finds They Can Become Good Investments. *New York Times* (May 21): A16.

ten Brock, Jacobus, Edward N. Barnhart, and Floyd W. Matson. 1954. *Prejudice, War and the Constitution*. Berkeley: University of California Press.

Teranishi, Robert T. 2010. *Asians in the Ivory Tower: Dilemmas of Racial Inequity in American Higher Education*. New York: Teachers College Press.

Third World Institute. 2007. *The World Guide*, 11th ed. Oxford: New Internationalist.

Thomás Rivera Policy Institute. 2009. *Majority/Near-Majority of First Graders in Top Ten U.S. Cities are Latino*. Released March 5.

Thomas, Curlew O., and Barbara Boston Thomas. 1984. Blacks' Socioeconomic Status and the Civil Rights Movement's Decline, 1970–1979: An Examination of Some Hypotheses. *Phylon* (March), 45: 40–51.

Thomas, Debie. 2013. My Parents Chose My Husband. *Slate* (August 16). Accessible at http://www.slate.com.

Thomas, Dorothy S., and Richard S. Nishimoto. 1946. *The Spoilage: Japanese-American Evacuation and Resettlement*. Berkeley: University of California Press.

Thomas, Oliver. 2007. So What Does the Constitution Say about Religion? *USA Today* (October 15): 15A.

Thomas, William Isaac. 1923. *The Unadjusted Girl*. Boston: Little, Brown.

Thomas, William Isaac, and Florian Znaniecki. 1996. *The Polish Peasant in Europe and America* (5 vols.), Eli Zaretsky, ed. Urbana: University of Illinois Press.

Thompson, Ginger. 2005. Uneasily, a Latin Land Looks at Its Own Complexion. *New York Times* (May 19): A5.

Thompson, Krissah. 2010. Montgomery Parents' "Study Circles" Aim to Close the Gap on Student Achievement. *Washington Post* (November 9).

Thornton, Russell. 1991. *North American Indians and the Demography of Contact*. Paper presented at annual meeting of the American Sociological Association, Cincinnati, OH.

Threadcraft, Shatema A. 2008. Welfare Queen. Pp. 1384–1386 in vol. 3, *Encyclopedia of Race, Ethnicity, and Society*, Richard T. Schaefer, ed. Thousand Oaks, CA: Sage.

Tice, Lindsay. 2007. Another Side of Brent Matthews. *Lewiston-Auburn Sun Journal* (April 29). Accessed April 16, 2012, at http://www.sunjournal.com/node/239728.

Time. 1974. Are You a Jew? (September 2), 104: 56, 59.

Timerman, Jacob. 2002. *Prisoner Without a Name, Cell Without a Number*. Madison: University of Wisconsin Press.

Tizon, Thomas Alex. 2004. Internment Lesson Plan Is Under Attack. *Los Angeles Times* (September 12): A21.

Toensing, Gale Courey. 2011. Recession-Proof Is in the Pudding. *Indian Country Today* (April 13): 28–31.

Tomaskovic-Devey, Donald, and Patricia Warren. 2009. Explaining and Eliminating Racial Profiling. *Contexts*, 8 (Spring): 34–39.

Tomlinson, T. M. 1969. The Development of a Riot Ideology among Urban Negroes. Pp. 226–235 in *Racial Violence in the United States*, Allen D. Grimshaw, ed. Chicago: Aldine.

Tonelli, Bill. 2004. *Arrivederci, Little Italy*. (September 27.) Accessed August 28, 2013, at http://nymag.com/nymetro/urban/features/9904/.

Tong, Benson. 2000. *The Chinese Americans*. Westport, CT: Greenwood Press.

Torkelson, Jason and Douglas Hartmann. 2010. White Ethnicity in Twenty-First-Century America: Findings from a New National Survey. *Ethnic and Racial Studies*, 33 (8): 1310–1331.

Torres, Lourdes. 2008. Puerto Rico. Pp. 1086–1090 in vol. 2, *Encyclopedia of Race, Ethnicity, and Society*, Richard T. Schaefer, ed. Thousand Oaks, CA: Sage.

Townsend, Sarah S. M., Hazel R. Markos, and Hilary Bergsieker. 2009. My Choice, Your Categories: The Denial of Multiracial Identities. *Journal of Social Issues*, 65 (1): 185–204.

Tran, My-Thuan. 2008. Their Nation Lives On. *Los Angeles Times* (April 30): B1, B8–B9.

Traoré, Rosemary. 2008. Africans in the United States. Pp. 38–40 in vol. 1, *Encyclopedia of Race, Ethnicity, and Society*, Richard T. Schaefer, ed. Thousand Oaks, CA: Sage.

Tredoux, Colin, and Gillian Finchilescu. 2010. Mediators of the Contact-Prejudice Relation among South African Students on Four University Campuses. *Journal of Social Issues*, 66 (2): 289–308.

Triev, Monica M. 2009. *Identity Construction Among Chinese-Vietnamese Americans Being, Becoming, and Belonging*. El Paso, TX: LFB Scholarly Publishing LLC.

Triplett, William. 2004. Migrant Farmworkers. *CQ Researcher* (October 8): 14.

Truman, Jennifer L. 2011. Criminal Victimization Survey. *BJS Bulletin* (September).

Tsui, Bonnie. 2011. The End of Chinatown. *The Atlantic* (December): 17–18.

Ture, Kwame, and Charles Hamilton. 1992. *Black Power: The Politics of Liberation*. New York: Vintage Books.

Turner, Margery Austin, Fred Freiburg, Erin Godfrey, Clark Herbig, Diane K. Levy, and Robin R. Smith. 2002. *All Other Things Being Equal: A Paired Testing Study of Mortgage Lending Institutions*. Washington, DC: Urban Institute.

Turner, Margery Austin, Fred Freiburg, Erin Godfrey, Clark Herbig, Diane K. Levy, Robin R. Smith et al. 2013. *Housing Discrimination Against Racial and Ethnic Minorities 2012*. Washington DC: The Urban Institute.

Turner, Ralph H. 1994. Race Riots Past and Present: A Cultural-Collective Approach. *Symbolic Interaction*, 17(3): 309–324.

Turner, Richard Brent. 2003. *Islam in the African-American Experience*, 2nd ed. Bloomington: Indiana University Press.

Two Bridges. 2013. *Celebrate the 5th Anniversary of New York City's Marco Polo Festival!* Accessed August 20, 2013, at http://www.twobridges.org.

Twohey, Megan. 2007. Outside, It's Suburban; Inside, It's Japan. *Chicago Tribune* (December 29): 1, 2.

Tyson, Ann Scott. 1996. Alabama Ferry to Bridge Racial Divide. *USA Today* (February 13), Sect. 4: 4.

Tyson, Karolyn. 2011. *Integration Interrupted: Tracking, Black Students, & Acting White After Brown*. New York: Oxford University Press.

Tyson, Karolyn, William Darity, Jr., and Domini R. Castellino. 2005. It's Not "a Black Thing": Understanding the Burden of Acting White and Other Dilemmas of High Achievement. *American Sociological Review* (August), 70: 582–605.

Uchitelle, L. 2003. Older Workers Are Thriving Despite Recent Hard Times. *New York Times* (September 8): A1, A15.

Ulrich, Roberta. 2010. *American Indian Nations from Termination to Restoration, 1953–2006*. Corvallis, OR: Oregon State University Press.

United Jewish Communities. 2003. *The National Jewish Population Survey 2000–01*. New York: United Jewish Community.

United Nations High Commission on Refugees. 2008. *2007 Global Trends: Refugees, Asylum-seekers, Returnees, Internally Displaced and Stateless Persons*. Geneva: UNHCR.

United States Border Patrol. 2012. *U.S. Border Patrol Fiscal Year Apprehension Statistics—Southeast Border Sectors*. Accessed January 29. 2013, at http://www.cbp.gov/xp/cgov/border_security/border_partol/usbp_statistics/.

U.S. English. 2013. *Official English*. Accessed August 9, 2013, at http://us-english.org.

van den Berghe, Pierre L. 1965. *South Africa: A Study in Conflict*. Middletown, CT: Wesleyan University.

———. 1978. *Race and Racism: A Comparative Perspective*, 2nd ed. New York: Wiley.

Vang, Chia Youyee. 2010. *Hmong America: Reconstructing Community in America*. Champaign: University of Illinois Press.

Vecsey, Taylor K. 2013. Arson Squad Probes Suspicious Shinnecock Gaming Authority Trailer Blaze. *Southampton Patch* (October 31). Accessed November 4, 2013, at http://southampton.patch.com.

Villarreal, Andrés. 2010. Stratification by Skin Color in Contemporary Mexico. *American Sociological Review*, 75 (5): 652–678.

Vincent, Louise. 2008. The Limitations of "Inter-racial Contact" Stories from Young South Africa. *Ethnic and Racial Studies*, 31 (November): 1426–1451.

Visitability. 2013. *Visitability*. Accessed November 10, 2013, at http://www.visit-ability.org.

Voo, Jocelyn, 2008. Arranged Marriage Gets High-Tech Twist. Accessed July 16, 2012, at http://articles.cnn.com/2008-04-23/living/web.arranged.marriages_1_cell-phones-marriage-profile?_s=PM:LIVING.

Wacquant, Loïc. 2007. *Urban Outcasts: A Comparative Sociology of Advanced Marginality*. New York: Polity.

Wagley, Charles, and Marvin Harris. 1958. *Minorities in the New World: Six Case Studies*. New York: Columbia University Press.

Waitzkin, Howard. 1986. *The Second Sickness: Contradictions of Capitalistic Health Care*, rev. ed. New York: Free Press.

Wald, Kenneth D. 2008. Homeland Interests, Hostland Politics: Politicized Ethnic Identity among Middle Eastern Heritage Groups in the United States. *International Migration Review* (Summer): 273–301.

Waldinger, Roger. 2007. *Between Here and There: How Attached Are Latino Immigrants to Their Native Country?* Washington, DC: Pew Hispanic Center.

Waldman, Carl. 1985. *Atlas of North American Indians*. New York: Facts on File.

Walgreens. 2013. *Recognizing Talent: Fucing Stereotypes*. Accessed September 23, 2013, at http://www.walgreens.com/topic/sr/recognizing_talent.jsp.

Wall Street Journal. 2011. Tiger Mom's Long-Distance Cub. (December 24).

Wallace, Jean E., and Fiona M. Kay. 2012. Tokenism, Organizational Segregation, and Coworker Relations in Law Firms. *Social Problems*, 59 (3): 389–410.

Waller, David. 1996. Friendly Fire: When Environmentalists Dehumanize American Indians. *American Indian Culture and Research Journal*, 20 (2): 107–126.

Wallerstein, Immanuel. 1974. *The Modern World System*. New York: Academic Press.

———. 2004. *World-Systems Analysis: An Introduction*. Durham, NC: Duke University Press.

Walzer, Susan. 1996. Thinking About the Baby: Gender and Divisions of Infant Care. *Social Problems* (May), 43: 219–234.

Wang, L. Ling-Chi. 1991. Roots and Changing Identity of the Chinese in the United States. *Daedalus* (Spring), 120: 181–206.

Wark, Colin, and John F. Galliher. 2007. Emory Bogardus and the Origins of the Social Distance Scale. *American Sociologist*, 38: 383–395.

Warner, W. Lloyd, and Leo Srole. 1945. *The Social Systems of American Ethnic Groups*. New Haven, CT: Yale University.

Warry, Wayne. 2007. *Ending Denial: Understanding Aboriginal Issues*. Orchard Park, NY: Broadview Press.

Washburn, Wilcomb E. 1984. A Fifty-Year Perspective on the Indian Reorganization Act. *American Anthropologist* (June), 86: 279–289.

Washington, Booker T. 1900. *Up from Slavery: An Autobiography*. New York: A. L. Burt.

Washington, Harriet. 2007. *Medical Apartheid: The Dark History of Medical Experimentation on Black Americans from Colonial Times to Present*. New York: Doubleday.

Watanabe, Teresa. 2007. Reclaiming Cultural Ties. *Los Angeles Times* (May 13): B1, B13.

Watanabe, Teresa, and Susana Enriquez. 2005. Church Redefined. *Los Angeles Times* (April 24): 54.

Waters, Mary. 1990. *Ethnic Options. Choosing Identities in America*. Berkeley: University of California Press.

Watson, Jamal E. 2004. Going Extra Mile to Worship. *Chicago Tribune* (August 8), sect. 4: 1, 4.

Wax, Murray L. 1971. *Indian Americans: Unity and Diversity*. Englewood Cliffs, NJ: Prentice Hall.

Wax, Murray L., and Robert W. Buchanan. 1975. *Solving "the Indian Problem": The White Man's Burdensome Business*. New York: New York Times Book Company.

Wax, Rosalie. 1967. The Warrior Drop-Outs. *Trans-Action* (May), 4: 40–46.

Weber, Max. 1947. *The Theory of Social and Economic Organization* [1913–1922], trans. by Henderson and T. Parsons. New York: Free Press.

Weinberg, Daniel H. 2004. Evidence from Census 2000 About Earnings by Detailed Occupation for Men and Women. *CENSR-15*. Washington, DC: U.S. Government Printing Office.

Weiner, Rebecca. 2008. *The Virtual Jewish History Tour*. Accessed September 8, 2008, at http://www.jewishvirtuallibrary.org/jsource/vjw/Argentina.html.

Weiner, Tim. 2004. Of Gringos and Old Grudges: This Land Is Their Land. *New York Times* (January 9): A4.

Weiser, Benjamin. 2013a. Swastikas, Slurs and Torment in Town's Schools. *New York Times* (November 8): A1, A20.

———. 2013b. Cuomo Orders Investigation into Claims of Anti-Semitic Acts in a School District. *New York Times* (November 8). Accessible at http://www.nytimes.com.

Welch, William M. 2011. More Hawaii Resident Identify as Mixed Race. *USA Today* (February 28).

Wessel, David. 2001. Hidden Costs of Brain Drain. *Wall Street Journal* (March 1): 1.

West, Darrel M. 2010. *Brain Grain: Rethinking U.S. Immigration Policy*. Washington, DC: Brookings Institution Press.

White, Jack E. 1997. I'm Just Who I Am. *Time* (May 5), 149: 32–34, 36.

White House. 2012. *Remarks by the President on the Nomination of Dr. Jim Kim for World Bank President*. (March 23.) Accessible at http://www.whitehouse.gov/photos-and-video/video/2012/03/23/president-obama-nominated-jim-yong-kim-world-bank-president#transcript.

Whitman, David. 1987. For Latinos, a Growing Divide. *U.S. News and World Report* (August 10), 103: 47–49.

Whittaker, Stephanie. 2006. Who Would You Prefer to Work For? *The Gayette (Montreal)* (November 4): 1.

Wickham, De Wayne. 1993. Subtle Racism Thrives. *USA Today* (October 25): 2A.

Wieberg, Steve. 2006. NCAA to Rename College Football Subdivisions. *USA Today* (August 3).

Wiesel, Elie. 2006. *Night* (trans. from French by Marion Wiesel). New York: Hill and Wang.

Wilder, Craig Steven. 2013. *Ebony & Ivory: Race, Slavery, and the Troubled History of America's Universities*. New York: Bloomsbury.

Wilkins, Amy C. 2012. Becoming Back Women: Intimate Stories and Intersectional Identities. *Social Psychology Quarterly*, 75 (2): 173–196.

Willeto, Angela A. 1999. Navajo Culture and Female Influences on Academic Success: Traditional Is Not a Significant Predictor of Achievement among Young Navajos. *Journal of American Indian Education* (Winter), 38: 1–24.

———. 2007. Native American Kids: American Indian Children's Well-Being Indicators for the Nation and Two States. *Social Indicators Research* (August), 83: 149–176.

Williams, Carol J. 2006. Puerto Rico Could Soon Get Real Vote on Status. *Los Angeles Times* (February 17): A15.

Williams, Carol J. 2007. Emotions Run High in Puerto Rican Debate. *Los Angeles Times* (April 26): A27.

Williams, Kim M. 2005. Multiculturalism and the Civil Rights Future. *Daedalus*, 134 (1): 53–60.

Williams, Patricia J. 1997. *Of Race and Risk. The Nation Digital Edition*. Accessed December 12, 1997, at http://www.thenation.com.

Williams, Timothy. 2012a. U.S. Will Pay A Settlement of $1 Billion To 41 Tribes. *New York Times* (April 14): A10.

———. 2012b. Sioux Racing to Find Billions to Buy Sacred Land in Black Hills. *New York Times* (October 4): A1, A20.

———. 2012c. $1 Million Each Year For All, Until Tribe's Luck Runs Out. *New York Times* (August 9): A1, A4.

———. 2013. Quietly, Indians Reshape Cities and Reservations. *New York Times* (April 14): 14.

Williams, Vernon J., Jr. 2008. Abolitionism: The Movement. Pp. 1–2 in vol. 1, *Encyclopedia of Race, Ethnicity, and Society*, Richard T. Schaefer, ed. Thousand Oaks, CA: Sage.

Willie, Charles V. 1978. The Inclining Significance of Race. *Society* (July–August), 15: 10, 12–13.

Willie, Charles V. 1979. *The Caste and Class Controversy.* Bayside, NY: General Hall.

Willoughby, Brian. 2004. *10 Ways to Fight Hate on Campus.* Montgomery, AL: Southern Poverty Law Center.

Wilson, William Julius. 1973. *Power, Racism and Privilege: Race Relations in Theoretical and Sociohistorical Perspectives.* New York: Macmillan.

———. 2011. The Declining Significance of Race: Revisited and Revised. *Annals of the American Academy of Arts and Sciences*, 140 (Spring): 55–69.

———. 2012. *The Declining Significance of Race: Blacks and Changing American Institutions.* 3rd ed. Chicago: University of Chicago Press.

Winant, Howard. 1994. *Racial Conditions: Politics, Theory, Comparisons.* Minneapolis, MN: University of Minnesota Press.

———. 2001. *The World Is a Ghetto: Race and Democracy Since World War II.* New York: Basic Books.

———. 2004. *The New Politics of Race: Globalism, Difference, Justice.* Minneapolis: University of Minnesota Press.

———. 2006. Race and Racism: Towards a Global Future. *Ethnic and Racial Studies* (September), 29: 986–1003.

Winerip, Michael. 2011. New Influx of Haitians, But Not Who Was Expected. *New York Times* (January 16): 15, 22.

———. 2013. Three Men, Three Ages. Which Do You Like? *New York Times* (July 23): B1, B5.

Winks, Robin W. 1971. *The Blacks in Canada: A History.* Montreal: McGill-Queen's University Press.

Winseman, Albert L. 2004. *U.S. Churches Looking for a Few White Men.* Accessed July 27, 2004, at http://www.gallup.com.

Winter, Richard, and Teresa Watanabe. 2007. LAPD Drops Its Plan to Map Muslim Community. *Los Angeles Times* (November 15): A1, A21.

Winter, S. Alan. 2008. *Symbolic Ethnicity.* Pp. 1288–1290 in vol. 3, *Encyclopedia of Race, Ethnicity, and Society*, Richard T. Schaefer, ed. Thousand Oaks, CA: Sage.

Wisniewski, Mary. 2012. Transformed by Immigration, and Illinois Farm Town Thrives. *Chicago Tribune* (July 15). Accessible at http://www.chicagotribune.com.

Withrow, Brian L. 2006. *Racial Profiling: From Rhetoric to Reason.* Upper Saddle River, NJ: Prentice Hall.

Witt, Bernard. 2007. What Is a Hate Crime? *Chicago Tribune* (June 10): 1, 18.

Woesthoff, Julia M. 2008. *Muslims in Europe.* Pp. 925–928 in vol. 2, *Encyclopedia of Race, Ethnicity, and Society*, Richard T. Schaefer, ed. Thousand Oaks, CA: Sage.

Wolfe, Ann G. 1972. The Invisible Jewish Poor. *Journal of Jewish Communal Services*, 48 (3): 259–265.

Women Work. 2011. *Women Work* (maintained by Pennsylvania Women Work). Accessed June 16, 2011, at http://pawomenwork.org/.

Wong, Janelle, S. Karthick Ramakrishnan, Taeku Lee, and Jane Junn. 2011. *Asian American Political Participation: Emerging Constituents and Their Political Identities.* New York: Russell Sage Foundation.

Woodward, C. Vann. 1974. *The Strange Career of Jim Crow*, 3rd ed. New York: Oxford University Press.

Working, Russell. 2007. Illegal Abroad, Hate Web Sites Thrive Here. *Chicago Tribune* (November 13): A1, A15.

World Bank. 2013a. *Work Bank Launches Initiative on Migration, Releases New Projections on Remittances Flows.* (April 19.) Accessible at http://www.worldbank.org.

———. 2013b. *World Databank.* Accessed August 7, 2013, at http://databankl.wpr;dbanl.org/data/views/tableview.aspx.

Wortham, Robert A. 2008. Du Bois, William Edward Burghardt. Pp. 423–427 in vol. 1, *Encyclopedia of Race, Ethnicity, and Society*, Richard T. Schaefer, ed. Thousand Oaks, CA: Sage.

Wozniacka, Gosia. 2011. United Farm Workers Fight Dwindling Membership. *Press Democrat* (Santa Rosa, CA) (April 20).

Wright II, Earl. 2006. W. E. B. Du Bois and the Atlantic University Studies on the Negro Revisited. *Journal of African American Studies*, 9 (4): 3–17.

Wright, Erik Olin. 2012. My Journey Into the Deaf World: A Visit to Gallaudet University. *Footnotes* (March): 11–12.

Writers Guild of America West. 2013. *Diversity on TV Writing Staffs: Writers Guild Releases Latest Research Findings.* (March 26.) Accessible at http://www.wga.org.

Wrong, Dennis H. 1972. How Important Is Social Class? *Dissent* (Winter), 19: 278–285.

Wu, Frank M. 2002. *Yellow: Race in America beyond Black and White.* New York: Basic Books.

Wyatt, Edward. 2009. No Smooth Ride on TV Networks' Road to Diversity. *New York Times* (March 18): 1, 5.

Wyman, Mark. 1993. *Round-Trip to America. The Immigrants Return to Europe, 1830–1930.* Ithaca, NY: Cornell University Press.

Xu, Jun, and Jennifer C. Lee. 2013. The Marginalized "Model" Minority: An Empirical Examination of the Racial Triangulation of Asian Americans. *Social Forces*, 91 (4): 1363–1397.

Yancey, George. 2003. *Who Is White? Latinos, Asians, and the New Black–Nonblack Divide.* Boulder, CO: Lynne Rienner.

Yemma, John. 2013. Teaching the Freedom to Believe. 2013. *Christian Science Monitor* (June 17): 5.

Young, Jeffrey R. 2003. Researchers Change Racial Bias on the SAT. *Chronicle of Higher Education* (October 10): A34–A35.

Yinger, John. 1995. *Closed Doors, Opportunities Lost: The Continuing Costs of Housing Discrimination.* New York: Russell Sage Foundation.

Zaidi, Arisha U., and Muhammad Shuraydi. 2002. Perceptions of Arranged Marriages by Young Pakistani Muslim Women Living in a Western Society. *Journal of Comparative Family Studies*, 33 (Autumn): 495–515.

Zambrana, Ruth Enid. 2011. *Latinos in American Society: Families and Communities in Transition.* Ithaca: Cornell University Press.

Zarembro, Alan. 2004. Physician, Remake Thyself: Lured by Higher Pay and Heavy Recruiting, Philippine Doctors Are Getting Additional Degrees and Starting Over in the U.S. as Nurses. *Los Angeles Times* (January 10): A1, A10.

Zeng, Zhen, and Yu Xie. 2004. Asian-Americans' Earnings Disadvantage Reexamined: The Role of Place of Education. *American Journal of Sociology* (March), 109: 1075–1108.

Zhao, Yilu. 2002. Chinatown Gentrifies, and Evicts. *New York Times* (August 23): A13.

Zhou, Min. 2009. *Contemporary Chinese America.* Philadelphia: Temple University Press.

Zhou, Min., and Carl L. Bankston, III. 1998. *Growing Up American: How Vietnamese Children Adapt to Life in the United States.* New York: Russell Sage Foundation.

Zia, Helen. 2000. *Asian American Dreams: The Emergence of an American People.* New York: Farrar, Straus & Giroux.

Zimmerman, Seth. 2008. *Immigration and Economic Mobility.* Washington, DC: Economic Mobility Project.

Zittrain, Jonathan. 2008. *The Future of the Internet and How to Stop It. With a New Forward by Lawrence Lessig and New Preface by the Author.* New Haven: Yale University Press.

Zogby, James. 2001. *National Survey: American Teen-Agers and Stereotyping.* Submitted to the National Italian American Foundation by Zogby International. Accessed June 3, 2008, at http://www.niaf.org/research/report_zogby.asp?print=1&.

———. 2010. *51% Expect Major Terror Attack This Year and 25% Plan to Fly Less.* (February 4.) Accessed March 2, 2011, at http://www.zogby.com.

Photo Credits

Index

Diné College (Navajo Community College), 160
disabilities, 372–7
  advocacy for rights and, 376–7
  Americans with Disabilities Act (ADA)
    and, 27, 376
  in contemporary society, 372–3
  famous people with, 373
  institutional discrimination and, 376
  labeling the disabled and, 373–6
  visitability and, 377
disability rights, advocacy for, 376–7
disabled, labeling, 373–6
discrimination, 15, 17, 33–6, 58–82
  affirmative action and, 72–6
  Chinese Americans and, 297–9
  Craigslist policy on discriminatory
    advertisements, 80
  defined, 33, 60
  economy and, 64–7
  in economy of women, 332–5
  eliminating, 67–9
  environmental justice and, 71–2
  gays and lesbians and, 379–80
  glass ceiling and, 77–9
  hate crimes and, 61–2
  housing, 68
  individual, 63
  institutional, 63–4
  Japanese Americans and, 297–9
  in job seeking, 59
  LaPiere's study of, 34–6
  median income by race and sex, 66
  Merton's typology and, 46
  relative *vs.* absolute deprivation in, 60–1
  reverse, 76–7
  Romanian experience, 60
  total, 60–1
  wealth inequality and, 69–71
displaced homemakers, 336
Ditka, Mike, 128
diversity training, 52–5
Dixon, Margaret, 371
Dublin, Frank, 54
Doherty, Carroll, 381
Dolan, Timothy, 132
Donoghue, Christopher, 252
Douglass, Frederick, 170, 174
Dreby, Joanna, 105
Drewery, Malcolm P. Jr., 189, 212
dry foot, wet foot, 217
dual or split labor market, 80, 222
Du Bois, W. E. B., 7, 8, 28, 43, 173–5, 183, 185,
  193, 200, 253
Dunham, Katherine, 354
Durkheim, Emile, 306
dysfunction, 15
Dyson, Michael, 191

E

early immigration, 87–90
  of Irish Americans, 119–22
  of Italian Americans, 122–25
  of Polish Americans, 125–8
Eastwood, Clint, 276
economic impact of immigration, 104–6
  contemporary social concerns, 96–9
  global, 104–6
  negative trends in, 97
  positive trends in, 98
  remittances and, 105
economy; *see also* economy of African
  Americans; economy of women; income
  of Asian Americans, 264–7
  of Chinese Americans, 285
  discrimination and, 64–7

  of Japanese Americans, 296
  of Latinos, 210–11
  of Mexican Americans, 234–5
  of Native Americans, 156–9
  of Puerto Ricans, 238–9
economy of African Americans, 193–5
  Black-White income gap and, 181, 197–8
  employment and, 196
  income and, 197–8
  wealth and, 198
economy of women, 329–37
  discrimination in, 332–5
  displaced homemakers and, 336
  executive advancement and, barriers to, 334
  feminization of poverty and, 335–6
  financial return on education for women
    and, 333
  glass ceiling and, 334
  in Japan, gender inequality in, 332
  mommy tax and, 338
  mommy track and, 335, 338
  occupational segregation by gender
    and, 330, 333
  pay equity and, 333–4
  ratio of women's to men's earnings
    by occupation, 330
  second shift and, 338
  sexual harassment and, 335
  women as a percentage of all workers
    in selected occupations, 331
education; *see also* education of African
  Americans; education of Native Americans
  of Arab Americans, 256
  of Asian Americans, 264–6
  bilingual, 96
  denominations and, 134
  of Jewish Americans, 313
  of Mexican Americans, 231
  of Muslim Americans, 256
  of Native Americans, 159–61
  Navajo way of learning and, 160
  of Puerto Ricans, 236
  reducing prejudice and, 47–56
  tracking, 190
  of women, 336–7
education of African Americans, 188–93
  acting white and, 191–2
  apartheid schools and, 190
  higher education of, 178, 192–3
  historically Black colleges and universities
    and, 192
  percentage of adults receiving college
    degrees, 189
  school segregation and, 190
  tracking and, 190
education of Native Americans, 159–61
  attainment and quality of, 159–61
  higher education of, 160–1
  kickouts or pushouts and, 159
  Navajo way of learning and, 159–60
  overview of, 159
Eisenhower, Dwight, 119
elderly, 367–72
  advocacy for rights and, 371–2
  ageism and, 368–70
  economic picture of, 370–1
  identifying, 368
  population in US (actual and projection
    1960–2060), 368
Elias, Sean, 11
Eligon, John, 262
Ellis Island, 90
Ellison, Keith, 203, 256–7
El Salvador, 220–221
El-Shabazz, Malik, 250

Embrick, David, G., 23, 43, 52, 254
emigration, 18
employment; *see also* economy of African
  Americans; economy of women;
  employment of African
Americans; income
  of Chinese Americans, 286
  discrimination in job seeking and, 59
  of Jewish Americans, 312–13
  occupational segregation by gender and,
    330, 333
Employment Assistance Program (EAP),
  144, 148–50, 164
employment of African Americans, 195
  occupations and, 195
Engel v Vitale, 134
English language acquisition, 212
environment
  immigration and, 106
  Native Americans and, 162–3
environmental justice, 71–2, 79, 163, 351
environmental refugees, 106
Equal Employment Opportunity Commission,
  67–68
Eriksson, Leif, 142
Eskimos, 350, 351
ethnic cleansing, 20
ethnic diversity, 112
  in Brazil, 353–6
  in Canada, 350–3
  Chinese Americans in Manhattan's Little
    Italy, 112
  five-nation comparison of, 347
  income distribution by race and, 355
  in Israel, 356–7
  in Mexico, 347–50
  "moment of silence", in public schools, 135
  national comparison, 347
  Protestants and, 132–4
  in Republic of South Africa, 359–63
  Roman Catholics and, 132
  studying Whiteness, 113–14
  White privilege, 36–7, 114
  worldwide, 346
ethnic groups
  defined, 6
  in United States, 3–4
ethnicity, 111–39; *see also* ethnic diversity;
  rediscovery of ethnicity
  ethnic paradox and, 115–16
  German Americans and, 117–19
  Irish Americans and, 119–22
  Italian Americans and, 122–25
  Polish Americans and, 125–28
  religion and the courts and, 134–6
  religious pluralism and, 128–34
  symbolic, 117
  third-generation principle and, 115
  whiteness and, 113–14
ethnic paradox, 115–16, 136, 362
ethnocentrism, 33
ethnonational conflict, 346
ethnophaulisms, 33
evacuees, 292
Executive Order 9066, 291–2, 295
exploitation theory, 38
expulsion, 20, 21, 79, 105, 137, 164, 185, 204,
  222, 280, 298, 321, 342, 364, 382
extermination, 20, 79, 105, 137, 164, 185, 204,
  222, 280, 298, 321, 342, 364, 382

F

Fairlie, Robert, 195
Fakih, Rima, 243
familism, 232–233, 289